CONTEMPORARY ESTATE PLANNING

CONTEMPORARY ESTATE PLANNING

TEXT AND PROBLEMS

JOHN R. PRICE
DEAN AND PROFESSOR OF LAW
UNIVERSITY OF WASHINGTON

LITTLE, BROWN AND COMPANY
BOSTON   TORONTO

Library of Congress Catalog Card No. 82-081493
ISBN 0-316-71856-4

Second Printing

HAL

Published simultaneously in Canada
by Little, Brown & Company (Canada) Limited

Printed in the United States of America

TO SUZANNE, JOHN, AND STEVEN

Summary of Contents

Contents

CHAPTER 1

An Overview of Estate Planning

CHAPTER 2

BASIC TRANSFER TAX LAWS AND ESTATE-PLANNING STRATEGIES

CHAPTER 3

Concurrent Ownership and Estate Planning

CHAPTER 4

WILLS AND RELATED DOCUMENTS

CHAPTER 5

THE GIFT AND ESTATE TAX MARITAL DEDUCTIONS

CHAPTER 6

Life Insurance

CHAPTER 7

PLANNING LIFETIME NONCHARITABLE GIFTS

CHAPTER 8

GIFTS TO CHARITABLE ORGANIZATIONS

CHAPTER 9

INTRAFAMILY TRANSFERS FOR CONSIDERATION

CHAPTER 10

Trusts

CHAPTER 11

CLOSELY HELD BUSINESS INTERESTS

CHAPTER 12

Post-Mortem Planning

PREFACE

This book is intended primarily for use in a problem oriented course or seminar on estate planning; however, it can be used successfully by lawyers for self study and reference purposes. It reflects my belief that a mix of text, examples, and problems is the most flexible, effective and economical way to teach a basic or an advanced estate-planning course to law students in their second or third years or to practicing lawyers. Ideally the course would be taken by students after ones on trusts and estates, personal income tax, and estate and gift tax. However, the text has been used successfully by students who have had none, or less than all, of those courses. Some other students have taken estate planning and one or more of the other courses concurrently. Because the text includes extensive references to the provisions of the Internal Revenue Code of 1954 and Treasury Regulations, a reader should have ready access to a suitable pamphlet edition or other compilation of the Code and Regulations.

The approach and coverage of the book allow it to be used in courses of varying length and sophistication, depending on the instructor's individual preferences. For example, the manuscript has been used in courses ranging from 30 to 60 classroom hours in length, including estate-planning courses or workshops; estate-planning seminars; and a combined course on the federal taxation of trusts and estates and estate planning. The organization of the book into chapters that deal with more or less discrete subjects enables the instructor to consider them out of sequence or to narrow the course coverage by omitting one or more of them.

The book is a product of my combined experiences as a lawyer specializing in estate planning and administration in a large law firm and as a teacher of those subjects for the past dozen years. Overall it expresses my concern that an estate planner provide clients with high quality personal services and comprehensive, fully integrated estate plans (what might be called "holistic" estate planning). At appropriate points the text includes references to practical planning and ethical considerations. Given the demand that lawyers be more efficient and the burgeoning interest in the ethical responsibilities of lawyers, it is particularly desirable to consider those dimensions of an estate-planning practice. Because of the migrant character of our population and the growing interest in community property and similar marital property regimes, the text includes discussions of community property considerations.

The book opens with an examination of the lawyer's role in estate planning (Chapter 1) and concludes with a review of the increasingly important post-mortem phase of estate planning (Chapter 12). In between, consideration is given to a wide range of important estate-planning problems and techniques, extending from nontax topics, such as the use of durable powers of attorney and living wills, to sophisticated tax devices, such as the private annuity and the charitable remainder trust. Considerable attention is devoted to life insurance, which is not adequately understood by most clients and receives little, if any, attention in most law school courses. Constraints of time and space required some hard choices regarding coverage. Thus, the text does not include a separate consideration of annuities or employee benefits, but the topics are discussed at various points, particularly in connection with private annuities and post-mortem planning.

A teacher's manual is available that discusses various ways of using the text, suggests solutions to problems contained in it, and offers a list of cases that might be assigned or used for discussion and analysis. The manual also includes some lengthy problems that might be assigned in lieu of, or in addition to, a final examination. Students have reacted favorably to the two or three long planning problems I usually assign instead of an examination or a research paper. Each of the long problems is based on an extensive set of facts concerning a fictional family at successive stages of development. For example, stage one may be set when the husband and wife are relatively young and have minor children; stage two when they are older, more affluent, and the children are in college; and stage three following the death of one or both of them. The problems are excellent learning tools that combine the advantages of simulation with those of take home examinations. They approximate the work of a lawyer in practice and require a careful analysis and discussion of complex factual and legal issues.

June, 1982   *John R. Price*
Seattle, Washington

ACKNOWLEDGMENTS

A large and varied group contributed directly or indirectly to the completion of this book. First, and foremost, are my wife, Suzanne, and our 2 sons, John and Steven, all of whom were a continual source of love, support, and encouragement. Second is my brother, Professor H. Douglas Price, of the Department of Government, Harvard University, who very early in our lives established a pattern of support, affection, and high scholarly achievement.

Over the years I have benefited from the valuable counsel, assistance, and encouragement of many colleagues at the University of Washington Law School and practicing lawyers in Seattle and elsewhere. I am particularly grateful to Ron Hjorth, Jack Huston, Bob Mucklestone, Gordon Schaller, John F. Sherwood, and Ken Schubert, all of whom read portions of the manuscript at various stages. My former deans, Dick Roddis and George Schatzki, and my colleague Don Chisum also gave me important support and encouragement.

Friends at a number of other schools also provided valuable inspiration, help, and encouragement. Doug Kahn of the University of Michigan Law School and Ed Halbach of the University of California at Berkeley read and made helpful suggestions regarding the content and organization of early versions of some chapters. More recently, Professors Joel Dobris and Bruce Wolk of the University of California at Davis used the manuscript in the class they taught together and gave me additional helpful suggestions and welcome encouragement. Finally, correspondence and conversations with several other teachers helped shape the content and scope of the book.

Students in my estate-planning classes and seminars since 1970 helped in the development and refinement of the manuscript as a teaching and research tool. Their comments while students and following graduation have been useful and reassuring. I am particularly grateful to James A. Harris, a 1982 graduate of the University of Washington Law School, for his superb help as a research assistant. During the winter term 1982 I was a visiting professor at the University of Michigan Law School, where I received outstanding research assistance from a third year law student, Bruce Boruszak.

The manuscript was prepared by several cheerful, cooperative, and very talented word processors: Jeri Miles and Bill Herman at the University of Washington and Chris Moulton at the Perkins law firm in Seattle. Throughout the protracted gestation period of this book the editors and staff of Little, Brown & Company have been most cooperative, encouraging, and patient — especially my manuscript editor, Elizabeth Collins; the assistant editor of the Law Division, Rick Heuser; and his predecessor, Jerry Stone.

Some of the discussion of life insurance trusts in Chapter 6 is based on a paper I wrote for the University of Miami's 14th Estate Planning Institute in 1980. The paper is copyrighted by the University of Miami and is used with permission of the University of Miami, Fourteenth Institute on Estate Planning (1980) published by Matthew Bender & Company. The graph at §6.3, which shows the risk and investment elements of a cash value life insurance policy, is reproduced from S. S. Huebner and Kenneth Black, Jr., Life Insurance 8 (9th ed. 1976), with permission from Prentice-Hall, Inc., Englewood Cliffs, N.J. An excerpt from Professor Sheldon Kurtz's article, Allocation of Increases and Decreases to Fractional Share Marital Deduction Bequest, 8 Real Prop., Prob. & Tr. J. 450, 460 (1973), is reprinted with the permission of the Real Property, Probate and Trust Section of the American Bar Association.

Citation Form and References

Citation form. Most citations follow widely used and perfectly orthodox forms, but for sake of brevity some short forms are used. Thus, sections of the Internal Revenue Code of 1954 are referred to by citing the section number alone (*e.g.,* §267). Similarly, references to sections of the Treasury Regulations are made by citing "Reg." followed by the numbers of the sections. Private letter rulings and technical advice memoranda are cited "LR" followed by the documents' 7-digit numbers. Each LR is assigned a 7-digit number, the first 2 of which indicate the year of its publication, the next 2 the week of its publication, and the final 3 the order of its publication in that week. Thus, LR 8235001 is the first document of the set published in the thirty-fifth week of 1982. Also for brevity and convenience, several recent tax acts are cited simply by reference to the year of their enactment. In particular, the Tax Reform Act of 1969 is the "1969 Act"; the Tax Reform Act of 1976 is the "1976 Act" and the Economic Recovery Tax Act of 1981 is the "1981 Act." References throughout the text regarding ethical issues are made to the Code of Professional Responsibility (Disciplinary Rules are cited DR and Ethical Considerations EC); the content of the proposed Model Code of Professional Responsibility is essentially the same.

Books, periodicals, and loose-leaf services. Each chapter includes a bibliography that cites helpful books, articles, and other resource materials. Nonetheless, at this point it may be helpful to mention some of the books, periodicals, and services with which an estate planner should have some familiarity.

A number of valuable texts and treatises are available that deal with various tax and nontax aspects of estate planning. They include the following:

T. Atkinson, Wills (2d ed. 1953)
A. J. Casner, Estate Planning (4th ed. 1980)
J. Farr & J. Wright, An Estate Planner's Handbook (4th ed. 1979)
J. K. Lasser, Estate Tax Techniques (1955 with annual supplements)
C. Lowndes, R. Kramer & J. McCord, Federal Estate and Gift Taxes (3d ed. 1974)

J. Mertens, Federal Gift and Estate Taxation (1959 with annual supplements)

R. Powell, Real Property (rev. ed. 1975 with annual supplements)

W. Reppy & W. de Funiak, Community Property Law in the United
States (1975)

R. Rice, Family Tax Planning (1960 with annual supplements)

A. Scott, Trusts (3d ed. 1967 with annual supplements)

R. Stephens, G. Maxfield & S. Lind, Federal Estate and Gift Taxation (4th ed. 1978)

L. Waggoner, Future Interests (West Nutshell Series 1981)

Papers presented at various tax institutes are also helpful in research and planning. Fortunately, the papers from the major institutes are re-printed each year, including those from the University of Miami's Institute on Estate Planning, New York University's Institute on Federal Taxation, and the University of Southern California's Tax Institute.

Current developments are discussed and articles of interest to estate planners appear regularly in a number of periodicals, including Estate Planning; Journal of Taxation; Real Property, Probate and Trust Journal; Tax Lawyer: Tax Advisor; Taxes; Tax Law Review; and Trusts and Estates. In addition, the BNA Tax Management portfolios include a number of very helpful volumes (*e.g.*, S. Simmons, Personal Life Insurance Trusts, 210-2d, BNA Tax Mgmt. Portfolio (1980) and W. Streng, Estates, Gifts and Trusts — Planning, 11-8th BNA Tax Mgmt. Portfolio (1979). Finally, the statutes, regulations, rulings, and cases relating to estate and gift tax laws are compiled in loose-leaf services published by Commerce Clearing House and by Prentice-Hall, Inc., both of which also publish similar compilations of federal income tax laws.

Contemporary Estate Planning

CHAPTER 1

AN OVERVIEW OF ESTATE PLANNING

1

Estate planning is not susceptible of precise definition; it is as broad as the human imagination. It involves the use and arrangement of property for and among the members of a family group under a planned design affording the greatest enjoyment to the whole group commensurate with sufficient conservation. It is still one of the privileges of this Republic. J. Farr & J. Wright, An Estate Planner's Handbook 1 (4th ed. 1979).

A. INTRODUCTION

§1.1.   The Lawyer's Role

The lawyer's principal role in estate planning consists of advising clients regarding the effective and economical organization and disposition of wealth. The advent of new forms of property, the burgeoning importance of will substitutes, and the growing complexity of the income and transfer tax laws have broadened the scope of estate planning to include much more than the preparation of a will. An appropriate estate plan may now involve a host of related documents including a will, a durable power of attorney, an instrument of transfer under the Uniform Anatomical Gifts Act, and a living will. *See* Chapter 4, *infra.* The plan may also call for creating or terminating cotenancies, making gifts outright or in trust, changing beneficiary designations in life insurance policies or employee benefit plans, acquiring new life insurance policies or transferring old ones, and changing investments or the form of a business enterprise. Accordingly, the lawyer must be competent in a number of important areas of substantive and tax law. In addition, the lawyer must be sensitive to the ethical demands of an estate-planning practice and alert to avoid acts of professional malpractice. The lawyer must also appreciate the human dimension of estate planning, which often requires the lawyer to deal with the client's innermost secrets. For most clients these include a fear of death, anxiety about seeing a lawyer, ambivalent feelings about some relatives, and uncertainty about the future. Above all, the lawyer must render the personal services that are required to meet the needs of the whole client. The lawyer's role demands that the client be recognized and respected and not treated as an anonymous object being processed on an assembly line. The lawyer may have dozens of clients, but the client probably has only one lawyer, who may be the only lawyer the client has ever consulted professionally.

Associating Others. In order to formulate a comprehensive plan for a client it may be desirable to associate a more expert lawyer or other estate planners with particular expertise, such as an insurance advisor, an accountant, a trust officer, or an investment counselor. Of course, the lawyer's duty of confidentiality to the client precludes involving another person without the consent of the client. *See* DR 4-101 and EC 4-2. If the client does approve, the others should be selected with care and an explicit arrangement should be made with them and the client regarding the payment of their fees, if any.

> A client is not bound to pay for the services of an assisting attorney whom he did not employ unless he has authorized the employment or consented to it in some binding fashion. Estate of Anderson v. Smith, 316 N.E.2d 592, 594, 83 A.L.R.3d 1153, 1156 (Ind. App. 1974).

(Without the full knowledge and consent of a client, the lawyer may not accept or retain any referral fee, commission, rebate, or discount from anyone on account of his or her dealings with the client. DR 5-107(A). The client is entitled to any commission, rebate, or discount that is paid to the lawyer. New York Bar Association Formal Ethics Opinions 107 (1969) and 107(a) (1970). Although advisors from other disciplines do become involved, the lawyer should oversee the formulation and execution of the estate plan because of its predominantly legal nature and because the lawyer is generally free of the self-interest that may affect the judgment of the insurance advisor and the trust officer.

§1.2. *Clients and Conflicts of Interest*

At the outset the lawyer must ascertain whether his or her representing a prospective client would conflict with the interests of other clients or potential clients. In all phases of estate planning the lawyer must bear in mind the identity of the client whom the lawyer represents and the extent of the duties that flow from the representation.

> [B]efore a lawyer may represent multiple clients, he should explain fully to each client the implications of the common representation and should accept or continue employment only if the clients consent. EC 5-16.

Consider, for example, the position of a lawyer who planned the estate of a woman and is later asked by her husband to plan his estate. Although the lawyer completed the planning job for the woman, without her consent the lawyer cannot use the information that was acquired through representing her in planning the husband's estate. *See* Panel Discussion, Professional Ethics, U. Miami 8th Inst. Est. Plan., Ch. 7 (1974). The lawyer's duties to the woman did not end when her will was executed. For example, the lawyer's duty of confidentiality continues after the estate plan is implemented. Fortunately, most clients recognize the value of coordinated planning and freely consent to the same lawyer representing others in the client's family. Of course, without the client's consent a lawyer may not disclose the content of documents he or she has prepared for the client. H. Drinker, Legal Ethics, 94, 136 (1953).

Conflicts and Separate Counsel. When the interests of potential clients do conflict, the lawyer should suggest that each of them be represented by separate counsel. In such a situation, there is some risk that a single lawyer will not adequately represent one or more of the clients. Such a failure can lead to a charge of malpractice or an attempt to invalidate any agreement into which the parties entered. Sending one of them to a partner or associate does not provide them with the necessary independent counsel. *See* Eckhardt, The Estate Planning Lawyer's Problems: Malpractice and Ethics, U. Miami 8th Inst. Est. Plan. ¶606.3 (1974).

> [P]arties interested in establishing an estate plan may be well advised to seek independent counsel, particularly in instances, such as this, where the wife is giving up certain rights. The utilization of independent counsel would forestall a challenge to the estate plan upon that basis. However, we decline to establish a requirement that independent advice must be sought or that a recommendation to seek independent counsel be expressed before such a plan is valid. Whitney v. Seattle First National Bank, 560 P.2d 360, 364 (Wash. App. 1977), *aff'd,* 579 P.2d 937 (Wash. 1978) (inter vivos widow's election to allow all of the community property to pass to testamentary trust under husband's will, of which she was life income beneficiary, is binding although she was not separately represented).

The representation of parties with conflicting interests is also undesirable because of its unseemly appearance. That is the thrust of Canon 9: "A lawyer should avoid even the appearance of professional impropriety."

Competence of Client. Before proceeding with an estate-planning matter the lawyer should be satisfied that the client is competent and not acting under duress or a discoverable form of undue influence. Particular care must be exercised if the lawyer is retained by a person other than the client, especially where the client is aged, ill, or of diminished capacity. The duties of the lawyer toward such a client are summarized in the following passage from Re Worrell, 8 D.L.R. 3d 36, 42-43 (Ontario Surr. Ct. 1969):

> I would suggest that in this day of speedy methods of transportation there should be no occasion when a solicitor should prepare a will without receiving his instructions from the testator. It is certainly improper for the solicitor to draft a will without taking direct instructions from the testator and then not to attend personally when the will is executed. For example, a son of an old client might come to the solicitor's office and advise that his

father, a widower, is in hospital and wants a will leaving his whole estate equally among his children. In such circumstances, the solicitor might properly, for convenience, engross such a will and attend on the testator, but should—under no circumstances—say to the testator: "I understand you want a will leaving your property thus and so and I have drawn such a will. Is this satisfactory?" This, especially with older people is a dangerous practice and the solicitor should, on attending the testator say: "I understand you want a will drawn and will you tell me how you wish your estate to go on your death." The asking of leading questions by a solicitor obtaining instructions from an elderly testator is a practice to be avoided. Too often the elderly person, if asked leading questions, will reply in the affirmative, but if simply asked "What property do you have?" or "How do you wish your estate to go on your death?" may exhibit complete lack of comprehension.

A similar caution has been urged by Professor Robert Lynn: "Generally speaking, an attorney should altogether avoid drafting a will for a person whom he does not personally interview." An Introduction to Estate Planning 57 (1975).

In the case of a disabled client or a "deathbed" will, the lawyer should use the meetings with the client to test for the presence of at least the minimum degree of competence required for the execution of a will. The typical test of testamentary capacity requires the testator to understand "(1) The nature and extent of his property, (2) The persons who are the natural objects of his bounty, and (3) The disposition which he is making of his property." T. Atkinson, Wills §51 (2d ed. 1953). Discussions with doctors, nurses, family members, and friends may provide additional useful information regarding the testator's mental condition. As a precautionary measure the lawyer may take statements from some of them regarding the testator's condition and use more witnesses than necessary when the will is executed. In order to establish the competency of the testator and the proper execution of the will, the lawyer may make a video tape of an interview of the testator and the execution of the will.

If the lawyer concludes that the client lacks the necessary testamentary capacity, some commentators believe that the lawyer must refuse to draw the will. H. Drinker, Legal Ethics 93 (1953). Others point out that, if the lawyer refuses to draw a will for a marginally competent client, the lawyer deprives the client of having a court determine the client's competency and the validity of the will. Of course, if the lawyer draws a will for the client of uncertain competency, there is no assurance that the validity of the instrument will ever be considered by a court. After the client has died, it would be unusual, and perhaps inappropriate, for the scrivener to inform interested parties of the testator's uncertain competency.

Certainly the benefit of all doubt should be given to the client and the determination of the fact left to the courts. In most such situations there is sufficient doubt to justify drafting the will. But where the lawyer is convinced that the client lacks the capacity he should not assume responsibility for preparing the will. To do so would give false assurance to the client and would be apt to cause litigation that might otherwise not occur. Miller, Functions & Ethical Problems of the Lawyer in Drafting a Will, 1950 U. Ill. L.F. 415, 426.

The validity of the will can be established during the client's lifetime in a few jurisdictions that provide for the ante-mortem probate of wills. In the absence of such a binding determination, the lawyer should preserve the prior will of a client who may lack testamentary capacity.

The lawyer should also discourage a client from making decisions regarding the disposition of property when the client is emotionally distraught or may be suffering from an "insane delusion." For example, a bereaved widow or widower should defer making large gifts or establishing irrevocable trusts. Here some procrastination may be justified: The lawyer may delay the preparation and execution of a new will or other dispositive documents until the client has had a chance to think things over and there has been an opportunity to reason with the client. An alert lawyer may be able to dissuade the client from taking unwise action. If the client insists that the lawyer help with a plan that is unjust, unwise, or vulnerable to being set aside, the lawyer is faced with a difficult choice: "Shall I refuse to assist my client in carrying out his plan and probably lose him as a client, or shall I assist him although I have serious reservations about it?"

The Code of Professional Responsibility does not provide a pat answer to the question. The response of any given lawyer will be colored by the lawyer's concept of morality, the lawyer's perception of the duties owed to a client, the nature of the plan, and the lawyer's own economic security. From an economic perspective, it is easier for a prosperous lawyer to refuse a client than it is for a new, financially insecure lawyer to do so. Hopefully, even a financially insecure lawyer will have a high enough regard for the profession to refuse the client rather than to assist him or her in using the law to achieve questionable goals. Edmond Cahn, the late legal philosopher, has written enthusiastically of the lawyer's exhilaration in refusing to represent a client who has asked the lawyer to do something wrong. Cahn, Introduction to Ethical Problems of Tax Practitioners, in Professional Responsibility in Tax Practice 15-16 (B. Bittker, ed., 1970).

The lawyer should also be careful not to influence a client to appoint a business associate or an institution with which the lawyer has some connection. A corporate fiduciary should be recommended, for example, only when in the best interests of the client. Even then, if the client asks for a recommendation, the lawyer would do well to recommend more than one institution. Any documents that are drawn should protect the client's interests and not unduly favor the corporate fiduciary.

In the past lawyers have too often been willing to subordinate the needs of their clients to the interests of the corporate fiduciary, particularly when the law firm has been recommended by the fiduciary. Whitman, Coping With Corporate Fiduciaries Declining to Serve, 115 Tr. & Est. 9, 52 n.7 (1976).

Along the same lines, if the client is considering the appointment of a corporate fiduciary, the lawyer should tell the client about any practices that corporate fiduciaries have of retaining the lawyer who prepares an instrument that names it as fiduciary. The client is entitled to know about such policies before a fiduciary is chosen.

One person may pay the cost of preparing a will or providing other legal services to another. Thus, a child may pay the cost of estate-planning services provided to his or her parent. However, the person for whom the will is prepared or the services are rendered is the client and is the person to whom the lawyer is responsible. Under DR 5-107(B), "[a] lawyer shall not permit a person who recommends, employs, or pays him to render legal services for another to direct or regulate his professional judgment in rendering such legal services."

Problem 1-1. Lawyer, L, has represented Client, C, for many years. In 1970 C executed a will prepared by L that left all of C's estate to 2 of C's 4 children. Later C and the other 2 children reconciled. In 1975 C destroyed the 1970 will with the intent that each child would take an equal share of C's estate by intestacy. C is now in the hospital terminally ill and incompetent to execute a new will. However, C recalls the 1970 will and has pleaded with L to prepare a new one for C that leaves all of C's property to the 4 children in equal shares. Should L prepare such a will and allow C to execute it although C presently lacks testamentary capacity? Somewhat similar facts were involved in Estate of Callahan, 29 N.W.2d 352 (Wis. 1947), which did not discuss the propriety of the lawyer's conduct.

B.　THE ESTATE-PLANNING PROCESS

§1.3.　An Introduction to the Two Phases

A brief look at the steps involved in the inter vivos and post-mortem estate-planning processes may help in understanding the various aspects of the lawyer's role in estate planning. The inter vivos and post-mortem phases are discussed separately in the following pages, but they are intimately related: The plan that is adopted during the inter vivos planning phase determines the disposition of the client's property that will be made at death and establishes the framework within which post-mortem planning must take place.

§1.4.   Inter Vivos Estate Planning

The inter vivos estate-planning process consists of at least 4 functionally distinct stages. In chronological sequence they are: (1) getting the facts; (2) helping the client choose a plan; (3) producing the required documents; and (4) implementing the plan. A fifth stage, providing continuing guidance, may be present depending on the nature of the plan that is adopted. In any case, the lawyer should encourage clients to review their plans periodically.

Stages of the Inter Vivos Estate-Planning Process

1. Getting the facts. In this stage the lawyer collects data by interviewing the client, examining documents, and gathering information from other sources.
2. Helping the client choose a plan. Here the lawyer analyzes the data, prepares tax estimates, and counsels the client regarding choice of plan.
3. Producing the required documents. Drafting the necessary documents and submitting them to the client and others for review are the main features of this stage.
4. Implementing the plan. In this stage the lawyer supervises execution of documents, transfers of property, and submission of necessary tax returns and advises the client and the fiduciaries regarding their duties to beneficiaries and others.
5. Continuing guidance. Finally, the lawyer provides advice to the client and the fiduciaries regarding accountings, tax returns, and changes in the law.

Each stage is important and presents the lawyer with a different set of challenging opportunities and responsibilities. However, the first stage is often considered to be the most important.

§1.5.   Getting the Facts

[T]he chief fault with most estate plans is that they are based upon incomplete facts and that emphasis is wrongly placed; insufficient attention is given to those things which in human affairs ought to come first. J. Farr & J. Wright, An Estate Planner's Handbook 2 (4th ed. 1979).

The lawyer cannot begin to advise the client regarding an estate plan until the lawyer has relatively complete information regarding the client's family, assets, and planning objectives. The necessary information may be collected more efficiently and effectively if the lawyer makes careful use of legal assistants, questionnaires, and checklists. One expert put the case for using questionnaires in these terms: "To elicit the requisite facts takes more than a good memory. Only a written questionnaire covering these facts in depth will do the job. There is simply too much that needs to be known, and memory, however good, is always fallible." Bush, Estate Planning: The Client Interview, N.Y.U. 33d Inst. Fed. Tax. 3, 4 (1975). The lawyer may, for example, send a new estate-planning client a letter confirming the appointment for the initial interview and describing the information the lawyer will need and the documents that the client should bring to the meeting. In appropriate cases, the letter may also ask the client to complete a questionnaire with basic data regarding the client's family and finances. However, if a questionnaire is too detailed or too demanding, it may deter the client from going forward and result in the client missing or cancelling the scheduled appointment with the lawyer. Either for that reason or out of personal preference, some lawyers prefer to obtain the necessary data from the client during the initial interview. Still others leave the collection of the data to a legal assistant, who may interview the client before the client meets with the lawyer.

Clients have generally reacted favorably to the use of legal assistants in estate planning. However, the lawyer should not involve them beyond the level that is acceptable to the client. Also, some clients are more reluctant to disclose intimate family and financial matters to a legal assistant than to a lawyer. In any case, the client may be more willing to provide the necessary information if the lawyer assures the client that the information will be held in strictest confidence by the lawyer and the lawyer's office staff. Under DR 4-101(D), a lawyer is required to "exercise reasonable care to prevent his employees, associates, and others whose services are utilized by him from disclosing or using confidences or secrets of a client. . . ." The interviewer should also recognize that it is difficult for some clients to discuss persons or events that have caused them pain. In those cases the lawyer must proceed with tact and compassion. Communication may be helped if the lawyer simply expresses sympathy and understanding or mentions similar experiences of his or her own.

The success of the first stage depends largely upon the ability of the lawyer to obtain the necessary information from the client — what the late Joseph Trachtman called "a benign species of cross examination." J. Trachtman, Estate Planning 5 (rev. ed. 1968). That task is facilitated if the law office environment and the lawyer's approach are designed to facilitate communication between the client and the lawyer. The lawyer should strive to eliminate any features of the office or his or her demeanor that may interfere with the establishment of a good relationship or the conduct of effective communication with the client. Comfort, privacy, and the lawyer's undivided attention are all conducive to effective communication. *See* A. Watson, The Lawyer in the Interviewing and Counselling Process 75 (1976). The task can also be helped if the lawyer tells the client in advance about information the lawyer will need.

Initial Letter to Client. A letter of the following type can be used to confirm an appointment with the client. It can also be used to raise some of the points the client(s) should think about prior to the initial conference and can list some of the documents that the client(s) should bring to the meeting.

Mr. and Mrs. Joseph L. Client
1500 Evergreen Lane, N.E.
Our Town, MA   02110

Dear Mr. & Mrs. Client:

This will confirm the appointment that we have at 2:00 P.M. next Thursday, November 16. As you may know, my office is located on the fourth floor of the Merchants' Exchange Building. Although you might find parking on the street, it may be more convenient for you to park in the lot located on the north side of our building.

Enclosed is a copy of the Confidential Estate-Planning Data form that I mentioned when we talked on the telephone. Please complete the form, as best you can, and bring it along to our meeting next Thursday. I know the form looks complicated, but most clients are able to complete the pertinent items without too much difficulty. Some of the questions call for readily available data, but others may require some digging to complete. In any case, you will find it unnecessary to complete all of the items. Please note that you should bring to our meeting copies of various documents, including your present wills, deeds, insurance policies, and trusts in which you have an interest. It will be important for me to see the documents sometime soon, but don't be too concerned if you won't have them all when you come in next Thursday.

Prior to our meeting you should give some thought to the persons you will each name as executor of your will (the executor is the person who will be in charge of administering your property and carrying out the terms of your will). You may each designate the other, but it is customary and desirable to name a relative, trusted friend, or financial institution to serve as successor should the need arise. Also, your wills should name an individual to serve as guardian of the person of your minor children should neither of you be able to act. In the unlikely event that both of you die leaving minor children, you will probably want to leave your property in trust for their benefit. Otherwise it would be necessary to appoint a guardian of the estate to manage the property of each minor, which is cumbersome and expensive. Accordingly, I recommend that you include in each of your wills a trust for the benefit of your children. If you do, the wills should name one or more trustees to manage the trust property and be responsible for carrying out the terms of the trust. The same person could serve as guardian of your minor children's persons and as trustee, except that a corporate trustee cannot act as guardian of the person. Finally, you should consider how you would like your property distributed should none of your children be living upon the death of the survivor of you two.

Looking forward to seeing you next week, I am,

Sincerely yours,

Confidential Estate-Planning Data Form. A sample of an estate-planning data collection form is printed at the end of this chapter, §1.20, *infra.*

The Psychological Setting. The lawyer also needs to take steps to deal with the problems that may arise because of the dominant position that lawyers generally occupy in dealing with clients. In most instances the lawyer is perceived to be the powerful professional and the client as the dependent party, who is in need of help. "The person being helped projects certain feelings and attributes onto the helper. This projection or transference may extend to the client's superficial dependence on the lawyer. The tendency of clients to become dependent or hooked on lawyers is related to the perception of the lawyer as an authority or parental figure. In addition to the transference of positive feelings that encourage dependency, the client may project negative feelings onto the lawyer, causing the client to be hostile and uncooperative." Elkins, The Legal Persona: An Essay on the Professional Mask, 64 Va. L. Rev. 735, 752-753 (1978). The relationship between the lawyer and client may develop better if they "interact openly and on an equal basis [which allows] both [to] seek recognition, appreciation, respect, and value in the other as a total being." *Id.* at 754.

The attitude and approach of the lawyer is also important to effective communication. Going to meet the client in the reception area and extending a warm greeting will help get the interview off to a good start. If the client is brought to the lawyer's office by a receptionist or secretary, the lawyer should at least come forward to meet the client instead of remaining behind a desk or table. Achieving the desired rapport may be quickened if office furniture is thoughtfully arranged, where possible allowing the lawyer to sit with the client. A desk, another symbol of the lawyer's power and authority, generally suggests an undesirable degree of separation; instead, the lawyer and client should sit together at a table.

Many lawyers use a round table for this purpose, which permits more flexible seating than a square or rectangular table. Natural and artificial lighting should also be considered when the seating is arranged — a client should be spared facing the sun or other harsh glares. Finally, the lawyer should assure that the conference with the client will not be interrupted by telephone calls or other intrusions. The client deserves the lawyer's undivided attention during the interview.

Facilitating Communication. During the interview the lawyer should be "tolerant and non-judgmental, neutral as to the subject matter, concerned as to the person. . . . You should certainly avoid what clients complain of most, appearing bored or indifferent or exhibiting a superior attitude." H. Freeman & H. Weihofen, Clinical Law Training: Interviewing and Counseling 18 (1972). Generally the flow of information from the client will be encouraged if the lawyer is attentive and responds to the client's statements with an indication that a statement has been heard and understood. A short verbal or nonverbal response, such as a nod, is generally sufficient. Another means of encouraging the flow of information is by responding with a question, such as "When did you and Fred move here?" The client will, as a rule, tell the lawyer what the client believes to be important, but the lawyer must be alert for verbal or nonverbal indications of a subject that needs to be explored in more detail. A failure to discuss one child may indicate a dissatisfaction with that child's development or with the child's perceived attitude toward the client. Sometimes the lawyer's benign cross-examination can help the client better understand his or her own feelings — which may lead to an improvement in family relations.

Client Objectives. It is axiomatic that the client's overall planning objectives should be established first, without regard to the tax consequences. At this stage the lawyer needs to acquire an accurate picture of the client's objectives and feelings about family members and the disposition of property. Throughout the process the emphasis should be on sound planning for the client and the client's family, an aim that may not be entirely consistent with tax minimization. Most of the counselling regarding the tax and nontax effects of attempting to achieve objectives in various ways occurs in the next stage.

Documents. In most cases the lawyer will need to examine a variety of documents, including the client's existing will, trusts in which the client has an interest, decrees of divorce or separate maintenance that affect the client or the client's spouse, employee benefits that include the client, and policies of insurance on the client's life or in which the client has an interest. The lawyer should also generally see any gift tax returns that have been filed and copies of income tax returns for recent years. As a matter of routine, a law-trained person should examine deeds, stock certificates, and other documents that affect title to property. Unfortunately, the average lay client cannot be expected to characterize properly the nature or extent of interests in property. Laymen are not generally aware of the distinctions between various forms of property ownership and do not appreciate the important substantive and tax law consequences that turn upon those distinctions. The need for reliable information regarding the manner in which clients hold title to property is illustrated by this example:

Example 1-1. H and W told Lawyer that they owned $250,000 in securities, but they did not tell Lawyer how they held title to the securities nor did Lawyer ask. At their request Lawyer prepared a will for each of them under which the survivor was given a life estate in the testator's property with remainder to other relatives of the testator. When H died it was found that substantially all of the securities stood in the name of H and W as joint tenants with right of survivorship. If the joint tenancies were validly created, W is entitled to the entire interest in the securities. Otherwise, the remainder interest in the securities over which H had power of testamentary disposition will pass under his will to his relatives. *See* Lambert v. Peoples National Bank, 574 P.2d 738 (Wash. 1978) (joint tenancies not validly created, securities were community property, one-half of which was subject to H's will) and Estate of Fletcher v. Jackson, 613 P.2d 714 (N.M. Ct. App. 1980) (joint tenancies upheld). If the joint tenancies are upheld, the remaindermen may assert a claim against Lawyer for loss of their interests in the securities.

The breadth of the lawyer's duty to collect data is suggested by Smith v. Lewis, 530 P.2d 589 (Cal. 1975) in which the California Supreme Court upheld a malpractice award of $100,000 against a lawyer for failure to assert the community character of military pension rights in a divorce action that took place in 1967. (Ironically, the United States Supreme Court subsequently held that military pension rights are not subject to division or equitable distribution under community property laws. McCarty v. McCarty, 453 U.S. 210 (1981). However, the general thrust of the opinion remains valid.) An attorney, the court said, "is expected, however, to possess knowledge of those plain and elementary principles of law which are commonly known by well informed attorneys, and to discover those additional rules of law which, although not commonly known, may readily be found by standard research techniques." 530 P.2d at 595. An analogous obligation to exercise diligence in ascertaining the existence of property and powers over the disposition of property and the state of beneficiary designations probably exists in the estate-planning field.

Associating Others. As indicated above, if a client's affairs involve legal matters beyond the competence of the lawyer, the lawyer should recommend associating counsel who are qualified to advise the client competently. This course of action is dictated by ethical considerations and by a concern for the lawyer's potential liability in not providing the client with competent advice. Canon 6 requires a lawyer to represent a client competently, a position further elaborated by DR 6-101:

> (A) A lawyer shall not:
> > (1) Handle a legal matter which he knows or should know that he is not competent to handle, without associating with him a lawyer who is competent to handle it.
> > (2) Handle a legal matter without preparation adequate in the circumstances.
> > (3) Neglect a legal matter entrusted to him.

However, as indicated above, the lawyer cannot associate others without the client's consent.

The California Court of Appeal upheld the following jury instruction in an action involving the liability of a general practitioner for damages resulting from the ineffectiveness of a short-term reversionary trust to relieve the grantor of the income tax liability for patent license payments made to the trustee by a corporation controlled by the grantor. Horne v. Peckham, 158 Cal. Rptr. 714, 719 (1979).

> It is the duty of an attorney who is a general practitioner to refer his client to a specialist or recommend the assistance of a specialist if under the circumstances a reasonably careful and skillful practitioner would do so.

In *Horne* the Court of Appeal upheld a judgment of almost $65,000 against the attorney-draftsman for legal malpractice in connection with the preparation of the trust instrument.

§1.6. *Helping the Client Choose a Plan*

> In assisting his client to reach a proper decision, it is often desirable for a lawyer to point out those factors which may lead to a decision that is morally just as well as legally permissible. He may emphasize the possibility of harsh consequences that might result from assertion of legally permissible positions. In the final analysis, however, the lawyer should always remember that the decision whether to forego legally available objectives or

methods because of non-legal factors is ultimately for the client and not for himself. In the event that a client in a non-adjudicatory matter insists upon a course of conduct that is contrary to the judgment and advice of the lawyer but not prohibited by the Disciplinary Rules, the lawyer may withdraw from the employment. EC 7-8.

After the facts are collected and analyzed, the lawyer will be in a position to counsel the client regarding the adoption of a plan for the organization and disposition of the client's property. Because the client's objectives may often be achieved by various methods, the lawyer should advise the client regarding the overall consequences of each of the principal methods under consideration. The relative convenience, reliability, flexibility, cost, and fairness of each should be explained. The lawyer and client should both understand that the adoption of a plan that minimizes state and federal taxes is not morally objectionable. As Judge Learned Hand pointed out, "Any one may so arrange his affairs that his taxes shall be as low as possible; he is not bound to choose that pattern which will best pay the Treasury; there is not even a patriotic duty to increase one's taxes." Helvering v. Gregory, 69 F.2d 809, 810 (2d Cir. 1934), *aff'd,* 293 U.S. 465 (1935). However, the lawyer should not attempt to force a tax-saving plan on a client.

The lawyer should also be sure that the client gives adequate consideration to the nontax consequences of the plans under consideration.

> In considering tax avoidance devices in estate planning the client should be counseled to consider not only tax-saving effects of any proposed scheme, but also its soundness in terms of flexibility. An inter vivos disposition, as by irrevocable trust, may give away assets that the client ought to retain against possible future needs, of himself or his widow in old age or in an emergency. The human, personal effects should also be considered. Although the scheme may save money, is it likely to disappoint children or other potential heirs, or otherwise create family discord? Is the tax liability that may be avoided worth the anxiety caused over whether the scheme may be questioned by the Internal Revenue Service, and perhaps held illegal? H. Freeman & H. Weihofen, Clinical Law Training: Interviewing and Counselling 306 (1972).

The lawyer may properly attempt to dissuade a client from a course of conduct that may hurt or disadvantage others. As stated in EC 7-8, it is permissible, desirable, and thoroughly professional for a lawyer to point out to a client the "factors which may lead to a decision which is morally just as well as legally permissible. He may emphasize the possibility of harsh consequences that might result from assertion of legally permissible positions."

Valuation of Assets. In preparing tax estimates and advising clients regarding estate-planning matters, the lawyer must keep in mind the

difference between the income tax basis of an asset and its value for gift
and estate tax purposes. The income tax basis of an asset is important in
some circumstances — such as advising a client regarding the consequences of a sale of the asset or in helping select property to give to a
family member or to a charity. On the other hand, the fair market value
of an asset is more important for gift and estate tax purposes — it determines the amount of a gift for gift tax purposes and the amount that
is includible in the gross estate for estate tax purposes. Fair market value
is defined in the regulations as "the price at which the property would
change hands between a willing buyer and a willing seller, neither being
under any compulsion to buy or sell and both having reasonable knowledge of relevant factors." Regs. §§20.2031-1(b), 25.2512-1. The regulations also provide detailed instructions for the valuation of particular
types of assets for gift and estate tax purposes. For example, Regs.
§§20.2031-2 and 25.2512-2 describe the way in which stocks and bonds
are valued and Regs. §§20.2031-8 and 25.2512-6 govern the valuation of
life insurance and shares in open-end investment companies (mutual
funds). The value of closely held stock may be controlled through a
recapitalization of the corporation or the use of a buy-sell agreement. *See*
Chapter 11, *infra.* Life estates, remainders, annuities, and other limited
interests transferred after December 31, 1970, are valued according to
actuarial tables set forth in Regs. §§20.2031-10 and 25.2512-9 that are
based on an assumed 6% rate of return and different mortality rates for
males and females. Transfers made prior to 1971 are valued according
to different actuarial tables, which assume a $3\frac{1}{2}\%$ return and the same
mortality rate for males and females. Regs. §§20.2031-7; 25.2512-5.

   Tax Estimates. If a client's estate is large enough to require a federal
estate tax return to be filed, it is generally desirable to prepare an estimate of the transfer tax consequences that would result from the implementation of each of the plans under consideration. The estimates
will indicate the tax cost of each plan and can be used to show the net
amount of property that would remain under each plan for distribution
to the client's beneficiaries. Whether the client is given only a summary of
the tax consequences or is also given the worksheets that were used in
preparing the estimates will depend in large measure on the sophistication and interest of the client. In any case, the client should be given a
written description of the plans under consideration and the overall tax
consequences of implementing each of them. In some cases it is also
important to point out the income tax and cash flow consequences of the
plans.

   The primary purpose of preparing tax estimates is to enable the client
to make an informed choice among various plans for achieving his or her
estate-planning goals. In some cases the estimates should be amplified to
indicate how particular assets would be disposed of under the various

plans. For example, life insurance proceeds and joint tenancy assets might pass outright to a surviving spouse under one plan, whereas under another plan they might pass into a trust for the surviving spouse. By tracing the disposition of significant assets under various plans, the lawyer will be in a better position to advise the client regarding the provisions that should be included in a will or trust. Such an analysis may indicate that most of the client's property will pass to the client's spouse outside the will, which may make it uneconomical to create a testamentary trust for the client's spouse. As an alternative the manner of holding title to property could be changed to eliminate the survivorship feature.

Standardized forms for the presentation of estimates can be easily devised. A worksheet that can be used to make a more detailed estimate of estate taxes is included, along with a form for estimating the pre-1982 maximum allowable marital deduction, at the end of this chapter, §§1.21-1.22, *infra.* Also, some commercial enterprises provide estate-planning calculations and analyses performed by computer. *See* Paffendorf, Computer Aid to Estate Planning, U. Miami 1st Inst. Est. Plan., Ch. 17 (1967). Somewhat similar services are available through some accounting firms and insurance companies.

Record of Advice to Client. It is important for the lawyer to make a contemporaneous written record of the advice that is given to a client and of the client's instructions to the lawyer. A record is particularly desirable if the client selects a plan that does not minimize the overall tax costs. For example, a married person with a large estate may choose not to make any substantial gift to his spouse in a form that qualifies for the marital deduction. In such a case the lawyer should be sure to give the client a letter describing the tax consequences of the plan as compared with a plan that includes a marital deduction gift. Without such evidence it may be very difficult to persuade the surviving spouse, the beneficiaries, or a court that the client received competent advice from the lawyer and that the client chose a plan that did not minimize death taxes. In other contexts the courts have often acknowledged that wills are commonly planned with the intent of reducing taxes: "It is well known that wills and testamentary trusts are customarily prepared in light of their probable tax consequences, and that, particularly where the testator is married, they are usually written to take advantage of the marital deduction." Mittleman v. Commissioner, 522 F.2d 132, 139 (D.C. Cir. 1975) (will construed to qualify for marital deduction). Similar risks exist if property is given to the surviving spouse in a way that will unnecessarily subject it to taxation upon his or her death. *See* Bucquet v. Livingston, 129 Cal. Rptr. 514 (Cal. App. 1976).

Gifts or Loans to the Lawyer. The lawyer should be aware of the risks that arise if the lawyer accepts a gift from a client or if the lawyer participates in the preparation of a will or trust for a nonfamily member of which the lawyer is a beneficiary. The rules stated in EC 5-5 should be taken as the minimum duty of the lawyer:

> If a client voluntarily offers to make a gift to his lawyer, the lawyer may accept the gift, but before doing so, he should urge that his client secure disinterested advice from an independent, competent person who is cognizant of all the circumstances. Other than in exceptional circumstances, a lawyer should insist that an instrument in which his client desires to name him beneficially be prepared by another lawyer selected by the client.

A lawyer who accepts a gift or participates in the preparation of a will that names the lawyer as a beneficiary may be the subject of an action to invalidate the gift or bequest *and* a disciplinary action. *See, e.g.,* Magee v. State Bar of California, 374 P.2d 807 (Cal. 1962). The lawyer should also not suggest that the lawyer be named in the instrument as fiduciary or lawyer for the fiduciary. EC 5-6.

Similarly, a lawyer should not borrow from a client — at least not without advising the client to seek independent legal advice. A lawyer who borrows from a client without recommending independent counsel may be subject to disciplinary proceedings. Giovanazzi v. State Bar of California, 619 P.2d 1005 (Cal. 1980). The Oregon Supreme Court has stated that "[i]t is an axiom that attorneys should not borrow or accept gifts from their clients unless the client has advice from independent counsel or a knowledgeable person. The transaction should be reduced to writing, fully explaining the circumstances." In re Hendricks, 580 P.2d 188, 190 (Ore. 1978).

§1.7. Sample Letter and Tax Estimates

Here are samples of the type of letter and tax estimates that might be sent to a client following the initial conference. The letter and estimates can be more or less detailed depending upon the circumstances.

Mr. and Mrs. Joseph L. Client
1500 Evergreen Lane, N.E.
Our Town, MA   02110

Dear Mr. and Mrs. Client:

In accordance with the discussion at our initial conference I have prepared estimates of the federal estate taxes on your estates under the two plans we discussed. The estimates are based on the data provided by the Confidential Estate-Planning Data Form that you brought to our meeting. Copies of the estimates are enclosed for your review and reference. For purposes of the estimates, the estate of the first spouse to die is allowed a unified credit at the 1982 level ($62,800) and the survivor's estate is allowed a credit at the 1987 level ($192,800). The estimates indicate that almost $90,000 in taxes could be saved by substituting the plan we discussed for the one you now have.

Under your existing wills when one of you dies, all of your property will pass outright to the survivor. As I explained to you, no federal estate tax will be payable upon the first death because of the unlimited marital deduction that is allowable to the estates of persons dying after 1981. However, the tax due from the survivor's estate is unnecessarily increased by passing the deceased spouse's property outright to the survivor. In particular, if Joe dies first, the present plan will subject an unnecessarily large amount of property to taxation when Mary dies.

Part A of Estimate 1 shows that no tax will be due on Joe's death. However, as shown in Part B, a tax of $74,430 would be due from Mary's estate (assuming that Mary lives until 1987 and the values remain constant). The tax on Mary's estate would be greater if she survives Joe, but dies before 1987 when the full increase in the amount of the unified credit becomes available. Under the alternate plan we discussed, the federal estate tax on Mary's estate is largely eliminated and the related state "pick up" tax is substantially reduced.

Estimate 2 shows the federal estate taxes that would be due if you adopt the alternate plan. Under it each of you leaves most of your property to a trust of which the survivor is entitled to receive all of the income and limited distributions of principal. In addition, the survivor could be given the power to control the distribution of the property among your descendants upon the survivor's death. The trust would be designed to qualify for the federal estate tax marital deduction to the extent the survivor, as executor of the deceased spouse's will, elects to treat the property transferred to the trust as "qualified terminable interest property." The election gives the plan additional flexibility without affecting the actual interests of the survivor in the trust. Of course, to the extent the deduction is claimed in the first estate the property of the trust is includible in the estate of the survivor. Again, no estate tax will be due if Joe dies first. More important, only about $850 in estate tax will be due if Mary dies after 1986 and the state pick up tax would be reduced by about $10,000 to $15,800.

If Mary dies first, no federal estate tax will be due unless the value of her property is worth more than $225,000 (or more than $600,000 if she dies in 1987 or later). However, the estate tax that will be due on Joe's death will be increased to the extent Mary leaves property to him outright or in other ways that would cause it to be subject to tax when he dies. Under the present circumstances any additional property that is included in Joe's estate will be subject to a marginal estate tax rate of 39%. Accordingly, Mary may want to leave her property in ways that will insulate it from taxation on Joe's death. For example, she might leave her jewelry outright to your children and her stocks and bonds to a trust for Joe and your children.

Please call me after you have reviewed the enclosures and are ready to meet again. At our next meeting we should be able to decide upon the details of an estate plan for you, after which I will begin to prepare drafts of the necessary documents.

Sincerely yours,

Estimate 1.   Federal Estate Tax
Mr. and Mrs. Joseph L. Client

This memorandum estimates the amount of the estate taxes that will be due upon deaths of Mr. and Mrs. Client, assuming that Mr. Client dies first, leaving all of his property outright to Mrs. Client.

Part A.   Tax on Mr. Client's Estate.

1. Gross Estate

Residence	$150,000	
Stocks and bonds	350,000	
Cash	50,000	
Tangible personal property	50,000	
Life insurance	200,000	
Total Gross Estate		$800,000

2. Deductions

Debts, funeral expenses, etc. (estimated)	$ 5,000	
Administration expenses (estimated at about 3% of gross estate)	25,000	
Marital deduction (amount allowable for property passing to Mrs. Client)	770,000	
Total Deductions		800,000

3. Taxable Estate (Gross Estate less Deductions)

		$ 0

4. Federal Estate Tax

Adjusted taxable gifts	$ 0	
Taxable Estate	0	
Tentative tax		$ 0
Less:		
Unified Credit (1982 amount)	62,800	
Credit for state death taxes		62,800
Estate tax due		$ 0

5. Amount available to beneficiaries from
    Mr. Client's estate:

Total Gross Estate		$800,000
Less:		
Debts and expenses	$ 30,000	
State death taxes	0	
Federal estate tax	0	30,000
Net amount available		$770,000

Part B.   Tax on Mrs. Client's Estate.

1. Gross Estate

Inherited from Mr. Client	$770,000	
Mrs. Client's stocks and bonds	100,000	
Jewelry and personal effects	25,000	
Total Gross Estate		$895,000

2. Deductions

Debts, funeral expenses, etc. (estimated)	$ 5,000	
Administration expenses (estimated at about 3% of gross estate)	25,000	
Total Deductions		$ 30,000

3. Taxable Estate (Gross Estate less
    Deductions) $865,000

4. Federal Estate Tax

Adjusted taxable gifts	$ 0	
Taxable Estate	865,000	
Tentative tax		293,150
Less:		
Unified Credit (1987 amount)	$192,800	
Credit for state death taxes	25,920	218,720
Estate tax due		$ 74,430

5. Amount available to beneficiaries from
    Mrs. Client's estate:

Total Gross Estate		$895,000
Less:		
Debts and expenses	$ 30,000	
State death taxes	25,920	
Federal estate tax	74,430	130,350
Net amount available		$764,650

Estimate 2.   Federal Estate Tax
Mr. and Mrs. Joseph L. Client

Below are estimates of the estate taxes that will be due from the estates of Mr. and Mrs. Client, assuming that Mr. Client dies first leaving a will creating a trust for Mrs. Client that qualifies for the marital deduction under §2056(b)(7). The portion of the trust with respect to which the election is made will be included in Mrs. Client's estate, but the balance will not.

Part A.   Tax on Mr. Client's Estate. Mr. Client's executor can make an election under §2056(b)(7) that will eliminate any estate tax on his estate yet shelter an amount equal to the credit equivalent from inclusion in her estate.

1.	Gross Estate		
	(as in Estimate 1, Part A, above)		$800,000
2.	Deductions		
	Debts, funeral expenses, etc.	$ 5,000	
	Administration expenses (estimated		
	at about 3% of gross estate)	25,000	
	Marital deduction (election to treat		
	this portion of trust as qualified		
	terminable interest property under		
	§2056(b)(7))	545,000	
	Total Deductions		$575,000
3.	Taxable Estate (Gross Estate less		
	Deductions)	$225,000	
4.	Federal Estate Tax		
	Adjusted taxable gifts	$ 0	
	Taxable Estate	225,000	
	Tentative tax		$ 62,800
	Less:		
	Unified credit (1982 amount)		62,800
	Estate tax due		$ 0
5.	Amount available to beneficiaries from		
	Mr. Client's estate:		
	Total Gross Estate		$800,000
	Less:		
	Debts and expenses	$ 30,000	
	State death taxes	0	
	Federal estate tax	0	30,000
	Net amount available		$770,000*

---

* The trust for Mrs. Client will be funded with the full $770,000, of which $545,000 is includible in her estate under Code §2044 by reason of the election Mr. Client's executor made under Code §2056(b)(7). The other $225,000 is not includible in her estate.

Part B.   Tax on Mrs. Client's Estate.

1. Gross Estate
    Marital deduction interest
        in trust under
        Mr. Client's will $545,000
    Mrs. Client's stocks and
        bonds   100,000
    Jewelry and personal
        effects   25,000
                                            ─────────
    Total Gross Estate $670,000
2. Deductions
    Debts, funeral expenses,
        etc. (estimated) $ 5,000
    Administration expenses
        (estimated at about 3%
        of gross estate) $ 20,000
                                      ─────────
    Total Deductions $ 25,000

3. Taxable Estate (Gross Estate
        less Deductions) $645,000
4. Federal Estate Tax
    Adjusted taxable gifts $ 0
    Taxable estate   645,000
    Tentative tax $209,450
    Less:
    Unified credit (1987
        amount) $192,800
    Credit for state death
        taxes   15,800   208,600
                                      ─────────   ─────────
    Estate tax due $ 850
                                                           ═════════

5. Amount available to bene-
    ficiaries from Mrs. Client's
    estate and trust under
    Mr. Client's will:
    (a) From Mrs. Client's
            estate
         Total Gross Estate $670,000
         Less:
             Debts and expenses $ 25,000
             State death taxes   15,800
             Federal estate tax   850   41,650
                                      ─────────
         Net amount available $628,350
    (b) From trust under
            Mr. Client's will
         Net amount distrib-
            utable under Mr.
            Client's will (Esti-
            mate 2, Part A 5) $770,000

Less:		
Marital deduction		
gift to trust for		
Mrs. Client	545,000	
Net amount available		$225,000
(c) Total from estate and trust ((a) & (b))		$853,350

(d)   Comparison with plan described in Estimate 1. If all of Mr. Client's property is left outright to Mrs. Client, a total of $764,650 will be available for distribution on her death. See Estimate 1, Part B 5. Under the plan described in this estimate the distributees will receive $853,350 or about $88,700 more.

§1.8.   Producing the Documents

How to get the document on paper and to the client for execution is generally not covered by any course in law school. "Clinical studies in law schools would expose law students to the many books and articles on the subject. The average lawyer newly admitted to practice opens his career with limited knowledge of the existence of systems and procedures that can be used in his estate planning practice, or even be adapted to his preferences."

There is a great difference between what attorneys actually do in their practice of drawing wills for clients and what they could do, or what they should do. They are well aware of what they could or should do, but don't do. Boucher, THE WILL-sey REPORT in Estate Planning: Systems and Technology 3,4 (ABA Sections of Economics of Law Practice and of Real Property, Probate and Trust Law, 1978).

One of the greatest opportunities for improving the lawyer's performance exists in the third stage — the production of documents. Advanced word processing and duplicating techniques allow lawyers to use forms to produce error-free documents quickly and economically. The objectives of automation in estate planning are described in this passage:

The objectives of the estate planner in installing a system of automation are: (1) cost control in increasingly complex computations and documents; (2) quality control over such computations and documents; (3) freeing himself for the highest functions for which he was trained and should be paid; (4) improving services to clients by delivery of advice and documents in shorter turn-around time; (5) increasing his own professional and job satisfactions by gaining time for doing those things which caused him to select the estate planning specialty. Brink, Automation in Estate Planning, N.Y.U. 32d Inst. Fed. Tax. 1, 4 (1974).

A lawyer should have a reliable file of forms to use in preparing estate-planning documents, whether or not an automated system is used to produce the documents. It is inefficient, costly, and downright dangerous to create each document from scratch. Too much time is required and there are too many opportunities to unintentionally include or exclude a provision or to draft a provision improperly. Developing and maintaining a repertoire of interchangeable forms also helps the lawyer to comprehend the purpose and function of each interrelated part as well as the whole. *See* Keydel, Automated Techniques for Preparation of Estate Planning Documents, U. Miami 4th Inst. Est. Plan., Ch. 6 (1970). Unacceptable risks are involved if the lawyer uses or alters forms without understanding their purpose or the effect of the alterations.

Once the lawyer and client have agreed upon a plan, they should set a target date for execution of the documents. In the meantime the lawyer should promptly prepare a draft of the documents and submit them to the client for review. In order to avoid the type of lengthy delays that clients often complain about, the lawyer can calendar reminders to prepare the documents. The lawyer will also find it more efficient to produce documents promptly. If the necessary documents are not prepared within a reasonable time, the lawyer may be liable for any loss suffered by the intended beneficiaries. In some jurisdictions, an action brought to recover losses caused by the negligent failure to prepare a document within a reasonable time will be dismissed in the absence of privity between the lawyer and the intended beneficiary. Victor v. Goldman, 344 N.Y.S.2d 672 (Sup. Ct. Rockland Cty. 1973), *aff'd mem.*, 351 N.Y.S.2d 956 (App. Div., 2d Dept. 1974). In contrast, under the California rule, which can only be expected to grow in influence, the lawyer is liable for any loss caused the intended beneficiaries by his or her negligence regardless of privity. "The duty . . . stems from the attorney's undertaking to perform legal services for the client but reaches out to protect the intended beneficiary." Heyer v. Flaig, 449 P.2d 161 (Cal. 1969); McAbee v. Edwards, 340 So. 2d 1167 (Fla. Dist. Ct. App. 1976).

The production of documents by most estate planners now depends heavily upon copying machines and automatic or electronic typewriters. However, the use of an advanced technology based upon optical scanners, computers, and mini-computers is growing. The relatively large capital cost involved in some new systems may lead individual lawyers or small law firms, in the interest of economy, to share equipment. If equipment is shared, each lawyer must be sure that the system protects the confidentiality of information regarding his or her clients.

The methods available to retrieve and reproduce forms are constantly evolving, but the particular method that a lawyer uses is relatively unimportant. Many systems are capable of quickly producing documents of acceptable quality and appearance. Firms that market and service word processing units and automated business machines will usually advise lawyers about the installation of word processing units and improving law office organization. They can also usually arrange for visits to offices that have systems in operation. Useful materials on those subjects are also available through bar association sections and committees on law office economics and management.

§1.9. Implementing the Plan

When the time comes to implement the plan, the lawyer should remain in charge. In particular, the lawyer should oversee the execution of documents, transfer of property, and filing of tax returns. Because of the possibility that documents might be altered or incorrectly executed, the lawyer should not ordinarily entrust them to clients for execution. A lawyer may advise an out-of-town client regarding the proper method of executing a will, but allowing a legal assistant to supervise the execution of a will may violate DR 3-101(A) ("A lawyer shall not aid a non-lawyer in the unauthorized practice of law"). New York Bar Association Formal Ethics Opinion 347 (1974). If a document prepared by a lawyer is not properly executed, the lawyer may be the subject of a malpractice action. *See, e.g.,* Ward v. Arnold, 328 P.2d 164 (Wash. 1958). The lawyer should also supervise title transfers, changes of beneficiary designation in insurance policies, and other acts necessary to implement the plan.

> **Example 1-2.** Client executed a short-term trust in Lawyer's office, under which the trust corpus would revert to Client 10 years and 1 day later. Lawyer gave Client oral instructions regarding the transfer of property to the trust. Client failed to transfer the property promptly, which caused the income of the trust to be taxed to Client under §673. Client will probably be dissatisfied with Lawyer whether or not Lawyer is liable to Client for any losses that arise because the property was not promptly transferred to the trust.

Because of the lawyer's position of leadership on the estate-planning team, the lawyer may be held liable for the failure of another team member to carry out a portion of the estate-planning program competently. For example, the lawyer may be held liable for the loss caused by the failure of the insurance advisor to prepare and have the client execute a change of beneficiary form in accordance with the plan. *See* Eckhardt, The Estate Planning Lawyer's Problems: Malpractice and Ethics, U. Miami 8th Inst. Est. Plan. ¶607.2 (1974).

After the documents are executed, the lawyer should provide the client with written instructions regarding the client's fiduciary duties under the plan, including any obligation to file tax returns. Ordinarily, the lawyer will assist in preparing any gift tax returns or other tax returns that are required at the time. The lawyer and client also need to reach a clear understanding regarding any continuing supervision or services the lawyer will provide. In some cases the lawyer may agree to inform clients regarding changes in the law that affect their plans.

> If the lawyer is willing to assume that burden, he is justified in charging for the service. If the client is not willing to pay for this service, the lawyer need not bear that burden. If the lawyer is not willing to assume that burden even with an annual retainer, he should so advise the client. Eckhardt, *supra* at ¶611.

In order to render a service of that type, the lawyer must be able to identify the clients who may be affected by a particular change in the law. The lawyer will have the capacity to do so if the contents of dispositive instruments are classified and recorded in a retrievable form on discs, tape, or punched or edge-notched cards. Even the simple edge-notched card can be used for other purposes in the law office, such as providing reminders of dates upon which tax returns are due or other important events will occur. *See* Furth, Manually Operated Mechanical Devices, in Computers and the Law (ABA Comm. on Law and Technology, 2d ed. 1969). Understandably, some lawyers prefer to limit their role to providing clients with periodic reminders that their estate plans should be reviewed.

§1.10.   *Subsequent Communications*

Providing clients with advice regarding changes in the law or reminders to review their wills is ethically appropriate. For example, Opinion 210 of the ABA Committee on Professional Ethics and Grievances (1941) states:

> It is our opinion that where the lawyer has no reason to believe that he has been supplanted by another lawyer, it is not only his right, but might even be his duty, to advise his client of any change of fact or law which might defeat the client's testamentary purpose as expressed in the will.
>
> Periodic notices might be sent to the client for whom a lawyer has drawn a will suggesting that it might be wise for the client to re-examine his will to determine whether or not there has been any change in his situation requiring a modification of his will.

New York Bar Association Formal Ethics Opinion 188 (1971) reaches the same conclusion: "An attorney may call the attention of his clients to facts which inure to their benefit in relation to matters regarding which he has been consulted, and the attorney may, in fact, have a duty to do so. EC 2-1, 3 and 4; DR 2-104(A)(1); *cf.* ABA Committee on Professional Ethics, Opinions, No. 213 (1941). There is no ethical objection to the will review program proposed [reminder that will is 5 years old and recommendation that it be reviewed]."

§1.11. Post-Mortem Estate Planning

Creative post-mortem planning can maximize the benefits the survivors will derive from a decedent's estate. The process is a challenging one that requires the lawyer to explore all of the opportunities that state and federal substantive and tax laws offer to minimize taxes and protect property from creditors. In a large estate the help of a competent accountant is almost indispensable. In order not to lose any tax-saving opportunities it is important to begin planning for the administration of an estate as soon after death as possible.

The stages of the post-mortem estate-planning process roughly parallel those of the inter vivos process. At the beginning an extensive amount of information must be collected regarding the decedent and the decedent's property. *See, e.g.,* Abel & Price, First Steps in Handling Decedent's Property, 1 California Decedent Estate Administration 207 (Cal. CEB 1970). If an estate administration proceeding is required, the lawyer will prepare the documents necessary to obtain appointment of the personal representative. Thereafter the lawyer will assist the representative to marshal and protect the decedent's property, publish notice to creditors, etc.

In the estate administration setting the lawyer represents the personal representative as a fiduciary and not as an individual. The lawyer does not directly represent the beneficiaries or creditors, whose interests may conflict with the overall interests of the estate. It is no doubt appropriate for the lawyer to point out to the personal representative the tax consequences that would follow if the personal representative made a timely waiver of any right to receive a fee. The lawyer should also advise the fiduciary fully regarding his or her duties and the restrictions that apply to their conduct (*e.g.,* impartiality, no self-dealing).

The lawyer may also communicate with the beneficiaries regularly regarding the progress in the administration of the estate. Indeed, a regular course of communications may forestall the common complaint that lawyers fail to inform beneficiaries regarding estate matters. *See* M. Sussman, J. Cates & D. Smith, The Family and Inheritance (1970). At an early stage the lawyer might inform the beneficiaries of their right to disclaim an interest in property they would otherwise be entitled to receive under the will or by intestate succession. If a beneficiary decides to disclaim, the lawyer should recommend that the beneficiary be represented by separate counsel. The lawyer may represent the fiduciary although the lawyer is a beneficiary, "unless, because of the factual situation surrounding the estate and the bequest, a conflict of interest (EC 5-5) or an appearance of impropriety (Canon 9) will arise." New York Formal Ethics Opinion 356 (1974).

No Self-Dealing. Neither the fiduciary nor the lawyer for the fiduciary is free to purchase assets of the fiduciary estate or to acquire the interests of beneficiaries. In some instances transactions between the fiduciary and the estate or trust may be valid and formally unobjectionable if they are approved by a court upon full disclosure. 2 A. Scott, Trusts §§170-170.11 (3d ed. 1967); ABA Informal Ethics Opinion C-804 (1964). As a general rule the lawyer should not enter into any personal transactions with a fiduciary estate or a beneficiary.

Cash Projection and Tax Planning. In the next stage the lawyer must analyze the data that have been collected and project the amount of cash the estate will need to support dependents, pay legacies, debts, taxes, and expenses, etc. The projection will be used to determine the estate's liquidity and to plan for the sale of assets, borrowing, or other steps that should be taken to meet any cash shortfall. Early in this stage the lawyer and fiduciary should consider the adoption of a tax year for the estate and the elections that must be made for tax purposes. The entire process requires a continuous consideration of the state and federal tax consequences of actions taken or planned. The sale and distribution of assets may begin in this stage, depending upon the circumstances of the estate and the beneficiaries.

Tax Returns. Filing the estate tax return and making the more important sales and distributions of assets take place in the third stage. When the return is prepared the lawyer and fiduciary must make some decision regarding the available elections (*e.g.,* alternate valuation of assets, use of alternatively deductible expenses). Throughout the proceedings the lawyer must also consider the options available under the local law, including the use of family awards and allowances and disclaimers.

The lawyer may be liable for any additional taxes, penalties, or interest that must be paid because a tax return is filed late. Cameron v. Montgomery, 225 N.W.2d 154 (Wis. 1975), Lohn's Estate, 269 A.2d 451 (Pa. 1970). However, a lawyer is not negligent in advising a client regarding an estate tax matter in accordance with the current understanding of the law among competent lawyers in the community, although the advice is subsequently determined to be incorrect. Smith v. St. Paul Life & Marine Insurance Co., 366 F. Supp. 1283 (M.D. La. 1973), *aff'd per curiam,* 500 F.2d 1131 (5th Cir. 1974) (erroneous advice that a judgment of possession under Louisiana law did not constitute a distribution for alternate valuation date purposes under the federal estate tax law). The lawyer "is not required to exercise perfect judgment in every instance." Ramp v. St. Paul Fire & Marine Insurance Co., 269 So. 2d 239 (La. 1972).

Closing the Estate. The final stage of the post-mortem process involves the audit of the estate's tax returns, the preparation of the necessary estate fiduciary accountings, and the closure of the estate. The lawyer must see that the fiduciary provides the beneficiaries with the necessary information regarding distributions and the bases of assets, that receipts are received for distributions, and that the fiduciary is properly discharged. If distributions are made to guardians or trustees, the lawyer should also provide them with some guidance regarding their duties.

Problem 1-2. Lawyer serves on the board of directors of the local private university, a position that provides her with a great deal of personal satisfaction and favorable publicity. Because of her experience and position in the community she is often consulted with regard to estate-planning matters. She believes strongly in the value of private educational institutions, the need for private philanthropy, and the desirability of taking advantage of the available charitable deductions for gift, income, and estate tax purposes. How free is she to encourage her clients to make gifts to charity? To private educational institutions in general? To the university with which she is connected?

Problem 1-3. This morning Lawyer, L, received an urgent telephone call from a client, Norma Thomas, for whom L had drawn a will several years ago. Norma asked L to prepare a new will for an elderly neighbor, Hedda Jones, whom she has befriended in recent years. According to Norma, Mrs. Jones has suffered a massive heart attack from which she is not expected to recover. However, she said that Mrs. Jones is alert and resting comfortably in the coronary care unit of the Good Shepherd Hospital, which is a few miles from L's office. L had drawn a will for Mrs. Jones several years ago that left her residuary estate to her daughter who lives in another state. Norma told L that Mrs. Jones wants to revoke her old will and leave her relatively small estate in equal shares to Norma and the minister of the church she formerly attended, who has been calling on her recently. Who is Lawyer's client in this matter? How should L proceed?

§1.12. Legal Ethics and Taxes

Lawyers must also be equipped to deal with the ethical issues that will confront them when they prepare tax returns or deal with the tax authorities. The lawyer's role is complicated by the fact that the lawyer's conduct toward the government is subject to the detailed regulations of Treasury Circular 230, 31 C.F.R. part 10 (1966). Thus, in tax practice the lawyer's conduct is governed by both the Code of Professional Responsibility and Treasury Circular 230 — which sometimes conflict. Fortunately, the basic rules do not also conflict.

The Code of Professional Responsibility requires a lawyer to represent a client zealously. *See* Canon 7. However, the lawyer may not participate in a fraud on the government by concealing or misrepresenting facts. In particular, DR 7-102(A)(5) provides that "in his representation of a client, a lawyer shall not knowingly make a false statement of law or fact." This position is buttressed by DR 1-102(A)(4), which prohibits a lawyer from engaging "in conduct involving dishonesty, fraud, deceit, or misrepresentation." Such conduct is also banned by the Treasury rules, the violation of which may cause the lawyer to be disbarred or suspended from practice before the IRS. 31 C.F.R. §10.51(a), (b), (d) (1979).

Where the facts or the law are uncertain, the lawyer may take positions that favor the client — provided that the lawyer acts in good faith.

> Both the disciplinary rules and the ethical considerations condone advancing positions in good faith to test adversary positions. Disciplinary Rule 7-102(A)(2) permits a lawyer to put forth a claim or defense "if it can be supported by good faith arguments for an extension, modification, or reversal of existing law." Ethical Consideration 7-22 provides that a lawyer may "in good faith and within the framework of the law, take steps to test the correctness of a ruling of a tribunal." Ethical Consideration 7-25 permits the lawyer to take "steps in good faith to test the validity of rules. . . ." Sax, Lawyer Responsibility in Tax Shelter Opinions, 34 Tax Law. 5, 37 (1980).

Under these rules a lawyer may not advise a client to claim deductions or credits that are clearly unwarranted. However, uncertain claims may be advanced if the facts are adequately disclosed in the client's return. Hard questions sometimes arise regarding the extent of the disclosure that must be made. Although the ethic may not be perfectly adhered to in practice, the lawyer should recommend full and fair disclosure of the facts regarding questionable positions. *See* Paul, The Lawyer As Tax Adviser, 25 Rocky Mt. L. Rev. 412 (1953), reprinted in Professional Responsibility in Federal Tax Practice 64, 79 (B. Bittker ed. 1970).

Ethical concerns and Treasury rules bar lawyers from advising their clients to play the "tax lottery" game by taking positions for which there is little or no legal support on the chance that their returns will not be audited by the IRS or the unsubstantiated position will not be discovered if their returns are audited. The complexity of the tax law, the relatively high tax rates, and the limited capacity of the IRS to audit returns all tempt lawyers and clients to participate in the tax lottery. Taxpayers are attracted to the lottery because of the small number of individual returns that are audited and the limited economic risk to the taxpayer. "Finally, even if the odds in the lottery come up against the taxpayer and the case is lost, as long as his original position finds sufficient protective coloration against the background of a confused or uncertain statute, the taxpayer is in danger of no greater penalty than simple interest for the tax money 'borrowed' from the Government." Ferguson, Tax Complexity and Compliance — One View from the Department of Justice, U. So. Cal. 30th Tax Inst. 871, 874 (1978).

Assistant Attorney General Ferguson also pointed out that the success of our system of self-assessment depends heavily upon the essential integrity and honesty of taxpayers and their professional advisors. "The system could not survive on a principle of hide-and-seek between the Service and taxpayers. If tax returns were to degenerate into mere first offers, signaling the beginning of a bargaining process, we might well be forced to abandon the income tax as our principal method of sharing the expense of government. Thus, the effective operation of our tax laws depends upon the lawyers, the accountants, and others engaged in the professional practice of tax counselling and return preparation to assure full and fair reporting of tax liabilities." *Id.* at 878.

Lawyers who are fair and reasonably open in their dealings with the tax authorities will find that their work and their words are more readily accepted than those of other lawyers. Here, in a sense, virtue is rewarded. Lawyers with a reputation of high integrity will also be rewarded by the esteem of their colleagues and the benefit of referrals from them. In order to protect their reputation, lawyers must insist on full and complete disclosure by their clients, some of whom may seek to take advantage of a lawyer's good reputation to sanitize a questionable position.

C. LAWYER'S FEES AND ESTATE PLANNING

The area of law which perhaps is most affected by the inflationary spiral and the resulting cost consciousness of the general public is that of estate planning. This results from a twofold attitude problem on the part of the general public: (1) perpetuation of the myth of the $50 will; and (2) the fact that current results are not available in connection with the drawing of a will. . . . [T]he estate lawyer is caught between his client on the one hand seeking rates which, in some cases, are based upon antiquated reasoning, and his partners on the other hand seeking to have estate planning services billed out at the same progressive rates at which the corporate law partner bills his corporate client. Callahan, How to Make Sure Fees for Estate Planning Compensate the Attorney for Work Done, 5 Est. Plan. 322 (1978).

§1.13. *Discussion with Client*

Clients are often fearful of the amount they will be charged for the services of a lawyer, but they are reluctant to broach the subject. They may be relieved if the lawyer raises the subject at the initial interview, which will generally serve the interests of both lawyer and client. Such a recommendation is made in EC 2-19:

> As soon as feasible after a lawyer has been employed, it is desirable that he reach a clear agreement with his client as to the basis of the fee charges to be made. Such a course will not only prevent later misunderstanding, but will also work for good relations between the lawyer and the client. It is usually beneficial to reduce to writing the understanding of the parties regarding the fee, particularly when it is contingent. A lawyer should be mindful that many persons who desire to employ him may have had little or no experience with fee charges of lawyers, and for this reason he should explain fully to such persons the reasons for the particular fee arrangement he proposes.

At the conclusion of the initial conference the lawyer may be able to give the client an estimate of the overall cost of the legal services to be performed for the client. If so, the lawyer should record the estimate and refer to it when a statement is prepared for the client. Prior to sending the client a statement, the lawyer should review the client's file to see if an estimate was given. A failure to review the file may cause unnecessary embarrassment and controversy if the lawyer sends the client a statement for a larger amount without a satisfactory explanation.

§1.14. *Determining Fees for Lifetime Estate-Planning Services*

The lawyer's fee for estate-planning services is usually based either on a fixed fee (*e.g.*, $250 for a will with marital deduction and family trusts) or on an hourly time charge (*e.g.*, $85 per hour). In a particular case the fee may also take into account a variety of other factors. EC 2-18 states that "[t]he fees of a lawyer will vary according to many factors, including the time required, his experience, ability, and reputation, the nature of the employment, the responsibility involved, and the results obtained. Suggested fee schedules and economic reports of state and local bar associations provide some guidance on the subject of reasonable fees." A more complete statement of the factors that should be considered in setting a fee is contained in DR 2-106(B).

Historically, lawyers have not been adequately compensated for lifetime estate-planning services. Minimum fee schedules printed in the 1970s and current ads for law clinics suggest charges of $25 for a "simple" will and $40 to $50 for substantially identical wills for husband and

wife. The nominal charge for the preparation of wills was often traceable
to the practice of using wills as "loss leaders." The lawyer's present loss in
drafting a will would be made up by the future compensation to be
received for acting as attorney for the client's personal representative.
That practice led some critics to charge that lawyers do not adequately
inform their clients about inter vivos trusts and other will substitutes that
might eliminate the necessity for an administration proceeding. The
charge may have some substance in states such as California, which base
the compensation of the personal representative's lawyer on the amount
of the estate subject to administration.

Lawyers are now usually compensated more reasonably for lifetime
estate-planning services. Clients who are accustomed to paying only a
small fee for estate-planning services object to the trend. However, it
may actually be in their interest to pay the lawyer at essentially the same
level the lawyer receives for other types of work. If so, the effort exerted
and the quality of the documents prepared by the lawyer should increase. Overall, the trend toward basing the amount of fees upon a
realistic hourly charge or a reasonable fixed fee is a desirable one, which
reduces or eliminates a potential conflict of interest. The lawyer's fee
should reflect the cost of providing the service to the client, including the
research and development of will and trust forms, the cost of sophisticated word processing equipment, and the use of legal assistants. In
preparing and presenting a statement, the lawyer should consider that
clients are more willing to pay substantial fees for estate-planning services if the lawyer shows them how the planning will save costs and taxes.
Of course, some of the projected savings may not occur until the client's
death. Tax estimates help show the savings that will result from the plan
recommended by the lawyer. Also, the client's reaction to the lawyer's
statement may be more favorable if it shows the portion of the fee that is
deductible for income tax purposes. *See* §1.17, *infra*.

§1.15. Determining Fees for Estate Administration Services

Until recently the compensation of a personal representative's lawyer was
usually based upon a fee schedule that was published by the local bar
association. Under them the amount of the fee was determined by applying a decreasing percentage scale to some measure of the value of the
decedent's property, typically either the property subject to administration, plus income received during probate, or the total gross estate for
federal estate or state inheritance tax purposes. In California the personal representative and the lawyer for the personal representative are
each entitled to a statutory fee for their ordinary services ranging from
4% on the first $15,000 to 1% on amounts of the total estate accounted for
in excess of $1,000,000. Cal. Prob. Code §§901, 910 (West 1981 Supp.).
The fee determined under such schedules sometimes bears little or no

relation to the time or expertise required, the results obtained, or the responsibilities undertaken. The trend is clearly away from rigid adherence to minimum fee schedules for the purpose of determining fees for estate administration services. Some local and state bar associations have abolished their recommended fee schedules. However, some fee schedules are still published as guides regarding the general fee practices in the local legal community.

The legality of most types of fee schedules under the Sherman Act is uncertain after the Supreme Court's decision in Goldfarb v. Virginia State Bar, 421 U.S. 773 (1975). *Goldfarb* held that a minimum fee schedule promulgated by a county bar association that was sanctioned by the state bar association was not exempt from the Sherman Act under the "learned profession" or "state action" exceptions. Rather, the Court concluded that it violated the Act because it resulted in the fixing of the prices of services that affect interstate commerce. The Court pointed out that a different issue would be involved in the case of a "purely advisory fee schedule issued to provide guidelines, or an exchange of price information without a showing of an actual restraint on trade." 421 U.S. at 781. The Court also did not pass on the legality of fee schedules prescribed by the state; however, the opinion did recognize the interest of the state in regulating the legal profession.

Widespread public and professional concern regarding the amount of fees charged in estate administration proceedings led to the adoption of the Statement of Principles Regarding Probate Practices and Expenses by the Real Property, Probate and Trust Section of the American Bar Association. The Statement, which appears at 8 Real Prop., Prob. & Tr. J. 293 (1973), is intended to provide guidelines to legislatures, courts, and bar associations when investigating, evaluating, and establishing standards with respect to the fees of personal representatives and their lawyers. It was adopted by the ABA House of Delegates in 1975.

The Statement evidences the shift away from rigid adherence to fee schedules and emphasizes the desirability of basing the compensation of the personal representative and his or her lawyers upon the value of services each actually renders. It calls for significant weight to be given the following factors:

A. The extent of the responsibilities assumed and the results obtained;
B. The time and labor required, the novelty and difficulty of the questions involved, and the skills required to perform the services properly;
C. The sufficiency of assets properly available to pay for the services.

Those factors are among the ones specified in DR 2-106(B) for use in determining the reasonableness of a lawyer's fee. The Statement also recognizes that a personal representative or attorney is entitled to compensation for services he is required to render in connection with non-probate property even though the owner of the property did not request the services. Accordingly, the personal representative could charge a surviving joint tenant with some of the cost of valuing and determining taxes on joint tenancy or trust property. Point 4 of the Statement allows an attorney to serve as personal representative and as counsel to the personal representative and to be compensated for his service in both capacities. Most jurisdictions allow an attorney to be compensated for serving in both roles, but California does not, unless authorized by the will. Duque & Watts, Fees & Commissions, in 1 California Decedent Estate Administration §18.10 (Cal. CEB 1970).

> **Problem 1-4.** Lawyer is a tax and estate-planning expert. Several times in recent years she has provided expert advice to Adam, a lawyer who lives in a rural area where he has a general practice. The work generally involved reviewing wills and trusts that Adam had drawn. In each case Lawyer billed Adam at a straight hourly rate (which is now $125). Last week Adam asked Lawyer to review an estate tax return for a large estate that was due to be filed on Friday. Adam had prepared the return, which he insisted had to be filed without any extensions.
>
> When Lawyer reviewed the return she found that the estate consisted primarily of valuable farm land that was left to a trust in a way that would allow it to be valued under the special use valuation method. The calculations she made indicated that the estate tax could be reduced by $200,000 if the special use method were used. She immediately called Adam, who said that he had heard of special use valuation but really didn't know much about it. He was delighted with her discovery and asked her to make the necessary revisions to the return. Lawyer did so at some inconvenience to herself and her clients and the revised return was filed on time.
>
> Lawyer has asked your advice regarding the fee she should charge Adam for working on the return. On the one hand she feels that her work is worth at least $20,000 (10% of the apparent tax saving). However, on the other hand, she devoted only about 12 hours to the job, which would indicate a basic fee of $1,500 at her hourly rate. She believes Adam would be shocked by a fee in excess of $2,500.

§1.16. Satisfying the Fee

In some cases clients have agreed to make specified testamentary gifts to their attorneys in lieu of paying for the lawyers' services currently. Arrangements of that type should generally be avoided because of the uncertainty of payment at any time, possible ethical violations, and the absence of any income tax advantages to the client or lawyer. For example, Wolder v. Commissioner, 493 F.2d 608 (2d Cir. 1974), held that a specific bequest to a lawyer pursuant to a contract with the decedent was income to the lawyer and deductible by the estate for estate tax purposes. "A transfer in the form of a bequest was the method that the parties chose to compensate Mr. Wolder for his legal services, and that transfer is therefore subject to taxation, whatever its label whether by federal or by local law may be." 493 F.2d at 612.

§1.17. *Income Tax Deductibility of Estate-Planning Fees*

It is often highly important for a client to know the extent to which the lawyer's fee, or any part of it, will be deductible for federal income tax purposes. If a significant portion of the fee will be deductible, the client may wish to take that factor into account in connection with the client's overall income tax planning. The client may wish to accelerate the payment into the current tax year or defer it to the next, depending upon a variety of tax considerations. The lawyer should, of course, attempt to accommodate the client's wishes to the extent it is feasible to do so.

The deductibility of fees for income tax purposes is largely governed by §212, which provides:

> In the case of an individual, there shall be allowed as a deduction all ordinary and necessary expenses paid or incurred during the taxable year. . . .
> (2) for the management, conservation, or maintenance of property held for the production of income; or
> (3) in connection with the determination, collection or refund of any tax.

There is a great deal of tension between this section and §262, which disallows deductions for "personal, living or family expenses" not otherwise expressly allowed. The regulations under §212 reflect the narrow view the IRS has usually taken regarding the deductibility of fees for lifetime estate-planning services. However, the regulations are not necessarily good predictors of the outcome of litigation in a disputed case. In general the courts have been more generous to taxpayers. *See, e.g.,* Carpenter v. United States, 338 F.2d 366 (Ct. Cl. 1964); Nancy R. Bagley, 8 T.C. 130 (1947), *acq.,* 1947-1 C.B. 1. Overall, the Court of Claims seems to be the most hospitable forum from the taxpayer's perspective.

The position of the IRS was relaxed somewhat in Rev. Rul. 72-545, 1972-2 C.B. 179, which held that a deduction is allowable for the portion of a lawyer's fee attributable to advice regarding the federal income, gift, and estate tax consequences of divorce. The ruling is based upon §212(3) and Reg. §1.212-1(1). The latter provides that:

> Expenses paid or incurred by an individual in connection with the determination, collection, or refund of any tax, whether the taxing authority be Federal, State or municipal, and whether the tax be income, estate, gift, property, or any other tax, are deductible. Thus, expenses paid or incurred by a taxpayer for tax counsel or expenses paid or incurred in connection with the preparation of his tax returns or in connection with any proceedings involved in determining the extent of tax liability or in contesting his tax liability are deductible.

Although the regulation speaks of deductions for the advice of tax counsel, the IRS has generally not allowed deductions for advice regarding the tax consequences of donative transfers.

Attorney's fees incurred in connection with a trade or business are deductible under §162. However, personal, living, and family expenses are not deductible by reason of §262. Specifically, the cost of preparing a will is a nondeductible personal expense. Estate of Helen S. Pennell, 4 B.T.A. 1039 (1926). Expenses incurred in connection with the defense or perfection of title to property are generally not deductible. *See* §263 (capital expenditures) and Reg. §1.212-1(k). On the other hand, if the expenses were incurred in connection with a contest that determines the amount of taxable income to be received by the taxpayer, the expenses are deductible under §212.

§1.18. Allocating the Fee

The lawyer should keep adequate records of the time devoted to various work performed for a client in order to permit the fee to be allocated to deductible and nondeductible parts. It is not enough to show that the work performed by the lawyer had some tax consequences. Instead, "the plaintiff must show that there is a reasonable basis for allocating a portion of his legal fees to tax counselling advice . . . this court has found that a good faith allocation by the attorney who performed the services may be sufficient to meet plaintiff's burden." Hall v. United States, 78-1 U.S.T.C. ¶9126, 41 A.F.T.R.2d 78-367 (Ct. Cl., Trial Judge 1978).

The majority and dissenting opinions in Sidney Merians, 60 T.C. 187 (1973), illustrate the confusion that exists with regard to the deductibility of fees for tax advice rendered in connection with estate planning. There, "[t]he legal services also included the preparation of wills for Dr. and Mrs. Merians, taking into consideration current requirements with respect to the qualification for the marital deduction; the establishment of an irrevocable trust for the primary benefit of Mrs. Merians; the transfer to that trust of certain corporate stock; the dissolution of the corporation; and the creation of a partnership, with the trust as a limited partner, to hold the real estate which the corporation had owned." In addition a life insurance trust for the benefit of the taxpayer's wife was created and gift tax returns were prepared and filed. An unitemized bill for 42.8 hours of legal services at $50 per hour was submitted and paid by Dr. Merians. The taxpayer contended that the fee pertained only to services regarding tax matters and was fully deductible under §212(3). The IRS stated in its brief that "there is a probability that some of the legal fee represented services which are deductible under section 212(3)" but contended that the amount could not be determined. Based largely upon the concession of the IRS that some portion of the fee was incurred for deductible services, a majority of the Tax Court allowed the taxpayer to deduct 20% of the total fee for legal advice regarding tax matters.

In establishing an estate plan, the court said, "choices made for personal non-tax reasons may have tax implications, but the consideration of such implications does not convert into tax advice the advice given concerning non-tax problems." Three judges concurred in opinions expressing the view that the taxpayer might also be entitled to deduct some of the fee under §212(2). Several dissenters believed the fee represented a personal expense that was not deductible. The principal dissent, by Judge Whithey, contended that only the portion of the fee attributable to the gift tax returns was deductible. The remainder, he contended, was entitled to a deduction neither under §212(2) nor §212(3). "However, expenses paid or incurred as in the instant proceeding for legal services in rearranging ownership of such property by means of a trust, or to minimize the taxation of such property at some time in the future are not deductible from gross income under section 212(2)." Furthermore, he urged, "the words of section 212(3), 'determinations, collections, and refunds,' connote an appraisal of tax liability on the basis of past or of settled events, not a molding of future events to reduce taxes." All in all, the decision did very little to clarify the issue.

Problem 1-5. Clara consulted Lawyer, L, in January regarding a gift of income-producing property that she planned to make to her son, Donald. L counselled Clara regarding the selection of the property to give, prepared the transfer documents, and supervised the execution and recording of the documents of transfer. L later assisted Clara in preparing a federal gift tax return (form 709) that reported the gifts. L's time records indicate that a total of 5 hours was devoted to Clara's affairs, of which 1 hour was attributable to preparation of the gift tax return. If L charges Clara $100 per hour, how much of L's fee would be deductible for federal income tax purposes?

Problem 1-6. Earlier this year Lawyer, L, prepared a revocable trust for Homer, under which all of the income is payable to Homer for life. The principal of the trust consists of income-producing securities, all of which were transferred to the trustee when the trust was executed. At the same time L prepared a simple pour over will and a so-called living will for Homer. L has allocated 6 hours to the preparation of the trust and advice regarding its tax consequences and 1 hour to the preparation of the other documents. If L charges $100 per hour, how much of the fee would be deductible by Homer for income tax purposes? Will the trustee's fees for administering the trust be deductible by Homer? How about the fees L charges the trust for legal services regarding administration of the trust? How would your answers differ if the trust were an irrevocable one in which Homer did not retain any interest?

§1.19. Deductibility of Post-Mortem Estate-Planning Fees

The fees of the personal representative and his or her lawyer are deductible for estate tax or income tax purposes, but not both. §642(g). *See* §12.15, *infra*. Under the regulations a portion of a deduction may be deducted for income tax purposes and the remainder for estate tax purposes. Reg. §1.642(g)-2. Under §2053 the fees are deductible whether they are incurred with respect to property subject to claims or not subject to claims. Regs. §§20.2053-3(c), -8. However, fees incurred by beneficiaries are generally not deductible by the estate (they are not administration expenses) or by the beneficiaries (they are personal in nature).

§1.20. Sample Estate-Planning Data Collection Form

Date _____

CONFIDENTIAL ESTATE-PLANNING DATA

I. General Information

	Client	*Client's Spouse*
Name	_____	_____
Occupation	_____	_____
Date and place of birth	_____	_____
Home address	_____	
	_____	Telephone _____
Bus. telephone:	_____	_____
Soc. Sec. No.	_____	_____

Date and place of marriage _____

Length of residence in this state _____

Prior residences during marriage _____

Prior marriages _____

    (Attach a copy of decree of dissolution and other documents
    regarding property settlement and custody of children.)

Describe any agreement between client and spouse regarding property
(ante-nuptial or post-nuptial agreements). _____

_____

(Attach a copy of any written agreement.)

II. Children

1.	2.
Name _____	Name _____
Date and place	Date and place
of birth and	of birth and
age _____	age _____
Soc. Sec. No. _____	Soc. Sec. No. _____
Address _____	Address _____
_____	_____
Occupation _____	Occupation _____
Name of spouse _____	Name of spouse _____
Names and ages	Names and ages
of children _____	of children _____
_____	_____
Special needs of	Special needs of
this child _____	this child _____
Note if adopted,	Note if adopted,
divorced, or	divorced, or
separated _____	separated _____

[Add further blanks for children as required.]

III. Parents, Brothers, and Sisters

1. Parents

	Client		*Client's Spouse*	
Names	_____		_____	
	_____		_____	
Address	_____		_____	
	_____		_____	
Health	M _____	F _____	M _____	F _____
Age or date of death	M _____	F _____	M _____	F _____
Estimated size of estate	M _____	F _____	M _____	F _____

2. Brothers and Sisters

	Client	*Client's Spouse*
Names and ages (or dates of death)	_____	_____
	_____	_____
	_____	_____
	_____	_____

3. Are any persons other than minor children dependent on client or client's spouse? If so, describe relationship and degree of dependency.

_____

_____

_____

IV. Gifts and Inheritances

1. Describe the date and amount of any large* gifts that have been made to client or client's spouse. _____

2. Describe any inheritance that client or client's spouse has received from any person. _____

3. Describe any gifts or inheritances that client or client's spouse expects to receive from any person. _____

4. Describe any large gifts that client or client's spouse has made to any person in any one year. _____

    Please attach a copy of any state or federal gift tax returns filed by client or client's spouse.

5. Describe any gifts that client or client's spouse expects to make to any person in any one year. _____

6. Attach a copy of any trust under which client or client's spouse is a beneficiary or holds any power of appointment.

7. Attach a copy of any will or trust agreement that has been executed by client or client's spouse.

V. Asset Information

1. Real property. At some point we will need to see copies of all deeds in order to verify the manner in which title to the property is held. Details

---

* For purposes of this form a "large" gift is one of more than $3,000 if made prior to 1982 or more than $10,000 if made after 1981. This ties in to the amount of the allowable annual per donee federal gift tax exclusion.

regarding each parcel of real property may be written on a separate sheet of paper and attached to this form. In each case indicate the net value of the asset.

	Client	Client's Spouse
a. Residence	_____	_____
b. Recreational property	_____	_____
c. Investment property	_____	_____
Total value of real property	_____	_____

2. Publicly traded stocks and bonds. Details regarding each issue of stock or series of bonds may be provided on an attachment. Again, we will need to verify the manner in which title to the securities is held.

	Client	Client's Spouse
Common stocks	_____	_____
Preferred stocks	_____	_____
Bonds and debentures	_____	_____
Tax-exempt bonds	_____	_____
Total value of stocks and bonds	_____	_____

3. Closely held stock. Give details regarding any interests you have in a corporation that is closely held (*i.e.*, the stock is not publicly traded).

4. Accounts in financial institutions.

	Client	Client's Spouse
Checking		
Bank name and location	_____	_____
Approximate balance	_____	_____
Savings		
Bank name and location	_____	_____
Approximate balance	_____	_____
Certificates of deposit		
Bank name and location	_____	_____
Amounts	_____	_____

5. Life insurance.

	On Life of Client	On Life of Client's Spouse
Company	_____	_____
Face Amount	_____	_____
Loans outstanding on policy	_____	_____
Type (term, ordinary life, or other)	_____	_____
Owner of policy	_____	_____
Beneficiaries designated in policy 1.	_____	_____
2.	_____	_____

[Repeat blanks as required for additional policies.]

6.   Tangible personal property.

	Client	Client's Spouse
Jewelry	_____	_____
Antiques	_____	_____
Art objects	_____	_____
Automobiles	_____	_____
Boats	_____	_____
Stamps, coins, or other collections	_____	_____

7.   Describe any employee benefit plans in which client or client's spouse has an interest. Indicate whether or not the plans are qualified plans under the federal income tax law, the approximate value of interests in the plans, and how payments will be made in the event of the death or retirement of the participant.

Client: _____

_____

Client's Spouse: _____

_____

8.   Describe any interests that client or client's spouse has in any other deferred compensation contracts or plans. _____

_____

9.   Describe any other assets in which client or client's spouse may have an interest. _____

_____

10. Describe any debts of client or client's spouse that are not reflected in any of the lists of assets. _____

_____

11. What is the approximate present net worth of client and client's spouse, excluding life insurance?

Client: _____
Client's Spouse: _____

12. Location of any safe deposit boxes maintained by client or client's spouse.

Client	Client's Spouse
_____	_____
_____	_____
_____	_____

13. List the resale value of club memberships of client and client's spouse.

Client: _____

_____

Client's Spouse: _____

_____

VI. Advisors

Please list the names, addresses, and telephone numbers of other persons who serve as advisors to client or client's spouse.

	Client	*Client's Spouse*
Other lawyers	_____	_____
	_____	_____
Stockbroker	_____	_____
	_____	_____
Investment counsellor	_____	_____
	_____	_____
Life insurance	_____	_____
	_____	_____
Accountant	_____	_____
	_____	_____
Real estate advisors	_____	_____
	_____	_____
Physician	_____	_____
	_____	_____
Dentist	_____	_____
	_____	_____
Minister, priest, rabbi, or other religious counselor	_____	_____
	_____	_____

§1.21. *Federal Estate Tax Worksheet*

The letter designation of items on this worksheet corresponds to their designation in the federal estate tax return (Form 706). If an estate does not include any community property, all entries in Part I should be made in the column headed "Total."

	One-half of Community Property	*Separate Property*	*Total*
I. Gross Estate:			
A. Real property			
B. Stocks and bonds			
C. Mortgages, notes, and cash			
D. Insurance on decedent's life			
E. Jointly owned property			

F.   Miscellaneous
     assets
G.   Transfers during
     lifetime
H.   Powers of
     appointment
I.   Annuities   _____   _____   _____
Total $ $
     Total gross estate $_____

II. Deductions:
     J.   Funeral expenses (§2053) (The
          amount allocable to decedent's
          estate differs from state to state
          where community property is
          involved) $_____
     K.   Administration expenses
          (§2053) (Entire amount attrib-
          utable to tax matters, including
          costs of appraisal, etc.)   _____
     L.   Debts, mortgages, and liens
          (§2053) (One-half of com-
          munity property debts, etc., and
          usually pro rata share of joint
          note where others are also
          liable)   _____
     M.   Casualty losses (§2054)   _____
     N.   Marital deduction (§2056)   _____
     P.   Charitable deduction (§2055)   _____
          Total deductions $_____

III. Computation of Estate Tax:
     A.   Taxable estate (total gross estate
          less total deductions) $_____
     B.   Post-1976 taxable gifts other
          than gifts includible in gross
          estate   _____
     C.   Total of (A) and (B)   _____
     D.   Tentative tax on (C) from rate
          schedule (§2001(c))   _____
     E.   *Less:*
          1.   Gift taxes paid on post-1976
               gifts   _____
          2.   Unified credit (§2010)   _____
          3.   Credit for state death taxes
               (§2011)   _____

4. Credit for gift tax on pre-
1977 gifts includible in
gross estate (§2012)   _____

5. Credit for tax on prior
transfers (§2013)   _____

6. Credit for foreign death
taxes (§2014)   _____   _____

F. Estate tax liability $ _____

The payment of the federal estate tax may be extended for reasonable cause (§6161) or to the extent attributable to a reversionary or remainder interest (§6163). *See* §§12.37 to 12.38, *infra.* Payments may be extended over a 15-year period to the extent the tax is attributable to an interest in a closely held business (*see* worksheet for §6166, §11.32, and §12.40, *infra*). Also, stock included in the decedent's estate may be redeemed under §303 (*see* worksheet for §303, §11.21, *infra*).

Some issues of United States Treasury bonds may be redeemed at par plus accrued interest in payment of the federal estate tax to the extent they are included in the decedent's gross estate. *See* §12.41, *infra.*

§1.22. Worksheet for Computing Maximum Allowable Federal Estate Tax Marital Deduction for Estates of Persons Dying Prior to January 1, 1982

I. Computation of deduction based on
adjusted gross estate (do not complete if estate consists entirely of
community property):

A. Gross estate $ _____

B. *Less:*

1. Community property (from
Estate Tax Worksheet)   _____

2. Expenses, debts, taxes, etc.,
allowed by §§2053 and 2054
(items II.J, K, and L from
Estate Tax Worksheet)*   _____   _____

C. Adjusted gross estate   _____

D. One-half of item (D)
(§2056(c)(1)(A)(ii))   _____

---

* Where estate includes community property, a portion of these items is deducted according to this formula:

$$\frac{\text{gross estate} - \text{community property}}{\text{total gross estate}} \times \text{§§2053 and 2054 items}$$

II.   Alternative "minimum" marital
      deduction:
      A.   Maximum amount
           (§2056(c)(1)(A)(i)) $ 250,000
      B.   Community property reduction:
           1.   Community property in-
                cluded in gross estate   _____
           2.   *Less:* portion of §§2053 and
                2054 deductions attrib-
                utable to community
                property

                community
                 property   ×   §§2053 and
                total gross   2054 items
                   estate   =_____   _____
      C.   Alternative minimum deduc-
           tion ((A) less (B)) $ _____

III. Maximum marital deduction:
      A.   Insert greater of I.D or II.C. $ _____
      B.   *Less:* Excess of gift tax marital deduction
           allowed for post-1976 gifts to spouse (other
           than gifts included in decedent's estate under
           §2035) *over* one-half of amount of post-1976
           gifts to spouse that are required to be included
           in gift tax return. (This reduction only applies
           where there are post-1976 gifts of separate
           property that total less than $200,000.)   =_____
      C.   Maximum marital deduction $ _____

BIBLIOGRAPHY

 I.   Legal interviewing and counselling:
          Freeman, H. & Weihofen, H., Clinical Law Training: Inter-
             viewing and Counseling (1972)
          Shaffer, T. & Redmount, R., Legal Interviewing & Counseling
             (1980)
          Watson, A., The Lawyer in the Interviewing and Counseling
             Process (1976)

 II. Collection of estate-planning data:
          Bush, Estate Planning: The Client Interview, N.Y.U. 33d Inst.
             Fed. Tax. 3 (1975) (includes an extensive form of question-
             naire)

Mucklestone, The Legal Assistant in Estate Planning, 10 Real Prop., Prob. & Tr. J. 263 (1975)

Wilkins, How an Attorney Can Use a Checklist to Better Organize an Estate Planning Practice, 5 Est. Plan. 30 (1978)

III. Professional responsibility:

Aronson, R. & Weckstein, D., Professional Responsibility (1980)

Comment, Considerations of Professional Responsibility in Probate Matters, 51 Neb. L. Rev. 456 (1972)

Drinker, H., Legal Ethics (1953)

Eckhardt, The Estate Planning Lawyer's Problems: Malpractice & Ethics, U. Miami 8th Inst. Est. Plan., Ch. 6 (1974)

Heckerling, Estate Planning Malpractice: What Standard of Care?, 16 Tr. & Est. 728 (1977)

Professional Responsibility in Federal Tax Practice (B. Bittker ed. 1970)

Symposium on Education in the Professional Responsibilities of Lawyers, 41 U. Colo. L. Rev. 303 (1969)

Wolfman, B. & Holden, J., Ethical Problems in Federal Tax Practice (1981)

IV. Deductibility of estate-planning fees:

Allington, Deductibility of Estate Planning Fees, 60 A.B.A.J. 482 (1974)

Comment, Considerations of Professional Responsibility in Probate Matters, 51 Neb. L. Rev. 456 (1972)

Gibbs, Post-Gilmore — Recent Trends in the Deductibility of Professional Fees, 23 S.W.L.J. 644 (1969)

Grisham, Deductibility of Legal Expenses for Income Tax Purposes, 26th U. So. Cal. 26th Tax Inst. 875 (1974)

Symposium on Education in the Professional Responsibilities of Lawyers, 41 U. Colo. L. Rev. 303 (1969)

Weaver, The Merians Decision: What Are Its Implications for Tax Planning Deductions, 39 J. Tax 348 (1973)

Wormser, Charging for Estate Planning — Methods and Problems, U. Miami 10th Inst. Est. Plan., Ch. 8 (1976)

CHAPTER 2

Basic Transfer Tax Laws and Estate-Planning Strategies

A. INTRODUCTION

§2.1. Scope

This chapter summarizes the main features of the gift, estate, and generation-skipping taxes and reviews some of the important basic estate-planning tax strategies. Depending upon the reader's background, the chapter may serve either as an initial orientation to the subject or as a refresher. In any case, it provides a useful preview to the remainder of the book, which explores the taxes in more detail and examines the various devices that can be used to carry out the basic planning strategies. The income taxation of trusts and estates is summarized in Chapters 10 and 12 and relevant income tax considerations are discussed throughout the book. Later materials also consider the major nontax considerations that bear on the selection and implementation of various estate plans.

The next part of this chapter opens with an historical note regarding the estate and gift taxes, which is followed by a brief discussion of the unified transfer tax system adopted in 1976. Subsequent parts review the highlights of the current gift and estate tax laws. Then the focus shifts to the generation-skipping tax, an important new tax added by the 1976 Act. The chapter closes with an examination of tax strategies commonly employed in estate planning.

B. UNIFIED TRANSFER TAX SYSTEM

§2.2. *Historical Note*

Federal inheritance taxes were imposed for 3 short periods between 1797 and 1902 in order to meet temporary fiscal emergencies. The federal estate tax was adopted in 1916, largely to finance the cost of military preparations for participation in World War I. *See* Eisenstein, The Rise and Decline of the Estate Tax, 11 Tax L. Rev. 223, 230-231 (1956). The tax has remained essentially the same, although refinements have been made over the years to meet new challenges and to deal with changed circumstances. For example, important changes have been made in the taxation of powers of appointment (§2041) and of life insurance (§2042). The adoption of a limited marital deduction in 1948, §2056, was perhaps the most important single change made between 1916 and 1976. The most sweeping changes in the federal transfer tax laws were made by the 1976 Act, which unified the gift and estate tax structure and added the generation-skipping tax, and by the 1981 Act, which removed the quantitative limits on the amount of the marital deduction.

The first federal gift tax was adopted in 1924 and repealed 2 years later. That short-lived tax was seriously flawed by the fact that it was calculated annually on a noncumulative basis. It was also weakened by a large annual exemption. The existing graduated, cumulative gift tax was adopted in more or less its present form in 1932. It was intended to help bolster federal tax revenues, which had sagged with the onset of the Great Depression, and to supplement the income and estate taxes. A gift tax provides valuable protection for income and estate taxes by imposing a tax on transfers that would deplete the amount of the donor's income and the size of the donor's estate. Perhaps because the gift tax was adopted at a later time, the gift and estate taxes were largely independent of each other until their unification in 1976.

The spur for unification was generated by the extraordinary preferences that the dual gift and estate tax system accorded to inter vivos gifts. The main preferences were attributable to 3 basic features of the dual system: First, although the gift and estate tax rate schedules had identical brackets, at each interval the gift tax rate was only 75% of the estate tax rate. Second, the gift tax was based only on the net value of the property transferred (*i.e.*, the gift tax on a transfer was not "grossed up" and included in the tax base). In contrast, the estate tax was based upon the total amount of the decedent's gross estate (*i.e.*, the estate tax itself was included in the tax base). Third, inter vivos gifts were usually not included in the donor's gross estate or otherwise included in the estate tax base.

Although the gift tax was calculated on the cumulative total of gifts made by the donor after June 6, 1932, gifts completed more than 3 years prior to death were generally not included in the donor's estate tax base. Where an inter vivos gift was included in the donor's gross estate, the donor's estate was allowed a credit for any gift tax paid (or due) on the gift. Despite the allowance of the credit, the amount of the gift tax was not included in the estate tax base. In fact, a deduction was allowed for any gift tax that was due but unpaid at the time of death. Deathbed gifts were strongly encouraged by the availability of the credit and the failure to include the amount of the gift tax in the donor's estate tax base.

The operation of the dual transfer tax system under the pre-1977 law is illustrated by the following example:

Example 2-1. X and Y each owned property worth $2,000,000. X made no gifts during his lifetime. Accordingly, when he died, his entire estate was subject to the old estate tax. Under the old rates an estate tax of $726,200 would be due from X's executor, which would leave his family with $1,273,800. Y made a lifetime gift of $1,000,000 to her family, which would be subject to a gift tax of $227,625. The remaining $772,385 would be subject to an estate tax of $220,035 when she died. Thus, taxes of $447,660 would be paid with respect to Y's transfers, leaving $1,552,340 for her family. By making lifetime gifts Y transferred almost $280,000 more to her family than X, who made no inter vivos gifts.

Commentators frequently charged that the preference shown for inter vivos gifts was unjustified and discriminatory and proposed various remedial steps, including the adoption of a unified transfer tax system. A form of unified transfer tax was advanced in the 1969 tax reform proposals that were published by the Treasury Department. Tax Reform Studies and Proposals, 91st Cong., 1st Sess. (Comm. Print 1969).

In 1976 Congress concluded that the dual transfer tax system was inequitable and undesirable, a situation that it sought to remedy by unifying the existing gift and estate tax systems. Staff, Joint Committee on Taxation, General Explanation of the Tax Reform Act of 1976 526 (1976) (hereinafter referred to as General Explanation of the Tax Reform Act of 1976). The unification largely eliminated the 3 features of the dual system, mentioned above, which were the main causes of the preferential treatment of inter vivos gifts. However, the changes do not require the gift tax paid on a transfer made more than 3 years prior to death to be grossed up and included in the tax base. The 1976 Act also left intact the annual gift tax exclusion, which sheltered annual gifts of $3,000 or less per donee from both the gift and the estate tax. Of course, the 1981 Act increased the amount of the annual exclusion to $10,000 per donee. By regularly making gifts within the amount of the exclusion an individual can transfer a substantial amount of property to the donees completely free of tax. The remaining incentives for making lifetime gifts are discussed in detail in §§7.7 to 7.11, *infra*.

§2.3.   *Unification under the Tax Reform Act of 1976*

The unification was achieved primarily by adopting a single, progressive rate schedule that applies to the cumulative total of lifetime and death-time taxable transfers. As explained below, it also applies in a limited way to the generation-skipping tax. *See* Part E, *infra*. As a result, substantially the same amount of tax will be due from taxpayers who make taxable transfers of equal total amounts, whether or not any of the transfers are made inter vivos. Thus, the large disparity in the tax imposed on the 2 taxpayers discussed in Example 2-1, *supra*, is eliminated under the new scheme. However, in order to avoid any retroactive effect, only the amount of post-1976 gifts is cumulated in calculating the tax. §2001(b)(2).

The unified rate schedule that was adopted in 1976, §2001(c), opened at a higher rate than the prior ones but the rates increased more slowly and ended at a lower rate than before. Also, the Act substituted a single unified credit for the lifetime $30,000 gift tax exemption and the $60,000 estate tax exemption. The unified credit, which applies to lifetime or deathtime transfers, increased in roughly equal annual increments from $30,000 in 1977 to $47,000 in 1981. The $47,000 credit was equal to the tax imposed on a taxable transfer of $175,625. The amount of a taxable transfer sheltered by the credit is called the "credit equivalent." The adoption of the unified credit eliminated the estate tax on about two-thirds of the estates that would otherwise have been required to file estate tax returns. The 1981 Act increased the unified credit in annual stages from $47,000 in 1981 to $192,800 in 1987 and thereafter, which further diminished the number of estates required to file estate tax returns. The increases in the unified credit and the credit equivalent are shown in Table 2-1. The increase in the amount of the

Table 2-1

Year	Unified Credit	Credit Equivalent
1981	$ 47,000	$175,625
1982	62,800	225,000
1983	79,300	275,000
1984	96,300	325,000
1985	121,800	400,000
1986	155,800	500,000
1987	192,800	600,000

unified credit also affects the lowest marginal rate at which any tax will be due from an estate. Specifically, the marginal rate is 32% for 1982; 34% for 1983, 1984, and 1985; and 37% for 1986 and 1987.

The 1981 Act also reduced the maximum gift and estate tax rates by 5% annually for the following 4 years. Between 1981 and 1985 the maximum rate will decrease from 70% to 50%. However, no reductions were made in the rates payable by estates of $2,500,000 or less. The effect of the reduction in the maximum rate is shown in Table 2-2.

Table 2-2

Year	Maximum Rate	Applies to Amounts Over
1981	70%	$5,000,000
1982	65%	4,000,000
1983	60%	3,500,000
1984	55%	3,000,000
1985	50%	2,500,000

The decrease in the maximum rate encourages wealthy persons to take advantage of the unlimited marital deduction to defer payment of the estate tax until the death of the surviving spouse. The reduction in the maximum rate alone can make the use of the unlimited marital deduction pay off handsomely where at least one spouse dies prior to 1985. For example, in the case of a decedent dying in 1982, the deferral of the tax could reduce the tax rate applicable to amounts in excess of $4,000,000 by 15% (from a maximum rate of 65% on the death of the first spouse to a maximum rate of 50% on the death of the surviving spouse after 1985).

Between 1981 and 1987 the "spread" between the lowest marginal rate at which any estate tax is payable and the maximum estate tax rate will shrink from 38% (70% − 32%) to only 13% (50% − 37%). This shrinkage will, in effect, increase the advantages of deferring the payment of any estate tax and decrease the advantages of equalizing the sizes of the spouses' estates. A consideration of the relative advantages of deferral and equalization must take other factors into account, including the effect of inflation on the amount of property subject to tax and the return that can be earned on taxes that are deferred.

The effect of the unification is most evident when it comes to calculating the estate tax due from the estate of a person who made taxable gifts after December 31, 1976. First a "tentative tax" is determined by applying the unified rate schedule, §2001(c), to the sum of the post-1976 taxable gifts and the taxable estate. Then, the estate tax is determined by subtracting the amount of gift tax paid on post-1976 gifts. Pre-1977 gifts are not included in the tax base and no credit is allowed for any gift tax paid with respect to them. The amount of the estate tax thus calculated is then reduced by the unified credit allowable for the year of the decedent's death. §2010(a). The unified credit is always allowed in the full amount because all post-1976 taxable gifts are included in the base upon which the estate tax is calculated, either as an adjusted taxable gift or as an item included in the donor's gross estate. Credits are also allowed against the estate tax for state death taxes (§2011); taxes paid on prior transfers (§2013); and for foreign death taxes (§2014).

Example 2-2. T made taxable gifts of $150,000 prior to 1977 and taxable gifts of $150,000 in 1981. T made no more gifts and died in 1985 leaving a taxable estate of $500,000. T paid a gift tax of $2,000 on the 1981 gifts because the tax on the gifts ($49,000) exceeded the amount of the unified credit allowed for that year ($47,000). The gift tax liability is calculated as follows:

Taxable gifts prior to 1977	$150,000
Taxable gifts in 1981	150,000
Lifetime total of taxable gifts	$300,000
Tentative tax on all taxable gifts	87,800
Less: Tentative tax on pre-1981 gifts	38,800
Gift tax on 1981 gifts	$ 49,000
Less: Unified credit	47,000
Gift tax payable for 1981	$ 2,000

An estate tax of $77,500 is due from T's estate, calculated as follows:

Post-1976 taxable gifts		$150,000
Taxable estate		500,000
Tax base		$650,000
Tentative tax		211,300
Less: Gift tax paid on post-1976 gifts		2,000
Estate tax		$209,300
Less:		
Unified credit	$121,800	
State death tax credit	10,000	131,800
Estate tax payable		$ 77,500

The unification of the gift and estate tax and the adoption of the generation-skipping tax (*see* §§2.19 to 2.26, *infra*) probably did improve the overall equity of the transfer tax system and sealed some loopholes. In addition, a great many estates were relieved of the need to file an estate tax return and to pay a federal transfer tax. Unfortunately, the changes increased the complexity of the transfer tax laws, which inevitably increased the compliance costs and the incidence of estate-planning malpractice. The amount of the unified credit in the years after 1987 probably will be indexed or other provisions will be made for periodic increases in order to offset the effects of inflation.

C.   FEDERAL GIFT TAX HIGHLIGHTS

§2.4.   Basic Nature of the Federal Gift Tax

This part presents a basic overview of the main features of the federal gift tax law. The tax and nontax considerations involved in making noncharitable gifts are reviewed in Chapter 7, *infra,* and those concerning charitable gifts are reviewed in Chapter 8, *infra.*

The federal gift tax is an excise tax imposed on the transfer of property by a gift during any calendar year. §2501(a)(1). It applies although the identity of the donee may not be known or ascertainable at the time of the gift. The donor is primarily liable for payment of the tax. §2502(d).

Neither the Code nor the regulations attempt to define the term "gift"; however, the regulations explain that the tax extends to "all transactions whereby property or property rights or interests are gratuitously passed or conferred upon another, regardless of the means or device employed." Reg. §25.2511-1(c). The tax applies to all gratuitous transfers, whether direct or indirect, whether outright or in trust, and whether the property transferred is real or personal, tangible or intangible. §2511(a); Reg. §25.2511-1(a).

> **Example 2-3.** Father, F, sold 1,000 shares of XYZ, Inc. common stock to his daughter, D, for $10 per share on a day when the mean price of the stock on an established exchange was $25 per share. F made a gift to D of $15 per share — the difference between the mean price of $25 per share and the price he received. The transaction was a part-sale, part-gift and not a bona fide business transaction. No income tax deduction is allowable when there is a "loss" on the sale or exchange of property between related taxpayers, §267. D's carryover basis in the stock is determined under §1015.

Exclusion for Payment of Tuition and Medical Expenses. The 1981 Act added §2503(e), which allows a gift tax exclusion for a tuition payment made directly to an educational institution described in §170(b)(1)(A)(ii) or for the payment of medical expenses (including medical insurance) directly to the individual or organization providing the services. Rev. Rul. 82-98, 1982-1 C.B. — . The exclusion is allowable regardless of the relationship, or absence of relationship, between the donor and the donee. Note that the exclusion applies only where the payment is made directly to the educational institution or medical services provider; reimbursement to the donee as intermediary does not qualify. Insofar as educational expenses are concerned, the exclusion extends only to tuition payments although a strong argument can be made for broadening it to cover other associated costs (*e.g.*, books and supplies; room and board). The exclusion for medical expenses extends to those described in §213. However, medical expense payments are excludable regardless of the percentage limitation of §213. The new exclusion is particularly welcome because most taxpayers were probably unaware that the payment of educational or medical expenses constituted a gift under the prior law except to the extent the payor was legally obligated to make the payment.

Completed Gifts. The gift tax applies only to completed gifts. A gift is complete as to any property over which the donor has so parted with dominion and control as to leave the donor with no power to change its disposition. *See* Reg. §25.2511-2. Thus, a gift is incomplete if the transferor retains a general or special power to appoint the property. In such a case the gift is completed if the transferor releases the retained power. *See* Estate of Sanford v. Commissioner, 308 U.S. 39 (1939). Along the same lines, a gift is not consummated by the delivery of the donor's own check or note. *See* Rev. Rul. 67-396, 1967-2 C.B. 351. Under that ruling the gift of a note is complete when it is paid or transferred for value and the gift of a check is complete when it is paid, certified, accepted by drawee, or is negotiated for value to a third person.

Gift Tax Exemption Replaced by Credit. With respect to transfers made prior to 1977, the donor could elect to use all or part of the lifetime gift tax exemption of $30,000 at any time. As a part of the unification of the gift and estate tax laws in 1976 the exemption was replaced by the unified credit, which must be used by the donor as a credit against the tax on gifts as they are made. Rev. Rul. 79-398, 1979-2 C.B. 338. This rule has particular significance in planning "net" gifts. *See* §7.24, *infra*.

§2.5. Annual Gift Tax Exclusion (§2503(b))

The continuing availability of the annual gift tax exclusion is a major reason for the popularity of inter vivos gifts. Under §2503(b) the first $10,000 of property or interests in property, other than future interests, given to each person is excluded in computing the donor's taxable gifts for the year. Prior to 1982 the exclusion was $3,000 per donee. The donor is not required to file a gift tax return if no gifts to any donee during the calendar year include a future interest or amount to more than $10,000 in value. §6019(a). In most other cases the donor must file a return. A return must also be filed for a donor to split gifts with his or her spouse under §2513 or to claim a gift tax marital deduction for qualified terminable interest property or a charitable deduction.

Future Interests. For purposes of §2503, "future interest" includes "reversions, remainders, and other interests or estates, whether vested or contingent, and whether or not supported by a particular interest or estate, which are limited to commence in use, possession or enjoyment at some future date or time." Reg. §25.2503-3(a). Thus, if X transfers Blackacre to A for life, remainder to B, the life interest transferred to A is a present interest, but the remainder transferred to B is a future interest. No annual exclusion is available with respect to the future interest given to B although it is indefeasibly vested, may be of great value, and is freely alienable by B.

The question of whether or not a particular interest constitutes a present or a future interest is primarily determined by the extent of the transferee's interest and not by the nature of the property. As Reg. §25.2503-3(a) explains, "The term has no reference to such contractual rights as exist in a bond, note (though bearing no interest until maturity), or in a policy of life insurance, the obligations of which are to be discharged by payments in the future. But a future interest or interests in such contractual obligations may be created by the limitations contained in a trust or other instrument of transfer used in effecting a gift."

The present interest/future interest question is most difficult to analyze in the case of transfers in trust. For gift tax purposes a transfer in trust is treated as made to the beneficiaries and not to the trust or the trustee. Helvering v. Hutchings, 312 U.S. 393 (1941). A transfer in trust qualifies for the annual exclusion to the extent the beneficiaries have the unrestricted right to the immediate use, possession, or enjoyment of the property or the income from it. Reg. §25.2503-3(b). That requirement is met to the extent the beneficiary has the power to withdraw the property transferred to the trust. The power, sometimes called a *Crummey* power, is discussed at §7.36, *infra*. Transfers to a trust for the benefit of a minor also qualify for the annual exclusion if the requirements of §2503(c) are met. *See* §7.35, *infra*.

A gift to a corporation is considered to be made to its shareholders. Reg. §25.2511-1(h)(1). However, unlike transfers to a trust, the transfer to a corporation is necessarily a gift of a future interest because the shareholders do not have a direct right or interest in property that is transferred to the corporation. *See, e.g.,* Heringer v. Commissioner, 235 F.2d 149 (9th Cir.), *cert. denied,* 352 U.S. 927 (1956); LR 7935115. The rule is based upon the fundamental distinction between the corporate entity on the one hand and the shareholder-owners on the other. A gift to a corporation may enhance the value of the stock owned by the shareholders, but it is not treated as a transfer of a present interest to them.

The annual exclusion for gifts to each donee is renewable, but not cumulative. One $10,000 exclusion is available annually to each donor with respect to gifts to a particular donee, whether or not gifts were made to the donee in any preceding years. Thus, gifts of present interests having a value of $10,000 or less are generally not subject to the gift or the estate tax.

§2.6. Gift Splitting (§2513)

In order to equalize the gift tax on gifts of community and noncommunity property, the law permits married persons to elect to treat all gifts made to third parties during the reporting periods as made one-half by each. §2513. For purposes of §2035 the actual donor and not the consenting spouse is regarded as the transferor. English v. United States, 284 F. Supp. 256 (W.D. Fla. 1968). The privilege of splitting gifts does not apply to community property, which is naturally "split" between the spouses from the outset. When a gift of community property is made to a person outside the community, each spouse is necessarily the donor of one-half of the property. Each spouse is considered to be the donor of one-half of the total value of community property gifts even in states that permit one spouse alone to make gifts of community property. Rev. Rul. 56-408, 1956-2 C.B. 600. However, as a matter of practice both spouses should join in making gifts of community property in order to avoid any uncertainty regarding the effectiveness of the gift.

In effect, §2513 doubles the exclusions available for gifts of noncommunity property made by a husband and wife to third parties. Gift splitting also allows the spouses to equalize the unified transfer tax rates that are applicable to each of them. Prior to the adoption of the unlimited marital deduction, gift splitting was more important. In order to be effective, both spouses had to signify their consent to split gifts for the period in question. If only one spouse was required to file a return, the consent of both spouses had to be signified on that return. Now spouses can achieve the same result by making a tax-free gift from the wealthier to the poorer spouse, after which each makes equal gifts to third parties.

> **Example 2-4.** H transferred $20,000 of his separate property to his son, S, on December 30. Neither H nor W made any other gifts during that year. The gift to S must be reported on H's gift tax return for the calendar year. The short form of the gift tax return, Form 709A, may be filed in such a case. If W signifies her consent on H's gift tax return the amount of the gift will be completely

offset by the annual exclusions available to H and W and no gift tax will be due. W is not required to file a return because she did not make any gifts during the year, and the gift she is considered to have made to S did not exceed her annual exclusion of $10,000 and was not a future interest. *See* Reg. §25.2513-1(c).

Where both spouses are required to file gift tax returns, the consent of each spouse to split gifts may be signified on either return. Reg. §25.2513-2(a)(1)(i). A decedent's personal representative may consent to split gifts made prior to the decedent's death. *See* §12.19, *infra.*

None of the property actually transferred by the donor spouse is includible in the gross estate of the consenting spouse. For estate tax purposes the consenting spouse is not treated as the transferor of property that was actually transferred by the other. Thus, property held by a consenting spouse as custodian under the Uniform Gifts to Minors Act at the time of death is not includible in her gross estate where the custodial property was actually transferred to the minor by the other spouse and the consenting spouse was only treated as the donor for gift tax purposes. Rev. Rul. 74-556, 1974-2 C.B. 300 (involving §2038). However, the amount of taxable gifts is taken into account in computing the consenting spouse's gift and estate tax liability.

Where the state gift tax law also permits gift splitting, the state and federal elections can be made independent of each other. Thus, gifts made by a couple could be split for federal, but not for state, purposes. In states that determine the gift tax in part according to the relationship between the donor and donee, the state gift tax may be lower in some cases if the gift is not split. Such a result may occur, for example, where the donor spouse is closely related to the donee, but the consenting spouse is unrelated to the donee. Thus, if a donor makes a gift to his or her parents, the state gift tax may be lower if the gift is not split with the donor's spouse, who would probably be considered to be unrelated to the donor's parents.

§2.7. *Charitable Deduction (§2522)*

The income, gift, and estate tax rules that apply to charitable gifts are reviewed in detail in Chapter 8, *infra*. In brief, §2522 allows an unlimited deduction for the value of gifts made by citizens or residents to charities described in §2522(a). Gifts made by a nonresident who is not a citizen of the United States are governed by the same rules as those applicable to citizens, except that they are subject to 2 additional restrictions: (1) Gifts made to a corporation qualify only if it is created or organized under the laws of the United States or a state or territory of the United States; and

(2) gifts to trusts, community chests, etc., qualify only if they must be used within the United States exclusively for religious, charitable, educational, scientific, or literary purposes, including the encouragement of art and the prevention of cruelty to children or animals. Reg. §25.2522(b)-1. With slight variations the same organizations are qualified donees under the income, gift, and estate tax laws. See §8.2, infra.

Planning outright gifts to charitable organizations is usually simple enough, although the valuation of some assets can present a problem. However, that problem is eased considerably if the donor obtains contemporaneous appraisals of the property by qualified experts. The planning becomes much more complex when the gift consists of less than the donor's entire interest in the property. In the case of such a "split gift," a deduction is generally allowed only if the gift takes the form of (1) a charitable remainder trust or pooled income fund (see §§8.20 to 8.24, infra); (2) a guaranteed annuity interest or unitrust interest (see §8.25, infra); (3) a nontrust remainder interest in a personal residence or a farm (see §8.15, infra); or (4) an undivided portion of the donor's entire interest (see §8.16, infra).

> **Example 2-5.** D transferred some property to the trustee of an irrevocable trust, the income of which is payable to her daughter, X, for life, remainder to a charity described in §2522(a). The gift of the remainder interest to the charity is not deductible for income, gift, or estate tax purposes because it is not in one of the approved forms. Prior to the changes made by the Tax Reform Act of 1969, federal tax deductions would have been allowed for the value of the charitable remainder interest.

Because of the complexity of the income, gift, and estate tax rules, gifts of split interests must be planned very carefully.

§2.8. Marital Deduction (§2523)

Section 2523 allows citizens and resident aliens an unlimited marital deduction for qualifying gifts made to a spouse. For gifts made prior to 1977 the deduction was limited to one-half of the value of the gift. The 1976 Act amended §2523 to allow a full deduction for the first $100,000 of noncommunity property given to a spouse after 1976. §2523(a)(2)(A). However, no deduction was allowed for the next $100,000 of post-1976 taxable gifts. Thereafter (i.e., to the extent post-1976 taxable gifts exceeded $200,000) a deduction of 50% was allowed. §2523(a)(2)(B). No gift tax marital deduction was allowable for gifts made prior to January 1, 1982, of community property (§2523(f)) or of nonqualifying terminable interests (§2523(b)). Beginning in 1982 a deduction was allowed on an elective basis for gifts of qualifying terminable interest property. *See* §2523(f) and §5.18, *infra*.

Under the pre-1982 law, the gift tax marital deduction was coordinated with the estate tax marital deduction by reducing the amount of the estate tax deduction where the deductions allowable under §2523 exceeded 50% of the value of the post-1976 gifts.

> **Example 2-6.** This example illustrates the application of the pre-1982 law. In 1979 W, who had not previously made any gifts, gave her husband, H, noncommunity property worth $103,000. No gift tax was due on the gift because of the combined effect of the annual exclusion ($3,000) and the marital deduction ($100,000). When W gave H an additional $103,000 in property in 1980, the annual exclusion sheltered the first $3,000 from tax, but the remaining $100,000 was subject to tax. W's unified credit offset the tax on the gift. If W made any other pre-1982 gifts to H, a 50% marital deduction would have been available. Thus, if W had given H another $103,000 in 1981, she would have been entitled to a marital deduction of $51,500 and an annual exclusion of $3,000, which would have resulted in a taxable gift of $48,500.

Gifts made after December 31, 1981, qualify for the unlimited marital deduction if the donee spouse receives a sufficient interest in the property. Also, the deduction is available on an elective basis for gifts of qualified terminable interest property. *See* §5.18, *infra*.

The overall gift and estate tax consequences of various interspousal gift programs should be estimated and given to the client for consideration before any substantial gifts are made. The estimates should indicate the tax consequences of making gifts of various amounts assuming, alternatively, that (1) the donor predeceases the donee and (2) the donee predeceases the donor. Although the effect of the gifts may seem obvious, the preparation of estimates provides a valuable check that may lead to a refinement of the plan.

Because of the progressive nature of the federal transfer tax, the overall gift and estate taxes are minimized if the sizes of the spouses' estates are equalized. A plan can easily provide for equalization if the wealthier spouse happens to die first. Lifetime interspousal gifts provide a hedge against the possibility that the poorer spouse will die first. Equalization is of little value unless the estate of one spouse is much larger than the estate of the other because the tax brackets are relatively large and the increase in rates is quite gradual after $100,000. For example, a rate of 34% applies to amounts between $250,000 and $500,000, a rate of 37% to the next $250,000, and a rate of 39% to amounts between

$750,000 and $1,000,000. Also, after 1985 the maximum rate will be 50% and the "spread" between the marginal rate applicable to amounts in excess of the credit equivalent (37%) and the maximum rate (50%) will be only 13%. Overall, the 1981 Act enhanced the advantages of deferral and decreased the importance of equalization. If gifts are made for purposes of equalization, the donee's estate should be planned so as to dispose of the donative property in a way that will not cause the property to be included in the donor's estate if the donee dies before the donor. For example, the donee might leave the property to their children or to a bypass trust for the benefit of the donor.

Substantial interspousal gifts are sometimes made to the poorer spouse so that the donee's estate can use the full amount of unified credit should the donee predecease the donor. If the poorer spouse died first, leaving a gross estate that had a value under the amount of the credit equivalent, the decedent's unified credit would be largely wasted. The estate of a poorer spouse can be built up without federal transfer tax cost by making gifts to the poorer spouse. Such a program might be undesirable, however, for other reasons (*e.g.*, the possibility of marital dissolution).

Summary. Gifts to a spouse may be used to achieve the same general tax goals served by other inter vivos gifts. *See* §§7.7 to 7.11, *infra*. In addition, however, they may (1) equalize the sizes of the spouses' estates; (2) create an estate for the "poorer" spouse, as a hedge against the donee's earlier death and consequent loss of the marital deduction to the donor; and (3) increase the size of the donee's estate to take advantage of the shelter provided by the donee's unified credit should the donee predecease the donor. Prior to 1982 inter vivos gifts were also made in order to maximize the amount of property that could be transferred to a spouse free of federal gift and estate taxes. Where the spouses' estates are entirely community, an interspousal lifetime gift program is seldom indicated. In that case their estates are equalized naturally, which eliminates most of the tax advantages of making interspousal gifts. Of course, in any case the tax on the death of the first spouse can be completely deferred under the unlimited marital deduction.

Inter vivos gifts to a spouse are not generally made for income tax purposes because the advantages of income splitting are already available by filing joint income tax returns. However, in some cases a gift may be helpful for income tax purposes. For example, a sale may be facilitated by transferring the property from one spouse, in whose hands the property is not a capital asset, to the other spouse, in whose hands it will be a capital asset. *See* §7.9, *infra.* The general tax factors discussed in §§7.12 to 7.17, *infra,* should also be considered in selecting property transfer to a spouse.

§2.9. Gift Tax Returns

A federal gift tax return (Form 709) is filed individually and not jointly or collectively with other taxpayers. §6019. A short form (Form 709A) can be used where a return is required only to split gifts between the spouses and the resulting gifts are within the amount of the allowable annual exclusions. As noted in §2.6, *supra*, it is necessary to file gift tax returns in order to take advantage of gift splitting under §2513. A return must be filed on or before April 15th of the year following the close of the calendar year in which the gifts were made. However, a return for the year that includes the death of the donor must be filed no later than the time for filing the donor's estate tax return (*i.e.*, 9 months after death). §6075(b)(3).

> **Example 2-7.** T made a gift of $50,000 to X on January 1 and died on January 15. A gift tax return reporting the gift to X is due at the same time as T's estate tax return (*i.e.*, October 15).

Community Property Gifts. A gift of community property to a person outside the marital community is considered to be 2 gifts — each spouse makes a gift of one-half of the whole value of the property. Accordingly, where community property is given to a third party, each spouse may be required to file a gift tax return. However, neither spouse is required to file a gift tax return where the gift is a present interest that does not exceed $20,000 in value.

> **Example 2-8.** H and W gave their daughter, D, $20,000 of community property cash last year. Because each of them was considered to have made a gift of $10,000 to D, they were not required to file any gift tax return respecting the gift. H and W would be required to file returns on or before April 15, however, if they had made any other gifts to D during the year. In January of this year H and W gave D community property worth $25,000. H and W are each required to file a return reporting a gift of $12,500 on or before next April 15.

Manner of Filing. The gift tax return may be hand carried to the office of the district director for the district in which the donor resides or else filed with a regional service center. See §6091 and the instructions for Form 709. Under §7503, if the last day prescribed for filing is a Saturday, Sunday, or legal holiday, the time is extended to the next succeeding day that is not a Saturday, Sunday, or legal holiday. A return is considered timely filed if it is mailed within the time allowed. The pertinent regulations provide generally that a document is deemed filed on the date of the postmark stamped on the cover in which it was mailed. Reg. §301.7502-1(a). Returns and other documents mailed to the IRS should be sent by registered mail, return receipt requested, if the date of mailing or receipt is important.

Payment and Penalties. Under §6151, the gift tax is required to be paid at the time the return is due. An extension of time within which to pay the tax may be allowed under §6161 in cases of "undue hardship." *See* §6161(a) and Reg. §25.6161-1(b). However, the donor's unified credit is available to offset the gift tax and must be used for that purpose to the full extent it remains available to the donor. Unlike the case of the $30,000 lifetime gift tax exemption available prior to 1977 under §2521, the donor has no option regarding the use of the credit. Any tax that is not paid when due is subject to an interest charge at the floating annual rate established under §6621 until it is paid. §6601. Also, an addition to tax will be imposed under §6651 unless the failure to pay the tax was for reasonable cause. The addition to tax is one-half of 1% if the failure is no longer than one month and an additional one-half of 1% for each month thereafter, to a maximum of 25%. A penalty of 5% of any underpayment resulting from negligent or intentional disregard of rules may be imposed. §6653(a)(1). In addition, a penalty of 50% of the amount of interest due under §6601 is imposed where the underpayment was due to negligent or intentional disregard of the rules. §6653(a)(2). If an underpayment is the result of civil fraud the penalty is 50%. Penalties are also imposed for willful failure to file a return on time and for willful attempts to evade or defeat payment of the tax.

Checks or money orders in payment of the tax should be drawn to the order of "Internal Revenue Service" and carry the donor's social security number.

Problem 2-1. Prior to 1977 W made taxable gifts of $350,000. Until this year all of W's subsequent gifts were within the allowable annual exclusions. During this year W registered stock that had a cost basis of $50,000 and a current value of $250,000 in the name of her husband, H. W also gave each of her children, X and Y, a cash gift of $100,000. Compute the gift tax on the gifts made by W this year assuming, alternatively, that the gifts are and are not split with H, who had previously made no gifts. What is H's basis in the stock? *See* §§2513, 2523, and 1015.

D. FEDERAL ESTATE TAX HIGHLIGHTS

Death taxes are ancient taxes. They were known to the Egyptians, as well as the Romans and Greeks. Even the complaints against them have a venerable pedigree. Pliny the Younger provides as good an example as any. He is among the earliest critics who have left summaries of their complaints. Pliny eloquently argued that a tax on the shares of direct heirs "was an 'unnatural' tax, augmenting the grief and sorrow of the bereaved." Almost two thousand years later the same argument was still being heard. For in 1898 Senator Allen forcefully inquired whether it was right "to stand with the widow and children at the grave side of a dead father to collect a tax," and then he sympathetically referred to the widow "in weeds" and the children "in tears." Eisenstein, The Rise and Decline of the Estate Tax, 11 Tax L. Rev. 223 (1956).

§2.10.   Nature and Computation of Tax

The federal estate tax is "neither a property tax nor an inheritance tax." Reg. §20.0-2(a). Instead, it is an excise tax imposed on the transfer of the entire taxable estate of the decedent. §2001(a). A decedent's taxable estate is determined by subtracting the deductions allowable under §§2053 to 2057 from the decedent's gross estate. As explained at §2.3, *supra,* the unified rate schedule, §2001(c), is used to calculate the amount of the estate tax. In brief, a tentative tax is calculated by applying the unified rate schedule to the sum of the decedent's taxable estate *plus* the amount of post-1976 taxable gifts made by the decedent. However, in order to avoid taxing the same property twice, gifts that are includible in the decedent's gross estate are not counted as post-1976 taxable gifts. *See* §2001(b). The gross amount of the estate tax is determined by subtracting the gift tax paid on the decedent's post-1976 taxable gifts from the amount of the tentative tax. The gross tax is then reduced by the unified credit allowable in the year of the decedent's death and any of the other credits allowed by §§2011 to 2014 that are appropriate. Most estates involve only the unified credit and the credit for state death taxes allowed by §2011.

§2.11.   Gross Estate

The property and interests described in §§2033 to 2044 are included in the gross estate, valued in accordance with §§2031 to 2032A. Although the gross estate includes the property subject to administration in a decedent's estate under state law, it is a much broader and more inclusive concept. As explained below, it may include property that the decedent no longer owned at death.

The scope of §§2033 to 2044 and §2046 is described in the following paragraphs, which are largely adapted from Reg. §20.2031-1(a).

1.   Property owned by a decedent at death is includible in the decedent's gross estate under §2033. The section extends to future

interests as well as present possessory interests. Section 2034 merely provides that the property is includible in the decedent's estate even though the decedent's surviving spouse has an interest in the property, such as dower or curtesy.

2. Property transferred within 3 years of death is generally not includible in the gross estate of a transferor who dies after December 31, 1981. A contrary rule applied to the estates of persons dying prior to 1982. §2035. Other lifetime transfers are includible under §§2036 to 2038 unless the transferor received full and adequate consideration for the transfer in money or money's worth. In general, §2036 requires the inclusion of property with respect to which the decedent retained either the use or income from the property or the power to designate who would receive its use or income. Property transferred by the decedent is includible under §2037 if it could be enjoyed by others only if they survived the decedent and the decedent retained a reversionary interest, the value of which immediately before the decedent's death exceeded 5% of the value of the property. The scope of §2038 is essentially the same as that of §2036 although §2038 speaks specifically of a power, retained by the decedent, to alter, amend, revoke, or terminate the transfer.

3. Sections 2039 through 2042 deal with special types of property and powers of appointment held by the decedent. Section 2039 requires the inclusion of certain interests in annuities and other payments made pursuant to a contract or other agreement under which the decedent had a right to receive payments for life or for a period not ascertainable without reference to his or her death. The law allows important exclusions for interests in qualified plans including Keogh plans and IRAs. See §§2.33 and 12.21, infra. Section 2040 governs the inclusion of interests in joint tenancies and tenancies by the entirety. Property subject to certain powers of appointment is includible in the power holder's estate under §2041. Finally, §2042 requires the inclusion of insurance receivable by the insured's executor or over which the insured retained any incident of ownership.

4. Under §2043 the amount includible in a decedent's estate under §§2035 to 2038 and 2041 is reduced by the amount of consideration in money or money's worth that the decedent received in the exchange for the transfer of the property or the release or exercise of the power. This section deals with cases in which the decedent received insufficient consideration in money or money's worth for the transfer, release, or exercise. The amount of consideration received by the decedent is "frozen" at the time of the transfer, while the value of the property transferred by the decedent is determined on the appropriate valuation date (i.e., the value

of the property included in the transferor's estate may increase or decrease after the date of the transfer, but the amount of the consideration is fixed on that date). Section 2045 merely provides that unless otherwise provided, §§2034 to 2042 apply to transfers, interests, and powers whenever made, created, exercised, or relinquished.

     5.   Under §2044 the gross estate of a surviving spouse includes any property for which a marital deduction was allowed as qualified terminable interest property under §2523(f) (gift tax) or §2526(b)(7) (estate tax). *See* §5.18, *infra*.

     6.   Section 2046 recognizes that a qualified disclaimer under §2518 does not constitute a transfer for purposes of the estate tax.

The scope and application of §§2035, 2036, and 2038 to 2041 are examined in more detail in §§2.14 to 2.18, *infra*. Particular attention is given to some of the traps created by those sections and how to avoid them. The life insurance section, §2042, is explored at length in Chapter 6, *infra*. Section 2044 and others concerning the marital deduction are discussed in Chapter 5, *infra*.

Valuation. Under §2031(a) property included in a decedent's gross estate is valued on the date of the decedent's death. Extensive regulations issued under §2031 describe the manner in which various types of property are to be valued, including annuities, life estates, terms for years, and remainders. *See* Reg. §20.2031-10. However, §2032 allows the executor to elect to value a decedent's gross estate on an alternate valuation date. If the election is made, any assets that are distributed, sold, exchanged, or otherwise disposed of within 6 months following death must be valued on the date of distribution, sale, or exchange. Any assets that are not distributed, sold, or exchanged within 6 months following death must be valued as of the date 6 months following the decedent's death. Changes in value due to the mere lapse of time are not taken into account for purposes of the alternate valuation. Section 2032A allows certain closely held farm and business interests to be valued specially at less than their fair market value. Alternate valuation and special use valuation under §2032A are described more fully in §§12.17 to 12.18, *infra*.

§2.12. Deductions

Sections 2053 to 2057 describe the deductions that are allowed against the gross estate in calculating a decedent's taxable estate. In brief, the sections provide as follows:

1. Section 2053 allows deductions for funeral and administration expenses and claims against the estate, including certain taxes and charitable pledges. Essentially the same deductions are allowable whether or not there is an estate administration. The personal representative may elect to deduct administration expenses either on the estate tax return or on the estate's income tax return. This, and other important post-mortem elections, are described in §12.15, *infra*.

2. A deduction is allowed by §2054 for the amount of uncompensated losses suffered during administration of the estate on account of fires, storms, shipwrecks or other casualties, or from theft.

3. Section 2055(a) allows a deduction for the value of charitable transfers of property included in the decedent's estate. However, if a transfer is made for both a charitable and a noncharitable purpose, a deduction is allowed for the value of the charitable interest only if the transfer takes one of the forms described in §2055(e)(2). The allowance of charitable deductions for such "split interests" is explored in more detail in Chapter 8, *infra*.

4. Prior to 1982 §2056 allowed a limited deduction for the value of property or interests in property that were included in the decedent's gross estate and passed from the decedent to the surviving spouse. However, the deduction was only allowed if the interest transferred to the surviving spouse was a "deductible interest." In broad terms, the pre-1982 deduction could not exceed the greater of $250,000 or one-half of the decedent's adjusted gross estate (the adjusted gross estate was defined as the value of the noncommunity property included in the decedent's estate, less the amount of §§2053 and 2054 deductions attributable to it).

An unlimited marital deduction is available to the estate of decedents dying after December 31, 1981. Thus, all of the property of a married person may be passed, free of tax, to or for the benefit of his or her surviving spouse. Also, beginning in 1982, the deduction was made available on an elective basis for part or all of the value of property in which the surviving spouse is given a qualifying income interest for life. §2056(b)(7). At the same time a marital deduction became available for the current interest in a qualifying charitable remainder trust given to a surviving spouse. §2056(b)(8).

5. Prior to 1982 a limited deduction was also allowed by §2057 for property included in the decedent's gross estate that passed to a surviving child under the age of 21. However, the deduction was only allowable if the decedent was not survived by a spouse and if the child had no known surviving parent. The deduction was limited to $5,000 multiplied by the excess of 21 over the age of the child at the time of the decedent's death. The so-called orphan's

deduction was repealed with respect to decedents dying after December 31, 1981, because of its complexity and the substantial increase in the amount of the unified credit.

A planner must have a good grasp of the rules regarding the charitable and marital deductions in order to advise clients competently regarding the formulation of estate plans. A comprehensive understanding of the deductions is also necessary in order to do an effective job of post-mortem planning. Of course, in some cases the inter vivos or post-mortem planning may require the assistance of an expert on the particular subject.

§2.13. Credits

Sections 2010 through 2016 deal with the credits that are allowable against the federal estate tax. The most important is usually the unified credit allowed the estate of each citizen or resident. A different rate of tax and a much smaller credit apply to the estates of nonresidents who are not citizens (§§2101 to 2102). As explained in §2.3, *supra*, by 1987 the unified credit will be equal to the tax imposed on a taxable transfer of $600,000. In addition to the unified credit, credits are allowed for:

1. State death taxes actually paid with respect to property in cluded in the decedent's gross estate. §2011. The credit ranges from an opening rate eight-tenths of 1% to 16% on a taxable estate in excess of $10,100,000. A growing minority of states impose only a death tax equal to the amount of the allowable federal credit, called a "pick up" tax.

2. A credit is allowed under §2012 for gift taxes paid on gifts made prior to January 1, 1977, where the same property is included in the donor's gross estate. The amount of any gift tax paid on post-1976 gifts is deducted in computing the amount of the estate tax itself. *See* §2001(b).

3. Section §2013 allows a credit for the estate tax paid with respect to the transfer of property to the decedent by or from a person who died within 10 years before or 2 years after the death of the decedent. There is no requirement that the transferred property be identified in the estate of the present decedent or that the property be in existence at the time of his or her death. The amount of the credit is limited to the lesser of (1) the amount of the tax attributable to the interest in the estate of the transferor or (2) the amount of the tax attributable to the interest in the estate of the present decedent. The full amount of the credit is allowable if the

present decedent died within 2 years of the time the property was transferred to him or her. Thereafter, the amount of the credit diminishes by 20% every 2 years, so that no credit is allowable if the transferor died more than 10 years preceding the death of the present decedent.

4. A credit is allowed under §2014 for the death taxes actually paid to any foreign country with respect to property situated in that country and included in the decedent's gross estate. The allowance of the credit may be affected by the terms of a gift and estate tax treaty between the United States and the foreign country imposing the tax.

5. Section 2015 relates to the allowance of the credits for state and foreign death taxes attributable to remainder or reversionary interests with respect to which the payment of the estate tax has been deferred under §6163(a). In essence, the section allows credits for the state and foreign death taxes if they are paid within the time for payment of the deferred portion of the estate tax. Note that the provisions of this section do not apply to deferrals under §§6166.

6. Finally, §2016 requires a person who receives a refund of any state or foreign death tax that was claimed as a credit under §§2011 or 2014 to notify the district director of the refund within 30 days of its receipt. The amount of the estate tax is then redetermined and the amount of any additional tax due by reason of the redetermination must be paid by the executor.

The unified credit is particularly important in planning relatively small sized estates. Otherwise, the credits are mainly significant only for preparing the federal estate tax return.

§2.14. Transfers within 3 Years of Death (§2035)

Under §2035 property transferred within 3 years of death generally is not includible in the estate of a transferor who dies after December 31, 1981. §2035(d). However, the value of property transferred within 3 years of death generally is included for the purpose of determining the qualification of the estate for special treatment under §§303, 2032A, and 6166. §2035(d)(3). Insurance on the life of the transferor and certain other property transferred within 3 years of death are includible in the transferor's gross estate. §2035(d)(2). Section 2035(c) requires the inclusion of the amount of any gift tax paid by the decedent or the decedent's estate on any gift made by the decedent or the decedent's spouse within 3 years of death. Prior to 1977 the law did not require such a "gross up," which encouraged deathbed gifts. The application of §2035 is illustrated by the following example:

> **Example 2-9.** In 1981 X gave stock worth $10,000 to her daughter, D, and a policy of insurance on X's life worth $2,500 to her son, S. X filed a gift tax return that reported the gift of stock because its value exceeded the amount of the then allowable gift tax exclusion ($3,000). X died in 1982 when the stock was worth $50,000. S received the insurance proceeds of $25,000. Under §2035(d), the gift of stock is not includible in X's gross estate, but the proceeds of the life insurance on X's life are includible.

§2.15. *Retained Interests and Powers (§§2036, 2038)*

Property transferred during lifetime is includible in a decedent's estate under §2036(a) to the extent the decedent retained "for his life or for any period not ascertainable without reference to his death or for any period which does not in fact end before his death — (1) the possession or enjoyment of, or the right to the income from, the property, or (2) the right, either alone or in conjunction with any person, to designate the persons who shall possess or enjoy the property or the income therefrom." Thus, this section extends to transfers, in trust or otherwise, under which the decedent-transferor retained the use or enjoyment of property or the right to designate the persons who could possess or enjoy the property or the income from it. The scope of §2038 is essentially the same as that of §2036(a)(2). Specifically, §2038 extends to any interest in property transferred by the decedent, in trust or otherwise, if the enjoyment of the property was subject, at the date of the decedent's death, to change through the exercise of a power by the decedent to alter, amend, revoke, or terminate the interest. Inclusion is also required if the decedent relinquished the power within the 3-year period ending on the date of the decedent's death. *See* §2038(a)(1) and Reg. §20.2035-1(b).

> **Example 2-10.** T purchased securities that were registered in T's name as custodian under the Uniform Gifts to Minors Act for T's 10-year-old nephew, N. The registration of the securities constituted an irrevocable gift subject to the gift tax. If T dies while acting as custodian, the securities are includible in T's gross estate under §2038 because of T's power under the Uniform Act to distribute the securities to N prior to the time when the custodianship would otherwise terminate. *See* §7.33, *infra.*

Section 2036 was broadened in 1976 and 1978 to require inclusion of stock in a "controlled corporation" that was transferred during lifetime if the transferor retained, directly or indirectly, the right to vote the stock alone or in conjunction with any person. The provision was adopted in order to overcome the effect of United States v. Byrum, 408 U.S. 125 (1972), which held that the power to control a corporation through a retained power to vote its stock did not require inclusion of the stock under §2036. For purposes of §2036(b), a controlled corporation is one in which the transferor at any time after the transfer of the property, and within 3 years of death, owned or had the right to vote stock that represented at least 20% of the combined voting power of all classes of stock. §2036(b)(2). The attribution rules of §318 apply for the purpose of determining whether the transferor owned the requisite interest in the stock. Also, for purposes of applying §2035, the relinquishment or cessation of voting rights is treated as a transfer of property made by the decedent. §2036(b)(3). The provisions of §2036(b) create a trap for the unwary and raise a host of complex issues that will require litigation to resolve. See McCord, The 1978 Anti-Byrum Amendment: A Cruel Hoax, U. Miami 14th Inst. Est. Plan., Ch. 12 (1980). A serious trap exists because §2036(b) requires inclusion of stock in a controlled corporation with respect to which the decedent retained the right to vote in any capacity (i.e., the section extends to stock over which the transferor held the right to vote solely in a fiduciary capacity — as trustee or custodian under the Uniform Gifts to Minors Act).

§2.16. Annuities and Other Death Benefits (§2039)

Section 2039 requires the inclusion of an annuity or other payment receivable by any beneficiary by reason of surviving the decedent under the terms of certain contracts or agreements to the extent that the annuity is attributable to contributions made by the decedent or the decedent's employer. However, benefits payable under qualified plans are excluded from the estate of an employee to the extent they are attributable to the employer's contributions. §2039(c). The exclusion does not apply if the payments are receivable by or for the benefit of the decedent's estate. See Reg. §20.2039-2(b). The exclusion is also lost if the benefit is received in a lump sum unless the recipient irrevocably elects to forego favorable income tax treatment of the payment (10-year averaging). See §2039(f) and §12.21, infra.

For planning purposes it is important to take the fullest possible advantage of the exclusions available under §2039. Particular care should be taken that the exclusion is not inadvertently lost — benefits should not be made payable to or for the benefit of the decedent's estate. Where the benefit is payable in a lump sum (all in one taxable year), the recipient should be made aware of the opportunity either to exclude the benefit from the decedent's gross estate or to take advantage of 10-year income averaging. Of course, the availability of the unlimited marital deduction makes it largely insignificant whether the benefits paid in a lump sum to the surviving spouse are or are not included in the decedent's estate. In general, a surviving spouse who receives a lump sum distribution has nothing to gain by making a §2039(f) election. Also, where the beneficiary is the decedent's surviving spouse, a lump sum distribution also escapes current income taxation if the surviving spouse rolls it over within 60 days into an IRA. *See* §§402(a)(7), 2039(f) and §12.21, *infra.*

In 1976 the exclusion for annuities under qualified plans was extended to payments receivable by beneficiary other than the decedent's estate under Keogh plans and individual retirement accounts (IRAs). §2039(c), (e). The exclusion applies, however, only to the extent that the contributions to the Keogh plan or IRA were deductible for income tax purposes at the time made. Also, a payment under an IRA does not qualify for the exclusion unless it provides for "a series of substantially equal periodic payments to be made to a beneficiary (other than the executor) for his life or over a period extending for at least 36 months after the date of the decedent's death." §2039(e).

§2.17. *Joint Tenancies* (*§2040*)

Joint tenancies and tenancies by the entirety are widely used, particularly by married persons, to hold title to property because each of the tenancies carries a right of survivorship. That is, upon the death of one tenant the decedent's rights in the property terminate and all rights in the property are owned by the survivor. The estate tax disadvantage of spouses holding property in joint tenancy form was largely eliminated by the adoption of the unlimited marital deduction.

Joint Tenants Other Than Husband and Wife. The 2 basic rules that govern the taxation of joint tenancies are stated in §2040(a). First, where the joint tenancy was acquired by the decedent and the other joint owner by gift, devise, or inheritance, the decedent's fractional interest in the property is included in the decedent's gross estate. This rule is simple and logical in its application, at least in states that permit a joint tenant to sever the joint tenancy and convert it into a tenancy in common with no right of survivorship. The second rule includes the entire value of the property in the decedent's gross estate except to the extent it is attributable to the contributions in money or money's worth made by the other tenant. For this purpose, the contributions of the other tenant are not taken into account to the extent they are attributable to money or other property acquired from the decedent for less than full and adequate consideration.

Example 2-11. T's will left Blackacre to T's children, A and B, as joint tenants with right of survivorship. T also left a cash gift of $100,000 to A, which A used to purchase Whiteacre in the name of A and B as joint tenants. The purchase of Whiteacre involved a gift from A to B of $50,000 (one-half of its total value). If A dies survived by B, a one-half interest in Blackacre and the whole interest in Whiteacre are includible in A's estate under §2040(a). Because the value of Whiteacre is included in A's gross estate, the amount of the prior taxable gift is not taken into account in computing the estate tax. *See* §2001(b). Otherwise, the same property would be taxed twice.

Qualified Joint Interests. In 1976 Congress added §2040(b), which provides that only one-half of the value of a "qualified joint interest" owned by a married person at death is includible in the decedent's estate, regardless of which spouse provided the consideration for the acquisition of the property. Such a fractional interest rule is fair, simple to understand, and easy to administer. It is also consistent with the adoption of the unified transfer tax system that substantially reduced the advantages of making lifetime gifts. However, §2040(b) originally applied only to a joint tenancy created after 1976 by one or both spouses that was treated as a gift. In addition, only the spouses could be parties to the tenancy. The Revenue Act of 1978 added provisions that allowed conversion of pre-1976 joint tenancies into qualified joint interests. *See* former §§2040(d), (e), and §3.15, *infra.* The 1981 Act repealed subsections (c), (d), and (e) and the qualified joint interest rule was made applicable to all joint tenancies between a husband and wife in which there was no other joint tenant.

The estate of the spouse first to die includes only one-half of the total value of qualified joint interests, including post-gift appreciation. Of course, the entire value of the property is includible in the estate of the surviving joint tenant.

For historical purposes it should be noted that the Revenue Act of 1978 also added §2040(c), which permitted the efforts of the decedent's spouse to be taken into account in determining the amount of jointly held farming or business property includible in the decedent's gross estate. This cumbersome elective provision allowed the value of the gross estate to be reduced by (1) the "adjusted consideration" of the spouse and (2) by 2% of the excess of the value of the property over the total adjusted consideration provided by both spouses for each year that the decedent's spouse participated materially in the operation of the farm or other business. The adjusted consideration was defined as the consideration furnished by a spouse plus interest computed at 6% per year from the date the consideration was furnished until the date of the decedent's death. The provision was intended to give a surviving spouse reasonable credit for the increase in the value of the joint tenancy property due to the surviving spouse's efforts.

Problem 2-2. When T died several years ago he left Blackacre to his son, S, and his daughter, D, as joint tenants with right of survivorship. Subsequently S contributed the $20,000 down payment on the $100,000 cost of Whiteacre, title to which was taken in the names of S and D as joint tenants with right of survivorship. Over the next 9 years S also contributed the full $10,000 annual payments on Whiteacre. Earlier this year S and W were married. Shortly after their marriage W transferred her farm, Greenacre (worth $200,000) into the names of S and W as joint tenants with right of survivorship. Assuming that none of the parties had made any other inter vivos gifts, what are the gift tax consequences of the transactions described above? If S died before any changes were made in the property ownerships, how would the various joint tenancies be treated for estate tax purposes in his estate?

§2.18. *Powers of Appointment (§2041)*

The flexibility of an estate plan is increased substantially by creating powers of appointment that allow changes to be made in the distribution of income and principal according to future conditions. However, transactions involving powers of appointment must be carefully planned because of their important tax consequences, particularly for estate tax purposes.

Under §2041 property over which a decedent possessed, exercised, or released a general power of appointment is usually includible in the decedent's gross estate. For purposes of §2041 a general power of appointment is one that may be "exercised in favor of the decedent, his estate, his creditors, or creditors of his estate." §2041(b)(1). Section 2041 does not apply, however, to powers that the decedent reserved over property he or she had transferred. *See* Reg. §20.2041-1(b)(2).

There are some important exceptions to the basic rules regarding the taxation of powers under §2041. To begin with, property subject to a general power of appointment created before October 22, 1942, is not includible in the decedent's gross estate unless the power is exercised. §2041(a)(1). Also, a power is not considered to be a general power of appointment if the power is exercisable only with the consent or joinder of (1) the creator of the power or (2) a person having a substantial adverse interest. §2041(b)(1)(C). Finally, a power limited by an ascertainable standard relating to the health, education, support, or maintenance of the power holder is not a general power of appointment. §2041(b)(1)(A).

Property subject to a post-October 21, 1942, general power of appointment is also includible in the decedent's estate if the power was exercised or released in such a way that the property would have been includible in the decedent's estate under §§2035 to 2038, had it been a transfer of property owned by the decedent. §2041(a)(2). Thus, property that had been subject to a general power of appointment is includible in the decedent's estate if the decedent released the power and retained the income, use, or control of the property.

> **Example 2-12.** At a time after October 21, 1942, G transferred property in trust to pay the income to X for life, then to distribute the principal to Y. The trust gave X a power to withdraw the trust principal whenever X chose to do so. X irrevocably released the power. The property of the trust is includible in X's gross estate under §2041(a)(2)—it is treated as if X had transferred property to the trust, reserving the income in the property for life. Of course, the release also involved a gift to Y of the value of the remainder interest. §2514(b).

The lapse of a general power created after October 21, 1942, is treated in the same way as a release. §2041(b)(2). Thus, property subject to a general power that lapses is includible in the power holder's estate if the power holder retained an interest or power described in §§2036 to 2038. However, lapses of powers during any calendar year are treated as releases only to the extent that the property subject to the power exceeds the greater of $5,000 or 5% of the value of the property out of which the exercise of the power could have been satisfied. Thus, a person can be given the noncumulative annual rights to withdraw the greater of $5,000 or 5% of the value of the trust without causing the property to be included in the power holder's gross estate. This rule, together with the exception for powers limited by ascertainable standards, allows an individual to hold important powers of withdrawal without requiring any of the trust principal to be included in his or her gross estate.

Property subject to a nongeneral power of appointment is not includible in the gross estate of the holder of the power. Accordingly, wills and trusts are frequently drafted to give a surviving family member a power to appoint the property to and among a class that excludes the holder of the power, his creditors, his estate, and the creditors of his estate. The power is often limited to the descendants of the donor of the power, which may be too restrictive. See §10.21, infra.

> **Problem 2-3.** T died earlier this year leaving property worth $500,000 in trust to pay the income each year to X and, upon the

death of X, to pay the principal to A and B in equal shares. The trust gives X the noncumulative right each year to withdraw $50,000 from the trust for her own use. Assuming that X is a 50-year-old female, what gift and estate tax consequences will occur if she fails to exercise the power this year? Trust income of $25,000 has been accumulated and is ready for distribution to X. If X directs that the accumulated income be added to the principal of the trust, how will the transaction be treated for gift and estate tax purposes?

E. GENERATION-SKIPPING TAX

Prior law imposed transfer taxes every generation in the case of families where property passed directly from parent to child and then from child to grandchild. However, where a generation-skipping trust was used, no tax was imposed upon the death of the child even where the child had an income interest in the trust, and substantial powers with respect to the use, management, and disposition of the trust assets. While the tax advantages of generation-skipping trusts were theoretically available to all, in actual practice these devices were more valuable (in terms of tax savings) to wealthier families. Thus, generation-skipping trusts were used more often by the wealthy. General Explanation of the Tax Reform Act of 1976, 564 (1976).

§2.19. Background and Scope of Tax

The 1976 Act added Chapter 13 to the Code, §§2601 to 2622, which was intended to plug the generation-skipping loophole, referred to in the quotation above, by imposing a new tax on certain transfers made by generation-skipping trusts. However, the tax will be only a relatively loose plug because of the grandchild exclusion, which will shield most generation-skipping transfers from the imposition of the tax. Also, wealthy taxpayers will often choose to avoid the tax, or blunt its effect, by adopting certain specialized planning techniques.

Congress intended the new tax to be substantially equivalent to the gift and estate taxes that would have been imposed had the property been transferred outright once in every generation. However, the tax only applies to transfers that are made by generation-skipping trusts and trust equivalents. Thus, it does not apply to transfers that are made outright, even though the transferees are more than one generation younger than the transferor.

Example 2-13. G's will specifically bequeathed securities outright to his great-grandchildren, X and Y. The securities were, of course, subject to the estate tax upon G's death. Although the bequests to X and Y effectively "skip" the generations of G's children and grandchildren, they are not subject to a generation-skipping tax.

A form of the generation-skipping tax proposed in 1969 would have subjected transfers, of the type described in Example 2-13, to a substitute additional tax. United States Treasury Department, Tax Reform Studies and Proposals, 91st Cong., 1st Sess., Part 3 at 388 *et seq.* (Comm. Prop. 1969). Under it, an additional tax would have been imposed on any transfer made outright or in trust to a person more than one degree of family relationship younger than the transferor.

The generation-skipping tax also does not apply to any transfer that is subject to the gift or estate tax. §2613(a)(4)(B). Accordingly, property transferred inter vivos or at death to a generation-skipping trust is not subject to any current generation-skipping tax liability — the tax is only imposed when a taxable distribution or a taxable termination takes place. *See* §2.21, *infra.*

When a taxable transfer occurs, the tax is determined by applying the marginal unified tax rate of the "deemed transferor" to the amount of the generation-skipping distribution or generation-skipping termination, as explained in §2.26, *infra.* For the purposes of the tax, the deemed transferor is generally the parent of the transferee who is more closely related to the grantor. *See* §2.22, *infra.* In the case of a taxable distribution, the tax base is the value of the property distributed, plus the amount of any generation-skipping tax paid with respect to the distribution; in the case of a taxable termination, the tax base is the entire value of the property subject to the intervening interest or power that terminated. The tax is calculated according to the unified transfer tax rate applicable to the deemed transferor, but the deemed transferor is not liable for the tax. Instead, §2603(a) imposes liability for the tax on the trustee of the generation-skipping trust and on any distributee of the property. Importantly, the imposition of the tax does not affect the calculation of the unified tax on any subsequent dispositions made by the deemed transferor.

Example 2-14. G died leaving his residuary estate in trust to pay the income to his niece, N, for life and upon her death to distribute the principal to her children. The trust is a generation-skipping trust, but the tax does not apply until N dies, when there will be a generation-skipping distribution to her children. As explained above, N is the deemed transferor of the distribution. The tax is then determined by applying the unified rate schedule to the sum of the distribution, the amount of N's estate tax base (*i.e.,* her taxable estate plus post-1976 taxable gifts), and the amount of all prior generation-skipping transfers of which N was the deemed transferor. The tax thus calculated is reduced by a tentative tax on the amount of such transfers other than the current distribution. Any unused part of N's unified credit is allowable as a credit against the tax. §2602(c)(3). Any tax due is payable by the trust and not by N's estate. Had a distribution of principal been made during N's lifetime to her children, the tax would have been determined by applying N's marginal unified tax rate to the amount of the distribution. However, the unified tax on subsequent transfers made by N would have been determined without taking the generation-skipping transfer into account.

The terminology and basic operation of the tax are explained in the following sections. Consideration is also given to some specialized techniques for avoiding the application of the tax.

§2.20.   Effective Date

In general, the generation-skipping tax applies to generation-skipping transfers made after June 11, 1976. However, there are 2 major exceptions to that rule. The tax does not apply to transfers made out of property that was held by a trust that was irrevocable on June 11, 1976. It also does not apply to any trust or will executed before June 12, 1976, that became irrevocable by reason of the death of the decedent before January 1, 1983, provided that the instrument was not amended after June 11, 1976, in any way that resulted in the creation of, or an increase in the amount of, a generation-skipping transfer. *See* Reg. §26.2601-1(b). Both rules will affect the treatment of transfers made under the instrument at any time. The regulations provide a useful indication of the IRS position regarding the exceptions. However, they will almost certainly be challenged by taxpayers who seek to escape the reach of the tax.

§2.21.   Generation-Skipping Trusts and Taxable Transfers

The tax only applies to certain transfers made by generation-skipping trusts, which are trusts that have younger generation beneficiaries who belong to 2 or more generations younger than that of the grantor. Thus, trusts that have beneficiaries who belong to only one generation younger than that of the grantor are not subject to the tax. For example, a trust that is established for the benefit of the grantor's spouse for life, remainder to their children, is not a generation-skipping trust. Accordingly, the tax does not apply to the transfer of the trust property to the children of the grantor following the death of the grantor's spouse. That result, of course, turns on the generational assignment of the grantor's spouse. As explained below, a husband and wife are always assigned to the same generation regardless of the difference in their ages.

Taxable Distribution. For the purposes of the tax, a generation-skipping transfer occurs when there is a distribution of trust principal to a younger generation beneficiary who is assigned to a generation younger than that of any other younger generation beneficiary. *See* §2.23, *infra.* Importantly, in applying this rule, a beneficiary who at no time has held anything other than a future interest is not considered to be a younger generation beneficiary. Thus, there cannot be a generation-skipping distribution unless there are younger generation beneficiaries with present interests or powers who are assigned to 2 or more younger generations.

> **Example 2-15.** G established a trust to pay the income and so much of the principal as the trustee deemed appropriate to G's niece, N. Upon the death of N the trust would continue for the benefit of her children, X and Y. The trust is a generation-skipping trust because it has beneficiaries who are assigned to 2 generations younger than that of G. However, a distribution of principal to N is not a generation-skipping distribution because X and Y do not hold present interests or powers and are not considered to be younger generation beneficiaries for the purpose of determining whether there was a generation-skipping distribution.

Income Exception. A distribution of current income to a younger generation beneficiary is not a taxable transfer. §2613(a)(1). However, if the distributions made during the taxable year of the trust exceed its trust accounting income, the trust is deemed to have distributed the income to the beneficiaries in descending generational order beginning with the beneficiaries of the oldest generation. §2613(a)(2); Prop. Reg. §26.2613-1(b). Thus, the distributions to the oldest generation of beneficiaries are treated as having been made out of income to the extent the trust has income, and the distributions to the other beneficiaries are treated as having been made out of principal. This rule is arbitrary, but it is administratively convenient and prevents an obvious form of avoidance.

> **Example 2-16.** A trust created by G directed the trustee to make discretionary distributions of income and principal to G's niece, N, and grandniece, GN. The trust had income of $40,000 for the taxable year, during which the trustee distributed $40,000 to N and

$20,000 to GN. The distribution to N is considered to consist entirely of income and the distribution to GN to consist entirely of corpus. Thus, the distribution to GN is a taxable distribution.

Taxable Termination. A taxable termination occurs when there is a termination, in accordance with the terms of the trust, of an interest or power of a younger generation beneficiary who is assigned to a generation older than that of any other younger generation beneficiary. §2613(b)(1); Prop. Reg. §26.2613-2(a). For example, a taxable termination occurs upon the death of a younger generation beneficiary where the trust continues in effect for the benefit of the deceased beneficiary's descendants. For the purpose of this rule, the assignment of a beneficiary's interest, with or without consideration, is not a taxable termination. As in the case of distributions, the termination of an interest or power of a person who at no time had anything other than a future interest or power in the trust is not a taxable termination.

Postponed Termination. Where 2 or more members of the same generation have interests or powers in the same trust, a termination generally does not occur until the termination of the interest or power of the last surviving member. §2613(b)(2); Prop. Reg. §26.2613-2(b)(1). This rule prevents the imposition of the tax more than once each generation. However, a taxable termination is not postponed if the remaining beneficiary's present interest or power is nominal. Prop. Reg. §26.2613-2(b)(3). Also, the termination of the interests or powers of one beneficiary is not postponed where the other beneficiaries have separate shares. Prop. Reg. §26.2613-5.

Example 2-17. G created a trust, the income and corpus of which is distributable in the trustee's discretion to G's adult children, M and N. Upon the death of the survivor of M and N, the principal is distributable to G's great-grandchildren, X, Y, and Z. Because M and N have substantial interests in the trust, the death of the first of them to die will not be treated as a taxable termination. Instead, the taxable termination for both M and N will take place upon the death of the survivor. Prop. Reg. §26.2613-2(b)(5), *Example (1)*. If M and N each held interests in, or powers over, substantially separate shares of the trust, the death of each would constitute a taxable termination. Prop. Reg. §26.2613-5.

Unusual Order of Termination. The statute also provides some relief in the case of an unusual order of termination. §2613(b)(2)(C); Prop. Reg. §26.2613-2(d). Thus, if a present interest or power held by a member of a younger generation of beneficiaries terminates first, the tax is postponed until the termination of the interests or powers of the beneficiaries who belong to older generations.

Example 2-18. G established a trust that gave the trustee discretion to distribute income and principal to G's niece, N, and grandniece, GN, for so long as they, or the survivor of them, should live. If GN predeceases N, the termination that took place when she died is postponed until N dies. When N dies, the tax will be imposed as if N died first; then a tax will be imposed with respect to the termination by reason of GN's death.

§2.22. *Grantor, Deemed Transferor, and Transferee*

The statute itself does not define the term "grantor," but it is defined in the regulations: "A grantor of a trust includes any person contributing or adding money or property directly or indirectly to a trust if the contribution is included in the Federal gross estate or is subject to a gift tax without regard to section 2503(b)." Prop. Reg. §26.2611-2(a). On its face the definition does not include property that is not included in the transferor's gross estate, such as qualified plan benefits that are paid to a trust but excluded from the decedent's estate under §2039(c). Where more than one person contributes property to a trust, the regulations treat each of them as a grantor of the trust in proportion to the value that the contribution made by that person bears to the value of all contributions to the trust.

Example 2-19. H and W each contributed $250,000 to a generation-skipping trust. Each of them is considered to be a grantor with respect to one-half the amount of any transfers made from the trust. If H added another $250,000 and the value of the original contributions had not changed, H is thereafter treated as the grantor of two-thirds of the trust assets. Prop. Reg. §26.2611-2(b).

Building on the basic definition given in the regulations, a person who releases a general power of appointment over trust property is treated as having contributed to the trust the property that was subject to the power. Thereafter that person would displace the original contributors as the grantor of the trust for purposes of the generation-skipping tax. However, where a general power of appointment lapses, the power holder is considered to be a grantor of the trust only to the extent that the lapse is subject to the gift or estate tax. That is, the power holder would become the grantor only to the extent that the value of the property with respect to which the power lapsed exceeds $5,000 or 5% of the value of the property out of which the exercise of the lapsed power could have been satisfied. This treatment of lapsed general powers is consistent with other aspects of the general policy toward "5 or 5" powers, which is reflected in §§2041(b)(2) and 2514(e). It also avoids the complications that would arise if the lapse of a "5 or 5" power were treated as a contribution to the trust. In drafting trusts and advising clients regarding powers of appointment, a planner must recognize that the failure to exercise a general power of appointment will cause a change in the identity of the grantor to the extent the value of the property exceeds $5,000 or 5% of the value of the trust. The change in grantors may also change the tax treatment of subsequent generation-skipping transfers.

> **Example 2-20.** When T died part of his estate passed to a trust over which his second wife, W, held a general testamentary power of appointment. In default of exercise of the power, the property will remain in trust for T's children by his first wife for life after which the trust principal will pass to their children (*i.e.,* T's grandchildren). If W does not exercise the power, she will be treated as the grantor of the trust. Unless W adopted T's children by his first wife, she will not be related to them or to their children. In such a case, the distributions to T's grandchildren would not qualify for the "grandchild exclusion." *See* §2.24, *infra.* The negative result illustrated in this example is avoided by limiting W's power to a special power of appointment, which would not cause the trust to be included in her gross estate.

Deemed Transferor. Under §2612(a)(1), the deemed transferor is generally the parent of the transferee who is more closely related to the grantor than the other parent. For this purpose, the regulations recognize that the parent related to the grantor by blood or adoption is more closely related than a parent related to the grantor only by marriage. Prop. Reg. §26.2612-1(a).

> **Example 2-21.** G created a trust to pay the income to his son, S, for life and to distribute the principal to S's children when S died. S was married to W when S died and the principal was distributed to his children. S is the deemed transferor of the distribution and not W, who was only related to G by marriage.

If neither parent of the transferee is related to the grantor, the deemed transferor is the parent "having a closer affinity to the grantor." The regulations explain that "a parent having closer affinity will be the person named in the grantor's will or trust instrument, or the lineal descendant of that person having the intervening interest or power in the trust." Prop. Reg. §26.2612-1(a). However, the regulations do not indicate which parent will be considered the deemed transferor where they are both named in the grantor's will but neither of them is related to the grantor. If neither parent is named in the grantor's will or trust instrument, the older parent is treated as the deemed transferor with respect to all of the property transferred. *Id.*

A parent of the transferee is not the deemed transferor where the parent is not a younger generation beneficiary and there is another ancestor of the transferee, related to the grantor, who is a younger generation beneficiary. In such a case, the latter person is treated as the deemed transferor. Thus, where a trust is created for the benefit of the grantor's child for life, remainder to the grantor's great-grandchildren, the child-beneficiary is treated as the deemed transferor of any distribution to the great-grandchildren.

Transferee. It is, of course, necessary to identify the transferee in order to determine whether there has been a generation-skipping transfer and to apply the other rules regarding the tax. Where there is a taxable distribution, the transferee is the person who receives the distributed property. Prop. Reg. §26.2612-1(b). In the case of a taxable termination that results in the distribution of trust property, the transferee is the person who receives the property or for whose benefit it is applied. But, if the property remains in trust after a taxable termination, the transferee is a person who has a present interest or power in the trust immediately after the termination. Note that for this purpose the persons who only have future interests or powers are disregarded.

> **Example 2-22.** G created a trust under which the income was payable to his niece, N, for life. The trustee was given the discretionary power to distribute principal to N or her descendants. Following the death of N the income of the trust was distributable in equal shares to the children of N who were living at the time the trust was created. Upon the death of each child, the share of the property from which the child was receiving income was distributable to and among the child's issue as the child should appoint. If the trustee distributed principal to one of N's children, the child would obviously be the transferee. When N died there would be a taxable termination, but not a distribution of trust assets. Each of her children would be treated as a transferee of the termination because they would all have present interests. Similar rules would apply to the determination of the transferees upon the death of one of N's children.

§2.23.   Beneficiary and Younger Generation Beneficiary

The determination of whether or not a trust is a generation-skipping trust depends upon a proper identification of the beneficiaries and the assignment of the beneficiaries to the proper generations.

The term "beneficiary" is broadly defined in the law to include any person who has a present or future interest or power in the trust.

§2613(c)(3); Prop. Reg. §26.2613-4(c)(3). For the purposes of the tax, a person has an "interest" in a trust if he or she has the right to receive income or principal or is a permissible distributee of income or principal. §2613(d)(1). Accordingly, if a trustee has discretion to distribute income to the grantor's children and grandchildren, the grantor's children and grandchildren all have present interests in the trust and are beneficiaries of the trust.

Power. Under §2613(d)(2) power is defined to mean "any power to establish or alter the beneficial enjoyment of the corpus or income of the trust." The term seems to include virtually all powers that may affect beneficial interests in the trust, including powers that are limited by an ascertainable standard. Presumably it also includes powers that must be exercised jointly. However, the term does not encompass purely administrative or managerial powers. Also, 2 important exceptions are carved out by the statute from the coverage of the term.

Under the first exception, a person is not treated as having a power if the person's only power is one "to dispose of the corpus of the trust or the income therefrom to a beneficiary or a class of beneficiaries who are lineal descendants of the grantor assigned to a generation younger than the generation assignment of such individual." §2613(e)(1); Prop. Reg. §26.2613-6. Thus, a child of the grantor may hold the power to make distributions of principal or income to the grantor's grandchildren. The exception is an important one that can easily be lost if any other persons are included in the class of permissible distributees or if the trustee is given any other nonmanagerial powers.

> **Example 2-23.** T left his residuary estate to his son, S, in trust to make discretionary distributions of income and principal to the issue of S. If S does not have any other present or future powers, the discretionary power to make distributions to the issue of S is not to be treated as a power. However, it would not fall within this exception if persons other than the grantor's lineal descendants were included in the class of persons to whom distributions could be made. Thus, the power would not fall within this exception if the testator's widow or siblings were included in the class of permissible distributees. Also, S might be treated as a beneficiary if he could exercise the discretionary power in a way that would relieve him of the legal obligation to support his children.

The second exception, added in 1978, applies in the case of "independent" trustees. §2613(e)(2); Prop. Reg. §26.2613-7. Under it, an individual trustee is not treated as having a power if he or she has no interest in the trust "other than as a potential appointee under a power of appointment held by another," is not "related or subordinate," and has no present or future power in the trust "other than a power to dispose of the corpus of the trust or the income therefrom to a beneficiary or a class of beneficiaries designated in the trust instrument." §2613(e)(2)(A). In the absence of this exception, an independent individual trustee who could make discretionary distributions or otherwise exercise any powers over the beneficial enjoyment of income or principal would be treated as a beneficiary.

The term "related or subordinate trustee" is broadly defined in §2613(e)(2)(B) to include certain relatives of the grantor or any beneficiary and employees of corporations or partnerships in which the interests of the grantor, the trust, or the beneficiaries are significant or in which the grantor or any beneficiary is an executive or a partner. The definition is generally broader than that of a related or subordinate party for purposes of the grantor trust rules. *See* §672(c).

Younger Generation Beneficiary. Not surprisingly, a younger generation beneficiary is any beneficiary who is assigned to a generation younger than that of the grantor. §2613(c)(1); Prop. Reg. §26.2613-4(c). For purposes of analysis it is helpful to develop a system of charting or otherwise designating the generational level of each beneficiary. The system might involve a simple chart, such as Chart 2-1, in which the names (or class designations) of the beneficiaries are inserted in the blocks opposite the appropriate generational designation. Thus, the generations might be designated as "G," "G + 1," "G + 2," etc. Other systems may be evolved for the same purpose. For example, my colleague Jack Huston has suggested that the grantor's generation might be designated as the "senior" generation and succeeding generations as the "junior," "sophomore," and "freshman" generations.

	Interests in the trust		Powers	
	Income	Principal	Income	Principal
Grantor's generation				
Grantor's plus one				
Grantor's plus two				
Grantor's plus three				

Chart 2-1

In general, to the extent possible beneficiaries are assigned to generations along family lines. §2611(c). Specifically, the descendants of a grandparent of the grantor, and their spouses, are assigned to generations in accordance with the family's actual structure. Prop. Reg. §26.2611-3(a). Thus, the grantor, the grantor's spouse, and their siblings all belong to the same generation (they are members of the "G" or the "senior" generation). The natural or adopted children of persons who belong to the grantor's generation are members of the first younger generation (the "G + 1" or the "junior" generation). Similarly, their grandchildren are members of the second younger generation (the "G + 2" or the "sophomore" generation).

Beneficiaries who are not descendants of the grantor's parents are assigned to generations according to a different regime. Such a beneficiary who was born no more than 12½ years after the grantor is assigned to the grantor's generation and one born between 12½ and 37½ years after the grantor is assigned to the first younger generation. §2611(c)(5). Under the rules, there is a new generation for each successive 25 years. See Prop. Reg. §26.2611-3(b). Note that a grantor's stepchildren are unrelated to the grantor and are assigned to generations according to their respective ages and not according to their relationship to the grantor's spouse.

§2.24. Grandchild Exclusion

The grandchild exclusion is one of the most important features of the generation-skipping tax. Indeed, the exclusion largely eliminates the significance of the tax for most taxpayers who wish to leave property in trust for more than one generation of descendants. Under §§2613(a)(4)(A) and (b)(5)(A), transfers to a grandchild of the grantor are not taxable to the extent of $250,000 per deemed transferor. See Prop. Reg. §26.2613-4(a). For purposes of the tax the deemed transferor is always the grantor's child who is also the parent of the grandchild to whom a transfer is made. §2612(a)(1).

The exclusion effectively shelters up to $250,000 that is transferred to each set of the grantor's grandchildren. According to the explanation of the Joint Committee's staff, only one grandchild exclusion is allowed with respect to each child of the grantor and the grantor's spouse: "All trusts established by a grandparent or his spouse for any child's children would be attributed to that child as deemed transferor; thus, only one $250,000 exclusion is to be allowed to flow through a child of the grantor (for the ultimate benefit of the grandchildren)." General Explanation of the Tax Reform Act of 1976, 572 n.9 (1976). However, another exclusion is available with respect to transfers made by the parents of the deemed transferor's spouse (i.e., the other set of grandparents). Note that the amount of the exclusion is not $250,000 per grandchild, nor is it directly related to the number of grandchildren who receive generation-skipping transfers. As the following example indicates, the exclusion can shelter a large amount of property from the tax:

Example 2-24. G left an estate of $1,000,000 (after taxes and expenses) in trust for his 4 children for life. Upon the death of each child a proportionate part of the trust property is distributable outright to the deceased child's children. By reason of the grandchild exclusion, as much as $1,000,000 may be transferred to G's grandchildren without incurring any generation-skipping tax liability. Of course, the full amount of a transfer will not be sheltered from the tax if more than $250,000 is transferred to the children of a particular child. That might occur if some of G's children do not leave surviving children or if the value of the trust property increases following G's death.

Vesting Requirement. In order to qualify for the exclusion the property must be transferred in a way that will cause it to be included in all events in the grandchild's gross estate if the grandchild dies at any time after the generation-skipping transfer. Prop. Reg. §26.2613-4(a)(1). According to the Report of the Conference Committee, the exclusion will be available for property that vests in a grandchild in such a way, "even where the property continues to be held in trust for the grandchild's benefit. . . ." S. Rep. No. 94-1236, 94th Cong., 2d Sess. 618 (1976). The requirement is met if the property passes outright to the grandchild, or to a custodian under the Uniform Gifts to Minors Act. It is also satisfied if the property is held in a trust that will either terminate in favor of the grandchild or the grandchild's estate (an "estate" trust) or be distributed as the grandchild appoints under a general power of appointment. However, where either of those trust forms is used, a separate trust or a separate share should be set apart for each grandchild at the time of the generation-skipping transfer. Otherwise the vesting requirement may not be satisfied. The planner should avoid subjecting an unnecessarily large amount of property of the trust to inclusion in the grandchildren's estates. For that reason, the amount that "vests" in the grantor's grandchildren upon the death of a child-beneficiary might be limited to the amount of the grandchild exclusion at the time.

The amount of a taxable distribution or termination is subject to the tax to the extent that it exceeds the grandchild exclusion. In effect, the excess is treated as if it were a transfer by the deemed transferor. If the same property is later distributed to the children of the deemed transferor, it will also be subject to the estate tax when they die.

Example 2-25. G left his residuary estate of $1,000,000 in trust to pay the income to his daughter, X, for life. Following her death, the property will be held in separate subtrusts for each of her children for life. In order to qualify for the grandchild exclusion each of her children is given a general testamentary power of appointment over his or her subtrust. When X dies the property of the trust will be subject to the generation-skipping tax at X's marginal unified tax rate to the extent it exceeds $250,000 in value (*i.e.*, $750,000 will be subject to tax). The entire value of each subtrust will also be subject to tax when a grandchild-beneficiary dies because of the grandchild's general power of appointment over the property. Otherwise the property would be subject to a generation-skipping tax at that time.

The planner should consider whether it is desirable to attempt to insulate the amount in excess of the grandchild exclusion from inclusion in the grandchildren's estates and let it be subject to a generation-skipping tax or vice versa. The total amount of tax payable will probably be the same unless the grandchild exercises the power by appointing to a surviving spouse or charity.

The result would be much the same if the trust limited the amount that will "vest" in the grandchildren to a total of $250,000 (or such larger amount as may be allowable as an exclusion) on the date of the generation-skipping transfer to them. The trust property in excess of that amount might be held in trust for their benefit and the benefit of subsequent generations. Unfortunately, in such a case, the death of a grandchild-income beneficiary would involve a taxable termination of the decedent's interest in the excess. That transfer would be fully taxable, as it would not qualify for the grandchild exclusion because the transferees would be the grantor's great-grandchildren.

The results might be improved if the deemed transferor were given a presently exercisable general power of appointment over the trust assets to the extent they exceed $250,000 in value. The excess would be includible in the deemed transferor's gross estate; however, a proper exercise of the power could prevent the excess from being subject to the estate tax when the deemed transferor's children die (*i.e.*, at the grandchildren level). The death of a child of the deemed transferor might involve a generation-skipping transfer under the appointment. The appointment, though, could be made in a way that would allow those transfers to qualify for the grandchild exclusion available at that level (the deemed transferor would have become the grantor by reason of the general power of appointment). Of course, the deemed transferor might want to appoint some of the property to his or her own estate for the purpose of paying the additional estate tax incurred by reason of the power.

Giving the deemed transferor a presently exercisable power of appointment would increase overall flexibility because it would start the perpetuities period running again. For purposes of the Rule Against Perpetuities such a power is comparable to an indefeasibly vested remainder and is exempt from the rule. *See* R. Lynn, The Modern Rule Against Perpetuities 123 (1966). Consistent with that treatment, the validity of an exercise of the power is measured from the time of exercise and not from the time the power was created.

§2.25. *Planning and Drafting Techniques*

Several basic planning techniques can be used to reduce or avoid the impact of the generation-skipping tax. The first, and perhaps the most important, is to take full advantage of the grandchild exclusion. Use of the exclusion can be combined with powers of appointment to preserve flexibility and to prevent too much property from being included in the grandchildren's estates. *See* §2.24, *supra.* Second, and probably next in importance, is the exception for distribution of current income, which can be used to deflect income to younger generations. Third is the postponement of imposition of the tax by creating trusts that have multiple beneficiaries in the same generation. Finally, and probably the least significant for most taxpayers, is the creation of a separate trust for each generation of beneficiaries ("layered" trusts). More exotic techniques may be used in special cases, such as conferring powers of appointment that will permit a change in the grantor of the trust.

Grandchild Exclusion. Trusts for the grantor's descendants should generally be drafted to qualify for the grandchild exclusion. Fortunately, the necessary requirements are met if the interest is transferred to the grantor's grandchildren in a form that will cause the interest to be included in the grandchild's estate. As explained above, the interest may pass to the grandchild outright, to a custodian under the Uniform Gifts to Minors Act, or to a trust that will terminate in favor of the grandchild's estate or over which the grandchild has a general power of appointment. Giving the grandchildren the necessary interest or power does not usually require any complicated drafting. *See, e.g.,* Article Eleven of the sample will, §4.22, *infra.*

Postponement of Tax. The imposition of the tax may be postponed by creating trusts that have multiple beneficiaries in the same generation. That may be done, for example, by giving the trustee the power to sprinkle the income of the trust among several beneficiaries, all of whom belong to the same generation. Of course where each beneficiary has a substantially separate and independent share, the shares are treated as separate trusts for purposes of applying the tax. *See* Prop. Reg. §26.2613-5. In order to preserve family harmony and promote fairness, it may be desirable to forego this type of postponement and, instead, to create separate trusts or separate shares.

Imposition of the tax may also be postponed if the beneficiary exercises a special power of appointment to create a present interest in a member of the beneficiary's own generation. Thus, a child, who is the income beneficiary of a trust that is intended to qualify for the grandchild exclusion, might appoint an income interest in the trust to the child's own spouse. The imposition of the tax would be postponed until the death of the spouse, when it would still qualify for the grandchild exclusion.

Income Exception. Some tax savings can also result if the trustee is given broad discretion to distribute income to more than one younger generation of beneficiaries. When the senior generation of beneficiaries does not need all of the income, the trustee may distribute it to one or more younger generations of beneficiaries. By doing so the trustee can limit the amount of property subject to the estate tax or the generation-skipping tax when the senior beneficiaries die. As mentioned above, the trustee cannot qualify for this exception by distributing income to the younger generation beneficiaries and principal to the older generation. *See* §2613(a)(2). Of course, in order to preserve flexibility, the trust should also permit the trustee to make discretionary distributions of principal. The planner should also be sure that the trust does not contain any boiler-plate or other provisions that might require the accumulation of income that is not distributed to the senior generation of beneficiaries. Similarly, the trust should not bar distributions of income to or for the benefit of the younger generations of beneficiaries. Instead, where the beneficiaries are minors, the trust might authorize the trustee to distribute income to custodians for them under the Uniform Gifts to Minors Act or to other trusts for their benefit.

Layered Trusts. By creating trusts for each generation of beneficiaries, the grantor may limit the amount that would be subject to estate or generation-skipping taxes at any generational level. The trusts would not be subject to the generation-skipping tax because they have only one younger generation of beneficiaries. In theory the grantor would attempt to transfer to each trust for a senior generation beneficiary an amount sufficient to meet that beneficiary's needs (in essence an annuity) and would transfer the balance of his or her property to trusts for the younger generations of beneficiaries. Of course, the use of layered trusts involves a risk that the provision made for the senior generation will be too large or too small. The risk that the trust will be too small is reduced somewhat by authorizing the trustee to distribute property from the trusts for the younger beneficiaries to the seniors if they need additional support. The approach is generally suitable only for very wealthy clients, who have sufficient property to fund adequately trusts for more than one generation of beneficiaries.

Problem 2-4. T died in 1982 survived by his wife, W, and his two minor children, X and Y. He left his entire estate to X as trustee. Under the terms of the trust W is entitled to the income for life together with so much of the principal as the trustee believes is in her best interests. The trust also gave W the noncumulative power to withdraw the greater of $5,000 or 5% of the principal of the trust each year. Upon W's death the principal of the trust will be distributed to those of the descendants of T and W who survive her. Is the trust a generation-skipping trust? If X predeceases W leaving children who survive W, does X's death involve a taxable transfer? Upon the death of W, will there be a taxable distribution from the trust to the children of X? If so, who is the deemed transferor? Would it qualify for the grandchild exclusion?

§2.26. Calculating the Tax

The generation-skipping tax is calculated by applying the marginal unified tax rate of the deemed transferor to the fair market value of the property transferred. §2602(a). The trustee may elect to value all of the property transferred in accordance with §2032 where the transfer is a taxable termination that occurs at the same time as the death of the deemed transferor (or at the same time as the death of a beneficiary assigned to a higher generation than the deemed transferor). §2602(d). Note that the alternate valuation applies only in the case of terminations — no alternate valuation is allowed in the case of distributions. According to the Joint Committee on Taxation, the trustee may elect to use the alternate valuation date whether or not the executor of the deemed transferor's estate also elected to use it for estate tax purposes. General Explanation of the 1976 Act 580. Importantly, the amount of any transfers of which an individual is the deemed transferor is not included in the deemed transferor's tax base for gift or estate tax purposes. Thus, the amount of the generation-skipping tax will be lower when the transfer is made during the lifetime of the deemed transferor than if it is made at or after the deemed transferor's death (or within 3 years preceding the deemed transferor's death as explained in the next paragraph).

Under §2602(e), transfers within 3 years preceding the death of the deemed transferor are deemed to have occurred after the death of the deemed transferor in accordance with the principles of §2035. Because of the 1981 changes in §2035, deathbed transfers may qualify for the lower tax rates that would apply if the amount of the deemed transferor's taxable estate were not taken into account.

Deductions. Section 2602(c) also allows 2 important deductions in determining the amount of the tax. First, a charitable deduction is allowed for the value of interests that are transferred to qualified charities. This deduction would be available, for example, in connection with an appointment made to a charity by a younger generation beneficiary pursuant to a special power of appointment. Second, where the transfer takes place at the same time as, or after, the death of the deemed transferor, certain expenses are allowable as deductions. In the case of a taxable termination, a deduction is allowed for items that are allowable as deductions under §§2053 and 2054 (*e.g.,* costs of administration, debts, and taxes). §2602(c)(5)(B). Where the transfer is by way of distribution, the deductions are limited to expenses incurred in connection with the determination, collection, or refund of the generation-skipping tax.

Credits. The amount of the tax may be reduced by 3 credits that are recognized by §2602(c). First, the trustee may offset the tax by any unused portion of the deemed transferor's unified credit where the transfer takes place at or after the death of the deemed transferor. §2602(c)(3). Thus, the deemed transferor's unified credit may not be used to offset the tax on transfers made during his or her lifetime. Second, the §2013 credit for prior transfers is allowable where the deemed transferor dies within 10 years of the creation of the trust. §2602(c)(4). Third, when the transfer takes place at or after the death of the deemed transferor, a credit is allowed for any estate, inheritance, legacy, or succession tax actually paid to any state or the District of Columbia with respect to the transferred property. §2602(c)(5)(B). Several states have adopted "pick up" taxes that are designed to be equal to the allowable credit. *E.g.,* Calif. Rev. & Tax Code §§16700-16950 (West 1981 Supp.); Colo. Rev. Stat. §39-23.5-106 (1981 Supp.).

Liability for Tax. The deemed transferor's marginal tax rate is used for purposes of calculating the tax, but neither the deemed transferor nor the estate of the deemed transferor is liable for the tax. Instead, the tax is payable out of the trust property. If the tax is not paid when due, the trustee is personally liable for the tax in the case of a taxable termination and the distributee is personally liable in the case of a taxable distribution. §2603(a). The tax imposed is a lien on the transferred property until paid or barred by the lapse of time. §2603(b).

Returns. A return must be filed with respect to all generation-skipping transfers regardless of the amount involved. General Explanation of the 1976 Act 581. The return is to be filed by the distributee in the case of a taxable distribution and by the trustee in the case of a taxable termination (§2621(c)(1)(A)) with the IRS office in which an estate or gift tax return of the deemed transferor must be filed. Temp. Reg. §26a.2621-1(c)(1). Where the transfer takes place during the life of the deemed transferor, the return must be filed within 6 months following the close of the taxable year of the trust in which the transfer took place. Where the transfer takes place during or after the same taxable year as the death of the deemed transferor, the return is due on or before the later of: (1) 6 months after the estate tax return of the deemed transferor is due, or (2) 6 months after the close of the taxable year during which the transfer took place. Temp. Reg. §26a.2621-1(c). In the case of a generation-skipping transfer, the regulations also require the trustee to file an information return, Form 706-B(1). Temp. Reg. §26a.2621-1(f). In addition, the trustee must complete and send Form 706-B(2) to each distributee who is required to file a generation-skipping tax return (Form 706-B).

F. BASIC LIFETIME ESTATE-PLANNING TAX STRATEGIES

§2.27. *Overview*

Where federal income or transfer taxes are significant factors in planning for a client, the client's estate plan will usually be based upon one or more of the estate-planning strategies described in this part. More sophisticated individual income tax strategies, such as ones involving tax-sheltered investments other than individual retirement arrangements (IRAs) and self-employed plans, are less commonly encountered. Post-mortem planning strategies are discussed in Chapter 12, *infra.*

The following lifetime strategies are discussed in this part:
1. shifting of income within the family
2. reducing the size of the estate
3. freezing the value of the estate
4. bypassing the estates of survivors and
5. deferring the payment of estate taxes.

As explained in the following sections, each of these general strategies can usually be carried out in a variety of ways. For example, income can be shifted within the family by making outright gifts, by transferring assets to irrevocable trusts (in which the grantor may retain a reversionary interest) and by certain other types of transfers. The estate-planning devices used to carry out a strategy for a particular client will vary, of course, depending upon the client's overall circumstances. As always, the content of an estate plan should be designed to carry out the client's tax and nontax objectives. This part concludes with summaries of the important tax shelters that individual retirement accounts offer to employees and that self-employed retirement plans offer to self-employed persons.

§2.28.   Shifting of Income within the Family

The progressive individual income tax rates encourage taxpayers to shift income within the family so that it is divided among as many separate taxpayers as possible, including individuals and trusts. A shift of income from family members who are subject to relatively high marginal income tax rates to members who are subject to lower rates can result in a substantial increase in the family's after-tax income. Such a shift is particularly helpful where the family is composed of parents with large taxable incomes and minor children who have little or no income. A variation on the basic approach involves creating additional taxpayers (trusts and corporations) with whom the family income may be split. Of course, the benefit derived from the use of trusts as separate taxpayers is limited by the throwback rules, §§665 to 668, which tax distributions of accumulated income as if the beneficiary had received the income as it was accumulated. See §10.2, infra.

Fortunately, clients can select from a variety of methods by which income can be shifted within the family. Some, such as an outright gift of property, are suitable if a client is willing and able to give up the property permanently. See §7.13, infra. Of course, where the donee is a minor, the gift should be made in a way that avoids the necessity of a guardianship. For example, the gift might be made to a custodian under the Uniform Gifts to Minors Act or to the trustee of a trust for the minor. See §§7.27 to 7.37, infra.

Income can also be shifted by several methods in which the donor retains an interest in the property. Perhaps the most popular is the short-term trust in which the grantor retains a reversionary interest that will take effect after 10 years or more. See §§7.38 and 10.26 to 10.32, infra. Aggressive clients with a surplus of cash may attempt to shift income by making interest-free demand loans to their children, other family members, or to trusts. Under the existing law such loans do not constitute gifts and may not require the lender to report any of the income earned by the borrower. See §7.19, infra. Income may also be shifted by more indirect means, such as by deflecting business or investment opportunities to a child. See §7.18, infra.

Assignment of Income

But this case is not to be decided by attenuated subtleties. It turns on the import and reasonable construction of the taxing act. There is no doubt that the statute could tax salaries to those who earned them and provide that the tax could not be escaped by anticipatory arrangements and contracts however skillfully devised to prevent the salary when paid from vesting even for a second in the man who earned it. That seems to us the import of the statute before us and we think that no distinction can be taken according to the motives lending to the arrangement by which the fruits are attributed to a different tree from that on which they grew. Lucas v. Earl, 281 U.S. 111, 114-115 (1930).

As indicated by a host of Supreme Court decisions, an assignment of income alone is not effective to shift the tax incidence from the assignor to the assignee. *E.g.,* Helvering v. Horst, 311 U.S. 112 (1940) (father taxable on bond interest where interest coupon detached and given to son prior to payment date); Lucas v. Earl, 281 U.S. 111 (1930) (husband remained taxable on personal service income that he contracted to give to his wife). In general, the law distinguishes between a gift of property, which is usually effective to shift the income from the property, and a gift of the "mere" right to receive income, which is usually not effective to shift the income. That distinction is the origin of the famous fruit and tree analogy that appears in the above quotation from Lucas v. Earl. However, differentiating between "property" and a "right to income" can be difficult in some cases. Because of that problem some arbitrary rules have grown up, as illustrated by the tax consequences of the assignment of the income interest in a trust.

In Blair v. Commissioner, 300 U.S. 5 (1937), the Supreme Court held that a life income beneficiary's gratuitous assignment of his interest in the trust income constituted a transfer of an equitable property interest sufficient to shift the income to the assignee. In a subsequent case the Court ruled that the transfer of one year's trust income was not sufficient to shift the income to the assignee. Harrison v. Shaffner, 312 U.S. 579 (1941). It reasoned that the donor "has parted with no substantial interest in property other than the specified payments of income which, like other gifts of income, are taxable to the donor." *Id.* at 583. Several later decisions held that assignments of trust income for 10 years or more would shift the income to the assignee. *E.g.,* Hawaiian Trust Co. v. Kanne, 172 F.2d 74 (9th Cir. 1949). In 1955 the IRS adopted that view, ruling that the trust income would be taxed to the assignee where it was transferred for a period of at least 10 years. Rev. Rul. 55-38, 1955-1 C.B. 389. The ruling is consistent with the grantor trust rules adopted in 1954, which permit the grantor to shift income by placing the property in trust for a period of 10 years or more. *See* §673 and §10.28, *infra.*

§2.29.   *Reducing the Size of the Estate*

Reducing the amount of property that is potentially includible in a client's gross estate is a primary estate-planning strategy. Outright lifetime gifts are the simplest and most direct way of achieving such a reduction. Of course, as a result of the unification of the gift and estate taxes in 1976, the amount of post-1976 taxable gifts is included in the tax base at the time of the donor's death. The unification of the taxes increased the importance of reducing one's estate by making inter vivos gifts that qualify for the gift tax annual exclusion. Under the unified transfer tax rate table, each $10,000 annual exclusion can be expected to save at least $3,200 in estate taxes ($10,000 × 32%, the lowest marginal unified tax rate applicable to amounts in excess of the credit equivalent) (in 1983 the marginal rate becomes 34%, in 1985 it grows to 37%). Importantly, even deathbed gifts may be excluded from the donor's gross estate. Under §2035 gifts other than interests in life insurance, made within 3 years of death, generally are not included in the donor's estate.

Taxable gifts (*i.e.*, ones in excess of the annual exclusion) can also help control the size of a client's gross estate. Although the amount of a taxable gift is includible in the donor's tax base, any subsequent appreciation in value of the transferred property is excluded. Also, any gift tax paid more than 3 years prior to death is not included in the donor's estate. In addition, by making a gift the donor removes post-gift income from his or her estate. Note that taxable gifts within the amount of the credit equivalent do not require any out of pocket tax cost.

> **Example 2-26.** Donor, D, made a gift of stock worth $235,000 to his son, S, in 1982. The gift did not require the payment of any gift tax — $10,000 was allowed as a gift tax exclusion and the tax on $225,000 was offset by D's unified credit. When D died in 1983 the stock he gave to S was worth $500,000. Because D made the gift of stock his transfer tax base was $275,000 smaller than it would have been without the gift. Of course, any income derived from the stock after the gift was made was also excluded from D's estate. By making the gift the estate tax payable by D's estate was reduced by at least $88,000 ($275,000 × 32%).

Gifts of some types of property may result in a disproportionately large reduction in value of the donor's estate. This may occur, for example, where a gift reduces the donor's stock holding in a closely held business to a minority interest, which may qualify for a discount in value. Similarly, a gift of an undivided interest in real property may reduce the value of the donor's retained interest. (The IRS is understandably reluctant to recognize a discount in either case.) The opportunity to effect such a tax-free reduction in the size of the donor's estate exists because the value of a transfer for gift tax purposes is measured by the value of the property transferred and not the amount by which the transfer reduces the value of the donor's estate. §2512. The United Kingdom's Capital Transfer Tax adopts the opposite rule — the amount of a chargeable transfer is the amount by which the transfer reduces the value of the transferor's estate. Finance Act 1975, §20(2).

The prospective size of a client's gross estate can often be reduced substantially by making a gift of insurance on the client's life, which may have little or no value for gift tax purposes. The assignment of group-term insurance can produce quite favorable results because of its low present value. See §6.59, infra. The overall estate tax savings can be increased if the insurance is transferred to an irrevocable trust and the insurance is insulated from inclusion in the estate of the insured's spouse. See §6.71, infra.

The size of the estate can also be controlled to a limited degree by making the maximum allowable contributions to qualified retirement plans and IRAs. Such contributions shelter income during the contributor's lifetime and, importantly, are generally excludible from the contributor's gross estate. The 1981 Act increased the amounts that can be contributed to self-employed (Keogh) plans (the lesser of $15,000 or 15% of employment income) and IRAs (the lesser of $2,000 or 100% of compensation). See §§404(e), 408(a), and §2.33, infra.

§2.30. Freezing the Value of the Estate

Many wealthy or prospectively wealthy clients seek to prevent any further growth in value of their estates through a so-called estate freeze. It is used most often where the client owns an interest in a closely held business or other unique asset that the client wishes to retain within the family. In the typical transaction, the client exchanges that asset for one with a fixed dollar value, such as preferred stock or a promissory note.

Where a family corporation is involved, an estate freeze often takes the form of a preferred stock recapitalization. See §§11.8 to 11.13, infra. In a typical recapitalization the controlling shareholder exchanges all of his or her common stock for preferred stock that has a fixed value. The rest of the common stock is owned by other, younger family members. The recapitalization leaves the entire equity interest, representing the entire growth potential of the corporation, in the hands of the younger shareholders. Importantly, the controlling shareholder may retain control after the recapitalization where the preferred stock carries the right to vote. Under another approach, a sole shareholder exchanges the outstanding common stock for voting preferred stock that is approximately equal in value to the present value of the corporation plus shares of a new class of common stock of little value that will be given to the younger generation family members.

The other principal methods of accomplishing an estate freeze are reviewed in Chapter 9. They include the installment sale, the private annuity, and the sale and leaseback. Of them, the installment sale is probably the least controversial and the most widely used. See §§9.3 to 9.7, infra. However, changes made by the Installment Sales Revision Act of 1980 have removed some of the income tax ploys that were formerly used. *See* §9.6, *infra*. The private annuity is used less often, perhaps because of its more controversial nature and more uncertain tax consequences. *See* §§9.8 to 9.14, *infra*. A typical private annuity transaction involves the transfer by a senior family member of appreciated property to a junior family member in exchange for the latter's unsecured promise to pay the transferor a specified annual amount for life. The sale and leaseback usually involves the sale of an office or office equipment by a doctor or other professional to family members or a trust for family members, from whom the property is leased back. Although it has some estate-freezing characteristics, it is primarily intended to redistribute income within the family.

§2.31. *Bypassing the Estates of Survivors*

Transferring property in a way that will not subject it to taxation upon the death of the transferee is one of the most fundamental strategies for limiting estate taxes. For example, the estates of married persons are often planned so the surviving spouse will receive the benefit of a portion of the deceased spouse's estate, but it will not be included in the survivor's estate. A qualified terminable interest property trust is the most popular and effective way to accomplish that result. The trust property is includible in the surviving spouse's estate only to the extent an election is made to claim the marital deduction in the estate of the first spouse to die. The balance of the property "bypasses" the surviving spouse's estate. (This is one type of bypass trust). Leaving the surviving spouse a legal life estate in the property is generally a much less satisfactory way of reaching this result than using a trust.

A bypass trust is simply one in which the surviving spouse or other beneficiary is given substantial interests, but not ones that would cause the trust property to be included in the beneficiary's estate. The beneficiary is commonly given a life income interest in the trust, although others are sometimes given the right to receive discretionary distributions of income or principal. (Of course, a trust that allows any distributions to others cannot qualify for the marital deduction.) In addition, the beneficiary may be given a limited power to invade corpus and a special testamentary power of appointment.

A bypass trust may be used to provide for the grantor's descendants. However, the tax incentive to attempt to bypass one or more generations of descendants was eroded somewhat by the adoption of the generation-skipping tax.

Prior to the adoption of the generation-skipping tax in 1976, wealthy individuals frequently established trusts that were designed to provide lifetime benefits to one or more generations of descendants without subjecting the trust property to taxation in the estates of one or more generations of descendants. Of course, the number of generations of estate tax levies that could be "skipped" by a trust is limited to some extent by the applicable Rule Against Perpetuities. Nonetheless, it is quite easy to draft a trust that skips one generation — for example, by a parent creating a trust to pay the income to a child for life and to distribute the principal to and among such of the trustor's issue as the child may appoint. Of course, under the generation-skipping tax the distribution that would take place upon the death of the child is taxable except to the extent it is shielded by the grandchild exclusion ($250,000 for each child of the grantor). *See* §§2613(a)(4), (b)(5), (b)(6). Wealthy individuals may now create bypass trusts for descendants only to the extent the trusts are sheltered by the grandchild exclusion. They may avoid the application of the generation-skipping tax to additional gifts by making separate gifts to or for the benefit of each generation of descendants or by creating layered trusts. Thus, gifts may be made outright to children and grandchildren or to trusts, each of which is created for the benefit of a single generation.

§2.32.   *Deferring the Payment of Estate Taxes*

Substantial savings can be achieved by deferring payment of estate taxes. The estate tax marital deduction, which is discussed in detail in Chapter 5, is the most important deferral option. In essence it allows the payment of the estate tax on a married person's entire estate to be deferred until the death of the surviving spouse. In the interim, the funds that would have been paid in estate tax on the death of the first spouse are available for use by the surviving spouse. The estate and gift tax marital deductions can also be used to equalize the sizes of the spouses' estates, which may reduce the overall estate tax burden because of the progressive nature of the estate tax.

> **Example 2-27.** W has an estate of $1,000,000, but her husband, H, owns only a nominal amount of property. If W dies in 1982, leaving all of her property in a form that does not qualify for the marital deduction, her estate will have to pay state and federal death taxes of at least $283,000 ($345,800 less the unified credit of $62,800). Of course, in that case, no tax would be due when H died. On the other hand, if W leaves all of her property to H in a form that qualifies for the marital deduction, no tax will be due from her estate. If the property retains the same value and H dies in 1987, his estate will be subject to a tax of about $153,000 ($345,800 less the unified credit of $192,800). If W's estate were allowed a marital deduction of $600,000 her estate would have to pay only $59,000

($121,800 less the unified credit of $62,800). In that case when H died in 1987 leaving an estate of $600,000 no tax would be due from his estate ($192,800 less the unified credit of $192,800). The combined use of the marital deduction and unified credits could reduce the overall tax from $283,000 to $59,000.

Another important deferral opportunity is extended to the estates of persons who own substantial interests in closely held businesses. Where the interest in a closely held business comprises a large enough part of a decedent's estate, the estate tax attributable to that interest may be paid over a maximum of 15 years under §6166. Deferral under §6166 is particularly attractive because the tax attributable to the first $1 million in value of the business is only subject to a 4% interest rate. *See* §6601(j) and §11.26, *infra*. The balance of the deferred tax is subject to an interest rate that is adjusted annually based on the prime rate quoted by commercial banks to large businesses. §6621.

Section 6166 allows the executor to defer making any payment on the principal amount of the tax until 5 years after the due date of the estate tax return, after which the tax is payable in equal annual installments over a period of not more than 10 years.

Lifetime planning decisions for clients who own interests in closely held businesses should be made in light of the important opportunity for deferral under §6166. For example, a client's gift program should be planned in a way that will leave a client's estate with a sufficient interest in the business to meet the requirements of §6166. *See* §7.10, and Chapters 11 & 12, *infra*. The same considerations may lead a client to transfer additional property to a corporation in order to increase the value of the client's stock holding and to reduce the nonbusiness portion of the client's estate.

§2.33. *Tax-Sheltered Retirement Contributions*

Qualified retirement plans and IRAs offer the ultimate tax shelter: Contributions are not taxed to the participant; earnings accumulate free of tax; and the value of benefits payable to the participant's survivors is generally not includible in the participant's gross estate. This section summarizes the rules applicable to the retirement shelters, IRAs, and self-employed retirement plans, which are available to a large number of clients on an optional basis. The importance of these devices was increased by the changes made by the 1981 Act. Of course, professionals and other self-employed persons who incorporate may take advantage of the less restrictive rules applicable to corporate qualified plans. However, the general subject of qualified plans and employee benefits is beyond the scope of this book. Life insurance and related employee benefits, such as death benefit only plans, are discussed in Chapter 6.

Individual Retirement Arrangements (IRAs). The limited retirement tax shelter first made available by the Employee Retirement Income Security Act of 1974 (ERISA) for contributions to IRAs by individuals who were not covered by any qualified plan was expanded by the 1981 Act to offer an important tax shelter to millions of employees and self-employed individuals. In order to encourage saving and to allow the accumulation of a retirement fund free of tax, the 1981 Act liberalized the rules applicable to IRAs by removing the requirement that the contributor not be covered by any other plan and by increasing the amounts of allowable contributions. Specifically, beginning in 1982 an employee or self-employed person may deduct contributions to an IRA to the extent of the greater of $2,000 or the amount of his or her earned income for the year, whether or not he or she is covered by a qualified plan. §219(b). An IRA can take the form of an individual retirement account, an individual retirement annuity, or a retirement bond, each of which is described below. Where the contribution also covers the individual's spouse, the dollar limit was increased from $1,750 to $2,250 if the couple files a joint income tax return for the year. §219(d). Alternatively, an individual who participates in a qualified plan of an employer, a government, or a governmental agency may deduct the amount of voluntary contributions to the plan, not to exceed the lesser of earned compensation for the year or $2,000. §219(e)(2). In order to be deductible, the plan must allow voluntary employee contributions, the contribution must be voluntary, and the employee must not have designated the contribution as nondeductible. §219(e)(2).

Importantly, an IRA is exempt from tax and the earnings on funds contributed to it accumulate free of tax. §408(e)(1). However, disqualification results if the owner of an individual retirement account engages in a prohibited transaction (§408(e)(2)) or the owner of an individual retirement annuity borrows any money under the annuity or through use of the annuity (§408(e)(3)). Taken together the deduction under §219 and the tax-free status of the accumulated earnings represent a substantial incentive to make annual contributions to an IRA. Note also that under §2039(f) the proceeds of an IRA are not included in the contributor's gross estate if they are payable as an annuity to a person other than the contributor's executor. For this purpose an annuity is an arrangement for a series of substantially equal periodic payments for life or for a period extending over a period of at least 36 months following the contributor's death. Of course, the beneficiary will have more flexibility if the benefit is payable in a lump sum. In this connection remember that the unlimited marital deduction will offset the inclusion of amounts paid outright to a surviving spouse. For a discussion of post-mortem planning considerations regarding qualified plans, *see* §12.21, *infra.*

Individual retirement account (§408(a)). An individual retirement account is a domestic trust or custodial account managed by a bank or other qualified person (§408(h)), created for the exclusive benefit of an individual or the individual's beneficiaries. The trust must be in writing and meet the requirements of §408(a), which, in brief, are as follows:

1. Contributions on behalf of any individual must be limited to $2,000 per year except for amounts rolled over from other IRAs and plans;
2. No part of the funds can be invested in life insurance contracts;
3. The assets of the fund cannot be commingled with other property except in common trust or common investment funds;
4. The interest of the contributor is nonforfeitable;
5. If the contributor (or the contributor's spouse who has begun to receive benefits) dies before complete payout, the balance must be distributed within 5 years or used to purchase an annuity for the beneficiary; and
6. Distributions to the contributor will commence before the end of the taxable year in which the contributor becomes 70½ years of age.

Amounts distributed to a contributor prior to age 59½ are subject to an additional special tax of 10% of the amount of the distribution that is included in the contributor's gross income. §408(f)(1). However, the additional tax does not apply to distributions made by reason of the contributor's death or disability.

A contributor may direct the investments made for the account. However, beginning in 1982 any amount invested in "collectibles" (defined as "any work of art; any rug or antique; any metal or gem; any stamp or coin; any alcoholic beverage, or any other tangible personal property specified by the Secretary for purposes of this subsection," §408(n)(2)) is treated as a distribution to the owner. §408(n)(1).

It is important to note that distributions from qualified plans of various kinds, IRAs, and retirement bonds may be rolled over into an individual retirement account without incurring any current income tax liability. *See* §§402(a)(5), (a)(7); 403(a)(4), (b)(8); 405(d)(3); and 409(b)(3)(C). The rollover must be made within 60 days of the date of the distribution to the contributor, or to the contributor's spouse in the case of a rollover by a surviving spouse under §402(a)(7). *See* §12.21, *infra*. A rollover of this type is not subject to the contribution limits of §408(a). The use of a rollover allows the distributee to control to a higher degree the time at which the distribution will be taxed for income tax purposes. In particular, the application of the tax may be deferred until withdrawals are made from the account (generally not before 59½ and not later than 70½).

In general, distributions from an IRA are includible in the gross income of the distributee as ordinary income. §§408(d), 409(b)(1). However, as noted above, distributions may be rolled over without the imposition of any tax. §408(d)(3). Also, under certain circumstances contributions in excess of the authorized amount may be returned to the contributor free of tax. §408(d)(4), (5). Finally, the transfer of an interest in an IRA to a former spouse under a divorce decree or related written instrument is not taxable. §408(d)(6). Instead, after such a transfer the former spouse is treated as the owner of the interest.

Individual retirement annuity (§408(b)). An individual retirement annuity is an annuity or endowment contract issued by an insurance company that is nontransferable by the owner. §408(b). In addition, the premiums are not fixed, the annual premium for any individual cannot exceed $2,000, and any refund of premiums must be used before the end of the following year to pay future premiums. §408(b)(2). Also, the interest in the annuity must be distributed to the contributor before the end of the year in which the contributor becomes $70\frac{1}{2}$ years of age or will be distributed over the life of the owner (and his or her spouse) or over a period not extending beyond the life expectancy of the owner and the owner's spouse. §408(b)(3). The interest of the owner must be nonforfeitable. §408(b)(5). Individual retirement annuities are also generally subject to the income and estate tax rules that apply to individual retirement accounts.

Retirement bonds (§409). A retirement bond is a special class of bonds issued by the United States Treasury for the purpose of allowing individuals a secure investment for the tax free accumulation of a retirement fund. The bonds may be purchased from Federal Reserve Banks and branches, from the Bureau of Public Debt, or through commercial banks and trust companies. However, the low interest rate payable on the bonds makes them relatively unattractive when compared with other available forms of investment. Under §409(a) retirement bonds are nontransferable; provide for payment of interest or redemption yield on redemption; bar payment of interest if redeemed within 12 months of issuance; limit the amount that may be purchased to $2,000 each year except for roll over contributions; and provide for payment of no interest after the contributor attains $70\frac{1}{2}$ years or after a date 5 years after the contributor's death.

Within the limits generally applicable to IRAs, investments in retirement bonds are deductible for income tax purposes in the year of purchase. Accordingly, the bonds have a zero basis and the entire proceeds are includible in gross income at the time of redemption unless the proceeds are reinvested in another bond or are rolled over into another IRA or qualified plan. §409(b). The proceeds of a redemption made before the investor becomes $59\frac{1}{2}$ years of age that are not reinvested or rolled over are subject to a special 10% excise tax unless the investor is disabled. §409(c).

Self-employed retirement plans (§401(c), (d). Self-employed persons, including partners, who choose not to incorporate and enjoy the benefits of a corporate retirement plan may create an important tax shelter by establishing an exempt retirement plan covering themselves and their employees, if any. Such plans, usually called Keogh Plans or H.R. 10 plans, were first authorized by the Self-Employed Individuals Tax Act of 1962. The plans are subject to the basic rules that apply to corporate qualified plans. In addition, plans that cover owner-employees must comply with the strict rules of §401(d). In particular, contributions for employees must be nonforfeitable at the time they are paid (§401(d)(2)(A)), and the plan must cover all employees with 3 or more years of service (for this purpose a year of service is one in which the employee works 1,000 hours or more) (§401(d)(3)). Perhaps most important, plans covering owner-employees cannot allow employer contributions on behalf of an owner-employee of any amount in excess of the allowable deduction. The 1982 Act increased the limit on contributions to defined benefit plans to the lesser of $15,000 or 15% of earned income. §404(e). Previously the dollar limit was $7,500. However, a contribution of the lesser of $750 or 100% of earned income may be contributed on behalf of an employee whose adjusted gross income for the year (determined without regard to any community property laws or the deduction allowable under §404(a)) is not more than $15,000. §404(e)(4). Defined benefit plans are subject to a different limit, calculated under regulations that are designed to insure reasonable comparability of tax favored retirement benefits regardless of the nature of the plan. §401(j).

Within the limits described above, contributions to self-employment retirement plans are deductible under §404 and the earnings of the plans are not subject to the income tax. Distributions are generally taxed as ordinary income when received by the recipient. §402(a). Death benefits are not taxed to the extent they constitute life insurance in excess of the cash surrender value of the policy at the time of the contributor's death. §72(m)(3)(c). The value of benefits receivable by a person other than the contributor's executor is generally excludible from the contributor's gross estate. See §2039(c) and §12.21, infra. As described in §12.21, a lump sum distribution is not excludible unless the recipient elects under §2039(f) to forego the favorable 10-year averaging for income tax purposes.

Distributions from self-employed retirement plans are subject to the same restrictions that generally apply to other qualified plans and IRAs. Thus, amounts may not be withdrawn by an owner-employee before the contributor becomes 59½ except in the case of death or disability. §401(d)(4)(B). Any amounts distributed to an owner-employee prior to that time are subject to a special additional 10% tax. §72(m)(5). Distributions may be made to other employees prior to age 59½ without penalty. Plans that cover owner-employees must provide for the distribution of benefits no later than age 70½. §401(a)(9). The distribution may be in the form of a lump sum, payments over the lifetime of the contributor or over the lifetimes of the contributor and his or her spouse, or over a period not longer than the lifetime of the contributor or the lifetimes of the contributor and his or her spouse. *Id.* If an owner-employee dies prior to the complete distribution of plan benefits to the contributor, balance must be paid out within 5 years after the contributor's death (or the death of the contributor's spouse) or be used to purchase an immediate annuity for the contributor's beneficiary payable for the life of the beneficiary (or for a period not extending beyond the life expectancy of the beneficiary). §401(d)(7).

Community Property

[W]e can appropriately reflect the realistic situation by recognizing that the husband's pension rights, a contingent interest, whether vested or not vested, comprise a property interest of the community and that the wife may properly share in it. *Marriage of Brown,* 544 P.2d 561, 570 (Cal. 1976).

The characterization of retirement benefits as community or separate property is important in some circumstances, such as the dissolution of marriage or death of a spouse. Thus far, most courts have applied the local community property laws, which recognize the community character of vested or unvested employee benefits accrued during marriage. *See, e.g.,* Marriage of Brown, 544 P.2d 561 (Cal. 1976) and DeRevere v. DeRevere, 491 P.2d 249 (Wash. App. 1971); Reppy, Community and Separate Interests in Pensions and Social Security Benefits After *Marriage of Brown* and ERISA, 25 U.C.L.A. L. Rev. 417 (1978). However, the Supreme Court has found that some federal retirement programs preempt state community property laws. McCarty v. McCarty, 453 U.S. 210 (1981)(military retirement benefits); Hisquierdo v. Hisquierdo, 439 U.S. 572 (1979) (Railroad Retirement Act). It is generally doubtful that the federal laws regarding qualified plans preclude the characterization of interests in the plans under local community property laws. In the absence of a more specific preemption, the courts should recognize the overriding local concern with family law matters. The gift and estate tax exclusions for the nonemployed spouse's community property interest in qualified plans (§§2517(c), 2039(d)) are consistent with the determination of the spouse's rights under local law.

BIBLIOGRAPHY

I. Gift tax. See the references listed in Chapters 7 and 8, *infra.*
II. Estate tax. See the references listed in the chapters that deal with the particular topic (*e.g.,* materials on the estate tax marital deduction are listed at the end of Chapter 5, and those dealing with life insurance are listed at the end of Chapter 6).

III.   Generation-skipping tax:

        Brush, The Generation-Skipping Transfer Tax: An Explanation and Analysis, 58 Taxes 451 (1980)

        Covey, R., Generation-Skipping Transfers in Trust (3d ed. 1978)

        Hodges, Generation Skipping Transfers and the Marital Deduction, 6 Est. Plan. 14 (1979)

        Horn, Planning Suggestions to Minimize the Effect of the Generation Skipping Tax, 5 Est. Plan. 130 (1978)

        McCaffrey, Planning for Generation Skipping Transfers, 14 Real Prop., Prob. & Tr. J. 722 (1979)

        McCaffey & Metrick, Planning for the Generation-Skipping Transfer, U. Miami 12th Inst. Est. Plan., Ch. 20 (1978)

IV.   Planning Strategies:

        Cooper, A Voluntary Tax? New Perspectives on Sophisticated Tax Avoidance, 77 Colum. L. Rev. 161 (1977)

CHAPTER 3

Concurrent Ownership and Estate Planning

A. Introduction

111

A.   INTRODUCTION

§3.1.   Scope

This chapter is concerned with the 3 principal forms of coownership of legal interests in property other than the partnership form. They are, in order of discussion: the tenancy in common; the joint tenancy and the tenancy by the entirety; and community property. Each section discusses the characteristics of the form, the methods by which it is created, the federal tax consequences of transactions involving its use, and planning suggestions. Some special survivorship forms of ownership of deposits in financial institutions and of United States savings bonds are considered in connection with the discussion of joint tenancies.

Throughout the chapter dominant consideration is given to coownership of property by spouses, who are most likely to own property together. Because of the differences in substantive and tax law treatment, it is imperative that the planner be aware of the characteristics of the principal forms of coownership. Community property is discussed in some detail because of its importance to present or past residents of the 8 community property states. Planners in noncommunity property states must also be aware of the basic characteristics of community property because of the migrant nature of our population. Under basic conflicts of law rules, the nature of a couple's interests in property is generally fixed at the time of acquisition and does not vary although they later move to a state with a different marital property regime.

B. TENANCY IN COMMON

§3.2. *Substantive Law Summary*

A tenancy in common is a form of concurrent ownership between 2 or more persons, in which each cotenant owns an undivided fractional interest in the property. The interests need not be equal, but each tenant has an equal right to occupy the whole of the property. The interest of each tenant is freely transferable and devisable. In the ordinary case there is no right of survivorship between the tenants. However, the instrument creating the tenancy may provide for survivorship interests. Although most states follow the general rules regarding tenancies in common, there are some variations. For example, Wisconsin recognizes a tenancy in common with an indestructible right of survivorship. Zander v. Holly, 84 N.W.2d 87 (1957); Sheedy & Sullivan, Nature of Cotenancies and Their Taxation — Death and Gift, 56 Marq. L. Rev. 3, 5 (1972). Oregon takes a similar approach. Or. Rev. Stat. §93.180 (1979); Holbrook v. Holbrook, 403 P.2d 12 (Ore. 1965). A corporation, trust, or other artificial legal entity may be a tenant in common, but not a joint tenant.

§3.3. *Creation*

A tenancy in common may be created by the express terms of a will, conveyance, or other instrument of transfer ("to X and Y as tenants in common"). However, more often it results from a transfer to 2 or more persons that does not specify the type of tenancy the transferor intended to create or the extent of each transferee's interest (*e.g.,* "to A, B, and C"). In many states, a transfer to 2 or more persons creates a tenancy in common and not a joint tenancy unless the instrument of transfer clearly manifests an intent to create a joint tenancy. *E.g.,* Cal. Civ. Code §683 (West 1981 Supp.); N.Y. EPTL §6-2.2(a) (McKinney 1980 Supp.). Those states have reversed the ancient constructional preference that favored joint tenancies. In them a conveyance to "X and Y jointly" would probably be characterized as a tenancy in common and not as a joint tenancy. Of course, property gratuitously transferred to a husband and wife may create a tenancy by the entirety in common law states that recognize that form of ownership. N.Y. EPTL §6-2.2(b) (McKinney 1980 Supp.).

By Termination of Joint Tenancy. A tenancy in common may also be created when a joint tenancy is severed, as it is when one joint tenant transfers an interest in the joint tenancy property to a third party.

Example 3-1. X devised Blackacre to his daughters, A and B, in a way that was sufficient to constitute them as joint tenants. Prior to the death of either of them, B conveyed her interest to her stepsister, C. Following the conveyance A and C own Blackacre as tenants in common. Each is free to dispose of her interest in the property by deed or will.

Also, property owned by a husband and wife as joint tenants or tenants by the entirety may be converted into a tenancy in common if their marriage is dissolved and the property is not otherwise disposed of in the decree of dissolution.

A joint tenancy may also be converted into a tenancy in common by an agreement of the tenants or a decree of a court that directly or indirectly terminates the right of survivorship. *E.g.*, Reilly v. Sageser, 467 P.2d 358 (Wash. App. 1970) (agreement eliminating survivorship feature); Mann v. Bradley, 535 P.2d 213 (Colo. 1975) (divorce property settlement agreement providing for sale of premises and division of proceeds upon occurrence of certain events evidences intent no longer to hold the property in joint tenancy). As suggested by *Mann* and other cases, property settlement agreements incident to marital dissolutions should provide expressly for the disposition of all of the property of the spouses.

Community Property States. Community property states recognize that married persons may hold title to property as tenants in common. In such a case, the interest of each spouse is owned as separate, not community, property. However, in some states a gratuitous transfer to a husband and wife ("to H and W") may be treated as their community property. Estate of Salvini, 397 P.2d 811 (Wash. 1964). In California and Texas property conveyed in that manner probably would be owned by the husband and wife as tenants in common. W. deFuniak & M. Vaughn, Principles of Community Property §69 (2d ed. 1971).

Upon the death of a spouse, the property formerly owned as community property may be owned by the surviving spouse and the deceased spouse's successors as tenants in common. This result occurs where the community property interest of the deceased spouse is devised to a person other than the surviving spouse or where the deceased spouse dies intestate and the surviving spouse is not entitled to receive all of the deceased spouse's share in the community property under the local law. *See, e.g.*, Pritchard v. Estate of Tuttle, 534 S.W.2d 946 (Tex. Civ. App. 1976).

Example 3-2. H and W owned Whiteacre as community property. H's will devised his interest in Whiteacre to their daughter, D. Following H's death W and D own Whiteacre as tenants in common.

The community property of a couple may also be converted into tenancy-in-common property upon the termination of their marriage, either according to the express terms of a decree of dissolution or by a decree of dissolution that does not dispose of the community property.

> If the marital relationship between the parties no longer exists by reason of divorce (dissolution), the prerequisite to community property is gone. Therefore, the former community property, if not changed from its community status by a transfer while the two were married and if not allocated by the divorce (dissolution) court, will be held by the former spouses as equal tenants in common. Cross, The Community Property Law in Washington, 49 Wash. L. Rev. 729, 818 (1974).

The same rule is followed in other community property states, including California (Tarien v. Katz, 15 P.2d 493 (Cal. 1932)) and Texas (Fox v. Smith, 531 S.W.2d 654 (Tex. Civ. App. 1975) (profit sharing plan)). The rule commonly extends to all forms of existing or inchoate community property that are not allocated by decree, including employee benefits and insurance policies. Accordingly, it is important to provide for the disposition of all of the community property of a husband and wife upon dissolution of their marriage.

§3.4. *Termination*

No gift occurs upon the termination of a tenancy in common if each tenant receives a share of the property or its proceeds proportional to his or her ownership interest in the tenancy. A gift does occur, however, if a tenant receives less than his or her proportional share.

> **Example 3-3.** X and Y each contributed one-half of the cost of acquiring Blackacre as tenants in common. They recently sold Blackacre for $100,000, of which X received $60,000 and Y received $40,000. The division involved a gift of $10,000 from Y to X unless the unequal division was made in the ordinary course of business. *See* Reg. §25.2512-8.

§3.5. *Miscellaneous*

The fractional interests of tenants in common in real property may be voluntarily or involuntarily partitioned into individually owned parcels. If a partition is not practical, a sale of part or all of the property may be required. Although the provisions vary somewhat from state to state, all states provide a form of action for partition of real property.

4A R. Powell, Real Property ¶609 (rev. ed. 1975). Personal property may also be partitioned by voluntary or involuntary action.

The interest of a tenant in common is usually subject to creditor's claims to the same extent as other individually owned property. That is, a creditor may reach the fractional interest of the debtor-tenant, but not the interest of any other tenant.

§3.6. Gift Tax

The creation of a tenancy in common may constitute a gift, depending upon the manner of acquisition and the extent of each tenant's interest in the property. A gift of course results where one tenant contributes a disproportionate amount of the purchase price. However, the acquisition, with the separate funds of one spouse, of an asset in the names of both spouses as tenants in common qualifies for the unlimited gift tax marital deduction.

> **Example 3-4.**   T provided the entire purchase price of Greenacre, title to which was taken in the names of T and X, who are not married. Under the local law T and X own Greenacre as tenants in common. When T purchased Greenacre, he made a gift of one-half of the purchase price to X. If T and X were married, the gift would qualify for the gift tax marital deduction under §2523.

Apart from the marital deduction, the creation of a tenancy in common between spouses is treated in the same way as the creation of the tenancy between unrelated parties.

> **Community Property.** The conversion of community property into a tenancy in common owned in equal shares by a husband and wife does not involve a taxable transfer for federal gift or estate tax purposes. Commissioner v. Mills, 183 F.2d 32 (9th Cir. 1950); Rev. Rul. 55-709, 1955-2 C.B. 609. After such a conversion presumably each spouse is free to dispose of his or her interest in the property by reason of the general rule that one spouse may transfer separate property without the consent of the other spouse. Because of the fiduciary relationship between the spouses, a conversion procured by fraud, undue influence, or other inequitable means is vulnerable to challenge by the disadvantaged spouse.

> **Example 3-5.** H induced W to participate in the formal conversion of their community property ranch into a tenancy in common for "tax reasons." Shortly thereafter, H transferred all of his interest in the ranch to his nephew and instituted dissolution proceedings

against W. The conversion would not involve any gift by H or W. However, it might be subject to challenge by W if it was to her disadvantage.

The transfer of property held by a husband and wife as equal tenants in common into a community property form of ownership should not involve a gift because each spouse owned a one-half interest in the property before and after the transfer. *See* Rev. Rul. 77-359, 1977-2 C.B. 24, discussed at §3.28, *infra*. As a general rule, no gift occurs where the value of the property interests owned by each spouse is not affected by the transfers.

§3.7. Estate Tax

In general, the interest of each tenant is includible in the tenant's gross estate under §2033 in accordance with basic estate tax principles.

> **Example 3-6.** T left Blackacre by will to "A and B in equal shares," which is effective under the local law to constitute A and B as equal tenants in common. The interests of A and B are freely transferable. Upon the death of either A or B, the value of a one-half interest in Blackacre is includible in the deceased tenant's estate.

The interest of the surviving tenant ordinarily is not includible in a deceased tenant's estate. In the case of a decedent who died prior to 1982, the survivor's share of the property would have been includible in the decedent's estate under §2035 where the decedent created the tenancy with his or her own property within 3 years of death.

It is important to note that the reach of §2040(a) may be blunted by converting a joint tenancy into a tenancy in common. (The unlimited marital deduction and the qualified joint interest rule of §2040(b) make it unnecessary for married joint tenants to attempt to avoid the application of §2040(a).) The courts and the IRS seem now to agree that §2040(a) applies only to property held in joint tenancy form at the time of a decedent's death. *See, e.g.,* Glaser v. United States, 306 F.2d 57 (7th Cir. 1962); Rev. Rul. 69-577, 1969-2 C.B. 173. Accordingly, the amount of property includible in a joint tenant's estate may be limited by converting a joint tenancy into a tenancy in common prior to the joint tenant's death. As indicated above, such a conversion will occur if one of the tenants transfers an interest in the property to another person or the survivorship feature is eliminated by agreement. Only a one-half interest in property is includible in a decedent's estate where it was originally acquired in joint tenancy form entirely with the decedent's funds, but the tenancy is severed prior to the decedent's death and the property is held as a tenancy in common at the time of the decedent's death. This rule applies even when the severance is made within 3 years of death.

Example 3-7. X, who is not married to Y, paid the entire cost of acquiring Blackacre, title to which was taken in the names of "X and Y as joint tenants." The purchase of the property involved a gift from X to Y of one-half of the value of Blackacre. If the title remains in that form, the entire value of Blackacre is includible in X's estate. However, only one-half of the value of Blackacre is includible in X's estate if the joint tenancy is terminated prior to X's death. The necessary termination might occur if Y's interest is transferred or if the tenants agree to hold the property as tenants in common.

§3.8. Income Tax

Neither the creation nor the termination of a tenancy in common usually involves any recognition of gain or other income tax consequences. The income from property owned as tenants in common is taxed to the tenants in accordance with their respective rights to the income under the local law. In the absence of a contrary agreement, each tenant is ordinarily entitled to a part of the income proportionate to his or her ownership interest in the property.

§3.9. Conclusion

The tenancy in common is used infrequently in planning and organizing the ownership of family wealth. However, individuals sometimes do convey or devise interests in real or personal property to children, or other family members, as tenants in common. The transfer of property to multiple parties as tenants in common is often preferable to its transfer to them as joint tenants. Overall, it is generally best if each transferee receives a fee interest in a separate parcel of property or the property is transferred to a trustee for the benefit of the intended donees. If a client contemplates transferring property to multiple parties as tenants in common the planner should tell the client about the problems that can arise regarding the management and disposition of undivided interests in real property. The relationship between the parties may be aggravated by the difficulty of obtaining a satisfactory partition or liquidation of one tenant's interest. The potential for additional problems is increased if the interests of the tenants are further fractionalized upon their deaths. Because the tenancy in common lacks a survivorship feature, it does not have the popular appeal of the joint tenancy or some of the other will substitutes. An inter vivos or testamentary trust provides a far more flexible and intelligent method of arranging title than a tenancy in common.

Individuals may choose to take title to investment property as tenants in common. If so, it is desirable for them to have an agreement regarding the partition or sale of the property if one, or both, wish to terminate their coownership of the property. Also, individuals associated in a professional practice may purchase an office building as tenants in common. For example, partners in a medical practice may acquire real property initially as tenants in common. Perry v. United States, 520 F.2d 235 (4th Cir. 1975), *cert. denied,* 423 U.S. 1052 (1976). However, the ownership of such a building by the partnership, or a corporation or trust created by the parties, is more typical.

All in all, the creation of a tenancy in common probably results more often from the absence of effective estate planning than from an intelligently formulated plan.

C. JOINT TENANCY AND TENANCY BY THE ENTIRETY

§3.10.   Introduction

The historical joint tenancy stressed the presence of the four unities — the unity of interest, the unity of title, the unity of time and the unity of possession. This meant that joint tenants had one and the same interest, accruing by one and the same conveyance, commencing at one and the same time, and held by one and the same undivided possession. The last of these four unities was alone prerequisite for a tenancy in common. All four of these unities, plus the additional fact of the tenants being husband and wife, characterized the tenancy by the entireties. 4A R. Powell, Real Property ¶615 (rev. ed. 1975).

The joint tenancy form of ownership is a very popular form of ownership, particularly between husband and wife. Hines, Personal Property Joint Tenancies: More Law, Fact and Fancy, 51 Iowa L. Rev. 582 (1966). The popularity of the joint tenancy is primarily attributable to the right of survivorship, which makes it a simple and effective probate avoidance device. Under it, when a joint tenant dies, the surviving joint tenant or tenants own the entire interest in the property by operation of law. Thus, a deceased tenant's interest is not subject to disposition by will or administration in the decedent's estate. The following commonly recognized advantages of the joint tenancy were identified by Professor Regis

Campfield in his article, Estate Planning for Joint Tenancies, 1974 Duke L.J. 669, 671–673:

a. Jointly held property oftentimes enjoys preferential treatment for state death tax purposes;
b. Jointly held property is free from the claims of creditors of either spouse;
c. Joint property expresses the idea of partnership in a marriage and reinforces family security and harmony;
d. Joint property reduces administration costs;
e. Joint property avoids probate delays;
f. Joint property avoids publicity;
g. Joint property is convenient; and
h. Joint property avoids fragmentation of ownership.

The principal disadvantages of joint tenancies spring from their general inflexibility and the inability of tenants to dispose of the property by will except upon the death of the survivor. The potentially adverse tax consequences of joint ownership by spouses were largely eliminated by the 1981 Act. However, the excessive use of joint tenancies may deprive a decedent's estate of needed cash, thereby causing problems of liquidity. It also deprives the survivors of income-tax-splitting opportunities to the extent the estate is eliminated as a separate income-tax-paying entity. *See* §4.4, *infra.* The principal vice of the joint tenancy is that the entire interest in the property passes to the surviving tenant outright — which makes it all subject to inclusion in the survivor's estate.

Joint tenancies are not complete will substitutes and should not be taken as such. It is almost invariably necessary for the tenants to have wills that dispose of other assets and the joint tenancy property if the testator is the survivor, to appoint guardians for minor children, etc.

Overall, the joint tenancy is neither an estate-planning panacea nor a disaster. It is reasonable for some persons with small estates to hold all of their property in joint tenancy and for most persons so to hold some of their property, such as checking or savings accounts. "All joint tenancies are not cursed. Ordinarily, there would not seem to be any real harm in spouses holding their house as joint tenants, or maintaining their household bank account in that manner." Manning, Planning for Problems Created by Various Types of Property and Ownership, N.Y.U. 30th Inst. Fed. Tax 623, 660 (1972).

§3.11. Features of Joint Tenancies

Most states allow 2 or more individuals to hold real or personal property in joint tenancy, under which each tenant owns an equal, undivided interest in the property. The joint tenancy is distinguished from the tenancy in common primarily by the right of survivorship. As mentioned above, the right of survivorship operates upon the death of one tenant so that the surviving tenant (or tenants) becomes the exclusive owner (or owners) of the property. Because of the survivorship feature, an artificial legal entity, such as a corporation, cannot be a joint tenant. However, individual trustees may hold trust property as joint tenants.

Joint tenancies were once favored by the law; however, now they are generally disfavored by both judicial decisions and legislative enactments. The law of many states provides that a joint tenancy may only be established by a written instrument that expressly declares the interest created to be a joint tenancy. *E.g.*, Cal. Civ. Code §683 (West 1981 Supp.); Nev. Rev. Stat. §111.065 (1979); Wash. Rev. Code §64.28.010 (1979). The courts have generally required complete compliance with such statutes in order to create a valid joint tenancy. Accordingly, a conveyance "to A and B jointly" would probably not create a joint tenancy. Instead, A and B would probably hold the property as tenants in common. *See* §3.3, *supra.*

Joint accounts in financial institutions are generally subject to special statutory provisions that impose different requirements. The accounts are often called joint tenancy accounts, but they ordinarily would not qualify under the common law definition for failure to satisfy the 4 unities. Unfortunately, the law in most states regarding joint accounts is confusing and unclear. However, there is hope: The law regarding multiparty accounts is effectively rationalized and clarified by Article VI, Part 1, of the Uniform Probate Code. In general, the UPC recognizes that a joint account belongs to the parties in proportion to their respective net contributions to the account. Under this approach, the interest of a party *passes* at death to the surviving account holder or holders. It rejects the joint tenancy theory that each tenant was seized of the whole from the inception of the joint tenancy. In the case of joint accounts the courts may be more willing to treat an ambiguous account as carrying a right of survivorship. For example, in a case involving the question of whether a right of survivorship attached to an account in the name of "A or B," the Washington Court of Appeals stated that "[w]e think the modern policy favors the avoidance of probate administration by use of joint tenancy survivorship rights." In re Estate of Bonness, 535 P.2d 823, 833 (Wash. App. 1975).

Simultaneous Death. Section 3 of the Uniform Simultaneous Death Act, 8 U.L.A. 605, 617 (1972), provides, in substance, that the tenancy is severed in case the joint tenants die simultaneously. Under it the undivided interest of each tenant is distributed as if he or she had survived the other.

Example 3-8. A and B, who own Blackacre as joint tenants, die simultaneously. The right of survivorship is inoperative. That is, one-half of Blackacre will be distributed in the estate of A as if A were the surviving joint tenant and the other half will be distributed similarly in the estate of B.

The estate tax consequences of a simultaneous death are discussed at §3.17, *infra*.

Creditor's Rights. The creditors of a joint tenant can ordinarily reach the tenant's undivided interest in the property until the tenant's death. (If a joint tenant's interest is taken in satisfaction of a tenant's debt, the joint tenancy is severed and the holding shifts to a tenancy in common.) The common law does not allow the creditors of a deceased joint tenant to reach the property unless an action was commenced prior to the tenant's death or the property was transferred into the joint tenancy in fraud of creditors. Of course, the limitation on the reach of creditors is meaningful only if the deceased tenant's estate is insolvent or the property of the decedent's estate is otherwise exempt from the reach of creditors. A 1966 California decision, Rupp v. Kahn, 55 Cal. Rptr. 108, 113 (Cal. App.), concluded that "the entire title held by a surviving joint tenant resulting from a conveyance by an insolvent without consideration, is subject to the debts of the transferor." The alleged insulation of joint tenancy property from the claims of creditors is often illusory.

Community Property. The community property states allow spouses to acquire and hold property in joint tenancy form. If a valid joint tenancy is created the interest of each spouse is properly characterized as separate property. The law of most community property states allows community property to be transmuted into joint tenancy ownership. However, the policy favoring community property may require the proponent of the joint tenancy to support the transmutation by clear and convincing evidence. Estate of Bogert, 531 P.2d 1167 (Idaho 1975).

Courts in several community property states have concluded that the joint tenancy and community property forms of ownership are mutually exclusive. In Estate of Cooke, 524 P.2d 176 (Idaho 1974), the court put it quite succinctly: "[P]roperty held in a joint tenancy between husband and wife is not community property. If a true joint tenancy exists, created according to statute, each spouse owns his or her respective interest as separate property." The same rule applies in Arizona (Collier v. Collier, 242 P.2d 537 (1952)), California (King v. King, 236 P. 912 (1915)), and New Mexico (N.M. Stats. §40-3-8(6) (1978)).

If the interest of each spouse is separate property, presumably each is free to make a gratuitous transfer of his or her interest to a person outside the marital community without the consent of the other spouse.

(Some community property states do not allow a spouse to make an inter vivos gift of community property without the consent of the other spouse. *See* §3.24, *infra*.) It is unclear why the courts have not allowed community property to be held in joint tenancy form, which would permit the survivorship feature to operate. The courts have recognized that community property may retain its character when it is transferred to an inter vivos trust or is made subject to some other survivorship arrangements. A creative approach to the community property-survivorship problem was recently taken in Nevada. Legislation effective July 1, 1981, allows a husband and wife to hold community property with right of survivorship. *See* §3.26, *infra*. Presumably the IRS will recognize the community property character of the property despite the survivorship feature.

§3.12. *Tenancy by the Entirety*

A tenancy by the entirety is essentially a joint tenancy between husband and wife. It was once favored by the law, but has declined in importance and is now recognized in less than half the states. 4A R. Powell, Real Property ¶621 (rev. ed. 1975). The tenancy is usually created in land, although some states permit personal property to be held in the same manner. The characteristics of the tenancy vary from state to state, particularly regarding the rights of the wife. In some states the husband alone is entitled to the income from the property and the wife cannot convey any interest in the property or cause a partition of it. The characteristics of the tenancy, of course, have an impact on its treatment for tax purposes. Thus, a gift to a husband and wife in North Carolina did not qualify for the annual exclusion as to the wife's interest because she had no enforceable interest in the rents, income, or profits from the property during coverture. Rev. Rul. 75-8, 1975-1 C.B. 309.

The tenancy is usually created by a conveyance of real property to a husband and wife, designated as such in the instrument of conveyance. For example, in states that recognize the tenancy, a conveyance of land to "H and W, husband and wife" is effective to create a tenancy by the entirety between them in the property. The outcome is less certain where other language is used or additional persons also receive interests under the conveyance. *See* 4A R. Powell, Real Property ¶622 (rev. ed. 1975). Where an instrument is ineffective to create a tenancy by the entirety, the transferees usually hold the property as tenants in common.

None of the community property states recognize the tenancy by the entirety. It is mentioned in a Washington statute that expressly abolishes the right of survivorship as an incident of the tenancy by the entirety (Wash. Rev. Code §11.04.071 (1979)), but it is not referred to in another statute that lists the permissible forms of joint ownership (Wash. Rev.

Code §64.28.020 (1979)). Statutes of the latter type have been construed as evidencing the unavailability of the tenancy by the entirety in the jurisdiction. Swan v. Walden, 103 P. 931 (Cal. 1909) (construing Cal. Civ. Code §686 (West 1954)).

At best the tenancy by the entirety is an anachronistic duplication of the joint tenancy; at worst it is an unjustifiable form of discrimination against women. The extent to which it will survive, and the characteristics it will have in the future, are uncertain. The characteristics of the tenancy favoring the husband have been attacked in several federal court actions. Klein v. Mayo, 367 F. Supp. 583 (D. Mass. 1973), *aff'd mem.*, 416 U.S. 953 (1974); D'Ercole v. D'Ercole, 407 F. Supp. 1377 (D. Mass. 1976). Although the attacks were unsuccessful, the Massachusetts statute was subsequently amended to eliminate the discrimination against wives.

For estate-planning purposes the significance of the tenancy depends upon its characteristics under the governing law. In most cases it will produce the same tax consequences as a joint tenancy, which may or may not be satisfactory for the circumstances of a particular couple. It can be used to obviate the necessity of an estate administration proceeding in another state in which the client owns real property or immovable personalty. However, it does not eliminate the need for a proceeding on the death of the surviving joint tenant. Overall, a revocable trust is better suited to help the clients avoid ancillary estate administration proceedings.

§3.13.   Gift Tax

The gift tax consequences of creating a joint tenancy depend upon whether the tenants are married to each other, the nature and valuation of the interests of the tenants, and the amount each tenant contributed toward the acquisition of the property. Property transferred into joint tenancy form qualifies for the unlimited gift tax marital deduction, §2523(d). In most states one tenant acting alone can sever the joint tenancy, thereby terminating the right of survivorship and converting the holding into a tenancy in common. Accordingly, in those states each tenant is considered to have an equal interest in the joint tenancy property regardless of age. In contrast, interests must be valued actuarially where the joint tenancy is not unilaterally severable.

> **Example 3-9.** X, a 78-year-old unmarried female, conveyed Blackacre into joint tenancy with right of survivorship with Y, a 45-year-old male. Under the local law (Michigan), when express words of survivorship are used a joint tenancy may be severed only with the consent of all of the joint tenants. Under Reg. §25.2512-9, the

value of an interest dependent upon the continuation of more than one life, a special factor must be used, based upon Table LN of paragraph (f) of Reg. §20.2031-10 with interest at 6%. The appropriate special factor will be given by the IRS upon request. The special factor to be used to value X's retained interest is .21388. Accordingly, the value of X's gift to Y is .78612 times the value of Blackacre. *See* LR 7946080 (Michigan law).

In states that allow the unilateral severance of joint tenancies, the creation of a joint tenancy does not involve a gift if each tenant makes an equal contribution toward the acquisition of the property. For example, no gift occurs if community property is used to acquire an asset in joint tenancy. However, a gift of one-half of the value of the property would occur where one person transfers previously owned property into a joint tenancy without any contribution by the other tenant or tenants. The same result occurs where one person provides the funds with which an asset is purchased and title is taken in the name of the donor and another as joint tenants.

Example 3-10. X, an unmarried man, purchased stock with his own funds, the certificates for which were issued in the names of X and Y as joint tenants with right of survivorship. The purchase of the shares involved a gift to Y of one-half of the fair market value of the stock.

The interest transferred to the donee constitutes a present interest that qualifies for the annual gift tax exclusion. As noted above, the interest qualifies for the marital deduction where the donor and donee are married. Section 2523(d) provides expressly that the survivorship interest of the donor and the right of severability do not constitute a retained interest for purposes of determining whether the interest was terminable under §2523(b).

Example 3-11. W paid $50,000 of her noncommunity property for securities that were issued in the names of W and H as joint tenants with right of survivorship. The total gift to H was $25,000, which qualifies for the annual exclusion and the marital deduction.

Exception to the General Rule — Revocable Transfers. There is an important exception to the basic rule that a transfer of property by a donor into joint tenancy with a donee is a present gift. It treats the creation of a joint tenancy in certain types of assets as a revocable transfer that does not involve a present gift. In those cases the donor has the right to recover the entire interest in the property at any time without obligation to the donee. Within this exception are joint bank accounts, joint United

States savings bonds (*i.e.*, ones acquired in the names of "donor or donee") (Reg. §25.2511-1(h)(4)), and joint accounts with brokerage firms where the securities are held by the firm in "street name" (*i.e.*, the securities are registered in the name of the firm's nominee) (Rev. Rul. 69-148, 1969-1 C.B. 226).

> **Example 3-12.** X created and deposited funds in a joint account in the name of X and Y at a financial institution. Under the local law X may withdraw the entire fund without the consent of Y. X did not make a gift at the time of the deposit of the funds, but does make a gift at any time Y withdraws funds without any obligation to account to X.

In general, where a donor places funds in a joint tenancy that allows the donor to withdraw the full amount without obligation to the donee, no gift takes place until the donee withdraws the funds for his or her own account. The same rule applies in some states that impose gift taxes. *E.g.*, California, Cal. Adm. Code Tit. 18, §15104.3(a).

Pre-1982 Exception — Transfers of Real Property to a Spouse. Prior to 1982 the creation of a joint tenancy in real property between husband and wife was not deemed a transfer for gift tax purposes regardless of the proportion of the consideration furnished by each spouse, unless the donor elected to treat the transaction as a gift by filing a timely gift tax return. *See* former §2515(a), (c). If the donor spouse did not treat the creation of the joint tenancy as a gift, the donor was treated as owner of the entire property for most gift and estate tax purposes. Thus, a gift took place if the joint tenancy was later terminated and the donor spouse did not receive all of the proceeds of the termination. Former §2515(b).

> **Example 3-13.** In 1979 W provided all of the funds used to purchase Blackacre, title to which was taken in the names of H and W as joint tenants with right of survivorship. W did not file a gift tax return treating the purchase of Blackacre as a gift. H and W sold Blackacre in 1981 for $100,000, one-half of which was paid to each of them. The sale constituted a termination of the joint tenancy under former §2515(b) and the payment of $50,000 to H was treated as a gift. Of course, the gift qualified for the gift tax exclusion and the pre-1982 gift tax marital deduction under §2523.

Under former §2515(a) additions to the value of the joint tenancy property or reductions in the indebtedness thereon were subject to the same election.

Under the pre-1982 law an election under §2515(c) also had important estate tax consequences. In brief, if creation of the joint tenancy was reported as a gift, each spouse was treated as owning a one-half interest in the property for estate tax purposes. Former §2040(b). Otherwise, the entire value of the joint tenancy property was includible in the donor spouse's estate if the donor died first. §2040(a). None of the value was includible in the estate of the donee spouse if he or she died first. As illustrated by the following example, reporting the creation of the joint tenancy as a gift was disadvantageous in some cases:

> **Example 3-14.** In 1978 W paid the entire $100,000 cost of acquiring Blackacre, title to which was taken in the name of "H and W as joint tenants with right of survivorship." W elected to report the creation of the joint tenancy as a gift under §2515. Because W had already made gifts of more than $100,000 to H, the purchase of Blackacre resulted in a taxable gift of $47,000 ($\frac{1}{2}$ × $100,000 − $3,000 annual exclusion). When H died in 1981, one-half of the value of Blackacre was included in his gross estate. Thereafter, W owned the entire interest in Blackacre — all of which is includible in her estate. Under the pre-1982 law W's election under §2515 caused the same one-half interest to be subject to transfer tax 3 times.

Disclaimer. The disclaimer of an interest in a joint tenancy does not involve a gift if the disclaimer constitutes a qualified disclaimer under §2518(b). According to Prop. Reg. §25.2518-2(d)(3), to be a qualified disclaimer

> of an interest in a joint tenancy (other than a revocable joint tenancy, such as a revocable joint bank account) or a tenancy by the entirety, the disclaimer
> (i) Must be made with respect to the entire interest in property which is the subject of the tenancy,
> (ii) Must be made within 9 months of the creation of the tenancy, and
> (iii) Must meet each of the remaining requirements in section 2518(b).

Presumably, the parenthetical exclusion of joint tenancy bank accounts is based on their unique character and the impossibility of the noncontributor effectively accepting an interest during lifetime without actually withdrawing funds from the account. A surviving joint tenant could not make a qualified disclaimer of a joint tenancy interest within 9 months of its creation if he or she had accepted "the interest or any of its benefits." See §2518(b)(3).

Under the 1981 Act a surviving joint tenant's interest in joint tenancy property can be validly disclaimed under §2518 regardless of whether the local law permits joint tenancy survivorship interests to be disclaimed. See §2518(c)(3). Briefly, a written transfer of the surviving joint tenant's entire interest in the property will be recognized as a qualified disclaimer, if

    1. The written transfer is received by the original transferor of the interest or the transferor's legal representative within 9 months of the original transfer (*see* §2518(b)(2));

    2. The surviving joint tenant has not accepted the interest or any of its benefits; and

    3. The interest is transferred to the same person(s) who would have received the interest if the transferor had made a qualified disclaimer of it (*i.e.,* the transfer cannot "redirect" the interest to another person).

The rule is particularly helpful because it is doubtful that the common law in most states allows a survivorship interest to be effectively disclaimed. *See, e.g.,* Bishop v. United States, 338 F. Supp. 1336 (N.D. Miss. 1970), *aff'd,* 468 F.2d 950 (5th Cir. 1972); Krakoff v. United States, 313 F. Supp. 1089 (S.D. Ohio 1970), *aff'd,* 439 F.2d 1023 (6th Cir. 1971). Statutes in some states permit a surviving joint tenant to disclaim the interest of a deceased joint tenant that would otherwise be owned by the survivor by right of survivorship. For example, the Uniform Disclaimer of Transfers Under Nontestamentary Instruments Act allows a surviving joint tenant or his or her representative to disclaim interests in joint tenancy: "A surviving joint tenant [tenant by the entireties] may disclaim as a separate interest any property or interest therein devolving to him by right of survivorship. A surviving joint tenant [tenant by the entireties] may disclaim the entire interest in any property or interest therein that is the subject of a joint tenancy [tenancy by the entireties] devolving to him, if the joint tenancy was created by the act of a deceased joint tenant [tenant by the entireties] and if the survivor did not join in creating the joint tenancy [tenancy by the entireties]." §1, 8 U.L.A. 33 (1981 Supp.).

    In appropriate cases, joint tenancy interests can be disclaimed in order to "fine tune" the amount of property passing to a surviving spouse for purposes of achieving the optimum estate tax marital deduction. Otherwise, a carefully constructed estate plan could be frustrated by the unwitting transfer of too much of their property into joint tenancies. Joint tenancies could be disclaimed, for example, in order to preserve the advantages of wills that include trusts that qualify for the elective marital deduction under §2056(b)(7), where a husband and wife held most of their property in joint tenancy form at the time of the death of the first spouse.

§3.14. Estate Tax: General Rule

Prior to 1976 all property held in joint tenancy at the time of a decedent's death was subject to inclusion in the decedent's estate under the provisions of §2040(a). Under that rule the entire value of jointly held property is included in the estate of a deceased joint tenant "unless the executor submits facts sufficient to show that property was not acquired entirely with consideration furnished by the decedent, or was acquired by the decedent and the other joint owner or owners by gift, bequest, devise, or inheritance." Reg. §20.2040-1(a)(2). Where the survivor contributed toward the acquisition of the joint tenancy, a proportionate part of its value is excluded from the decedent's estate. This "proportionate contribution" rule applied whether or not the creation of the joint tenancy was treated as a gift. The proportionate contribution rule continues to apply to all joint tenancies except to ones between husband and wife. See §3.15, infra.

The application of the basic rule is illustrated in the following example.

> **Example 3-15.** O and P each provided one-half of the cost of purchasing securities, certificates for which were issued in their names as joint tenants. Upon the death of either O or P, one-half of the value of the securities is includible in the decedent's gross estate.

However, if the decedent had given the survivor the money or other property that the survivor contributed toward the cost of acquiring the property, the entire value of the property is includible in the decedent's gross estate. The rule is the same where the property contributed by the survivor toward the acquisition increased in value between the date of the gift to the survivor and the acquisition of the joint tenancy property. Reg. §20.2040-1(c)(4).

The contribution of the surviving joint tenant toward the cost of acquiring joint tenancy property, although derived from a gift received from the decedent, is taken into account in some cases. Specifically, any income received by the survivor on property given to him or her by the decedent and applied toward the acquisition of the joint tenancy property is counted as a contribution by the survivor. Reg. §20.2040-1(c)(5). Gain received by the survivor on property given to him or her by the decedent is also taken into account. Thus, "[w]hen the transfer to the joint tenancy consists of proceeds realized by the survivor upon a sale of property acquired with monies transferred from the decedent, the sale proceeds attributable to appreciation in value during the survivor's ownership of the acquired property are considered the survivor's individual contribution to the joint tenancy for purposes of section 2040." Rev. Rul. 79-372, 1979-2 C.B. 330; see also Estate of Marcia P. Goldsborough, 70 T.C. 1077 (1978).

Gifts to Decedent and Survivor as Joint Tenants. Where an asset was gratuitously transferred to the decedent and others as joint tenants, only the decedent's pro rata share of the property is includible in the decedent's estate. Thus, where Blackacre was devised to A and B as joint tenants, only one-half of the value of Blackacre is included in the estate of the first of them to die. For additional examples see Reg. §20.2040-1(c)(7),(8). The proportionate interest includible in the gross estate of a deceased tenant is increased, however, if he or she made subsequent unreimbursed contributions in connection with the property (*e.g.*, additions or improvements).

§3.15. Estate Tax: Joint Tenancies between Husband and Wife (§2040(b))

In view of the unlimited marital deduction adopted by the committee bill, the taxation of jointly held property between spouses is only relevant for determining the basis of property to the survivor (under sec. 1014) and the qualification for certain provisions (such as current use valuation under §2032A, deferred payment of estate taxes under secs. 6166 and 6166A, and for income taxation of redemptions to pay death taxes and administration expenses under sec. 303). Accordingly, the committee believes it appropriate to adopt an easily administered rule under which each spouse would be considered to own one-half of jointly held property, regardless of which spouse furnished the original consideration. H.R. Rep. No. 97-201, 97th Cong., 1st Sess. 160 (1981).

The 1976 Act added §2040(b), which first introduced the concept of the "qualified joint interest" between husband and wife, one-half of which is includible in the estate of the joint tenant first to die. For purposes of §2040 a qualified joint interest is a joint tenancy (or tenancy by the entirety) in which the husband and wife are the only tenants. The 1981 Act eliminated the requirement that the creation of the joint tenancy must have been treated as a gift for gift tax purposes. The more complex rules of subsections 2040(c), (d), and (e) were repealed by the 1981 Act.

Treatment as a qualified joint interest under §2040(b) usually results in no particular advantage or disadvantage because the unlimited marital deduction is available to the estate of the spouse first to die. Of course, it does result in a stepped-up basis of the portion included in the decedent's estate.

Example 3-16. W paid $50,000 for stock that was issued in the name of "H and W as joint tenants with right of survivorship." The purchase of the stock resulted in a gift of $25,000 to H, which qualified for the annual gift tax exclusion and the marital deduction. When W died one-half of the value of the stock was included in her gross estate, but the interest qualified for the estate tax marital deduction. When H dies, the full value of stock will be includible in his estate. The results would have been the same had H predeceased W.

Essentially the same tax treatment applies to property acquired by the spouses as tenants in common where the interest of the spouse first to die is left to the surviving spouse. In such a case the interest of the spouse first to die is included in his or her estate, but an offsetting marital deduction is allowable.

Former §2040(d). The Revenue Act of 1978 allowed spouses to convert pre-1977 joint tenancies into qualified joint interests by reporting the conversion in a gift tax return filed for any quarter of 1977, 1978, or 1979. As noted above, this provision, along with subsections 2040(c) and (e), was repealed by the 1981 Act. The amount of the gift at the time of conversion depended upon whether the original creation of the joint tenancy had been treated as a gift. Where the donor furnished all of the consideration and the creation of the tenancy was not treated as a gift, a conversion under former §2040(d) resulted in a gift equal to one-half of the total value of the property. Former §2040(d)(5). In contrast, where the creation of the tenancy was treated as a gift, the amount of the gift taking place by filing the return was limited to one-half of the post-acquisition appreciation in value of the property. Former §2040(d)(4).

Example 3-17. In 1955 H paid $50,000 for real property, title to which was taken in the name of "H and W as joint tenants with right of survivorship." H did not elect to treat the acquisition of the property as a gift. The property was worth $150,000 in 1978 when H elected to file a gift tax return under §2040(d). The conversion resulted in a gift of one-half of the total value of the property, or $75,000. However, the gift qualified for the annual exclusion and the marital deduction.

Example 3-18. The facts are the same as in Example 3-17, *supra*, except that H treated the creation of the joint tenancy as a gift in a timely-filed 1955 return. When H elected to convert the property into a qualified joint interest, he made a gift of $50,000 (one-half of the total post-1955 appreciation in value).

Former §2040(e). For a time spouses could change a pre-1977 joint tenancy into a qualified joint interest by proceeding under §2040(e). Until it was repealed by the 1981 Act, §2040(e) required the termination of the pre-1977 joint tenancy and creation of a new one between the spouses. In addition, the donor was required to elect to subject the transaction to §2040(d) in a gift tax return filed with respect to the calendar quarter in which the "new" joint tenancy was created. Former §2040(e)(1). The amount of the gift arising from the creation of a new joint tenancy was calculated in accordance with the rules applicable to elections under former §2040(d).

§3.16. Estate Tax: Eligible Joint Interests (Former §2040(c))

The concept of the eligible joint interest was added by the Revenue Act of 1978 in order to allow a limited reduction in the value of joint interests held with a surviving spouse in real or tangible personal property used as a farm or in any other trade or business. A joint tenancy (or tenancy by the entirety) qualified as an eligible joint interest only if it was created by one or both spouses and did not include any other person. This subsection allowed the value of an eligible joint interest to be reduced by an amount, not to exceed $500,000, on account of contributions made by the surviving spouse. Former §2040(c)(2)(B). However, in no event could the election result in the inclusion of less than 50% of the value of the eligible joint interest. Former §2040(c)(2)(A). For purposes of the reduction, the survivor's contributions consisted of (1) contributions actually made plus 6% simple interest from the time made and (2) an amount equal to the excess of the value of the eligible joint interest over the total consideration furnished by either or both spouses, increased by 6% simple interest and multiplied by 2% for each year (not to exceed 25) that the surviving spouse materially participated in the farm or other business. The latter figure was called the "section 2040(c) value."

> **Example 3-19.** In 1946 H purchased a farm for $50,000, title to which was taken in the names of "H and W as joint tenants with right of survivorship." The farm was worth $500,000 when H died in 1981 (35 years later) survived by W. W materially participated in the operation of the farm in each year, but did not make any out of pocket contribution towards its acquisition. H's executor was allowed to elect to reduce the value includible in his estate on account of the farm to $327,500 (a reduction of $172,500) computed as follows:
>
> | | | |
> |---|---:|---:|
> | Value of eligible joint interests | | $500,000 |
> | Adjusted consideration furnished by W | $0 | |
> | Adjusted consideration furnished by H | | |
> | Purchase price | 50,000 | |
> | Simple interest at 6% for 35 years | 105,000 | |
> | Total consideration furnished by H | | |
> | and W | | 155,000 |

Value of eligible interest less adjusted consideration		345,000
Percentage reduction for years of W's material participation (2% × maximum of 25 years)		.50
Section 2040(c) value		$172,500
Amount includible in H's gross estate Value of eligible joint interest		$500,000
Less:		
Contributions made by W, plus 6% interest	$0	
Section 2040(c) value	172,500	172,500
Amount includible		$327,500

Prior to the adoption of §2040(c) some courts had recognized the value of the services contributed by the surviving spouse toward the acquisition of joint tenancy property. Thus, in Estate of Everett Otte, 31 T.C.M. 301 (1972), the Tax Court treated the value of the surviving spouse's labor on the farm as "an adequate and full consideration in money or money's worth in the acquisition of her one-half interest in all the real and personal property enumerated in decedent's federal estate tax return and included in the latter's taxable gross estate." 31 T.C.M. at 305. In essence, the Tax Court allowed the personal services of the surviving joint tenant to be taken to account for the purpose of determining the proportionate contributions under §2040(a). In comparable cases where the title is held in the name of the decedent alone, the surviving spouse may be treated as owning a full one-half interest in the property under a partnership rationale. Craig v. United States, 451 F. Supp. 378 (S.D. 1978) (mem.). *See also* Messinger, Section 2040(c): More Complexity and Limited Relief in Taxation of Jointly Held Interests of Spouses, 34 Tax Law. 89 (1980). The *Otte* rationale may continue to have some viability, particularly where the decedent's interest does not pass to the surviving spouse (or does not pass in a way that qualifies for the marital deduction).

Essentially the same tax treatment applies to property acquired by the spouses as tenants in common where the interest of the spouse first to die is left to the surviving spouse. In such a case the interest of the spouse first to die is included in his or her estate, but an offsetting marital deduction is allowable.

§3.17. Estate Tax: Simultaneous Deaths

Adverse estate tax consequences may occur if joint tenants other than a husband and wife die simultaneously. Under §3 of the Uniform Simultaneous Death Act, "[w]here there is no sufficient evidence that two joint tenants or tenants by the entirety have died otherwise than simultaneously the property so held shall be distributed one-half as if one had survived and one-half as if the other had survived." 8 U.L.A. 605, 617 (1972). In 2 revenue rulings the IRS has asserted that if the Act is applicable, the entire value of the property is includible in the gross estate of the tenant who provided all of the consideration paid to acquire the property and one-half is includible in the estate of the other tenant. Rev. Ruls. 66-60, 1966-1 C.B. 221, 76-303, 1976-2 C.B. 266. The IRS analysis no longer applies in the case of a husband and wife because of the joint interest rule of §2040(b). In other cases the adverse effect should be reduced by the availability of the previously taxed property credit under §2013. The rule also could be avoided if the sole contributor were deemed to be the survivor.

In Rev. Rul. 66-60, 1966-1 C.B. 221, the government asserted that the full value of the property was includible under §2040 in the gross estate of the tenant (H) who provided the full consideration and one-half was includible under §2033 in the estate of the other tenant (W) because the survivor had the power under the Act to dispose of one-half of the property. The analysis was changed by Rev. Rul. 76-303, 1976-2 C.B. 266, which held that §2040 applies only if the other tenant survives. Accordingly, only the value of the one-half of the property with respect to which W was considered to have survived was includible in H's estate under §2040. The full value of that one-half was includible because there was no evidence that W had furnished any consideration for the acquisition of the property. However, none of the value of the one-half interest, with respect to which H was deemed to be the survivor, was includible in W's estate under §2040 because H provided all of the consideration for the property.

Rev. Rul. 76-303 also held that one-half of the value of the property was includible in each tenant's gross estate under §2033: "[S]ince each is considered to have survived as to one-half of the property, each is considered to have acquired an absolute, sole ownership interest in one-half of the property before death. Thus, the value of one-half of the property is includible in each of their gross estates under section 2033 of the Code." Under this approach the one-half interest included in H's estate should have qualified for the marital deduction. In other instances a previously taxed property credit should be available to the survivor's estate under §2013.

Of course, the 2 rulings under discussion antedated the adoption of the qualified joint interest rule. Accordingly, they only involved the proportionate contribution rule and did not indicate that any different result would occur if the joint tenants were husband and wife. In the case of the simultaneous deaths of a husband and wife after 1981, presumably one-half the total value of the joint tenancy property would be included in each spouse's estate under §2040(b). If each such interest is disposed of as if the decedent's spouse did not survive, then no marital deduction would be available. In such a case it would be difficult to uphold the inclusion of any additional amount of the property in either spouse's estate. On the other hand, if a marital deduction were allowed for the one-half included in one spouse's estate, then the full value of the property should be included in the other spouse's estate under §2033.

The position taken in Rev. Rul. 76-303 might also be contested on the basis of the Tax Court's holding in Estate of Nathalie Koussevitsky, 5 T.C. 650 (1945), *acq.,* 1945 C.B. 4, that when §2040 is applicable no section other than §2035 may also be applied. The contest might be assisted by the general hostility of the courts to the operation of §2040.

§3.18. Estate Tax: Termination of Joint Tenancies

As noted above, the proportionate contribution rule of §2040(a) is restricted if the joint tenancy is terminated, even though the termination occurs within 3 years of death. According to the regulations, §2040 applies to property "held jointly at the time of the decedent's death by the decedent and another person or persons with right of survivorship." Reg. §20.2040-1(a). Most important, the courts have held that §2040 has no application to property transferred before the decedent's death. *E.g.,* Glaser v. United States, 306 F.2d 57 (7th Cir. 1962). Where the creation of the joint tenancy was treated as a gift, a severance allows one-half of the post-gift appreciation to escape taxation on the death of the donor. (Of course, this result will occur without a severance where the tenants are husband and wife and the joint tenancy is a qualified joint interest under §2040(b). *See* §3.15, *supra.*) A severance can backfire if the donee tenant predeceases the donor. In such a case the proportionate contribution rule of §2040(a) no longer applies and the full value of the donee's interest in the property is includible in the donee's estate.

In the past some commentators complained that the treatment given terminated joint tenancies was unduly favorable and was based on an unnecessarily narrow construction of the statute. *See* C. Lowndes, R. Kramer & J. McCord, Federal Estate & Gift Taxes 284-285 (3d ed. 1974); *see also* Campfield, Estate Planning for Joint Tenancies, 1974 Duke L.J. 669, 707-708. Given the unification of the transfer tax system and the adoption of the unlimited marital deduction, it is hard to become too concerned over the issue. The present treatment is undesirable in the sense that it represents a triumph of form over substance and places a premium on obtaining sophisticated estate-planning advice. Overall, the estate tax law would be much simpler and more straightforward if the law merely required the inclusion of a proportionate interest in the property upon the death of any joint tenant.

Example 3-21. X paid the full $100,000 cost of acquiring Black-acre, title to which was taken in the name of X and his brother, Y, as joint tenants with right of survivorship. The purchase of Black-acre resulted in a gift of $50,000 from X to Y, which qualified for the annual gift tax exclusion. The joint tenancy in Blackacre was severed a week before X died, when it had a value of $200,000. As a result, X and Y held Blackacre as tenants in common. The sever-ance did not result in a gift, because X and Y each already owned a full one-half interest in Blackacre. Estate of Sullivan v. Commis-sioner, 175 F.2d 657 (9th Cir. 1949). X's estate includes one-half of the value of Blackacre at the time of his death ($100,000). The amount of the original taxable gift is probably includible in X's tax base as a post-1976 adjusted taxable gift. *See* §2001(b).

Example 3-22. The facts are the same as in Example 3-21, *supra.* However, instead of severing the joint tenancy and holding Black-acre as tenants in common, X and Y transferred their interests to a trust from which each was entitled to receive one-half of the income and to dispose of one-half of the principal. Only one-half of the trust property is includible in X's gross estate under §2036, on account of his reserved life estate. Rev. Rul. 69-577, 1969-2 C.B. 173. The same result would follow if they transferred Blackacre to other parties, reserving life estates to themselves. United States v. Heasty, 370 F.2d 525 (10th Cir. 1966). Presumably the adoption of §2035(d) does not affect the outcome in this case.

§3.19.   *Income Tax*

The creation of a joint tenancy does not ordinarily have any immediate income tax consequences. However, the transfer of some special types of assets may generate some income tax liability. In particular, the transfer of property into joint tenancy probably constitutes at least a partial dis-position of installment obligations under §453B and investment recap-ture (section 38) property under §47(a). The creation of a joint tenancy ordinarily should not involve recapture of depreciation under §§1245 or 1250 because recapture does not take place in the case of transfers by gift.

In some unusual cases the creation of a joint tenancy may be treated as a taxable event and result in the recognition of gain by one or more taxpayers. As one author indicates, "[t]axable gain may also be realized upon creation of the joint tenancy if it is created by an exchange of property owned by one of the joint tenants where the property ex-changed does not constitute a like kind property within section 1031 —

for example, where corporate stock owned by one joint tenant is exchanged for real estate which is conveyed in joint tenancy." Young, Tax Incidents of Joint Ownership, 1959 U. Ill. L.F. 972, 977.

> **Example 3-23.** X, who owned ABC stock with a basis of $100 and a fair market value of $1,000, converts that stock into a joint tenancy with Y; and in exchange Y converts XYZ stock, which has a basis and a fair market value of $1,000, into joint tenancy with X. In effect X transfers an asset with a basis of $50 (a one-half interest in the ABC stock) in exchange for an asset worth $500 (a one-half interest in the XYZ stock). Presumably the gain is taxable to X at the time of the exchange. Y has no gain or loss as a result of the transaction.

If the exchange involved stock in the same corporation, the transaction might not be taxable by reason of §1036. *See* Rev. Rul. 66-248, 1966-2 C.B. 303, which holds that the conversion by a husband and wife of equal amounts of common stock in the same corporation from separate to community was nontaxable.

Income from Joint Tenancy Property. In the absence of an agreement to the contrary, each joint tenant is usually entitled under the local law to an equal share of the income from joint tenancy property. *E.g.,* Lipsitz v. Commissioner, 200 F.2d 871 (4th Cir.), *cert. denied,* 350 U.S. 845 (1955) (applying Maryland law). The income attributable to each tenant is determined by reference to the state law — not necessarily according to the extent of the contributions the tenant made toward acquiring the asset. As indicated above, an unequal distribution of income may constitute a taxable gift from one tenant to the other.

Income Tax Deductions. Conceptually a tenant should be entitled to deduct the taxes and interest the tenant pays only to the extent it exceeds the tenant's right to reimbursement from other tenants. *See* 3 A. J. Casner, Estate Planning 836 (4th ed. 1980). However, a tenant may be entitled to deduct the amount of taxes and interest the tenant actually pays on joint tenancy where the tenants are jointly and severally liable to make the payments. Rev. Rul. 71-268, 1971-1 C.B. 58, followed such a rule in the case of a tenancy by the entirety where the husband and wife filed separate income tax returns. On the other hand, the ruling may merely evidence a more liberal policy of allowing deductions to married persons who make payments without regard to any right of reimbursement. *See* Young, Tax Incidents of Joint Ownership, 1959 U Ill. L.F. 972, 988. Where the joint tenants are husband and wife, the allocation of income and expenses is unnecessary if they file joint income returns.

Basis. The basis of the joint tenants is determined according to the ordinary rules applicable to acquisitions by purchase (§1012); gift (§1015); and inheritance (§1014).

Example 3-24. X provides the entire purchase price of Redacre, title to which is taken in the name of X and Y as joint tenants. X has made a gift of a half-interest in Redacre to Y. Y's basis in the property is one-half of X's cost basis, increased under §1015(d)(6) by the portion of any gift tax paid that is attributable to the appreciation element. However, in no event can Y's basis exceed the fair market value of the interest on the date of the gift.

Under §1014(b)(9) the basis of a surviving joint tenant is determined by the federal estate tax valuation in the decedent's estate to the extent that the property is includible in the decedent's estate. Rev. Rul. 56-215, 1956-1 C.B. 324.

Example 3-25. F and G each paid $5X as the cost of acquiring Orangeacre, title to which was taken in their names as joint tenants. The property increased in value from $10X at the time of acquisition to $20X on the date of F's death. One-half the then value of Orangeacre ($10X) is includible in F's gross estate. G's basis in the property is $15X, a composite of G's cost basis ($5X) and the federal estate tax valuation of the interest included in F's estate ($10X).

However, a survivor will not receive an increase of basis merely by failing to rebut the presumption of §2040 that all of the property is includible in the gross estate of the first tenant to die. Richard v. Madden, 52 T.C. 845 (1969), *aff'd per curiam,* 440 F.2d 784 (7th Cir. 1971). Note also that the alternate valuation date cannot be used unless the decedent's estate was required to file an estate tax return. Reg. §20.2032-1(b); Rev. Rul. 56-60, 1956-1 C.B. 443.

Community Property. In the case of a validly created joint tenancy in property acquired with community property funds, only one-half of the property is includible in the estate of the spouse first to die. In such cases there has been some uncertainty as to whether the basis of the survivor's interest in the property might also be determined by the federal estate tax value of the interest included in the decedent's estate. Under §1014(b)(6) the survivor's interest in community property is also considered to have been acquired from the decedent and, hence, its basis is determined by reference to the federal estate tax value of the decedent's interest. Where the federal estate tax value in the decedent's estate exceeds the otherwise determined basis of the survivor in the property (*e.g.,* its cost), the rule of §1014(b)(6) operates in the taxpayer's favor. In such cases the survivor's basis is increased without any tax cost whatever.

A higher basis is of obvious advantage in the case of depreciable property, in case of sale, etc.

Because planners have focused on the use of the rule to increase the survivor's basis, it is commonly referred to as the "free step up" of the survivor's basis. The applicability of §1014(b)(6) to joint tenancy property acquired with community funds is questionable. As noted above, §3.11, *supra,* the courts of several community property states have held that community property that is transferred to a validly created joint tenancy loses its character as community property. In addition, federal tax cases applying California law have held that the basis of the surviving spouse is not affected by the death of a spouse in the case of community property converted to joint tenancy property (Bordenave v. United States, 150 F. Supp. 820 (N.D. Cal. 1957)) and tenancy in common property (Murphy v. Commissioner, 342 F.2d 356 (9th Cir. 1965)). In *Murphy,* the Ninth Circuit said, "[W]e think congress did not intend that the surviving spouse in a community property state should get a new basis for the one-half separate interest that the survivor owns in former, but converted, community property. There will, however, in such case be a new basis for the one-half interest that is in the decedent's estate, just as is true in Dr. Murphy's estate." 342 F.2d at 360.

Placing community property in joint tenancy form may jeopardize a tax-free increase of the survivor's basis in the property. On the other hand, if it appears that the federal estate tax value of community property on the death of one spouse will be lower than its adjusted basis, a "step down" of the survivor's basis in the property could be averted if the property is transferred into a joint tenancy, partitioned, or otherwise converted into a tenancy in common. *See* §3.29, *infra.*

Termination. The conversion of joint tenancy property into property held as tenants in common or otherwise separately held by the tenants probably does not constitute a taxable event. Dickinson, Federal Income Tax Treatment of Divisions of Property: Marital Property Settlements, Estate and Trust Distributions and Other Transactions, 18 Kan. L. Rev. 193, 229 (1970). This view is supported by Rev. Rul. 56-437, 1956-2 C.B. 507, which held that "[t]he conversion, for the purpose of eliminating a survivorship feature, of a joint tenancy into a tenancy in common is a nontaxable transaction for Federal income tax purposes." A termination involving a transfer of the entire interest in the property to one tenant would not involve any immediate income tax consequences if it was treated as a gift under §102.

§3.20. State Death Taxation of Joint Tenancies

The death tax laws of many states tax property held in joint tenancy under a proportionate contribution rule similar to §2040(a). *E.g.,* Cal.

Rev. & Tax. Code §13671 *et* seq. (West 1981 Supp.); Idaho Code §14-402(5) (1979); Texas Tax-Gen. Ann. art. 14.011 (Vernon 1980 Supp.) (however, in absence of evidence to the contrary, it is assumed that each tenant contributed equally to the joint tenancy). No particular rule is in effect in the states that impose only a "pick up" tax equal to the maximum credit allowable under federal estate tax law for state death taxes paid. The death tax laws of some states favor joint tenancies and tenancies by the entirety by taxing only a pro rata portion of the property upon the death of a tenant even though he or she contributed the entire purchase price. Oregon joined the group in 1975 by adopting legislation that presumes that a surviving spouse owned one-half of property the decedent owned separately and property they held as joint tenants. Or. Rev. Stat. §118.010(2)(b) (1979). A few states do not impose any death tax on joint tenancy property. *E.g.*, Renz' Estate, 61 N.W.2d 148 (Mich. 1953).

§3.21. Conclusion

Tax and nontax considerations dictate that joint tenancies should be used cautiously, if at all. It may be satisfactory for a couple to hold their home and some bank accounts in joint tenancy form. However, in order to avoid bloating the survivor's estate, it may be unwise to pass large amounts of property outright to the survivor. Often assets may better be held in individual ownership and left to a trust for the surviving spouse and their children. Effectuating such a plan may require the termination of some existing joint tenancies, which must be planned with a view toward the gift tax consequences. It may be entirely satisfactory for a couple whose combined estates are less than the credit equivalent to hold all of their property in joint tenancy form. In any case, each spouse should have a back-up will that will (1) dispose of any assets not held in joint tenancy in case the testator dies first, (2) dispose of the testator's share of the assets in case of simultaneous death, and (3) dispose of all of the assets in case the testator is the survivor.

There are some valid nontax reasons for a couple to hold title to the family home and some accounts at financial institutions in joint tenancy form. First, holding property in that form expresses confidence in the marriage and in the ability of the survivor to deal with the property. Second, in many states joint tenancy bank accounts are not "frozen" on the death of a tenant and, thus, are fully and immediately available to the surviving spouse. Third, in some states the fees of the personal representative and the personal representative's attorney are based upon the amount of property accounted for in the estate proceeding, which does not include joint tenancy property, life insurance, and other property that passes outside of the proceeding.

Problem 3-1. Prior to 1982 W paid the full $25,000 cost of acquiring Greenacre, to which she and her husband, H, took title as joint tenants with right of survivorship. No gift tax return was filed with respect to the purchase. Recently the marriage of W and H was dissolved. The decree of dissolution allocated all of their property between them except Greenacre, which had increased to $100,000 in value. Under the local law, a dissolution converts unallocated joint tenancy property into property held by the former spouses as tenants in common. What are the gift and estate tax consequences of the conversion? *See* Rev. Rul. 80-241, 1980-2 C.B. — .

Would the consequences have been any different if Greenacre had been allocated to them in equal shares under the decree? *See* §2516. Under United States v. Davis, 370 U.S. 65 (1962), the transfer by one spouse of appreciated property to the other spouse in exchange for a release by the transferee of all claims and rights against the transferor arising out of the marital relationship is a taxable event. The transferee is considered to have relinquished marital rights equal in value to the property received under the decree. Accordingly, the transferee has no gain or loss and has a basis in the property equal to its fair market value on the date of the transfer. *See* Rev. Rul. 67-221, 1967-2 C.B. 63. Would W be required to recognize a gain on the conversion of Greenacre in this problem?

D. COMMUNITY PROPERTY

There is no single community property "system" in the United States. Arizona, California, Idaho, Louisiana, Nevada, New Mexico, Texas and Washington, of course, draw their community property laws from a common source — the civil law of marital property developed in Spain and brought to North America by Spanish colonists. While the legal fundamentals of community property are similar in the eight states, their legislatures and courts have resolved several problems differently. By varying degrees the states have reworked and refined their community property systems into unique bodies of law. Louisiana still closely adheres to the civil law rules. Elsewhere, notably California, there have been infusions of English common-law principles and extensive statutory "modernization" to meet changing economic and social conditions. W. Reppy & W. de Funiak, Preface to Community Property in the United States at v (1975).

§3.22. *Scope and History*

A brief overview is provided here of the community property laws in effect in our 8 community property states, including their origins, their basic characteristics, and their general tax consequences. It is meant to provide a broad sketch of American community property systems and not a statement of the law of any particular state. The relationship of community property to specific subjects is considered in later portions of the book. For example, the community property aspects of the gift and estate tax marital deductions are discussed in Chapter 5, community property issues concerning life insurance are covered in Chapter 6, and the use of the community property widow's election is explored in Chapter 9. In general, each chapter includes a separate discussion of the relevant community property considerations.

Community property is a civil law system of marital property under which each spouse owns a one-half interest in property acquired during marriage. The system was introduced by early settlers from France and Spain. When the colonies of France and Spain were freed of foreign rule, all of them retained the civil law marital property system. Curiously, all of them except Louisiana abandoned the civil law in favor of the English common law as their basic system of jurisprudence. Community property systems were adopted later in Idaho and Washington, perhaps due to the influence exerted by California.

Eight states in the South and West now have community property systems of marital property (Arizona, California, Idaho, Louisiana, Nevada, New Mexico, Texas, and Washington). While the systems vary somewhat from state to state, they all treat a husband and wife as partners with respect to property onerously acquired during marriage. Of course, the marital community ceases to exist upon the death of a spouse or dissolution of the marriage. Until recently a husband generally had greater managerial powers over community property than his wife. However, legislative changes made in the 1970s extended to each spouse essentially the same powers to manage and control community property.

§3.23. An Introduction to Planning with Community Property

Important property rights and tax consequences are affected by the characterization of property as separate or as community property. Accordingly, one of the planner's first jobs is to determine the character of the property owned by a married person. If the character of some items is uncertain, the planner may recommend that spouses enter into an agreement specifying their respective interests in those items. Of course, the planner should be alert to the tax consequences of interspousal agreements as well as the ethical implications of representing both spouses. The planner may also recommend that the status of some items be changed by agreement, conveyance, or partition. Thus, assets held in joint tenancy may be converted into community property in order to preserve the step up in basis that is available for community property under §1014(b)(6) on the death of one spouse. *See* §3.19, *supra,* and §3.29, *infra.*

Once the character and ownership of the items is properly arranged, the spouses should be given some guidance regarding the maintenance of that arrangement. In particular, they should be advised to keep the separate and community property completely segregated. Thus, separate and community property funds should be kept in separate bank accounts and securities registered in proper forms. Some extra care is required in the states (Idaho, Louisiana, and Texas) that characterize the income derived from separate property as community property. In them, the interest paid on a separate property bank account should be withdrawn at regular intervals and deposited in a community property account. Caution must also be exercised with respect to the reinvestment of the dividends on separately owned mutual funds shares.

The transfer of property to a revocable inter vivos trust may be the best way to preserve its separate or community property character. The transfer of community property to a properly drafted revocable trust should not cause any change in its character. However, in order to preserve the character of the property, such a trust should specify that the property transferred to the trust will remain community property. The provisions of the trust regarding revocation, distribution of income, and other matters should, of course, be consistent with the character of the property transferred to the trust. Thus, a trust of community property should be revocable by the joint action of husband and wife, the income should be payable to them as community property, and the property should retain its community character in the event of revocation. As an alternative one spouse could hold a power of revocation with respect to community property that would be exercisable on behalf of both spouses.

Under California law, community property transferred to a revocable inter vivos trust retains its character if the trust meets the requirements of Cal. Civ. Code §5113.5 (West 1981 Supp.). The requirements generally follow those of an earlier revenue ruling, Rev. Rul. 66-283, 1966-2 C.B. 297, that applied California law. *See also* Katz v. United States, 382 F.2d 723 (9th Cir. 1967) (California law). Idaho has a similar law. Idaho Code §32-906A (1979).

Two principles dominate estate planning in community property states. The first is to take advantage of the change in the income tax basis of all of the community property under §1014(b)(6) upon the death of a spouse. Since §1014(b)(6) applies to the extent property is held as community property at the time of a spouse's death, this principle simply requires that the spouses avoid forms of ownership that do not involve a step up in basis of all of the couple's property (*e.g.,* tenancies in common and joint tenancies). Overall, it is generally desirable to hold property in which both spouses have an interest as community property.

The second principle is to avoid subjecting an unnecessarily large amount of property to taxation upon the death of the surviving spouse. It is most commonly observed by executing wills that leave each testator's property to a qualified terminable interest property trust (*i.e.*, in a way that will cause it to be included in the surviving spouse's estate only to the extent the marital deduction is claimed in the estate of the first spouse to die (*see* §2056(b)(7) and §2.31, *supra*). Some clients attempt to reduce the amount of property subject to tax on the surviving spouse's death and gain some other tax advantages by using a community property widow's election plan. *See* §9.21 to 9.34, *infra*. However, a widow's election plan is unsuitable for most clients because of its rigidity, complexity, and uncertain income tax consequences. *See* §9.23, *infra*.

§3.24. *Separate and Community Property*

The community property states all define separate property as the property owned by a spouse prior to marriage and all property acquired after marriage by gift, inheritance, devise, or bequest. All other property acquired during marriage by a husband or wife is their community property. This "negative" definition of community property is simple to understand and provides the key to answering most questions regarding the characterization of property. It is important to note that marriage itself does not cause any previously owned property to become community property. Quite the contrary: Property owned prior to marriage retains its separate character unless it is changed by agreement or conduct of the parties.

The characterization of an item of property as separate does not mean that only one spouse owns an interest in it. Each spouse may own a separate property interest in the same asset. For example, a husband and wife may own an asset as tenants in common or as joint tenants — both of which are separate property forms of ownership. The ownership interests of the spouses in cotenancy property may approximate their interests in community property, but there are important tax and nontax differences.

Each spouse is generally free to dispose of his or her separate property inter vivos or at death without restriction. However, California and Idaho do give the nonacquiring spouse an interest at death or dissolution of marriage in property acquired during marriage while the couple resided in a noncommunity property state that would have been community property had they been domiciled in California (or Idaho). This "quasi-community property" is discussed further at §3.31, *infra*.

Each spouse owns an equal, undivided one-half interest in all community property. Consistent with that concept of ownership, each spouse has the power of testamentary disposition over only one-half of the community property — the other one-half belongs to the other spouse. California, Idaho, and Washington prohibit one spouse from making a gift of community property without the consent of the other spouse. Cal. Civ. Code §5125(b) (West 1981 Supp.); Wash. Rev. Code §26.16.030(2) (1979); Koenig v. Bishop, 409 P.2d 102 (Idaho 1965). The other states appear to permit a spouse to make reasonable gifts of community property that do not injure or defraud the other spouse. Reppy & de Funiak, *supra* at 338-344; W. de Funiak & M. Vaughn, Principles of Community Property §122 (2d ed. 1971). In order to reduce the potential for conflict, both spouses should consent in writing to any significant gifts of community property.

The character of property as separate or community generally persists through sales, changes in form, and reinvestments. Thus, the proceeds from the sale of an item of separate property and any property purchased with the proceeds would be separate property. In all states the income derived from community property is community. Likewise, in most states the income from separate property is separate. However, in Idaho, Louisiana, Texas, and perhaps Arizona, the income from separate property is community property. Idaho Code §32-906(1) (1980 Supp.); La. Civ. Code Ann. art. 2339 (West Supp. 1981). Until 1980 Texans could not overcome that rule, which caused some estate tax complications under §2036. *See* §6.24, *infra.* However, under the 1980 Amendment of Article XVI, Section 15 of the Texas constitution, the income from the spouses' separate property is community property unless the spouses otherwise agree in writing. *See* Vaughan, Texas Amends Its Constitution and Its Community Property System, 8 Community Prop. J. 59 (1981).

Basic Presumption. In all community property states property acquired during marriage, or owned at the time of dissolution of the marriage, is presumed to be community property. Rebuttal of that presumption generally requires clear, cogent, and convincing evidence to the contrary. The presumption is the basis of the rule that commingled property is community in nature (*i.e.*, any separate property component is lost if it cannot be traced). "In the absence of any statutory qualification, this presumption in favor of community property is given effect regardless of whether the title to the property is taken in the name of one or the other or both of the spouses. Doctrines of the common law relative to presumptions existing when property is purchased by one spouse and taken in the name of the other or in the names of both are not entitled to recognition under a system in which the presumption is that an acquisition is community property of husband and wife." W. de Funiak & M. Vaughn, Principles of Community Property §60 (2d ed. 1971).

Special Problems of Characterization. Certain types of property present particularly difficult problems of characterization. Perhaps the most serious concerns the appreciation in value during marriage of stock owned prior to marriage in a closely held business. Most community property states "first attempt to ascertain whether the community estate has been fairly compensated for the community efforts, by way of salary or otherwise. If this is the case, the entire appreciation will be awarded to the owner-spouse's separate estate." Weekley, Appreciation of a Closely-Held Business Interest Owned Prior to Marriage — Is It Separate or Community Property?, 7 Community Prop. J. 261, 279 (1980). Where the community was not fairly compensated for the owner-spouse's efforts, some part of the appreciation will be treated as community property.

Sticky problems can also arise where separate and community funds are both used to acquire an asset. Where an asset is purchased with a lump sum payment that is made up of community and separate funds, proportionate interests in the asset are held as community and separate property respectively.

> **Example 3-26.** Blackacre was purchased by H and W for $10,000, of which $3,000 was community and $7,000 was W's separate property. In the absence of a contrary agreement, in most community property states, H and W would own a 30% interest in Blackacre as their community property and the balance would be the separate property of W.

Different results may occur where a spouse contracts to buy an asset prior to marriage, but some post-marriage payments on the asset are made from community property. In some states the asset would be treated as separate because it was separate at the time the purchasing spouse first acquired an interest in it (this is called the "inception of title" rule). In those states the community has a right of reimbursement for the payments made from community property. *E.g.*, McCurdy v. McCurdy, 372 S.W.2d 381 (Tex. Civ. App. 1963), *writ refused*. Although the community may be reimbursed, it is generally not entitled to recover any interest on the community funds that were invested in the property. *Id.* In contrast, other states apply the proportionate ownership rule to property acquired with mixed deferred payments, just as in the case of lump sum payments. *E.g.*, Gudelj v. Gudelj, 259 P.2d 656 (Cal. 1953). Thus, if community funds are used to make one-third of the payments on property that was originally acquired as the separate property of one spouse, a one-third interest in the property is held as community property.

The characterization of life insurance acquired with mixed community and separate funds also varies among the states. *See* §§6.9 to 6.12, *infra*. California and Washington generally characterize life insurance according to the proportion of the premiums paid from each source, while the other states usually follow an inception of title approach under which the insurance retains its original character. However, in the latter case, the other estate would be entitled to reimbursement for premiums paid from it.

§3.25. Agreements Regarding Character of Property

The community property states generally allow a husband and wife to enter into agreements regarding the character of their property. *See, e.g.,* Cal. Civ. Code §5103 (West 1970); Nev. Rev. Stat. §123.070 (1979); Wash. Rev. Code §26.16.120 (1979). The restrictions formerly imposed by the Texas constitution were largely removed by a 1980 amendment of Article XVI, Section 15. *See* Vaughan, Texas Amends Its Constitution and Its Community Property System, 8 Community Prop. J. 59 (1981). Some of the states, including California, also recognize oral agreements regarding the ownership of personal property. Spouses may use an agreement to change the character of property from separate to community or vice versa. However, such changes may have important tax consequences. *See* §§3.28 to 3.29, *infra.* Of course, spouses may also partition community property into equally owned units of separate property. Perhaps most important, an agreement can be used to clarify the rights of the spouses in their property where its separate or community property character is uncertain. An agreement could be used, for example, to fix the character of commingled property or to establish the separate or community character of property that is nominally joint tenancy. Because of the inherent conflict in the spouses' economic interests, each party to an agreement should be encouraged to obtain independent counsel.

§3.26. Agreements Governing Disposition of Property at Death

Idaho and Washington have statutes that expressly permit a husband and wife to enter into written agreements regarding the disposition of property at death. Idaho Code §15-6-201 (1979); Wash. Rev. Code §26.16.120 (1979). An agreement subject to the Idaho law may extend to separate and community property, but the Washington law applies only to community property. In both states the agreement is effective to pass the property outright to the surviving spouse without the necessity of any estate administration proceeding. The Idaho statute is simply an expanded version of UPC §6-201, which treats as nontestamentary a variety of arrangements that were often previously challenged as testamentary in nature. Professor Richard Effland has suggested that the amended form of UPC §6-201 adopted in Arizona will sustain interspousal agreements regarding the status and disposition of property at death. Estate Planning under the New Arizona Probate Code, 1974 Ariz. St. L.J. 1, 19.

An agreement of the type under discussion is not itself a sufficient estate plan, even for a couple with a relatively small estate. The agreement should be supplemented with a will to dispose of any property not subject to the agreement and to dispose of all of the property upon the death of the survivor. Also, the agreement is not a complete will substitute — it probably cannot be used to nominate guardians for minor children, direct apportionment of taxes, exercise powers of appointment, dispose of property subject to administration in other states, etc. Finally, property subject to such an agreement probably cannot be set apart to a surviving spouse as a family award or family allowance that is exempt from creditors. Presumably a surviving spouse could disclaim the right to receive the decedent's interest in the property subject to the agreement, which would subject the property to administration in the deceased spouse's estate. See §2518 and §§12.26 to 12.29, infra.

Spouses in community property states are generally free to contract regarding the content or revocability of their wills. However, contractual wills often give rise to serious tax and nontax problems. See §4.5, infra. In most cases clients should be encouraged to use another device, such as an inter vivos trust, instead of contractual wills.

A unique approach adopted by Nevada in 1981 allows the creation of a survivorship right in community property. Specifically, Nev. Rev. Stat. §111.064 provides:

> 2.   A right of survivorship does not arise when an estate in community property is created in a husband and wife, as such, unless the instrument creating the estate expressly declares that the husband and wife take the property as community property with a right of survivorship. This right of survivorship is extinguished whenever either spouse, during marriage, transfers his interest in the community property.

An approach of the type evidenced by the statute increases the number of methods by which a husband and wife can provide for each other yet avoid probate. The law regarding survivorship community property will probably develop more or less parallel to that applicable to joint tenancies. Presumably a dissolution of the parties' marriage would terminate the survivorship feature and constitute the parties tenants in common with respect to the property. Under the statute the survivorship feature is extinguished if either spouse transfers his or her interest in the property. However, there is no indication that a spouse could overcome the survivorship feature by a provision in his or her will. The statute also does not deal with any rights a deceased spouse's creditors may have against the property. The statute provides a shortcut way to pass community property to the surviving spouse without the necessity of an estate administration proceeding, which would be required to pass community property to the survivor under the intestate succession law. It also allows the spouses to avoid the income tax basis disadvantage of putting their property into joint tenancy form. *See* §3.29, *infra*.

§3.27. Estate Tax

Community property is includible in the estate of a deceased spouse to the extent of the decedent's one-half interest. In this connection it is important to note that the characterization of property is governed by the applicable state law and not by federal rules. For example, the amount of property includible in the estate of a deceased spouse may be affected by the terms of a property agreement between the spouses if such agreements are allowed under the local law, as they generally are. Of course, an agreement between the spouses is effective to characterize their property only if the requirements of state law are satisfied. Some states demand more than others to overcome the presumption that property acquired during marriage is community property. In some states an oral agreement may suffice, but in others more is required. For example, Kern v. United States, 491 F.2d 436 (9th Cir. 1974), held that under Washington law the presumption was overcome only if the evidence of separate property ownership was clear, definite, and convincing.

The Code and regulations include some special rules regarding the inclusion of community property in the gross estate in order to preserve the equity of the estate tax. Thus, where the nonemployed spouse dies first, §2039(d) exempts the decedent's community property interest in the portion of a qualified plan that is attributable to the employer's contributions. Also, the regulations recognize that only one-half of the proceeds of community property life insurance is ordinarily includible in the estate of the insured spouse. Reg. §20.2042-1(b)(2). Similarly, where the noninsured spouse dies first, only one-half of the value of a community property policy is includible in the decedent's estate. Reg. §20.2042-1(c)(5). Although it is largely no longer of much significance, the IRS has recognized that only one-half of the value of joint tenancy property acquired with community property funds is includible in a deceased spouse's estate. Rev. Rul. 55-605, 1955-2 C.B. 328 (Nevada).

Deductions. Deductions are allowable under §2053 for expenses of administration, funeral expenses, and debts, to the extent they are chargeable to the decedent's share of the community property under the local law. Thus, where only the decedent's one-half of the community property is subject to administration, the estate is allowed a deduction for the full amount of the administration expenses. On the other hand, where all interests in the community property are administered, the deduction is limited to one-half of the expenses of administration that are not specifically allocable to the decedent's share of the community property. Expenses that relate only to the decedent's share of the community property are fully deductible. Thus, the attorney's fees and other expenses incurred in connection with the determination of federal and state death taxes are fully deductible. Lang's Estate v. Commissioner, 97 F.2d 867 (9th Cir. 1938). Likewise, the costs of appraising the decedent's interest in the community property are fully deductible. Ray v. United States, 385 F. Supp. 372 (S.D. Tex. 1974), *aff'd per curiam on other issues,* 538 F.2d 1228 (5th Cir. 1976).

Funeral expenses are deductible under §2053 only to the extent the decedent's estate is liable for their payment. Accordingly, one-half of the funeral expenses are deductible in a state that makes them a charge against the entire community property. Lang's Estate v. Commissioner, *supra;* Rev. Rul. 70-156, 1970-1 C.B. 190. The IRS has ruled that the expenses are fully deductible in the states that changed their laws to provide that funeral expenses are charged entirely to the decedent's share of the community property. Rev. Rul. 71-168, 1971-1 C.B. 271 (California); Rev. Rul. 69-193, 1969-1 C.B. 222 (Texas).

Deductions for losses and charitable transfers are of course limited to the decedent's interest in the lost or transferred property. *See* §§2054, 2055.

Marital Deduction. An unlimited marital deduction is allowable to the estates of decedents dying after December 31, 1981, regardless of the community or separate character of the decedent's property. That is quite a change from the pre-1982 law. Prior to 1977 no marital deduction was allowable to an estate composed entirely of community property. Technically, the deduction was limited to 50% of the adjusted gross estate, which is the gross estate reduced by the sum of (1) the §2053 and §2054 deductions attributable to the decedent's separate property, and (2) the decedent's interest in the community property. For decedents dying after 1977 and before 1982 a limited marital deduction was allowed with respect to community property. During the 1977 to 1982 period the marital deduction was limited to the greater of 50% of the adjusted gross estate or $250,000. §2056(c)(1)(A). However, the alternate $250,000 amount was reduced to the extent the community property included in the decedent's estate exceeded its pro rata share of the §2053 and §2054 deductions. §2056(c)(1)(C). Accordingly, no marital deduction was allowable where a community property estate had a value of $250,000 or more, net of §2053 and §2054 deductions.

Credits. The unified credit and the credits for state death taxes, taxes on prior transfers, and foreign death taxes are allowable with respect to property included in the decedent's estate, whether it is community or separate in nature.

§3.28.   Gift Tax

Taxable gifts may result from transfers of community property to third parties. Transactions between spouses that affect their respective ownership interests in community property generally qualify for the gift tax marital deduction. §2523. For federal and state gift tax purposes, a gift of community property to a person outside the community is generally treated as 2 gifts — one by each spouse and each for one-half of the total value of the property transferred. Accordingly, each spouse is treated as a donor of the property, whose transfer may qualify for the annual gift tax exclusion.

> **Example 3-27.** In 1982 H and W gave $20,000 of community property cash to their daughter, D. For gift tax purposes H and W are each considered to have made a gift of $10,000 to D. The gifts of course involve present interests that qualify for the annual gift tax exclusion. Accordingly, if neither H nor W makes any other gifts to D in 1982, neither is required to report the gifts to D on a federal gift tax return.

A gift also takes place if one spouse transfers all of his or her interest in a community property asset to the other spouse, who would then own the entire interest in the asset as separate property. Such a transfer of community property qualifies for the gift tax annual exclusion and marital deduction. It would be unnecessary to file a gift tax return with respect to such a gift. §6019.

Transfer of Separate into Community Property. Where one spouse transfers separate property into community property, the transferor makes a gift to the other spouse of an amount equal to one-half of the value of the transferred property. That results because each spouse owns a one-half interest in the property after the transfer. Where both spouses transfer separate property into community property, "a single gift will take place with respect to the conversion of the separately owned properties and the value of the single gift will be the net difference between the value of the husband's (or the wife's) separate property before its conversion into community property and the value of the husband's (or the wife's) interest in the community property resulting from the conversion." Rev. Rul. 77-359, 1977-2 C.B. 24. Such a gift should also qualify for the gift tax annual exclusion and marital deduction. Louisiana law was changed in 1981 to permit spouses to transmute separate property into community property. La. Civ. Code art. 2443.1.

Example 3-28. W transferred $100,000 of her separate property cash into a community property form of ownership with her husband, H. The transfer involved a gift from W to H of one-half of the amount transferred ($100,000 × ½ = $50,000). Such a transfer qualifies for the gift tax annual exclusion and marital deduction. If H had also transferred $50,000 of his separate property into a community property form of ownership with W, the transfers by W and H would be aggregated for purposes of determining the gift tax consequences. After the transfers were made each spouse would own a community property interest worth $75,000 (½ × ($100,000 + $50,000)). H would not have made a gift since he transferred property worth $50,000 and received an interest worth $75,000. W would have made a gift of $25,000, since she transferred property worth $100,000 and received an interest worth only $75,000.

Partition of Community Property into Separate Property. The partition of community property into equal shares of separate property does not involve a gift because each spouse continues to own an interest of equivalent value. Probably no gift occurs if each spouse receives either an equal interest in each asset or the whole interest in assets of the same total value. As indicated in §3.29, *infra,* either type of division should not require any recognition of gain. The result should be the same regardless of the type of separate property ownership. Thus, a transfer of community property into joint tenancy or tenancy in common does not involve a gift. In 1981 Louisiana changed its laws to allow spouses to partition community property into separate property. La. Civ. Code arts. 2336, 2341.

Conversion of Future Income into Separate Property. An agreement that the future income of each spouse will be his or her separate property may constitute a gift. The gift might not take place when the agreement is executed because of the impossibility of valuing the interests involved. *Cf.* Rev. Rul. 69-346, 1969-1 C.B. 227. Presumably gifts would occur over time as income is earned by one or both spouses. Here, again, the analysis is largely of academic interest since the gifts should qualify for the gift tax marital deduction.

Example 3-29. H and W entered into an agreement, valid under the local law, that the employment income of each spouse will be the separate property of the spouse who earns it. It was impossible to determine the gift tax consequences at the time the agreement was made. In the following year H was unemployed and W received employment income of $25,000. H may be treated as having made a gift of $12,500 to W if the agreement was effective to cause the entire $25,000 to be treated as W's separate property. Such a gift should qualify for the gift tax annual exclusion and marital deduction.

§3.29. Income Tax

In general the income tax law follows the state law characterization of income and expenditures. Thus, the income earned by a married couple in a community property state is naturally "split" between them. Given the progressive character of the income tax rates, the split of community property income between the spouses was of great advantage to couples who lived in community property states so long as the federal law required each spouse to file a separate income tax return. The significance of community property in that regard was largely eliminated in 1948 when Congress enacted a legislative package that sought to equalize the overall tax treatment of community and noncommunity property. Part of that package gave married persons the option to report their combined income on a single ("joint") income tax return, where it would be taxed at preferential rates.

Conversion of Separate into Community Property. Some conversions of separate into community property may result in the realization of gain. A conversion by only one spouse is a gift by that spouse, which is not a taxable event. However, a conversion by both spouses of separate property into community property may involve the realization of gain. No realization takes place "provided that the separate conversions by husband and wife are determined to be gifts under Section 102 of the Code." LR 7821150. Most conversions probably satisfy the requirement of Commissioner v. Duberstein, 363 U.S. 278 (1960), that a gift in the statutory sense of §102 must proceed from a detached and disinterested generosity out of affection, respect, admiration, charity, or like impulses. If a conversion qualifies as a gift under §102, no gain is realized and, presumably, each spouse will have a basis in the assets equal to one-half of the sum of the adjusted bases of the property that was formerly held as separate property. Such a conversion could not result in a loss because of §267, which bars the deduction of a loss on transfers between related taxpayers including spouses.

Conversion of Community into Separate Property. Three methods by which community property may be converted into separate property do not involve a taxable event. First, a gift by one spouse of his or her one-half interest in a community property asset to the other spouse is not taxable by reason of §102. However, any gift of some types of assets, such as installment obligations, triggers the recognition of gain or loss. *See*

§453B. Second, the conversion of a community property asset into one that the spouses own as equal tenants in common or as joint tenants is not taxable. *See* Commissioner v. Mills, 183 F.2d 32 (9th Cir. 1932); Rev. Rul. 56-437, 1956-2 C.B. 507 (conversion of joint tenancy in stock into tenancy in common, or partition and issuance of separate stock certificates is not taxable). Third, a division of community property by which each spouse receives the entire interest in assets of approximately equal value is not taxable. LR 8016050. An unequal in kind division of community property is also nontaxable if the transfer of the excess property to one spouse is regarded as a gift under §102.

Most of the law regarding the taxability of conversions of community property has been generated by cases involving the consequences of marital dissolutions. It is summarized in Rev. Rul. 76-83, 1976-1 C.B. 213, which holds that no gain or loss results from the approximately equal division of the fair market value of community property. *See also* Jean C. Carrieres, 64 T.C. 959 (1975), *aff'd per curiam*, 552 F.2d 1350 (9th Cir. 1977), *acq.* (result only), 1976-2 C.B. 1. The ruling involved an agreement that called for each spouse to receive community property of equal value. "However, certain community assets cannot feasibly be partitioned between the taxpayers because the nature of the assets makes them incapable of division, they are associated with a particular liability, or they are part of a business venture that can be managed by only one of the taxpayers. Under the terms of the settlement agreement, certain assets will be assigned to the husband and certain other assets of approximate equal value will be assigned to the wife. The remaining community assets will be equally partitioned between the taxpayers." Insofar as the basis of assets is concerned, the ruling holds that an asset allocated entirely to one spouse retains its community basis. A spouse's basis in a partitioned asset is equal to the percentage of the asset received by the spouse multiplied by the community property basis of the asset. "For example, if corporate stock that has a community basis of $15,000 is partitioned so that the husband receives 40 percent of the stock and the wife receives the remaining 60 percent of the stock, the basis of the stock received by the husband will be $6,000 (40 percent of $15,000) and the basis of the stock received by the wife will be $9,000 (60 percent of $15,000)."

Basis Following Death of a Spouse. The characterization of property as community or separate is also important when it comes to determining the basis of property following the death of a spouse. Under §1014(b)(6), the survivor's share of the community property has a basis equal to its fair market value on the valuation date applicable to the deceased spouse's estate for federal estate tax purposes (*i.e.,* either on the date of the decedent's death or on the alternate valuation date under §2032). Thus, the survivor's share of the community property benefits from a free "step up" in basis where the community property has appreciated in value. On the other hand, the survivor's share suffers a decrease in basis ("step down") if the estate tax value in the decedent's estate is below its immediately preceding adjusted basis. In contrast, the basis of a survivor's separate property is not changed by reason of the decedent's death. It is readily apparent, then, that the survivor's basis in a jointly owned asset depends upon whether it was held as community property or as equally owned units of separate property (*e.g.*, tenancy in common or joint tenancy).

Obviously it is advantageous to hold an appreciated asset in community property form, which allows the basis in both halves of it to be increased ("stepped up") on the death of the first spouse to die. Presumably the step up is available with respect to Nevada's form of survivorship community property. *See* Nev. Rev. Stat. §111.064 (1981) and §§3.11 and 3.26, *supra*. Of course, a "full" step up in basis is also available where the entire interest in an asset is included in a deceased spouse's estate.

> **Example 3-30.** H and W purchased 100 shares of stock at $10 per share with their community property funds. H bequeathed his interest in the stock to W, who survived him. The stock had a value of $100 per share on the estate tax valuation date applicable to H's estate. Accordingly, H's estate included a value of $5,000 attributable to the stock ($\frac{1}{2} \times \$100 \times 100$). W's one-half interest in the stock was increased to $5,000 under §1014(b)(6). Accordingly, W has a basis of $10,000 in the 100 shares.

In the case of separate property, only the decedent's interest in the property is affected by §1014. Thus, the survivor's basis in assets that stood in joint tenancy form will vary according to whether they were held in true joint tenancies and are the separate property of the spouses or they were their community property. Where an asset is recognized as community property that was merely held in joint tenancy for convenience only, the basis in both halves of the asset is changed to its federal estate tax value in the decedent's estate. On the other hand, only the decedent's interest in a "true" (*i.e.*, separate property) joint tenancy will be affected by the decedent's death. *See* Murphy v. Commissioner, 342 F.2d 356 (9th Cir. 1965); Bordenave v. United States, 150 F. Supp. 820 (N.D. Cal. 1957). A community property characterization might result if either the attempt to establish the joint tenancy fails to comply with the requirements of the local law or the husband and wife used the joint tenancy form for convenience without intending to create a valid joint tenancy with right of survivorship. By way of illustration, had the stock in Example 3-30, above, been held by H and W in a true joint tenancy, W would have had a basis of only $5,500 in the stock following H's death.

That figure is the sum of W's share of the original cost basis ($500) plus the basis of H's one-half share determined under §1014 ($5,000).

Where the value of community property has declined below its adjusted basis, §1014(b)(6) could cause a decrease in the basis of both halves of the property. However, that result can be avoided by partitioning the property prior to the death of a spouse. If that is done, the survivor's basis in one-half of the property is unaffected by the decedent's death. Only the decedent's one-half share of the property suffers a decrease in basis. This opportunity is recognized in Rev. Rul. 68-80, 1968-1 C.B. 348: "There is nothing in the Internal Revenue Code or regulations that would indicate that section 1014(b)(6) of the Code relating to 'community property held' was intended to include separate property that had previously been converted from community property to separate property. Accordingly, W's unadjusted basis in her undivided one-half interest in the Virginia property held as tenant in common at H's death is her cost. Her unadjusted basis in the undivided one-half interest she acquired by inheritance from H is its fair market value at the time of H's death." An inter vivos gift of one spouse's share in community property that has declined in value would produce essentially the same result: The donee's original interest in the property would retain its adjusted basis unaffected by the gift or the donor's death and the donee's basis in the gifted share would be limited to its fair market value on the date of the gift for the purpose of determining loss. See §1015(a).

The effect of §1014(b)(6) on a client's estate plan should be carefully considered, particularly if the client is terminally ill. An appropriate shift into or out of the community form of ownership may leave the surviving spouse with a higher basis in jointly owned property.

Appreciated Property Acquired from a Decedent. The 1981 Act added §1014(e), which provides that the stepped-up basis rules of §1014 do not apply to appreciated property acquired by the decedent by gift within a year of death where the property passes directly or indirectly from the donee-decedent to the original donor or the donor's spouse. The Ways and Means Committee recommended this provision because of a concern that §1014 would otherwise encourage taxpayers to transfer appreciated property to a terminally ill person in hopes of receiving the property back upon the death of the donee, complete with a stepped-up basis. The concern was more acute because of the adoption of the unlimited marital deduction.

> The donor-heir might pay gift taxes on the fair market value of the gift (unless it qualified for the marital deduction or the amount of the gift is less than the donor's annual exclusion or unified credit) but will pay no income tax on the appreciation. . . . [U]pon the death of the donee-decedent, the donor-heir could receive back the property with a stepped-up

basis equal to its fair market value. The stepped-up basis would permanently exempt the appreciation from income tax. H.R. Rep. No. 97-201, 97th Cong., 1st Sess. 188 (1981).

Section 1014(e) probably bars any step up in the basis of the surviving spouse in property that he or she transferred into community property within a year preceding the death of the donee spouse.

Example 3-31. W owned separate property with a basis of $50,000 and a fair market value of $500,000. Within a year preceding H's death W transferred the property into a community property form of ownership with H. Thereafter H owned a one-half interest with a basis of $25,000 and a value of $250,000. When H died he left to W the community property created by W's transfer. H's one-half interest ($250,000) was includible in his estate under §2033, but W's basis in it remained $25,000. It is unclear whether the basis of W's one-half interest would be stepped up under §1014(b)(6).

The basis in H's one-half of the property would have been stepped up if H had left it outright to someone other than W. In such a case presumably W's one-half interest in the property would also receive a stepped-up basis. Again, it is unclear whether the basis of either share would be stepped up if H left his one-half interest to a trust in which W had an interest.

§3.30. Conflict of Laws: Basic Rules

A marital property interest in a chattel, or right embodied in a document, which has been acquired by either or both of the spouses, is not affected by the mere removal of the chattel or document to a second state, whether or not this removal is accompanied by a change of domicile to the other state on the part of one or both of the spouses. The interest, however, may be affected by dealings with the chattel or document in the second state. Restatement (Second), Conflict of Laws §259 (1971).

Under basic conflict of laws principles, the character of property acquired by a husband and wife while domiciled in one state is not changed if they move to another state. However, their rights in the property may be affected by the move, as indicated in the discussion of quasi-community property. §3.31, *infra.*

Applying the basic rule, property acquired as community property in California will be recognized as community property if the couple move to a noncommunity property state such as Colorado. People v. Bejarano, 358 P.2d 866 (Colo. 1961). Other noncommunity property states may treat imported community property as converted into a more familiar common law form of ownership, such as a tenancy in common. Edwards

v. Edwards, 233 P. 477 (Okla. 1924); Depas v. Mayo, 49 Am. Dec. 88 (Mo. 1848). Even that approach may lead to an acceptable resolution of tax and nontax problems if the couple's new domicile recognizes that each spouse has a one-half interest in the imported community property. Unfortunately, the tax authorities and courts have not always recognized the ownership interest of each spouse in the imported community property. *See, e.g.*, Commonwealth v. Terjen, 90 S.E.2d 801 (Va. 1956). (The court recognized that property imported from California retained its community character, but erroneously failed to recognize the wife's interest in the property because it was a "mere expectancy.")

Several noncommunity property states have addressed the problem of providing for the proper disposition of community property upon the death of a spouse by adopting the Uniform Disposition of Community Property Rights at Death Act, 8 U.L.A. 61 (1972). The Act, approved as a Uniform Act in 1971, was adopted by New York in 1981, effective September 1, 1981. New York Laws 1981, Ch. 187, adding EPTL §§6-6.1 through 6.67. The Act defines the rights, at death, of a married person in community property that was acquired before the couple took up domicile in a noncommunity property state. In brief, it recognizes the right each spouse has under the community property law to dispose at death of one-half of the community property, the other one-half of which belongs to the surviving spouse. The Commissioners' Prefatory Note states that the Act was intended "to preserve the rights of each spouse in property which was community property prior to the change of domicile, as well as in property substituted therefore where the spouses have not indicated an intention to sever or alter their 'community' rights. It thus follows the typical pattern of community property which permits the deceased spouse to dispose of 'his half' of the community property while confirming the title of the surviving spouse in 'her half.'" 8 U.L.A. 61 (1972). The Act is in effect in Colorado, Hawaii, Kentucky, Michigan, New York, and Oregon. Professor Stanley Johanson has argued persuasively that the Act provides an appropriate solution for the most commonly encountered problems regarding imported community property. Johanson, The Migrating Client: Estate Planning for the Couple from a Community Property State, U. Miami 9th Inst. Est. Plan. ¶831 (1975).

When a couple move from a noncommunity property state to a community property state, the property formerly owned by each spouse is generally characterized as his or her separate property. Thus, property acquired with the earnings of a husband while the couple was domiciled in a noncommunity property state is generally treated as his separate property following their move. This treatment works well enough in most instances. However, as a result of the move, the nonacquiring spouse loses any right to dower, curtesy, or an elective share that was provided by the state of their former domicile. Perhaps more important, except for California and Idaho, the community property states do not provide any substitute for the protection lost as a result of the move. The concept of quasi-community property provides a limited solution to this problem in California and Idaho.

§3.31. Conflict of Laws: Quasi-Community Property

Quasi-community property is property acquired during marriage while the spouses were domiciled in a noncommunity property state that would have been community property had they been domiciled in California (or Idaho) at the time of acquisition. Cal. Civ. Code §4803 (West 1981 Supp.); Idaho Code §15-2-201(b) (1979). Upon termination of the marriage by dissolution or death of the acquiring spouse, each spouse is generally treated as having a one-half interest in the quasi-community property. Thus, upon the death of the acquiring spouse, one-half of the quasi-community property is subject to the decedent's disposition and the other one-half belongs to the surviving spouse. Cal. Prob. Code §201.5 (West 1981 Supp.); Idaho Code §15-2-201(a) (1979). The validity of the California statute was upheld in Addison v. Addison, 399 P.2d 897 (Cal. 1965). Upon dissolution of marriage Arizona also recognizes that "property acquired by either spouse outside the state shall be deemed to be community property if the property would have been community property if acquired in this state. . . ." Ariz. Rev. Stat. §25-318 (1980 Supp.).

California and Idaho could have dealt with the problem by giving the nonacquiring spouse the same rights in the property that the nonacquiring spouse would have had under the law of the place of acquisition. However, that approach would be more complicated and would involve difficult problems of tracing. Tracing would be particularly hard if the couple lived in several noncommunity property states prior to their move to California (or Idaho). California earlier tried to deal with the problem by adopting a statute that converted the separate property of a married person to community property when they established a domicile in California. That approach was struck down in Estate of Thornton, 33 P.2d 1 (Cal. 1934), as an unconstitutional taking of the acquiring spouse's property without due process of law and as a violation of the acquiring spouse's privileges and immunities by penalizing the acquiring spouse for making a change of domicile.

For federal tax purposes quasi-community property is treated as the separate property of the acquiring spouse. Accordingly, the entire interest in quasi-community property is includible in the gross estate of the acquiring spouse. Estate of Frank Sbicca, 35 T.C. 96 (1960).

BIBLIOGRAPHY

  I. General:
        Committee Report, Property Owned With Spouse: Joint Ten-
        ancy, Tenancy by the Entireties and Community Property,
        11 Real Prop., Prob. & Tr. J. 405 (1976)
 II. Joint tenancy:
        Campfield, Estate Planning for Joint Tenancies, 1974 Duke
           L.J. 669
        Manning, Planning for Problems Created by Various Types of
           Property and Ownership, N.Y.U. 30th Inst. Fed. Tax. 623
           (1972)
        Maxfield, Some Reflections on the Taxation of Jointly Held
           Property, 34 Tax Law. 47 (1980)
        Messinger, Section 2040(c): More Complexity and Limited Re-
           lief in Taxation of Jointly Held Interests of Spouses, 34 Tax
           Law. 89 (1980)
III. Community property:
        Crehore, Community Property — Quasi-Community Prop-
           erty — A Caveat for Common Law Practitioners, N.Y.U.
           34th Inst. Fed. Tax. 1685 (1976)
        Johanson, The Migrating Client: Estate Planning for the
           Couple from a Community Property State, U. Miami 9th
           Inst. Est. Plan., Ch. 8 (1975)
        O'Connell, Estate and Tax Planning Using a Revocable Trust
           Funded with Community Property, 1 Est. Plan. 110 (1974)

CHAPTER 4

Wills and Related Documents

> While it is increasingly popular to support the estate plan in its main parts upon inter vivos instruments, particularly the revocable living trust, the historic keystone of the arch is the will. Of all legal instruments the will is probably the most familiar; almost every person ought to have one, and every member of the bar is likely to be required, from time to time, to prepare one. Thus the estate plan may consist only of a will: for a person of modest means and "normal" family, possibly a simple will; for a person of moderate or substantial means, with or without some family member needing special attention, possibly a will with trust provisions. The estate plan may consist of several instruments, including a revocable or irrevocable trust; but there always is a will. J. Farr & J. Wright, An Estate Planner's Handbook 129 (4th ed. 1979).

A.   INTRODUCTION

§4.1.   Summary

This chapter opens with a review of some of the main reasons why most adults should have wills, followed by a discussion of some of the advantages of conducting an estate administration proceeding and the disadvantages of joint or contractual wills. The main portion of the chapter consists of an examination of a form of a will for a married person with a contingent trust for the testator's children. Each provision of the will is followed by comments regarding relevant tax and nontax considerations. More complex dispositive devices, such as marital deduction trusts, widow's election trusts, and charitable remainder trusts, are discussed in later chapters. The chapter concludes with a discussion of some of the other documents a client may wish to execute along with a will, including the durable power of attorney (§4.33), the gift of bodily parts under the Uniform Anatomical Gift Act (§4.34), and the so-called living will (§4.35).

As the quotation from Farr and Wright indicates, almost every adult should have a will. Even though the bulk of a client's wealth may pass under the terms of inter vivos trusts, retirement plans, life insurance policies, joint tenancies, and other will substitutes, a will is needed to provide "backup" protection. A will can control the disposition of assets that are not effectively disposed of by will substitutes, dispose of after-acquired assets, and perform some important functions that other instruments often cannot perform. For example, a will — and typically no other instrument — may be used to:

1. disinherit children in favor of a spouse, or otherwise deviate from the local intestate succession law;
2. appoint guardians of the person and estate of minor children;
3. consolidate assets in inter vivos or testamentary trusts for post-mortem management;
4. exercise testamentary powers of appointment;
5. direct the source from which debts and death taxes should be paid;
6. achieve income and transfer tax savings by giving survivors limited interests in testamentary trusts;
7. dispose of the proceeds of policies of insurance on the life of the testator if the beneficiary does not survive him or her; and
8. vary the consequences of simultaneous death or require the beneficiaries to survive the testator for a limited period.

The available data and the limited wealth of most American families suggest that most wills are drawn for persons of modest wealth and relatively simple estate plans. For example, the principal goals of parents with young children are usually (1) to transfer all of their property to the surviving parent or, if neither of them survives, to a contingent trust for their children; and (2) to appoint guardians of the person for their minor children. Their needs may be met by a "simple" will, a durable power of attorney, and a living will.

§4.2. Avoiding Intestacy

The vast majority of decedents in both common law and community property states possess or control very limited amounts of property. For example, data for 1972 indicate that a quarter of all United States citizens owned no property of any significant value, 55% had a net worth of less than $5,000, and only 7% had a net worth in excess of $60,000. Estate and Gift Tax Hearings Before the House Comm. on Ways and Means, 94th Cong., 2d Sess. 108, 115 (Committee Print, 1976) (statement of James D. Smith). As a result of the substantial increase in the amount of the unified credit made in 1981, few individuals need to be seriously concerned about the impact of federal gift and estate taxes. However, most individuals do need to be concerned about providing in the most economical and efficient way for the welfare of their spouses, children, and other dependents.

If neither parent survives, the welfare of minor children is generally best served by consolidating all of the parents' wealth either in an inter vivos trust (through the use of a "pour over" will) or in a testamentary trust. When allowed by local law, life insurance proceeds and other nonprobate assets may be made payable to the trustee of the trust. In any event, the expense, delay, and inconvenience of a guardianship of a minor's share of an estate should be avoided. These plans are discussed in more detail in connection with Article Nine of the model will. *See* §4.19, *infra.*

Most married persons who die testate transfer all of their property at death to the surviving spouse, whether they reside in a community or a common law property state. M. Sussman, J. Cates & D. Smith, The Family and Inheritance 89-90, 143-144 (1970); Price, The Transmission of Wealth at Death in a Community Property Jurisdiction, 50 Wash. L. Rev. 277 (1975). Wills are usually needed to achieve that result because in many circumstances the intestate succession laws do not allocate all of a deceased spouse's property to the surviving spouse. A surviving spouse is entitled to a deceased spouse's entire share of the community property in all cases under the law of some community property states — California, Idaho, Nevada, New Mexico, and Washington — but not of others. For example, a surviving spouse is entitled to all of the community property under the intestate succession law of Texas only if the decedent is not survived by descendants.

Under the succession law of most community property states the noncommunity property of a deceased spouse is divided between the surviving spouse and the decedent's surviving descendants, parents, and issue of parents. The alternate provisions of the Uniform Probate Code (UPC) recommended for adoption in community property states allocate all of the community property to the surviving spouse. UPC §2-102A. The UPC also allocates all of the decedent's noncommunity property to the surviving spouse if the intestate is not survived by descendants or parents. When married persons move from a common law property state to a community property state, or vice versa, the property they owned prior to the move retains its original character in the absence of some action on their part to change it. *See* §3.30, *supra.*

Under the law of most common law property states, the surviving spouse is also generally not entitled to all of a decedent's estate if the decedent was survived by any descendant or parent. *E.g.*, N.Y. EPTL §4-1.1. In such a case the UPC allows the surviving spouse the first $50,000 and one-half of the balance of the decedent's estate, except where the decedent was survived by issue who are not issue of the surviving spouse. UPC §2-102. When married persons move from a community property state to a common law property state, the community property they bring with them may retain that character, although courts have encountered some difficulty in properly characterizing the property. *See* Johanson, The Migrating Client: Estate Planning for the Couple from a Community Property State, U. Miami 9th Inst. Est. Plan., Ch. 8 (1975). Under the Uniform Disposition of Community Property Rights at Death Act, 8 U.L.A. 61 (1972), which has been adopted by some common law property states, one-half of the community property brought into a common law property state is confirmed to the surviving spouse and one-half is subject to the deceased spouse's power of testamentary disposition. *See* §3.31, *supra*.

§4.3. Why Have an Estate Administration Proceeding — Protecting the Survivors' Economic Interests

A client may assume his or her best interests lie in "avoiding probate" entirely. Unless informed otherwise, the client will not understand that the cost and delay of an estate proceeding may be relatively small — often more than offset by the advantages of such a course. For example, having such a proceeding makes it mandatory for the claims of creditors to be filed within a statutory period — typically 4 months from the first publication of notice to creditors — or they are forever barred. *See, e.g.*, Cal. Prob. Code §700 (West 1981 Supp.), UPC §3-803. This protection may be particularly valuable in the case of a decedent engaged in business or professional activities that might generate lingering contract or tort liabilities. In some cases a lawyer may be negligent if he or she fails to advise a client that creditors' claims may be barred by conducting an estate proceeding and publishing the requisite notice. Also, family awards and allowances that are available to a surviving spouse and minor children under the law of most states insulate a small amount of property from creditors' claims. *See* §12.23, *infra*. Finally, in recent years the cost and delay of estate administration proceedings have been reduced by the UPC and other streamlined estate administration procedures.

§4.4. Income Splitting between Estate and Survivors

One of the important advantages of conducting a proceeding arises from the fact that a decedent's estate is treated as a separate taxable entity for income tax purposes. However, it is important to understand that the income tax does not "track" the estate tax in a very important respect: The income from an asset included in the gross estate is not necessarily taxed to the estate. The post-mortem income from property that passes to a survivor without estate administration is normally taxed entirely to the survivor and not to the decedent's estate. A leading text explains the point in this way:

> During the estate's recognized period of existence, the property treated as a part of the estate for income tax purposes does not necessarily include all assets in which the decedent had some interest at death. However, property subject even temporarily to administration is usually within the Subchapter J estate. Thus, many of the tax consequences . . . hinge not so much on the nature of the decedent's interests in property generating income after his death as on the degree to which the property is subject to the custody or management of his personal representative. C. Ferguson, J. Freeland & R. Stephens, Federal Income Taxation of Estates and Beneficiaries 11 (1970).

Thus, the post-mortem income generated by property that the decedent and a survivor held as joint tenants is taxed entirely to the survivor. However, for most nontax purposes joint tenancy property is not considered to pass through the decedent's estate. An asset held in joint tenancy and the income generated by it belong exclusively to the survivor by reason of the form of ownership.

The post-mortem income from the decedent's share of the community property that is subject to an administration proceeding is taxed to the decedent's estate. The remaining one-half is taxed to the surviving spouse. That rule applies even if the local law subjects all of the community property to administration upon the death of one spouse.

The message is relatively short and simple — if there is no estate administration there is no separate taxable entity and no opportunity for income splitting.

§4.5. Contractual Wills

A husband and wife, siblings, or other relatives often ask for wills that contain more or less reciprocal provisions. In such a case the clients need to decide the extent to which they want to restrict the survivor's right to dispose of the property inter vivos or change the dispositive provisions of his or her will. See Article Sixteen, §4.26, infra. This subject must be raised, although the lawyer should conduct the discussion in a tactful way that neither promotes discord between the clients nor generates undue concerns. The lawyer must also be alert to the conflict-of-interest problems that may arise if the parties wish to bind the survivor in some respect. In a word, their interests may be adverse. See §1.2, supra.

In any case, wills that contain reciprocal provisions should generally state whether or not they were executed pursuant to any agreement. If so, the agreement should be set forth in the wills or in a supplemental instrument. The same practice should be followed whether the parties execute separate instruments with reciprocal provisions (mutual wills) or a single instrument (a joint will). The statement should be made even though the governing law may, like the UPC, make it difficult to prove will contracts. Under UPC §2-701 will contracts entered into after its effective date may "be established only by (1) provisions of a will stating material provisions of the contract; (2) an express reference in a will to a contract and extrinsic evidence proving the terms of the contract; or (3) a writing signed by the decedent evidencing the contract. The execution of a joint will or mutual wills does not create a presumption of a contract not to revoke the will or wills." However, despite the best efforts of the testators to clarify their intent, when contractual wills are executed the potential for litigation remains high.

Uncertain Tax Consequences. The uncertain federal and state tax consequences of contractual wills also make them generally undesirable. For example, the interests in property that pass to a surviving spouse under a contractual will may or may not qualify for the marital deduction. In the case of decedents dying after 1981 a marital deduction is available on an elective basis for a qualifying income interest left to a surviving spouse for life. See §2056(b)(7) and §5.18, infra. No deduction was available to the estate of a person dying before 1982 if the survivor received an interest only equivalent to a life estate in the decedent's property with a power to consume. Estate of Opal v. Commissioner, 450 F.2d 1085 (2d Cir. 1971). In such a case the surviving spouse received a terminable interest that was not deductible under the pre-1982 law. In addition, upon the death of the first spouse to die, the surviving spouse may be treated as having made a taxable gift of a future interest in his or her property to the beneficiaries named in the contractual wills. LR 7810001. The imposition of a gift tax at the time of the death of the first spouse to die is also consistent with Rev. Rul. 69-346, 1969-1 C.B. 227, which holds that in the case of a binding inter vivos widow's election, a gift of the survivor's remainder interest in the community property takes place at the time of the husband's death, when it is first possible to value the remainder interest in the property that she became obligated to transfer at the time she executed the election. See §9.24, infra. Presumably no gift takes place if the survivor retains a power to consume or appoint his or her share of the property. See Reg. §25.2511-2(c).

Trusts Are Preferable. In view of the substantive law problems and uncertain tax consequences of contractual wills, an inter vivos or testamentary trust is almost invariably a better way to provide for survivors. Importantly, a trust may avoid the uncertainty that inheres in contractual arrangements regarding a variety of matters, including the scope of the survivor's authority to dispose of assets during his or her lifetime. Also, in the case of a trust, the legal title to the trust property is vested in the trustee, who may manage and invest the assets in accordance with the terms of the trust. A trust may also more effectively limit the control that one of the parties may exert over the property. Of course, a trust may avoid the necessity of establishing a guardianship should one or both of the parties become incompetent. However, in such a case the trustee must be given sufficient discretionary powers to distribute income and principal to the survivors in order to meet their needs.

Conditional Wills. Wills may be made conditional on the occurrence or nonoccurrence of a specific event. Conditional wills should generally be avoided, however, because of their potential for litigation. For example, a "condition" may be construed by some courts as an indication of the reason the will was made. Generally a client's needs are better met by a "regular" will, which may include conditional bequests. *See* T. Atkinson, Wills §83 (2d ed. 1953).

B. ORGANIZATION AND CONTENT OF WILLS

§4.6. *General*

Professionally prepared wills are usually arranged so that the articles, or paragraphs, that deal with related subjects appear together. A will typically contains provisions that (1) identify the testator and the testator's family, revoke earlier wills, and define terms; (2) dispose of the testator's property; (3) appoint fiduciaries including guardians and trustees; (4) enumerate the powers and duties of fiduciaries and contain directions regarding the payment of debts and taxes; and (5) provide for execution by the testator and witnesses. Many lawyers prefer to locate the articles appointing fiduciaries and enumerating their powers in the fore part of the will, before the dispositive provisions, on the theory that the identity of the fiduciaries and the extent of their powers should be dealt with at the outset. The substance — not the particular order of these materials — is what is important.

The following sections contain the provisions that might be included in a "typical" will for a married client of modest means. After making some specific gifts, the will gives all of the client's property to his wife if she survives him, otherwise to a contingent trust for their children. Each provision is followed by a comment concerning its substantive and tax law consequences. The comments also point out why some other commonly encountered provisions should be used sparingly, if at all. The provisions are presented for the purpose of discussion and analysis and are not intended for use without the professional assistance of a competent lawyer.

As a convenience some lawyers provide clients with a table of contents of wills or trusts that are drawn for them. Such a guide is particularly helpful to a client if it includes a brief summary of the content of each article of the will or trust. A few lawyers go beyond that and attach a chart to each will or trust they prepare, which shows how various types of property will be disposed of under the client's estate plan. In any case, the client must be cautioned regarding the impact of any changes in the way in which property is held, in beneficiary designations, etc. *See* §4.31, *infra.*

§4.7. Introduction

WILL OF JOHN Q. CLIENT

I, John Q. Client, also known as John Quincy Client, a resident of ―――――――――― , ―――――――――― ,
         (*city*)   (*state*)
declare this to be my will.

Comment. The introduction (or exordium clause) of a will indicates the name or names by which the testator is known. This may help the personal representative to identify, collect, and transfer the testator's property. The declaration may also help establish the place of the decedent's residence. Although not determinative, it is some indication of the testator's understanding and intent. T. Atkinson, Wills §147 at 819 (2d ed. 1953). The recitation may be helpful in dealing with procedural issues, such as the jurisdiction and venue of courts. Normally the courts of the state of a decedent's domicile have jurisdiction over most estate administration matters. Within a state the venue is laid in the county in which the decedent was domiciled.

The determination of domicile is sometimes also significant for death tax purposes. In general, the state of a decedent's domicile has jurisdiction to tax all of the decedent's property except real property and tangible personal property located in other states. Most states have enacted laws that are intended to relieve the double tax burdens that might be imposed if 2 or more states determine that the decedent was a domiciliary. However, any conceivable conflict regarding the place of a client's domicile should be eliminated through planning, if at all possible.

The declaration that the instrument is the testator's will indicates that the testator is aware of the character and purpose of the instrument and evidences the necessary testamentary intent. The introduction may also include a clause revoking all prior wills, but a revocation clause is perhaps more properly the subject of a separate article. In either case the revocatory provision is equally effective.

Some lawyers favor a more elaborate caption and clause, perhaps to satisfy clients' expectations regarding the formality and quality of their wills. Thus, the caption may read: "LAST WILL AND TESTAMENT OF JOHN Q. CLIENT" and the exordium: "IN THE NAME OF GOD, AMEN, I, JOHN Q. CLIENT, also known as JOHN QUINCY CLIENT, a resident of ————————, ————————, being of sound mind and body and sound and disposing memory and not acting under fraud, duress, or undue influence, do make, publish, and declare the following to be my last will and testament, to wit. . . ." A recitation setting forth the soundness of the testator's mind, etc., is of little value and may even create suspicion that the testator's lawyer was uncertain about his or her testamentary capacity. Nonetheless, language of that kind still crops up in form books . . . and wills.

§4.8. Revocation

Article One: I revoke all wills and codicils previously made by me.

Comment. A complete disposition of the testator's property in a later will revokes the provisions of a former one by inconsistency. However, it is more straightforward and orderly to include an express revocation of earlier testamentary documents. There is no virtue in leaving the issue even slightly uncertain when it can easily be nailed down.

§4.9. Disposition of Remains

Directions regarding funeral arrangements and the disposition of remains are sometimes included in a will. The inclusion of directions ordinarily does no harm; however, they should also be included in a letter or other writing more readily accessible than the will. Perhaps the best solution is for the client to give a separate statement to the executor named in the will or to another reliable person. The statement, and perhaps the client's will, should refer to any burial plot the client owns and any funeral arrangements the client has made. As Professor Thomas Shaffer has observed, the will is perhaps the worst place to put directions regarding the disposition of the testator's remains: "Most families, when stricken by the death of a close relative, will abstain from reading the will until after the funeral. This is the result of grief, appearances, decency or ritual." The Planning and Drafting of Wills and Trusts 176 (2d ed. 1979).

If a client wishes to make a gift of part or all of his or her body for medical research or organ transplantation, the intended donee institution should be consulted regarding the acceptability of the intended gift, the form in which the gift should be made, and any other requirements the donee may impose. All states have enacted some form of the Uniform Anatomical Gift Act, section 4 of which authorizes gifts to be made by will, card, or other writing signed by the donor and two witnesses in the donor's presence. 8 U.L.A. 30, 31 (1972). *See* §4.34, *infra*.

§4.10. Payment of Debts

Wills frequently include a direction that "my executor shall pay all of my just debts as soon as practicable after my death." Such a direction is superfluous and can lead to a variety of wholly unnecessary disputes. For example, a controversy may concern the necessity of exonerating requests of encumbered property or the necessity of paying debts that are barred by the statute of limitations, etc. With respect to exoneration, UPC §2-609 provides that "[a] specific devise passes subject to any mortgage interest existing at the date of death, without right of exoneration, regardless of a general directive in the will to pay debts." As indicated below, designating the source of funds that should be used to pay debts, expenses of administration, and taxes may be desirable, rather than relying on the local law regarding abatement. *See* Article Fifteen, §4.25, *infra*. Such a specification is permissible under UPC §3-902.

§4.11. Extent of Testator's Property

If a husband and wife have had some contact with a community property state during their marriage, their wills might include provisions that specify the extent to which their property, or specific items of it, is community in nature. Although such a recitation is not determinative of the property's character, it is some evidence of the testator's understanding. Also, a discussion of the matter of community property, if it had not been previously broached between the lawyer and involved parties, is encouraged by such a provision. In order to fortify the effect of any other oral or written agreement between a husband and wife, it may be desirable to include a statement in their wills regarding the character of the property they own. The statement may be particularly appropriate where their property is entirely community in nature. For example, the will might state, "I declare that all of the property in which I have an interest is the community property of me and my wife." Except in cases in which there is an intent to put a surviving spouse to an election, the will might also recite, "I hereby declare that I do not intend to put my wife to any election regarding the disposition of her interest in our community property and I expressly confirm to her the one-half interest therein that belongs to her by reason of law."

Uncertain language may require the surviving spouse to elect whether to accept the benefits provided under the decedent's will and consent to the decedent's disposition of the entire community interest in a particular asset or to reject the benefits and retain a one-half interest in all of the community property. An election may be required if, for example, the will leaves "all items of property which bear both my name and my wife's name to my wife" and "all other property to my children." In Estate of Patton, 494 P.2d 238 (Wash. App. 1972), the court held that such provisions required the wife to elect whether to receive the entire interest in assets that stood in both their names and consent to the transfer of the entire interest in all other community property to the decedent's children, or to retain her half of the community property and receive no benefits under the will. If a surviving spouse elects against the will, the surviving spouse should not be entitled to receive an intestate share in any of the property that is undisposed of by the will as a result of the election.

The will may also confirm that the residence of the husband and wife is held by them as joint tenants and that he intends the property to belong exclusively to her if she survives him. The provision is particularly appropriate if the will leaves the testator's residuary estate to persons other than the surviving spouse — such as children by a prior marriage. The residue would be increased to the extent of one-half of the value of the residence if it was determined to be held by them as tenants in common or owned by them as community property. For example, under the law of some community property states, assets that are acquired in joint tenancy form with community property funds remain the spouses' community property if the spouses did not actually intend to create a valid joint tenancy. Also, property placed in joint tenancy form will retain its community character if the joint tenancy was not created in compliance with the local law. See §3.11, supra.

§4.12. Family Status and Definitions

> Article Two: I declare that I am married to Jane Martin Client (my "wife") and that I now have three children, namely, Karen Ann Client (born August 1, 1973), Samuel Martin Client (born April 15, 1975), and John Rogers Client (born November 7, 1978). Refer-

ences in this will to "my children" are to them and any children later born to or adopted by me.

The term "descendants" refers to all naturally born or legally adopted descendants of all degrees of the person indicated.

Comment. The introduction and identification of the testator's spouse and children establishes the testator's family circumstances at the time the will was executed. It also helps a reader by clarifying the relationship of the persons mentioned in the will, resolves ambiguities that might otherwise be caused by the use of terms such as "wife" and "children," and avoids the pretermission of children by naming all existing children and using a class term to include children who are later born to or adopted by the testator. The recitation also tends to establish that the testator knew "the objects of his bounty" at the time the will was executed, which is one of the elements of the traditional test of testamentary capacity. By including the dates of the children's births the client and the lawyer will be led to consider problems that might arise by reason of their minority, such as the need for guardians of their persons. The dates may also be helpful to the court, tax authorities, and others who may be called upon to deal with the instrument. The possible pretermission of descendants of a testator's deceased children under the law of some states (*e.g.*, Cal. Prob. Code §§71, 90 (West 1981 Supp.)) suggests the desirability of also mentioning the testator's grandchildren by name or class (*e.g.*, descendants).

The term "descendants" is used in the instrument rather than "issue" because the former term is more understandable to lay persons. It is defined to include both naturally born and adopted persons of all degrees. A client may wish to exclude either all adopted persons or ones who are adopted after a specified age, such as 18. In some cases a restriction may be appropriate in order to prevent an adult from being adopted primarily for the purpose of qualifying to receive property under a will or trust. The definition is broad enough to include children born to unmarried parents. Under the Uniform Parentage Act, 9A U.L.A. 579 (1979), and similar laws a child's status is recognized regardless of whether the child's parents ever intermarry. Accordingly, it may be wise to expressly include or exclude children born to unmarried parents in order to avoid their pretermission. Unless a term such as "descendants" or "issue" is adequately defined it may require construction by a court — a form of resolution that should be avoided.

In general, "heirs" is a term that should not be used in any dispositive instrument. Its inappropriateness lies in the fact that the trustor usually intends to describe a definite, more limited class of persons (*e.g.*, children or descendants). Even if the term appears to be proper, a more precise description of the intended beneficiaries is preferable. This point is elaborated in the comment on Article Nine, §4.19, *infra*. Finally "heirs" should not be used in order to avoid any lingering possibility that the Rule in Shelley's Case or the testamentary branch of the Doctrine of Worthier Title might be applied to gifts made in the will.

§4.13. Gift of a Specific Item of Personalty

Article Three: I give my gold-plated skateboard to my friend Samuel Gompers if he survives me. However, if the skateboard is not a part of my estate at the time of my death for reasons other than an inter vivos gift to Samuel Gompers, I give him the sum of five hundred dollars ($500) in place of the skateboard if he survives me.

Comment. A gift to an individual beneficiary should ordinarily be expressly conditioned, as here, upon the beneficiary surviving the testator. Under such a provision, if the beneficiary does not survive the testator the property will be disposed of as a part of the testator's residuary estate. The gift would not pass to the beneficiary's surviving descendants under the anti-lapse statute because of the express requirement of survivorship. Of course, anti-lapse statutes often apply only to a gift made to a relative of the testator who predeceases the testator but leaves lineal descendants who do survive the testator. *See, e.g.*, UPC §2-605; Cal. Prob. Code §92 (West 1956); N.Y. EPTL §3-3.3 (McKinney 1967); Wash. Rev. Code §11.12.110 (1979). If a specific gift not conditioned on survivorship fails because the beneficiary predeceases the testator and the anti-lapse statute does not apply, the subject of the gift will pass as a part of the testator's residuary estate under the common law and under the provisions of many statutes. *E.g.*, UPC §2-606.

Problem 4-1. T died leaving a will that included a bequest of "my gold watch to my uncle Harold" and gave the entire residuary estate to a charitable organization. Harold did not survive the testator, but his wife, Wilma, and two children, Adam and Claude, did survive him. Under the law of your jurisdiction, who is entitled to receive T's watch? How would the watch be disposed of if Harold had survived T, but validly disclaimed the bequest?

Ademption. Under the common law, a specific gift is adeemed and fails entirely if the property does not exist at the time of the testator's death. Thus, if the property is lost, sold, stolen, destroyed, or otherwise disposed of prior to the testator's death, the gift fails and the beneficiary is not entitled to receive any other property in place of it. Where the property was insured, the right to any insurance recovery generally becomes an asset of the residuary estate. However, under some statutes the legatee of a specific gift is entitled to any proceeds unpaid at the time of the testator's death on fire or casualty insurance on the property. *E.g.*, UPC §2-608; N.Y. EPTL §3-4.5 (McKinney 1967). In all cases in which a client indicates a desire to make a specific gift, the lawyer should ask whether he or she wishes to make any alternative gift to the beneficiary if the particular property is not owned by the client when the client dies. In appropriate cases, the will should include a substitutional gift, as in Article Three. The testator's intent regarding the matter should be specified in the will, although the same result might be reached under existing statutes or decisional law. The reasons are obvious why these should not be relied upon — the law might change or the testator might be domiciled in another jurisdiction at the time of death.

Lapse. The lawyer also needs to know how the client wishes to dispose of the property if the intended beneficiary does not survive the client. Lawyers cannot rely on the immortality of the beneficiaries any more than on their own. They cannot assume that (1) the named beneficiary will survive the testator or (2) a distribution in accordance with the provisions of the local law (or the testator's intent as determined by the court) will serve the interests of the client or the client's family. An early Connecticut decision described the problem in this passage (Bill v. Payne, 25 A. 354 (Conn. 1892)):

> It frequently happens that legatees die during the lifetime of the testator. The testatrix could have provided for such a contingency by giving it to the survivors, or to other parties. She did neither. There is, therefore, some presumption that she intended that the law should settle the matter. That presumption is strengthened by the fact that she had an opportunity to change her will after one or more of the legatees had died, and failed to do so.

In short, a will should include appropriate provisions dealing with the premature death of the beneficiaries.

Simultaneous Death. A will should also include some direction regarding the disposition of the property in the event of the simultaneous death of the testator and the intended beneficiary. In that way the client's intent will be clear, constructional problems will be avoided, and the lawyer will be protected against serious criticism and liability for failure to draft an unambiguous bequest.

A direction that the client's spouse should be deemed to survive the client in the event of simultaneous death may be appropriate if it is important for the client's estate to qualify for the federal estate tax marital deduction. For marital deduction purposes the estate tax regulations allow survivorship to be governed by a presumption provided by the instrument or the local law in the event of simultaneous death. Reg. §20.2056(e)-(2). *See* §5.14, *infra*.

Survivorship for Specified Period. Many lawyers routinely condition gifts upon the beneficiary surviving the testator by a specified number of days. In general the practice is a good one. The condition may be imposed with respect to an individual gift or all gifts. For example, a will might provide that:

> For the purposes of this will a beneficiary is deemed to survive me only if the beneficiary is living on the sixtieth day following my death.

A survivorship requirement of this type prevents the same property from being subjected to the cost and delay of multiple estate administrations and possibly greater tax burdens. It also prevents the property from passing in an uncontrolled manner if the beneficiary survives the testator for only a short time. For example, without such a provision under Article Three, if Gompers survived the testator for only a short time, the skateboard would be distributed from Client's estate to Gompers' personal representative. The skateboard would be disposed of as an asset of Gompers' estate, totally uncontrolled by John Q. Client's will. The item might pass to a person who had no appreciation or use for it.

Survivorship of more than 180 days is usually not required because (1) distributions are often made within 180 days following death and (2) a gift to a spouse may qualify for the marital deduction if it is conditioned on the death of the surviving spouse within 6 months of the testator's death and the surviving spouse survives that period. Reg. §20.2056(b)-3(a). A lengthier survivorship period would disqualify the gift for the marital deduction. §2056(b)(3).

Note that the UPC requires survivorship of 120 hours in the case of intestate succession (UPC §2-104) and testate dispositions unless otherwise provided in the will (UPC §2-601). The requirement alleviates some of the problems of the "almost simultaneous death," but does not deal with the problems that arise if the beneficiary survives for more than 5 days.

§4.14.   Cash Gifts

> Article Four: I give two thousand dollars ($2,000) to the Regents of the University of _____, to be used for such of the general educational purposes of the University as they deem proper. However, if the total inventory value of the property

of my estate subject to administration less liens and encumbrances is less than fifty thousand dollars ($50,000), then the amount of this gift shall be reduced to an amount that bears the same relation to two thousand dollars ($2,000) as such adjusted inventory value of my estate bears to fifty thousand dollars ($50,000).

Comment. The aggregate amount of cash gifts generally should be limited in a way that protects the residuary estate from undue diminution if the testator's estate shrinks in value after the will is executed. Without this safeguard an unexpectedly large part of the estate might be required to pay cash gifts if the client's estate shrinks in value because of business reversals, large unforeseen expenses, lifetime gifts, or any other reason. If the will contains a number of cash bequests, the limitation can be modified to apply to all of them. In the case of multiple cash gifts, the limitation could be expressed as a percentage of the testator's net estate subject to administration. In such a case, it should also provide for a pro rata reduction of each legacy if the percentage limit is exceeded.

Charitable Deduction for Tax Purposes. Remember that in order to qualify for a federal estate tax charitable deduction, a gift of less than the taxpayer's entire interest in the property to a charity must be either an undivided portion of the property, a remainder interest in a personal residence or farm, a charitable remainder trust, a charitable income interest, or a pooled income fund. §2055(e)(2). In order to qualify for a charitable deduction, a gift of a remainder interest in trust must meet the stringent rules of §664. *See* §8.20, *infra.* A gift of a life estate to a surviving spouse, remainder to charity, qualifies for the elective marital deduction under §2056(b)(7), but does not qualify for a charitable deduction by the testator's estate. The property is includible in the surviving spouse's estate under §2044 to the extent the marital deduction is claimed. The survivor's estate will be entitled to an offsetting charitable deduction under §2055 if §2044 is amended as proposed to treat the survivor as the transferor of such property. A gift, not in trust, of a remainder interest in a personal residence or farm does qualify for the charitable deduction. *See* §8.15, *infra.*

Satisfaction. A cash gift or other general legacy may be satisfied in whole or in part by an inter vivos gift to the legatee. Under the UPC a satisfaction occurs "only if the will provides for a deduction of the lifetime gift, or the testator declares in a contemporaneous writing that the gift is to be deducted from the devise or is in satisfaction of the devise, or the devisee acknowledges in writing that the gift is in satisfaction." UPC §2-612. If a client intends an inter vivos transfer to discharge a bequest included in the client's will, the client should execute a new will or a codicil rather than rely on the proper application of this doctrine.

Distribution in Kind. There is some disagreement among commentators regarding the extent to which an executor should be authorized to distribute estate assets in kind in satisfaction of pecuniary legacies.

Such authority does give the executor more flexibility. However, if property is distributed in satisfaction of a pecuniary gift, the estate will realize a taxable gain in the amount by which the date of distribution value of the property exceeds its estate tax value. Reg. §1.661(a)-2(f)(1). A distributee will take a basis in the property equal to the amount of the pecuniary claim that was discharged by the distribution. *See, e.g.,* Lindsay C. Howard, 23 T.C. 962, 966 (1955), *acq.* 1955-2 C.B. 6. If it appears that a testator's estate may not be sufficiently liquid to pay pecuniary gifts without difficulty, it may be preferable to rely directly upon specific gifts rather than to burden the executor with the problem of deciding whether and how to make distributions in kind in satisfaction of the pecuniary gifts.

Problem 4-2. T's will included a cash bequest of $10,000 to B, who survived T, and gave T's executor authority to satisfy cash gifts by distributing assets in kind. The executor distributed 100 shares of ABC, Inc. stock to B in satisfaction of the gift. The shares, which had been purchased by T several years before for $2,000, had the values shown below on the dates indicated:

Date of death	$ 8,000
(federal estate tax value)	
Date of distribution, 18	
months following death	$10,000

What was the estate's basis in the shares? How much gain, if any, did the estate realize when the shares were distributed? What basis will B have in the shares? *See* §12.32, *infra.*

Forgiveness of Indebtedness. An indebtedness owed the testator may be forgiven conditionally or unconditionally by an appropriate provision in the will. Because the forgiveness is essentially equivalent to a cash bequest, the former debtor may be obligated to contribute toward the payment of the state death tax and, depending upon the provisions of the testator's will and the local law, a portion of the federal estate tax. If the estate is insolvent a forgiveness directed in the will may not be effective. However, where the note or other obligation provides for forgiveness of the debt, it might be an effective nontestamentary provision. *See* UPC §6-201. Alternatively, the testator might bequeath the note to the obligor. Note, however, that the forgiveness or other cancellation of an installment obligation triggers recognition of gain under the installment sale rules. *See* §9.6, *infra.*

§4.15. *Tangible Personal Property*

Article Five: I give all of my clothing, furniture, furnishings and effects, my automobiles, and other tangible personal property of every kind except jewelry to my wife if she survives me. If my wife does not survive me, I give such tangible personal property excluding automobiles to those of my children who survive me, to divide among themselves as they may agree. If my children do not agree regarding the disposition of the personal property within sixty (60) days of my death, I direct my executor to divide the property among them in shares as nearly equal in value as practicable, having due regard for the personal preferences of each child. The share of any child who is a minor at the time the property is distributed may be delivered without bond to the child's guardian or to any suitable person with whom the child resides or who has custody or control of the child.

Comment. The disposition of the testator's interest in tangible personal property may pose problems if a number of beneficiaries must agree upon its distribution. If the property might pass to a minor, the will should attempt to obviate the need to have a guardian of the estate appointed for the minor. For example, the will might provide that the property otherwise distributable to a minor may be delivered to the guardian of the minor's person or to other suitable persons. Where minors are involved, automobiles, boats, and airplanes generally should be excluded from the gift. Because of its value jewelry is excepted from this article and is disposed of expressly in Article Six, §4.16, *infra*. Otherwise jewelry could be included within the scope of this article.

The executor or another responsible adult may be authorized to sell such of the items of a minor's share of the personal property as the executor believes is in the best interest of the child. In that way the insurance, storage, and other costs of retaining "white elephants" can be avoided and the proceeds invested for the minor, possibly in conjunction with a contingent testamentary trust.

The scope of this article may be further refined by specifically excluding money, precious metals (including coins) and unmounted gems held for investment, evidences of indebtedness, documents of title, and securities and property used in trade or business. Otherwise some beneficiaries might contend that those items are included in a bequest of "tangible personal property."

Testamentary Gifts to Custodians for Minors. Note that the form of the Uniform Gifts to Minors Act that is in effect in some states allows testamentary gifts of a security, life insurance policy, annuity contract, or money to a custodian for a minor. *E.g.,* Cal. Prob. C. §186 et seq. (West 1982 Supp.); Fla. Stat. Ann. §710.02 (West 1981 Supp.); Tex. Rev. Civ.

Stat. Ann. art. 5923-101, §2(a) (Vernon 1980 Supp.); and Wash. Rev.
Code §21.24.020(1) (1979). Note, however, that each gift must be made
to one minor — there cannot be multiple beneficiaries of a custodianship. The device is particularly useful in making gifts of small amounts
of cash or securities to minors without requiring a full-blown trust or the
appointment of a guardian for the minor. The version of the Act in effect
in some states permits fiduciaries to distribute qualifying types of property to a custodian for a minor although the gift was not made directly to
the custodian in the will or trust. *E.g.*, Ill. Ann. Stat. ch. 110½, §202
(Smith-Hurd 1978); N.Y. EPTL §7-4.8 (McKinney 1980 Supp.).

Specific Gifts and Cash Legacies. Casting gifts in the form of specific
bequests or cash legacies will prevent a distribution of the property from
carrying out the distributable net income of the estate to the beneficiaries. §663(a)(1). Such gifts may be distributed to the beneficiaries
without adverse income tax consequences and without affecting the estate's income-splitting role.

Specific gifts to a surviving spouse are particularly useful to preserve
income splitting in community property states where the income from
community property is naturally divided between the estate of the deceased spouse and the surviving spouse.

Example 4-1. H died survived by his wife, W, leaving a will that
gave W a cash legacy, his interest in their tangible personal property, and the residue of his estate. All or any part of the cash and
the personalty may be distributed to W without carrying out to her
any of the estate's distributable net income for federal income tax
purposes. In contrast, a distribution of the residue to W would
carry out to her the distributable net income of the estate for the
year of distribution, which would be taxed to her rather than to the
estate. *See* §§12.30 to 12.31, *infra*.

Nonspecific Gifts. The basis of property that is distributed in kind in
satisfaction of nonspecific gifts is increased to its fair market value at the
time of distribution to the extent its value is included in the gross income
of the beneficiary. Reg. §1.661(a)-2(f)(3). This approach may be used to
achieve a tax-free increase in the basis of the estate's appreciated assets.
See §12.32, *infra*.

Example 4-2. H left his residuary estate to W, who survived him.
The distributable net income of H's estate this year will be $20,000,
all of which is attributable to dividends and interest. The estate also
owns 100 shares of ABC, Inc. common stock that has a basis of $75
per share and a present value of $100 per share. The income of the
estate will be split between W and the estate if $10,000 in cash is

distributed to her. However, in that case, the basis of the ABC stock will remain at $75 per share. The income would also be split if the 100 shares of ABC stock are distributed to W (*i.e.*, it would carry out $10,000 of distributable net income to her). However, under Reg. §1-661(a)-2(f)(3) she would have a basis of $100 per share in the stock. The cash might be distributed to W without income tax consequences to her at a later time when the estate has no distributable net income.

§4.16. Disposition of Tangible Personal Property in Accordance with Testator's Subsequent Directions

Article Six: I give all of my jewelry to my wife, which I request her to dispose of as she believes would be in accordance with my wishes. I do not intend this Article in any way to obligate my wife to dispose of the jewelry to any other persons.

[Article Six: (UPC states) I give all of my jewelry to the persons and in the shares designated on a written statement I intend to prepare at a later time.]

Comment. The problem of drafting provisions designed to control the disposition of a large number of items of personalty to a changeable number of beneficiaries is virtually insoluble in states that do not recognize holographic wills and do not have a specific statute, such as UPC §2-513, that authorizes reference to a list prepared later by the testator.

Incorporation by Reference. In most jurisdictions other than New York, a testator may incorporate in the will an extrinsic writing by reference, provided the writing exists at the time the will is executed, is adequately described, and is mentioned in the will with the intent to incorporate it. *E.g.*, UPC §2-510. Thus, this theory allows a will to incorporate a list or other existing writing that the testator intends to govern the distribution of property. For a survey of the doctrine, see Incorporation by Reference — The Later Days, 7 Real Prop., Prob. & Tr. J. 502 (1972). Writings that are incorporated cannot be effectively changed after execution of the will unless the changes comply with the required testamentary formality. Uncertainties regarding the law and the risk that the incorporated document may be altered or destroyed suggest that private documents should generally not be incorporated. However, statutes, regulations, etc., may be incorporated to good effect — particularly when the draftsman wants to "freeze" the provision in its present form.

Facts or Acts of Independent Significance. An alternate doctrine allows a testator to control the disposition of property by appropriate reference to facts or acts of independent significance. UPC §2-512. Under this doctrine a testator could provide for a gift to a particular legatee of "all of the art objects listed on the fine arts rider to my fire and casualty insurance policy." Subsequent changes in the items listed on the rider would generally be recognized in making distribution of the testator's estate because of the independent significance of the list. Similarly, the identity of a beneficiary may be determined by independently significant facts: "I give one hundred dollars ($100) to each person who is employed by J. Q. Client, Inc. at the time of my death."

Overall, incorporation by reference and reference to acts of independent significance are probably less satisfactory in dealing with the problem than the execution of a new testamentary instrument when the testator wishes to make changes in the disposition of the property. However, the preparation of a codicil or a new will may involve unacceptable additional cost. Also, codicils can cause considerable confusion where the testator leaves several that are not consistent.

Bequest with Request. In order to meet this problem some testators bequeath their tangible property to one person with a request that the beneficiary dispose of it as the beneficiary believes is in accordance with the testator's wishes. Under this approach the testator's wishes regarding the disposition of the property are usually expressed to the beneficiary in letters or other writings that may be changed by the testator from time to time. Although the gift does not impose a legal obligation on the person to dispose of the property in the way indicated by the testator, it generally works and clients are usually satisfied with it.

The state and federal transfer taxes are generally computed on the theory that the beneficiary named in the will receives outright ownership of the personalty. If the beneficiary gives some of the property to others, the beneficiary has made a gift, which may produce some gift tax liability. Consistent with that approach, the beneficiary and not the estate will be entitled to a charitable deduction for any property the beneficiary transfers to charity.

Informal Lists. In states that have adopted the UPC, the disposition of tangible personalty may be dealt with by a direct, yet informal, method:

> Whether or not the provisions relating to holographic wills apply, a will may refer to a written statement or list to dispose of items of tangible personal property not otherwise specifically disposed of by the will, other than money, evidences of indebtedness, documents of title, and securities, and property used in trade or business. To be admissible under this section as evidence of the intended disposition, the writing must either be in the handwriting of the testator or be signed by him and must describe the items and the devisees with reasonable certainty. The writing may be re-

ferred to as one to be in existence at the time of the testator's death; it may
be prepared before or after the execution of the will; it may be altered by
the testator after its preparation; and it may be a writing which has no
significance apart from its effect upon the dispositions made by the will.
UPC §2-513.

If a client intends to utilize this procedure, the lawyer should provide the
client with written instructions regarding the preparation and alteration
of the statement. Also, the client should be warned that the statement
may be ineffective if the client resides in a non-UPC state at the time of
death. Coins and currency should not be disposed of under this provision because the section applies to items "other than money." If the
section were construed narrowly the informal disposition of items of
numismatic value might be ineffective. The client should keep any
statement of this type with the will, or in a place known to the lawyer and
the person named as executor. If a client wishes to change the disposition
that is provided for in a statement, a new one should be prepared and
signed and the old one destroyed in order to avoid any uncertainties
regarding the intent of the change or the identity of the person who
made it.

As a precaution, items of substantial value should not be disposed of
by an informal list. For example, valuable jewelry should be disposed of
in the will and any changes made by codicil. If that is done, the transfer
tax consequences will also be more straightforward.

§4.17. Gifts of Corporate Securities

Article Seven: I give one hundred (100) shares of the common stock
of ZYX, Inc., which I now own, as the same may be hereafter
increased or decreased by reason of stock dividends, stock splits,
mergers, consolidations, or reorganizations (but disregarding rights
to purchase stock, whether exercised or not), to my brother,
Horace M. Client, if he survives me. If I do not own a sufficient
number of shares of the stock at the time of my death to satisfy this
gift in full, then the gift shall be limited to the number of shares, if
any, owned by me.

Comment. Stock Splits, Stock Dividends, and Other Corporate Changes. A
gift of securities should specify whether the testator intends to give the
legatee only the particular securities then owned by the testator (a
specific bequest) or the specified quantity of the named securities
whether or not the testator owns any at the time of his death (a general
bequest). A specific gift of the type illustrated above, or as indicated by
the use of the possessive pronoun "my" in describing the shares, typically

carries with it any lifetime increase in the quantity of securities attributable to stock splits, but not those attributable to stock dividends. *See* T. Atkinson, Wills §135 (2d ed. 1953).

The terms of this article generally parallel the provisions of UPC §2-607. However, even though the existing law may carry out the client's present intent without elaboration, the will should specify the effect that should be given to changes in the number of shares owned by the client. If the will contains multiple gifts of the same issue of securities the testator may wish to reduce them all proportionately if the quantity of securities owned at death is insufficient to satisfy all of the gifts in full.

Problem 4-3. T's will contained the following provision:

"I give 100 shares of the common stock of Adams, Inc. to my son Sam, if he survives me, and I give my 100 shares of Baker, Corp. common stock to my daughter Doris, if she survives me."

T did not own any Adams, Inc. common stock at the time the will was executed or when T died. The 100 shares of Baker, Corp. common stock that T owned when the will was executed are represented by 150 shares of Cosmos, Ltd. common stock, 100 of which were acquired when Baker, Corp. was merged into Cosmos, Ltd., and the other 50 of which were received by T as stock dividends. Must the executor acquire 100 shares of Adams, Inc. stock for Sam? How many, if any, of the shares of Cosmos, Ltd. is Doris entitled to receive?

§4.18.   Gifts of Residence and Policies of Life Insurance

Article Eight: If my wife survives me, I give her all of my interest in:

(a)   any property we use as our principal place of residence at the time of my death that does not otherwise pass to her upon my death by right of survivorship or otherwise, together with my interest in all policies of insurance thereon including the right to receive the proceeds of all claims thereunder that are unpaid at the time of my death; and

(b)   all policies of insurance on her life and on the lives of our children.

Comment. It is not strictly necessary to include a specific devise of residential real property to the surviving spouse who is also the residuary legatee. However, a specific devise may reassure the spouses that the survivor will receive their residential property and continue to have the right to occupy it regardless of whether title to it is held by them in a survivorship form. It may also provide some greater flexibility in making distributions to the survivor from the estate. See the discussion of §663, §4.15, *supra*.

Exoneration. The question of whether an encumbrance on any specifically bequeathed or devised property must be discharged by payment from the residuary estate should also be specified. Under the UPC and the law of most states, an encumbrance is not required to be exonerated unless the testator specifically directs that the obligation be paid. UPC §2-609 provides that "[a] specific devise passes subject to any mortgage interest existing at the date of death, without right of exoneration, regardless of a general directive in the will to pay debts." Under California law a mortgage, deed of trust, or other lien must be discharged if it is collateral security for the testator's personal obligations. *See* Estate of Bernal, 131 P. 375 (Cal. 1913).

Insurance on Realty and Personalty. The testator's interest in insurance on real or personal property should also be given to the beneficiaries in order to give them the benefit of paid-up insurance and to provide them with continued protection. The will should also specify whether the devisee is entitled to receive the proceeds of insurance claims that exist, but are unpaid at the time of the testator's death. UPC §2-608(a)(3) and statutes in some other states give the beneficiary the right to the unpaid insurance proceeds in such cases. *See, e.g.,* N.Y. EPTL §3-4.5 (McKinney 1967). The provision could also deal specifically with the disposition of the proceeds of any sale or condemnation of the property that remain unpaid at the time of the testator's death.

Insurance on the Lives of Others. A testator's interest in policies of insurance on the lives of others should also receive special attention, particularly if the insured also owns an interest in the policies. Of course, if the noninsured spouse holds the entire interest in the policies for the purpose of keeping the proceeds out of the gross estate of the insured spouse, the noninsured spouse should leave the policies to a trust or a person other than the insured spouse. The insured generally should not serve as trustee of a trust that owns policies on the insured's life, which might cause inclusion of the proceeds of the policies in the insured's gross estate. *See* §6.18, *infra.* Ordinarily minors should not be given an outright interest in life insurance policies or proceeds, because a guardian might have to be appointed to deal with the insurance company on their behalf. If the testator's interest is given to a trustee of a trust in which the insured does not have an interest, the insured's interest might also be transferred to the trustee in order to reduce the size of the insured's gross estate. Techniques for dealing with life insurance in estate planning are discussed in more detail in Chapter 6, *infra.*

Change of Beneficiary – Life Insurance. An attempt to change a life insurance beneficiary designation by a provision in the insured's will is generally ineffective — and even where effective, should not be relied upon in any case. The current beneficiary designations on policies in which the client has an interest must be examined. The lawyer should also advise the client to review the designations if any of the named beneficiaries die or if the circumstances of the testator or the beneficiaries change substantially. A life insurance beneficiary designation is almost never affected by a change in the insured's family circumstances. *See* Parotaud, Should Implied Revocation Be Applied to a Life Insurance Beneficiary Designation, 25 Fed. Ins. Counsel Q. 357 (1975). A unique Michigan statute does provide that the designation of the spouse of the insured as beneficiary is revoked if they are divorced. Mich. Stat. Ann. §25.131 (1974).

Revocation by Change of Circumstances. Divorce and annulment are the only changes in family circumstances that revoke testamentary provisions under UPC §2-508. However, in most states a pre-nuptial will is revoked as to a surviving spouse who is not mentioned or provided for in a property settlement agreement or in the will. A will for a person who is contemplating marriage should mention or provide for the intended spouse in a way that will protect the will from revocation if the marriage takes place and the testator predeceases his or her spouse. "A reasonably prudent attorney should appreciate the consequences of a post-testamentary marriage, advise the testator of such consequences, and use good judgment to avoid them if the testator so desires." Heyer v. Flaig, 449 P.2d 161, 165 (Cal. 1969).

§4.19. Residuary Gift

Article Nine: All of my property that is not effectively disposed of by the foregoing provisions of this will, including all property over which I hold a power of appointment [excluding all property over which I only hold a power of appointment] (my "residuary estate"), shall be disposed of as follows:

    (1) If my wife survives me, I give my residuary estate to her.

    (2) If my wife does not survive me, but I am survived by one or more children who are under the age of twenty-one (21) years at the time of my death, I give my residuary estate to my trustee to hold in trust for the benefit of my descendants as provided in Article Ten.

    (3) If I am survived by descendants, but not by my wife or any children who are under twenty-one (21) years of age at the time of my death, I direct my executor to divide my re-

siduary estate into as many shares of equal value as are required to carry out the following provisions:

(a) I give one (1) such share to each of my children who survives me and has attained twenty-one (21) years of age at the time of my death; and

(b) I give one (1) such share to the descendants who survive me of any child of mine who fails to survive me, such descendants to take by right of representation subject, however, to the provisions of Article Eleven hereof.

(4) If I am not survived by my wife or by any of my descendants, I give one-half (½) of my residuary estate to the persons entitled to receive the noncommunity property of my wife under the laws of the State of _____ now in effect, as if she had died intestate at the time of my death not survived by a spouse, the shares of such persons also to be determined by said laws; and I give one-half (½) of my residuary estate to the persons entitled to receive my noncommunity property under the laws of the State of _____ now in effect, as if I had died intestate, not survived by any spouse, the shares of such persons also to be determined by said laws now in effect.

Comment. Should the Residuary Clause Exercise All Powers of Appointment? The residuary estate is described in this article in a way that attempts to exercise any power of appointment the testator may have. If that approach is adopted some lawyers would prefer to include the word "appoint" (*viz.*, "I give, devise, bequeath, and appoint . . ."). The bracketed alternate language should be used if the lawyer and client conclude that the attempt should not be made. Commentators are hopelessly divided on the question of whether or not a residuary clause should attempt to exercise unknown powers of appointment. *See* Rabin, Blind Exercise of Powers of Appointment, 51 Cornell L.Q. 1 (1965). Perhaps, as Professor Edward Rabin suggests, the exercise of unknown powers could be made dependent upon the nontaxability of the exercise for federal estate tax purposes. A client who is given the choice may prefer to attempt the exercise in order to pass the absolute maximum amount of property to the residuary beneficiaries named in the will.

Of course, there is some danger that a blind exercise may cause additional property to be included in the testator's gross estate. Property subject to a pre-1942 general power of appointment is not includible in the donee's gross estate unless the power is exercised. §2041(a). Of course, in some instances, a pre-1942 power may be exercised by the donee's will although the will does not manifest any intent to exercise the power. Stewart v. United States, 512 F.2d 269 (5th Cir. 1975). Such a result is attributable to the overly broad language of the instrument that created the power regarding the manner in which it could be exercised.

The effect of the inclusion may be ameliorated if the executor recovers the estate tax attributable to inclusion of the appointive property from the recipients of the property. *See* §2207. However, the recovery of a proportionate amount of the estate tax will not completely offset the increase in estate taxes where the inclusion of the property drives the taxable estate into higher brackets, which increases the effective rate of the tax.

Many lawyers object to preparing a will that exercises powers without knowing what the tax effects of the exercise will be and what provisions the donor of the power may have included in the instrument for disposition of the property in default of exercise of the power. If a client holds an interest in a trust, the lawyer should review the terms of the trust carefully in order to ascertain the extent of the client's interest and whether or not the client holds a power of appointment over the trust property. A lawyer cannot safely rely upon a client's impression regarding the extent of the client's interest in a trust or the existence of a power of appointment.

Whatever decision is made regarding the blind exercise of powers, the will should state expressly whether or not the testator intends to exercise any powers. Without an express indication of the testator's intent, an ordinary residuary clause may exercise a general power if there is any evidence the testator intended to exercise it. UPC §2-610; Cal. Prob. Code §§125, 126 (West 1981 Supp.); Cal. Civ. Code §1386.2 (West 1981 Supp.). The will should eliminate any opportunity for a court to clamber into the testator's armchair in order to ascertain the testator's intent on the subject. The law of the testator's domicile may not recognize a residuary clause as effective to exercise a power, but it may be recognized by the law of the jurisdiction in which the trust is being administered. For example, in Estate of Coffin, 499 P.2d 223 (Wash. App. 1972), a garden variety residuary clause was recognized by the trustee of a Massachusetts trust as effective to dispose of property that was subject to a general testamentary power of appointment. In that case the failure of the lawyer who drafted the will to discover the existence of the power, which might have led to a charge of malpractice, instead led to an award of substantial additional attorney's fees for dealing with the foreign trustee.

All to the Surviving Spouse? The article gives the entire residuary estate to the testator's wife if she survives him. Such a disposition is in accordance with the wishes of most testators. However, it will subject all of the couple's property to taxation upon the surviving spouse's death. If the combined estates of the spouses are large enough to generate any federal estate tax liability on the survivor's death, the will might provide that any interest disclaimed by the surviving spouse would pass to a trust in which the surviving spouse has a qualifying income interest for life. In such a case the surviving spouse might disclaim an amount equal to the credit equivalent in the decedent's estate and allow it to fall into the trust. As an alternative the surviving spouse might disclaim all of the outright gift and allow the estate tax consequences to be controlled by the executor's election with respect to the trust under §2056(b)(7). *See* §5.18 regarding the availability of the marital deduction in such cases. In such a case any property disclaimed by the surviving spouse would fall into the trust where it would be subject to the executor's election regarding the marital deduction. *See* §2056(b)(7) and §5.18, *infra.* Property with respect to which the election is made is includible in the surviving spouse's estate under §2044, but the other property of the trust (*e.g.,* an amount equal to the deceased spouse's credit equivalent) would not be included in his or her estate.

A legal life estate may constitute a qualified income interest for life for purposes of the elective marital deduction under §2056(b)(7). *See* §5.18, *infra.* However, under almost all circumstances the use of a legal life estate with remainder over is an unsatisfactory way of disposing of interests in real or personal property. Legal life interests create wholly avoidable problems of defining the rights of the owners *inter se* and of managing and disposing of the property. Also, the remaindermen may contest the ability of the life tenant to sell, lease, or otherwise dispose of the property and demand security and accountings. *See, e.g.,* Lehner v. Estate of Lehner, 547 P.2d 365 (Kan. 1976). A trust is almost always a better choice because of its flexibility and the variety of interests that can be given to the surviving spouse.

Apparently the §2056(b)(7) election will be available if a surviving spouse is given the following interests in a trust: (1) A lifetime income interest; (2) a power to draw down the greater of $5,000 or 5% of the trust corpus annually; (3) a special testamentary power to appoint the corpus of the trust to and among the testator's descendants; and (4) a power to invade corpus in accordance with an ascertainable standard (*e.g.,* to provide the surviving spouse with support in the survivor's accustomed manner of living, with education, including college and professional education, and with medical, dental, hospital, and nursing expenses). *See* Reg. §20.2041-1(c)(2). An independent trustee could also be given the power to invade trust corpus for the survivor's benefit without adverse impact. Importantly, a trust also better protects the interests of the remaindermen.

Married persons with relatively small estates almost invariably transfer all of their property to their spouses at death in community and noncommunity states:

   . . . 42 of the 44 males (95.45 percent) who died with community property agreements or wills in effect transferred substantially all of their property to their widows outright. There was virtually no indication that spouses of either sex used dispositive instruments to deprive the surviving spouse of any of the property the couple had accumulated during marriage. Price, The Transmission of Wealth at Death in a Community Property Jurisdiction, 50 Wash. L. Rev. 277, 316-317 (1975).

The same pattern has been observed in noncommunity property states. *See* Dunham, The Method, Process and Frequency of Wealth Transmission at Death, 30 U. Chi. L. Rev. 241, 252-253 (1963), and M. Sussman, J. Cates & D. Smith, The Family and Inheritance 86-89 (1970). Under the law of some states, estate administration costs may be substantially reduced if the surviving spouse is entitled to receive all of the decedent's property and it is unnecessary to have any formal administration proceedings. Cal. Prob. Code §202 (West 1981 Supp.); Tex. Prob. Code §155 (Vernon 1980). Texas law provides several alternatives to formal administration of a decedent's estate, including the admission of a will to probate as a muniment of title. Tex. Prob. Code §89 (Vernon 1980). *See also* Hudspeth, Texas Marital Property Laws as They Relate to Estate Administration, 36 Tex. B.J. 293 (1973); Gardner, When and How to Avoid or Simplify Administration of an Estate, 35 Tex. B.J. 695 (1972).

A "Pot" Trust, or a Separate Trust for Each Child? The testator's will could adopt any of a variety of patterns for distributing the residuary estate to descendants if the testator's spouse does not survive. The article places the entire residuary estate in a single trust if any of the testator's children are under 21 at the time of the testator's death. For a parent with a modest-sized estate a single "pot" trust for minor children is preferable to a separate trust for each child. The trust in this article will continue until the youngest living child is 21 or older. Some clients will want to provide for such a trust if any of their children are under age 25 or 30. The concept is more important than the particular age chosen.

Under the distributive provisions of the trust, Article Ten, §4.20, *infra*, the trustee will be free to use the entire income and principal of the trust flexibly to meet the needs of the testator's descendants. However, the primary emphasis will be on providing for the support and education of the children who are under 21 at the time. The older children will probably be more self-sufficient and more nearly through with their formal education. Of course, a modified approach would be called for if the testator has a child with special needs. Overall the clients are probably most concerned with providing for their children in the best possible way.

A testator with sufficient wealth to provide adequately for the needs of each child may prefer to divide the residuary estate into equal shares for the children at the time of the testator's death. That may also be an acceptable plan if the testator's children are older, their educational expenses have been substantially met, and they are more or less independent. Under this approach, one share could be distributed outright to each child over, say, 25, and one share held in a separate trust for each child under that age. In any case the lawyer should describe the alternatives fully to the clients and counsel them regarding the choice that seems best suited to their needs. The lawyer should not routinely squeeze clients into a particular type of estate plan or a particular form of trust that the lawyer happens to have available.

Consolidating the Client's Property in One Trust. If neither parent survives, the most economical and efficient management of the property will result if the probate assets are consolidated with life insurance proceeds and other nonprobate property. Under one approach the client's will creates a testamentary trust for the benefit of minor children if the client's spouse does not survive and the policies of insurance on the client's life are made payable to "the trustee named or to be named" in the will as contingent beneficiary. State statutes often permit such a beneficiary designation to be made without losing otherwise available exemptions of the insurance from creditors' claims and the local death tax. *E.g.*, Cal. Prob. Code §175 (West 1981 Supp.); Ill. Ann. Stat. ch. 110½, §4-5 (Smith-Hurd 1978); N.Y. EPTL §13-3.3 (McKinney 1980 Supp.); Tex. Ins. Code §3.49-3 (Vernon 1980 Supp.); Wash. Rev. Code §48.18.452 (1979).

If the local law does not expressly permit a testamentary trustee to be named as beneficiary, the desired consolidation could be achieved by establishing an inter vivos trust and naming the trustee as secondary beneficiary of the life insurance policies. Such a trust is generally recognized as valid although the trust is not funded during the lifetime of the insured and the trustee merely has the right to receive the insurance proceeds upon the insured's death. *See* §6.7, *infra*. If such a trust is created, the testator's residuary estate should be "poured over" to the trust if the testator's spouse does not survive.

Statutes authorizing pour overs, modeled on the Uniform Testamentary Additions to Trust Act, are in force in most states. *E.g.*, UPC §2-511; Cal. Prob. Code §170 *et seq.* (West 1981 Supp.); Nev. Rev. Stat. §163.220 *et seq.* (1979); N.M. Stat. Ann. §46-5-1 *et seq.* (1978); N.Y. EPTL §3-3.7 (McKinney 1967); Tex. Prob. Code §58a (Vernon 1980); Wash. Rev. Code §11.12.250 (1979). The following paragraph might be included in the will when a pour over plan is used:

(b) If my wife does not survive me and I am survived by any of my descendants, I give my residuary estate to the trustee, acting at the time of my death, of the trust created by the agreement dated January 1, 1981, between me and my wife as trustors and Horace M. Client as trustee, as the trust shall exist at the time of my death, to be added to and administered in all respects as property of the trust. I expressly direct that the trust shall not be considered to be a testamentary trust.

Other nonprobate assets, such as the balance due on notes, might also be made payable to the trustee if the testator's spouse does not survive. Such a provision for payment is treated as nontestamentary by UPC §6-201, but may be required to comply with testamentary formalities in other states.

Discretionary Distributions. The total income tax burdens of the beneficiaries may be lighter if one trust is created and the trustee is given the power to "sprinkle" the income among them. Ordinarily a beneficiary should not serve as trustee of a discretionary trust because of the potentially adverse income, gift, and estate tax consequences. *See* §10.24, *infra.* In determining the time and amount of distributions the trustee can take into account the income tax position of the beneficiaries. The income tax bite may be smaller if most of the income is distributed to the children, who will have little or no other income, leaving a relatively small amount to be taxed to the trust. The fact that the throwback rules do not apply to income accumulated prior to the time the beneficiary attains 21 is helpful in this regard. §665(b). Of course, in some cases that fact will favor the establishment of separate trusts.

The discretionary nature of the trust also allows the trustee to distribute property in kind, which may be used to give the beneficiary a basis in the property equal to its current value without subjecting the gain to the income tax. *See* Reg. §1.661(a)-2(f) and §12.32, *infra.*

If none of the testator's children are under 21, one share of his residuary estate will go to each living child and one share to the descendants of each deceased child. However, the share allocable to the descendants of a deceased child who are under 21 is subject to a very simple minors' trust under Article Eleven, §4.21, *infra.* The provision should obviate the necessity of establishing a guardianship of the estate of a minor descendant.

Ultimate Disposition of Residue. Most wills should include a "wastebasket clause," which disposes of the testator's residuary estate in the event the testator's spouse, descendants, and other specifically designated beneficiaries fail to survive the testator. If neither spouse nor descendants survive, a client may wish to divide the residuary estate equally between the client's surviving relations and those of the client's spouse. This article includes a form that gives one-half of the residue to the persons who would have been entitled to succeed to the wife's property by intestate succession, had she died unmarried at the time of the testator's death, and the other one-half is similarly given to the testator's intestate successors.

In effect, the gift recognizes the contribution each spouse made to acquiring the property and makes a logical division of the property between the surviving relatives of each spouse. The form avoids the problems that could arise if the gift were made to the "heirs" of the client and the client's spouse: It specifies (1) the time at which the class of persons is to be ascertained, (2) the law that is to govern the identification of class members, and (3) the shares they are to take. The identification of the persons and shares should be made under the law in effect at the time the will is executed, which is known, rather than the law as it may exist at a later time, which is unknown. The testator might choose to base the distribution upon the intestate succession law of another state. *See* UPC §2-602. However, a lawyer should hesitate to draft such a provision unless the lawyer knows exactly what the result will be. The disposition of one-half of the residuary estate to the persons who are entitled to receive the testator's noncommunity property under the intestate succession law in effect at the time the will is executed might be subject to the testamentary branch of the Doctrine of Worthier Title. However, the doctrine has been abolished in many states either legislatively or judicially and the Restatement, Property §312(2) (1940) states that it is no longer a part of American law. In any event, the application of this branch of the doctrine would very seldom have any significance.

§4.20. Trust Provisions

Article Ten: The property I have given to my trustee to hold for the benefit of my descendants as provided in this Article shall be held and administered as follows:

(1) The trustee shall pay to or apply for the benefit of my children and their respective spouses and descendants so much of the net income and principal of the trust as the trustee shall deem proper for their support, education, and general welfare, taking into account other sources of funds known to the trustee to be available to them for such purposes. However, in making decisions hereunder, I direct the trustee to prefer children of mine who are under twenty-one (21) years of age at the time of any payment or application of trust funds and to consider that the preservation of principal for ultimate distribution to my beneficiaries is of secondary importance.

I direct the trustee to reimburse fully the guardian of the person of a child of mine for all reasonable expenses incurred by the guardian in caring for and sheltering the child. In short, I do not intend the guardian to bear any financial burden whatsoever by reason of acting as such.

The trustee may pay or apply the income and principal of the trust unequally among my children and their respective spouses and descendants and may exclude one or more of my children and their respective spouses and descendants in making any payment or application of trust funds.

Any net income of the trust that is not expended pursuant to the provisions of this paragraph shall be accumulated and added to the principal of the trust at such times as the trustee determines.

(2) The trust shall terminate when there are no living children of mine under twenty-one (21) years of age ("then"). When the trust terminates I direct the trustee then to divide the property of the trust into as many shares of equal value as are required to carry out the following provisions:

   (a) I give one (1) such share to each of my children who is then living;

   (b) I give one (1) such share to then living descendants of each of my children who is then deceased, such descendants to take by right of representation subject, however, to the provisions of Article Eleven.

Provided, that, if none of my descendants are then living, I give all such property to the persons and in the shares described in Article Nine (4), as if my wife and I had died at the time of termination of the trust.

Comment. As indicated above, this article is designed to give the testator's children the maximum protection the testator can provide. Thus, the trustee is given very broad discretionary powers to use both the income and principal of the trust for the support and education of the testator's children and their dependents. In making distributions, however, the trustee is instructed to consider particularly the needs of minor children. The trustee is also directed to consider other funds that are available to the beneficiary from any source. Finally, the trustee is directed to reimburse the guardian of the person of a child for all reasonable expenses incurred by reason of the guardianship. Some clients may wish to provide expressly that the trustee should pay the costs incurred by the guardian in acquiring furniture or enlarging, remodeling, or renovating the guardian's residence to accommodate the testator's minor children.

This article provides that the trust will terminate when there are no living children of the testator under 21, but a client could just as well choose 25 or 30. Upon termination an equal share of the trust property will be distributed to each living child of the testator and to the living descendants of deceased children. The article does not provide a share for the surviving spouses of deceased children, but some clients may wish to do so. Unfortunately the needs of in-laws are almost totally overlooked in the planning process. If no descendants survive, the ultimate substitutional takers are the persons, determined in accordance with Article Nine (4), §4.19, *supra,* who would be the heirs of the testator and his wife as of the time of termination.

§4.21.   *Trust for Minors*

Article Eleven: If the property of a trust or any of my residuary estate would be distributable to a person who is under the age of twenty-one (21) at such time, then I direct that in lieu of being paid or distributed to such person, the property shall be held or retained by my trustee, in trust, as a separate trust fund for such person ("the beneficiary"). The trustee shall pay or apply so much of the income and principal of the trust for the benefit of the beneficiary as the trustee shall deem proper for support, maintenance, and education, taking into account all other funds available for such purposes and known to the trustee. The trust shall terminate when the beneficiary attains the age of twenty-one (21) or sooner dies. Upon termination, the trustee shall pay over the property of the trust to the beneficiary if he or she is then living, otherwise, to such persons, including the beneficiary's estate or creditors of the beneficiary's estate, as the beneficiary shall by will appoint. In default of such appointment such property shall be distributed to the then living descendants of the beneficiary, by right of representation, or, if the beneficiary leaves no then living descendants, to the person or persons then living who would have been entitled thereto if the beneficiary had predeceased the event that caused the property to be set aside in this trust.

Comment. This article establishes a simple, but very flexible, trust to receive and administer property that would otherwise be distributed to persons under the age of 21.

In large measure it is intended to eliminate the need to appoint guardians of their estates and to provide them with the benefit of a more flexible property arrangement. The article is added out of an excess of caution — its provisions will come into play very rarely. Under most circumstances the testator's estate will be distributed either to a surviving spouse or to their children. Note that by giving the beneficiary a general power of appointment, the transfer of the property to the trust will qualify for the grandchild exclusion to the generation-skipping tax. *See* §2.24, *supra*.

The provisions of this article do not give rise to any problem under the common law Rule Against Perpetuities. The interests will all ultimately vest when a beneficiary (whose parent was living at the time of the testator's death) attains age 21 or sooner dies. If a greater age is used, the provisions may cause a violation of the rule. Hence, a savings clause might be included in such cases. *See* §10.38, *infra*.

§4.22. *Provisions Applicable to All Trusts*

Article Twelve: (1) I appoint my brother, Horace M. Client, as trustee of each trust hereunder. If he shall fail or cease to act for any reason, I appoint _____ to serve as trustee in his place.

(2) I expressly confirm to the trustee named herein and any successor trustee, all of the powers contained in Chapter _____ of the laws of the State of _____ , as they now exist, which I incorporate by reference. In addition, I confer upon my trustee the following additional powers. . . .

(3) I direct that no bond shall be required of my trustee or any successor trustee for any purpose.

(4) If more than one trust is created by this will, the trustee is authorized to hold, manage, and invest the assets of the trusts as one unit, maintaining the separateness of the trusts by a bookkeeping and not a physical segregation of assets.

(5) I direct that no interest of any beneficiary in the income or principal of any trust created by this will may be anticipated, assigned, or encumbered, or be subject to any creditor's claims or legal process prior to its actual distribution to the beneficiary.

Comment. Successor Trustee. When an individual is appointed trustee, the will generally should appoint a successor. The first-named individual may not survive the testator or termination of the trust. Of course, the adult beneficiaries could be given the power to appoint someone other than one of themselves as successor trustee. The appointment of a successor could involve some delay and unpleasantness unless one is named in the will. Also, where multiple trustees are appointed, the survivor(s) could be given the power to fill any vacancy in the trusteeship.

Trustee's Powers. This will meets the problem of defining the trustee's powers by incorporating the existing state statutory provisions, which is satisfactory if the statutes give adequate powers to trustees. Of course, if the local law gives a trustee adequate powers, it is not necessary to incorporate them. However, some lawyers prefer to do so, in order to "freeze" the applicable law and to call the powers to the attention of the trustee and others. The latter objective is, of course, better served by including a complete statement of powers in the will. Unfortunately, the UPC does not include a list of trustees' powers. If the local law doesn't provide an adequate list, the will may incorporate either the laws of another state or the Uniform Trustees' Powers Act, which has served as a model for statutes adopted in many states in recent years. The Act is briefly reviewed in Horowitz, Uniform Trustees' Powers Act, 41 Wash. L. Rev. 1 (1966). The jurisdictions that have enacted the Uniform Act or statutes based on it are listed at 8 U.L.A. 589 (1972). Before a lawyer drafts a will that incorporates a list of powers, the list should be reviewed carefully to determine whether it is necessary to make any additions or deletions based upon the needs of the particular client.

The trustee will often need additional powers if the trustee is expected to deal with special types of property or with special situations, such as agricultural property, mineral interests, income-producing real property, or a business that may be continued following the testator's death. Also, it may be necessary to include special provisions regarding the allocation of receipts and disbursements between principal and income, particularly where income-producing real property is involved, and to give some specific directions to the trustee regarding depreciation and other charges. In some cases, clients will also want small stock dividends allocated to income instead of to principal as provided in the Uniform Principal and Income Act (1962 Revised Act) §6(a), 7A U.L.A. 444 (1978). *See* §10.37, *infra*.

Insofar as deletions are concerned, an informed client may wish to negate the provisions of statutes that authorize a trustee to retain all assets transferred to the trustee, including stock issued by a corporate trustee. *See* Uniform Principal and Income Act (1962 Revised Act) §3(c)(1) 7A U.L.A. (1978). The client also may not wish to relieve the trustee of the duty to diversify investments (Nev. Rev. Stat. §163.280 (1979)), or to allow the trustee to invest in common trust funds and shares of regulated investment companies. It is questionable whether a professional fiduciary should be insulated from liability for the retention of assets, however they were acquired by the trust. After all, a trustee is compensated in part for the prudent management and investment of the trust assets. Also, because of the potential conflict of interest, in most cases a corporate trustee should not be authorized to acquire or retain its own stock. If a client owns particular assets that the client desires the trustee to retain, his or her wishes should be expressed clearly in the will. In such a case the lawyer should not rely upon the general statutory authorization.

The client should weigh carefully whether to deny a trustee authority to invest in common trust funds operated by a corporate fiduciary, or to invest in mutual funds. One consideration is that a corporate trustee may decline to serve or may charge higher fees if its power to invest the assets of a modest-sized trust is so restricted. Also, the assets of the trust may not be as broadly diversified if the trustee is prohibited from investing in common trust funds. In order to facilitate diversification without making unduly small investments and without incurring the cost of investment counsel, perhaps the individual trustee of a small to medium-sized trust should be permitted to invest in mutual funds.

A lawyer may prefer to set forth the trustee's powers in full in the will. The provisions of the Uniform Trustees' Powers Act, or the statutory provisions of a state such as Florida, New York, or Virginia, could serve as a good base from which to work. Once evolved, basically the same statement of powers could be modified as required and used in other wills. As in the case of other forms, it should be used intelligently and not mindlessly included as boiler plate.

Trustee's Bond. Paragraph (3) waives any requirement that a bond be required of the trustee. The provision accords with the probable intent of most testators, who prefer to save the cost of a fiduciary bond and rely upon the good faith of the trustee they have selected. State statutes commonly exempt corporate trustees from posting bonds. A client might wish to require a bond of a successor trustee in a case such as this, where a successor is not named in the will. Again, this is a matter that should be put to the client for decision.

Unified Management of Trust Assets. Paragraph (4) authorizes the trustee to hold and manage the assets of trusts under the will as a single unit. In this way the trustee may achieve some economies of scale and greater diversification of the assets of each trust. The necessary segregation of the assets of the trusts can be adequately maintained on the books of the trust. In addition, the assets of the trusts may always be physically segregated if it becomes desirable to do so.

Spendthrift Clause. The last provision in this article makes the interest of each beneficiary inalienable to the extent permitted by local law. Most states recognize spendthrift restrictions to some extent. In some states income and principal interests can be made spendthrift, while in others only income, or some portion of income, can be protected in this way. Although the interest of a beneficiary may be inalienable because of its discretionary character, it may be desirable to make it spendthrift as well. The addition of this paragraph somewhat increases the probability that the beneficiaries will receive the intended benefits of the trust. Also, in the case of modest-sized estates, there are usually not any countervailing tax considerations that would support the omission of a spendthrift provision. The use of spendthrift clauses is also discussed at §10.19, *infra*.

In order to prevent the trust administration expenses from becoming too large in relation to the size of the trust, a provision might also be included that would authorize the trustee to terminate any trust if its principal value falls below a specified minimum amount (say, $10,000) at the end of any accounting period. If a trust is terminated for that reason, the trustee could be directed to distribute the fund to each beneficiary who is 18, otherwise to a custodian for the beneficiary under the Uniform Gifts to Minors Act. A guardianship should be avoided because the associated expenses could easily exceed the costs of continuing the trust. Since 1973 California has authorized judicial modification or termination of a trust in such circumstances upon petition of the trustee or any beneficiary. Cal. Prob. Code §1120.6 (West 1981 Supp.). Along the same lines, the planner may also wish to include a provision authorizing the trustee to merge substantially identical trusts that have the same beneficiaries. While the effect of such a provision may be uncertain, it might be sufficient to enable a court to authorize the merger of such trusts, which could reduce overall trust administration expenses.

§4.23. Guardian of Minor Children

Article Thirteen: If my wife does not survive me, or for any reason fails to qualify or ceases to act as guardian of the person of any of my children who are minors at the time, I appoint my brother, Horace M. Client, as guardian of the person [and estate] of such minor child. If he fails to qualify or ceases to act as such guardian at any time during the minority of any of my children, I appoint my sister, Louise Client Smith, now of San Francisco, California, as guardian of the person [and estate] of such minor children. I direct that no bond be required of the guardian for any purpose. I expressly authorize the guardian to change the place of residence of any minor child of mine from time to time to any place within or without the state in which the child resides at the time of my death or later.

Comment. The law of many states permits a surviving parent to make a testamentary appointment of a guardian for a minor child. UPC §5-201; Tex. Prob. Code §117 (Vernon 1980); Wash. Rev. Code §11.88.080 (1979). For obvious reasons only individuals may serve as guardians of the person. Although a trust or custodianship is used to provide for the management of the minor's property, a guardian of the minor's estate may be appointed to deal with additional assets that are excluded from the trust or custodianship. The same person, another individual, or a corporate fiduciary may be appointed guardian of the minor's estate. The appointment of a guardian of the person of a child is normally not required if a parent survives — a surviving parent is ordinarily entitled to the care and custody of a minor child.

Although the law of most states does not require a bond of the guardian of a minor's person, the imposition of a bond should be expressly waived in order to settle the matter clearly. The Texas law does require a bond of the guardian of the person, not to exceed $1,000. Tex. Prob.

Code §193 (Vernon 1980). Because of the possibility of the death of both parents as a result of a common accident, it is wise for clients to consider appointing guardians for their minor children. Before their wills are prepared the clients should discuss the topic with the prospective guardians. If the prospective guardians are not family members, the clients must consider whether the provisions of the will should be disclosed to family members. A discussion might relieve problems that could arise if, for example, the family members contested the appointment made in the will. On the other hand, broaching the subject of appointing a nonfamily member could generate an intrafamily controversy.

Often the state law allows a minor over the age of 14 to participate in the guardianship proceedings and to nominate a person to serve as his or her guardian. If the clients' children are 14 or older at the time the wills are prepared, the clients might discuss the subject with them — thus creating a valuable opportunity for parents and children to examine their feelings about each other, family friends, and, importantly, about death. Some clients will readily accept this suggestion — others will reject it or merely not carry it through.

Some jurisdictions allow the appointment of nonresident guardians. If the local law does not permit such an appointment, it may be difficult to meet the needs of some clients. However, a possible solution is to appoint a resident as coguardian with the nonresident. The authorization to change the place of residence of a minor child may provide some additional flexibility, although it is given to guardians by some existing statutes. *See, e.g.,* UPC §5-312(a)(1).

§4.24. Appointment of Executors

> Article Fourteen: I appoint my wife as executor of this will. If my wife does not survive me or otherwise fails or ceases to act as executor, I appoint my brother, Horace M. Client, to serve as executor in her place. I authorize my executor to serve without bond and to administer and settle my estate without the intervention of any court to the maximum extent permitted by the applicable law.

Comment. The lawyer can help a client select an executor by explaining the role of an executor in an estate administration and the pros and cons of having an individual executor, a corporate executor, or coexecutors.

One factor to bear in mind is the cost. If a family member is appointed, either the executor will waive the right to receive a fee or the fee paid will remain within the family. If a nonfamily member is appointed, a substantial fee may pass outside the family.

Where a decedent's personal representative was compensated, the cost was often substantial. However, in most cases in the sample the personal representative was a relative of the decedent who served without compensation. Sometimes a personal representative related to the decedent was paid — perhaps to minimize the aggregate estate and income taxes payable by the estate and the survivors. Even in those cases, the funds stayed within the decedent's family. Unrelated persons served as personal representatives in a small number of cases. Price, The Transmission of Wealth at Death in a Community Property Jurisdiction, 50 Wash. L. Rev. 277, 324-325 (1975); *see also* Kinsey, A Contrast of Trends in Administrative Costs in Decedents' Estates in a Uniform Probate Code State (Idaho) and a Non-Uniform Probate Code State (North Dakota), 50 N.D.L. Rev. 523, 524-527 (1974).

A fiduciary may waive the right to compensation without adverse gift or income tax consequences, provided it is done in a timely fashion. *See* §12.10, *infra*. For federal tax purposes the necessary intention to serve gratuitously is indicated if the fiduciary makes a formal waiver of any right to compensation within 6 months of appointment. *See* Rev. Rul. 66-167, 1966-1 C.B. 20 and Rev. Rul. 70-237, 1970-1 C.B. 13.

The basic fee of a corporate fiduciary is often determined by applying a percentage scale to some measure of the value of the property for which it must account, such as the inventory value. Current fee schedules can usually be obtained upon request by a lawyer from corporate fiduciaries. A typical schedule establishes a minimum fee of $500 and rates of 5% on the first $5,000; 3% on the next $45,000; 2½% on the next $200,000, and 2% on the next $250,000, etc. Some corporate fiduciaries now use schedules that base their fees principally on an hourly charge for the time of trust department personnel at rates comparable to the hourly charge for a beginning lawyer.

Lawyer-Fiduciary. The lawyer who prepares a will should not suggest directly or indirectly that the will appoint him or her as a fiduciary. *See* EC 5-6. The lawyer should also explain that the appointment of an individual as executor or trustee may require the lawyer to do more post-mortem legal work, as a result of which the lawyer's compensation might be greater than if a corporate fiduciary were appointed. On the other hand, the additional cost of legal services may be much less than the fee of a corporate fiduciary.

Corporate Fiduciary. It is impossible to generalize about the desirability of appointing a corporate fiduciary — the quality of its performance depends in large measure on the individual administrator assigned to the estate or trust. The lawyer can influence the fiduciary's performance to some degree, but, after all, the lawyer is retained by the fiduciary, not vice versa. In order to make a full disclosure, perhaps a client should be told of any policy the corporate fiduciaries under consideration may have regarding the employment of lawyers who draw instruments appointing them as fiduciaries. A corporate fiduciary may decline appointment, particularly if it did not review and approve of the terms of its appointment prior to the testator's death.

Family-Member Fiduciary. The availability, willingness, and ability of a family member to serve as executor must also be considered. After the death of a family member, the grief of the survivors may be relieved by devoting some time to the details of the executor's job. In some cases the lawyer can play a valuable role by assigning the survivors a reasonable amount of information gathering and other work. Clients often conclude that a surviving spouse should be appointed executor, recognizing that the survivor may decline to serve in favor of a child or other alternate named in the will. The lawyer should recognize that a surviving spouse or other client may become emotionally attached to and overly dependent on the lawyer and his or her advice. A lawyer should be sympathetic, while at the same time recognizing and discouraging the signs of such dependence.

A client may be less reluctant to appoint an individual fiduciary if the fiduciary is given express authority to retain accountants, investment counselors, or others whose services might assist in the administration of the estate. In essence, the services of a corporate fiduciary can be approximated if an individual executor is provided with adequate professional assistance. It is particularly appropriate to include such authorization where a family member who is unlikely to accept a fee is named as the fiduciary.

Exculpatory Clause. A testator may wish to exculpate an individual personal representative from liability for official acts except in cases of willful misconduct or gross negligence. As a general proposition, corporate fiduciaries and other professionals who are fairly compensated for their services should not be relieved of liability for their acts or omissions.

Coexecutors. The relationship between coexecutors can be a difficult one. A common cause of conflict involves the division of responsibilities and compensation. The advantages of having coexecutors, including continuity in the event one dies or otherwise ceases to serve, should be balanced against the potential disadvantages, including possible disputes over the custody and management of assets and over fees. A corporate fiduciary understandably wants custody of all of the estate's assets and to receive full compensation for its services. An argument against appointing coexecutors who may both seek compensation is that each may receive a full commission in some states. *See* N.Y. SCPA §§2307, 2309 (McKinney 1980 Supp.).

The law commonly requires the concurrence of both (or all) coexecutors to bind the estate, which can cause some delays and require the reference of some matters to the court for instructions. Some problems are avoided if the will authorizes one executor to act during the absence or disability of the other.

Executor's Bond. In most instances no bond is required of a personal representative under the UPC (*see* §§3-602 and 3-605). Under New York law no bond is required except where called for by the will, where the nominee is a nondomiciliary, or where the nominee does not possess the degree of responsibility demanded of a fiduciary. N.Y. SCPA §710 (McKinney 1967). In many states a bond is still routinely required of individual personal representatives unless it is waived. Cal. Prob. Code §541 (West 1981 Supp.); Tex. Prob. Code §§194, 195 (Vernon 1980). However, statutes generally excuse corporate fiduciaries from the requirement of posting bond. Fiduciary bonds, which each year cost from $5 to $10 per $1,000, are often an unnecessary expense that may deprive the surviving family members of needed funds. A client should, of course, be given the option of requiring a bond of fiduciaries but, in most cases, the additional cost should be avoided.

Alternate or Successor Executor. An alternate or successor executor should be appointed in wills that name individual executors. The first-named executor may not survive the testator, may decline to serve, or may not complete the administration of the estate. The need to name a successor is indicated by the fact that roughly 10% of the individual executors named in a sample of Washington wills failed to survive the testator. Price, The Transmission of Wealth at Death in a Community Property Jurisdiction, 50 Wash. L. Rev. 277, 325 n.130 (1975). Although a corporate executor might decline to serve or later resign, it is less necessary to name a successor to a corporate fiduciary. If a successor is not named, the will should establish a procedure for the selection of one (*e.g.*, "a successor executor may be designated by a majority of my surviving adult children").

Compensation of Executors. A will may provide the amount of compensation to be paid to a fiduciary, which binds a fiduciary who accepts appointment without objection. Under some circumstances, it may be desirable to include such a provision in the will. However, the fiduciary may choose not to accept appointment or may seek to be freed of the restriction.

The states have a wide variety of arrangements for establishing the compensation of fiduciaries. For example, California and New York have established statutory rate scales, while other states expect the courts to establish the "reasonable" compensation of executors and trustees.

Under Reg. §20.2053-3(b)(2) a bequest in lieu of commissions is not deductible by the estate. However, an amount of compensation fixed in the will is deductible to the extent it does not exceed the amount allowable under the local law. The payment, but probably not the bequest, will be income to the executor.

Authority to Settle Estate without Court Supervision. Unsupervised administration of estates is the norm under the UPC without any specific form of authorization. The expanded powers given to personal representatives under UPC §3-715, and recent changes in the laws of many states, largely eliminate the need to set forth the powers of the decedent's personal representative. Again, however, in special cases it may be desirable to give the personal representative specific powers with regard to particular assets. Some lawyers confer upon the personal representative the same powers that are given the trustee.

The powers of personal representatives in California were expanded by enactment of the Independent Administration of Estate Act, but no truly independent administration is authorized. *See* Cal. Prob. Code §591 *et seq.* (West 1981 Supp.). For over a century the law of Texas has allowed a testator to provide that his estate be settled without any action of the court other than the probating and recording of his will, and the return of an inventory, appraisement, and list of claims against the estate. Tex. Prob. Code §145 (Vernon 1980). Commentators have observed that virtually all well-drafted wills prepared in Texas direct that the estate be settled by independent administration. One suggested that the Texas courts would probably consider that "the plaintiff could make out a prima facie case of malpractice against a lawyer who drew a will that omitted independent administration." Saunders, A Texas View of Independent Administration and Other Devices for Probate Flexibility, UPC Notes No. 10, 3 (1974). The Washington experience with the unsupervised administration of estates has also been very good. *See* Fletcher, Washington's Non-Intervention Executor — Starting Point for Probate Simplification, 41 Wash. L. Rev. 33 (1966). Because of the mobility of our population and the possible enactment of similar legislation in other states, Article 14 authorizes the executor to settle the estate without court intervention.

§4.25. Directions Regarding Debts, Expenses of Administration, and Taxes

Article Fifteen: (1)   I direct my executor to pay all expenses of administration and all inheritance, estate, succession, and similar taxes ("death taxes") that become payable by reason of my death other than the estate tax attributable to property included in my gross estate by reason of I.R.C. §2044 from the assets of my residuary estate, whether or not the expenses of administration or death taxes are attributable to property passing under this will.

(2) I authorize my executor to exercise all elections available under federal and state laws with respect to (a) the date or manner of valuation of assets, (b) the deductibility of items for state or federal income or death tax purposes, and (c) other matters of federal or state tax law, in accordance with what my executor believes to be in the best interests of my estate. I relieve my executor of any duty to make any adjustment to the shares or interest of any person who may be adversely affected by all such elections.

Comment. A properly drawn will or trust should include a provision definitely establishing the fund from which expenses of administration and death taxes should be paid. The necessary estimates of taxes and expenses must be made and reviewed with the client to be sure that the client's dispositive plan will not be frustrated by charging the items in accordance with the client's directions. Directions should be included although they accord with the existing local law.

Source of Funds to Pay Federal Estate Tax. The executor is obligated to pay the federal estate tax (§2002) but the source from which the tax is paid is generally determined by state law. Many states including Arizona, Texas, and Washington follow the common law rules that call for payment of the entire amount of the tax from the decedent's residuary estate. Others have adopted rules that require the tax to be apportioned among the recipients of the decedent's property. Apportionment rules are usually statutory, *e.g.*, UPC §3-916; Cal. Prob. Code §970 *et seq.* (West 1981 Supp.); N.Y. EPTL §2-1.8 (McKinney 1967), but some states have adopted them by judicial decision. All states recognize that a testator may direct the tax to be satisfied from a different source by appropriate direction in the will. A will provision dealing with the subject must be carefully drafted in order to prevail over the local rule:

> [A]pportionment of the taxes is the general rule to which exception is to be made only when there is a clear and unambiguous direction to the contrary. Ambiguities are to be resolved in favor of apportionment. In re Armstrong's Estate, 366 P.2d 490, 494 (Cal. 1961).

The tax clause generally should not provide for payment from the residue of the taxes attributable to property that is includible in the testator's estate by reason of §2044 (*i.e.*, property for which a gift or estate tax marital deduction was previously allowed as qualified terminable interest property). Unless otherwise directed in the surviving spouse's will, the estate tax attributable to that property is recoverable by the surviving spouse's executor from the recipients of the property. §2207A. *See* §12.36, *infra.*

The substantial volume of litigation regarding the effect of particular provisions indicates the problems lawyers have had in drafting adequate provisions. For example, the term "estate" often appears in tax clauses without specifying whether it refers to the gross estate for tax purposes, the "probate" estate, or some other measure of property. Unfortunately the cost of the litigation is almost always borne by the hapless beneficiaries and not the lawyer who drew the will.

If multiple dispositive instruments are involved, all of the directions for the payment of taxes should be consistent and comply with the requirements of local law. Inconsistent provisions contained in a will and a trust may cause tax and substantive law problems that require judicial resolution. Estate of Brenner, 547 P.2d 938 (Colo. App. 1976). The local law may deny effect to directions regarding payment of taxes if they are not included in the will. For example, a provision of an inter vivos trust that directs the trustee to pay "any and all of the Federal Estate Tax for which no other provision for payment has been made" may not be given effect. Hill v. Nevada National Bank, 545 P.2d 293, 294 (Nev. 1976).

In drafting a provision regarding the payment of taxes it should be borne in mind that stock that is entirely relieved of the obligation to pay death taxes and funeral and administration expenses may not qualify for redemption under §303. For that reason closely held stock that might be redeemed should not be used to satisfy a marital deduction bequest or be treated as qualified terminable interest property. §2056(b)(7). In some instances, the problem can be avoided by making the closely held stock expressly subject to a pro rata portion of taxes and expenses. Such a provision might be effective even as to stock that does not stand in the decedent's name (*e.g.,* in a joint tenancy or a trust). *See* United States v. Goodson, 253 F.2d 900 (8th Cir. 1958) (Minnesota law construed to allow will to impose obligation of contributing to the estate tax on trust beneficiaries and joint tenants).

Power to Make Non-Pro Rata Distributions. In general, the executor should be authorized to make non-pro rata distributions to beneficiaries who are entitled to share equally in a pool of assets (*e.g.,* the residuary estate). The IRS has recognized that an equal, but non-pro rata, distribution to beneficiaries was not a taxable event where the decedent's will authorized such a distribution. LR 8119040. If a non-pro rata distribution is made with the consent of the beneficiaries, but without authorization by the testator, the beneficiaries may be treated as having made a taxable exchange. *See* §12.33, *infra* and Rev. Rul. 69-486, 1969-2 C.B. 159.

Example 4-3. T's will gave his residuary estate equally to A and B but did not authorize his executor to make non-pro rata distributions. In accordance with an agreement between A and B, asset 1 was distributed entirely to A and asset 2 was distributed entirely to B. A may be treated as having exchanged a one-half interest in asset 2 for B's one-half interest in asset 1.

The same concern regarding non-pro rata distributions applies to trusts as well.

Tax Payments and the Marital and Charitable Deductions. Special care should also be exercised in drafting directions regarding the payment of taxes if the client is passing to a surviving spouse property that is intended to qualify for the federal estate tax marital deduction:

> In the determination of the value of any property interest which passed from the decedent to his surviving spouse, there must be taken into account the effect which the Federal estate tax, or any estate, succession, legacy, or inheritance tax, has upon the net value to the surviving spouse of the property interest. Reg. §20.2056(b)-4(c)(1).

The marital deduction is allowable only to the extent of the net value of property passing to the surviving spouse. Reg. §20.2056(b)-4(a). The allowance of the charitable deduction is similarly limited: "Section 2055(c) in effect provides that the deduction is based on the amount actually available for charitable uses, that is, the amount of the fund remaining after the payment of all death taxes." Reg. §20.2055-3(a). The typical apportionment statute meets the problem by providing that allowances shall be made for exemptions and deductions that are available by reason of the relationship of the recipient to the decedent or by reason of the purposes for which the gift is made. *See, e.g.,* UPC §3-916(e)(2).

Interests in Qualified Plans. The estate tax exclusion for qualified employee benefits, §2039(c), is lost if the benefits are subject to a legally enforceable obligation that they be used to pay taxes, debts, or other charges against the employee's estate. The exclusion is not lost, however, if the benefits are payable to a trustee who is empowered, but not required, to use the funds to pay debts, taxes, or other charges against the estate. Rev. Rul. 77-157, 1977-1 C.B. 279. The ruling analogizes employee benefits to insurance proceeds and follows the approach of Reg. §20.2042-1(b). Under the latter, the voluntary power to apply the insurance proceeds to the payment of obligations of the insured's estate will not cause them to be included in the insured's gross estate. *See* §6.14, *infra* and Brorby, Designation of Inter Vivos or Testamentary Trustee as Beneficiary of Employee Benefits, 24 Tax Law. 141 (1970).

Payment of State Inheritance Tax. State inheritance taxes are usually payable by the decedent's executor, but are charged against the interest of each person who receives property from the decedent. Thus, they are naturally apportioned. However, a testator may direct that the inheritance tax should be borne instead by the residuary estate. If so, the provision will probably be treated as an additional gift to the beneficiaries whose obligation to pay the inheritance tax is relieved. However, clients, if consequences are adequately explained to them, will often choose to relieve specific gifts from the burden of inheritance taxes.

Statutes Relating to Payment of Federal Estate Tax. The laws regarding the source of payment of the federal estate tax are reviewed in §12.36, *infra,* in connection with the discussion of post-mortem planning. As indicated above, the testator is free to choose the way in which the tax burden is allocated. In the absence of direction the executor may collect a portion of the federal estate tax from insurance beneficiaries and others. *See* §§2205 to 2207A.

Power to Make Tax Elections. The second clause of this article is intended to alert the executor to valuable tax elections that should be considered and to relieve the executor from the obligation of making adjustments that might otherwise be required if alternatively deductible expenses, paid from the residuary estate, are claimed on the fiduciary income tax return rather than on the estate tax return. *See* §12.15, *infra.* The authorities generally indicate that the residuary estate should be reimbursed for the additional estate tax that results from the election to claim the expenses as income tax deductions. Even so, the persons entitled to the income will receive some benefit from the election in many instances. The provision in the will merely relieves the executor from any obligation to make the adjustment, which could require a complicated accounting; but it does not preclude making the adjustment.

§4.26. Wills Not Pursuant to Contract

Article Sixteen: The terms of this will and the will executed on this date hereof by my wife are essentially reciprocal in nature, that is, my wife is the principal beneficiary of this will and I am the principal beneficiary of my wife's will. The wills are not executed pursuant to any agreement between us. Accordingly, they may be changed or revoked at any time as each of us chooses.

Comment. As indicated above, the lawyer may wish to counter the uncertainty that may arise regarding the revocability of reciprocal wills by including a clarifying statement in the wills. Of course if the clients intend to have a binding agreement for the disposition of their wealth upon the death of the survivor, a different course of action is called for. In such a case the interests of a couple might be better served by establishing an inter vivos trust of substantially all of their property, which could become partially or totally irrevocable upon the death of the first spouse to die. This arrangement parallels the widow's election will that is sometimes used in community property states. *See* §§9.21 to 9.33, *infra.*

(In the typical widow's election will, the survivor receives the entire benefit of the property in the trust for life, with the remainder to others upon the survivor's death.) An independent individual or corporate fiduciary could assure that the survivor receives the intended benefits, yet protect the interest of the remaindermen. Even if a trust were utilized it is difficult to provide the remaindermen with the intended degree of protection and adequately provide for the surviving spouse. However, the trustee could be given the power to invade the corpus of the trust for specified needs of the survivor. Of course, the income, gift, and estate tax consequences of such an alternative must be carefully considered.

§4.27. No Contest Clause

An "in terrorem" clause, providing that gifts to a beneficiary shall be void if the beneficiary contests the will, is routinely included by many lawyers. Such a provision is generally not contrary to public policy insofar as it seeks to prohibit contests that are not made in good faith or have no reasonable cause. However, usually such a clause should be omitted. It may not always serve to protect the integrity of the testator's actual will. Little or nothing prevents the clause from being placed in a will by a person who does exercise undue influence over a testator and wants to prevent a contest.

§4.28. Execution

In witness whereof, I have signed this will on, _____ , 19_____ , at _____ .

_____

John Q. Client

_____

_____

_____

(witnesses)

On the date last above written John Q. Client declared to us that the foregoing instrument, consisting of _____ pages including this page, was his will and requested us to act as witnesses thereto. He thereupon signed his will in our presence, all of us being present at the same time. At his request and in the presence of each other we signed our names as witnesses thereto and signed this attestation clause.

_____

residing at_____

_____

residing at_____

_____

residing at_____

Comment. The testimonium clause should indicate both the date and place of execution. Those facts, while not required, are often helpful in passing on the validity and effect of the instrument.

Although the law of most states requires only 2 witnesses, several require 3. The use of 3 witnesses increases the probability that at least 1 witness will survive the testator and be available to testify if needed. Also, it is preferable to use 3 witnesses rather than to rely upon the application of a choice of law rule that recognizes the validity of a will executed in accordance with the law of the place of execution. Most states do have a statute such as UPC §2-506 that upholds wills that were executed in accordance "with the law at the time of execution of the place where the will was executed, or of the place where at the time of execution or at the time of death the testator is domiciled, has a place of abode or is a national."

Totally disinterested adults should serve as witnesses. Although the UPC does not invalidate a gift to an interested witness (UPC §2-505), the law of most states deprives an interested witness of benefits under the will except to the extent the witness would receive property from the decedent if the will were not established. The credibility of a witness may be affected if the witness is also a beneficiary under the will. The lawyer who drew the will and the persons appointed as fiduciaries generally are not disqualified from acting as witnesses, but may prefer not to do so.

Attestation Clause. An attestation clause, such as the one included above, should be provided for signature by the witnesses if the local law does not provide for the use of self-proving affidavits or if one is not used for some reason. The clause is not necessary for the validity of the will, but the recitation it contains of the facts required to establish due execution usually supports a presumption that the instrument was validly executed. The use of such a clause also makes it difficult for the witnesses later to disavow the facts of due execution recited in it.

§4.29. Self-Proving Affidavit

The attestation clause is now supplanted in many states by an affidavit of due execution that the witnesses can generally complete either at the time the will is executed or later. Completion of the affidavit simplifies the proof of the will by recording the necessary facts in a form that is admissible as evidence. A self-proved will may be admitted to probate without the testimony of the subscribing witnesses. The specific content of the form must comply with the applicable law, which varies somewhat. Compare UPC §2-504 and Cal. Prob. Code §329 (West 1981 Supp.) with Tex. Prob. Code §59 (Vernon 1980). Under some statutes the testator and the witnesses execute the affidavit, under others only the witnesses.

§4.30. Execution Ceremony

The execution ceremony should be conducted by the lawyer in a way that meets the requirements of the law of the place of execution *and* the law of the most demanding state currently in effect. It should also be done in a manner that satisfies the client's expectations: What may have become routine for the lawyer is for most clients an extremely significant event.

First of all, the lawyer should be satisfied that the client is competent and has read and understood the will. *See* §1.2, *supra.* Three adults who are not beneficially interested in the will should be asked to serve as witnesses and be present throughout the entire execution ceremony. *See* §4.28, *supra.* The client should initial each page in the margin or at the bottom of the page and also fill in the date and place of execution in the testimonium clause. The lawyer should then ask the testator, "Do you declare this to be your will and ask the 3 persons present with us to act as witnesses to the will and to your signature?" The testator should answer affirmatively in a voice clearly audible to all 3 witnesses.

At this point the testator should sign the will in the space provided at the end of the instrument in full view of all of the witnesses. Then each witness should sign the will in the space provided immediately below the testator's signature. The testator and all of the witnesses should observe each other's signatures. Under the UPC it is not necessary for (1) the witnesses to see the testator sign the will (if the testator acknowledges the signature to them), (2) the testator to observe the witnesses sign, or (3) the witnesses observe each other sign. UPC §2-502.

If a separate attestation clause is used, the witnesses should then complete and sign it. If the local law provides for making a will self-proving by the use of an affidavit of due execution, it should be executed by the witnesses in lieu of an attestation clause. In that case a notary must acknowledge the witnesses' signatures, and in some cases the testator's signature as well. The execution of affidavits such as this is facilitated if one or more persons in the lawyer's office is a notary public.

The lawyer may retain the original will for safekeeping if requested by the client to do so. If the lawyer does retain the original, he or she should give the client a receipt and make the document available to the client upon request. Some courts and bar association ethics committees have disapproved of lawyers retaining original wills. *E.g.*, State v. Gulbankian, 196 N.W.2d 733 (Wis. 1972). Overall, the retention of wills by lawyers is a valuable service that should be made available to clients. In this way the client's will is safeguarded, yet is readily available to the testator or the executor named in the will.

Only one copy of a will should be executed by the testator and the witnesses. It should be placed by the person having custody of it, usually the testator or the lawyer, in a safe place known to others. Multiple copies should not be executed because of the difficulty of accounting for all of them and the presumption of revocation that may arise if all of the executed copies cannot be produced. However, at least in Oklahoma, "today perhaps far the greater number of wills are executed in duplicate," which "is to be encouraged." Estate of Shaw, 572 P.2d 229, 231, 232 (Okla. 1977) (presumption of revocation of will caused by disappearance of duplicate traced to testator's possession is overcome by production of other executed copy and proof of due execution).

Conformed copies of the will with the date, place of execution, and signature blocks typed in or photocopies of the will should be sent to the testator for reference. If the testator is given the original document, he or she should be cautioned not to attempt to make changes in it or to execute a subsequent instrument intended to have testamentary effect without professional assistance. The testator should also be reminded of the necessity of reviewing the will periodically and of considering the need for changes if the testator's family or economic circumstances change substantially.

§4.31. *Sample Letter to Client*

Mr. and Mrs. John Q. Client
1000 Green Street
Seattle, Washington 98105

Dear Mr. and Mrs. Client:
    Enclosed is a folder that contains photocopies of the documents you executed in my office yesterday, together with a roster of the names, addresses, and telephone numbers of your principal advisors including your accountants, doctors, and brokers. In accordance with your instructions, we have placed the executed copies of your wills and durable powers of attorney in our safe deposit box [office vault] for safekeeping. Those documents are, of course, available to you at any time. As you

requested, we mailed the executed copies of your living wills to your principal physician, Dr. Martin A. Smith.

Periodic review. As I mentioned to you, we recommend that you review your wills and basic estate plan every 3 to 4 years to be sure that they continue to meet your needs. I have made a note on my calendar to send you a reminder in 3 years if I don't hear from you in the meantime. Please let me know if you want to make any changes in the wills or other elements of your plan before then.

Changes in circumstances. We also recommend that you review your wills and basic plan if there are any substantial changes in your personal or financial circumstances. Such a review should be made, for example, if there are any changes in your family as a result of births or deaths, marriages or divorces. A review is also indicated if you plan to move to another state or if the size or composition of your estate changes substantially. You should also be alert for any events that might affect the suitability or availability of the executors, trustees, and guardians who are named in your wills.

Forms of property ownership. In order for your estate plan to be effective, you should continue the present methods of property ownership and the present beneficiary designations in your life insurance and employee benefit plans. The transfer of property into another form of ownership, such as a joint tenancy with right of survivorship (*e.g.*, John Q. and Jane M. Client, as joint tenants), or the change of beneficiary designations would affect the distribution of your property and could have adverse tax consequences. Please check with me before you acquire or dispose of substantial assets, including life insurance.

Gifts. Please also let me know if you plan to make any gifts of more than $10,000 in value to one person in any calendar year. The maximum tax benefits are obtained by carefully planning substantial gifts. Particular attention should be given to the method by which gifts are made (*e.g.*, outright or in trust), the selection of the property to be transferred, and the time at which the gifts are made.

Please call me if you have any questions or would like to consult with me further regarding your plans.

Sincerely,

C. ADDITIONAL DOCUMENTS

§4.32. *General*

The lawyer should also be prepared to counsel clients regarding a variety of additional documents they may wish to execute. Three that have come into prominence in recent years are discussed in the following pages: the power of attorney that either becomes effective or does not terminate when the principal becomes incompetent (the so-called durable power of attorney), an instrument of gift under the Uniform Anatomical Gift Act, and the living will. The durable power of attorney is available in a growing number of states to protect against the necessity of a guardianship if the principal becomes incompetent. An increasingly large number of clients are interested in making gifts of their bodies or parts of their bodies for medical education, research, or transplantation. The Uniform Anatomical Gift Act provides a useful way of carrying out their wishes. Many clients are also anxious to execute a living will or similar document that expresses their wishes regarding the medical care they should receive in the event they become terminally ill and incompetent.

§4.33. Durable Power of Attorney

The National Conference included sections 5-501 and 5-502 in Uniform Probate Code (1969) (1975) concerning powers of attorney to assist persons interested in establishing noncourt regimes for the management of their affairs in the event of later incompetency or disability. The purpose was to recognize a form of senility insurance comparable to that available to relatively wealthy persons who use funded, revocable trusts for persons who are unwilling or unable to transfer assets as required to establish a trust. Commissioners' Prefatory Note, Uniform Durable Power of Attorney Act, 8 U.L.A. 70 (1981 Supp.).

In recent years more than 30 states have adopted legislation that allows a person to execute a power of attorney that will not be affected by any future physical disability or mental incapacity. Although the laws vary somewhat from state to state, they are largely traceable to the sections of the UPC that provide for a durable power of attorney. *See* UPC §§5-501 *et seq.* In 1979 the National Conference of Commissioners on Uniform State Laws promulgated a separate act, the Uniform Durable Power of Attorney Act, which is identical to the revised provisions of the UPC. 8 U.L.A. 70 (1981 Supp.). A revised form of the Durable Power of Attorney Act was adopted in California, effective January 1, 1982. The revised California Act provides for court enforcement of the duties of the attorney in fact, which is not authorized by the Uniform Act. *See* Cal. Civ. Code §§2400-2423 (West 1982 Supp.).

Under the UPC a person may specify that the power will become or remain effective in the event the maker should later become disabled. UPC §5-501. In the absence of such a statute, the usefulness of a power of attorney in estate planning is limited by the common law rule that a power of attorney is terminated by the death *or* incompetency of the principal. In states that have adopted the concept, it is possible to use a durable power of attorney to provide for the management of the principal's property in the event the principal becomes incompetent, in lieu of a guardianship or custodianship. The durable power is superior to other devices because it avoids the publicity, delays, and expense that are otherwise incurred. The power also eliminates the need to account to the court and to obtain court approval for actions concerning the sale or other use of the principal's assets. A durable power is also superior to joint bank accounts and similar arrangements, which may spawn conflicting claims to the funds on deposit — even prior to the principal's death.

The death of the principal terminates a durable power, just as it would terminate an ordinary power. However, actions taken in good faith by the attorney in fact under a durable or nondurable power without knowledge of the principal's death bind the successors in interest of the principal. UPC §5-504(a). Also, under UPC §5-504(b), "[t]he disability or incapacity of a principal who has previously executed a written power of attorney that is not a durable power does not revoke or terminate the agency as to the attorney in fact or other person, who, without actual knowledge of the disability or incapacity of the principal, acts in good faith under the power."

Creation and Revocation. Some states require that a durable power be executed with the same formality as a will and that it be recorded. *E.g.,* S.C. Code §32-13-10 (1980 Supp.). In order to create a durable power the UPC simply requires that the attorney in fact be designated in a writing that contains "the words 'This power of attorney shall not be affected by subsequent disability or incapacity of the principal,' or 'This power of attorney shall become effective upon the disability or incapacity of the principal,' or similar words showing the intent of the principal that the authority conferred shall be exercisable notwithstanding the principal's subsequent disability or incapacity." UPC §5-501.

Under the UPC if a conservator, guardian, or other fiduciary of the principal's estate is appointed after the execution of a durable power of attorney, the attorney in fact is required to account to the appointee. In addition, the appointee will have all of the powers the principal would have had to revoke, suspend, or terminate the power of attorney. UPC §5-503(a). The potential for conflict between the attorney in fact and the conservator is eliminated if the attorney in fact is also nominated in the durable power to serve as the principal's conservator or guardian. *See* UPC §5-503(b). Such a nomination will discourage others from applying for appointment as conservator or guardian and will secure the authority of the attorney in fact against upset in the event it becomes necessary or desirable to appoint a conservator or guardian for the principal. It is often wise to designate one or more successor attorneys in fact lest the first-named person predecease the principal or otherwise be unable to act.

Scope and Use. A durable power may confer as few or as many powers on the attorney in fact as the principal wishes. However, a durable power probably cannot authorize the attorney in fact to exercise powers that are personal and nondelegable, such as the power to make a will, to exercise a power of appointment, etc. Because a power of attorney is useful only to the extent it can be used to carry out transactions with other persons, many clients will choose to give the attorney in fact broad general powers to act with respect to their property. The acceptability of such a power of attorney is generally enhanced if it includes both a statement of the general powers that the attorney in fact may exercise and a list of the specific powers that the attorney in fact is most likely to need.

The needs of some clients are better met by a limited form of durable power, which merely authorizes the attorney in fact to fund a revocable trust of which the principal and the principal's spouse are the current beneficiaries. The typical plan involves a revocable trust, a pour over will, and a limited durable power of attorney. If the principal becomes incapable of managing property, the attorney in fact is authorized to transfer the principal's assets to the trustee for administration in accordance with the terms of the trust. Any additional assets of the principal that may be subject to testamentary disposition will be added to the trust under the terms of the pour over will.

Planners have evolved 2 general approaches to executing and funding the trust. Under one approach, the trust agreement is presently executed and the trust is either funded with some assets or the trustee is named as beneficiary of policies of insurance on the client's life. In this case the durable power permits the client's other assets to be added to the trust. Under the second approach, a form of revocable trust agreement is attached to the durable power of attorney, which the attorney in fact is authorized to execute on behalf of the principal in the event of incompetency. Of course, the durable power also authorizes the attorney in fact to transfer the principal's assets to the trustee to be held and managed as a part of the trust. Either approach should be satisfactory, although the former is, perhaps, more in accord with prior practice.

"Springing Powers." Under the UPC it is possible to execute a durable power of attorney that will become effective upon the incapacity of the principal. Such a "springing power" is helpful to clients who want the protection that a durable power provides, yet are reluctant to execute a presently effective power. The problem remains of defining when the principal becomes incapacitated; and it is typically addressed by making the power effective when the trustee receives a written certification of incapacity from the principal's attending physician. Under a common alternative, the responsibility of determining the incompetency of the principal rests with one or more persons named in the instrument, who

typically include a family member and the principal's attending physician.

Conclusion. A durable power of attorney can provide clients with important, low cost protection against the legal complications of physical or mental incapacity. Under the circumstances, "the possibility of naming an agent under a durable power should be discussed with any client for whom the lawyer is preparing a will or providing estate planning services." Moses & Pope, Estate Planning, Disability and the Durable Power of Attorney, 30 S.C.L. Rev. 511, 525-526 (1979).

§4.34. Anatomical Gifts

Clients frequently wish to donate part or all of their bodies to be used following their deaths to help the living and to contribute to medical education and research. Advances in medical science have made it possible to use a variety of a decedent's body parts, including corneas, kidneys, pituitary glands, and skin. The making of such gifts is facilitated by the Uniform Anatomical Gift Act ("the Act"), 8 U.L.A. 15 (1972), which is in effect in every state and the District of Columbia. The Act helps significantly by establishing legal procedures for making anatomical gifts and by providing for the resolution of conflicting interests. However, it does not attempt to deal with some issues, such as the time at which death occurs. The Act also avoids some other controversial points, such as the legality of selling body parts and the tax consequences of anatomical gifts.

Under §2(a) of the Act, any person 18 years of age and of sound mind may give all or any part of his or her body to certain specified donees. Further, in the absence of actual notice of the decedent's contrary intention, certain other persons may give all or part of the decedent's body to the specified donees. In order of priority the other persons are (1) spouse; (2) adult children; (3) parent; (4) adult brother or sister; (5) guardian of the deceased; or (6) person authorized or obligated to dispose of the body. §2(b). A donee may not accept the gift if the donee has actual knowledge that the gift was opposed by the decedent or is opposed by a member of the same or a prior class. Thus, the wishes of the decedent are recognized as paramount.

Donees. The donees to whom gifts may be made under the Act include hospitals, surgeons, dentists, medical or dental schools, organ banks, or storage facilities for the purpose of education, research, therapy, or transplantation. In addition, a gift may be made to a specified individual for therapy or transplantation. §3. Also, a gift may be made without specifying the donee, in which case the attending physician may accept the gift. §4(c). However, in order to avoid any conflict of interest in the latter case the attending physician is prohibited from participating in the removal or transplantation of a part.

Ways of Making a Gift. There are several ways of making a gift under the Act. The donor may make an anatomical gift by will, which is effective immediately upon death without the need for probate. Indeed, such a gift is effective even though the will is found to be invalid for testamentary purposes. §4(a). A gift may also be made by a document signed by the donor in the presence of two witnesses who must sign the document in the donor's presence. §4(b). As in the case of a will, the document need not be delivered during the donor's lifetime. The Act specifically provides that the document may be in the form of a card designed to be carried on the person. §4(b). A suitable form is printed on the back of driver's licenses in some states. Survivors who are authorized to make gifts of a decedent's body may do so by a signed document, or by telegraphic, recorded telephonic, or other recorded message. §4(e). Finally, the document or will may designate the physician or surgeon to carry out the appropriate procedures. §4(d).

Donee organizations such as eye banks, hospitals, and medical schools will usually supply donor cards and literature upon request. The cards typically have space for the donor to designate a gift of "any needed organs or parts," or "only the following organs or parts." They also usually permit a whole body donation for medical education or research purposes.

There is generally a shortage of suitable anatomical gifts. However, a donee is not obligated to accept a gift. The gift of a body or organs may not eliminate the responsibility of the decedent's estate or of surviving family members to pay the cost of cremation or burial.

Revocation and Amendment. There are also several means by which a gift may be revoked or amended. Where the will or other document has been delivered to the donee, the donor may revoke or amend the gift by (1) a signed statement delivered to the donee; (2) an oral statement made in the presence of two witnesses and communicated to the donee; (3) a statement made during a terminal illness or injury to a physician and communicated to the donee; or (4) a signed card or document found on the donor's person or among the donor's effects. §6(a). Where the will or other document has not been delivered, the gift may be revoked in any of the same 4 ways, or by mutilation, cancellation, or destruction of the document and all executed copies thereof. §6(b). Finally, any gift may be revoked or amended in the same manner that a will may be revoked or amended. §6(c).

Action by Others. A donee may accept or reject an anatomical gift. If the donee accepts a gift of the entire body, subject to the terms of the gift the donee may arrange for embalming or other funeral services. If only part of the body is accepted, the donee is required to remove the part without unnecessary mutilation. After the removal of a part or parts of the decedent's body the remainder is subject to the control of the surviving spouse, next of kin, or other person who is obligated to dispose of the decedent's body. §7(a). Under §7(b), the physician who determines the time of death may not participate in the removal or transplantation of any part. The Act further provides that good faith compliance with the terms of the Act precludes any civil or criminal liability. §7(c). Finally, the Act provides that it is subject to the laws regarding autopsies. §7(d).

Planning. Many clients are understandably squeamish when it comes to discussing anatomical gifts and the disposition of their remains. At the same time, however, most of them appreciate receiving an explanation of the power they have over the post-mortem disposition of their bodies. The subject is typically discussed during an initial office conference or in an early letter to the client. In order to avoid any uncertainty or conflict, the client's wishes should be recorded in an appropriate instrument whether or not the client plans to make any anatomical gifts. As explained in §4.9, *supra,* a client's wishes should usually be contained in an instrument other than a will, which may not be read until after funeral or memorial services are held and cremation or burial has taken place. Also, the client may be more willing to communicate his or her wishes to family members and others if they are set forth in a document other than a will. A client should be encouraged to inform close relatives and intended donees of his or her plans. The disclosure is particularly important if the client intends to provide a bodily part for purposes of transplantation, which may require some pre-mortem preparation and certainly prompt post-mortem action. Also, a donee may be reluctant to accept an anatomical gift where it appears that the spouse or next of kin may object.

A simple donor card is usually sufficient to record a client's anatomical gifts. The card is free, easy to complete, and convenient. A copy of the card should be given to the executor named in the client's will, to the client's spouse, and, perhaps, to the client's parents or adult children. The client may also want to record his or her wishes regarding funeral or memorial services. Such a document, which may be captioned "burial instructions" or "direction for disposition of remains," may be executed at the same time as the will. At a minimum it should be dated and signed by the client. Although witnesses are not required by local law, many lawyers have it witnessed by the same persons who witnessed the client's will.

The text of a common form of a donor's card that complies with the provisions of the Act is set forth below:

UNIFORM DONOR CARD

_____

(Print or type name of donor)

In the hope that I may help others, I hereby make this anatomical gift, if medically acceptable, to take effect upon my death. The words and marks below indicate my desires. I give

(a) ☐ any needed organs or parts

(b) ☐ only the following organs or parts _____

Specify the organ(s) or part(s) for the purpose of transplantation, therapy, medical research, or education.

(c) ☐ my body for anatomical study if needed. _____

Limitations or special wishes, if any

_____

[Reverse side]

Signed by the donor and the following 2 witnesses in the presence of each other.

Signature of Donor _____

Date of Birth of Donor _____ Date Signed _____

City and State _____

Witness _____

Witness _____

§4.35. *The Living Will*

We might start by asking what a living will is, and what it is not. It is a separate document in which a person expresses a wish that his life should not be prolonged by artificial, extraordinary or heroic measures. The definition may vary, but that is generally the intent. A living will is not a last will and testament. You should be aware that a living will probably is not legally effective unless it is made so by legislation in your State. Opinions on the desirability of living will legislation differ considerably. . . . Statement of R. N. Houghton, Panel Discussion on Legal Problems of the Aged and Infirm, 13 Real Prop., Prob. & Tr. J. 1, 22 (1978).

In the wake of the Karen Quinlan case many states have adopted legislation that recognizes the effectiveness of a living will, or directive to physicians as it is sometimes known. Unfortunately, the laws are far from uniform. However, in general, they permit a competent adult to direct in writing that in the event of terminal illness his or her life shall not be prolonged by artificial, extraordinary, or extreme medical treatment. The laws thus sanction passive euthanasia, or the failure to provide medical care, which permits death to occur naturally. Some laws, such as the California Natural Death Act, allow only a terminally ill person to give such directions. Cal. Health & Safety Code §7187 (West 1981 Supp.). The California Natural Death Act, and similar natural death acts, include the text of the directive to physicians that may be used. It is important to note that neither the California Act, nor the legislation adopted in most other states, permits anyone to execute a living will on behalf of a minor or incompetent person. Thus, in most states it is not possible to use the statutory procedure if the patient did not execute a living will prior to incompetency.

The laws generally provide immunity against civil or criminal liability for specified persons who carry out the patient's instructions. However, the persons to whom immunity is given and the circumstances under which it is given vary considerably. "Some statutes provide immunity only for physicians; others provide it for physicians, nurses and medical institutions; whereas others, such as the Arkansas statute, provide immunity to any person who acts in reliance on the living will." *Id.*, Real Prop., Prob. & Tr. J. at 23. Also, some statutes prescribe penalties for the concealment, destruction, falsification, or forgery of a living will.

The laws and the problems the statutes address are complex and controversial. Nonetheless, most clients appreciate being advised regarding the extent to which they can direct the medical care they will be given if they become incompetent. In states that have adopted legislation, documents should be carefully prepared to comply with its terms. In other states the client may wish to execute a form of living will, such as the very popular one published by the Euthanasia Educational Council, New York, N.Y., the text of which is set forth below.

Although a living will may not itself have any legal force, it does provide a valuable expression of the client's wishes, which may provide the maker's family members and attending physicians with the guidance they need. As a matter of routine a copy of the document should be given to the client's regular physician. If that is done, the document will be readily available in the event of illness or emergency. In addition, some members of the maker's family should also be told about the document.

FORM OF LIVING WILL PUBLISHED BY
EUTHANASIA EDUCATIONAL COUNCIL
NEW YORK, N.Y.

To my family, my physician, my lawyer, my clergyman, to any medical facility in whose care I happen to be, to any individual who may become responsible for my health, welfare or affairs:

Death is as much a reality as birth, growth, maturity, and old age — it is the one certainty of life. If the time comes when I, _____ can no longer take part in decisions for my own future, let this statement stand as an expression of my wishes, while I am still of sound mind.

If the situation should arise in which there is no reasonable expectation of my recovery from physical or mental disability, I request that I be allowed to die and not be kept alive by artificial means or "heroic measures." I do not fear death itself as much as the indignities of deterioration, dependence and hopeless pain. I, therefore, ask that medication be mercifully administered to me to alleviate suffering even though this may hasten the moment of death.

This request is made after careful consideration. I hope you who care for me will feel morally bound to follow its mandate. I recognize that this appears to place a heavy responsibility upon you, but it is with the intention of relieving you of such responsibilities and of placing it upon myself in accordance with my strong convictions, that this statement is made.

Signed _____

Date _____
Witness _____
Witness _____
Copies of the request have been given to

_____
_____
_____
_____

BIBLIOGRAPHY

I.   Wills:
        Atkinson, T., Wills (2d ed. 1953)
        California Will Drafting (Cal. CEB 1965)
        Estate Planning for the General Practitioner (Cal. CEB 1979)

Martin, The Draftsman Views Wills for a Young Family, 54 N.C.L. Rev. 277 (1976)

Report, A Sample Simple Will, 15 Real Prop., Prob. & Tr. J. 569 (1980)

Report, Proposed Uniform Acts for a Statutory Will, Statutory Trust and Statutory Short Form Clauses, 15 Real Prop., Prob. & Tr. J. 837 (1980)

Shaffer, Nonestate Planning, 42 Notre Dame Law. 153 (1966)

Shaffer, T., The Planning and Drafting of Wills and Trusts (2d ed. 1979)

Wilkins, R., Drafting Wills and Trust Agreements in [various states] (looseleaf binder, first published for South Carolina in 1971)

II. Durable powers of attorney:

Huff, The Power of Attorney — Durable and Nondurable: Boon or Trap?, U. Miami 11th Inst. Est. Plan., Ch. 3 (1977)

Moses & Pope, Estate Planning, Disability, and the Durable Power of Attorney, 30 S.C.L. Rev. 511 (1979)

III. Anatomical gifts:

Best, Transfers of Bodies and Body Parts Under the Uniform Anatomical Gift Act, 15 Real Prop., Prob. & Tr. J. 806 (1980)

Comment, "How to Do It" Donation of Bodies or Body Parts Under the Texas Anatomical Gifts Act, 27 Baylor L. Rev. 141 (1975)

Randall & Randall, The Developing Field of Human Organ Transplantation, 5 Gonz. L. Rev. 20 (1969)

Weissman, Why the Uniform Anatomical Gifts Act Has Failed, 116 Tr. & Est. 264 (1977)

IV. Living wills:

Akers, The Living Will: Already a Practical Alternative, 55 Tex. L. Rev. 665 (1977)

Comment, The Living Will — Death With Dignity or Mechanical Vitality, 10 Cum. L. Rev. 163 (1979)

Comment, The Right to Die a Natural Death and the Living Will, 13 Tex. Tech. L. Rev. 99 (1982)

Panel Discussion, Legal Problems of the Aged and Infirm — The Durable Power of Attorney — Planned Protective Services and the Living Will, 13 Real Prop., Prob. & Tr. J. 1 (1978)

CHAPTER 5

THE GIFT AND ESTATE TAX MARITAL DEDUCTIONS

225

The achievement of the purposes of the marital deduction is dependent to a great degree upon the careful drafting of wills. Jackson v. United States, 376 U.S. 503, 511 (1964).

We are not aware of any cases or guidelines establishing in a civil case a standard for the reasonable, diligent and competent assistance of an attorney engaged in estate planning and preparing a trust with a marital deduction provision. We merely hold that the potential tax problems of general powers of appointment in inter vivos or testamentary marital deduction trusts were within the ambit of a reasonably competent and diligent practitioner from 1961 to the present. Bucquet v. Livingston, 129 Cal. Rptr. 514, 521 (Cal. App. 1976).

A. INTRODUCTION

§5.1. Scope

The gift and estate tax marital deduction provisions are among the most important and the most complex provisions of the federal transfer tax laws. Our nomadic population and the increased importance of the marital deduction provisions make it necessary for lawyers in common law and community property states to know when and how to make gifts that qualify for the marital deduction.

This chapter opens with a review of the history and of the general contours of the marital deduction provisions. Next, the basic requirements of the deductions are examined in detail, with special attention to the terminable interest rule and its most important exceptions — the life income-general power of appointment trust, the estate trust, and the qualified terminable interest property trust. The issues involved in planning for use of the marital deduction are explored later in the chapter. Included among them are the general objectives of testamentary and inter vivos marital deduction gifts and the advantages and disadvantages of the principal types of formula marital deduction clauses. A related subject, the community property widow's election, is discussed in Chapter 9 in connection with an overall review of transfers for consideration.

§5.2. The Past

From the inception of the estate tax in 1916 until 1942, the estate tax burdens imposed on residents of common law states and those imposed on residents of community property states were not equal. The inequality arose from the federal recognition of the natural "estate splitting" of property onerously acquired by a couple living in a community property state. For example, if a family's material wealth was all attributable to a husband's earnings during marriage, only one-half of it was subject to the estate tax on his death if it had been earned in a community property state. In contrast, all of it was taxed if he had earned it during marriage in a common law state.

In 1942 Congress attempted to remedy the problem by bringing the treatment of residents of community property states more into line with that accorded residents of common law states. The estate tax amendments enacted that year required all of the community property to be included in the gross estate of the spouse first to die except to the extent it was attributable to the services or property of the survivor. This approach ordinarily required all of the community property to be included in the gross estate of the husband. If the wife died first, one-half of the community property was ordinarily includible in her gross estate because of a provision that called for the inclusion of community property over which a decedent held a power of testamentary disposition. The 1942 solution was unpopular with couples in community property states and did not improve the position of couples in common law states.

On the income tax side, couples living in community property states were benefited by the natural splitting of their income: Each spouse was taxed on one-half of the community property income. In contrast, the income of each spouse living in a common law state was fully taxable to the recipient alone. The advantage offered by estate-splitting was enough to lead 6 jurisdictions to adopt community property systems between 1945 and 1947 (Hawaii, Michigan, Nebraska, Oklahoma, Oregon, and Pennsylvania). The "new" community property jurisdictions all reverted to common law systems soon after the Revenue Act of 1948 was passed. The 1948 Act extended the principal tax benefits enjoyed by residents of community property states to residents of common law states. Equalization of advantages was at the heart of the marital deduction provisions from 1948 through 1981. It proved to be more acceptable and durable than equalization of the disadvantages.

The 1948 changes affected the transfer taxes and the income tax. For estate tax purposes, only the decedent's one-half interest in the community property was includible in his or her gross estate. Estate tax parity was achieved by allowing a deduction for transfers to a surviving spouse, limited ordinarily to 50% of the noncommunity property included in the deceased spouse's estate. Technically, the deduction was limited to one-half of the decedent's adjusted gross estate. (The adjusted gross estate was a concept that existed solely for the purpose of determining the maximum allowable marital deduction. *See* former §2056(c).) The adjusted gross estate was defined as the gross estate less (1) the value of all community property included in the decedent's estate and (2) the portion of §2053 and §2054 deductions allocable to the noncommunity property.

> **Example 5-1.** H died in 1981 leaving a gross estate of $800,000 in noncommunity property. A total of $40,000 in deductions was allowed under §2053. H left $25,000 to a charity, for which a deduction was allowable under §2055, and the balance of his estate to his wife, W. The maximum allowable marital deduction was limited to

$380,000 (one-half of H's adjusted gross estate) computed as follows:

Gross estate	$800,000
Less:	
Deductions under §2053	40,000
Adjusted gross estate	760,000
Maximum marital deduction	$380,000

If the expenses allowable as deductions under §2053 were not claimed on H's estate tax return, H's adjusted gross estate would have been $800,000 and the maximum allowable deduction $400,000.

In general, a deduction was allowable with respect to property transferred to a surviving spouse if the interest transferred to the survivor was sufficient to cause it to be includible in his or her gross estate. By taking advantage of these provisions, a married person could halve the amount of noncommunity property that would be subject to tax at death.

The 1948 gift tax changes allowed a couple to "split" gifts made to third parties and treat them as made one-half by each. It also introduced a deduction for up to 50% of the value of gifts of noncommunity property made to the donor's spouse. Finally, the 1948 Act allowed couples to reduce their income tax liability by filing a joint return on which their combined income was taxed at preferential rates.

The purpose of the 1948 legislation is recounted in the following passage from United States v. Stapf, 375 U.S. 118, 128 (1963).

The 1948 tax amendments were intended to equalize the effects of the estate taxes in community property and common-law jurisdictions. Under a community property system, such as that in Texas, the surviving spouse receives outright ownership of one-half of the community property and only the other one-half is included in the decedent's estate. To equalize the incidence of progressively scaled estate taxes and to adhere to the patterns of state law, the marital deduction permits a deceased spouse, subject to certain requirements, to transfer free of taxes one-half of his noncommunity property to the surviving spouse. Although applicable to separately held property in a community property state, the primary thrust of this is to extend to taxpayers in common-law states the advantages of "estate splitting" otherwise available only in community property states. The purpose, however, is only to permit a married couple's property to be taxed in two stages and not to allow a tax-exempt transfer of wealth into succeeding generations. Thus, the marital deduction is generally restricted to the transfer of property interests that will be includible in the surviving spouse's gross estate.

As the quotation indicates, the estate tax marital deduction adopted in 1948 allowed a portion of the tax otherwise payable upon the death of one spouse to be deferred until the death of the survivor. It did not allow the tax to be entirely avoided.

Quantitative Limits on the Marital Deduction, 1977-1982. In 1976 Congress liberalized the marital deduction provisions in order to increase the amount of property an individual could leave to a surviving spouse free of estate tax and to allow freer interspousal lifetime transfers. The 1976 Act amended §2056(c) to allow a new minimum marital deduction of $250,000. Under the amendment an estate was allowed to claim a deduction of $250,000 or 50% of the adjusted gross estate, whichever was larger. The $250,000 minimum deduction, reduced by the amount of community property included in the gross estate, was available to estates composed entirely of community property. However, because of the reduction, the $250,000 minimum deduction was not a major factor in planning community property estates.

The 1976 Act also amended §2523 to allow a greater current deduction for post-1976 gifts to a spouse. Under the change a full marital deduction was allowed for the first $100,000 of qualifying transfers to a spouse; no deduction was allowed with respect to the next $100,000; and a maximum deduction of 50% was allowed to the extent the post-1976 gifts exceeded $200,000. §2523(a). As before, no gift tax marital deduction was allowed for transfers of community property. Former §2523(f). Finally, the maximum allowable estate tax deduction was reduced by the amount by which the gift tax marital deduction that had been allowed the decedent under §2523 exceeded 50% of the value of the property transferred (*i.e.*, where the post-1976 gifts were less than $200,000). Former §2056(c)(1)(B).

The approach taken in 1976 represented a compromise between the proponents of an unlimited marital deduction of the type proposed in the Treasury Department's 1969 gift and estate tax reform proposals (U.S. Treas. Dept., Tax Reform Studies and Proposals, 91st Cong., 1st Sess., pt. 3 at 357 *et seq.* (Comm. Print 1969)) and those who wanted little or no change in the deductions. Proponents argued that an unlimited deduction would leave more property for the support of the surviving spouse; provide more flexibility in planning transfers; and simplify the law. Opponents countered that an unlimited deduction would merely increase the tax benefits already available to wealthy taxpayers, whose surviving spouses were amply protected by the law. They noted that even under the pre-1977 law a substantial amount of property could be transferred to a spouse inter vivos and at death without incurring any federal transfer tax liability. As noted below, the proponents of the unlimited marital deduction carried the day in 1981 when their proposal was adopted effective with respect to decedents dying after December 31, 1981.

§5.3. The Present

With relatively little fanfare the 1981 Act removed all quantitative limits on the marital deduction and relaxed the qualitative restrictions to allow 2 additional types of interests to qualify for the gift and estate tax deductions. The changes closely parallel 2 of the key recommendations made in the Treasury's 1969 tax reform proposals.

> It does not appear, then, that transfers of property between husband and wife are appropriate occasions for imposing tax. An especially difficult burden may be imposed by the tax when property passes to a widow, particularly if there are minor children. The present system of taxing transfers between spouses does not accord with the common understanding of most husbands and wives that the property they have accumulated is "ours." Furthermore, the distinctions drawn by existing law between transfers which qualify for the marital deduction and those which do not qualify have generated drafting complexities, artificial limitations upon dispositions, and considerable litigation.

> Under the [proposed] unified transfer tax there will be an exemption for the full amount of any property that passes to a spouse, either during the life of the transferor spouse or at his or her death. However, property received by the transferee spouse will, of course, become part of his or her taxable estate, unless consumed. U.S. Treas. Dept., Tax Reform Studies and Proposals, 91st Cong., 1st Sess., pt. 3, 358 (Comm. Print 1969).

The quantitative change was brought about by repealing §2056(c) (which limited the amount of the estate tax deduction as noted above), §2523(a)(2) (which limited the amount of the gift tax deduction), and §2523(f) (which disallowed any gift tax deduction for gifts of community property). Accordingly, beginning in 1982, gift and estate tax marital deductions became allowable for the full value of property that passes to a spouse in a qualifying way. As a result of the repeals, the gift and estate tax marital deduction provisions no longer differentiate between community and noncommunity property. Deferral of the tax on the death of the first spouse to die is a valuable option, particularly during the period the unified credit is increasing (through 1987) and the highest marginal tax rate is shrinking (through 1985).

Qualitative Changes. Important qualitative changes were also made by the 1981 Act. Most important, the Act added §§2056(b)(7) and 2523(f), which allow elective marital deductions with respect to qualified terminable interest property (QTIP), which is property in which the donee spouse is given a "qualifying income interest for life." To constitute such a qualifying income interest the donee spouse must be entitled to all of the income from the property for life, payable annually or at more frequent intervals, and no person can have the power to appoint any of the property to any person other than the surviving spouse during his or her lifetime. §§2056(b)(7)(B)(ii), 2523(f)(2). In essence the changes allow a marital deduction for a simple life income interest, provided that no one can divert any of the property to another person during the surviving spouse's lifetime. The lifetime and post-mortem planning opportunities created by the changes are enhanced by the fact that the deductions are not automatically allowable with respect to qualifying income interests for life. Instead, the donor, or the decedent's executor, may elect whether or not to claim a marital deduction with respect to the property in which the donee spouse has a qualifying income interest for life. Such an election can be made with respect to a specific portion of the property. §2056(b)(7)(B)(iv). The elective feature makes it possible to "fine tune" the amount of the estate tax marital deduction after the death of a spouse, when much more is known about the circumstances of the decedent's estate and of the surviving spouse. Of course, the portion of the property for which a deduction is claimed is includible in the donee spouse's estate under new §2044 unless the property is disposed of during his or her lifetime.

The 1981 Act also added provisions that allow gift and estate tax deductions for current interests in charitable remainder trusts that are transferred to a spouse. §§2056(b)(8); 2523(g). See §5.19, *infra*. Since the inception of the charitable remainder trust rules in 1969, gift and estate tax deductions have been allowed for the value of qualifying charitable remainder interests. See §§2055(e)(2), 2522(c)(2) and §8.20, *infra*. However, prior to 1982 no deductions were allowable with respect to the noncharitable current interest in such trusts. Given the shift to an unlimited marital deduction, Congress thought it was desirable to extend the deduction to this type of interest.

Transitional Rule. The changes in the marital deduction provisions made by the 1981 Act generally apply with respect to gifts made, or decedents dying, after December 31, 1981. However, under §403(e)(3) of the 1981 Act, the unlimited marital deduction generally does not apply to property passing under a will or trust executed prior to September 13, 1981, "which contains a formula expressly providing that the spouse is to receive the maximum amount of property qualifying for the marital deduction allowable by Federal law." Accordingly, "old" instruments that contain maximum marital deduction formula clauses will be governed by the pre-1982 law (*i.e.*, the marital deduction will be limited to the greater of one-half of the adjusted gross estate or $250,000). The unlimited marital deduction does apply to a pre-September 13, 1981, instrument if (1) the formula is amended after September 12, 1981, to refer to the unlimited marital deduction or (2) the state enacts a statute "which construes this type of formula as referring to the [unlimited] marital deduction allowable by Federal law." Act §403(e)(3)(C), (D). States will be reluctant to enact such a statute because of the palpable uncertainty regarding the decedent's intention in such a case. Congress enacted the transitional rule in order to avoid the constructional problems that would otherwise exist, the resolution of which might frustrate the testator's intent. "The committee is concerned that many testators, although using the formula clause, may not have wanted to pass more than the greater of $250,000 or one-half of the adjusted gross estate (recognizing the prior law limitation) to the spouse." S. Rep. 97-144, 97th Cong., 1st Sess. 128 (1981).

The adoption of the unlimited marital deduction in 1981 probably was unrelated to the experience in other countries. However, it is notable that the United Kingdom made a similar change in 1975, when it switched from an estate duty that allowed only a limited exemption for property transferred to a spouse at death, to a capital transfer tax (CTT) that totally exempts most transfers between spouses. Finance Act of 1975, Sched. 6, para. 1(1). CTT is a unified transfer tax — in essence a progressive rate scale is applied to the cumulative total of all nonexempt gratuitous transfers during lifetime and at death. The cumulative feature and the inclusion of the tax in the amount of lifetime transfers for purposes of computing the tax ("grossing up") may deter lifetime transfers of wealth to persons other than a spouse. Prior to the CTT, inter vivos transfers were not subject to tax, although the estate duty reached most gifts made within 7 years of a donor's death. British commentators have pointed out that individuals must consider a number of factors and settle their priorities before deciding how much of their estates should go to a surviving spouse. G. S. A. Wheatcroft and G. D. Hewson, Capital Transfer Tax 110-112 (1975). They believe that in most cases individuals will divide their property between their children and their surviving spouse in order to equalize the amount of property subject to tax on the death of each spouse.

§5.4. *The Future*

Probably no significant changes will be made in the marital deduction provisions in the near future. Predictions are hazardous, but since the unlimited marital deduction provisions were adopted in 1981, it seems safe to assume that they will remain in effect for some time. However, some minor changes and, hopefully, some further simplifications may occur. The sheer complexity of the marital deduction provisions is enough to warrant further simplification. Some of the fine distinctions between deductible and nondeductible interests were relaxed by the 1981 Act; yet some of the remaining distinctions are hard to justify in terms of equity, administrative convenience, or other considerations of tax policy. The excessive technicalities of the law are particularly objectionable because of the hazards and substantial direct and indirect compliance costs they impose on taxpayers. The difficulties of complying with the technicalities are sometimes compounded by the "hidebound position taken by the Commissioner." Estate of Smith v. Commissioner, 565 F.2d 455, 458 (7th Cir. 1977). The principal direct costs are payments of additional fees to personal representatives and attorneys in connection with disputes spawned by the present law. The indirect costs, which are generated by the additional loads placed upon the IRS, the Department of Justice, and the courts, are also substantial.

B. DETAILS OF THE MARITAL DEDUCTION

§5.5. Basic Requirements

The following 5 requirements must be met in order for a gift of an interest in property to qualify for the estate tax marital deduction. Listed in more or less ascending order of complexity and capacity for creating problems, they are:

1. the decedent was a citizen or resident of the United States;
2. the interest in property is included in the decedent's gross estate;
3. the decedent is survived by a spouse;
4. the interest "passes" to the decedent's surviving spouse; and
5. the interest is a deductible one (*i.e.*, it is not a nondeductible terminable interest).

The first 3 requirements ordinarily do not pose any particularly difficult problems. Unfortunately, the fourth and more often the fifth requirements do spawn disputes over the allowability of a deduction. In part the volume of litigation reflects the extent to which the IRS has insisted upon full compliance with some very technical provisions of the law.

Gift Tax. Section 2523 imposes similar requirements in connection with the gift tax marital deduction: A citizen or resident is entitled to a deduction for a gift of a deductible interest in property to his or her spouse. In order to qualify for the deduction the donor and the donee must be validly married at the time of the transfer. This places a premium on knowing when a gift is complete, particularly in cases that involve antenuptial agreements. The main differences between the gift and estate tax deductions are mentioned in the course of a detailed review of the estate tax provisions.

§5.6. Citizen or Resident

The citizenship and residence of a client are usually clear and will not be the subject of controversy upon his or her death. The overall consequences of establishing citizenship and residence should be carefully considered when a client has ties to more than one country. In general, ambiguous relationships should be resolved one way or another before a problem arises — either by firmly establishing the relationship or by clearly severing it. The existing tax treaties do not completely eliminate the additional transfer taxes that may result if a client has ties to 2 or more countries. Similarly, tax complications that result from the ownership of assets in more than one jurisdiction should be avoided. The cautious use of trusts and corporations allows some multijurisdictional problems to be avoided. *See* §10.10, *infra.*

§5.7. Inclusion in the Gross Estate

The includibility of property in a decedent's gross estate is also usually clearly determined under other Code sections. Although an otherwise qualifying interest passes to the surviving spouse in a requisite way, no deduction is allowed unless the interest is included in the decedent's gross estate and is not otherwise deductible. For example, amounts for which a deduction is allowed under §2053 for commissions paid to the surviving spouse as personal representative are not also deductible under §2056. Reg. §20.2056(a)-2(b)(2).

> **Example 5-2.** H designated W as the recipient of benefits payable under a qualified retirement plan. The interest received by W is deductible only to the extent it is included in H's gross estate. Thus, the value of any portion excluded from H's estate under §2039 does not qualify for the marital deduction. *See* Reg. §20.2056(e)-1(a)(6).

Similarly, no deduction is allowed for property the decedent gave inter vivos to his or her spouse unless the property is included in the decedent's gross estate.

§5.8. Surviving Spouse

Neither the Code nor the regulations define "surviving spouse." However, it is clear that the decedent and the transferee must be married at the time of the decedent's death. In that connection the IRS has ruled that "[t]he marital deduction is not allowed with respect to transferred property if the decedent was not married to the transferee at the time of death even though the decedent may have been married to the transferee at the time of the transfer." Rev. Rul. 79-354, 1979-2 C.B. 334 (gift made to spouse within 3 years of decedent's death, but donee predeceased donor). The same ruling allowed a marital deduction for a gift made within 3 years of the donor's death to a person other than the donor's spouse where the donor and donee were married at the time of the donor's death.

For federal estate tax purposes the marital status of a decedent is determined under the law of the state of his or her domicile. Estate of Goldwater v. Commissioner, 539 F.2d 878 (2d Cir.), *cert. denied,* 429 U.S. 1023 (1976); Estate of Spalding v. Commissioner, 537 F.2d 666 (2d Cir. 1976); Estate of Steffke v. Commissioner, 538 F.2d 730 (7th Cir.), *cert. denied,* 429 U.S. 1022 (1976).

> **Example 5-3.** H married W in 1946. H obtained a Mexican divorce from W in 1958. In 1959 H participated in a marriage ceremony with P. A court of the state in which H was domiciled later declared the Mexican divorce to be invalid. Thereafter H died, leaving his entire estate of $300X to P. W claimed and received an elective share of $100X from H's estate. The marital deduction is limited to the amount that passed to W, who was H's surviving spouse under the applicable state law (*i.e.,* no marital deduction is allowable for the property left to P).

As the example indicates, questions of status are extremely important in resolving issues both of tax law and of substantive property law. For the purposes of the marital deduction, presumably the marital relation continues although the spouses are living apart if their marriage has not been formally dissolved.

§5.9.   Interests "Passed" to the Surviving Spouse

A deduction is allowed only for interests that "pass" to the surviving spouse. The ways in which interests in property are considered to pass to a surviving spouse are listed in §2056(c). They include interests passing by (1) bequest or devise; (2) inheritance; (3) dower or curtesy; (4) inter vivos transfer; (5) joint tenancy or right of survivorship; (6) the exercise or nonexercise of a power of appointment; and (7) policies of insurance on the decedent's life. A decedent commonly passes property to a surviving spouse in several of the ways listed in the statute.

A controversy involving the passing requirement may arise when a surviving spouse elects against the decedent's will or, less commonly, when he or she receives (or surrenders) an interest in a decedent's estate in connection with a will contest. Any dower, statutory share, or other property a surviving spouse receives as a result of an election against the will is considered to pass from the decedent to him or her. However, any interest a surviving spouse is required to give up as a result of an election is not considered to pass from the decedent to him or her. Reg. §20.2056(e)-2(c). The value of the right of a surviving spouse to elect against the decedent's will and to receive a statutory share of the decedent's estate is not includible in the surviving spouse's gross estate if the surviving spouse dies without making the election. Rev. Rul. 74-492, 1974-2 C.B. 298. The cited ruling holds that the right is neither a property interest includible under §2033 nor a general power of appointment includible under §2041. Under it, "the election to take under the husband's will is treated as a disclaimer or renunciation of the alternative rights of the widow provided under state statute."

An interest is also considered to pass from the decedent to the surviving spouse if it is received as a result of a bona fide recognition of his or her enforceable rights in the estate. The necessary showing is ordinarily provided by a court decree upon the merits in an adversary proceeding following a genuine and active contest. Consistently, an interest in property is not considered to have passed to the surviving spouse to the extent he or she assigns or surrenders it in settlement of a controversy. *See* Reg. §20.2056(e)-2(d).

The regulations point out that the surviving spouse must receive the beneficial interest in the property in order to qualify for the deduction. Reg. §20.2056(e)-2(a). Thus, no deduction is allowed for property transferred to the spouse as trustee for others. Along the same lines, the deduction is limited to the net value of the interests that pass to the spouse. Section 2056(b)(4) requires the amount of death taxes, encumbrances, and any other obligations imposed by the decedent with respect to the passing of an interest to be deducted in computing the value of the interest received by the surviving spouse. This limitation on the amount of the deduction and the consequences of a "widow's election" in a community property state are discussed in United States v. Stapf, 375 U.S. 118 (1963). In *Stapf* the Court properly concluded that a deduction was allowable only to the extent the value of the interests received by the decedent's widow exceeded the value of the interests she was required to transfer to others.

Family Awards and Allowances. The regulations recognize that a widow's allowance or other family award payable during the administration of an estate constitutes property that passes from a decedent to the recipient. However, as explained below, §5.10, *infra,* no deduction is permitted if the allowance is a nondeductible terminable interest. *See* Reg. §20.2056(b)-1(g)(8). For example, in Jackson v. United States, 376

U.S. 503 (1964), the Court concluded that the California widow's allowance was not a deductible interest because the widow "did not have an
indefeasible interest in property at the moment of her husband's death
since either her death or remarriage would defeat it." 376 U.S. at 507.
Family allowances typically do not qualify for the deduction under the
terminable interest rule. Note, Widow's Allowances and Marital
Deductions — The Date-of-Death Rule, 63 Mich. L. Rev. 924 (1965).
However, homestead allowances and awards in lieu of homestead that
vest immediately at death do qualify for the marital deduction. *See,
e.g.,* Rev. Rul. 72-153, 1972-1 C.B. 309 (Washington); Comment, Federal
Estate and State Inheritance Tax Aspects of the Family Allowance, the
Homestead and the In Lieu of Homestead Awards, 37 Wash. L. Rev. 435
(1962).

The IRS has ruled that the Arizona homestead allowances of a cash
sum and the exempt property allowance, which are based on UPC §§2-
401 and 402, both qualify for the marital deduction. Rev. Rul. 76-166,
1976-1 C.B. 287. Note that they qualify although the surviving spouse
must survive the decedent by 120 hours and must elect to claim them. In
contrast, the value of a family allowance made to a surviving spouse
under UPC §2-403 is a terminable interest that does not qualify for the
deduction.

Disclaimers. The use of disclaimers in post-mortem planning is reviewed in some detail at §§12.26 to 12.29, *infra.* At this point it is important to note that the amount passing to the surviving spouse may be
increased or decreased by "qualified disclaimers." Under §§2046 and
2518 qualified disclaimers are recognized for purposes of the estate, gift,
and generation-skipping taxes.

A "qualified disclaimer" is defined in §2518(b) as a written, unequivocal, and unqualified refusal to accept an interest in property
(including a power with respect to property) that is received by the
transferor of the interest or the transferor's legal representative not later
than 9 months after the day on which the transfer creating the interest
was made. A disclaimer is not qualified if the disclaimant accepted the
property or any benefits from it prior to making the disclaimer. As a
result of the disclaimer, the interest must pass to the decedent's surviving
spouse or a person other than the disclaimant. Also, the disclaimant
cannot direct the transfer of the property to another person.

Qualified disclaimers may prevent a surviving spouse from receiving
"too much" property from the decedent's estate. In particular, disclaimers can adjust the amount of property that passes to the surviving spouse
so the decedent's unified credit is not wasted and the surviving spouse's
estate is not unnecessarily enlarged. Disclaimers may also be used to
increase the amount of property passing to the surviving spouse in ways
that qualify for the marital deduction. Disclaimers made by other persons of property that the surviving spouse becomes entitled to receive

are recognized as passing from the decedent to the surviving spouse if the disclaimers are made in accordance with the provisions of §§2046 and 2518. Prop. Reg. §20.2056(d)-1.

§5.10.   A Deductible Interest (i.e., Not a Nondeductible Terminable Interest)

[W]hile the terminable interest rule is, indeed, a thicket, the Congressional purpose of disqualifying terminable bequests was certainly not to elevate form over substance. It was, instead, to prevent the wholesale evasion of estate taxes which the skillful employment of terminable interests could have easily achieved. Allen v. United States, 359 F.2d 151, 153-154 (2d. Cir.), *cert. denied*, 385 U.S. 832 (1966).

The so-called terminable interest rule of §2056(b) is intended to assure that property for which a marital deduction is allowed in the estate of the spouse first to die will be included in the gross estate of the surviving spouse except to the extent the surviving spouse consumes or disposes of it during his or her lifetime. Accordingly, where the interest involved will be includible in the surviving spouse's estate, some courts have declared that "the Commissioner's dependence on any literal statutory language arguably contrary should not prevail, for in such an instance, form may not be elevated over substance." Estate of Smith v. Commissioner, 565 F.2d 455, 459 (7th Cir. 1977).

The basic terminable interest rule bars a deduction for an interest in property only where (1) the interest passing from the decedent to the surviving spouse is terminable (*i.e.*, it will terminate on the occurrence or nonoccurrence of an event or contingency); (2) the decedent also passed an interest in the same property to another person for less than adequate and full consideration in money or money's worth; *and* (3) the other person or his or her successors may possess or enjoy the property *after* the surviving spouse's interest terminates. §2056(b)(1). The rule does not bar a reduction unless all 3 of the elements are present. Practically the same rule applies to inter vivos transfers. *See* §2523(b).

Properly drafted formula marital deduction bequests and equalization clause bequests (*i.e.*, ones that give the surviving spouse interests in the deceased spouse's property sufficient to equalize the sizes of their respective taxable estates) do not violate the terminable interest rule. In the case of the equalization clause, the interest that the surviving spouse receives is not terminable — its value remains uncertain until the survivor's estate is valued, just as the value of a formula gift remains uncertain until certain valuations are made.

Terminable Interest.   The first requirement of the rule is satisfied only if the interest given the surviving spouse is a terminable interest. For this purpose the regulations explain that "[a] 'terminable interest' in property is an interest which will terminate or fail on the lapse of time or on the occurrence or failure to occur of some contingency. Life estates, terms for years, annuities, patents, and copyrights are therefore terminable interests. However, a bond, note, or similar contractual obligation, the discharge of which would not have the effect of an annuity or a term for years, is not a terminable interest." Reg. §20.2056(b)-1(b).

> **Example 5-4.** H devised Blackacre to W for life, remainder to his son S. The life interest that H passed to W is a nondeductible terminable interest because it will terminate upon W's death and Blackacre will be owned by S or his successors, who did not pay fair and adequate consideration for the remainder interest. However, the life interest may constitute a qualifying income interest for life, for which H's executor might elect to claim a deduction under §2056(b)(7). *See* §5.18, *infra.*

Interest Passed to Another Person. The second requirement is met only if an interest in the same property passes for less than full and adequate consideration from the decedent to a person other than the surviving spouse. §2056(b)(1)(A). For the purposes of the terminable interest rule, "it is immaterial whether interests in the same property passed to the decedent's spouse and another person at the same time, or under the same instrument." Reg. §20.2056(b)-1(e)(1).

> **Example 5-5.** H gave Blackacre to S, reserving the use of the property for a 20-year term. H died during the term and bequeathed his interest to his surviving spouse, W. The interest passed to W is a nondeductible terminable interest because S, who did not pay full and adequate consideration for his interest in Blackacre, will possess it after the term expires.

> **Example 5-6.** H sold a remainder interest in Blackacre to his son, S, for full and adequate consideration, reserving a joint and survivor life estate to himself and W. If W survives H, the interest W received from H is a deductible terminable interest. Although W's interest is terminable and the property will be enjoyed by S or his successors upon her death, S paid full and adequate consideration for the interest he received from H.

> **Example 5-7.** H bequeathed a patent to W. The interest given W will terminate upon the lapse of time. However, it is a deductible interest because no other person received any interest in the patent from H.

This requirement of the rule is not satisfied if the surviving spouse exercises the right to claim an absolute interest in the decedent's property, whether the elective right is conferred by the decedent's will or by state statute. In such cases the interest is not terminable and no interest in the property passes to any other person. Estate of Neugass v. Commissioner, 555 F.2d 322 (2d Cir. 1977) (will provision); Rev. Rul. 72-7, 1972-1 C.B. 308 (Virginia commuted dower); Rev. Rul. 72-8, 1972-1 C.B. 309 (Florida award of absolute dower interests).

Subsequent Enjoyment. The third requirement is present only if the other person to whom an interest was transferred or that person's successors may possess or enjoy the property *after* the termination of the surviving spouse's interest. §2056(b)(1)(B). Thus, a deduction may be allowed where the surviving spouse will possess or enjoy the property upon the termination of another interest.

> **Example 5-18.** H devised Blackacre to S for life, remainder to W. H's estate will be allowed a deduction for the value of the remainder interest determined in accordance with the applicable actuarial tables (Reg. §20.2031-7 for pre-1971 transfers and Reg. §20.2031-10 for post-1970 transfers). The interest devised to S is terminable, but the interest transferred to W is not. No one is entitled to possess or enjoy the property *after* W as a result of H's transfer.

Executor Purchase and Unidentified Asset Rules. Two subsidiary rules also restrict the allowability of a marital deduction. One, the executor purchase rule, §2056(b)(1)(C), prohibits a deduction for any terminable interest that "is to be acquired for the surviving spouse pursuant to the directions of the decedent, by his executor or by the trustee of a trust."

> **Example 5-9.** H bequeathed $100,000 to W subject to a direction that his executor use the funds to purchase an annuity for W. The bequest is a nondeductible interest. Note that if H had purchased a joint and survivor annuity under which payments were to be made to W after his death, the interest of W would be deductible. Also, note that W could use an outright bequest to purchase an annuity without jeopardizing the marital deduction. *See* Reg. §20.2056(b)-1(g), *Examples (3)* and *(4).*

Note that if the executor is directed to purchase a terminable interest for the surviving spouse, the last 2 requirements of the terminable interest rule are not satisfied. Nonetheless, no deduction is allowed.

The other rule, often called the unidentified or "tainted" asset rule, is also intended to assure that interests for which a marital deduction is allowed will be included in the surviving spouse's gross estate.

§2056(b)(2). Under this rule a deduction is not allowed to the extent that an interest given the survivor may be satisfied with assets (or their proceeds) that are nondeductible. For example, Reg. §20.2056(b)-2 indicates that a bequest to a surviving spouse of one-third of the decedent's residuary estate does not qualify for the marital deduction to the extent the residuary estate includes nondeductible interests that might be assigned to the surviving spouse. A marital deduction gift can be insulated from challenge under this rule if the will or other governing instrument prohibits the fiduciary from satisfying the gift with nondeductible interests.

Contractual Wills. Where it is important to obtain a marital deduction upon the death of the first spouse to die, the clients should be wary of entering into any contract that binds the survivor to dispose of the property received from the decedent in a particular manner. The deductibility of an interest depends upon the terms of the agreement and the nature of the interest passing to the surviving spouse. Under the pre-1982 law interests that passed to the surviving spouse under a contractual will frequently failed to qualify for the marital deduction because of the terminable interest rule. For example, in Estate of Opal v. Commissioner, 450 F.2d 1085 (2d Cir. 1971), no deduction was allowed for the interest that passed to the surviving spouse under a joint will because the interest was essentially a life estate with a power to consume. No marital deduction was allowed because the survivor did not have the requisite power to appoint to herself or to her estate. Of course, had the decedent died after 1981, presumably the decedent's executor could have elected to treat the property as qualified terminable interest property and claimed a marital deduction under §2056(b)(7). *See* §5.18, *infra.*

§5.11. Exceptions to the Terminable Interest Rule

Several important exceptions to the terminable interest rule allow transfers to a surviving spouse to qualify for the marital deduction although all 3 elements of the rule are present. The exceptions apply to transfers under which:

1. The interest of the surviving spouse will terminate if he or she dies within 6 months of the decedent or as a result of a common disaster (§2056(b)(3), §5.12);
2. The entire interest in the property will pass to the surviving spouse *or* to his or her estate (the so-called estate trust exception) (§2056(b)(1) and Reg. §20.2056(e)-2(b), §5.13);
3. The surviving spouse will receive all of the income from the property for life and will have a general power of appointment

over it (the "life interest-general power of appointment" exception) (§2056(b)(5)). Another subsection of the Code allows a deduction where the surviving spouse receives similar interests in the proceeds of insurance on the decedent's life (§2056(b)(6)) (§§5.14 to 5.17);

4. The surviving spouse will receive all of the income from the property for life and no one, including the surviving spouse, has the power to appoint any part of the property to any person other than the surviving spouse during the surviving spouse's lifetime (§2056(b)(7))(§5.18); or

5. The surviving spouse is the only noncharitable beneficiary of a charitable remainder annuity trust or a charitable remainder unitrust as defined in §§664, 2056(b)(8), §5.19.

The exceptions permit much greater flexibility in providing for the surviving spouse than would otherwise be possible. The fourth of the listed exceptions (for so-called qualified terminable interest property) provides a simpler and most welcome method of providing for a surviving spouse. In any case, great care must be taken in planning and drafting marital deduction trusts to be sure that the exacting requirements of the Code and regulations are met. Much of the litigation related to the exceptions involves instruments that include either inappropriate boiler-plate or provisions, otherwise acceptable, that have been altered in an uninformed way.

§5.12. Limited Survivorship

Under §2056(b)(3) a limited survivorship requirement may be imposed upon a transfer to a surviving spouse without jeopardizing the marital deduction. An interest will not be considered a terminable interest "if (1) the only condition under which it will terminate is the death of the surviving spouse within 6 months after the decedent's death, or her death as a result of a common disaster which also resulted in the decedent's death, and (2) the condition does not in fact occur." Reg. §20.2056(b)-3(a). The provision allows an individual to provide for an alternate disposition of property if the testator's spouse survives for only a short period of time. If the spouse does not survive the specified period, the testator's will and not the will of the surviving spouse controls the disposition of the property. Such a provision can be used to avoid the additional costs that would be incurred if the same property passed through two successive estates.

Example 5-10. H died leaving a will that gave his residuary estate to W if she survived him by 6 months, otherwise to X. If W survives H by less than 6 months H's estate will not be entitled to a marital deduction with respect to the residuary estate. However, if W survives H by 6 months, the contingent interest of X is extinguished and W is the only person to whom H transferred an interest in the property. In such a case, the residuary gift qualifies for the marital deduction under the exception provided for in §2056(b)(3).

For purposes of this rule the IRS has indicated that a month is measured from a given day in one calendar month to the corresponding numbered day in the next month. Rev. Rul. 70-400, 1970-2 C.B. 196. The ruling allowed a marital deduction for a gift to a surviving spouse which was conditioned upon survivorship for 6 months where the decedent died on January 1 and his widow died on July 2 (*i.e.,* the spouse survived the decedent by more than 6 months).

The exception also permits the use of a gift that will equalize the size of the spouses' taxable estates if they die within 6 months of each other. However, the objective of equalizing the sizes of the spouses' estates may be better achieved by giving the surviving spouse interests in qualifying terminable interest property. Under §2056(b)(7) the deceased spouse's executor is allowed to make the necessary election to claim a marital deduction with respect to part or all of the interests on the estate tax return of the spouse who died first (*i.e.,* the election need not be made until 9 months after his or her death). In effect, §2056(b)(7) allows the estates to be equalized if the spouses die within 9 months of each other.

Simultaneous Death. In the event of the spouses' simultaneous deaths, the regulations provide that a presumption of survivorship provided by the local law, the decedent's will, or otherwise will be respected for marital deduction purposes:

> If the order of the deaths of the decedent and his spouse cannot be established by proof, a presumption (whether supplied by local law, the decedent's will, or otherwise) that the decedent was survived by his spouse will be recognized as satisfying paragraph (b)(1) of §20.2056(a)-1, but only to the extent that it has the effect of giving to the spouse an interest in property includible in her gross estate under Part III of subchapter A of Chapter II. Reg. §20.2056(e)-2(e).

Under the basic rule stated in Section 1 of the Uniform Simultaneous Death Act, if there is no sufficient evidence that persons have died otherwise than simultaneously and no contrary directions were given by the decedents, the property of each decedent is disposed of as if he or she survived the other. 9 U.L.A. 608 (1972).

Example 5-11. H and W died under such circumstances that there was no sufficient evidence that they died other than simultaneously. In the absence of contrary direction in the will of H, his property will be disposed of as if he survived W. Similarly, the property of W will be disposed of as if she survived H. As a result neither estate is entitled to a marital deduction. However, the IRS would respect a provision in the will of either spouse that the other spouse should be deemed to have survived the testator in the event of their simultaneous deaths.

A substantial tax savings can be achieved through the proper use of such a clause (*e.g.,* if the gross estate of one spouse is much larger than that of the other and the will of the wealthier spouse makes gifts to the poorer spouse that equalize the sizes of their taxable estates). Where the dispositive plans of a husband and wife are harmonious, the wealthier spouse should consider including a simultaneous death clause sufficient to equalize the sizes of their taxable estates in such event. The approved language for a survivorship provision is, "if she [he] shall survive me for a period of six months." *See* Rev. Rul. 70-400, 1970-2 C.B. 196.

The Uniform Probate Code extends the concept of requiring survivorship for a limited period to provide that an heir, and in the absence of a contrary direction a devisee, will be deemed to have predeceased a decedent unless the heir or devisee survives the decedent by 120 hours or more. UPC §§2-104, 2-601. The provisions of both the Uniform Simultaneous Death Act and the Uniform Probate Code may be overridden by a contrary direction in an individual's will. Neither provision jeopardizes the allowance of a marital deduction for interests that pass to the decedent's spouse. Rev. Rul. 76-166, 1976-2 C.B. 287.

The marital deduction is not preserved under §2056(b)(3) if the gift is contingent upon an event other than survivorship for a period of 6 months or less. Also, no deduction is allowed if the gift is conditioned upon the occurrence or nonoccurrence of an administrative contingency such as admission of the decedent's will to probate, distribution of the decedent's estate, etc.

> A decedent devised and bequeathed his residuary estate to his wife if she was living on the date of distribution of his estate. The devise and bequest is a nondeductible interest even though distribution took place within 6 months after the decedent's death and the surviving spouse in fact survived the date of distribution. Reg. §20.2056(b)-3(d), *Example (4)*.

A gift intended to qualify for the marital deduction should not require survivorship for more than 6 months or survivorship of the occurrence or nonoccurrence of an event.

§5.13.   *Estate Trust*

A second and possibly unintended exception to the terminable interest rule allows a marital deduction for interests that pass entirely to the surviving spouse or to his or her estate. The basic terminable interest rule denies a deduction for an interest passing to a surviving spouse *only* if an interest in the same property also passed "from the decedent to any person other than such surviving spouse (or the estate of such spouse)." §2056(b)(1). The parenthetical language has led to an interpretation of §2056 that allows a marital deduction for the full value of an interest that passes from the decedent to the estate of a surviving spouse, although the survivor receives little if any lifetime benefit from the property.

> [T]here are two types of transfers that may qualify a limited interest passing to the surviving spouse, such as a life estate, for the marital deduction. The first, which is illustrated in examples (i), (ii), and (iii) of section 20.2056(e)-2(b)(1) of the regulations, is the estate trust, that is a trust that provides that the income is payable to the surviving spouse for a term of years, or for life, or is to be accumulated, with all of the undistributed trust property passing to the surviving spouse's executor or administrator at her death. In these cases the interest to the surviving spouse qualifies for the marital deduction for the reason that she does not get a nondeductible terminable interest. No one other than the surviving spouse or her estate takes any interest in the property passing from the decedent. Rev. Rul. 72-233, 1972-2 C.B. 530.

Thus, a deduction is allowed for interests transferred in trust although the lifetime benefits of the surviving spouse are limited provided that the trust property is ultimately distributable to the surviving spouse's personal representative. Thus, the trustee of such a trust can be given the discretionary power to accumulate the income of the trust and to retain unproductive assets. Rev. Rul. 68-554, 1968-2 C.B. 412.

The IRS has ruled that a trust that provides for the payment of the corpus to the testamentary appointee of the surviving spouse, and in default of exercise thereof to his or her estate, does not qualify for the marital deduction. Rev. Rul. 75-128, 1975-1 C.B. 308. According to the ruling the trust failed to qualify because the surviving spouse held a testamentary power of appointment over the property. Under Reg. §20.2056(e)-3 the possible appointees of such a power are considered persons to whom the deceased spouse passed an interest in the property.

The operation of Rev. Rul. 75-128 might be avoided if the decedent's will were construed to pass the absolute interest in the trust property to the personal representative of the surviving spouse, subject to the general testamentary power (*i.e.*, if the power were considered to be a "power appendant"). In such event the power should not be recognized at all. Where a person is given an absolute interest in property, any power also given to the same person is an invalid power appendant or a "lesser included interest," which may be disregarded. *See, e.g.*, V American Law of Property §23.13 (1952); Restatement, Property §325 (1940); Note, Appendant Powers of Appointment in the United States, 50 Harv. L.

Rev. 1284 (1937). In any event, note that the deduction might be preserved in such a case if the surviving spouse made a qualified disclaimer of the power. *See* §2518. There is no evident policy or revenue reason to support the unnecessarily technical position taken in Rev. Rul. 75-128. Professors Douglas Kahn and Lawrence Waggoner have expressed the same criticism of Rev. Rul. 75-128. D. Kahn & L. Waggoner, Federal Taxation of Gifts, Trusts and Estates ¶5-46 (2d ed. 1982).

Thus far the estate trust exception has functioned most often to "save" the marital deduction for trusts that do not qualify for the life estate-power of appointment exception because of deficient draftsmanship. *See, e.g.,* Rev. Rul. 72-333, 1972-2 C.B. 530. However, the estate trust can be very useful in some cases. As mentioned above, it allows a trustee to be directed to retain unproductive property, such as stock in a closely held corporation, without jeopardizing the allowance of the marital deduction. Rev. Rul. 68-554, 1968-2 C.B. 412. In contrast, no deduction is allowable where the trustee of a life estate-power of appointment trust is directed to retain unproductive property, unless the surviving spouse could compel the trustee to make the property productive or to convert it within a reasonable time. Reg. §20.2056(b)-5(f)(4) and (5).

An estate trust is also attractive because of the limitless range of provisions it allows to be made for the lifetime benefit of the surviving spouse. If the surviving spouse is expected to have a large income, the potential income tax savings of an estate trust make it preferable to an outright gift or a life interest-power of appointment trust. The spouse could be adequately protected if the trustee were authorized to make discretionary distributions of income to him or her as needed to provide for care and support, to meet emergencies, etc. Of course any income accumulated by the trustee would be initially taxed to the trust and subject to the throwback rules when it is distributed to the surviving spouse or to his or her estate. *See* §§665 to 667. Under those rules an accumulation distribution is taxed as if the distributee had received equal amounts of the accumulated income in the years it was accumulated. *See* §10.2, *infra.* Where an accumulation distribution is made to the surviving spouse's estate, little or no additional income tax is likely to be due because (1) the estate did not exist during the accumulation period and it necessarily had no other income and (2) the estate is entitled to a credit for the income tax paid by the trust on the accumulation distribution.

An estate trust may also permit the trustee to achieve a tax-free increase in the basis of property by distributing appreciated property to the surviving spouse. The basis of an asset received from a discretionary trust is "its fair market value at the time it was paid, credited, or required to be distributed, to the extent such value is included in the gross income of the beneficiary." Reg. §1.661(a)-2(f)(3). Such a distribution is deductible by the trust and includible in the distributee's gross income to the extent of the trust's distributable net income. *See* §10.2, *infra.* Thus, the unrealized gain in a distributed asset can be converted into basis without being subject to tax.

For a variety of reasons the estate trust is not widely used. First, most lawyers are not familiar with the device. Second, some commentators are concerned about the validity and effect of a gift to the estate of a named person. *See* Fox, Estate: A Word to Be Used Cautiously, If at All, 81 Harv. L. Rev. 992 (1968); Huston, Transfers to the "Estate of a Named Person," 15 Syracuse L. Rev. 463 (1964); and Browder, Trusts and the Doctrine of Estates, 72 Mich. L. Rev. 1507, 1517 (1975).

Third, and most important, the required distribution of the trust property to the surviving spouse's personal representative has some serious disadvantages. Most arise from the fact that the property will be subject to (1) claims of creditors against the estate of the surviving spouse; (2) claims of a subsequent spouse to an elective share under the law of common law property states, should the surviving spouse remarry; (3) family awards; and (4) increased costs of estate settlement (particularly executor's commissions and attorney's fees). A distribution of property to the estate of the surviving spouse also involves some risk that the property will ultimately go to unintended takers (*e.g.*, the intestate successors of the surviving spouse). In addition, property distributed to the surviving spouse's estate may be subject to the state death tax although it might not be taxed under other circumstances (*e.g.*, if the surviving spouse held only a qualifying income interest for life and no power of appointment). Finally, a spouse may react negatively to a plan that does not assure him or her of all of the trust's income, but instead gives the trustee the discretionary power to make distributions.

§5.14. *Life Interest-General Power of Appointment Trust*

Section 2056(b)(5) was unquestionably the most important exception to the terminable interest rule until the 1981 Act's addition of the exception for qualified terminable interest property. *See* §5.18, *infra.* Under this exception a deduction is allowed for an interest that passes to a surviving spouse, to the extent the surviving spouse is entitled for life to all of the income from it (or a determinable portion of it) and the surviving spouse also holds a general power of appointment over it (or a corresponding part of it). As stated in Reg. §20.2056(b)-5(a) this exception applies only if all of the following 5 requirements are met:

1. The surviving spouse is entitled for life to all of the income from the entire interest, or a specific portion of the entire interest, or to a specific portion of all the income from the entire interest;
2. The income is payable to the surviving spouse annually or at more frequent intervals;

3. The surviving spouse is given the power to appoint the entire interest or the specific portion to himself or herself or to his or her estate;
4. The power in the surviving spouse is exercisable by him or her alone and (whether exercisable by will or during life) must be exercisable in all events; and
5. The entire interest or the specific portion is not subject to a power in any other person to appoint any part to any person other than the surviving spouse.

The exception is available whether the interests involved are legal or equitable (*i.e.*, in trust). As a matter of planning, however, the exception is used almost exclusively in connection with trusts.

The use of this type of trust calls for very careful draftsmanship. A failure to satisfy any one of the requirements completely will deprive the estate of the spouse first to die of the deduction, although the surviving spouse is given sufficient interests in the property to cause it to be included in his or her estate.

Example 5-12. H died leaving his residuary estate to a trust in which W had the requisite life income interest. Under the trust W held a power exercisable jointly with her son, S, to appoint the corpus of the trust to whomever she wished. The power is not exercisable by W alone and in all events. Accordingly, under the pre-1982 law H's estate was not entitled to a marital deduction, but the corpus of the trust would be included in W's gross estate under §2041. No deduction would be allowable under the post-1981 law unless the power to appoint to persons other than W during her lifetime was effectively disclaimed and H's executor elected to treat the property as qualified terminable interest property under §2056(b)(7).

§5.15.   Specific Portion

If the right to income or the power of appointment or both is limited to a specific portion of the property passing from the decedent, the marital deduction is allowable to the extent of the specific portion. In determining whether a surviving spouse holds the requisite income interest and power of appointment over a "specific portion," the regulations require that they relate to either a fractional or percentile share of a property interest. Reg. §20.2056(b)-5(c). However, it has been held that the right to receive a regular payment of a specific dollar amount of income constitutes a right to the income from a specific portion. Northeastern Pennsylvania National Bank & Trust Co. v. United States, 387 U.S. 213

(1967); C. Lowndes, R. Kramer & J. McCord, Federal Estate and Gift Taxes §17.18 (3d ed. 1974).

Only a portion of the trust may qualify for the deduction if the survivor's power of appointment is limited. A deduction is not available to the extent the property might be applied by the trustee in satisfaction of debts, taxes, or other expenses even though none of it is actually used for those purposes. Estate of Wycoff v. Commissioner, 506 F.2d 1044 (10th Cir. 1974), *cert. denied,* 421 U.S. 1000 (1975); Rev. Rul. 79-14, 1979-1 C.B. 309. For that reason, the governing instrument usually prohibits charging any taxes or expenses against the marital deduction gift.

The IRS has ruled that no deduction was allowable with respect to an otherwise qualifying marital deduction trust, the income from which was to be used to accumulate $10,000 within 2 years of the decedent's death to provide for the education of his grandchildren. Rev. Rul 77-444, 1977-2 C.B. 341. "Unlike *Northeastern Pennsylvania National Bank* and *Gelb* [Gelb v. Commissioner, 298 F.2d 544 (2d Cir. 1962)], it is not possible in the instant case to determine any 'specific portion' as to which the income right of the surviving spouse relates." *Id.*

In some cases it may be advantageous and economical for a client to establish a single trust, a specific portion of which qualifies for the marital deduction under §2056(b)(5) and the remainder of which does not. For example, savings in trustee's fees and administrative costs may result and greater diversification of investments may be possible if only one trust is created. However, care must be exercised in funding the trust and allocating interests in it. Specifically, the surviving spouse's share should not include interests that do not qualify for the marital deduction.

§5.16.   Frequency of Payment of Income

The trust instrument should ordinarily require income to be paid to the surviving spouse more often than annually for the convenience and protection of the beneficiary as well as to qualify for the marital deduction. For example, a trust might provide that "the trustee shall pay the net income of the trust to my surviving spouse in quarterly or more frequent installments." Although an instrument does not include any express directions regarding frequency of payment, a trust may nonetheless qualify for the marital deduction. Under the regulations, "silence of a trust instrument as to the frequency of payment will not be regarded as a failure to satisfy the condition . . . that income must be payable to the surviving spouse annually or more frequently unless the applicable law permits payment to be made less frequently than annually." Reg. §20.2056(b)-5(e). The statutory requirements are satisfied if the surviving spouse is given "substantially that degree of beneficial enjoyment of the trust property during her life which the principles of the law of trusts accord to a person who is unqualifiedly designated as the life beneficiary of a trust." Reg. §20.2056(b)-5(f). The survivor's right to income cannot be directly limited by the trustee's discretion or otherwise. However, a trustee may be given some indirect control through the exercise of administrative powers, such as ones concerning the allocation of receipts and disbursements between principal and income. Reg. §20.2056(b)-5(f)(3). The determination of whether a particular trust meets the statutory requirement is based upon an overall consideration of the terms of the trust.

In general, the regulations require the income to be distributed currently. Reg. §20.2056(b)-5(f)(8). An interest will not satisfy this requirement to the extent that the income must be or may be accumulated. Reg. §20.2056(b)-5(f)(7). Thus, no deduction is allowed with respect to a testamentary trust that provides that after "the net income from the trust for the past year has been determined . . . such income shall be quarterly paid to my wife as long as she may live. . . ." Rev. Rul. 72-283, 1972-1 C.B. 311. A deduction will not be denied, however, "merely because the spouse is not entitled to the income from the estate assets for the period before distribution of those assets by the executor, unless the executor is . . . authorized or directed to delay distribution beyond the period reasonably required for administration of the decedent's estate." Reg. §20.2056(b)-5(f)(9). Consistent with that regulation, a deduction was allowed for interests in a trust to be funded upon the settlor's death with assets from an inter vivos trust, where the trust instrument delayed funding the trust for a reasonable time until after the payment of all probate expenses and death taxes. Rev. Rul. 77-346, 1977-2 C.B. 340. In such cases, the delay in payment of the income is taken into account in valuing the interest passing to the surviving spouse. Reg. §20.2056(b)-4(a).

A trust also will not qualify for the marital deduction under §2056(b)(5) if the distribution of income to the surviving spouse is discretionary in the event the survivor becomes incompetent. *See, e.g.,* Estate of Frank E. Tingley, 22 T.C. 402 (1954), *aff'd sub nom.,* Starret v. Commissioner, 223 F.2d 163 (1st Cir. 1955). Similarly, no deduction was allowed where the trust gave the surviving spouse all of the income except such amounts as the trustee considered to be necessary to maintain the decedent's parents in their customary standard of living. Rev. Rul. 79-86, 1979-1 C.B. 311. In such a case the surviving spouse does not have an unqualified right to receive income from any specified portion of the trust — all of the income could be diverted from the surviving spouse to the support of the decedent's parents. A marital deduction may also be denied if the distribution of income to the survivor will terminate or become discretionary upon the occurrence of some event such as the bankruptcy of the survivor or the attempted alienation of the beneficiary's interest in the trust. However, the deduction is not threatened merely because the instrument contains an orthodox spendthrift clause (*e.g.*, "that the right of the surviving spouse to the income shall not be subject to assignment, alienation, pledge, attachment or claims of creditors." Reg. §20.2056(b)-5(f)(7)).

Draftsmen should also exercise care in authorizing the trustee to retain the assets transferred in trust. As previously indicated, such a provision may jeopardize the deduction to the extent of the unproductive assets. *See* Reg. §20.2056(b)-5(f)(4), (5). The deduction is allowable, however, if the surviving spouse is given the power to require the trustee to "make the property productive or convert it within a reasonable time." Reg. §20.2056(b)-5(f)(4).

§5.17.   Power of Appointment

The surviving spouse must have a power exercisable alone (without the required joinder of any other person) and in all events (not contingent upon any event) "in favor of such surviving spouse, or of the estate of such surviving spouse, or in favor of either, whether or not in each case the power is exercisable in favor of others." *See* §2056(b)(5); *see also* §2523(e). A power will satisfy the requirement if it is exercisable during the lifetime of the surviving spouse (*e.g.*, an unlimited power to invade), by will, or by a combination of inter vivos and testamentary powers. The regulations recognize that the requirement may be satisfied by a combined power:

> [T]he surviving spouse may, until she attains the age of 50 years, have a power to appoint to herself and thereafter have a power to appoint to her estate. However, the condition that the spouse's power must be exercisable in all events is not satisfied unless irrespective of when the surviving spouse may die the entire interest or a specific portion of it will at the time of her death be subject to one power or the other (subject to the exception in §20.2056(b)-3, relating to interests contingent on survival for a limited period). Reg. §20.2056(b)-5(g)(1)(iii).

If the surviving spouse has a power of the type required by the statute, it is immaterial that the survivor also holds other powers over the interest, such as a noncumulative power of the type described in §§2041(b)(2) and 2514(e) to draw down the larger of $5,000 or 5% of the corpus each year. Of course, a "5 or 5" power to draw down provides the survivor with some additional independence and protection. A noncumulative 5 or 5 power given to a surviving spouse constitutes a power sufficient to support a marital deduction equal to the greater of 5% of the corpus of the trust or $5,000 even though the survivor is not given any other power of appointment over the trust corpus. Estate of Jean C. Hollingshead, 70 T.C. 578 (1978). Although the surviving spouse was entitled to all of the income of the trust for life, the deduction was limited to the amount subject to appointment under the 5 or 5 power at the time of the decedent's death because "any excess over 5 percent is not 'exercisable * * * in all events.' " 70 T.C. at 580. No marital deduction is allowable where the surviving spouse only holds a 5 or 5 power and no income interest. LR 8202023.

A presently exercisable 5 or 5 power of withdrawal allows the surviving spouse to reduce the amount of property includible in his or her gross estate by withdrawing property and making annual gifts within the annual gift tax exclusion. Although all of the trust property may be included in the surviving spouse's estate in any case, the testator may wish to limit the surviving spouse's right of withdrawal in order to assure the preservation of the trust principal for some time. As the entire ordinary income of the trust will be taxed to the surviving spouse, the existence of the power will not disadvantage him or her for income tax purposes. See §678. The income tax flexibility of the trust is reduced if the surviving spouse is given an unlimited inter vivos general power of appointment. In that event the capital gains of the trust will also be taxed to him or her. See §678(a)(1).

The mental incapacity of the surviving spouse under state law to exercise the power of appointment does not affect the allowance of the deduction under §2056(b)(5). If the trust otherwise qualifies, "the fact that the spouse is presently incapable of exercising a power of appointment over the interest by virtue of State law regarding legal incapacity does not require disallowance of the deduction." Rev. Rul. 75-350, 1975-2 C.B. 366 (testamentary power); Rev. Rul. 55-518, 1955-2 C.B. 384 (inter vivos power). The former ruling is based upon a determination that the phrase "in all events does not refer to those events that State law has determined to be sufficient to deprive a person of control of his or her property during a period of physical or mental incompetency. Otherwise, in view of the fact that any given person may become legally incompetent during his or her lifetime, no trust could ever qualify under §2056(b)(5)." 1975-2 C.B. at 368. However, if the existence of the power is restricted by the terms of the instrument, the trust would not satisfy the requirements of §2056(b)(5).

The IRS position has been rejected by some lower courts, but has been upheld by every appellate court that has passed on the issue. For example, in Fish v. United States, 432 F.2d 1278, 1280 (1970), the Court of Appeals for the Ninth Circuit held "the matter of the decedent's competency to be immaterial." See also Estate of Alperstein v. Commissioner, 613 F.2d 1213 (2d Cir. 1979), cert. denied sub. nom., Greenberg v. Commissioner, 446 U.S. 918 (1980); Estate of Bagley v. United States, 443 F.2d 1266 (5th Cir. 1971); Estate of Gilchrist v. Commissioner, 630 F.2d 340 (5th Cir. 1980); Pennsylvania Bank & Trust Co. v. United States, 597 F.2d 382 (3d Cir.), cert. denied, 444 U.S. 980 (1979). The same conclusion has been reached in cases concerning the inclusion of property in the estate of a minor under §2041. Estate of Rosenblatt v. Commissioner, 633 F.2d 176 (10th Cir. 1980); Rev. Rul. 75-351, 1975-2 C.B. 368 (property includible in estate of minor who held general testamentary power of appointment even though the minor could not execute a will under local law).

§5.18.   Qualified Terminable Interest Property (QTIP)

As noted above in §5.3, the 1981 Act also created new gift and estate tax exceptions to the terminable interest rule for property in which the transferor's spouse is given a qualifying income interest for life. §§2056(b)(7), 2523(f). In simple terms the new exception allows a marital deduction at the election of the donor or the transferor's executor, for part or all of the value of property in which the transferee spouse is given a qualifying income interest for life. The deduction is allowable only if no one has the power to appoint any of the property to a person other than the surviving spouse during his or her lifetime. The most important features of the new exception are that it is elective and it can be claimed with respect to part or all of the transferred property in which the transferee spouse is given the requisite interest. Naturally, any property for which a marital deduction is claimed under §§2056(b)(7) or 2523(f) is includible in the estate of the transferee spouse. §2044. The basis of the property so included in the surviving spouse's estate will be adjusted if §1014(b) is amended as proposed in the Technical Corrections Act of 1982. Also, the property is subject to a gift tax if the transferee spouse makes an inter vivos disposition of all or any part of the qualifying income interest. §2519(a).

Overall, the QTIP exception is most similar to the one for a life interest-general power of appointment trust. However, in the case of a QTIP, the transferee spouse need not be given any control over the ultimate disposition of the property. Indeed, as explained below, the surviving spouse should not be given a general power of appointment over a QTIP. A client may choose to give the transferee spouse some power over the ultimate disposition of the trust fund without adverse tax results. For example, a transferee spouse could safely be given a testamentary power to appoint the property to and among a limited class of persons, such as those of the transferor's issue who are living at the time of the transferee spouse's death. Of course, as noted above, no one can be given the power to appoint the property to anyone other than the transferee spouse during his or her lifetime.

The trust could be made a bit more flexible by allowing the transferee spouse to make withdrawals subject to an ascertainable standard (§§2041(b)(1)(B), 2514 (c)(1), §10.22, infra), or limited each year to the greater of $5,000 or 5% of the principal value of the trust (§§2041(b)(2),

2514(e), §10.23, *infra*). Giving the transferee spouse an unlimited power of withdrawal or other general power of appointment could jeopardize the tax advantage of a qualified terminable interest trust because it might require all of the property subject to the power to be included in the transferee spouse's estate under §2041. Indeed, if the transferee spouse's interest in the trust meets the requirements of both §§2056(b)(5) and (7), it is not clear that the decedent's executor could elect to treat the property as qualified terminable interest property under §2056(b)(7). Such a choice should be permitted, as there is no compelling reason to hold that the exceptions are mutually exclusive. In any event, all property over which the surviving spouse holds a general power of appointment is includible in his or her estate under §2041. Such inclusion might result although the deceased spouse's executor claimed a marital deduction with respect to less than all of the property. That is, the provisions of §2041 might override those of §2044 in such a case. Caution should be exercised in this regard until the uncertainties are clarified by regulations or otherwise.

> **Example 5-13.** H died in 1982 leaving his entire $500,000 estate to a trust from which W was entitled to receive all of the income for life. In addition, W was given a testamentary general power of appointment over the trust. H's executor elected under §2056(b)(7) to claim a marital deduction with respect to $275,000 of the trust property. The tax on the other $225,000 was offset by H's unified credit of $62,800. When W died a few years later the trust property was worth $1,000,000. If §2041 controls, the full $1,000,000 is includible in W's estate. On the other hand, if §2044 controls, only $550,000 of the trust is includible in W's estate ($275,000/$500,000 × $1,000,000).

Key Definitions. Several key definitions are at the heart of the QTIP exception and provide some guidance regarding the planning opportunities it offers.

Qualified terminable interest property. "Qualified terminable interest property" is defined as property passing from the decedent in which the surviving spouse receives qualifying income interest for life and with respect to which the decedent's executor makes an election under §2056(b)(7). §2056(b)(7)(B)(i). If the interest passing to the surviving spouse is a qualifying income interest for life, a deduction should be allowable — neither the passing nor the election requirement should pose any particular difficulty. Note, however, that the election "shall be made by the executor, on the return of tax imposed by Section 2001. Such an election, once made, shall be irrevocable." §2056(b)(7)(B)(v). (For this purpose the definition of the term "executor" provided in §2203 will control. The executor is the decedent's personal representative, or if none is appointed, qualified, or acting, then any person in actual or constructive possession of his or her property.) The election must be made on the return; it is not required to be made by the time fixed for filing the return (*i.e.*, normally 9 months after the decedent's death).

Qualifying income interest for life. Under §2056(b)(7)(B)(ii) a qualifying income interest for life must satisfy 2 basic requirements. First, the surviving spouse must be entitled "for life to all of the income from the entire interest, or all of the income from a specific portion thereof, payable annually or at more frequent intervals." H.R. 97-201, 97th Cong., 1st Sess. 161 (1981). Income interests for a term of years or until remarriage do not satisfy this requirement. However, a legal life estate or other nontrust interest may qualify if it gives the surviving spouse "rights to income which are sufficient to satisfy the rules applicable to marital deduction trusts under present [pre-1982] law." *Id.* Accordingly, some guidance regarding the application of this requirement can be gleaned from the existing regulations, *e.g.*, Reg. §20.2056(b)-5(f)(4). In particular, care should be exercised if the trustee is authorized or directed to retain unproductive property (unimproved real property, closely held stock, life insurance, etc.). In such a case the trust should permit the surviving spouse to require the trustee to dispose of unproductive property or to convert it to productive property within a reasonable time.

Second, no one (including the transferee spouse) can have a power to appoint any part of the property subject to the qualifying income interest to any person other than the transferee spouse during his or her lifetime. As the House Ways and Means Committee pointed out, "This rule will permit the existence of powers in the trustee to invade corpus for the benefit of the spouse but will insure that the value of the property not consumed by the spouse is subject to tax upon the spouse's death (or earlier disposition)." H.R. 97-201, 97th Cong., 1st Sess. 161 (1981). Powers over the trust corpus are permitted provided that they are "exercisable only at or after the death of the surviving spouse." §2056(b)(7)(B)(ii). Note that the limitation restricts the time a power is exercisable and the nature of the interest subject to the power.

> **Example 5-14.** W died leaving a trust from which H was entitled to receive all of the income payable annually or at more frequent intervals. In addition, H was given the power, exercisable by deed or will, to appoint the remainder following his life income interest. The text of §2056(b)(7)(B)(ii) and of the House Committee Report both indicate that the possible exercise of the power during the surviving spouse's lifetime would bar a deduction from being allowed for the property unless he or she effectively disclaimed the power or its lifetime exercise.

Under §2519 the disposition by gift, sale, or otherwise of all or part of the qualifying income interest in any property is treated as a transfer of the property subject to the gift tax. According to the House Report, "[i]f the property is subject to tax as a result of the spouse's lifetime transfer of the qualifying income interest, the entire value of the property, less amounts received by the spouse upon disposition, will be treated as a taxable gift by the spouse under new Code sec. 2519." H.R. 97-201, 97th Cong., 1st Sess. 161 (1981). Any tax paid by the donor with respect to such a transfer may be recovered from the person receiving the transfer. §2207A(b). Where the tax is entirely offset by the donor's unified credit it is unclear whether the statute gives the donor the right to recover any of the tax. Where some tax is recoverable, presumably the transaction will be taxed as a net gift (*i.e.*, the amount of the gift will be reduced by the gift tax paid by the donee, *see* §7.24, *infra*). In order to guard against inadvertently subjecting the property to the gift tax, the spouse should be restrained from disposing of all or any part of the income interest without the consent of the trustee or another responsible party. Such a spendthrift provision is permissible in the case of life interest-general power of appointment trusts. Reg. §20.2056(b)-5(f)(7). Spendthrift clauses are discussed at §10.19, *infra*.

Property. The statute recognizes that the term "property" includes an interest in property. §2056(b)(7)(B)(iii). More important, it provides that "[a] specific portion of property shall be treated as separate property." §2056(b)(7)(B)(iv). The latter definition together with the statements in the House Committee Report indicate that the election can be made (and a marital deduction taken) with respect to less than all of the property in which the surviving spouse has a qualifying income interest for life. The term "specific portion" will probably be construed in a manner consistent with the existing regulations under §2056(b)(5). *See* Reg. §20.2056(b)-5(b), (c). A fractional or percentage interest in property qualifies under those regulations. Accordingly, it should be possible to make the §2056(b)(7) election with respect to fractional or percentage interests in property transferred to a trust in which the surviving spouse has a qualifying income interest for life. Perhaps the election could run to specific items of property transferred to such a trust and to the proceeds of any disposition thereof. *See* Reg. §20.2056(b)-5(c), *Example* (2). However, an election with respect to specific assets should be avoided until clarifying regulations are promulgated.

A trust would be even more flexible if the executor's election could determine the portion of the trust from which the surviving spouse was entitled to receive the income for life. If it were possible to do so, the election could determine the extent of the interests of the surviving spouse and others in the income of the trust. The statute is also not entirely clear on the point. However, it seems likely that the surviving spouse must have a qualifying income interest for life in the entire trust in order to enable the transferor's executor to make an election with respect to any portion of the property transferred to the trust. The payment of all of the income to the surviving spouse can cause substantial income tax liabilities to be incurred — which would be avoided if the income were payable to others. The receipt of the income will also augment the size of the surviving spouse's estate to some extent.

Example 5-15. H left his entire estate in trust, the income from which is payable to W for life, remainder to those of their issue who survive W. H's executor can elect to claim a marital deduction with respect to a specific portion of the property by making a timely election under §2056(b)(7). If the trust provided W was entitled only to receive the income from the portion of the trust with respect to which H's executor made a QTIP election, it is doubtful that a deduction would be allowable under §2056(b)(7). In such a case W's right to the income would be dependent on the election by H's executor, who, in effect, holds a special power of appointment over the property.

Use in Connection with Disclaimers. Note that the opportunity to disclaim property exists independent of the §2056(b)(7) election. Thus, the surviving spouse may disclaim the right to receive property outright and cause the property to fall into a trust in which he or she has a qualifying income interest for life and with respect to which the executor may make a §2056(b)(7) election. Of course, a surviving spouse could also disclaim part or all of his or her interest in the trust. The disclaimed interest would pass according to the terms of the trust or, if none, according to the local law. Of course, it is essential for the surviving spouse and the executor to coordinate their planning with regard to the use of disclaimers and the §2056(b)(7) election. *See* §§12.26 to 12.29, *infra.*

Example 5-16. W died in 1982 leaving her entire $900,000 estate to H outright, provided that any property H disclaimed would pass to a QTIP trust for his benefit. The trust provided that upon H's death the trust would terminate and the trust property would be distributed to their then living issue by right of representation. H disclaimed the right to receive any of W's estate outright. Accordingly, all of her property passed to the trust. H also disclaimed all rights in one-fourth of the trust, which had a value equal to the credit equivalent ($225,000). Accordingly, a one-fourth interest in the trust property passed outright to the issue of H and W. The remainder of W's property remained in trust for H. W's executor elected under §2056(b)(7) to claim a marital deduction with respect to all of the property held in the trust. When H dies all of the trust property is includible in his gross estate under §2044.

Authorization to Make Election. A will or trust that contains a QTIP gift to a surviving spouse should include an appropriate provision regarding the exercise of the executor's election to claim a marital deduction with respect to part or all of the property. The inclusion of such a provision should reduce the potential for conflict among the survivors and should insulate the executor from liability resulting from exercise of the election. The provision may take the form of a direction that the executor make the election with respect to all of the property or an authorization to make the election with respect to part or all of the property according to some criteria. A provision directing exercise of the election gives the executor less flexibility in planning post-mortem strategy. However, the results may be varied somewhat through the exercise of disclaimers by the surviving spouse and others. Overall, it is probably more desirable to authorize the executor to make the election with respect to part or all of the property as he or she believes will be in accordance with the best interests of the surviving spouse and other beneficiaries, taking into account the sizes of the decedent's and the surviving spouse's estates, the health and life expectancy of the surviving spouse, the amount of property passing to the surviving spouse, and other beneficiaries under other provisions or arrangements, etc.

Tax on Surviving Spouse's Death. Unless otherwise directed in the surviving spouse's will, the estate tax attributable to the property included in his or her estate under §2044 is recoverable by his or her executor from the recipients of the property. §2077A(a). Thus, the inclusion of the property in the surviving spouse's estate ordinarily will not increase the amount of estate tax payable by the surviving spouse's executor from the surviving spouse's property. Under §2207A(a)(1) the surviving spouse's executor has the right to recover the entire additional amount of tax incurred by reason of the inclusion of the qualified terminable interest property in the surviving spouse's gross estate. The right of recovery extends to any penalties and interest attributable to the additional taxes. §2207(c). Where the §2044 property is distributed to more than one person, the right of recovery may be asserted against each of them. §2207A(d).

Example 5-17. H died in 1982 leaving an estate of $500,000 to a QTIP trust. His executor elected to claim the marital deduction with respect to $275,000 of the property. Accordingly, no estate tax was paid by H's estate. When W died in 1986 her estate consisted of $500,000 in addition to which $500,000 was includible in her estate under §2044. W's will did not contain any directions regarding the source of payment of the estate tax. The tax on W's $500,000 in property was entirely offset by the unified credit of $155,800. W's estate is subject to a tax of $190,000, all of which is recoverable by W's executor from the distributees of the QTIP property.

Tax on estate of $1,000,000	$345,800
Less:	
Tax payable without inclusion of QTIP property	155,800
Tax payable by QTIP distributees	$190,000

As noted before, similar right of recovery applies with respect to the gift tax imposed on the inter vivos disposition of part or all of a qualifying income interest. §2207A(b). It is recoverable by the transferee spouse (the donor of the qualifying income interest) from the recipients of the property.

Problem 5-1. W died 8 months ago by reason of which H received outright gifts from her of property worth $250,000. In addition, assets worth $600,000 will pass to a trust from which H is entitled to receive the income for life. H was given the noncumulative power to withdraw the greater of $5,000 or 5% of the value of the principal of the trust each year. Apart from that power no one holds any power to appoint any of the trust property during H's lifetime. However, upon his death the trust property will pass to whomever he appoints by will. In default of exercise of the power, the assets will be distributed to the then living issue of H and W. H's estate has a present value of $800,000 including the $250,000 he received from W's estate. H is 60 years old and in good health. He enjoys an ample income, which he expects to continue under an excellent retirement plan provided by his employer. Based primarily on the gift and estate tax consequences, what course of action would you recommend to H individually and as executor of W's will? If H died within 9 months following W's death leaving a will that gave all of his estate to their children outright, what advice would you give to W's successor executor and to H's executor?

§5.19.   *Current Interest in Charitable Remainder Trust*

If any individual transfers property outright to charity, no transfer taxes generally are imposed. Similarly, under the unlimited marital deduction provided in the committee bill, no tax generally will be imposed on an outright gift to the decedent's spouse. As a result, the committee finds no justification for imposing transfer taxes on a transfer split between a spouse and a qualifying charity. Accordingly, the bill provides a special rule for transfers of interest in the same property to a spouse and a qualifying charity. H.R. 97-102, 97th Cong., 1st Sess., 162 (1981).

The 1981 Act also created an exception to the terminable interest for the current interest in charitable remainder trusts where the surviving spouse is the only noncharitable beneficiary. §§2056(b)(8). A corresponding gift tax exception applies where the donor's spouse and the donor are the only noncharitable beneficiaries. §2523(g). Accordingly, a transfer to a charitable remainder unitrust qualifies for a charitable deduction under §2055 (or §2522) for the value of the charitable remainder interest and a marital deduction under §2056 (or §2523) for the value of the current (annuity or unitrust) interest. A gift tax return is not required on account of the marital deduction gift, but one probably is required to claim the charitable deduction.

A footnote in the House Committee Report suggests that the same overall result might follow where the surviving spouse is given a qualifying income interest for life with remainder to charity. H.R. 97-201, 97th Cong., 1st Sess., 162 (1981):

> The general rules applicable to qualifying income interests may provide similar treatment where a decedent provides an income interest in the spouse for her life and a remainder interest to charity. If the life estate is a qualifying income interest, the entire property will, pursuant to the executor's election, be considered as passing to the spouse. Therefore, the entire value of the property will be eligible for the marital deduction and no transfer tax will be imposed. Upon the spouse's death, the property will be included in the spouse's estate but, because the spouse's life estate terminates at death, any property passing outright to charity may qualify for a charitable deduction.

As the committee noted, the surviving spouse's estate may be entitled to a charitable deduction for the value of the property included in his or her estate under §2044 that passes to a charity upon his or her death. The deduction will be available if §2044 is amended as proposed to provide that property included in a decedent's estate under §2044 is treated as passing from the decedent.

The allowance of the charitable deduction to the surviving spouse's estate under §2056(b)(8) rescues some trusts that inadvertently fail to satisfy the charitable remainder trust rules. It would also simplify and, perhaps, encourage the creation of such trusts. On the other hand, it could be argued the allowance of the deduction allows the parties to avoid the stringent rules that have applied to charitable remainder trusts since the Tax Reform Act of 1969. See §664(d). Of course, those rules were adopted largely to assure that the value of the charitable remainder for which the grantor was allowed one or more tax deductions would in fact be received by the charity. In the case under discussion the grantor is not allowed any charitable deduction at all. Instead, the charitable deduction is deferred until the death of the surviving spouse when the actual value of the property passing to charity will be known.

§5.20. Which Form of Trust — Summary

The particular circumstances of the clients and their desires will determine which form of marital deduction trust, if any, should be used. In the past many lawyers and clients preferred the life interest-general power of appointment trust because it did not require the trust property to be subject to estate administration upon the death of the surviving spouse. In addition, the surviving spouse's general power of appointment could be limited to one that was exercisable at his or her death. Following the adoption of the 1981 Act many lawyers and clients have opted for QTIP trusts (*i.e.*, ones in which the surviving spouse is given a qualifying income interest for life). As noted above, such a trust is essentially a life interest-general power of appointment trust shorn of the power of appointment. Lawyers feel comfortable using a trust of the QTIP variety because it more closely resembles the traditional form of family trust. On the other hand, the estate trust is useful in some circumstances, particularly where the surviving spouse does not need to be assured of additional lifetime income. The charitable remainder trust is also useful to clients in special circumstances (*e.g.*, ones with no children and a strong desire to benefit one or more charities). Of course, all 4 types of trusts provide for the management of property during the surviving spouse's lifetime. With the exception of the estate trust they can also insulate the trust property from the surviving spouse's creditors.

Savings Clauses. The IRS and the courts should give effect to a clause that expresses the decedent's intent that the provisions of the instrument be interpreted and applied so as to sustain the allowance of the marital deduction. Such a clause may save a marital deduction where a particular power, duty, or discretion of the trustee might otherwise bar the deduction. For example, Rev. Rul. 75-440, 1975-2 C.B. 372, held that a disqualifying power to invest in nonincome-producing property applied to the residuary trust, but not to the marital deduction trust because of the decedent's intent expressed in a savings clause. A savings clause is generally ineffective to overcome the effect of a disqualifying power that is clearly applicable to the trust intended to qualify for the marital deduction. The IRS and some courts have refused to recognize "condition subsequent" clauses that purport to revoke powers that apply to the trust in the event the powers are determined to prevent allowance of the marital deduction. Thus, in Rev. Rul. 65-144, 1965-1 C.B. 422, the IRS refused to give effect to a clause that attempted to revoke the powers of the trustee to the extent necessary to make the interest deductible for federal tax purposes.

Overall, it is worthwhile to include a savings clause in an instrument that is intended to generate a marital deduction. *See* Johanson, The Use of Tax Savings Clauses in Drafting Wills and Trusts, U. Miami 15th Inst. Est. Plan., Ch. 21 (1982). The clause provides some assurance that the instrument will be interpreted and applied in a sympathetic way. However, such a clause should not be relied upon to provide any protection against disqualifying provisions that clearly apply to the gift intended to support the marital deduction. A savings clause might be drafted along these lines:

> I intend that the property given to the trustee of the trust shall qualify for the marital deduction. Accordingly, I direct that all provisions of this will shall be interpreted and applied in a manner consistent with my intention.

C. PLANNING FOR USE OF THE MARITAL DEDUCTION

> It is important to keep in mind the main objectives — always to chart a plan which keeps foremost the special needs and personalities and relationship of the interested parties. The practitioner does not deal with symbols *H* and *W* and estates of dollars in cash. He is concerned with particular individuals and their families and particular combinations of assets and liabilities. Much of the "buzzing, blooming confusion" about taking or not taking the marital deduction and how to do it may disappear if taxes are considered after, and not before, the main objectives are analyzed. What would the testator want to do apart from the marital deduction? How far is he led away from that by the tax law? J. Trachtman, Estate Planning 82 (rev. ed. 1968).

§5.21. *Approaching the Planning Job*

In formulating an estate plan, the lawyer and the client should give priority to sound planning for the welfare and security of the client and the client's family. A host of primarily nontax factors need to be considered in the process, including the age, health, ability, marital status, wealth, and feelings of the members of the client's family. For example, in some cases all of a client's estate will need to be made available to the surviving spouse for his or her support and in others it will not. The circumstances of the client and the client's family will also determine whether gifts to the surviving spouse are made outright or in trust and what choice of assets is made to fund the gifts. After the general contours of a plan are worked out, the lawyer should give more direct attention to tax planning, including the use of the marital deduction, to conserve the family's property.

In order to make the necessary tax analysis, the lawyer needs to know the size and composition of the estates of both spouses and the objectives of their dispositive plans. Those factors influence to a great degree the extent to which overall tax benefits will result from the use of the marital deduction and from other dispositions of the client's property. Consideration must be given to the effect of a plan upon the amount of estate tax due upon the death of each spouse and to the various income tax matters, including the bases of assets.

> **Example 5-18.** W's estate is worth \$2,000,000 and H's is worth \$275,000. If H dies after 1982 no estate tax will be due upon his death, but any property he leaves to W will be subject to a marginal estate tax rate of 49% when she dies. In this case, H's unified credit is wasted to the extent his property passes in a way that will require it to be included in W's estate. Of course, H and W may not be concerned about the size of the survivor's estate, particularly if all of their property will pass to charity upon the death of the survivor.

In any case, the lawyer should prepare estimates of the state and federal tax consequences of the plans under consideration. The estimates, which should take into account the possibility that either spouse may die first or that they will die simultaneously, provide a good check on the merits of a plan from the transfer tax perspective. While estimates are helpful for purposes of analysis, the lawyer and client need to remember that they are only estimates — informed guesses about exceedingly uncertain future events.

§5.22. General Objectives

Several general objectives of marital deduction tax planning can be identified that may be helpful in formulating and analyzing estate plans that involve use of marital deduction gifts. The objectives are:

1. To equalize the sizes of the spouses' estates and to pay the least total amount of estate tax;
2. To defer the payment of any estate tax until the death of the surviving spouse; and
3. To insure that the estates of both spouses will take full advantage of the unified credit.

The objectives are not equally important and are not always entirely compatible. For example, equalizing the sizes of the spouses' estates may not minimize the amount of tax due on the death of the first spouse to die. The value of the objectives should also be kept in mind — they merely suggest general approaches that may reduce tax costs, but which must yield to the circumstances and desires of particular clients.

§5.23. Equalizing the Spouses' Estates and Minimizing Overall Taxes

The tax advantage that flows from equalizing the amount of property subject to tax in each spouse's estate is a product of the progressivity of the unified tax rate schedule (§2001). From the transfer tax point of view the optimum result is achieved when both estates are subject to the same marginal tax rate. A greater combined estate tax is paid if one of the estates is subject to a higher marginal rate than the other. However, the importance of equalization is often overemphasized — the transfer tax brackets are generally quite broad, the rate increases rather slowly, and the gap between the lowest rate at which any tax will be paid and the highest marginal rate is shrinking. It must also be balanced against the importance of deferring the payment of any tax until the death of the surviving spouse.

Equalization Clauses. The size of the gross estates of the spouses may be closely equalized as of the appropriate valuation date if the wealthier spouse dies first, leaving the surviving spouse an amount equal to the difference in value of their estates on the estate tax valuation date applicable to the decedent's estate. A proper simultaneous death clause can be combined with an equalization clause to provide the optimum tax result if the spouses die simultaneously. Professor Casner has suggested that such an equalization clause should apply when the surviving spouse dies within 6 months of the first spouse to die. *See* 4 A. J. Casner, Estate Planning 1377 (4th ed. 1980). The necessary equalization can also be achieved through the use of a QTIP trust, which does not require an election to be made until the estate tax return is filed (*i.e.*, at least 9 months after death). *See* §5.18, *supra.* Disclaimers can also be used to adjust the amount of property received by the surviving spouse, which presumably will be included in his or her estate. *See* §§12.26 to 12.29, *infra.*

The IRS first contended that the interest given the survivor under an equalization clause is a terminable interest. However, the contention was rejected by the courts, Estate of Charles W. Smith, 66 T.C. 415, *nonacq.*, 1978-1 C.B.3, *aff'd*, 565 F.2d 455 (1977); Estate of Fritz L. Meeske, 72 T.C. 73 (1979), *aff'd sub nom.*, Estate of Laurin v. Commissioner, 645

F.2d 8 (6th Cir. 1981, consolidated appeal). The courts considered that the necessary interest unquestionably passed to the survivor and would be included in her gross estate. In their view only the value of the interest depends upon the subsequent valuation of assets, etc. In early 1982 the IRS abandoned the contention and conceded that a marital deduction gift subject to an equalization clause was not a terminable interest. Rev. Rul. 82-23, 1982-1 C.B.

The key clause of the will upheld in the *Smith* case read as follows:

> (b) There shall then [after allocation of the Residual Portion] be allocated to the Marital Portion that percentage interest in the balance of the assets constituting the trust estate which shall when taken together with all other interests and property that qualify for the marital deduction and that pass or shall have passed to Settlor's said wife under other provisions of this trust or otherwise, obtain for Settlor's estate a marital deduction which would result in the lowest Federal estate taxes [on] Settlor's estate and Settlor's wife's estate, on the assumption Settlor's wife died after him, but on the date of his death and that her estate were valued as of the date on (and in the manner in) which Settlor's estate is valued for Federal estate tax purposes; Settlor's purpose is to equalize, insofar as possible, his estate and her estate for Federal estate tax purposes, based upon said assumptions. 66 T.C. at 418.

As noted above, the use of an equalization clause or a QTIP trust is particularly appropriate where both spouses are expected to die within a relatively short time period.

Community Property Estates Are Already Equalized. The ownership of community property is naturally equalized by operation of state laws. Accordingly, in most cases the total estate tax burden on community property is minimized if little or no property is passed to a surviving spouse in a way that will cause it to be included in the survivor's gross estate. However, many clients prefer to transfer enough of their community property to the surviving spouse in order to defer payment of any estate tax until the death of the survivor.

Under the most common plan a client with a substantial community property estate leaves most of it to a trust that meets the requirements of §2056(b)(7). The interests given to the surviving spouse are not sufficient to cause the property to be included in his or her gross estate apart from the portion with respect to which the executor elects to claim the marital deduction. §2044. Thus, the surviving spouse typically receives a life income interest in the trust; the noncumulative right to draw down the greater of $5,000 or 5% of the value of the trust each year (§2041(b)(2)); the power to invade the corpus of the trust limited by an ascertainable standard relating to the survivor's health, education, support, or maintenance (§2041(b)(1)(A)); and a testamentary power to appoint the trust property to a limited class of persons, excluding herself, her creditors, her estate, and creditors of her estate (§2041(b)(1)). Of course, a trustee other than the surviving spouse can be given the power to make discretionary distributions of corpus to the surviving spouse. Under this approach the executor can elect to claim a marital deduction for a portion of the property transferred to the trust according to the circumstances as they exist at the time the estate tax return is filed for the spouse who died first.

§5.24. *Minimizing Tax – Deferring Payments*

The needs of the family may be served best by a plan that defers payments of any estate tax until the death of the surviving spouse. Now that the unlimited marital deduction is available, it is easy to achieve that goal. However, such a deferral may unreasonably delay the time at which any of the property will be available to the client's children or other younger generation beneficiaries. The plan should not "waste" the unified credit of the spouse first to die by giving all of his or her property outright to the surviving spouse. Such a waste could be avoided to the extent the surviving spouse disclaims interests in the property. The goal is better achieved, however, by using a QTIP trust or a marital deduction formula clause. In either case the plan preserves the maximum amount of property during the surviving spouse's lifetime. Also, by eliminating the need to pay any tax, the estate of the first spouse to die is relieved of the necessity to liquidate additional assets, which could require the recognition of capital gains.

Where each spouse owns a substantial amount of property the total amount of transfer taxes ultimately payable by their estates may be increased by deferring the payment of any tax until the death of the surviving spouse. First, an increase might result because of the progressivity of the estate tax. However, the progressivity of the tax was greatly reduced by the 1981 Act, which dramatically increased the amount of the unified credit and reduced the maximum rate to 50% beginning in 1985. Taken together those changes shrank the spread between the lowest marginal rate at which any tax will be payable and the maximum rate to 13%. *See* §2.3, *supra*. Second, the tax might be greater on the surviving spouse's death because of an increase in the value of the assets or because of his or her accumulation of income. This risk is easily exaggerated — it is impossible to foresee the composition or value of the surviving spouse's estate or the rates or other provisions of the tax laws that will be in effect at the time of his or her death. (The substantial transfer tax changes made by the 1976 and 1981 Acts were largely unanticipated even in the years they were adopted.) Also, the amount and value of property includible in the surviving spouse's estate may be controlled by careful estate planning, including gifts, installment sales, corporate recapitalizations, etc. In this connection it should be noted that the increase in the unified credit, which may continue beyond 1987, allows a relatively large amount of property to escape taxation entirely.

After 1984, when the highest marginal estate tax rate will be 50%, the largest amount of additional tax that could result from the use of the unlimited marital deduction is $129,200 if the values remain constant. That amount represents the difference between the tentative tax on an estate of $2.5 million ($1,025,800) and the tentative tax on 2 estates of $1.25 million ($448,300 × 2 or $896,600).

> **Example 5-19.** H died in 1982 leaving an estate of $500,000 to a trust in which W had a qualifying income interest for life. No tax will be due from H's estate if his executor elects to claim a deduction with respect to $275,000 of the property passing to the trust. If the value of the property remains constant no estate tax will be due from W's estate if she dies after 1982. Indeed, because of the steady increase in the amount of the unified credit available to her estate no tax may be due from her estate even if the value of the trust property increases substantially.

§5.25. *Taking Advantage of the Unified Credits*

In general a spouse should not provide in his or her will for a larger gift to the other spouse than is necessary to eliminate the testator's estate tax liability. That is, none of a client's unified credit should be allowed to go to waste. Instead, the estate of each spouse should make maximum use of the "shelter" provided by the unified credit. Of course, this point generally concerns only married clients whose combined gross estates are likely to exceed the amount of the credit equivalent allowable to one person.

> **Example 5-20.** H died in 1982 leaving an estate of $350,000 to W, who owned about $150,000 in property. A marital deduction was allowable for the full amount of H's gift to W. Accordingly, no tax was payable by H's estate. However, all of their property is potentially includible in W's estate. If the value of the property remains constant no tax will be due if W dies in 1986 or 1987. Some tax would be due from W's estate if she died prior to 1986. Should the value of the property increase after H's death, some tax would be due from W's estate if she dies in 1986 (when the credit equivalent will be $500,000), etc. H could have preserved the use of his unified credit, and sheltered $225,000 in property from taxation on her death, by leaving it in a form that would not be subject to taxation on W's death. For example, H might have left his entire estate to a

QTIP trust with respect to which the shelter could have been preserved by an appropriate election by H's executor.

As indicated by Example 5-20, the "shelter" provided by the unified credit may be preserved in a variety of ways. Some clients prefer to make a formula gift of an amount equal to the credit equivalent in a way that insulates the property from tax on the death of the surviving spouse. Others prefer to leave substantially all of their property outright to the surviving spouse and to rely upon him or her to adjust the amount of the gift through the use of disclaimers. Probably the most popular approach is based on a QTIP trust, in which the surviving spouse has a qualifying income interest for life. Its success of course depends upon an appropriate election being made under §2056(b)(7).

If one spouse has a relatively large estate and the other spouse has an estate significantly smaller than the amount of the credit equivalent, the wealthier spouse may make inter vivos gifts to the poorer spouse in order to assure the use of the donee-spouse's full unified credit. For example, a gift might be made to a QTIP trust for the benefit of the poorer spouse. Perhaps the donor spouse could retain a successive life income interest in the trust should the donor survive the donee. Better yet, the poorer spouse could exercise a special power of appointment over the trust and transfer it to a QTIP trust for the original donor. In such a case presumably an election could be made by the donee's executor that might cause part or all of the property to be excluded from the donor's estate upon his or her subsequent death. Of course, the basis of the property is not increased under §1014 if the donee spouse dies within one year of the original gift and leaves the property to the donor spouse. §1014(e).

Problem 5-2. H died earlier this year leaving his $1,000,000 estate to a trust in which his widow, W, was given a qualifying income interest for life. Under the terms of the trust any portion of the trust with respect to which W disclaims the income interest will pass outright to their 3 adult children. Upon W's death any remaining trust property will be distributed to their then living issue, by right of representation. W is 65 years old and in good health. She believes that the income from her own $1,000,000 estate should be sufficient to provide adequately for herself. However, she is unwilling to disclaim all interests in H's estate. Advise W regarding the tax and nontax factors she should consider in deciding what election to make under §2056(b)(7) as executor of H's will. In this connection provide her with a simple estimate of the estate consequences of (1) claiming no deduction and (2) claiming a deduction sufficient to reduce the tax payable by H's estate to zero. For this purpose assume that no deduction will be available to either estate other than the marital deduction, if any, allowed to H's estate. The estimate should assume alternatively that W dies one year after H during which the value of all of the property remained constant and that W dies 5 years later during which all of the property doubled in value.

D. THE GIFT TAX MARITAL DEDUCTION

§5.26. *Overall Considerations*

The adoption of the unlimited marital deduction eliminated many of the tax advantages of making inter vivos gifts to a spouse. Formerly lifetime gifts to a spouse were widely used to equalize the size of the estates of the donor and donee and to maximize the amount of property that could be passed to a spouse free of tax. Nonetheless, lifetime gifts to a spouse retain some tax advantages, particularly where one spouse has a small estate (*i.e.*, one smaller than the amount of the credit equivalent).

Of course, the desirability of making substantial gifts to a spouse should depend in large measure upon the stability of the marriage and other nontax factors. In the nature of things very few individuals will make an inter vivos gift of a substantial portion of their wealth to a spouse under any circumstances. In some cases a large gift may help to cement the relationship between the spouses by providing tangible evidence of the donor's affection for, and confidence in, the donee. The desirability of each spouse's having control over some assets and of holding others in the names of both spouses should also be recognized. However, an unanticipated dissolution proceeding may negate the "tax advantages" of gifts including inter vivos assignments of life insurance policies (Moser v. Moser, 572 P.2d 446 (Ariz. 1977)); private annuities (Stanger v. Stanger, 471 P.2d 1126 (Idaho 1977)); and other estate-planning devices (Marriage of Hadley, 565 P.2d 790 (Wash. 1977), agreements regarding status of assets as community or noncommunity property).

§5.27. *General Objectives of Inter Vivos Gifts*

Some of the general objectives of making inter vivos gifts also apply in planning gifts to a spouse.

First, an interspousal gift removes from the donor's estate any future appreciation in value of the property transferred. Of course, the significance of this objective was reduced by the adoption of the unlimited marital deduction — tax-free gifts can be made to a spouse at any time regardless of their value.

Second, such a gift may reduce the value of the nonbusiness assets owned by the donor so the business holdings retained by the donor will constitute a large enough proportion of his estate to qualify for the special tax benefits of §§303, 2032A, or 6166. However, gifts made within 3 years of the donor's death are brought back into the donor's estate for purposes of §§303, 2032A, and 6166. §2035(d)(3). Inter vivos gifts to a spouse can also serve to equalize the sizes of the spouses' estates and to create an estate for a "poor" spouse in order to take advantage of the unified credit if the donee should predecease the donor. Gifts to a spouse will generally yield little, if any, income tax benefit because married persons almost always benefit from filing joint income tax returns.

§5.28. Equalizing Estates by Lifetime Gifts

The general importance of equalizing the sizes of the spouses' estates was reviewed in §5.23, *supra*. Lifetime equalization may be undertaken to ensure that the wealthier spouse will be able to transfer some property at lower tax cost via the poorer spouse's estate. If inter vivos gifts are made, the spouses' dispositive instruments should be reviewed to be sure the provisions are compatible with the gifts. For example, it may be necessary to scale down the amount of the gifts made to the donee in the donor's will to avoid unduly increasing the donee's estate. Also, the donee should plan to dispose of the gifted property in a tax-sensitive way consistent with their overall dispositive goals. In particular, the donee spouse should prevent the gifted property from returning the assets to the donor or otherwise causing them to be included in the donor's gross estate.

As a result of the adoption of the unlimited marital deduction it is no more advantageous to make lifetime equalizing gifts than it is to do so at death if the wealthier spouse dies first. However, inter vivos gifts are an effective hedge against the possibility that the opportunity to equalize will be lost by the unexpected prior death of the poorer spouse.

The sizes of the estates may be equalized without depriving the donor of substantial current value by making gifts of life insurance. For example, the spouse with the smaller estate may be given policies of insurance on the other spouse's life or funds with which to acquire new policies. Alternatively, the insurance might be transferred to an irrevocable life insurance trust. *See* §§6.18 to 6.74, *infra*.

§5.29. Using Lifetime Gifts to Take Advantage of the Poorer Spouse's Unified Credit

Where the estate of one spouse substantially exceeds the amount of the credit equivalent and the estate of the other is substantially less than the

credit equivalent, steps should be taken to assure that the shelter provided by the poorer spouse's credit is fully utilized.

> **Example 5-21.** W's estate is worth $1,000,000 while H's estate is
> worth only $50,000. If H predeceases W, most of his unified credit
> will be wasted. W should consider making a substantial gift to H,
> which he could leave to a QTIP trust for the benefit of W if he
> predeceases her.

Some commentators have pointed out that there are tax advantages to
transferring property to a terminally ill spouse whose estate is less than
the credit equivalent. Paster, Gifts Made to Dying Spouse Can Cut Estate
Tax and Boost Up the Basis of Appreciated Property, 4 Est. Plan. 238
(1977). However, as noted above, the bases of appreciated assets given to
the decedent within a year of death are not increased if the decedent
transfers them back to the original donor (or his or her spouse).
§1014(e). Also, the lawyer should recognize that some clients will react
negatively to using tax advantages they perceive as derived from the
spouse's illness and imminent death. Also, if such a gift is made, it may be
necessary to change the content of the donee's will in order to take full
advantage of the tax savings plan. Query: What reactions might the
donee and the donee's children have toward the proposal? Toward the
lawyer and the donor?

If the technique is used, highly appreciated assets (*i.e.*, ones with low
bases) should normally be the subject of the gift. Their bases would be
increased the most by the stepped-up basis the assets would acquire
upon the donee's death under §1014.

E.   EXPRESSING A MARITAL DEDUCTION GIFT — FORMULA AND NONFORMULA GIFTS

§5.30.   *Overview*

Property may pass to a surviving spouse in a variety of ways that qualify
for the marital deduction. *See* §2056(c) and §5.9, *supra.* Because property
commonly passes to a surviving spouse and others under several will
substitutes (*e.g.*, joint tenancies, life insurance beneficiary designations,
multi-party bank accounts), the planner must carefully review, analyze,
and organize the client's property. During the era of the limited marital
deduction, estate plans often sought to achieve the optimum estate tax
result by providing in the client's will for a formula gift to the surviving
spouse of an amount equal to the maximum allowable marital deduction.

Two basic formulae were developed in response to the problem of transferring precisely the right amount of property to the surviving spouse (or to a qualifying trust) to support the maximum marital deduction. (Any excess distribution to the surviving spouse would be subject to tax in the testator's estate and in the estate of the surviving spouse. Thus, the formulae sought to avoid "overfunding" the marital deduction gift.)

Both formulae gave the surviving spouse property equal in value to the maximum allowable marital deduction *less* the value of all other property for which the deduction was available. One formula gave the surviving spouse *an amount* of property equal to the maximum allowable marital deduction (the so-called pecuniary formula); the other gave the survivor *a fractional interest* in a designated portion of the testator's estate (the fractional share formula). Both types of formulae can be adapted for use in connection with the unlimited marital deduction. *See* §§5.33-5.34, 5.44, *infra.* The revised formulae are designed to preserve the testator's unified credit by limiting the amount of property passing to the surviving spouse in ways that would require the inclusion of the property in the estate of the surviving spouse.

Before turning to a consideration of the formulae it should be noted that no formula may be needed in some cases. First, it is unnecessary to use a formula when the shelter provided by the testator's unified credit will not be needed (*i.e.,* where the value of their combined estates will be less than the amount of the credit equivalent). In such a case the testator may choose to leave all of his or her estate outright to the surviving spouse. Thus, the plan for a young couple whose estates are small may provide for an outright gift of all of the testator's property to the surviving spouse, with a contingent gift to a trust for their minor children. Such a plan is discussed in detail in Chapter 4, *supra.* Of course, this approach involves some speculation about the value the couple's property will have and the amount of the unified credit that will be available to the surviving spouse's estate.

Second, although their estates may be large enough to generate some tax on the death of the surviving spouse, the testator may choose to rely upon the surviving spouse's use of qualified disclaimers to adjust the amount of property that passes to him or her. In its simplest form this approach merely involves an outright gift of the testator's entire estate to the surviving spouse with no special provision for the disposition of any property disclaimed by the surviving spouse. In such a case the distribution of any disclaimed property would be determined by the local law. For example, if the surviving spouse disclaims a one-half interest in the testator's residuary estate, the interest would pass to the testator's intestate successors. In order to assure that the disclaimed property will pass to others, the surviving spouse should also disclaim the right to receive any interest in the property by intestate succession. It should be recognized that the surviving spouse may be incompetent to execute a valid disclaimer, which can jeopardize the plan unless an affective disclaimer can be made by a guardian or other personal representative. Also, the surviving spouse may be unwilling to disclaim any property because it will pass outright to others and will not be directly available to support him or her.

Under a more sophisticated approach the testator's will provides for the disposition of any property disclaimed by the surviving spouse. The will might call for any disclaimed property to pass outright to designated persons or to a trust in which the surviving spouse has a qualifying income interest for life. Under such an approach the surviving spouse is entitled to the income from the disclaimed property for life and the testator's executor can control the amount of the marital deduction through exercise of the election under §2056(b)(7). As a further embellishment such a plan might provide that any interest in the trust that is disclaimed by the surviving spouse will pass outright to designated persons (or to trusts for their benefit).

The third situation in which a formula is unnecessary is if the testator is willing to leave the bulk of his or her estate to a QTIP trust, thus relying upon the executor's election under §2056(b)(7) to produce the optimum tax result. Here again, the testator could provide for the disposition of any interest in the trust that is disclaimed by the surviving spouse.

> **Example 5-22.** W died in 1982 leaving her $500,000 estate outright to H if he survived her, otherwise to those of their adult children who survive her. W was survived by H and their two adult children, S and D. H disclaimed the right to receive property from W's estate that had a value equal to the amount of the credit equivalent available to W's estate ($225,000). The disclaimed property passed directly to S and D and is not includible in H's gross estate. W's unified credit offset the amount of tax due from her estate on the disclaimed property.

> **Example 5-23.** H died in 1985 leaving his estate of $750,000 to a trust in which W had a qualifying income interest for life. H's executor elected under §2056(b)(7) to claim a marital deduction with respect to an interest in the trust that had a value of $350,000 (a $\frac{7}{15}$ths interest). The election took advantage of H's unified credit by sheltering part of the trust from inclusion in W's estate (*i.e.*, the other $\frac{8}{15}$ths interest in the trust is not includible in W's estate).

Fourth, the testator may choose to approximate the effect of a formula clause by making a pecuniary nonmarital gift of an amount equal to the credit equivalent and leaving the balance of his or her estate to the surviving spouse. While this approach may not yield the optimum tax result, it is simple and easy to understand. The nonmarital pecuniary gift might be expressed along these lines:

> If my wife survives me, I give to A, B, & C Trust Company, in trust, subject to the terms of Article Ten [a nonmarital trust], an amount equal to the sum set forth below opposite the year of my death:

1982	$225,000
1983	275,000
1984	325,000
1985	400,000
1986	500,000
1987 and thereafter	600,000

The amount of such a gift would more closely approximate the credit equivalent if it were reduced by the amount of the testator's adjusted taxable gifts (*i.e.*, taxable gifts made after 1976).

Overall, the most flexible plan involves the creation of a QTIP trust for the surviving spouse with provision for the disposition of any interest in the trust that he or she disclaims. In that way the choice regarding the size of the marital deduction can be fixed after many more facts are known. However, as noted above, §5.18, *supra*, the use of a QTIP may cause unnecessary income taxes to be paid and may bloat the size of the surviving spouse's estate.

§5.31. An Assessment of Formula Provisions

Both the pecuniary and the fractional share clauses automatically adjust for changes in the composition and value of the testator's estate prior to death and in the amount of property that passes under will substitutes. The use of a formula clause is a reasonably effective way to ensure the proper division of property between transfers that are designed to preserve the testator's unified credit and ones to the surviving spouse that qualify for the marital deduction. Although a formula clause is capable of producing good results, it is not a universal panacea and is not a substitute for careful work by the planner. The use of a formula clause does not relieve the lawyer of the obligation to review, analyze, and organize the client's estate in the most careful and deliberate way. Because of the significance of the changes made by the 1981 Act planners should exercise caution in drafting formula gifts of any kind. It is not safe to rely upon formulae that were sufficient under the pre-1982 law, particularly in the case of formula pecuniary nonmarital gifts. For example, it is unclear how Rev. Proc. 64-19 might apply to such a gift and whether a "minimum worth" pecuniary clause would support the allowance of a marital deduction for the value of the residue determined according to estate tax values. *See* §5.39, *infra.*

It is also important to appreciate the limitations of formula provisions: No mere formula clause can provide absolute protection against transferring too little or too much property to the surviving spouse. Too little may be transferred to the surviving spouse if the bulk of a client's estate passes to other persons under will substitutes and the probate estate is inadequate to satisfy the formula gift to the surviving spouse. Conversely, too much may pass to the surviving spouse if assets in excess of the amount of the maximum allowable deduction pass to the surviving spouse under will substitutes that are not subject to the limitations expressed in the formula clause.

Caution must also be exercised because the amount of property that passes under a formula provision may be too small to warrant the establishment of a trust. For that reason the planner should consider providing that the gift will pass to the surviving spouse outright if its value is below a certain amount. A small trust can be a nuisance, involving unnecessary expenditures of time and money preparing accountings, keeping records, and filing fiduciary income tax returns. The expense could be considerable if a corporate trustee is appointed and insists on payment of a minimum annual fee of, perhaps, $750 or $1,000.

To put matters further into perspective, the general disadvantages of formula provisions should be mentioned. First, by their very nature formula clauses are complicated and difficult to draft, explain, understand, and administer. Because of their complexity it is easy to make a costly mistake at any step along the way. Second, the use of a formula marital deduction clause may require multiple valuations of assets and more complex accountings, which can delay settlement of an estate and impose additional costs of administration. Delay may also result because the exact amount of the gift may not be known until the valuation of property included in the gross estate is finally determined upon audit of the estate tax return. Third, the use of a formula may cause controversies between the surviving spouse and other beneficiaries regarding the proper exercise of elections by the fiduciary that affect the amount of the gifts to the surviving spouse and others. Among these elections are those regarding the use of the alternate valuation date (§2032); the specific use valuation of assets (§2032A); and the return upon which alternatively deductible items are claimed for tax purposes (§642(g)). As noted in §5.32, *infra,* an election to claim an alternatively deductible item as an income tax deduction will affect the amount of a nonmarital pecuniary formula gift.

§5.32.   Planning a Formula Pecuniary Gift

A formula pecuniary gift is generally simpler to understand and easier to administer than a fractional share gift. In the pre-1982 era pecuniary formula gifts were used more often than fractional share gifts. Because of their advantages they will probably continue to be more popular than fractional share gifts. Presumably a nonmarital gift could be expressed as the pecuniary amount and a marital deduction allowed for the value of the residuary gift. The question is significant primarily because the amount of the pecuniary gift will remain fixed although the overall value of the estate may increase or decrease. Viewed conversely, the gains or losses will all be allocated to the nonpecuniary share (usually the residuary estate). The difference is illustrated by the following simplified example:

> **Example 5-24.** W's will made a formula pecuniary gift to H and left the residue of her estate to a discretionary trust for H and their children. W's estate had a federal estate tax value of $1,000,000, of which H was entitled to receive $500,000 by reason of the formula gift. Under the terms of W's will the gift to H could be satisfied by distributing assets in kind provided they were valued for that purpose according to their values on the date of distribution. The value of the assets of the estate increased to $2,000,000 on the date of distribution. None of the increase is allocable to H's gift. Note, however, that a decrease in the value of the estate's property would reduce the amount passing under the nonmarital gift (*i.e.*, the portion in the trust, sheltered by W's unified credit).

It is also significant that gain is realized on the transfer of appreciated property in kind in satisfaction of a pecuniary gift. *See* §5.37, *infra*. Accordingly, a larger gain may be realized where the amount passing under the formula pecuniary gift is larger than the amount passing under the residuary clause. For that reason it may be preferable to use formula pecuniary language to describe the share (marital or nonmarital) that is expected to be smaller.

Credits. In computing the amount of a pecuniary gift the formula should take into account the decedent's unified credit, the offset allowed under §2001(b)(2) for gift taxes paid with respect to post-1976 gifts, and the state death tax credit (at least to the extent the state credit does not increase the amount of tax payable to any state). Expressed in that way the credits operate positively to shelter property from taxation without causing any increase in the amount of taxes payable by either spouse's estate.

Example 5-25. H died in 1982 leaving an estate of $500,000. His will made a formula pecuniary gift to W of the smallest amount which, if allowable as a marital deduction, would result in the payment of no federal estate tax, taking into account other deductions and the unified credit and the state death tax allowed to his estate. The residue of H's estate was left to a nonmarital trust. H's estate was entitled to no deductions apart from the marital deduction. However, it paid a state inheritance tax of $1,945. H's unified credit shelters a transfer of $225,000 to the nonmarital trust. The state death tax credit of $1,945 shelters an additional $6,080 (*i.e.,* the combined unified and state death tax credits shelter a total of $231,080). Since the state inheritance tax of $1,945 was payable in any event, the total taxes payable by reason of H's death were not increased by giving recognition to it in determining the amount of the pecuniary gift.

Richard Covey has cautioned that the state death tax credit should only be taken into account to the extent it does not require the payment of any additional state death tax. R. Covey, The Marital Deduction and the Use of Formula Provisions (2d ed., 1978) 164. The point is significant because recognition of the credit would result in the payment of an avoidable state death tax in states that impose only a pick up tax. (A "pick up" tax is a state death tax equal to the amount of the maximum allowable estate tax credit for state death taxes). Such a pick up tax is in effect in a number of states including Alabama, Alaska, Arkansas, Colorado, Florida, and Washington. Of course, the payment of some state death tax in such a case shelters an additional amount of property from taxation on the surviving spouse's death. In essence, the recognition of the credit in such a case involves the payment of a state tax at the marginal estate tax rate applicable to amounts in excess of the credit equivalent. The following variation of Example 5-25, *supra,* illustrates the point:

Example 5-26. The facts are the same as in Example 5-25, except that the state in which H was domiciled at death imposed only a state pick up tax. Had the formula pecuniary gift taken into account only the unified credit, it would have sheltered $225,000 and no pick up tax would have been payable. (Under §2011 (f) the state death tax credit "shall not exceed the amount of tax imposed by §2001 reduced by the amount of the credit provided for in §2010.") Recognition of the state death tax credit requires the payment of a pick up tax of $1,945. Payment of the tax does shelter an additional $6,080 from taxation on the surviving spouse's death. Note, however, that the cost of the shelter is the imposition of a tax at an effective rate of 32%. Perhaps it would be better to take full advantage of the unlimited marital deduction and forego the payment of the pick up tax and the shelter it provides.

Charge Nonmarital Share for Principal Expenses for Which No Estate Tax Deduction Is Claimed. A marital deduction is allowable only with respect to the net amount passing to the surviving spouse. §2056(b)(4). That rule does not cause a problem where the formula gift to the surviving spouse includes a proper adjustment for deductions charged against principal and *allowed* for federal estate tax purposes. *See* §5.33, *infra*. Administration expenses and other items that are deductible for federal estate tax purposes should not be taken into account to the extent they are claimed on the estate's income tax return. A formula that takes allowable expenses into account could require the payment of some estate tax through the allocation of too much property to the nonmarital share.

> **Example 5-27.** H died in 1982 leaving an estate of $500,000. His will contained a pecuniary formula marital deduction gift to W and left the residue of his estate to a nonmarital trust. The formula provided that the amount of the marital gift should be calculated by taking into account the unified credit and all other deductions *allowed* to his estate. H's estate paid a total of $25,000 in administration expenses and other items that were deductible under §2053. However, all of the items were claimed as deductions on the estate's income tax return. The amount of the pecuniary marital gift is equal to the difference between the gross estate ($500,000) and the amount of the credit equivalent ($225,000) or $275,000. Had the expenses been claimed as deductions on the estate tax return, the marital gift would have been reduced to $250,000, which represents the excess of the gross estate over the total of the deductions allowed for estate tax purposes ($25,000) and the credit equivalent ($225,000). If the formula had provided that allowable deductions would be taken into account, some estate tax would have been due had the items been claimed as income tax deductions (*i.e.,* too much property would have passed to the nonmarital trust).

§5.33. Model Formula Pecuniary Marital Deduction Gift

A formula pecuniary marital deduction gift could be expressed in a variety of ways. Language such as the following reflects the points discussed above and should suffice as a nonresiduary formula gift:

> If my wife survives me, I give to [her or to a trust for her benefit] the smallest amount, which if allowable as a marital deduction for federal

estate tax purposes in the matter of my estate will result in no federal estate tax being due from my estate, taking into account all other deductions allowed to my estate for federal estate tax purposes and the amount of the unified credit, the amount of gift tax payable with respect to post-1976 taxable gifts, and the state death tax credit. However, the state death tax credit shall only be taken into account to the extent that it does not increase the amount of tax payable to any state.

The formula should also contain directions regarding the funding of the marital gift and the valuation of assets. *See* §§5.35 to 5.41, *infra.*

§5.34.   Model Formula Pecuniary Nonmarital Deduction Gift

A formula nonmarital deduction gift could be expressed along these lines:

If my wife survives me, I give to [the nonmarital trust or other beneficiaries] an amount equal to the excess of (1) the amount upon which the tentative tax calculated under I.R.C. §2001(c) is equal to the sum of the unified credit, the amount of gift tax payable with respect to post-1976 gifts, and the state death tax credit (but the state death tax credit shall be taken into account only to the extent that it does not increase the amount of tax payable to any state) over (2) the amount of post-1976 taxable gifts made by me other than gifts includible in my gross estate; the amount of property includible in my gross estate for which no charitable or marital deduction or casualty loss deduction is allowed; and the amount of administration expenses and other expenses incurred in connection with the settlement of my estate that are charged against principal and are not allowed as deductions for federal estate tax purposes.

In this case the formula should also be fleshed out by appropriate provisions regarding funding and valuation of property.

§5.35.   Directions Regarding Funding a Pecuniary Marital Deduction Gift

Various options are available for specifying the manner in which a formula pecuniary gift should be satisfied. If nothing is said on the subject, the fiduciary may be obligated by local law to satisfy the gift in cash. The liquidation of assets that would ordinarily be required to satisfy the gift in cash might be inconvenient and cause the estate to incur unnecessary capital gains taxes. Whatever the local law may be, it is generally desirable to authorize the fiduciary to satisfy the gift by distributing assets in kind. The fiduciary needs the flexibility such a provision confers in order to be able to select and distribute the most appropriate assets, taking into account the circumstances of the estate and the beneficiaries.

Stock distributed in kind in satisfaction of a pecuniary marital deduction bequest is redeemable under §303 if the fiduciary has discretion to distribute assets in kind and the qualifications of §303 are met. Rev. Rul. 70-297, 1970-1 C.B. 66. Under Reg. §1.303-2(f) stock distributed in satisfaction of a specific monetary bequest does not qualify for redemption under §303. In drafting a marital deduction gift it is also important to note that several of the requirements of §303 were changed by the 1976 and 1981 Acts. Under one change, redemption is available "only to the extent that the interest of the shareholder is reduced directly (or through a binding obligation to contribute) by any payment of" death taxes and funeral and administration expenses. §303(b)(3).

§5.36.   Valuation of Assets Distributed in Kind

The fiduciary should be given some guidance regarding the valuation of any assets that are distributed in kind in satisfaction of a pecuniary formula bequest. Of necessity some specific value must be assigned to each asset. The principal valuation methods and the income and estate tax consequences of each are described in the following sections.

Thus far the IRS has not required the income tax basis of an asset to be taken into account in valuing the asset in connection with an in kind distribution. Accordingly, neither the value of an asset nor the amount of the marital deduction has been adjusted merely because the asset will have a basis in the hands of the distributee that is less than its value for purposes of distribution. Similarly, no adjustment has been required when the assets distributed included a component of income in respect of a decedent. Thus, a marital deduction has been allowed without reduction for future income tax liability that might arise upon payment of installment notes distributed in satisfaction of the marital deduction gift. LR 7827008. Consistent with that result the Tax Court has not allowed a decedent's estate to discount the value of installment notes on account of the possible income tax payable on collections made on the notes in the future. Estate of G. R. Robinson, 69 T.C. 222 (1977).

At some point the IRS might require the distribution of assets that fairly reflect the overall appreciation or depreciation in value of all assets available for distribution. Beyond that, the tax consequences are probably too speculative and uncertain to take into account. The speculative and uncertain nature of the future income tax consequences has caused California courts generally to ignore them in connection with the allocation of community property assets in dissolution proceedings. See Comment, Future Tax Consequences in Community Property Divisions: An Analysis of the California Approach, 24 U.C.L.A. L. Rev. 1354 (1977).

§5.37.   Value on the Date of Distribution ("True Worth")

Unless the fiduciary is directed to value the assets that are distributed in kind in some other manner, the fiduciary may be obligated to value them at their fair market values on the date or dates of distribution. Such a requirement, which is commonly called a "true worth" provision, may be expressly imposed by the terms of a will or trust. A true worth provision assures that the value of the property distributed in satisfaction of the gift will have a total market value on the date or dates of distribution exactly equal to the amount of the marital deduction. If the assets of the estate appreciate in value, the rule acts as a ceiling; and if they decline, it acts as a floor. A true worth provision could be used in connection with a pecuniary marital or nonmarital gift.

> **Problem 5-3.** W died in 1982 leaving an estate that consisted of assets A, B, and C, each of which was worth $200,000 on the estate tax valuation date and $300,000 on the date of distribution. W made no taxable gifts during her lifetime and her taxable estate is $600,000. What value must the assets that are distributed in kind have on the date of distribution in order to satisfy a "true worth" pecuniary formula gift of the smallest amount that, if allowed as a marital deduction, would result in no estate tax being due from W's estate — taking into account only the unified credit? What value must the assets have if each asset had a value of only $150,000 on the date of distribution?

As noted above, §5.32, if the assets of the estate appreciate substantially in value between the estate tax valuation date and the date of distribution, a true worth provision marital deduction gift limits the value of property that can be distributed in satisfaction of the marital deduction gift and would be subject to inclusion in the estate of the surviving spouse. In such a case a larger amount of property would pass under the other provisions of the will or trust. Of course, as Problem 5-3 illustrates, if the assets of the estate decline in value, the floor comes into effect and a smaller amount passes to the other beneficiaries.

"Sale" at a Gain. Under the true worth rule assets that are distributed in satisfaction of the gift must be valued again on the date or dates of distribution. The extra valuation may be time-consuming and costly where the estate includes items difficult to value. A trust or estate recognizes gain if a pecuniary gift is satisfied by distributing an asset that has a date of distribution value greater than the asset's estate tax value. The gain is generally limited to the amount by which the fair market value of the property on the date of distribution exceeds its estate tax value. Note that §1040 limits the amount of gain taxed to a trust or estate when

special use property is distributed to a qualified heir in satisfaction of a pecuniary bequest. In such a case the gain is limited to the amount by which the date of distribution value of the property exceeds its estate tax value, determined without regard to §2032A (*i.e.*, its fair market value on the estate tax valuation date). §1040(a). Where such a distribution is made, the qualified heir's basis in the property is equal to the basis of the estate or trust immediately before the distribution plus the amount of gain recognized by the estate or trust as a result of the distribution. §1040(c).

Language of this type could be used to express a true worth valuation requirement:

> I authorize my executor to satisfy this gift by making distributions in cash or in kind, or part in cash and part in kind, provided that each asset that is distributed in kind shall be valued at its fair market value on the date it is distributed.

"Sale" at a Loss — §267. If the value of an asset is lower on the date of distribution than its basis, the fiduciary must decide whether to sell the asset to a third party or distribute it to a beneficiary in a transaction that will be treated as a sale. In the former case the fiduciary may unquestionably take advantage of the loss on the fiduciary income tax return, while in the latter case the deduction may be prohibited by §267. That section bars a deduction for a loss incurred in a sale or exchange directly or indirectly between related taxpayers, including a fiduciary of a trust and a beneficiary of the trust. However, it does not bar a deduction for a loss on a sale between an estate and a beneficiary of the estate. Estate of Hanna v. Commissioner, 320 F.2d 54 (6th Cir. 1963); Rev. Rul. 77-439, 1977-2 C.B. 85.

The true worth provision is probably used more often than any other, although it requires an additional valuation of assets and may result in recognition of gain by the fiduciary. Planners are attracted by its relative simplicity and the downside protection it gives to the surviving spouse.

§5.38. Estate Tax Value

Some wills and trusts attempt to provide additional flexibility by directing that assets must be valued at their respective estate tax values. Under such a provision a distribution does not result in gain or loss because the basis of each asset was increased to its federal estate tax value under §1014. However, the rule tempted fiduciaries to allocate assets that had declined in value to the marital share and assets that had increased in value to the other beneficiaries. The object of such an allocation was to reduce the amount of property includible in the estate of the surviving spouse. (In the case of a pecuniary nonmarital gift the fiduciary would be tempted to make the reverse allocation.) The IRS responded by issuing Rev. Proc. 64-19, 1964-1 C.B. 682, which sets forth the conditions under which a marital deduction is allowed for a pecuniary gift that the fiduciary is authorized to satisfy by distributing assets in kind at their federal estate tax values.

Rev. Proc. 64-19 provides that when an instrument allows or requires a fiduciary to distribute assets in kind in satisfaction of a pecuniary marital deduction gift, and specifies that the assets distributed in kind must be valued at their values as finally determined for federal estate tax purposes, a marital deduction will be allowed only if (1) the fiduciary "must distribute assets, including cash, having an aggregate fair market value at the date, or dates, of distribution amounting to no less than the amount of the pecuniary bequest or transfer, as finally determined for Federal estate tax purposes," or (2) the fiduciary "must distribute assets, including cash, fairly representative of appreciation or depreciation in the value of all property thus available for distribution in satisfaction of such pecuniary bequest or transfer." In effect federal estate tax values can only be used if the integrity of the marital deduction is protected by the alternative requirements quoted above. Presumably the principles of Rev. Proc. 64-19 will apply where a pecuniary formula is used to express the nonmarital gift.

The Revenue Procedure also noted that the problem it addressed did not arise in some other cases. In particular, it noted that the problem was not present:

1. In a bequest or transfer in trust of a fractional share of the estate, under which each beneficiary shares proportionately in the appreciation or depreciation in the value of assets to the date, or dates, of distribution.
2. In a bequest or transfer in trust of specific assets.
3. In a pecuniary bequest or transfer in trust, whether in a stated amount or an amount computed by the use of a formula, if:
   (a) The fiduciary must satisfy the pecuniary bequest or transfer solely in cash, or
   (b) The fiduciary has no discretion in the selection of assets to be distributed in kind, or
   (c) Assets selected by the fiduciary to be distributed in kind in satisfaction of the bequest or transfer in trust are to be valued at their respective values on the date, or dates, of their distribution. §401, Rev. Proc. 64-19, 1964-1 C.B. at 684.

However, Rev. Proc. 64-19 does not sanction the use of devices in those cases that operate to diminish the value of the interests that are transferred in satisfaction of a marital deduction gift. In particular, it does not authorize the fiduciary to select and distribute assets on a non-pro rata basis in satisfaction of a formula fractional share gift.

Under Rev. Proc. 64-19 a fiduciary may be given authority to satisfy a pecuniary marital deduction gift that requires the use of the federal estate tax value of the assets by only 1 of the 2 approved methods. The fiduciary may not be given a choice between them. Most commentators favor the "minimum value" method; *see* Polasky, Marital Deduction Formula Clauses in Estate Planning — Estate and Income Tax Considerations, 63 Mich. L. Rev. 809, 832 (1965) (cited hereafter as Polasky). The other method, which is commonly called either the "fairly representative" or "ratable sharing" provision, is more cumbersome and is less well understood by planners, courts, and the IRS.

§5.39.   Estate Tax Value: "Minimum Value" Provisions

Under this method the assets distributed in kind must have an aggregate fair market value on the date or dates of distribution of no less than the amount of the pecuniary marital deduction gift. The effect of this approach is to specify a floor beneath which the value of the assets distributed in kind cannot fall (an amount equal to the pecuniary gift), but no ceiling. A minimum worth provision should not be used in connection with a pecuniary formula nonmarital gift because of the possibility that the value of a residuary marital deduction gift could be attritioned by allocating "too much" to the pecuniary nonmarital gift.

> **Example 5-28.** H's estate is composed of assets A, B, and C, each of which has an estate tax value of $300,000 and a date-of-distribution value of $400,000. H's will makes a formula pecuniary gift to W of an amount that is determined to be equal to $450,000. Under an estate tax minimum value provision, a combination of the assets worth at least $450,000 on the date of distribution must be transferred in satisfaction of the gift. However, assets having a date-of-distribution value of as much as $600,000 could be distributed. On the other hand, if the assets fell to a value of $200,000 each on the date of distribution, the fiduciary would still be obligated to distribute to W assets with a date-of-distribution value of at least $450,000.

A minimum worth provision can be used in conjunction with a pecuniary marital deduction gift. It is useful where the client wishes to authorize the fiduciary to allocate some of the increase in value of assets to the marital deduction gift. On the other hand, if the client doesn't want to put the fiduciary in the position of having to decide whether the marital deduction gift or other beneficiaries will benefit from an increase in the value of the estate's property, the provision should not be used.

A minimum value provision might read,

> I authorize my fiduciary to satisfy this gift by making distributions in cash or in kind or part in cash and part in kind, provided that the aggregate fair market value of the cash and other assets on the date or dates of distribution shall be no less than the amount of the gift as finally determined for federal estate tax purposes.

A minimum value marital deduction gift complies with Rev. Proc. 64-19. It should also eliminate the possibility that the estate will recognize capital gain or loss upon the distribution of assets in kind. According to Professor Polasky, the no gain or loss occurs because "the ultimate value of the bequest is not ascertainable until distribution; and the receipt of assets cannot be said to be in satisfaction of a fixed dollar amount bequest or claim." Polasky at 867.

A somewhat similar provision used by some planners requires assets distributed in kind to be valued at the lower of their federal estate tax or date of distribution values. This variation also establishes a floor, but no ceiling. Under it the marital deduction gift can participate in an overall appreciation in value of the assets of the estate, but will not suffer from an overall decline. In such a case the distribution of assets in kind in satisfaction of the gift should not give rise to gain because the value of each asset for purposes of distribution is limited to its federal estate tax value. Presumably the estate would incur a deductible loss if depreciated assets were distributed.

§5.40. Estate Tax Value: "Fairly Representative"

A requirement that the assets distributed in satisfaction of the marital deduction gift fairly reflect the appreciation and depreciation in value of the estate's assets may be imposed by local law or the instrument itself. In either case, the requirement satisfies Rev. Proc. 64-19. A fairly representative clause should be safe to use in conjunction with a formula marital or nonmarital gift under the 1981 Act.

The following language could be used to impose a fairly representative requirement:

> I authorize my fiduciary to select and distribute in satisfaction of this gift assets included in my gross estate (or the proceeds of their disposition), including cash, which have an aggregate fair market value fairly representative of the distributee's proportionate share of the appreciation or depreciation in value, to the date or dates of distribution, of all property then available for distribution.

A fairly representative clause assures that the marital deduction gift
and other gifts will be treated fairly when it comes to making distributions: All will share ratably in any overall increase or decrease in the
value of the assets available for distribution. However, a ratable allocation is most important where the surviving spouse will not also receive
the benefit of the nonmarital share. In contrast, where the surviving
spouse will receive the benefit of both shares, it is more efficient from the
tax perspective to use a clause that permits the distribution of assets
having as low a value as possible in satisfaction of the marital deduction
gift. By doing so the size of the surviving spouse's gross estate can be
kept down.

The primary disadvantage of the fairly representative approach is its
difficulty of application, particularly where distributions are made at
different times to multiple beneficiaries. It is administratively complex
and fraught with problems for the fiduciary. Its use can increase the
amount of the fiduciary's commissions and the amount of the attorney's
fees.

Problem 5-4. H's will contains a formula pecuniary marital deduction formula clause gift to W expressed in the same way as the one
at §5.33. His gross estate consisted of the assets that had a value of
$1,250,000 for federal estate tax purposes. Expenses of administra-
tion and other costs deductible under §2053 amount to $50,000
and will be taken as income tax deductions; only the marital deduction will be claimed on the federal estate tax return.

(a) Assuming that H had made no taxable gifts and lived in a
state that imposes only a pick up tax, what amount will be claimed
as a marital deduction?

(b) If the assets of the estate have the values listed below on the
date they are distributed, what is the total value of the assets that
must be distributed in satisfaction of the gift to W (and what is the
value of the assets to be distributed to the residuary trust) under a
true worth provision? Under a fairly representative clause? In
either case could the distributions be made without incurring any
net capital gain?

Asset	Federal Estate Tax Value	Date of Distribution Value
A	$100,000	$200,000
B	200,000	400,000
C	200,000	100,000
D	400,000	500,000
E	100,000	350,000
F	200,000	150,000

(c)   How would your answers differ if each asset had declined
25% in value between the federal estate tax valuation date and the
date of distribution?

§5.41.   Directions Regarding Allocation of Assets to the Marital Deduction Gift

The amount of the marital deduction is subject to reduction under the
terminable interest rule if any disqualified assets (or their proceeds)
could be distributed in satisfaction of the marital deduction gift. Accordingly, instruments that include a formula gift typically require the
fiduciary to satisfy the marital deduction portion with assets that qualify
for the deduction. For example, an instrument might provide, "This gift
shall be satisfied only with assets or the proceeds of assets with respect to
which a federal estate tax marital deduction is allowable." Without such a
provision, the marital deduction would be disallowed to the extent that
nondeductible interests were included in the pool of assets from which
the gift could be satisfied. *See* §5.10, *supra.*

Closely Held Stock. If the client owns closely held stock that it might be
desirable to redeem under §303, the fiduciary should be directed not to
use the stock to satisfy the marital deduction gift. *See* §5.35, *supra.*

Income in Respect of a Decedent. Generally speaking, income in respect
of a decedent (IRD) items should not be distributed in satisfaction of a
pecuniary formula bequest because the distribution will trigger recognition of income by the estate. Under §691(a)(2) income must be reported
if an IRD item is sold or exchanged. However, income is not triggered by
the distribution of an IRD item in satisfaction of a specific bequest. Thus,
a planner has some flexibility in planning for the distribution of IRD
items. In some cases it may be preferable to have the estate bear the tax
and permit the surviving spouse to receive the income free of tax. In
other cases it is preferable for the surviving spouse to be taxed on the
income, which in effect reduces the size of his or her estate.

The income tax cost of IRD is ameliorated somewhat by the deduction
that is available under §691(c) for the estate tax paid with respect to the
IRD. Of course, if a marital deduction formula works properly the estate
will pay no estate tax.

§5.42.   Planning and Drafting a Formula Fractional Share Gift

The beneficiary of a fractional share gift is entitled to receive the
specified fractional interest in each asset that is included in the pool

against which the fraction is applied. The beneficiary is also entitled to receive a proportionate part of the income generated by the asset pool.

Example 5-29. H bequeathed one-half of his residuary estate to W. When H's estate is distributed, W is entitled to receive an undivided one-half interest in each asset included in H's residuary estate, together with one-half of the income derived from it. If the death taxes, costs of administration, and like items are payable from the nonmarital share of the residue, W may be entitled to a larger proportionate interest in each asset and a larger proportion of the income after those items are paid.

A nonformula fractional share gift (*e.g.*, one-half of my residuary estate) may have a value that is more or less than the amount of the optimum marital deduction. Also, such a gift does not include any mechanism for adjusting the amount of the fraction on account of property that passes outside the will or trust. The absence of a self-adjusting mechanism makes this type of gift too unreliable for general use in marital deduction planning.

In contrast, a formula fractional share gift produces a marital deduction that is precisely equal to the amount necessary to eliminate the payment of any estate tax by the decedent's estate. Exceptions occur if either the gift is overfunded by nontestamentary transfers or the pool of assets against which the fraction is applied is too small to fund the gift fully. A formula fractional share gift also allows each beneficiary to participate in any overall change in the value of the residuary estate or other pool of assets from which the gift will be satisfied. Thus, the fraction serves 2 purposes.

> First, it describes the proportionate share of the residuary estate that is to be qualified for the marital deduction. Necessarily this will produce an *amount,* expressed in dollars, to be claimed on the estate tax return. Second, once constituted, the fraction will be applied to actually allocate the aliquot shares of the described residuary estate to the marital and nonmarital trusts at the distribution date. Polasky, *supra,* at 841.

As the composition and value of the residuary estate will change between the estate tax valuation date and the date or dates of distribution, the value of the assets actually distributed in satisfaction of the gift may be more or less than the amount of the marital deduction.

Example 5-30. W died leaving a will that made a formula fractional share gift to H. According to the federal estate tax value of the assets of W's estate, which governed for the purpose of the formula gift, H was entitled to receive $\frac{5}{9}$ths of W's residuary estate. Accord-

ingly, H was entitled to receive a ⅗ths fractional interest in each
asset, regardless of its value on the date or dates of distribution.

A fractional share gift should be used sparingly where community
property is involved. The management of the property could be complicated if it is fractionalized further by distributing part of a deceased
spouse's share to a marital deduction trust for the surviving spouse and
part to others or to another trust. Where community property is involved, a pecuniary formula is preferable.

Drafting a formula fractional share gift requires the lawyer to focus
on 2 problems: (1) formulating the language with which to express the
fraction itself, and (2) determining and describing the residue or other
pool of assets against which the fraction will be applied (the multiplicand).

§5.43. Expressing the Fraction

The fraction itself may be referred to in several ways that qualify for the
marital deduction. All of them should use the federal estate tax value of
assets for purposes of the numerator, the denominator, and the multiplicand. The numerator is the amount of property to be passed to the
surviving spouse. (A "reverse" formula could be devised, which would be
based upon the maximum amount of property that could be passed to
persons other than the surviving spouse or charities without incurring
any estate tax.) The denominator is the residuary estate or other pool of
assets against which the fraction is applied. In order to preserve the
fractional character of the gift, the denominator must also reflect the
estate tax value of the assets. *See* Polasky at 842, n.116. In drafting the
gift, the lawyer must be sure that the same definition of the residue is
used both for the denominator and the multiplicand. If so, the value of
the gift will be the same whether the residue is constituted before the
payment of cash legacies, expenses, debts, and taxes; before the payment
of taxes (a "pre-tax" provision); or after the payment of all of those items
(a "true residue" provision).

The numerator, denominator, and multiplicand are most often defined expressly in a fractional share gift, as in the model below.

§5.44. Model Formula Fractional Share Gift

A formula fractional share gift might be expressed along these lines:

> If my wife survives me, I give to [her or to a trust for her benefit] a fraction
> of my residuary estate, determined after payment of all pecuniary gifts,

expenses of administration, debts, and death taxes that are properly chargeable against my residuary estate. The numerator of the fraction shall be the smallest amount which, if allowable as a marital deduction for federal estate tax purposes in the matter of my estate, will result in no federal estate tax being due from my estate, taking into account all other deductions allowed for federal estate tax purposes, the unified credit, the amount of gift tax payable with respect to post-1976 taxable gifts, and the state death tax (but only to the extent that the latter credit does not increase the state death tax payable to any state). The denominator of the fraction shall be the federal estate tax value of my residuary estate so determined. For the purposes of this gift, my residuary estate shall include only assets that would qualify for the federal estate tax marital deduction if they were distributed outright to my spouse.

Of course the gift can be made outright to the surviving spouse or in trust. For reasons that are explained below, the multiplicand and the denominator are defined as the residuary estate *after* the payment of all pecuniary gifts, expenses of administration, debts, and death taxes (a true residue provision). The final sentence of the gift is included to prevent loss of any portion of the deduction under the unidentified (tainted) asset rule if the residue includes any terminable interests.

§5.45. Directions Regarding Allocation of Income and Capital Gains and Losses

When a formula fractional share gift is used, the manner in which the income and capital gains and losses will be allocated is uncertain unless some specific directions are included in the instrument. Even statutes that deal with the general problem of allocating income between various residuary beneficiaries, such as N.Y. EPTL §11-2.1 (McKinney, 1980 Supp.), do not provide a clear answer. *See* Covey, *supra* §5.32, at 33-41. Insofar as the allocation of income is concerned,

> an informal survey of corporate fiduciaries suggests varying approaches not necessarily keyed to the particular definition of the residue. Some apply the fraction produced by the formula while others allocate to the marital share only that amount of income which the average rate of return would produce on the calculated marital share. Polasky at 849-850.

The allocation problems are illustrated in the following example:

Example 5-31. W left an estate that was valued at $1,100,000 for federal estate tax purposes and a will that made a formula fractional share gift of her residuary estate to H. Expenses of administration and debts of $100,000 were paid at the same time from the nonmarital share of the residue. H's fractional share was one-half under the true residue provision that was contained in W's will. Income of $50,000 was earned by the estate prior to the payment of the expenses and debts. To be equitable, the nonmarital share should receive all of the income that was earned from the funds used to pay expenses, debts, and taxes. Accordingly, the nonmarital share should be entitled to $\frac{6}{11}$ths of the income earned prior to payment of those items. Income earned thereafter should be allocated according to the formula fraction (*i.e.*, one-half to the marital share and one-half to the other residuary beneficiaries). Of course, convenience tempts the fiduciary to allocate all of the income on the basis of a single fraction.

In an actual case the allocation is likely to be complicated by the payment of debts, expenses, and other items at various times and by the receipt of income at intervals that don't nicely coincide with those times. The same problem exists with respect to the allocation of capital gains and losses, which are frequently incurred to raise funds with which to pay expenses, debts, and taxes.

If the fiduciary is directed to allocate all income and capital gains according to the fraction determined under a true residue provision, the marital share will receive more of those items than it would under the strictly equitable approach. It is important to note that such a provision will inflate the survivor's gross estate to the extent of the excess. However, this approach is infinitely simpler to administer than one that calls for allocation according to the equitable approach and requires almost continuous revision. A provision that requires allocation according to a formula based upon a residue constituted prior to the payment of expenses, debts, and taxes would achieve essentially the same results as the equitable approach and is subject to the same objection.

§5.46. Why Use a True Residue Provision?

Use of a true residue provision is generally preferable to any other definition of the residue for purposes of the fractional share gift. In general, the use of a true residue provision increases the fiduciary's ability to select and dispose of assets in satisfaction of pecuniary legacies, expenses of administration, debts, and taxes. The increased flexibility that such a provision allows the fiduciary is generally desirable.

> Shrinking the residue to which the fraction is to be applied obviously increases the percentage interest of the marital share in the remaining available assets, since the numerator stays the same while the denominator diminishes. Further, shrinking the defined residue gives the executor an

increasing power to choose assets to satisfy the general pecuniary legacy and other non-residue obligations and a concomitant power to affect the makeup, in terms of the specific assets remaining, of the pool to which the fractional share will be applied. . . . Polasky at 844-845.

Also, a true residue provision requires fewer adjustments to the fraction and is generally easier to administer. Finally, the need to trace assets of the estate for purposes of distribution can be eliminated if a true residue provision is used. In other cases it might be necessary to trace all of the assets that were originally included in the residuary estate in order to determine the portion of each asset that should be distributed to the marital and nonmarital shares. *See* 4 A. J. Casner, Estate Planning 1397 (4th ed. 1980).

The fraction will change, whatever residuary definition is used, if a non-pro rata distribution is made to a residuary beneficiary. For that reason disproportionate distributions should generally be avoided when a fractional share gift is used in an instrument. If a true residue provision is used, the fraction will not have to be adjusted when pecuniary legacies, expenses of administration, debts, and taxes are paid. Adjustments will be required, however, if the fraction is originally computed according to the value of the residuary estate prior to the payment of those items. In such a case the payment of each such item is in effect a distribution to the nonmarital share, which has the obligation to make those payments. Accordingly, the fraction must be adjusted every time the estate pays an item that is properly chargeable to the residue.

The complexity of recomputing the fraction discourages many planners from using formula fractional share gifts. The steps involved in determining the initial and final fractions are described in the following passage:

1.   Determine the initial fraction. The numerator and denominator are based upon estate tax values as of the decedent's death if the executor does not elect the alternate valuation method. The denominator must be reduced by all administration expenses, whether or not claimed as an estate tax deduction and, if a true residuary clause is utilized, by estate taxes. If the executor elects the alternate valuation method, the assets of the residuary estate must be valued as of the appropriate alternate valuation date.

2.   Divide the numerator by the denominator in order to determine the initial percentage interest of the marital share in increases and decreases of the estate until the first tax payment or distribution, whichever occurs first if a pre-tax residuary clause is utilized, or the first distribution if a true residuary clause is utilized.

3.   As of the date of any tax payment or distribution, determine the fair market value of the undistributed residuary estate, including cash, and subtract therefrom any unpaid administration expenses taken into account

in determining the initial denominator. Determine any net appreciation or depreciation by subtracting therefrom in the case of the first revaluation the denominator of the initial marital fraction or, in the case of any revaluation other than the first, the denominator of the initial marital fraction increased or decreased by any tax payments, distributions, increases or decreases taken into account in all prior revaluations resulting in a change in the denominator. Allocate to the marital share its percentage interest in the difference, if any, applicable to the period during which such appreciation or depreciation occurs.

4.   Subtract from the denominator the amount of the tax payment if a pre-tax residuary clause is utilized or, in the case of distributions, subtract from the denominator the total amount of distributions (whether or not made to the surviving spouse) and from the numerator only that amount of the distribution passing to the surviving spouse.

5.   After allocating the increases or decreases and subtracting the tax payments or distributions, divide the resulting numerator by the resulting denominator to determine the revised fractional interest of the marital share in the undistributed assets of the residuary estate.

6.   With each succeeding tax payment or distribution, apply the principles set out in 3, 4 and 5 above. Kurtz, Allocation of Increases and Decreases to Fractional Share Marital Deduction Bequest, 8 Real Prop., Prob. & Tr. J. 450, 460 (1973).

As Professor Sheldon Kurtz indicates in the foregoing passage, the fraction must be recomputed "at each tax payment and distribution in the case of a pre-tax residuary clause and at each distribution in the case of a true residuary clause." *Id.* at 460.

Problem 5-5. H died earlier this year leaving a will that made a formula fractional share gift to W of the type described in §5.44 while giving the balance of his residuary estate to a nonmarital trust. His gross estate had a value of $975,000 for federal estate tax purposes, including a house held in joint tenancy with W that had a total value of $150,000, survivorship bank accounts with W in the amount of $25,000, and life insurance payable to W in the amount of $75,000. Debts, costs of administration, etc., payable from the residuary estate came to $80,000. What is W's initial fractional interest in the residue, assuming that H made taxable gifts of $100,000 during his lifetime, that he died in a state that imposed only a pick up tax, and that the marital deduction is the only deduction that will be claimed for federal estate tax purposes? How would the fraction be affected by an interim distribution of assets worth $100,000 to the nonmarital trust just prior to which the residuary assets remaining after payment of debts, etc., had a value of $750,000?

§5.47. Income Tax Aspects of a Formula Fractional Share Gift

A distribution in satisfaction of a fractional share gift does not cause the fiduciary to recognize any gain or loss. Reg. §§1.661(a)-2(f)(1), 1.1014-4(a)(3). This rule is generally beneficial for taxpayers and is an important reason for using a fractional share formula. Of course, its value depends upon the nature of the property involved and the relative income tax positions of the surviving spouse and the estate. A distribution in satisfaction of a fractional share gift does carry out the distributable net income of the estate, which may increase the distributee's basis in the property. Reg. §1.661(a)-2(f)(3).

Under the changes made by the 1976 Act, closely held stock may be redeemed under §303 only to the extent that the interest of the redeeming shareholder is reduced by payment of death taxes and funeral and administration expenses. The marital share, of course, is not reduced by the payment of those items. Accordingly, stock that the parties may wish to redeem under §303 should not be included in the pool of assets subject to the marital deduction formula gift.

§5.48. Summary — Choosing between a Formula Pecuniary Gift and a Formula Fractional Share Gift

"The choice between a formula pecuniary marital deduction gift and a fractional share marital deduction gift is not an easy one." 4 A. J. Casner, Estate Planning 1433 (4th ed. 1980). The fractional share gift has a slight edge when it comes to fairness and security against manipulation. Under a formula fractional share gift the share of each beneficiary fluctuates with changes in the composition and value of the residue, rather than being based upon a fixed amount. Of course, the actual value of the items distributed in satisfaction of a pecuniary gift depends in part upon the type of valuation clause that is used. From the income tax perspective the fractional share gift has the advantage because the distribution of assets does not involve the realization of any gain. However, when appreciated assets are distributed in kind in satisfaction of a pecuniary gift, only the gain in value that takes place between the estate tax valuation date and the date of distribution is realized. The fractional share gift will also enjoy an advantage if a portion of the income taxes attributable to sales made in order to generate funds with which to pay debts, expenses of administration, and taxes may be absorbed by the marital share without requiring any adjustment.

The formula fractional share gift has two major disadvantages. First, the fiduciary does not have as broad a power to select and allocate assets to the marital share as in the case of the pecuniary gift. This shortcoming may be alleviated if the fiduciary is given authority to make non-pro rata distributions of assets in kind. However, the tax consequences of giving the fiduciary such authority are uncertain: The IRS could argue that it converts the gift into a pecuniary one, which would require the fiduciary to recognize gain or loss upon the distribution of assets. *See* Rev. Rul. 60-87, 1960-1 C.B. 286. Second, the administration and acounting for a fractional share gift is much more complicated.

> The fraction itself is easily arrived at — initially. The problem is, that each time a non-pro rata distribution is made the fraction must be recalculated. The numerator and denominator are originally computed using federal estate tax values. The estate is then revalued at each partial distribution, reduced by all unpaid principal charges, and the fraction then recast in terms of current market values. The numerator is reduced by distributions to the spouse and the denominator is reduced by distributions to the spouse and other beneficiaries, payment of expenses (whether or not deductible), and the like. A new fraction is then arrived at which is to be used for the period until the next partial distribution. Rosen, How to Select the Proper Formula Clause to Fit Testator's Desires and Minimize Taxes, 3 Est. Plan. 20, 25 (1975).

In contrast, the administration of a formula pecuniary gift is usually very simple. Often the only complication is that the assets distributed in kind in satisfaction of the gift must be valued again at the time of distribution.

BIBLIOGRAPHY

Casner, A. J., Estate Planning (4th ed. 1980)

Covey, R., The Marital Deduction and the Use of Formula Provisions (2d ed. 1978)

Friedman, Choosing the Proper Formula Marital Bequest, 58 Taxes 632 (1980)

Hastings, Coordinating the Marital Deduction, Orphan's Deduction and Estate Tax Credits, U. Miami 14th Inst. Est. Plan., Ch. 19 (1980)

Kurtz, Impact of the Revenue Act of 1978 and the 1976 Tax Reform Act on Estate Tax Marital Deduction Formulas, 64 Iowa L. Rev. 739 (1979)

Polasky, Marital Deduction Formula Clauses in Estate Planning — Estate and Income Tax Considerations, 63 Mich. L. Rev. 809 (1965)

Trapp, Appreciation, Depreciation, and Basis in Drafting and Funding Marital Deduction Formula Bequests, U. Miami 13th Inst. Est. Plan., Ch. 3 (1979)

CHAPTER 6

LIFE INSURANCE

The life insurance industry directly affects most families in this country. Seventy-two percent of the adult population of the United States and over 90 percent of all husband and wife families own some form of life insurance. In 1977, Americans purchased $367 billion of additional life insurance coverage bringing the total of life insurance coverage to almost $2.6 trillion. Insured families paid an average of over $500 a year in premiums and had approximately $37,000 insurance in force. FTC Staff, Report on Life Insurance Cost Disclosure 5 (1979) (hereinafter referred to as the FTC Report).

A. INTRODUCTION

§6.1. Background

In order to plan estates adequately, a lawyer must be familiar with the basic substantive and tax law regarding life insurance. As the quotation above indicates, a lawyer will seldom see a client whose life is not insured under at least one policy. Indeed, for many families insurance is the largest single investment apart from the family residence and is the largest single liquid asset that is available upon the death of the head of the family. A good grasp of the basic tax laws is necessary to advise clients regarding the consequences of both simple and complex insurance transactions. The existing federal tax laws offer some important opportunities for removing a very substantial amount of life insurance from the gross estate of the insured at little or no gift or income tax cost. Whatever the size of a client's estate, the lawyer also needs to know the basic types of life insurance policies and the advantages and disadvantages of different forms of ownership and different types of beneficiary designations. The estate plan recommended for a client may involve the transfer, surrender, or retention of existing policies or the acquisition of additional insurance. The recommendations regarding life insurance will depend upon a variety of factors, including the client's age, health, family circumstances, and investment objectives. A lawyer should also recognize his or her own limitations, however, and be reluctant to assume the role of investment counselor or insurance advisor. It is often advisable to suggest involving an experienced and reliable insurance advisor when the selection of additional insurance or special types of policies are involved. Note that many insurance advisors charge hourly fees for their services.

This chapter includes a review of the basic types of life insurance; a discussion of the gift, estate, and income tax consequences of transactions involving life insurance; an examination of the characteristics of some special types of life insurance; and a consideration of the basic objectives and techniques of planning with life insurance.

Basically, life insurance is a contractual arrangement for spreading among all members of a group the risk of suffering economic loss upon the death of any member of the group. This is accomplished by each person in the group paying a relatively small amount each year into a pool in consideration of the promise by the operator of the pool to pay a larger amount to designated persons upon the death of any group member during that year. In practice the risk pools are operated by insurance companies subject to state laws and the supervision of state insurance commissioners. The beneficiary designated in the insurance contract is ordinarily not subject to change by will. However, a contrary conclusion was reached in Connecticut General Life Insurance Co. v. Peterson, 442 F. Supp. 533 (W.D. Mo. (1978)).

Before going further it may be helpful to review the terms that are commonly used to designate the parties to a transaction involving life insurance. The *insurer* is the company that issues a life insurance policy and the *insured* is the person whose life is insured and upon whose death a specified sum is payable under the terms of the policy. An insured may, or may not, have been the *applicant,* who originally applied for issuance of the policy. Upon the death of the insured the death benefit (policy proceeds) is payable to the *beneficiary* designated in the policy or in a change of beneficiary form. If the primary beneficiary is an individual, it is wise to designate a secondary, or contingent, beneficiary to whom the proceeds will be paid if the primary beneficiary does not survive the insured. Under the terms of modern policies the *owner,* who may or may not be the insured, has the unrestricted right to change the beneficiary unless the beneficiary has been irrevocably designated. The irrevocable designation of a beneficiary in effect makes that person the owner of the policy but is seldom done because the substantive and tax law consequences are not entirely clear.

As a rule the lawyer or a legal assistant should assemble data regarding all existing policies of insurance on the client's life for purposes of analysis and future reference. Reliable data regarding some items of information, such as the beneficiary designations, current policy values, and outstanding loan balances may only be available from the insurers. The necessary information is usually provided promptly by the insurer in response to a letter signed by the owner of the policy that encloses an appropriate data collection form. A form letter can be used for that purpose. The use of a data collection form is convenient and assures that the necessary data will be obtained for each policy.

The data form should generally contain the following items: (1) insurer and number of policy; (2) type of policy (term, ordinary life, endowment, etc.); (3) face amount; (4) amount of premium and source of payment; (5) dividend option selected; (6) accidental death benefit; (7) waiver of premium in event of disability; (8) original applicant; (9) current owner of policy; (10) successive owner of policy (if designated); (11) current beneficiary designation; (12) current cash surrender value; and (13) amount of policy loans, if any, and interest rate. The lawyer should also record the place where the client keeps the policies. Some additional data should be collected for special types of policies and when policies have been assigned to a trust. It is important to know the current status of beneficiary designations, policy loans, etc., in order to integrate life insurance fully into the client's estate plan. To preserve the integrity and value of a plan, the client should be cautioned not to change beneficiary designations, to assign policies, or to take other significant action with respect to life insurance without consulting the lawyer in advance.

§6.2. *Basic Functions of Life Insurance*

Life insurance is usually purchased in order to provide funds with which to (1) pay taxes, costs, and expenses of an illiquid estate; (2) fund a buy-sell agreement or other business-related transaction; or (3) support the dependents of the insured. In any case, the ownership and beneficiary designations can often be arranged so that none of the proceeds are includible in the insured's gross estate even though the insured pays the premiums. Cash value life insurance (ordinary life insurance, limited-pay life and endowment insurance) is also sometimes acquired as a personal investment because the earnings on the reserve of the policy can accumulate free of tax until withdrawal. Finally, life insurance is often purchased in the business setting as an employee benefit. For example, an employer may provide employees with §79 group-term insurance as a fringe benefit. *See* §§6.53 to 6.59, *infra.*

Additional insurance is often not needed to fund the costs of final illness and funeral, debts, death taxes, and administration expenses. However, life insurance is a popular way for persons with illiquid estates to provide funds with which to meet those costs. In specific cases it may be purchased to avoid the forced liquidation of the decedent's interest in a closely held business or other illiquid assets such as unimproved real property. Insurance may be needed although the immediate post-mortem demand for funds can be reduced through special use valuation under §2032A, redemption of stock under §303, or deferral of estate tax payment under §§6166. *See* §§11.14 to 11.21, 11.26 to 11.32, and §12.18, *infra.* Liquidity can, of course, be provided although the insurance is not includible in the insured's gross estate. An irrevocable life insurance trust is often used for this purpose. *See* §6.71, *infra.*

Life insurance is also sometimes purchased in order to provide funds with which to finance the acquisition of the decedent's interest in a partnership, closely held corporation, or other business enterprise. The amount needed for this purpose can be ascertained if the purchase price is fixed by the terms of a buy-sell agreement or is based upon a formula set forth in the agreement. Otherwise the amount may be roughly esti-mated. Regardless of the form of the agreement (*e.g.*, cross-purchase or entity purchase), the ownership of the insurance and the beneficiary designations should be carefully arranged to preserve the available in-come and estate tax advantages. The use of buy-sell agreements is dis-cussed at §§11.3 to 11.7, *infra.*

How Much Insurance? Most often life insurance is purchased to pro-vide for the dependents of the insured following his or her death. For this purpose some companies and agents recommend carrying insurance equal to 5 or 6 times annual earnings or spending "at least" a specified percentage of gross or net income for cash value insurance. Unfortu-nately, these simple formulae are not reliable because they have no necessary relation to the actual financial needs or circumstances of the family. Similarly, the emphasis on ordinary life insurance instead of term insurance is often misplaced.

> The bias of many agents in favor of whole life insurance also contrib-utes to the problem of underinsurance. The insurance needs of some people, especially young families with modest incomes and several small children, can be met only through the purchase of term insurance. Yet, in many cases, they may be sold insurance by an agent who has a strong philosophical and financial bias in favor of whole life insurance. FTC Re-port 93.

For the same premium a much larger amount of term insurance can be puchased on the life of a relatively young person, which generally better protects a typical young family. By way of illustration, for a male aged 35, the annual premium cost of a $50,000 5-year renewable and converttible term policy is about $200, while the annual premium on a $25,000 ordinary participating life policy is about $600. The annual cost of group-term insurance is often lower than individual term. For example, $50,000 of 5-year renewable and convertible group-term insurance is available through the American Bar Endowment, for an annual premium of about $185. In any case, it pays to shop carefully before purchasing life insurance — the price of comparable policies may vary by as much as 300%.

The amount of insurance needed to protect the family can be based upon a projection of the family's needs and an estimate of the resources that will be available to the family. A rough estimate is the best we can do because we don't know when the insured will die or what the future will bring in terms of family circumstances or general economic conditions. The extent of the imponderables is illustrated by the difference between assuming the family's needs will be affected by a 4%, 6%, or 10% rate of inflation. However, a fairly useful estimate can be made under the approach recommended by Consumers Union in a very helpful paperback book, The Consumers Union Report on Life Insurance: A Guide to Planning & Buying the Protection You Need 33-48 (rev. ed. 1977). This approach is based on the preparation of a family balance sheet that includes estimates of what the family needs to maintain its standard of living if the insured were to die tomorrow and the resources, including Social Security and pension payments, the family would have available to meet those needs. Perhaps recognizing that most Americans are under-insured, several insurance companies offer to make essentially the same calculations for prospects who provide the necessary financial data. Programs of this type are generally helpful to clients because they take into account the latest developments, such as changes in the Social Security benefit formulae, that may not be readily available to individuals.

Under the Consumers Union approach the family's needs are estimated first, including (1) the decedent's final expenses (costs of last illness and funeral, debts, estate administration expenses, and death taxes, etc.); (2) the family's basic income requirements (costs of food, clothing, recreation, etc., net of Social Security benefits and pension payments); (3) the children's education fund (cost of making higher education available to children); and (4) the surviving spouse's retirement fund (to provide for retirement of surviving spouse). Some of the calculations are a bit complex. For example, the estimate of the family's income needs should reflect the variance in the level of Social Security benefits payable, since this amount will be tied to the ages of the surviving spouse and children; it should reflect a discount (or inflation) factor that should be used when the needs are future ones, such as the cost of food and housing. The family assets are then estimated, including cash on hand and other liquid assets, such as securities, insurance proceeds, and other death benefits and equity in real estate. The insurance needed by the family is the amount by which the family's estimated needs exceeds the family's estimated assets. Unfortunately the estimates rapidly become obsolete because of changes in the family structure (number and age of children), the family fortunes, and the provisions of retirement programs, including Social Security.

Some consideration should also be given to purchasing insurance on the life of a nonemployed spouse. Insurance can be used to meet the liquidity needs that may arise if the nonemployed spouse dies first, particularly where he or she owns an estate of substantial value that produces little income. Of course, the needs were reduced somewhat by the adoption of the unlimited marital deduction in 1981. The proceeds from this kind of insurance protection may also be excluded from the employed spouse's estate where the policies are owned by their children or the trustee of an irrevocable life insurance trust. *See* §6.73, *infra*. They may also help offset the additional costs that may be incurred by a surviving spouse for child care, etc., or by the inability to file joint income tax returns.

§6.3. Types of Life Insurance

The second kind of life insurance complexity stems from the proliferation of policy types. It is not surprising that there is virtually an infinite variety of life insurance policy types, because businesses in every industry (other than the monopolies) engage in product differentiation in an attempt to avoid price competition.

But the proliferation in life insurance has reached very large proportions. There are many so-called specialty policies. These usually are designed to fit an elaborate sales presentation, rather than to perform real services for the buyer. There are also many different policies of the so-called conventional types — so many, indeed, that it is difficult to distinguish between conventional policies and specialty policies. J. M. Belth, Life Insurance: A Consumer's Handbook 180-181 (1973).

At base all life insurance policies are term insurance, which provides insurance protection alone for the specified period; cash value insurance, which combines insurance protection with an investment element; or a combination of term and cash value insurance. Term and cash value insurance are very different — each meets the needs of some persons, but neither meets the insurance needs of everyone. On the one hand, term insurance provides maximum insurance protection for the premium dollar. On the other, cash value insurance provides insurance protection and a fund that is sheltered from creditors, the earnings on which accumulate free of tax to the policy owner.

The main differences between term and cash value insurance arise from the fact that the premium on term pays only for the cost of insurance protection during the term, while the premium on cash value insurance usually remains level for the entire premium payment period. Because mortality increases with age for adults, the cost of term insurance increases with the age of the insured. What is very economical term insurance protection at age 30 or 35 can become very expensive at age 60. The premium cost of cash value insurance is initially much greater than term, but is typically much less in later years. The excess of the annual premium on cash value insurance over mortality losses, costs, and company profit is accumulated in a policy reserve used to offset the cost of insurance protection in later years and to fund the policy's surrender and loan value. Thus, in the case of cash value insurance, the amount at risk (the insurance element) decreases over time as the size of the reserve increases. In contrast, the entire amount of a term policy usually remains at risk throughout the term.

The general relationship between the amount at risk and the investment component of a typical cash value policy (an ordinary life policy) on the life of a 30-year-old male is illustrated by Graph 6-1. The graph may help to understand the basic economics of cash value insurance. Unfortunately it cannot be used to determine whether cash value insurance is appropriate for a particular client.

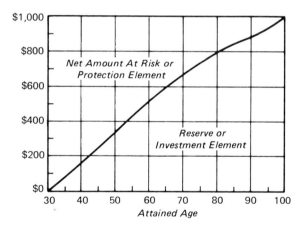

Reprinted from S. S. Huebner and Kenneth Black, Jr., *Life Insurance* 8 (9th ed. 1976), with permission of Prentice-Hall, Inc., Englewood Cliffs, N.J.

Graph 6-1

§6.4. *Cash Value Insurance*

In an age of inflation, whole-life is almost a caricature of the kind of product a buyer should wish to avoid: it is a long-term promise to pay, denominated in fixed dollars; it develops savings, in the form of "cash values," on which a policy holder earns only low rates of interest; and for all these wonderful things, the buyer gets to pay extra, laying out much more per dollar of insurance than he would if purchasing the main alternative product, term insurance, which includes no savings feature. Loomis, Life Isn't What It Used to Be, Fortune, 86, 87 (July 14, 1980).

The most common form of cash value insurance is ordinary life, which is also called straight life or whole life. Cash value policies are also sometimes called "permanent" insurance to distinguish them from term insurance that is issued for a specified term of years (*e.g.,* 1, 5, or 10 years). Of course term insurance is typically renewable without further evidence of insurability until the insured reaches an advanced age. With ordinary life, both the amount of insurance and the premium usually remain level for the duration of the policy. Premiums are payable until the insured dies or the policy matures when the insured attains a very advanced age, usually 99 or 100. If the insured lives to maturity, the face amount of insurance is paid to the policy owner and the policy terminates. Limited-pay life is a variation that involves payment of premiums for a limited period — usually a fixed number of years or until the insured attains a specified age. Policies on which premiums are payable for 20 years ("twenty-pay-life") or until the insured reaches age 65 ("pay-to-sixty-five") are common examples of limited-pay policies. The premium on a limited-pay policy is higher than on an ordinary life policy in the same amount, but the cash value of the limited-pay policy usually builds up faster. The final major form is the endowment policy, which provides for payment of the face amount to the policy owner when the insured attains a specified age, usually planned to coincide with the time of retirement. Premiums are payable until the policy endows or the insured dies. Of course, if the insured dies prior to endowment the face amount of insurance is payable to the designated beneficiary. The premiums on endowment policies are usually very high — substantially higher than on either of the other forms.

Variable life insurance is a slightly different type of ordinary life insurance that is now available. It has a level premium and a death benefit that may increase or decrease, but not below a specified minimum amount, in accordance with the investment experience of the individual account established for the policy. Another type of variable policy may also become available, one on which the death benefit remains constant, but the amount of the premium varies according to the success of investments attributable to the policy. The variable life plans described in Rev. Rul. 79-87, 1979-1 C.B. 73, provide for the net annual premium to be allocated to a separate account, which is invested primarily in equity securities in the discretion of the insurer. The cash surrender value, and presumably the loan value, may also increase or decrease depending upon investment experience, but with no guaranteed minimum. Whether or not variable life insurance will succeed in protecting the real value of the death benefit from the ravages of inflation is unknown, but at least the face amount is guaranteed. From the investment perspective, variable insurance is comparable to a mutual fund, which may offer a more direct and less expensive way of investing in equity securities. See also the discussion of universal life insurance at §6.63, *infra*.

§6.5. Term Insurance

Term insurance, which may be issued either on an individual or a group basis, provides insurance protection for the period specified in the policy, which is usually a term of 1, 5, or 10 years. It is often called "pure" insurance, because it does not involve any investment component or nonforfeiture values. Unlike cash value insurance, term insurance does not provide any loan or surrender value that can be reached in case of financial emergency. Viewed in its simplest terms, the full face amount of the insurance is at risk each term.

If term insurance is guaranteed renewable, it may be continued for successive terms without further evidence of insurability until final termination of the coverage, usually at age 65 or 70. If the amount of the term insurance remains the same, the premium will increase with each renewal as the insured grows older. If the insurance is not guaranteed renewable, the insurance protection will lapse at the end of the term and a new policy will be issued only upon showing evidence of insurability. Guaranteed renewability is desirable in order to be able to continue the insurance regardless of the state of the insured's health. Term insurance is also often convertible during the term into any regularly issued form of endowment or whole life policy issued by the insurer. In case of conversion the premium on the new policy is usually based upon the insured's attained age at the time of conversion and not the insured's age at the time the term policy was originally issued. A conversion right is also generally desirable because it can be used to continue the insurance on a permanent basis. Overall, renewable and convertible term insurance is often the best buy for a relatively young person who wants to obtain the maximum amount of life insurance protection at the lowest cost.

Basically, the cost of term insurance is determined by the amount of death benefits the insurer expects to pay for the group of insured lives according to its mortality tables and the projected amount of other costs and expenses. Because the mortality rate for adults increases with age, the cost of a fixed amount of life insurance increases as the insured grows older. By way of illustration, based upon the Commissioner's 1958 Standard Ordinary Mortality Table, an insurer would expect 3 persons out of a group of 1,000 aged 35 to die over a 1-year period. Accordingly, the insurer would have to charge a premium of \$30 merely to cover the cost of death benefits that would be payable under \$10,000 1-year term policies issued to a group of 1,000 persons of that age. Based upon the same table the insurer would expect 4 persons to die in a year out of a group of 1,000 persons aged 40; 6 persons out of a group aged 45; 9 out of a group aged 50; 13 out of a group aged 55, and 20 out of a group aged 60. In order to cover the death benefit alone, the annual premium on a \$10,000 1-year term policy would be at least \$40 at age 40, \$60 at age 45, \$90 at age 50, \$130 at age 55, and \$200 at age 60.

Decreasing Term. In the case of decreasing term insurance the premium remains the same over time, but the face amount of insurance decreases. Decreasing term is often used to provide for payment of the balance of a mortgage if the primary breadwinner in a family dies prior to its satisfaction. Terms of from 5 to 30 years are usually available for this purpose, depending somewhat upon the age of the insured at the time of issue. However, it is usually less expensive for an individual to buy decreasing term directly than it is to buy the insurance through the mortgagor or other creditor.

Group-Term. Very economical guaranteed renewable and convertible group-term insurance is often available through an employer, professional associations, or other membership groups. Many group plans do not require evidence of insurability for persons under age 40 who buy a limited amount of group-term coverage when the plan is first made available or during some subsequent enrollment periods. In many cases group-term insurance fits well into an estate plan because of its low cost, its general assignability, and its small value for gift tax purposes.

§6.6. Common Policy Riders

Insurers typically offer at least 2 riders that can be added at a small increase in cost to most term and cash value policies — the accidental death benefit rider and the waiver of premium rider.

Accidental Death. Under the accidental death benefit rider, commonly called the "double indemnity clause," an additional death benefit equal to the face amount will be paid in the event the insured dies as the result of an accidental injury. Some clauses provide for triple indemnity if the insured dies as a result of injuries suffered while riding on a bus, train, plane, or other licensed public conveyance. The cost of the rider is usually about one dollar per year for each thousand dollars of accidental death benefit, but it is questionable whether it is a wise purchase for most persons. In truth, a double indemnity rider does not provide insurance protection that can be relied upon in all cases to meet the needs of the survivors. Instead, it is essentially a gamble that the insured will die as the result of an accident, which is highly unlikely in any given case.

Waiver of Premium. The typical waiver of premium rider provides that the insurer will waive payment of all premiums falling due under the policy while the insured is totally and permanently disabled prior to a certain age — usually 65. This type of rider also typically comes into effect only if the disability occurs prior to age 60 or 65 and it lasts for 6 months or more. The value of the rider depends largely upon the limitations applicable to it and its cost, both of which vary substantially from policy to policy. Stripped to its essentials, the rider is a mini-disability policy. The cost of the rider varies with the age and occupation of the insured and from company to company. Some advisors consider the rider to provide useful additional protection against disability. However, the same coverage might be available at lower cost by increasing the amount of disability insurance carried by the insured instead of purchasing the waiver of premium provision.

§6.7. *Participating and Nonparticipating Policies*

Policies upon which the insurer may pay annual dividends, usually beginning after the second or third policy year, are called participating policies. Most cash value policies issued by mutual insurance companies and some issued by stock companies are participating policies. Some term policies are also participating, but most are not. Although participating policies generally do not guarantee that any dividends will be paid, the amounts paid in dividends can be quite substantial.

The initial premium on participating policies is generally higher than for nonparticipating policies, but the long run cost of participating policies is often much lower. In effect, the dividends represent a refund of excess premiums previously paid on a policy and part of the income derived from investing the excess. Consistent with that analysis, dividends are not taxable income until the amount recovered by the policy owner exceeds the premiums or other consideration paid for the policy. *See* §6.41, *infra.* For purposes of setting the premium on nonparticipating policies some insurers assume a rate of return of only 2 to 3%, which makes the premium actually exceed the premium on participating policies after a short time. The Federal Trade Commission (FTC) staff has pointed out that "[n]on-participating cash value insurance policies are a low-yield, fixed-dollar saving medium, uniquely unsuited to cope with accelerating inflation." FTC Report at 37.

Participating cash value policies generally give the policy owner 4 options regarding the use of the dividends: (1) to receive payment of the dividend in cash; (2) to apply the dividends against current premium costs; (3) to leave the dividends with the company at interest; or (4) to use the dividends to purchase additional paid-up insurance. Ordinary life policies issued in recent years generally include a fifth dividend option, which permits the dividends to be used to purchase 1-year term insurance. The fifth dividend option is a key feature of some plans, such as the minimum deposit plans discussed at §6.61, *infra,* and is very useful, particularly if the option can be exercised without further evidence of insurability.

It is often tempting to take dividends in cash or to apply them in reduction of the amount of the premium necessary to continue a policy. However, these may be poor choices. Instead, the dividends might better be used to buy additional paid-up insurance or 1-year term insurance that will help maintain the real value of the insurance protection provided by the policy against the attrition of inflation. There is usually little or no reason to leave dividends at interest with the insurer at a low guaranteed rate of interest, especially since the interest is fully taxable.

§6.8. *Life Insurance Agents*

Life insurance agents most often recommend that prospects buy ordinary life insurance instead of term insurance. This recommendation may be based upon a sincere belief in the superior quality of ordinary life insurance and on the importance of life insurance as an investment. Ordinary life and term are different types of insurance, but both are generally sold by the same companies, which indicates that they are both reliable. Objectively speaking, it is doubtful (1) whether ordinary life is inherently superior and (2) whether cash value life insurance is a wise investment for most persons, particularly during periods of high inflation. Individual life insurance purchasers would usually be much better off financially if they bought term insurance and invested the difference in ways that provided a better return than a cash value policy. For example, certificates of deposit, money market funds, or high quality bonds generally provide a much higher, and equally secure, return. However, some purchasers of term insurance would not save the difference, and, of those who did, some would make poor investments. In contrast, cash value life insurance involves forced savings that are readily available. Of course, before buying a policy the client should be satisfied that the insurer is reliable and financially sound.

Agents are also inevitably influenced somewhat by the higher commissions paid on sales of cash value life insurance. An agent typically receives a commission of between 55 and 60% of the first year's premium on an ordinary life policy and about 35 to 40% on a term policy. FTC Report at 86. Because the premium rate for ordinary life is often several times that of term insurance, the agent has a powerful incentive to oversell ordinary life insurance.

§6.9. *Community Property*

If a married client lived in a community property jurisdiction at any time during his or her marriage, the lawyer must be aware of the need to characterize the client's life insurance as separate or community property. The proper characterization is important for tax and nontax purposes. For example, under the law of most community property states the character of a policy determines the extent to which the insured spouse has the power, acting alone, to designate the beneficiary. The character of a policy may also affect the disposition of the policy in the event the marriage is dissolved. Perhaps most important, it determines the extent to which the interests in the policy, or its proceeds, are subject to state and federal gift and death taxes. In general the state law characterization of a policy is accepted and followed for federal tax purposes. *E.g.*, Scott v. Commissioner, 374 F.2d 154, 157 (9th Cir. 1967).

Happily, insurance is often characterized without difficulty — it is either entirely community or entirely separate under the rules of all community property states. By way of illustration, a policy purchased by the insured prior to marriage is entirely separate property if the insured makes all subsequent premium payments from separate property. Conversely, a policy purchased during marriage is entirely community property if all premiums are paid with community funds.

Serious problems of characterization may arise when premiums on a policy are paid partly with separate funds and partly with community funds. In those cases the community property states apply a variety of rules. The 3 main rules are: (1) the inception-of-title rule, (2) the apportionment rule, and (3) the risk payment doctrine. A lawyer who understands the basic features of those rules will be able to recognize and deal with most common problems of characterization — even though the law in most states is still evolving and the outcome in certain circumstances is uncertain.

§6.10. *Community Property: Inception-of-Title Rule*

The inception-of-title rule is generally applied by Arizona, Louisiana, New Mexico, and Texas to determine the character of cash value life insurance. Under it the insurance policy and its proceeds retain the original character of the policy regardless of the source of subsequent premium payments. Thus, if a policy is acquired prior to marriage, the policy remains separate property although some later premiums are paid

with community property funds. However, in such a case the community
is usually entitled to reimbursement out of the insurance proceeds for
premiums that were paid with community funds. *See, e.g.,* McCurdy v.
McCurdy, 372 S.W.2d 381 (Tex. Civ. App., 1963, writ refused). The
community's claim for reimbursement is reflected as a reduction in the
amount of the insurance that is includible in the insured's gross estate.
Thus, where the community paid $12,000 of the premiums on a
$100,000 separate policy, $88,000 was includible in the insured's estate
as insurance (§2042) and one-half of the reimbursement was includible
as "owned" property (§2033). Rev. Rul. 80-242, 1980-2 C.B. 276. On the
other hand, if the separate property funds of one spouse are used to pay
premiums on a community owned policy without the intention of making a gift to the other spouse, the spouse whose funds were used is
entitled to reimbursement for one-half of the amount of the payments.
Comment, Community and Separate Property Interests in Life Insurance Proceeds: A Fresh Look, 51 Wash. L. Rev. 351, 356 (1976).

This rule is criticized in W. deFuniak & M. Vaughn, Principles of
Community Property §79 (2d ed. 1971), as inconsistent with basic principles of community property. The authors favor the apportionment
rule, which allocates interests in a policy according to the portion of the
premiums that were paid with separate and community funds respectively.

§6.11. Community Property: Apportionment Rule

California and Washington apportion both cash value and term policies
between separate and community according to the character of the
funds used to pay the premiums. Modern Woodman of America v. Gray,
299 P. 754 (Cal. App. 1931); Small v. Bartyzel, 177 P.2d 391 (Wash.
1947). The application of this rule to cash value policies is consistent with
the basic principle that "where separate or community property is used
to acquire other property, the latter partakes of the same nature as that
of the property used for its acquisition." W. deFuniak & M. Vaughn,
Principles of Community Property §79 (2d ed. 1971). It is questionable
whether the same rule should apply to term policies: The payment of a
premium on a term policy merely provides insurance protection for that
period — when the term ends the policy has no value in the ordinary
case. Of course, the renewal right may have substantial value if the
insured is terminally ill or is no longer insurable. Logically, at the expiration of the term there is no asset that is properly subject to apportionment. As explained below, the risk payment doctrine does a more
satisfactory job of characterizing the proceeds of term insurance.

Example 6-1. H, a resident of California, purchased a $25,000 non-
participating cash value life insurance policy on which he paid 5

annual premiums prior to his marriage to W. Five subsequent premiums were paid with their community property funds. Under the apportionment rule at the end of 10 years the policy is one-half the separate property of H and one-half the community property of H and W.

Thus far neither Idaho nor Nevada has adopted a general characterization rule. Often in the past Idaho courts have followed California or Washington precedents while Nevada courts have frequently followed Texas law.

§6.12. Community Property: Risk Payment Doctrine

The inception-of-title states (Arizona, Louisiana, New Mexico, and Texas) and Idaho characterize the proceeds of term insurance under the risk payment doctrine. Under that doctrine life insurance proceeds are characterized as separate or community according to the source of the last premium payment. For example, if the last premium on a term policy was paid with community property funds, the proceeds of the policy are characterized as entirely community property. This approach recognizes that the current protection provided by term insurance depends entirely upon the last premium payment. *See* Phillips v. Welborn, 552 P.2d 471 (N.M. 1976). "Premium payments in years gone by are not considered important. This is in contrast to the necessity of knowing the sources of past years' premium payments before applying the inception of title and apportionment rules." Comment, Community and Separate Property Interests in Life Insurance Proceeds: The Risk Payment Doctrine in State Courts and Its Federal Estate Tax Consequences, 52 Wash. L. Rev. 67, 69 (1976). Because each premium payment provides only insurance protection for the period and does not contribute cumulatively to the value of a term policy, it seems more appropriate to apply the risk payment doctrine.

> **Problem 6-1.** Five years before H and W married, H purchased a nonparticipating $25,000 ordinary life policy on which the annual premium was $500. Soon after they were married W purchased a $25,000 nonparticipating ordinary life policy on which the annual premium was $400. All of the subsequent premiums on both policies were paid with the earnings of H and W, which were community property under the governing state law. In addition, W's job, which she took 2 years after their marriage, provides her with $50,000 of group-term insurance. Assuming that H and W have been married for 5 years, how would the ordinary life policies be characterized under the inception-of-title rule? Under the apportionment rule? What characterization would be given the group-term policy under the 3 rules?

B. ESTATE TAXATION OF LIFE INSURANCE

§6.13. History

Since 1918 life insurance has been subject to special estate tax rules, with substantial changes being made in 1942 and 1954. In brief, between 1918 and 1942 the proceeds of life insurance policies were includible in the estate of the insured if the insurance had been taken out by the insured decedent. The proceeds were fully includible if they were receivable by the executor of the insured, but they were includible only to the extent they exceeded $40,000 if they were receivable by others. Because of uncertainties about the criteria that should be used in determining when insurance had been taken out by the decedent, the Revenue Act of 1942 repealed that requirement. At the same time Congress also repealed the $40,000 exemption and changed the law regarding the inclusion of life insurance receivable by other beneficiaries to require inclusion if the insured had paid premiums on the insurance or held incidents of ownership in the policy at the time of death. Under the first ground of inclusion, called the premium payment test, insurance was includible in the insured's gross estate in the proportion that premiums paid by the insured bore to the total premiums paid on the policy.

> **Example 6-2.** In 1943 X paid the first $1,000 premium on a $50,000 policy on his life and then irrevocably assigned all of his interests in it to Y. Thereafter X paid 4 more annual premiums and Y paid 5. When X died in 1952 the $50,000 proceeds were paid to Y. Under the premium payment test one-half of the proceeds were includible in X's gross estate because he had paid one-half of the total premiums. Under the current provisions of §2035 presumably none of the premiums paid by X would be included in his gross estate and none of the proceeds would be included under §2042. As noted below, insurance transferred by the insured within 3 years of death is included in the insured's estate under §2035(d)(2).

The 1954 Code eliminated the premium payment test, but retained the incidents of ownership rule with one minor change. Accordingly, since 1954 insurance receivable by other beneficiaries has not been includible in the insured's gross estate merely because the insured paid some of the premiums. This change opened an important loophole, but the unification of the gift and estate tax laws in 1976 reduced its significance. Under the unified tax structure the amount of any post-1976 taxable gifts, including ones that result from premium payments during the lifetime of the insured, are included in the donor's tax base at death. Also, the proceeds of policies transferred by the insured within 3 years of death are included under §2035. Under the changes made by the 1981 Act premiums paid by the insured within 3 years of death generally are not included. *See* §6.22, *infra.*

§6.14. Insurance Receivable by or for the Benefit of the Estate (§2042(1))

Under §2042(1) insurance on a decedent's life is included in the insured's gross estate to the extent it is "receivable by the executor." However, insurance is not includible if it is payable to the estate in form and the state law requires it to be paid to the insured's surviving spouse or children. Webster v. Commissioner, 120 F.2d 514 (5th Cir. 1941).

Section 2042(1) requires inclusion although the insured neither held any incidents of ownership in a policy nor paid any premiums on it. Thus, the proceeds of a policy owned and controlled by a third party are includible if they are payable to the decedent's personal representative for the benefit of the estate. Draper v. Commissioner, 536 F.2d 944 (1st Cir. 1976). The rule may seem inconsistent with the basic estate tax approach of taxing only property owned by the decedent at death or transferred by the decedent with some retained interest or control over it, but it is consistent with the treatment of general powers of appointment under §2041.

> **Example 6-3.** X purchased a policy on the life of her brother, B, and paid all of the premiums on the policy until B's death. The proceeds were paid to B's personal representative in accordance with the terms of the policy. The proceeds are fully includible in B's gross estate although he neither paid any premiums on the policy nor had any incidents of ownership in the policy.

Insurance is also considered to be receivable by the executor if it is paid to a creditor in satisfaction of a loan or other indebtedness of the insured. Bintliff v. United States, 462 F.2d 403 (5th Cir. 1972); Reg. §20.2042-1(b)(1). Thus, the proceeds of "creditor" life insurance are includible in the gross estate of the insured to the extent they are applied in satisfaction of the insured's debts.

Proceeds receivable by other beneficiaries are includible under §2042(1) to the extent they are subject to a legal obligation to apply the proceeds for the benefit of the estate. Thus, although the property of a trust would not otherwise be includible in the insured's gross estate, the insurance receivable by a trustee is includible to the extent it must be used to pay debts, taxes, and other expenses of the insured's estate. In such a case the proceeds should not be includible if the trustee is merely authorized, or given discretion, to expend the corpus of the trust in satisfaction of the estate's obligations. *Cf.* Rev. Rul. 73-404, 1973-2 C.B. 319, and Estate of Joseph E. Salsbury, 34 T.C.M. 1441 (1975) (both of which dealt with a comparable issue involving exclusion of qualified plan proceeds under §2039(c)). In order to preserve the estate tax benefit of an insurance trust, the trustee should be prohibited from using the proceeds to pay obligations of the estate. Planning with irrevocable life insurance trusts is discussed at §6.71, *infra.*

Insurance owned by a person other than the insured and payable to a revocable trust created by the insured is not includible in the insured's gross estate under §§2041 or 2042. Margrave v. Commissioner, 618 F.2d 34 (8th Cir. 1980); Rev. Rul. 81-166, 1981-1 C.B. 477. The cited ruling recognizes that the policy owner's revocable designation of the trustee as beneficiary of the insurance does not constitute a gift. However, the payment of the proceeds to the trust may involve a gift to any others who are beneficiaries of the trust (*e.g.*, the remaindermen). Where the policy owner is an income beneficiary of the trust, the portion of the trust corpus attributable to his or her contributions to the trust (*i.e.*, the policy proceeds) is includible in his or her gross estate under §2036(a)(1). *See* Rev. Rul. 81-166, *supra.*

§6.15. Insurance Receivable by or for the Benefit of the Estate: Community Property Policies

If a policy was owned as community property, only the decedent's one-half interest in the proceeds is generally includible in the insured's gross estate under §2042(1). Reg. §20.2042-1(b)(2). The other one-half of the proceeds is not includible in the insured's estate because it belonged to the surviving spouse from the outset. However, if the full amount of the proceeds were paid to the insured's personal representative for the benefit of the estate, the full amount might be includible in the insured's gross estate. This issue could be presented if the noninsured spouse consented to the designation of the insured's personal representative as beneficiary and the proceeds were all available for payment of debts, taxes, and expenses of the estate. In contrast, the share of the proceeds attributable to the surviving spouse's community interest in the policy is not includible in the insured's gross estate where the survivor has the right to recover it from the estate. *See* Reg. §20.2042-1(b)(2).

§6.16. Incidents of Ownership (§2042(2))

We hold that estate tax liability for policies "with respect to which the decedent possessed at his death any of the incidents of ownership" depends on a general, legal power to exercise ownership, without regard to the owner's ability to exercise it at a particular moment. Commissioner v. Estate of Noel, 380 U.S. 678, 684 (1965).

The very phrase "incidents of ownership" connotes something partial, minor, or even fractional in its scope. It speaks more of possibility than probability. United States v. Rhode Island Hospital Trust Company, 355 F.2d 7, 10 (1st Cir. 1966).

Insurance proceeds are includible in the insured's gross estate under §2042(2) if, at the time of death, the insured possessed *any* incident of ownership in the policy, exercisable alone or in conjunction with any other person. The most common problems encountered under this subsection have been concerned with determining what constitutes an incident of ownership and under what circumstances an incident is considered to be exercisable by the insured.

Policy Facts and Intent Facts. Whether or not an individual possesses an incident of ownership in a policy is determined in most instances according to the terms of the policy (the "policy facts") and not the intention of the parties (the "intent facts"). Commissioner v. Estate of Noel, 380 U.S. 678 (1965). Accordingly, if a policy permits the insured to exercise an incident of ownership, the proceeds of the policy are includible in the insured's gross estate. Some courts have recognized an exception, however, where the insurance contract does not reflect the instructions of the parties, "as where an agent, on his own initiative, inserts a reservation of right to change a beneficiary contrary to the intentions which had been expressed to him." United States v. Rhode Island Hospital Trust Co., 355 F.2d 7, 13 (1st Cir. 1966).

What Are Incidents of Ownership. The term "incidents of ownership" is not defined in the Code, but the regulations describe the types of interests that are treated as incidents of ownership for purposes of §2042(2):

[T]he term "incidents of ownership" is not limited in its meaning to ownership of the policy in the technical legal sense. Generally speaking, the term has reference to the right of the insured or his estate to the economic benefits of the policy. Thus, it includes the power to change the beneficiary, to surrender or cancel the policy, to assign the policy, to revoke an assignment, to pledge the policy for a loan, or to obtain from the insurer a loan against the surrender value of the policy, etc. Reg. §20.2042-1(c)(2).

The portion of the regulation that links incidents of ownership to the economic benefits of a policy has caused some confusion. In one view a power is not an incident of ownership unless it can be exercised for the benefit of the insured. A competing view is that a power can constitute an incident of ownership although it cannot benefit the insured or the estate of the insured. For example, the courts have divided on the question of whether the bare power to select a settlement option under an employer-provided insurance plan is an incident of ownership. In Estate of Lumpkin v. Commissioner, 474 F.2d 1092 (5th Cir. 1973), the proceeds of a group-term policy were included in the gross estate of the insured because he had the power to vary the time at which the benefits would be paid. The court reasoned that inclusion under §2042 was justified by analogy to §§2036 and 2038 (which require the inclusion of property over which a decedent retained the power to vary the time of enjoyment). Critics hastened to point out that §§2036 and 2038 deal with property transferred by a decedent and that the insured in *Lumpkin* had never held or transferred any interest in the policy. Inclusion of the proceeds of the same group-term policy was rejected by the Third Circuit, Estate of Connelly v. Commissioner, 551 F.2d 545 (1977), which held that the insured's right "to select a settlement option with the mutual agreement of his employer and the insurer did not give him a substantial degree of control sufficient to constitute an incident of ownership." *Id.* at 552. The IRS has announced that it will not follow the *Connelly* decision outside the Third Circuit. Rev. Rul. 81-128, 1981-1 C.B. 469.

Powers to Terminate Membership in Group Plans. The power to cancel employer-provided insurance by terminating employment is not an incident of ownership. Landorf v. United States, 408 F.2d 461 (Ct. Cl. 1969). Rev. Rul. 69-54, 1969-1 C.B. 221 indicated otherwise, but the position was abandoned in Rev. Rul. 72-307, 1972-1 C.B. 307. The latter ruling recognized that "[a]n insured's power to cancel his insurance coverage by terminating his employment is a collateral consequence of the power that every employee has to terminate his employment." It continued to say that "[t]he examples in section 20.2042-1(c) of the regulations, on the other hand, concern powers that directly affect the insurance policy or the payment of its proceeds without potentially costly related consequences. Where the power to cancel an insurance policy is exercisable only by terminating employment, it is not deemed to be an incident of ownership in the policy." In light of this ruling it was surprising that the IRS later contended that an employee's right to convert group insurance to individual insurance upon the termination of employment was an incident of ownership. The contention was rejected by the Tax Court, which said that "[i]f quitting one's job is too high a price to pay for the right to cancel an insurance policy, it is likewise too high a price to pay for the right to convert to another policy." Estate of James Smead, 78 T.C. 43, 52 (1982).

Problem 6-2. W purchased a group policy through her university's alumnae association and assigned all her interest in the insurance to an irrevocable life insurance trust of which her sister, S, was the trustee and her adult children, A and B, were the beneficiaries. The group policy provided that the insurance coverage would continue as long as the insured remained a member of the association and the annual premiums were paid. S continued to pay the premiums until W died 4 years after the assignment. Are the proceeds includible in W's estate under §2042(2)? Would the issue be the same if the insurance were provided by a group in which the insured was required to retain membership in order to practice a profession (*e.g.*, membership in an integrated bar)?

In Rev. Rul. 79-46, 1979-1 C.B. 303, the IRS ruled that an employee's power to prevent cancellation of insurance coverage by purchasing the policy from his employer for its cash surrender value if the employer elected to terminate the policy was an incident of ownership. That position was rejected in Estate of John Smith, 73 T.C. 307 (1979), because of the contingent nature of the power: "Whatever rights Smith may have acquired under paragraph seven of his employment agreement were contingent ones dependent on an event which never occurred and over which he had no control." Of course, had Smith controlled his corporate employer through direct or indirect ownership of more than 50% of its stock, the incidents of ownership held by it would have been attributed to him. *See* Reg. §20.2042-1(c)(6) and §6.19, *infra*. A contingent power of the type involved in *Smith* must be distinguished from a power that is jointly exercisable by the insured and another person. *See, e.g.,* Commissioner v. Estate of Karagheusian, 233 F.2d 197 (2d Cir. 1956).

Negative or "Veto" Powers. A negative power, such as a power to prevent another person from changing the beneficiary, surrendering the policy, or exercising another incident of ownership, is itself an incident of ownership. *Eleanor M. Schwager,* 64 T.C. 781 (1975); Rev. Rul. 75-70, 1975-1 C.B. 301. Thus, when a policy is owned by another person, the insured generally should not have the right to veto a change in beneficiary, a surrender of the policy, or an assignment of it. However, an earlier case held that the power to veto a sale of assets by the trustee of an irrevocable life insurance trust was not an incident of ownership. Estate of Carlton v. Commissioner, 298 F.2d 415 (2d Cir. 1962). If such a power must be included in a trust, it should not extend to insurance on the power-holder's life because of the possibility that it would be considered to be an incident of ownership in policies held by the trustee.

§6.17.   *Incidents of Ownership: Reversionary Interests (§2042(2))*

The term "incidents of ownership" includes a reversionary interest in a policy or its proceeds, whether arising by the express terms of the policy or other instrument or by operation of law, if the value of the reversionary interest exceeded 5% immediately before the death of the insured. §2042(2). However, the insured is not considered to have an incident of ownership in a policy if the power to obtain the cash surrender value existed in some other person immediately before the insured's death and was exercisable by such other person alone and in all events. Reg. §20.2042-1(c)(3). The regulations also provide that the terms "reversionary interest" and "incidents of ownership" do not include the possibility that the decedent might receive a policy or its proceeds through the estate of another person, or as a surviving spouse under a statutory right of election or a similar right. *Id.*

The reversionary interest rule was applied in Rev. Rul. 76-113, 1976-1 C.B. 277, to a marital property settlement agreement under which the insured was required to name his former spouse a beneficiary of several life insurance policies for so long as she lived and remained unmarried. When the insured died the proceeds were paid to his former spouse as beneficiary. The proceeds of the policies were includible in the insured's gross estate because the possibility that his former spouse would predecease him or remarry prior to his death exceeded 5% immediately prior to his death. Under the terms of the decree the policies would return to the insured or to his estate or would be subject to a power of disposition by him if his former spouse predeceased him or remarried prior to his death. The ruling recognizes that in some cases an offsetting deduction is allowable under §2053 when the proceeds are includible in the insured's estate. For example, where the decree requires the payment of a specified sum upon the insured's death to a former spouse and the insured provided for payment of the obligation by purchasing insurance, a deduction is allowable under §2053(a)(3) as a claim against the insured's estate. Also, where the insurance proceeds that are included in the decedent's estate are paid to a former spouse in satisfaction of an indebtedness created in settlement of the decedent's marital obligations, the obligation is deductible under §2053(a)(4). If the obligation to provide the insurance is embodied not in a divorce decree, but in a property settlement agreement, a deduction is allowed only if the agreement was contracted bona fide and for an adequate and full consideration in money or money's worth, as required by §2053(c)(1). *Gray v. United States*, 541 F.2d 228 (9th Cir. 1976). Where the divorce court lacks power to alter the terms of the settlement, the obligation is deemed to be created by the property settlement agreement and not by the divorce decree. *Id.*

Rev. Rul. 78-379, 1978-2 C.B. 238, denied a deduction under §2053 for insurance proceeds that were paid to the insured decedent's minor children pursuant to a property settlement agreement and divorce decree under which the decedent's obligation to provide child support terminated at death. However, the ruling recognizes that a deduction is allowable if the divorce court has power to change the property settlement agreement because it is then a judicially imposed obligation.

Similarly, a deduction should be allowed if an obligation to provide life insurance is imposed in a support decree. LR 8128005.

In order to avoid the reach of the reversionary interest rule, the trust or other instrument governing the ownership of the policy should not allow the insurance to return to the insured or become subject to the insured's control. For example, a rider might be added to the policy specifying that the policy would be owned by a person other than the insured if the former spouse dies or remarries prior to the death of the insured. Note, too, that a decree of divorce or a property settlement agreement may sufficiently divest the insured spouse of the incidents of ownership so that the policy proceeds will not be includible in his or her gross estate. Estate of Theodore E. Beauregard, Jr., 74 T.C. 603 (1980).

§6.18. Incidents of Ownership Held in a Fiduciary Capacity

The regulations require the inclusion of the proceeds of a policy over which the insured held an incident of ownership as trustee, whether or not the incident could be exercised for the insured's own economic benefit. Reg. §20.2042-1(c)(4); Rev. Rul. 76-261, 1976-2 C.B. 276. The regulation has been upheld by two cases in the Fifth Circuit in which the incidents of ownership could not be exercised for the benefit of the insured-fiduciary. Rose v. United States, 511 F.2d 259 (1975); Terriberry v. United States, 517 F.2d 286 (1975), *cert. denied*, 424 U.S. 977 (1976). Decisions by several other courts uphold inclusion in the estate of an insured-fiduciary *only* if the power could be exercised for the benefit of the insured-fiduciary. Estate of Skifter v. Commissioner, 468 F.2d 699 (2d Cir. 1972); Estate of Fruehauf v. Commissioner, 427 F.2d 80 (6th Cir. 1970); Hunter v. United States, 624 F.2d 833 (8th Cir. 1980); Estate of Gesner v. United States, 600 F.2d 1349 (Ct. Cl. 1979). Ultimately the issue will be settled by Congress or the Supreme Court. In the meantime, the insured should not hold any incidents of ownership in a policy as executor or as trustee. The power to exercise control over a policy on the life of a trustee should be vested solely in a cofiduciary or some other party.

The government might also seek to apply §2042(2) to insurance over which the decedent held an incident of ownership as custodian for a minor or as guardian for an incompetent. Accordingly, it is best not to appoint the insured to any fiduciary office with respect to policies on his or her own life.

§6.19. Attribution of Incidents of Ownership

Under Reg. §20.2042-1(c)(6) incidents of ownership held by a corporation of which the decedent was the sole or controlling shareholder are attributed to the decedent to the extent the proceeds are not paid to or applied for the benefit of the corporation. However, the power to surrender or cancel group-term life insurance as defined in §79 will not be attributed to a decedent "through his stock ownership." *Id.*

In general the proceeds of a policy are includible in the gross estate of a sole or controlling shareholder to the extent that they are paid to a personal beneficiary rather than to the corporation. Rev. Rul. 76-274, 1976-2 C.B. 278 (*Situation 1*). In applying §2042(2) it makes no difference whether the decedent was the sole shareholder or the controlling shareholder — in either case the decedent held the power to affect the disposition of the proceeds through exercise of control over the corporation. Estate of Milton L. Levy, 70 T.C. 873 (1978) (the full amount of proceeds paid to a personal beneficiary was included in the estate of the 80.4% shareholder).

Proceeds paid to or for the benefit of the corporation are not attributed to the decedent under §2042 because they are taken into account in establishing the value of the decedent's stock under §2031. *See* Reg. §20.2031-2(f).

> **Example 6-4.** D owned a controlling interest in ABC, Inc., which owned 2 policies of insurance on D's life. When D died the proceeds of Policy One were paid to her father, F, in accordance with the beneficiary designation in the policy. The proceeds of Policy Two were paid to ABC, Inc. Under §20.2042-1(c)(6) the proceeds of Policy One are includible in D's gross estate, but the proceeds of Policy Two are not. However, the proceeds of Policy Two are taken into account in valuing D's shares of ABC, Inc. stock. The proceeds along with other corporate assets are subject to any applicable discount that is applied in valuing D's shares. Estate of John L. Huntsman, 66 T.C. 861 (1976), *acq.*, 1977-1 C.B. 1.

In effect the provisions of §2042(2) and §2031 are mutually exclusive — the proceeds of a policy may be includible under either, but not both, of the sections.

For purposes of §2042 a decedent is the controlling shareholder only if the decedent owned stock that represented more than 50% of the combined total voting power of the corporation. In making that determination a decedent is treated as owning only the stock the legal title to which was held at the time of death, by (1) the decedent, or an agent or nominee of the decedent; (2) the decedent and another person jointly (but only to the extent that the decedent furnished the total consideration for purposes of §2040); (3) the trustee of a voting trust to the extent of the decedent's interest; and (4) the trustee of any other trust of which the decedent was treated as the owner under §§671 to 678. Reg. §20.2042-1(c)(6).

Incidents of ownership attributed to a controlling shareholder under

Reg. §20.2042-1(c)(6) are not subject to fiduciary duties to minority shareholders or creditors that would preclude including the insurance in the shareholder's gross estate. Estate of Milton L. Levy, 70 T.C. 873 (1978). A controlling shareholder owes fiduciary duties to minority shareholders and creditors, but some incidents held by the corporation over the insurance could be exercised in a variety of significant ways without violating those duties (*e.g.*, the right to borrow against the policy).

Stock Held as Community Property. Where the stock of a corporation is all owned by a husband and wife as their community property, it is unclear whether either spouse can be considered to be a controlling shareholder for purposes of attributing the incidents of ownership held by the corporation. In Estate of Elizabeth Lee, 69 T.C. 860 (1978), *nonacq.*, 1980-1 C.B. 2, the Tax Court held that the decedent's one-half community interest in 80% of the stock of a closely held corporation would be valued separately as a 40% minority interest. A contrary result reached by a panel of the Fifth Circuit, Estate of Bright v. Commissioner, 619 F.2d 407 (5th Cir. 1980), was overturned when the issue was considered en banc, 658 F.2d 999 (5th Cir. 1981). Despite the outcome in those two cases, the IRS will probably continue to raise the issue.

If the *Lee* and *Bright* cases are followed, less value may be included in the gross estate of a shareholder if corporate-owned insurance is paid to the shareholder's personal beneficiaries than if it were payable to the corporation. In the former case the entire amount of the insurance may escape inclusion in the shareholder's estate, whereas in the latter the insurance would be taken into account in valuing the shareholder's interest in the stock.

Insurance Owned by a Partnership. Insurance owned by a partnership is not includible in the gross estate of a deceased partner where the proceeds are applied for the benefit of the partnership. Estate of Frank H. Knipp, 25 T.C. 153 (1955), *aff'd*, 244 F.2d 436 (4th Cir.), *cert. denied*, 355 U.S. 827 (1957) (appeal involved other issues); *nonacq. on insurance issue*, 1956-2 C.B. 10, *withdrawn and acq. in result substituted*, 1959-1 C.B. 4. If the proceeds are instead payable to a personal beneficiary designated by the insured, they are includible. The reciprocal trust doctrine, discussed below, probably does not require inclusion of policies that are cross-owned by partners. Rev. Rul. 56-397, 1956-2 C.B. 599.

§6.20.   Reciprocal Trust Doctrine and Life Insurance

The "reciprocal trust" or "crossed trust" doctrine was developed to determine who would be treated as the grantor of related trusts for tax purposes. Under the doctrine, where 2 or more trusts are created by

related parties and the nominal grantor of one trust is the beneficiary of
another trust, the trusts are uncrossed. That is, each person is treated as
the grantor of the trust of which he or she is the beneficiary if the trusts
are "interrelated, and . . . the arrangement, to the extent of mutual
value, leaves the settlors in approximately the same economic position as
they would have been in had they created trusts naming themselves as
life beneficiaries." United States v. Estate of Grace, 395 U.S. 316, 324
(1969).

> **Example 6-5.** In 1980 H transferred 1,000 shares of ABC, Inc. to a
> trust of which W was named trustee and income beneficiary. At the
> same time W transferred 1,000 shares of ABC, Inc. to an identical
> trust of which H was the trustee and income beneficiary. The chil-
> dren of H and W were the remaindermen of both trusts. The trusts
> will be "uncrossed" by the reciprocal trust doctrine and H will be
> treated as the grantor of the trust of which he was the trustee and
> income beneficiary and W will be treated as the grantor of the other
> trust. Upon H's death the property of the trust of which he is
> treated as the grantor is includible in his gross estate under
> §2036(a)(1).

The doctrine may be applied although the grantors do not retain any
economic interest in the trusts. *Id.* Thus, the doctrine was applied in
Estate of Bruno Bischoff, 69 T.C. 32 (1977), where each nominal grantor
appointed the other as trustee with discretion to distribute trust property
to the beneficiaries, who were the grandchildren of the grantors. It has
also been applied where donors appoint each other as custodians of gifts
made under the Uniform Gifts to Minors Act. *See* §7.33, *infra.*

The government contends that the reciprocal trust doctrine should
also apply where a husband and wife each buy and own a policy of
insurance on the other's life. The doctrine was applied in Rev. Rul.
67-228, 1967-2 C.B. 331, where a husband and wife domiciled in Texas
each used community property funds to purchase substantially identical
policies of insurance on the life of each other and designated the unin-
sured spouse as the owner and beneficiary. The ruling concluded that in
such circumstances,

> [T]he presumption under Texas law that the policies are community prop-
> erty will prevail unless it is clearly shown that the transfers were not recip-
> rocal and that gifts were intended. Accordingly, as a community asset,
> one-half of the value of the property received as insurance on the life of
> the husband upon his death is includible in his gross estate under the
> provisions of section 2042 of the Code. Furthermore, one-half of the value
> of the policy on the life of the wife is includible in his gross estate under
> section 2033 of the Code as his interest in the community asset. 1967-2
> C.B. at 333.

In Estate of Dorothy C. Wilmot, 29 T.C.M. 1055 (1970), the court refused to consider a belated argument by the government that the reciprocal trust doctrine should be applied to policies each spouse owned on
the life of the other.

It is reasonable to apply the reciprocal trust doctrine where the insured and another person acquire similar policies on each other's lives
and the insured in fact has the power to designate the beneficiary of the
policy that is nominally owned by the other person. The doctrine should
not apply where the policies are owned by business associates in connection with a buy-out agreement. Rev. Rul. 56-397, 1956-2 C.B. 599. These
rules roughly parallel the ones under which the incidents of ownership
held by a corporation or partnership are attributed to the insured. It is
questionable whether the doctrine should apply merely because a husband and wife, or 2 other parties, each purchase a policy on the life of the
other. As some commentators have pointed out, the mutual acquisition
of life insurance policies by a husband and wife involves the acquisition
of new wealth and not the rearrangement of existing wealth. Elisaberg,
The Estate Taxation of Life Insurance: A Survey of Recent Developments, U. So. Cal. 26th Tax Inst. 1, 62-66 (1974). The cross-ownership of
life insurance policies should be recognized as a legitimate estate-
planning tool. Of course, the incentive for cross-ownership of insurance
by a husband and wife is greatly reduced by the availability of the unlimited marital deduction.

§6.21.   Transfer of a Policy within 3 Years of Death (§2035)

In general, gifts made within 3 years of the death of a donor who dies
after December 31, 1981, are not generally includible in the donor's gross
estate. §2035(d). However, insurance transferred by the insured within 3
years of death is includible in the estate of the insured. §2035(d)(2). This
result is consonant with the regulations issued prior to the 1981 Act,
under which the proceeds of a policy the insured gave away within 3
years of death are includible in his or her gross estate. See Reg.
§20.2035-1(a).

The outcome under §2035 is relatively clear where a policy owned by
the insured was transferred gratuitously within 3 years of his or her
death. Uncertainty arises where the insured participates in the acquisition of a policy in the name of another person within 3 years of his or her
death. Under some circumstances the acquisition of the policy in the
name of another person and the subsequent payment of premiums by
the insured constitute a transfer by the insured. For example, the insured was treated as having acquired and transferred a policy that was
issued to a trust at the instance of the insured within 3 years of death and
with respect to which the insured paid the premiums directly or indirectly.

The purpose of section 2035 "is to reach substitutes for testamentary dispositions and thus to prevent the evasion of the estate tax." United States v. Wells, 283 U.S. 102, 117, 51 S. Ct. 446, 451, 75 L. Ed. 867 (1931). An insured pays the premiums on a life insurance policy in order to leave the proceeds to his beneficiaries; thus where a policy is both procured at the behest of the decedent within the statutory period and where all the premiums are paid by the deceased in contemplation of death [within 3 years of death], the gift must necessarily be one of the property interest in the policy. . . . In short, what is intended with the purchase of a life insurance policy in circumstances like these is the passing of the proceeds at death. That is the equivalent of a testamentary disposition, and its taxation is precisely the object of section 2035. First National Bank of Oregon v. United States, 488 F.2d 575, 577 (9th Cir. 1973). *See also* Detroit Bank & Trust Co. v. United States, 467 F.2d 964 (6th Cir. 1972), *cert. denied,* 410 U.S. 929 (1973).

Inclusion in such case appropriately extends to the whole proceeds and not merely the amount of the premiums paid by the insured within 3 years of death.

Money given away by a decedent within 3 years of death is not includible under the general rule of §2035 if the donee independently chooses to use the funds to purchase a policy on the donor's life. "If on the other hand, decedent had given money to her children, and they, entirely on their own volition, had chosen to purchase an insurance policy on her life, it would be equally clear that only the money would have been 'transferred.' " Estate of Inez G. Coleman, 52 T.C. 921, 923 (1969), *acq.,* 1978-1 C.B. 1.

The gross estate does not include property that is transferred within 3 years of death in "any bona fide sale for an adequate and full consideration in money or money's worth." For this purpose presumably the consideration would be adequate in ordinary cases if it were equal to the value of the policy determined under Reg. §20.2031-8(a)(2) (cost of comparable contracts or interpolated terminal reserve). However, the regulation by its terms applies to the valuation of a life insurance policy on the life of a person other than the decedent. Under the primary regulation governing valuation, "all relevant facts and elements of value as of the appropriate valuation date shall be considered." Hence, it may be necessary to consider the physical condition and insurability of the insured at the time of transfer. For example, in Estate of James Stuart Pritchard, 4 T.C. 204 (1944), the terminally ill insured did not receive adequate or full consideration when he sold a $50,000 policy on his life to his wife for its cash surrender value of $10,483. Note that if a policy is sold for full value, the income tax exclusion of the proceeds might have been lost. *See* §101(a) and §6.36, *infra.*

The present form of §2035 requires inclusion of the full proceeds of a policy that is transferred within 3 years of death together with any gift tax paid by the transferor or the transferor's estate. *See* §2035(d)(2). The general inclusionary rule of §2035(a) applies to the transfer of an interest that would have been included in the transferor's gross estate under §2042 "if such interest had been retained by the decedent." §2035(d)(2). Had the transferred interest (the insurance) been retained by the decedent, the insurance would have been included in the decedent's estate under §2042(2). However, as explained below, there is a possibility that part of the proceeds is excludible where some post-assignment premiums are paid by another person. The general rule of §2035(b)(2), which permits the exclusion of transfers within 3 years of death for which no gift tax return was required (*i.e.*, ones within the annual gift tax exclusion), does not apply to "any transfer with respect to a life insurance policy." Accordingly, the proceeds of a policy transferred by the insured within 3 years of death are includible even though the value of the policy was within the allowable gift tax exclusions at the time of the transfer and no gift tax return was required to be filed. This result is consistent with the prior law and the unique character of life insurance. The application of §2035 to group-term insurance is examined at §6.59, *infra*.

Part of the proceeds of a policy transferred within 3 years of death may be excluded from the insured's estate if some of the post-assignment premiums are paid by a person other than the insured. Thus, the Tax Court has held that the insured's estate was not required to include a portion of the proceeds that bore the same relation to the total proceeds as the premium payments made by the assignee bore to the total amount of premium payments. Estate of Morris R. Silverman, 61 T.C. 338 (1973), *acq.*, 1978-1 C.B. 2, *other issues affirmed*, 521 F.2d 574 (2d Cir. 1975). In effect the court adopted the proportional premium payment rule that the government advanced in Rev. Rul. 67-463, 1967-2 C.B. 327, and abandoned in Rev. Rul. 71-497, 1971-2 C.B. 329.

> **Example 6-6.** D irrevocably assigned a $100,000 policy on his life to his sister, S, within 3 years of his death. D paid 3 $1,000 premiums on the policy prior to the assignment and S paid 2 post-assignment premiums of $1,000 each. Following D's death the proceeds were paid to S. Under *Silverman* only $\frac{3}{5}$ of the total policy proceeds are includible in D's gross estate. The entire proceeds would have been includible if D had continued to pay the premiums.

It is curious that the government acquiesced in the Tax Court's decision in *Silverman* 5 years afterward. The Court of Appeals did not pass upon the proration issue because the government did not appeal that portion of the Tax Court's decision. Indeed, the appellate court admitted "some uneasiness about the proper basis for holding that . . . [the assignee's] payments in the last six months of his father's life changes the result from the situation where a decedent continues to pay the premiums until death." 521 F.2d at 577. It also questioned whether the assignee's payment of a portion of the premiums justified excluding a proportionate part of the proceeds rather than the actual amount the assignee paid in premiums. Where the insured dies within 3 years of making a gift of insurance on his or her life, a portion of the proceeds equal to the amount of any post-gift premiums paid by the assignee should be excluded from the insured's gross estate. The exclusion of a larger amount under the *Silverman* rule is difficult to justify.

Insurance on the Life of a Person Other Than the Decedent. Insurance transferred by a decedent within 3 years of death is generally not includible in the decedent's gross estate where the insurance is on the life of another person. In such a case the insurance is not subject to the rules of §2042 that are made applicable to transfers within 3 years of death by §2035(d)(2). Instead the insurance on the life of another person is subject to the same rules that apply to cash, securities, or other property transferred by the decedent within 3 years of death. A ruling issued prior to the 1981 Act reached a contrary conclusion. It reasoned that the language of §2035(b) did not support exclusion of the insurance in such a case. Rev. Rul. 81-14, 1981-1 C.B. 456. The ruling was questionable and appears to be overturned by the provisions of §2035(d)(1). Insurance should be treated differently under §2035 according to the identity of the insured. The transfer of insurance on the transferor's life, which could reduce the size of the transferor's estate by an amount much larger than the value of the insurance at the time of transfer, should be subject to a more stringent rule. The transfer of insurance on the life of another person does not pose the same risk and should, therefore, be subject to the same rules that apply to the transfer of ordinary types of property.

§6.22. Premiums Paid within 3 Years of Death (§2035)

Prior to its amendment in 1976, §2035 required the inclusion of premiums paid within 3 years of death and in contemplation of death. "[T]he value of any premiums paid by the decedent in contemplation of death within three years of death [on policies transferred more than 3 years prior to death] is includible in his gross estate under section 2035 of the Code." Rev. Rul. 71-497, 1971-2 C.B. 329. This rule required inclusion whether or not the premium payments were within the annual gift tax exclusion. The 1976 Act amended §2035 to allow exclusion of gifts made within 3 years of death that were not required to be reported on a gift tax return. §2035(b). Under the 1978 amendment the exclusion was made inapplicable to transfers "with respect to life insurance." However, according to the House Ways and Means Committee's Report that accompanied the 1978 Act, the exclusion of §2035(b) is available with respect to "any premiums paid (or deemed paid) by the decedent within 3 years of death to the extent that such payments would not have resulted in the inclusion of the proceeds of the policy in the decedent's gross estate under the prior law." The reference in the statement to the prior law is a bit confusing because the prior law was concerned with the subjective issue of whether the transfer was made in contemplation of death. However, the statement generally supports exclusion of premium payments made within 3 years of death if no gift tax returns were required with respect to them. The pre-1982 law is illustrated by the following example:

> **Example 6-7.** In 1977 X assigned one policy he owned on his life to his daughter, D, and another to his son, S. X continued to pay the premiums of $2,500 per year on D's policy and of $3,500 per year on S's policy until his death in 1981. No federal gift tax returns were required with respect to the payments on D's policy, but returns were filed for the payments on S's policy. Neither the proceeds of D's policy nor the premiums paid on it within 3 years of death are includible in X's gross estate. The policy was transferred more than 3 years prior to death and the premium payments were within the exclusion of §2035(b). The proceeds of the policy assigned to S are not includible in X's gross estate, but the premiums paid by X within 3 years of death are includible. Note that if X had died after December 31, 1981, none of the payments would have been included in his estate.

Under the general rule of §2035(d)(1) mere premium payments made within 3 years of the donor's death are generally not includible in the donor's estate. That outcome reflects the general rule applicable to gifts and is simpler to understand and administer. Of course, inclusion could result if the premium payments would otherwise be includible under §§2036, 2037, 2038, 2041, or 2042. *See* §2035(d)(2).

§6.23. Transfer of Incidents of Ownership within 3 Years of Death (§2042(2))

Section 2042(2) requires inclusion of the proceeds of policies over which the insured "possessed at his death any of the incidents of ownership." Section 2035(d)(2) seems to require inclusion where the insured transferred a policy more than 3 years prior to death, but retained an incident of ownership that he or she gave up within 3 years of death. Regulations issued prior to the adoption of the 1981 Act state that the proceeds are includible under §2035 if the insured transferred incidents of ownership over the policy in contemplation of death. Reg. §20.2042-1(a)(2). The position taken by the regulation is sound and consistent with §2035(d)(2) and other Code provisions, such as §2038(a)(1).

§6.24. Retained Life Interest (§2036)

Insurance may be included in the gross estate of a person other than the insured who directly or indirectly transfers a policy in which the transferor retains a life interest. The insurance proceeds are includible, for example, where a noninsured owner transfers a policy to the trustee of a trust in which he or she retains a life interest. Inclusion also results where the insurer holds the proceeds of a policy pursuant to an election made by the beneficiary to receive the income for life and to pay the principal to others following the beneficiary's death. Pyle v. Commissioner, 313 F.2d 328 (3d Cir. 1963). However, the insurance proceeds are not included in the beneficiary's estate where such a settlement option was chosen by the insured and not the beneficiary. Estate of Idamay Swift Minotto, 9 T.C.M. 556 (1950).

> **Example 6-8.** H's life was insured under 2 policies that he owned. Under Policy One the proceeds were payable outright to his wife, W, upon his death or according to a settlement option selected by her. After H died W elected an option under which she received the interest for life, remainder to their children. The proceeds of Policy Two were subject to the same option, but it had been selected by H. The proceeds of Policy One are includible in W's gross estate, but not the proceeds of Policy Two. In effect, W transferred the proceeds of Policy One to the insurer, but she did not transfer the proceeds of Policy Two.

Two decisions have allowed insurance proceeds to be excluded from the estate of a person other than the insured who paid premiums on policies in which he or she held substantial interests. In the first, Goodnow v. United States, 302 F.2d 516 (Ct. Cl. 1962), the insured's wife paid premiums on policies that the insured had transferred to a revocable trust in which the wife had a life interest. The insured predeceased his wife and the proceeds of the policies were paid to the trustee. Following the wife's death the Court of Claims upheld exclusion of the proceeds from her estate. In the court's view, she did not retain an interest in the same property that she transferred to the trust (*i.e.*, the premiums). Although the analysis is shallow, it was followed in City Bank of Cleveland v. United States, 371 F.2d 13 (6th Cir. 1966), with respect to policies for which the insured had selected an option that called for the payment of interest to his wife for life, remainder to his children, and the insured's wife had the power during the lifetime of the insured to change the beneficiary designation and to exercise other incidents of ownership. The wife had paid most of the premiums but, the Court said, "payment of [the] premiums by her did not make the insurance policies taxable as a transfer with a retained life income under §2036(a)(1)." 371 F.2d at 16.

The rationale of *Goodnow* and *City Bank of Cleveland* cannot reasonably be extended to the payment of premiums on policies held by an *irrevocable* trust in which the premium payor has a life interest. In such a case payment of the premiums is clearly a transfer with a retained life interest. Accordingly, where the insured predeceases the premium payor, the proceeds are includible in the gross estate of the premium payor.

Community Property. In community property states a portion of the insurance is includible in the gross estate of the noninsured spouse where a community property policy is transferred to the trustee of an inter vivos trust in which the noninsured spouse holds a life income interest. United States v. Gordon, 406 F.2d 332 (5th Cir. 1969) (Texas law). In *Gordon* the court recognized that the noninsured spouse, who survived the insured, was a grantor of the trust to the extent of her community interest in the policy. Importantly, however, the court allowed her estate a consideration offset under §2043(a), which reduced the amount includible in her estate by the actuarial value of the life estate she received in the share of the insurance proceeds that the husband transferred to the trust. The court reasoned that a consideration offset was allowable here on the same theory that it is allowed in the more traditional widow's election cases — the surviving spouse exchanged a remainder interest in her share of the proceeds for a life income interest in the insured's share. *See* §§9.21 to 9.34, *infra* for a discussion of the widow's election.

A special problem arises under the community property laws of some states. In Idaho and Louisiana the income from a spouse's separate property is characterized as community property; in Texas income from separate property is the spouses' community property unless they agree otherwise. *See* §3.24, *supra*. In these states, where one spouse transfers a community property interest in a marital asset to the other spouse as the donee's separate property, the income subsequently generated by that asset is community property. The IRS had argued that the transfer of a community property interest to one's spouse under such circumstances was a transfer with a retained life estate under §2036(a)(1) because the income is still treated as community property. The Tax Court accepted this argument (Estate of Charles J. Wyly, 69 T.C. 227 (1977); Estate of Winston Castleberry, 68 T.C. 682 (1977); Estate of Ray McKee, 37 T.C.M. 486 (1978)) but it was rejected by the Fifth Circuit. In reversing both *Wyly* and *Castleberry*, the Fifth Circuit court held that §2036 does not require inclusion in such cases. Estate of Wyly v. Commissioner, 610 F.2d 1282 (1980).

The IRS subsequently conceded the issue insofar as Texas is concerned. Rev. Rul. 81-221, 1981-2 C.B. — . The Fifth Circuit's reversal was predicated upon 2 views: First, under Texas community property law, the donor's interest was not sufficient to be characterized as a "right" within the meaning of §2036(a)(1). Second, the donor's interest in the transferred property was brought about solely by operation of the Texas community property law and, thus, was not a "retention" within the meaning of §2036. The *Wyly* decision did not involve policies of life insurance, but the rationale is the same. In fact, the IRS raised, then abandoned, the application of the theory to life insurance in the *McKee* case, preferring instead to pursue an incidents of ownership argument under §2042(2). *See* §6.17, *supra.* The problem for residents of Texas was also relieved by the 1980 amendment of Article XVI, Section 15 of the Texas constitution. *See* §3.24, *supra*.

§6.25. State Death Taxes

The provisions of the applicable state death tax laws should also be taken into account in planning transactions involving life insurance. Life insurance proceeds receivable by the insured's personal representative are generally taxable, as they are for federal purposes under §2042(1). Proceeds paid to other beneficiaries may also be subject to tax as they are under federal law (*e.g.*, N.Y. Tax Law §249-r(8) (McKinney 1966)), or they may be partly or totally exempt. For example, California allows a $50,000 exemption (Cal. Rev. & Tax. Code §13724 (West 1981 Supp.)) and Indiana allows an unlimited exemption (Ind. Code Ann. §6-4.1-3-6 (Burns 1978)). Some states that allow an exemption expressly extend it to proceeds that are paid to the trustee of an inter vivos or testamentary trust, except to the extent the proceeds are used for the benefit of the estate.

A state death tax saving may result from the careful selection and designation of the insurance beneficiary. A special opportunity exists, for example, in states that allow an exemption for insurance paid to a named beneficiary and calculate the tax according to the relationship of the decedent to the transferee of property. In those states insurance proceeds should be made payable to the person who would be subject to the highest inheritance tax rates upon the client's death. Thus, insurance proceeds should be made payable to more remotely related persons and assets that are subject to the tax should be bequeathed to closer relatives.

Example 6-9. Client wishes to leave $50,000 to his cousin, C, and the residue of his estate to his wife and children. In states that impose an inheritance tax and allow an insurance exemption, the overall state death tax will be lower if $50,000 in life insurance is made payable to C, rather than C being given a testamentary gift.

§6.26. Generation-Skipping Tax

Life insurance is generally subject to the same generation-skipping rules as any other property. The rules expressly apply to any arrangement, including insurance and annuities, that has substantially the same effect as a generation-skipping trust. §2611(b). Thus, the generation-skipping tax extends to insurance settlements under which the beneficial enjoyment is split between 2 or more generations younger than that of the transferor.

> **Example 6-10.** The insurance payable by reason of X's death was retained by the insurer under an option that called for the payment of interest only to the insured's nephew, N, for life and the payment of the principal sum to N's children upon his death. The agreement is an arrangement substantially equivalent to a generation-skipping trust. Accordingly, the tax will apply to the distribution of principal to N's children. When the distribution is made N will be treated as the deemed transferor. *See* §§2.19 to 2.26, *supra.*

The application of the generation-skipping transfer tax rules to life insurance and annuity contracts requires careful consideration of selection of a settlement option and the creation of trusts. *See* Note, Application of the New Generation-Skipping Tax to Life Insurance Proceeds: A Headache for Everyone Involved, 30 U. Fla. L. Rev. 586 (1978).

> **Problem 6-3.** Four years prior to his death in 1982 H assigned a $50,000 ordinary policy on his life to his wife, W. At the time the policy had an interpolated terminal reserve of $2,000. H continued to pay the annual premium of $1,200 from his earnings. In 1980 H transferred $2,000 to the independent trustee of an irrevocable trust for the benefit of his children, D and S. The trustee used $1,800 of the gift to purchase a $100,000 5-year term policy on H's life. Under the terms of the trust each child had the noncumulative right each year to withdraw the lesser of $3,000 or one-half of the value of the property transferred to the trust during the year. The $1,800 premium for 1981 was paid by the trustee from funds H gave to the trustee several years prior to 1980. When H died the proceeds of the $50,000 ordinary life policy were paid to W, and the proceeds of the other policy were paid to the trustees. Assum-

ing that H and W had always lived in a noncommunity property
state, which of the premiums and insurance proceeds are includible
in H's gross estate?

C.   GIFT TAXATION OF LIFE INSURANCE

§6.27.   *General*

A gift of an interest in life insurance is generally subject to the same gift
tax rules as a gift of any other type of property. Thus, a gift may occur
when a policy is assigned, when a premium is paid, or when the policy
proceeds are settled. Reg. §25.2511-1(h)(8), (9). The valuation of interests in life insurance is governed by special rules in the regulations,
which have been upheld in litigation. Reg. §25.2512-6(a). No gift occurs
when the policy owner revocably designates a beneficiary. Rev. Rul. 81-
166, 1981-1 C.B. 477.

Annual gift tax exclusions are generally available for outright transfers of life insurance, but exclusions are generally not available when
insurance is transferred to an irrevocable trust. Reg. §25.2503-3(c), Examples (2), (6).

An outright assignment of a policy may qualify for the gift tax charitable deduction (§2522) or marital deduction (§2523).

§6.28.   *Valuation of Policies*

For gift tax purposes the value of a life insurance policy is established by
the cost of the particular policy or of comparable policies on the date of
the transfer. Reg. §25.2512-6(a). The cost of a comparable new policy
better reflects value than a policy's cash surrender value. Guggenheim v.
Rasquin, 312 U.S. 254 (1941).

> **Example 6-11.** X paid $85,000 for a single-premium life insurance
> policy with a face amount of $100,000 and immediately assigned it
> to his daughter, D. The policy had a cash surrender value of
> $77,000 at the time of issue and transfer. For gift tax purposes H
> made a gift of property worth $85,000 to D.

Term and Group-Term Insurance. The valuation of term and group-
term insurance presents a different problem. In the ordinary case their
value depends principally upon the amount of the premium and the
length of time for which the premium has been paid in advance.

Example 6-12. On January 1 X paid the annual premium of $1,000 on a $150,000 term policy on his life. X assigned the policy to Y on June 30. For gift tax purposes the term policy will probably be considered to have a value of $500, which represents the portion of the premium that is attributable to the unexpired insurance coverage. However, if X were terminally ill, the insurance would have a much larger value.

In the case of employer-provided group-term insurance, the value of the gift may be determined according to the Table I cost of the insurance, Reg. §1.79-3(d)(2), which is used for income tax purposes. *Cf.* Rev. Rul. 76-490, 1976-2 C.B. 300. *See* §6.59, *infra.* That is a practical solution to the problem of valuing group-term insurance when it is not possible to identify the actual premium cost attributable to the particular insurance that was assigned. However, the mere fact that the Table I cost is used for income tax purposes does not require that it be used for gift tax purposes.

Single-Premium and Paid-Up Policies. A single-premium policy or a paid-up policy that has been in effect for some time has a value equal to the current cost of a policy of the same amount on the life of a person the age of the insured. Reg. §25.2512-6(a), Example (3).

Other Policies — Interpolated Terminal Reserve. The value of a policy that has been in effect for some time and on which further premium payments are to be made generally cannot be determined through the cost of comparable contracts. In such cases the regulations provide that the value is determined by adding the interpolated terminal reserve on the date of the gift and the portion of the premium last paid that covers the period following the date of the gift. Reg. §25.2512-6(a). The application of that rule is illustrated by Example (4) of that regulation:

A gift is made four months after the last premium due date of an ordinary life insurance policy issued nine years and four months prior to the gift thereof by the insured, who was 35 years of age at the date of issue. The gross annual premium is $2,811. The computation follows:

Terminal reserve at end of tenth year	$14,601.00
Terminal reserve at end of ninth year	12,965.00
Increase	1,636.00
One-third of such increase (the gift having been made four months following the last preceding premium due date), is	545.33
Terminal reserve at end of ninth year	12,965.00
Interpolated terminal reserve at date of gift	13,510.33
Two-thirds of gross premium ($2,811)	1,874.00
Value of gift	$15,384.33

Policy Subject to a Loan. The value of a policy is reduced by the amount of any loan outstanding against the policy, including accrued interest. Prior to 1982 loans were frequently taken out against policies in advance of transfer in order to reduce the value of the gift to an amount within the allowable annual exclusions. The increase in the amount of the annual exclusion made by the 1981 Act will probably result in fewer loans being taken out for that purpose. Of course, it may be desirable to borrow against cash value policies in any case.

Physical Condition of Insured. For purposes of valuation, "all relevant facts and elements of value at the time of the gift shall be considered." Reg. §25.2512-1. In some cases this may require the physical condition and insurability of the insured to be taken into account. *See* United States v. Ryerson, 312 U.S. 260, 262 (1941), and Estate of James Stuart Pritchard, 4 T.C. 204 (1944) (estate tax case discussed at §6.21, *supra*).

Form 712. The insurer should be asked to provide a completed copy of Form 712 for each policy that is transferred. A completed Form 712 contains detailed financial data regarding the policy, which is used to value it for gift and estate tax purposes. The instructions for preparation of gift tax returns require that a Form 712 be attached to the gift tax return for each policy that is transferred.

§6.29. Annual Exclusion

The complete, irrevocable assignment of a life insurance policy to a single donee qualifies for the annual exclusion because it gives the donee all of the interests in the policy. An exclusion is available although the principal performance under the contract, payment of the face amount of insurance, will take place at a future time, if at all. Reg. §25.2503-3(a). As indicated by Example (6) of that regulation, the payment of a premium on a policy owned outright by another person also qualifies as a gift of a present interest.

Multiple Donees. The transfer of a policy to multiple donees should qualify for the annual exclusion unless the donor has manifested an intent that the donees must act together in order to deal with the policy. Skouras v. Commissioner, 188 F.2d 831 (2nd Cir. 1951) (no annual exclusions allowed where donees must act together). Logically an exclusion should be available if each donee has the right to transfer or otherwise deal with his or her interest independent of the other owners of the policy.

Where the policy is transferred to a trust, an annual exclusion is not available if the beneficiaries of the trust must act together in order to obtain the present use or benefit of the insurance or other assets that are transferred to the trust. Ryerson v. United States, 312 U.S. 405 (1941). Annual exclusions are available, however, with respect to assets transferred to a trust where each beneficiary of the trust has a *Crummey* power, which permits him or her, acting alone, to withdraw a proportionate part of the assets. *Crummey*, or demand powers, are discussed in more detail at §7.36, *infra*. The IRS has recognized that annual exclusions may be claimed for the minor beneficiaries' interests in an irrevocable life insurance trust funded with only $1 and a $150,000 term policy. The trust gave each of the insured's children the right to withdraw the lesser of (1) $3,000 in trust assets or (2) one-half of the assets of the trust. In addition each child was given the power to revoke the trust, in which case the assets would be equally distributed to the children. LR 7935091. *See also* LR 7826050.

Transfer to Trusts. The general rules regarding the availability of an annual exclusion for interests in trusts apply in the case of insurance trusts. Because the beneficiaries of a trust are the donees of property transferred to a trust, Helvering v. Hutchings, 312 U.S. 393 (1941), an annual exclusion is only available if the donees receive a present interest under the trust. In order to qualify as a present interest the beneficiary must have the unrestricted right to the use, possession, or enjoyment of the trust property or its income. Reg. §25.2503-3(b). As indicated in Example (2) of Reg. §25.2503-3(c), an annual exclusion is not available if the benefits under the trust are payable only upon the death of the insured.

Although the beneficiary is given an immediate income interest in a trust, an annual exclusion is generally not available where the trust holds only life insurance policies, which produce no income, or where all of the income must be used to pay premiums. Rev. Rul. 69-344, 1969-1 C.B. 225; Jesse S. Phillips, 12 T.C. 216 (1949). However, an annual exclusion is available if the beneficiary may withdraw the principal of the trust at any time. Harbeck Halsted, 28 T.C. 1069 (1957), *acq.*, 1958-2 C.B. 5. An annual exclusion is also available to the extent the beneficiary holds a *Crummey* power that allows the beneficiary to withdraw property that is added to the trust within a limited period following its transfer to the trustee. Note that the annual exclusion is limited to the amount that can be withdrawn under a *Crummey* power — which prior to the 1981 Act was generally limited to the previously allowable $3,000 annual exclusion. Trusts often limited the beneficiary's power of withdrawal to the lesser of "the amount allowable as an exclusion under IRC §2503(b) or the value of the property transferred to the trust." The increase of the annual exclusion from $3,000 to $10,000 could distort the trustor's intent if the beneficiary were allowed to withdraw additions of up to $10,000. Accordingly, the 1981 Act included a transitional rule under which the increased annual exclusion does not apply to powers created prior to September 13, 1981, that are defined by reference to the §2503(b) gift tax exclusion unless the instrument containing the power is amended after September 12, 1981, or the state enacts a statute applicable to such trusts that provides such powers shall be construed by reference to the increased gift tax exclusion. Act §441(c). In short: Do not rely upon a formula *Crummey* power created prior to September 13, 1981, to uphold an annual exclusion in the increased amount.

The gift of a policy to a minor under the Uniform Gifts to Minors Act or to a §2503(c) minor's trust that authorizes the distribution of principal qualifies for an annual exclusion. Before a policy is transferred to a custodian the lawyer should check the local version of the Gifts to Minors Act to be sure that it authorizes the custodian to receive and hold insurance policies.

§6.30. Transfer of a Policy

An irrevocable assignment is generally used to transfer interests in an existing policy from the present owner to the intended donee. Insurers will generally provide assignment forms upon request; however, the forms should be reviewed carefully to be sure that they comply with the terms of the policy and will effectively transfer all incidents of ownership in it. If an insured-owner retains any interest in the insurance, an assignment may be incomplete *and* the policy proceeds will be includible in the insured's gross estate under §2042(2). If any part of the policy is, or may be, community property, both spouses should join in the assignment. Otherwise, in some community property states, the nonconsenting spouse has the power to invalidate the gift in whole or in part.

Irrevocable Beneficiary Designation. The irrevocable designation of a beneficiary is sometimes used instead of an assignment, but it is less satisfactory because its effects are generally uncertain. The economic interests of an irrevocably designated beneficiary probably are entitled to protection against unilateral action by the designated owner of the policy in most cases. However, the extent to which such a beneficiary may exercise control over the policy is not well defined in most states. "The law of West Virginia and other jurisdictions with regard to the right of irrevocably designated beneficiaries to exercise options of a life insurance policy without the consent of the insured is unclear at best." Morton v. United States, 457 F.2d 750, 754 (4th Cir. 1972). The IRS may assert that an insured who is named as owner of a policy has an incident of ownership although another person is irrevocably designated as the beneficiary.

Charitable and Marital Deductions. A gift tax charitable or marital deduction is available if all of the interests in a policy are transferred outright to a qualifying donee. No charitable deduction is available, however, where a charity is given a split interest in a policy. §2522(c)(2). In particular, no deduction is allowed where the charity is given the cash surrender value of a policy and the donor retains the right to designate the recipient of the difference between the face amount of the policy and the cash surrender value. Rev. Rul. 76-200, 1976-1 C.B. 308. A marital deduction is generally not available for a policy transferred in trust unless the donee spouse has the requisite life income interest plus the right to compel the trustee to convert the policy into income-producing property. §2523(e), (f); Reg. §25.2523(e)-1(f)(4). Of course, a marital deduction under §2523(e) is available only if the donee spouse also has a general power of appointment. However, a deduction is available under §2523(f) on an elective basis where the donee receives a qualifying income interest for life.

§6.31. Payment of Premiums

The payment of a premium on a policy in which the premium payor has no interest constitutes a gift to the owner of an amount equal to the payment. There is a gift of that amount although benefits are payable under the policy only upon the death of the donor and the donee must survive the donor in order to receive the proceeds of the policy. Reg. §25.2511-1(h)(8). The value of the gift is the amount of the premium payment, not the resulting increase in the cash surrender value of the policy. There may be no gift, however, if the insured retains an interest in the policy or some control over it. The identity of the premium payor is largely irrelevant — the payment of a premium by a person other than the policy owner generally involves a gift.

> **Example 6-13.** The life of X is insured under a policy owned by his daughter, D. This year the annual premium of $5,000 was paid by D's brother, B. By paying the premium B made a gift of $5,000 to D. The gift qualifies for the annual gift tax exclusion. Reg. §25. 2503-3(c), Example (6).

No gift is involved, however, where a premium is paid in order to protect the interests of the premium payor. Thus, there is no gift where the principal beneficiary of an insurance trust pays the premiums on policies held by the trustee in order to prevent lapse or diminution in the amount of insurance coverage. Grace R. Seligmann, 9 T.C. 191 (1947), acq., 1947-2 C.B. 4.

The use of community property funds to pay premiums on a policy owned by one or both spouses as separate property ordinarily does not involve a gift. Under the apportionment rule, which is applied in California and Washington, the use of community property funds establishes a community property ownership interest in the policy in the absence of a contrary agreement. *See* §6.11, *supra*. This is undesirable where the objective is to exclude all of the insurance from the estate of the insured. In the inception-of-title states — Arizona, Louisiana, New Mexico, and Texas — there is no gift because the community is entitled to reimbursement for premiums on separately owned policies that were paid with community funds. *See* §6.10, *supra*.

A marital deduction may be allowed for the payment of premiums on a policy held in trust for the benefit of the premium payor's spouse if the trust otherwise meets the requirements of §2523. However, no deduction is available unless the donee has the right to compel the trustee to convert the policy into income-producing property. Estate of Charles C. Smith, 23 T.C. 367 (1954).

§6.32. *Payment of Proceeds*

When a policy is owned by a person other than the insured, a gift occurs if the proceeds are paid to a third person.

> **Example 6-14.** X owned a $10,000 policy on the life of Y that designated X's daughter, D, as beneficiary. Upon Y's death the $10,000 policy proceeds were paid to D. The payment of the proceeds constituted a gift of $10,000 from X to D. The gift qualifies for the annual exclusion.

The owner of a policy likewise makes a gift where the proceeds are paid to a trust for the benefit of other persons. Goodman v. Commissioner, 156 F.2d 218 (2d Cir. 1946); Rev. Rul. 81-166, 1981 1 C.B. 477. In that case the availability of the annual exclusion depends on the terms of the trust.

Community Property Insurance. A gift may also take place where the proceeds of a community property life insurance policy are paid to a person other than the surviving spouse. This rule is stated in Reg. §25. 2511-1(h)(9):

> Where property held by a husband and wife as community property is used to purchase insurance upon the husband's life and a third person is revocably designated as beneficiary and under the State law the husband's death is considered to make absolute the transfer by the wife, there is a gift by the wife at the time of the husband's death of half the amount of the proceeds of such insurance.

The regulation was applied in Cox v. United States, 286 F. Supp. 761 (W.D. La. 1968), which held that the surviving spouse made a gift of one-half of the proceeds of community property life insurance policies to third party beneficiaries. The result is consistent with the item theory of community property that recognizes that each spouse owns an undivided one-half interest in each community asset. However, the item theory approach was not applied in a later case, Kaufman v. United States, 462 F.2d 439 (5th Cir. 1972), where the surviving spouse received $175,000 in proceeds from community property policies on her husband's life and their daughter received $72,000 in proceeds from other community property policies. The government contended that the surviving spouse made a gift of $36,000 to the daughter by permitting the entire proceeds of $72,000 in community property insurance to be paid to her. The court rejected that argument and instead appeared to apply an aggregate theory of community property: "[S]ince the wife received more than her share of the total community insurance proceeds, no gift can be constructively presumed." *Id.* at 441.

The risk that the payment of part of the proceeds of community property policies to a person other than the surviving spouse may involve a gift by the survivor is eliminated if the survivor receives at least one-half of the proceeds of each policy. The other portion of the proceeds is treated as a transfer by the decedent that does not involve a gift by the survivor.

Example 6-15. H's life was insured under 2 $100,000 community property policies. One of the policies designated H's wife, W, as beneficiary and the other designated his daughter, D, as beneficiary. Upon H's death $100,000 in proceeds was paid to W and $100,000 to D. Under the item theory applied in *Cox* the surviving spouse made a gift of $50,000 by permitting the full amount of the proceeds of the second policy to be paid to D. No gift would be involved, however, under the rationale of *Kaufman*. No gift would occur under either theory if the proceeds of each policy had been paid one-half to W and one-half to D.

The *Cox* approach is more consistent with the prevalent item theory of community property law, but the *Kaufman* approach is preferable because it is more equitable and treats similarly situated taxpayers in the same way.

Problem 6-4. A $100,000 ordinary life insurance policy on W's life was issued to her as owner when she married H 6½ years ago. At all times the policy has designated W's mother, M, as the primary beneficiary. Each year H paid the annual premium of $2,000 from his earnings. The terminal reserve of the policy at the end of year 6 was $12,000 and at the end of year 7 it will be $13,750.

(a) Assuming that H and W live in a noncommunity property

state, and have made no other gifts to each other of any significance, did the premium payments require any gift tax returns to be
filed? What would be the gift tax consequences if W assigns the
policy to the trustee of an irrevocable trust, the income of which
would be payable after her death to their 2 minor children, A and
B? In such a case, would any gifts occur as H paid future premiums?
How could the trust be drafted to ease the gift tax problems?

(b) How would your answers differ if H and W had always lived
in a community property state?

D. INCOME TAXATION OF LIFE INSURANCE

§6.33. Introduction

Transactions involving life insurance often have important federal income tax consequences. This part discusses the income tax aspects of
many transactions, including the payment of policy proceeds; payment
of premiums; and the sale, surrender, or exchange of insurance policies.
The income tax aspects of split-dollar, group-term, and minimum-
deposit insurance are reviewed in Part E, §§6.49 to 6.65, *infra,* along with
other aspects of those types of insurance that are of concern to estate
planners.

§6.34. Payment of Proceeds

In general, amounts received under a life insurance policy by reason of
the death of the insured are not included in the recipient's gross income.
§101(a)(1). However, part or all of the proceeds may be included where
the policy had been transferred for value (§101(a)(2)) or the policy was
held by a qualified retirement plan (§72(m)(3)(C)). Also, the proceeds
may be includible in the gross income of a separated or former spouse of
the insured if the requirements of §§71 or 682 are met. §101(e); Reg.
§1.101-5. Additional amounts paid because of the deferred payment of
the proceeds are generally not excluded from income. §101(c), (d). Insurance proceeds paid to a shareholder-beneficiary under a corporate
owned policy on which the corporation paid the premiums from its
earnings and over which the corporation held the right to designate the
beneficiary are taxed as a dividend to the recipient. Rev. Rul. 61-134,
1961-2 C.B. 250. The proceeds are only taxed under that rule where the
recipient is a shareholder. LR 8144001.

The general exclusion of §101(a) applies to all death benefits having the characteristics of life insurance, including endowment contracts, accident and health policies, double and triple indemnity provisions, paid-up additions, etc. Reg. §1.101-1(a). The entire amount of the death benefit payable on a variable life insurance policy is excludible under §101(a) although the amount of the benefit may increase or decrease, but not below a stated minimum, in accordance with the investment experience of the separate account for the policy. Rev. Rul. 79-87, 1979-1 C.B. 73. The exclusion is available whether the payment is made to the estate of the insured or to another beneficiary. Likewise, it is available whether the payment is made directly to an individual or in trust. *Id.* Importantly, the exclusion is not dependent upon the proceeds being subject to the estate tax. Thus, the proceeds are not includible in the beneficiary's gross income whether or not the insurance is included in the gross estate of the insured.

> **Example 6-16.** The life of W was insured under a policy owned by her husband, H, which designated their child, C, as beneficiary. The policy provided for the payment of an additional amount equal to the face amount of the policy if the insured died as the result of accidental injuries. W died in an automobile accident and C was paid the face amount of the policy plus the additional benefit. Although none of the insurance was included in W's gross estate, the payments made to C are excluded from C's gross income.

The general exclusion extends only to the amount payable as a death benefit at the time of the insured's death. It does not apply to interest paid because of a delay in payment of the death benefit.

§6.35. Settlement Options (§101(c), (d))

Most policies permit the insured or the beneficiary to elect to have the proceeds paid in a lump sum under one or more settlement options. The 2 principal options are the interest only option and the installment option. Under the former the beneficiary is entitled to receive only interest on the proceeds at a guaranteed rate (which, under some policies, is augmented by "excess" interest) until the principal amount is withdrawn or paid out. The installment option usually provides for payment of a fixed amount either for a specified period (*e.g.,* $250 per month for 10 years) or for the life of the beneficiary, with a certain number of payments guaranteed.

Where the proceeds are held subject to an option under which only interest is paid on a current basis, the beneficiary is taxed on the interest. §101(c). For this purpose it makes no difference whether the beneficiary has the right to withdraw the principal. This rule applies to payments made of interest earned on proceeds that are held without substantial diminution of principal during the period the interest payments were made or credited. Reg. §1.101-3(a). If the payments include a substantial amount of principal, the distributions are subject to §101(d) and not §101(c). Whether (c) or (d) applies is usually significant only in determining whether interest payments to a surviving spouse qualify for the $1,000 annual exclusion of §101(d)(1)(B), which is only available with respect to payments subject to §101(d).

Where payments are made under an installment option, the principal portion of each payment is not included in the beneficiary's income. §101(d). The principal component of each payment is determined by prorating the amount held by the insurer with respect to the beneficiary over the period for which payments will be made. The amount held by the insurer is usually the amount payable as a lump sum in discharge of the insurer's obligation under the policy; however, if the policy had been transferred for valuable consideration, the total amount held by the insurer cannot exceed the amount of consideration paid, plus any premiums or other amount subsequently paid by the transferee. Reg. §1.101-4(b)(3).

> **Example 6-17.** The proceeds of a $100,000 policy on the life of W are payable to her mother, M, in 10 annual installments of $11,500 each. Under the basic rule of §101(d), $10,000 of each payment is excludible from M's income ($100,000/10 = $10,000). The other $1,500 of each payment is taxable as interest.

A surviving spouse of an insured person may exclude up to $1,000 of the interest that is received each year under one or more installment options (§101(d)(1)(B)). As indicated above, this exclusion is not available where the payments are made pursuant to an interest only option. By way of illustration, if the installment payments in Example 6-17 were payable to W's surviving spouse, he could exclude from his income $1,000 of the interest component of each payment. A surviving spouse is only entitled to exclude a total of $1,000 for each year payments are received under installment elections.

§6.36.   Transfer for Value (§101(a)(2))

Where a policy is transferred for value, the proceeds are generally taxable except to the extent of the consideration paid plus premiums and other amounts subsequently paid by the transferee. §101(a)(2). This limitation on the availability of the general exclusion was apparently intended to discourage trafficking in life insurance policies for profit.

However, there are 2 important exceptions to the transfer-for-value rule. The rule does not apply (1) where the basis of the policy for the purpose of determining gain or loss is determined in whole or in part by reference to the basis of the policy in the hands of the transferor (§101(a)(2)(A)), or (2) where the transfer was made to the insured, a partner of the insured, a partnership of which the insured is a partner, or to a corporation in which the insured is a shareholder or officer (§101(a)(2)(B)).

The question of whether the transfer of a policy subject to a loan involves a transfer for consideration is unsettled. Some commentators argue that the assignment of a policy subject to a loan is not a transfer for value because a policy loan merely allows the insurer to apply the policy proceeds first to discharge the loan and does not involve any personal liability on the part of the owner. Walker, Life Insurance from the Standpoint of the Federal Corporate and Personal Income Tax, Gift Tax and Estate Tax, U. So. Cal. 18th Tax Inst. 543, 576 (1966). On the other hand, the government apparently views the transfer of an encumbered policy as a transfer for value — perhaps based upon Crane v. Commissioner, 331 U.S. 1 (1947). The government's position is reflected in Rev. Rul. 69-187, 1969-1 C.B. 45. In it the insured transferred a policy to his wife that had a cash surrender value of $85,000, but was subject to a loan of $75,000. The ruling concluded that the proceeds were not includible in the wife's gross income. The ruling is unsettling because it stated that the policy had been transferred in part for consideration and in part as a gift (*i.e.*, the basis was determined in part by reference to the basis of the transferor).

The first exception to the transfer-for-value rule also applies where a policy is transferred from one corporation to another in a tax-free reorganization, as a result of which the transferor's basis in the policy carries over to the transferee. Reg. §1.101-1(b)(5), Example 4.

The second exception is particularly important in planning business transactions. Under it, the transfer-for-value rule does not apply where the transferee is the insured, a partner of the insured, a partnership in which the insured is a partner, or a corporation in which the insured is a shareholder or officer. §101(a)(2)(B). However, the superficial breadth of the exception is misleading — it does not protect a wide variety of fairly common transfers, among which are:

1. Shareholder A transfers a policy insuring A's life to Shareholder B in exchange for a similar policy on B's life, or for other consideration;
2. An employee or director of a corporation, who is not a shareholder or officer, transfers a policy on his or her life to the corporation in exchange for cash or other valuable consideration; and,
3. A corporation sells a policy insuring the life of an employee to the

employee's spouse for a payment equal to its cash surrender value. *See* Estate of Rath v. United States, 608 F.2d 254 (6th Cir. 1979).

This exception does not protect transfers for value that are made to relatives of the insured.

> **Example 6-18.** Father, F, applied for and paid the premiums on a $25,000 policy on the life of his daughter, D. Subsequently F transferred the policy to his son, S, in exchange for a cash payment equal to its cash surrender value of $3,000. S paid an additional $3,000 in premiums prior to D's death. S will probably be taxed on $19,000 of the $25,000 in proceeds he received ($25,000 − $6,000). Alcy S. Hacker, 36 B.T.A. 659 (1937); Bourne Bean, 14 T.C.M. 786 (1955).

Of course, it is possible that a transfer that is not within this exception may nonetheless fall within the scope of the first one. Thus, if any part of the transferor's basis carries over to the transferee, as it would in the case of a partial gift, the first exception would insulate the proceeds from taxation.

> **Problem 6-5.** X assigned a $100,000 cash value life insurance policy to his son, S, at a time when X was in good health. The policy, which had been issued 10 years earlier, had a cash surrender value of $13,800 and an interpolated terminal reserve of $14,100 on the date of the transfer. At the time of the transfer the policy was subject to a loan equal to its cash surrender value. Assuming that X paid premiums in excess of $14,100 prior to the transfer, and S paid premiums of $5,000 afterward, to what extent are the proceeds excludible from S's gross income when X dies? Would the outcome be any different if X paid some of the subsequent premiums or if X had been terminally ill at the time of the assignment?

§6.37. *Policy Purchased by a Qualified Plan*

The proceeds of an insurance policy purchased by a qualified retirement plan on the life of an employee may not be included in the income of the plan beneficiary under §101(a) when they are distributed. However, they may be taxable under §72. If the employee paid the premiums, or the cost of the insurance was taxed to the employee under §72(m)(3)(B), the proceeds are excluded to the extent they exceed the cash surrender value of the policy immediately prior to the employee's death. §72(m)(3)(C). An amount of the proceeds equal to the cash surrender value qualifies for the $5,000 exclusion under §101(b) and the balance of it is taxable under the rules of §72. On the other hand, if the employee did not pay the premiums directly and they were not taxed to the employee under §72(m)(3), no part of the proceeds paid to the plan beneficiary as a death benefit qualifies for the exclusion under §101(a). Reg. §1.72-16(c)(4).

The rollover of a policy on an employee's life from one qualified plan to another does not constitute a transfer for value. LR 7906051.

§6.38. Premium Payments

Premiums paid on personal (*i.e.*, nonbusiness) insurance are generally not deductible for income tax purposes. To begin with, premiums paid by a taxpayer on policies insuring the premium payor's life are considered to be nondeductible personal expenses. Reg. §1.262-1(b)(1). Premium payments made on policies insuring the lives of family members are also subject to that rule. In addition, premiums on policies insuring the life of another person are not deductible if the proceeds would be excluded from the premium payor's gross income under §101(a). §265(1); Jones v. Commissioner, 231 F.2d 655 (3d Cir. 1956).

A deduction is allowed under §215(a) for premium payments that constitute income to a spouse or former spouse of the insured under §71. In order to obtain the deduction, the policy must generally have been assigned to the former spouse in connection with a legal separation, dissolution of marriage, or decree of separate maintenance — the mere designation of the former spouse as beneficiary is not sufficient. Henry B. Kelsey, 27 T.C.M. 337 (1968), *aff'd mem.*, 1969-2 U.S.T.C. ¶9619, 23 A.F.T.R.2d 69-1481 (2d Cir. 1969).

Subject to the percentage limitations of §170, a charitable deduction is allowed for premiums paid on a policy that is owned by a charity or a charitable trust. Eppa Hunton IV, 1 T.C. 821 (1943), *acq.*, 1943 C.B. 12. Where an income tax charitable deduction is sought the planner should not rely upon the mere irrevocable designation of the charity as beneficiary. *See* §6.30, *supra.*

Where premiums are paid at a discount in advance, the interest earned on the advance payment or the increment in value is includible in the gross income of the premium payor in the year or years the premiums are due. Rev. Rul. 66-120, 1966-1 C.B. 14. On the other hand, an additional premium charge that is imposed when a premium is paid on a semi-annual, quarterly, or monthly basis is not deductible as an interest charge under §163. Rev. Rul. 79-187, 1979-1 C.B. 95.

Under §162 an employer may deduct the premiums paid on life insurance policies on the lives of its officers and employees. The premiums are deductible business expenses if the payments are in the nature of additional compensation, the total amount of compensation paid to an officer or employee is not unreasonable (§162(a)), and the employer is not directly or indirectly the beneficiary (§264(a)(1)). Rev. Rul. 56-400, 1956-2 C.B. 116. No deduction is allowed for the payment of premiums on policies insuring lives of shareholders that constitute dividend distributions rather than the payment of compensation for services. In such cases, the amount of the dividends is includible in the shareholder's income. Also, no deduction is allowed if the employer is entitled to receive any of the proceeds of a policy under a split-dollar plan or otherwise. §264(a)(1); Rev. Rul. 66-203, 1966-2 C.B. 104.

In general, the premiums paid by an employer on a policy insuring the life of an employee are includible in the employee's gross income where the proceeds are payable to the beneficiary designated by the employee. Reg. §1.61-2(d)(2)(ii)(a). Under such circumstances the premiums paid by the employer constitute additional compensation to the employee. N. Loring Danforth, 18 B.T.A. 1221 (1930). Special provisions of §79 allow an employee to exclude the cost of up to $50,000 of employer-provided group-term insurance. *See* §§6.54 to 6.60, *infra.*

Qualified Plans (§72(m)(3)). The cost of current life insurance protection provided an employee under a qualified retirement plan is includible in the employee's income if the proceeds are payable directly or indirectly to the participant or the participant's beneficiary. §72(m)(3). Rev. Rul. 79-202, 1979-2 C.B. 31. If the trust has a right as a named beneficiary to retain any part of the proceeds, the premiums are not taxed to the employee. Under the regulations, the proceeds are considered to be payable to the participant or the participant's beneficiary if "the trustee is required to pay over all of such proceeds to the beneficiary." Reg. §1.72-16(b)(1).

The amount of life insurance protection provided in any year is the excess of the death benefit payable over the cash surrender value of the policy. Reg. §1.72-16(b)(3). The cost of the protection is determined under the table of one-year term premiums set forth in Rev. Rul. 55-747, 1955-2 C.B. 228 (the so-called P.S. 58 cost).

Example 6-19. The trustee of Employer's qualified pension plan, which provides a death benefit of $10,000, purchased a $10,000 ordinary life insurance policy on the life of Employee, who was 50 years old. The premium for the first year was $250, at the end of which the cash value of the policy was $0. The plan provided Employee's beneficiary with $10,000 of insurance protection. The P.S. 58 cost of $1,000 insurance for a person 50 years of age is $9.22. Employee must report $92.20 as income for the year (10 × $9.22).

§6.39. Grantor Trusts (§677(a)(3))

The income of a trust is taxed to the grantor of a trust to the extent it may be used without the consent of an adverse party to pay premiums on policies insuring the life of the grantor or the grantor's spouse. §677(a)(3). *See* §10.32, *infra.* This rule is intended "to prevent the avoidance of tax by the allocation of income through a trust device to the payment of life insurance premiums, which are universally recognized as a normal expense of protecting dependents but which are personal, as distinguished from business, expenses, and are therefore not deductible from gross income." Arthur Stockstrom, 3 T.C. 664, 668 (1944). The income of the trust is not taxed to the grantor merely because the trustee is authorized to pay premiums on policies insuring the life of the grantor or the grantor's spouse. Rather, the application of the statute depends upon the actual existence of policies upon which premiums might have been paid from trust funds. Corning v. Commissioner, 104 F.2d 329 (6th Cir. 1939).

The deductibility of interest paid by a trustee on a policy loan is discussed in §6.41, *infra.*

§6.40. Policy Loans

Under most cash value life insurance policies the owner may borrow up to the cash surrender value of the policy on the sole security of the policy. Although the payment to the owner is called a loan, there is no personal liability to repay it. The Tax Court in J. Simpson Dean, 35 T.C. 1083, 1085 (1961), *nonaqc.*, 1973-2 C.B. 4, commented on this feature of life insurance policies:

> Insurance policy loans are unique because the borrower assumes no personal liability to repay the principal or to pay interest on the amount borrowed. Such loans are based on the reserve value of the insurance policies involved. If either the principal or the interest is not repaid, it is merely deducted from the reserve value of the policy. Since the insurance company "never advances more than it already is absolutely bound for under the policy it has no interest in creating personal liability."

In Williams v. Union Central Life Insurance Co., 291 U.S. 170, 179-180 (1934), the Supreme Court said, "While the advance is called a 'loan' and interest is computed in settling the account, 'the item never could be sued for,' and in substance 'is a payment, not a loan.'"

Under some circumstances, the excess of the amount borrowed on a policy over the premiums paid is includible in the gross income of the borrower. The clearest case occurs when a policy is terminated for failure to pay on the loan or interest. Then the amount of the outstanding loan is an amount received under the contract for purposes of §72(e)(1)(B) and is includible in the borrower's gross income to the extent it exceeds the premiums and other amounts paid on the policy. Where the policy is not terminated or surrendered, the excess is not includible in the borrower's gross income if the transaction is treated as establishing a debtor-creditor relationship between the borrower and the insurer. In a related context the Tax Court held that a policy loan made against an employee annuity contract was not includible in the borrower-employee's income because it was not "an amount received under the contract" within the meaning of §72(e)(1)(B). Robert W. Minnis, 71 T.C. 1049 (1979), *nonacq.*, 1979-2 C.B. 2. The *Minnis* opinion rejected Rev. Rul. 67-258, 1967-2 C.B. 68, which held that money received by an employee as a loan against the value of an annuity contract prior to the annuity's starting date was a taxable advance.

Cash value policies issued prior to 1970 generally provide that loans carry an interest rate of 5% or less, while policies issued later commonly specify rates of 8% or more. Recently some companies have indicated that they intend to pay lower dividends on participating policies that carry rates of interest below the current rate unless the owners agree to a policy amendment that makes the current rate applicable to the policy. Also, some companies are studying the use of variable loan rates in lieu of fixed rates. A policy owner can generally turn a profit by borrowing on older policies and investing the funds in a higher-yielding certificate of deposit, money market fund, or other secure investment. Sometimes owners borrow against their policies in order to pay policy premiums. In fact, many policies provide for an automatic loan, up to the remaining loan value of the policy, to pay any premium that is not timely paid. It is also common for an owner to borrow on a policy that the owner intends to transfer in order to reduce its value for gift tax purposes. However, there is some risk that the transfer of a policy subject to a loan equal to its full cash value might be treated as a transfer for value, which could subject the proceeds to taxation under §101(a)(2). *See* §6.36, *supra*.

§6.41. *Deductibility of Interest on Policy Loans: General*

Subject to the provisions of §264, interest payments made by a cash basis policy owner on an outstanding policy loan are generally deductible in the year of payment under §163. However, no deduction is allowed for interest paid on transactions that lack economic substance apart from the possible benefit of an income tax deduction. Knetsch v. United States, 364 U.S. 361 (1960); Carpenter v. Commissioner, 322 F.2d 733 (3d Cir. 1963), *cert. denied,* 375 U.S. 992 (1964).

A taxpayer is entitled to deduct interest that is paid or accrued during the time the taxpayer owns the policy. The owner's "obligation" to pay interest does not survive the assignment of the policy to another person. J. Simpson Dean, 35 T.C. 1083 (1961), *nonacq.*, 1973-2 C.B. 4. Accordingly, interest that accrues and is paid after an assignment is deductible only by the assignee. Agnes I. Fox, 43 B.T.A. 895 (1941).

Where a policy has been transferred to a trust, interest payments made by the trustee may be deductible by the grantor where the grantor is treated as the owner of the trust property under the grantor trust rules. *See* §6.39, *supra.* This possibility has spawned the creation of "defective" trusts — ones that contain provisions that will cause the grantor to be treated as the owner under §§671 to 677 and thus report the items of income, deductions, and credits attributable to the trust. A defective trust may be drafted in a way that produces that result but will not cause the trust to be included in the grantor's gross estate. In LR 7909031, for example, a nonadverse trustee was given the power to pay the income and principal of the trust to the grantor's wife, which is sufficient to require the grantor to be treated as owner of the trust assets under §677(a) but will not cause the assets to be included in the grantor's estate.

Where interest is deducted from the original amount of the loan, or is unpaid and is added to the principal amount of the loan, an interest deduction is allowed to a cash basis taxpayer only when the interest is actually paid. Rev. Rul. 73-482, 1973-2 C.B. 44.

> **Example 6-20.** O, a cash basis taxpayer, borrowed $10,000 against a cash value policy last year. At the time the insurer deducted $1,000 as interest on the loan for the first year and paid O the $9,000 balance.The $1,000 interest "payment" is not deductible on O's income tax return for last year. This year O paid the insurer $10,000 in full satisfaction of the loan. O is entitled to claim an interest deduction for $1,000 on O's return for this year. The same rule applies if the annual interest on a policy loan is not paid and is, instead, added to the principal amount of the loan: A deduction is allowed when the full amount of principal and accumulated interest is paid.

This rule gives taxpayers some flexibility in timing the interest deduction. A taxpayer may prefer to have the interest go unpaid and add it to principal until a year in which the taxpayer's income will be subject to higher income tax rates and he or she can take maximum advantage of the deduction.

§6.42. Interest on Policy Loans: Limitations of §264

Under §264(a)(2) no deduction is allowed for amounts paid as indebtedness incurred directly or indirectly to purchase or continue in effect a single premium life insurance, endowment, or annuity policy purchased after March 1, 1954. Under Reg. §1.264-2 a contract is considered to be a single premium one if substantially all of the premiums are paid within 4 years from the date on which it was purchased or if an amount is deposited after March 1, 1954, with the insurer for the payment of a substantial number of future premiums. No deduction is allowed for interest paid on a bank loan secured by a single premium annuity policy purchased after 1954. Rev. Rul. 79-41, 1979-1 C.B. 124. As the ruling points out, "One who borrows to buy a single premium annuity contract and one who borrows against such a contract already owned are in virtually the same economic position."

Interest is also generally not deductible when paid in connection with a policy issued after August 6, 1963, under a purchase plan that contemplates the systematic direct or indirect borrowing of all or part of the increase in cash value of the policy. §264(a)(3). This limitation has reduced the attractiveness of the so-called financed life insurance or minimum deposit plan, which depends heavily upon the deductibility of interest payments made on indebtedness incurred to make premium payments. Minimum deposit insurance is explained at §6.61, *infra*. *See also* Hutchins, Financed Life Insurance — Obtaining Interest Deductions under Minimum Deposit Plans, 24 Tax Law. 101 (1970).

Exceptions to §264(a)(3). The 4 exceptions to the general rule of §264(a)(3) are explained next. The first and most important exception, the so-called four-in-seven exception, applies if any 4 of the first 7 annual premiums are paid without incurring any indebtedness in connection with the policy. §264(c)(1). For this purpose a new 7-year period starts to run if there is a substantial increase in the amount of the premium. §264(c). This exception allows the deduction of interest paid on an indebtedness incurred in connection with fewer than 4 of the first 7 annual premiums. Also, once the four-in-seven exception is satisfied, the deductibility of interest on policy loans is not restricted by §264(a)(3). The IRS applies the four-in-seven rule literally — it must be satisfied within the initial 7-year period without any violation of the rule. Thus, if O borrowed against a post-August 6, 1963, policy for 4 of the first 7 years, the exception is not available even if the full amount of the loan is repaid within the 7-year period. Rev. Rul. 72-609, 1972-3 C.B. 199.

The second exception is the "de minimis" one, which applies if the total amount paid or accrued under plans that contemplate the systematic borrowing of cash values is $100 or less. §264(c)(2). It is obviously of limited significance.

Under the third, the "unforeseen events" exception (§264(c)(3)), a deduction is allowed for interest paid on indebtedness incurred because of an unforeseen substantial loss of income or an unforeseen substantial increase in financial obligations. For the purposes of this rule a loss of income or increase in financial obligations is not unforeseen if it was, or could have been, foreseen at the time the policy was purchased. Reg. §1.264-4(d)(3).

The fourth, the "trade or business" exception (§264(c)(4)), applies if the indebtedness was incurred in connection with the taxpayer's trade or business. However, the indebtedness must have been incurred to finance business obligations and not the acquisition of cash value life insurance. Specifically, borrowing to finance business life insurance, such as keyman, split-dollar, or stock redemption plans, is not considered to be incurred in connection with the taxpayer's business. Reg. §1.264-4(d)(4). In contrast, borrowing to finance business expansion, inventory, or capital improvements does qualify under this exception.

§6.43. Dividends

As indicated previously, dividends generally constitute a partial premium refund. See §6.7, supra. Accordingly, a dividend is includible in the policy owner's income only to the extent that it, together with all previous excludible payments received under the policy, exceeds the total cost of the policy (i.e., premiums and other consideration). Reg. §1.72-11(b)(1). Under that rule a dividend is not includible in gross income in most cases. Of course, excludible dividends are deducted from the consideration paid or deemed paid for the purpose of computing the exclusion ratio under §72. Id. Also, only the net amount of premiums paid is taken into account in determining gain on amounts not received as annuities under a policy. §72(e)(1).

Interest paid or credited on dividends left with the insurer is includible in the gross income of the policy owner. The interest is includible in the owner's income for the year in which the owner may withdraw it. Reg. §1.61-7(d); Rev. Rul. 57-441, 1957-2 C.B. 45 (interest on dividends under converted United States Government Life Insurance or a National Service Life Insurance policy is not an exempt benefit within the meaning of the World War Veterans Act of 1924).

The distribution under a special reserve provision of a life insurance contract was a nontaxable return of premiums where it was less than the total premiums paid under the policy. Ned W. Mosely, 72 T.C. 183 (1979), acq., 1980-1 C.B. 1. In Mosely, the Tax Court refused to allocate the premiums paid by the taxpayer between the special reserve and the death benefit provisions.

§6.44. Sale, Surrender, or Exchange of Insurance Policies: General

The following general principles apply in determining the income tax consequences of transactions involving life insurance policies:

Basis. For the purpose of determining gain the basis of a policy is the net amount of premiums or other consideration the taxpayer has invested in it, but for the purpose of determining loss the basis is the cash surrender value of the policy.

Gain. With the exception of the tax-free exchanges described in §1035 ordinary gain is recognized when one policy is exchanged for another policy.

Loss. The excess of premiums paid over the value of property received upon the sale, exchange, or surrender of personal insurance is not deductible.

§6.45.   Sale of Policy — Gain and Loss

In the ordinary case, the excess of the proceeds received upon the sale of a policy over the premiums paid is taxable as ordinary income. Gallun v. Commissioner, 327 F.2d 809 (7th Cir. 1964). Analytically the courts have treated the excess as attributable to the earnings generated by the investment component of the policy essentially equivalent to interest and taxable as ordinary income. "[A]ccepting the effectiveness of the transaction as the sale of a capital asset, . . . we are, nevertheless, dealing here with the receipt as part of the purchase price — and in addition to any amount attributable to the property sold — of an amount representing income which has already been earned and which would have been ordinary income if and when received by the vendor." Estate of Gertrude H. Crocker, 37 T.C. 605, 612 (1962). The gain that would have been ordinary income cannot be transformed into capital gain through the simple expedient of a sale or transfer. First National Bank of Kansas City v. Commissioner, 309 F.2d 587 (8th Cir. 1962).

> **Example 6-21.** X had paid premiums of $12,000 on a policy insuring his life that he sold for $15,000. The $3,000 excess of the amount received over the premiums paid is ordinary income to X.

"Loss" on Sale. The excess of the premiums paid for a policy over the amount realized upon the sale of the policy is not deductible. Century Wood Preserving Co. v. Commissioner, 69 F.2d 967 (3d Cir. 1934). The reason is simple — the excess is considered to be attributable to the nondeductible cost of insurance protection provided over the period preceding the sale. Keystone Consolidated Publishing Co., 26 B.T.A. 1210 (1932). In essence the courts have taken the position that there is no loss.

§6.46.   Surrender of Policies

Ordinary income is realized to the extent the proceeds received upon surrender, refund, or maturity of a policy exceed the net amount of all premiums or other consideration paid. §72(e). The gain is not taxed currently if the policyholder elects, within 60 days of the time the lump sum becomes payable under the contract, to receive an annuity in lieu of a lump sum. §72(b). In the case of such an election, the annuity payments are taxed to the recipient in accordance with the basic income tax rules applicable to annuities (*i.e.,* a proportionate part of the total amount received each year is a tax-free return of capital and the balance is taxable income).

When a policy is surrendered, the gain realized is ordinary income and not capital gain. Some courts have reached that result because the surrender, refund, or maturity of a policy is not a sale or exchange. Avery v. Commissioner, 111 F.2d 19 (9th Cir. 1940) (maturity of endowment policy); Bodine v. Commissioner, 103 F.2d 982 (3rd Cir.), *cert. denied,* 308 U.S. 276 (1939) (surrender of annuity policy). It is true that capital gain treatment is available under §1222 only when there is a sale or exchange of a capital asset. However, as indicated in §6.45, *supra,* the sale of an insurance policy also generates ordinary income and not capital gain.

When a policy is surrendered the taxpayer may receive less than the total amount of the premiums and other considerations he or she paid for it. In general, no deduction is allowed for the difference. London Shoe Co. v. Commissioner, 80 F.2d 230 (2d Cir. 1935), *cert. denied,* 298 U.S. 663 (1936); Standard Brewing Co., 6 B.T.A. 980 (1927). Some cases disallowed a deduction because the "loss" was not incurred in a transaction that was entered into primarily for profit as required by §165(c)(2). Industrial Trust Co. v. Broderick, 94 F.2d 927 (1st Cir.), *cert. denied,* 304 U.S. 572 (1938) (single premium nonrefund annuity contract was purchased for reasons of security and not profit); Arnold v. United States, 180 F. Supp. 746 (N.D. Texas 1959) (endowment policies purchased to provide life insurance protection until maturity when they would provide secure source of income); Rev. Rul. 72-193, 1972-1 C.B. 58. Deductions were denied in other cases because the cash surrender value was equal to the taxpayer's capital investment. London Shoe Co. v. Commissioner, *supra.* Any excess of premiums paid over cash surrender value represented the nondeductible cost of the insurance protection provided by policy. For example, in *Standard Brewing Co., supra,* at 984, the court said:

> To the extent that the premiums paid by the petitioner created in it a right to a surrender value, they constituted a capital investment. To the extent they exceeded the surrender value, they constituted a payment for earned insurance and were current expenses. . . . The surrender value of the policy was the measure of the investment and upon the surrender there was no capital lost.

This result is consistent with the denial of a deduction for premiums paid on personal life insurance and on policies maintained on the lives of officers or employees of which the employer is a beneficiary.

§6.47. Exchange of Policies under §1035

Under the special nonrecognition rules of §1035, no gain or loss is recognized on certain exchanges of insurance policies. Specifically, under §1035(a) no gain or loss is recognized in the following exchanges:

A contract of life insurance for another contract of life insurance or for an endowment or annuity contract; or

A contract of endowment insurance (a) for another contract of endowment insurance which provides for regular payments beginning at a date not later than the date payments would have begun under the contract exchanged, or (b) for an annuity contract; or

An annuity contract for an annuity contract.

The nonrecognition rule also applies when a life insurance endowment or fixed annuity policy is exchanged for a variable annuity policy. Rev. Rul. 68-235, 1968-1 C.B. 360. For the rule to apply, however, the contracts must relate to the same insured, although they may be issued by different insurers. Rev. Rul. 72-358, 1972-2 C.B. 473.

When there is a tax-free exchange, the policy received has the same basis as the policy transferred. §1031(d). If other property is also received, the new contract has the same basis as the old, adjusted as provided in §1031(d). Specifically, the basis is (1) decreased by the amount of money and the fair market value of other property received and (2) increased by the amount of gain recognized on the exchange. When a new policy and other property are received, any gain arising from the transaction is recognized, but not in excess of the total value of the money and other property received. §1031(b). In such an exchange no loss is recognized. §1031(c).

> **Example 6-22.** T exchanged a life insurance policy upon which T had paid premiums of $40,000 for a life insurance policy that had a replacement value of $40,000 and cash of $5,000. The full amount of T's $5,000 gain is recognized in the year of the exchange. T's basis in the new policy is $40,000 as indicated in Reg. §1.1031(d)-1(b). If the new policy received by T were worth only $35,000, the $5,000 "loss" would not be recognized. However, the new policy would have a basis of $40,000.

§6.48. Exchange of Policies Not within §1035

Other exchanges are subject to the general rules regarding the recognition of gain or loss upon the sale or exchange of property. Thus, gain or loss is recognized when an endowment or annuity contract is exchanged for a life insurance contract. Gain or loss is also recognized when an annuity contract is exchanged for an endowment contract. Reg. §1.1035-1(c). Because of this rule a taxpayer cannot avoid the taxation of earnings that have accrued on an endowment or an annuity policy by exchanging it for a life insurance policy. The accrued earnings will be taxed to the owner unless the owner dies prior to the maturity of the policy. These rules reduce the flexibility a taxpayer has in dealing with investments in endowment or annuity policies, but they are consistent with other income tax principles.

> **Example 6-23.** In 1975 T paid $20,000 for a single premium endowment contract that would pay $30,000 to T in 1985 or to his beneficiary if he died before then. T exchanged the policy in 1984, when it had a cash value of $29,000, for a single premium paid-up life insurance policy that had a cash surrender value of $23,000. The same policy would cost $29,000 if purchased on the life of a person of T's age, sex, and medical history. As a result of the exchange T must recognize a gain of $9,000.

For the purpose of determining gain, the fair market value of a single premium life insurance policy received by the taxpayer is the amount a person of the same age, sex, and condition of health as the insured would have to pay for a life policy with the same company at the date of the exchange. Here again, the measure of value is not the cash surrender value of the policy. Charles Cutler Parsons, 16 T.C. 256 (1951); W. Stanley Barrett, 42 T.C. 993 (1964), aff'd, 348 F.2d 916 (1st Cir. 1965) (matured endowment policies exchanged for paid-up life insurance policies); Rev. Rul. 54-264, 1954-2 C.B. 57 (exchange of single premium endowment policy for paid-up life insurance policy and cash).

E.   SPECIAL TYPES OF LIFE INSURANCE

§6.49.   Introduction

Several of the most important types of special life insurance are described in this part, including split-dollar, group-term, and minimum-deposit insurance. These types of insurance are important to planners because they are often included in executive compensation packages and insurance proposals made to clients. Each of them has some special advantages and is subject to some special tax rules. Universal life insurance and death benefit only plans are also reviewed. The part concludes with a discussion of gifts of life insurance under the Uniform Gifts to

Minors Act and the application of the Uniform Simultaneous Death Act
to life insurance.

§6.50.   Split-Dollar Life Insurance: General

A split-dollar life insurance plan is designed to make a substantial
amount of life insurance available to the insured, or to the insured's
assignee, at little or no cost. The concept of split-dollar is based upon a
division of the interests in a cash value policy between a financing party
(usually an employer) and the insured (usually the employee). Under it
the cash surrender value is controlled by the financing party and the risk
portion is controlled by the insured or the insured's assignee. Although
split-dollar may be used in a variety of contexts, it is most commonly used
to provide insurance to key employees.

Typically, the financing party pays an amount of the premium equal
to the increase in the cash surrender value of the policy, and is entitled to
recover the full cash surrender value. The insured or the insured's assignee pays the balance of the premium, if any, and is entitled to name
the beneficiary of the risk portion of the insurance (the difference between the face amount and the cash surrender value). Although the
insured may be required to pay a large part of the premium in the first
year or two, the insured's share of the premium rapidly decreases. Some
policies are designed to build up cash value more rapidly to avoid this
problem. The financing party and the insured may split the premium
cost between them in different ways, which may produce more favorable
overall income tax consequences. For example, the employee may be
paid a "bonus" equal to the portion of the premium that he or she must
pay. In order to prevent the risk portion from declining as the cash value
increases, the dividends declared on participating policies may be
applied under the fifth dividend option to buy term insurance equal to
the increase in the cash value.

The 2 common types of split-dollar arrangements, the endorsement
system and the collateral assignment system, are described in the following excerpt from Rev. Rul. 64-328, 1964-2 C.B. 11, 12:

> In the endorsement system, the employer owns the policy and is responsi-
> ble for payment of the annual premiums. The employee is then required
> to reimburse the employer for his share, if any, of the premiums. Under
> the collateral assignment system, the employee in form owns the policy and
> pays the entire premium thereon. The employer in form makes annual
> loans, without interest (or below the fair rate of interest), to the employee of
> amounts equal to the increases in the cash surrender value, but not exceed-
> ing the annual premiums. The employee executes an assignment of his
> policy to the employer as collateral security for the loans. The loans are

generally payable at the termination of employment or the death of the employee.

The arrangements for the ownership of the policy and premium payments can, of course, be tailored to meet the needs of the parties.

The "split" of the premium payments and the other details of a particular split-dollar plan can also vary according to the needs of the parties. The employee might, for example, pay only an amount equal to the P.S. 58 cost of the risk element. *See* §6.51, *infra*. Alternatively, the employer might pay the employee a "bonus" equal to the portion of the premium taxed to the employee (the P.S. 58 cost). Of course, the interests of the financing party or of the insured can be held by a trust or an individual other than the insured. Also, the parties may enter into an agreement regarding the use of the proceeds (*e.g.*, to fund a stock purchase). Finally, dividends may be used in whole or in part to reduce the premium cost, to buy paid-up insurance, or to buy term insurance. As indicated above, if dividends are used to buy term insurance, the amount of insurance subject to the insured's control will not diminish as the cash value of the policy increases.

§6.51. *Split-Dollar Life Insurance: Income Tax Consequences*

Since 1964 the economic value of an employer-provided split-dollar plan has been includible in the gross income of an insured employee. Rev. Rul. 64-328, 1964-2 C.B. 11. The value of the plan is equal to the one-year term cost of the life insurance protection provided to the employee, less any amount paid by the employee. Because the plan is provided as an incident of employment, its value is includible in the gross income of the employee although control over the risk portion had been assigned to the employee's spouse or another person. Rev. Rul. 78-420, 1978-2 C.B. 67. The value attributed to the employee must also include the amount of any policyholder dividend paid to the employee or applied toward the purchase of additional term or paid-up insurance. Rev. Rul. 66-110, 1966-1 C.B. 12. If the insured is a shareholder and not an employee, the value of the insurance protection is treated as a taxable distribution from the corporation to the shareholder. Rev. Rul. 79-50, 1979-1 C.B. 138.

The cost of the insurance protection provided under a split-dollar arrangement is based upon the P.S. 58 cost that is set forth in Rev. Rul. 55-747, 1955-2 C.B. 228. *See* Table 6-1, below. However, the insurer's actual one-year term rates may be used where the current published premium rates regularly charged by the insurer are lower than the P.S. 58 costs. In some instances the regular term premiums are lower. How-

Table 6-1
Uniform One Year Term Premiums for $1,000 Life Insurance Protection

Age	Premium	Age	Premium	Age	Premium
15	$1.27	35	$ 3.21	55	$13.74
16	1.38	36	3.41	56	14.91
17	1.48	37	3.63	57	16.18
18	1.52	38	3.87	58	17.56
19	1.56	39	4.14	59	19.08
20	1.61	40	4.42	60	20.73
21	1.67	41	4.73	61	22.53
22	1.73	42	5.07	62	24.50
23	1.79	43	5.44	63	26.63
24	1.86	44	5.85	64	28.98
25	1.93	45	6.30	65	31.51
26	2.02	46	6.78	66	34.28
27	2.11	47	7.32	67	37.31
28	2.20	48	7.89	68	40.59
29	2.31	49	8.53	69	44.17
30	2.43	50	9.22	70	48.06
31	2.57	51	9.97	71	52.29
32	2.70	52	10.79	72	56.89
33	2.86	53	11.69	73	61.89
34	3.02	54	12.67	74	67.33
				75	73.23

ever even where they are not, the insured employee receives a valuable benefit.

A premium paid by an employer who has an interest in the cash surrender value of a policy is not deductible because the employer is "directly or indirectly a beneficiary under such policy" within the meaning of §264(a). Rev. Rul. 66-203, 1966-2 C.B. 104. In contrast, reasonable salary payments to employees are deductible. Because of that, the total after-tax cost of a split-dollar plan may be lower if the employer increases the employee's salary and the employee uses the increase to pay a greater part of the premium. The optimum tax result is often produced when the employee pays an amount of the premium equal to the P.S. 58 cost of the insurance provided under the plan, which eliminates any amount from inclusion in the employee's income. An employer may cooperate by paying the employee a "bonus" equal to the portion of the premium to be paid by the employee or a "double bonus" equal to that amount plus the income tax that the employee must pay on it.

In the ordinary case the proceeds paid when the insured dies are not included in the gross income of the employer or the beneficiary. Rev. Rul. 64-328, 1964-2 C.B. 11. However, some portion of the proceeds may be taxable if the insurance has been transferred for value.

§101(a)(2). Such a transfer might take place, for example, if the policy is sold by the employer to the spouse of the insured. *See* Estate of Rath v. United States, 608 F.2d 254 (6th Cir. 1979).

§6.52.   *Split-Dollar Life Insurance: Gift Tax Consequences*

Neither the original acquisition of employer-provided split-dollar insurance nor the payment of subsequent premiums usually involves a gift for federal gift tax purposes. However, as each premium is paid by the employer, the employee does make an indirect gift of the P.S. 58 cost where the insurance element is subject to the control of a third party. Rev. Rul. 78-420, 1978-2 C.B. 67 (policy owned by spouse of employee). The gift in such a case may qualify for the annual exclusion. Rev. Rul. 76-490, 1976-2 C.B. 300; *but see* Rev. Rul. 79-47, 1979-1 C.B. 312. The payment of premiums may also involve gifts where a split-dollar plan is used in a nonbusiness setting. The transfer of a split-dollar policy that has been in effect for some time involves a gift, as does the subsequent payment of premiums on the policy. Rev. Rul. 81-198, 1981-2 C.B. — .

> **Example 6-24.** Under a private split-dollar plan Mother, M, pays a portion of the premium on an ordinary policy on the life of her daughter, D, equal to the increase in cash surrender value of the policy, and D pays the balance. As each premium is paid, M makes a gift of the P.S. 58 cost of the insurance protection over which D has control, less the amount of the premium paid by D.

If all interests in the insurance are assigned to a qualified charity or charitable trust, presumably the assignment and the subsequent premium payments attributable to the employee would qualify for the income and gift tax charitable deduction. In contrast, no deductions are allowed where the sole owner of a policy attempts to take advantage of the different interests in a policy by assigning only the cash surrender value to a charity. Thus, where the insured owned the entire interest in a policy, the irrevocable assignment of the cash surrender value does not qualify for the charitable deduction for income or gift tax purposes because only a portion of the donor's interest was transferred. The cash surrender value does not constitute an undivided interest as required in the case of split gifts of outright interests. Rev. Rul. 76-143, 1976-1 C.B. 63 (income tax); Rev. Rul. 76-200, 1976-1 C.B. 308 (gift tax). The rules applicable to charitable gifts are reviewed in detail in Chapter 8.

§6.53.   *Split-Dollar Life Insurance: Estate Tax Consequences*

None of the proceeds paid to the employer is usually includible in the gross estate of the insured employee. However, where the insured was the controlling shareholder of the employer corporation, the portion of the proceeds paid to the employer is included as an asset of the corporation in valuing the stock owned by the insured. Reg. §20.2031-2(f); Estate of John Huntsman, 66 T.C. 861 (1976), *acq.,*1977-1 C.B. 1.

The proceeds payable to the beneficiary of the insurance component of the policy are includible in the insured's gross estate under §2042(1) if they were paid to the employee's estate or under §2042(2) if the employee held any of the incidents of ownership at the time of his or her death. For this purpose, the incidents of ownership held by a corporation are attributed to the estate of the controlling shareholder under Reg. §20.2042-1(c)(6) except to the extent the proceeds are payable to the corporation or are otherwise taken into account in valuing the insured's stock. Estate of Alfred Dimen, 72 T.C. 198 (1979), *aff'd mem.* (unpublished opinion) (2d Cir. 1980). Unless the insured was a controlling shareholder that portion of the proceeds is not includible in the insured's gross estate where the insured irrevocably assigned all incidents of ownership in the policy more than 3 years prior to death or the incidents of ownership were originally acquired by a third party directly from the employer. Rev. Rul. 76-274, 1976-2 C.B. 278 (*Situation 3*) and Rev. Rul. 76-421, 1976-2 C.B. 280.

The proceeds of insurance held in an irrevocable trust under a "private" split-dollar plan are includible in the estate of an insured who retains the right to borrow against the cash surrender value of the policy. Rev. Rul. 79-129, 1979-1 C.B. 306. Specifically the entire proceeds are includible in the estate of the insured where the insurance was assigned to an irrevocable trust, but the insured retained the right to borrow against the insurance. However, the balance remaining at the time of the insured's death of the funds transferred by the insured to the trust to pay premiums is not includible in the insured's estate. Rev. Rul. 81-164, 1981-1 C.B. 458.

Problem 6-6. Zeke is a 40-year-old executive in, and a 10% shareholder in, GO-GO Games (3-G), a closely held electronic video games manufacturer. 3-G pays the entire cost of a $250,000 policy on Zeke's life under a traditional split-dollar plan (*i.e.,* Zeke is entitled to designate the beneficiary of the insurance except for an amount equal to the aggregate premiums paid by 3-G, which is recoverable by 3-G). When the plan was instituted 3 years ago Zeke assigned his interest in the policy to his wife, W, who is currently designated as beneficiary of the insurance element of the policy. This year 3-G made its fourth annual premium payment of $8,000, which increased the cash surrender value of the policy by $6,000 to $22,000. What are the gift and income tax consequences of the premium payment? If W survives Zeke, how will the proceeds be treated for estate tax purposes?

§6.54.   Group-Term Life Insurance: General

The relatively low cost of group-term insurance and the favorable income tax treatment it is given make it a common and important fringe benefit. First, the cost of employer-provided group-term insurance is generally deductible as a business expense under §162 unless the employer is a beneficiary under the policy (§264(a)). Second, the employee is not taxed on the cost of $50,000 of coverage. §79(a)(1). Third, the cost of group-term insurance in excess of $50,000, determined under the favorable Table I rate schedule set out in Table 6-3, is includible in the gross income of an active employee except to the extent the employee contributed to the cost of the coverage. Fourth, the cost of group-term insurance in excess of $50,000 is not includible where the employer or a charity is the beneficiary under the policy. §79(b)(2). However, no charitable deduction is allowable under §170 with respect to a policy that has been assigned or is payable to a charity. Reg. §1.79-2(c)(3). Fifth, the cost of group-term insurance in excess of $50,000 is not includible in the gross income of a retired or disabled former employee. §79(b)(1). Of course, the preferential provisions of §79 do not apply to insurance in excess of the maximum amount allowable of group-term insurance under the applicable state law. Reg. §1.79-1(e).

The provisions of §79(a) govern the income taxation of the cost of group-term life insurance whether or not the employee has assigned his or her interest in the insurance. Rev. Rul. 73-174, 1973-1 C.B. 43. Each time the employer pays a premium on the insurance, the employee receives additional compensation. Rev. Rul. 76-490, 1976-2 C.B. 300 (gift tax).

Spouses and Children. In general the cost of employer-provided group-term life insurance on the life of an employee's spouse and children is includible in the employee's gross income. Here again, the cost is calculated under the favorable Table I rate schedule. Reg. §1.79-3(d)(2). However, the cost of up to $2,000 of group-term insurance on their lives is considered incidental and is not includible in the employee's gross income. Reg. §1.61-2(d)(2)(ii)(b). The amount of group-term insurance on the life of the employee's spouse or children is not taken into account in applying the rules of §79 since it is not insurance on the life of the employee. Reg. §1.79-3(f)(2).

The basic income tax consequences of employer-provided group-term insurance is summarized in Table 6-2.

§6.55.   Group-Term Life Insurance: Basic Requirements

In order to qualify as group-term life insurance it must be part of a group-term insurance plan that meets the technical requirements set out

Table 6-2

Taxpayer	Cost of Group-Term Insurance on Employee's Life		Cost of Group-Term Insurance on Employee's Spouse or Children	
	Up to $50,000	In excess of $50,000	Up to $2,000	In excess of $2,000
Employer[1]	Deductible by employer	Deductible by employer	Deductible by employer	Deductible by employer
Active employee	Not includible in gross income	Includible[2] in gross income	Not includible in gross income	Includible in gross income
Retired or disabled employee	Not includible in gross income	Not includible in gross income	Not includible in gross income	Includible in gross income

1. The results set forth here apply if the cost is a reasonable and necessary business expense and the employer is not directly or indirectly a beneficiary of the policy.
2. The cost would not be includible if the employer or a charity were the beneficiary.

in the regulations issued under §79. The basic requirements set forth in Reg. §1.79-1(a) are:

The insurance provides a general death benefit that is excludible from gross income under section 101(a).

The insurance is provided to a group of employees under a policy carried directly or indirectly by the employer.

The amount of insurance provided to each employee is computed under a formula that precludes individual selection and is based on factors such as age, years of service, compensation, or position.

Health and accident insurance and other policies that do not provide a general death benefit do not satisfy the first requirement. In general the group life insurance must be provided to at least 10 full-time employees in order to meet the second requirement. Reg. §1.79-1(c)(1). However, term insurance provided to a group of less than 10 employees will qualify if it is provided to all full-time employees, the amount of insurance is computed either as a uniform percentage of compensation or on the basis of coverage brackets established by the insurer, and evidence of insurability affecting an employee's eligibility is limited to a medical questionnaire completed by the employee. Reg. §1.79-1(c)(2). Term insurance provided to a group of less than 10 employees will also qualify if it is provided under a common plan of 2 or more unrelated employers, the insurance is restricted to and mandatory for all employees who belong to or are represented by an organization (such as a union) that carries on substantial activities in addition to obtaining insurance, and evidence of insurability does not affect an employee's eligibility. Reg. §1.79-1(c)(3).

§6.56. Group-Term Life Insurance: Plans That Include Permanent Benefits

The final form of the revised §79 regulations, adopted in April, 1979, Reg. §1.79-1, makes it difficult to combine qualifying group-term insurance and permanent benefits on a tax-free basis. Under the new regulations, no part of a life insurance policy that includes permanent benefits will be treated as group-term life insurance unless the requirements of Reg. §1.79-1(b)(1) are met. In brief that regulation requires that (1) the policy or the employer designate in writing the amount of the death benefit that is group-term life insurance, which must not be less than an amount determined under a formula set forth in Reg. §1.79-1(d)(3); (2) the employees must be free to decline or drop the permanent benefit; and (3) the amount of the group-term life insurance must not be reduced if the employee declines or drops the permanent benefit. If a group-term life insurance policy also provides permanent benefits, the cost of the permanent benefits, reduced by the amount contributed by the employee toward their cost, is includible in the employee's gross income. Reg. §1.79-1(d)(1).

§6.57. Group-Term Life Insurance: Who Are "Employees"?

Group-term life insurance may be provided only to employees. The common law rules for determining the existence of an employer-employee relationship provide the primary guide for resolving the question of whether or not a particular individual is an employee. Reg. §§1.79-0, 31.3401(c)-1. Clearly, a sole proprietor or partner is not an employee. A director of a corporation is also not an employee of the corporation. Reg. §31.3401(c)-1(f), *accord*, M. A. Enright, 56 T.C. 1261 (1971). Similarly, a trustee, executor, or other fiduciary is generally not considered to be an employee. Rev. Rul. 69-657, 1969-2 C.B. 189.

§6.58. Group-Term Insurance: Determining the Amount Includible in Income

The cost of any group-term life insurance that is includible in the gross income of an employee is determined according to the Table I rate schedule set forth in Table 6-3 below, and not by the actual cost of the insurance. For the purpose of determining the cost of group-term insurance an employee over 64 is considered to be in the 5-year age bracket of 60 to 64. Reg. §1.79-3(d)(2).

The following example illustrates how the cost of group-term insurance is calculated under Table I.

Table 6-3
Uniform Premiums for $1,000 of
Group-Term Life Insurance Protection
(Table I, Reg. §1.79-3(d)(2))

5-Year Age Bracket	Cost per $1,000 of protection for 1-month period
Under 30	8 cents
30 to 34	10 cents
35 to 39	14 cents
40 to 44	23 cents
45 to 49	40 cents
50 to 54	68 cents
55 to 59	$1.10
60 to 64	$1.63

Example 6-25. Employer, Inc. pays the entire cost of a $100,000 group-term life insurance on the life of its general counsel, X, who is 45 years old. X has designated her husband as beneficiary of the insurance. The amount included in X's gross income for the taxable year is calculated as follows:

Amount of group-term insurance	$100,000	
Less: Tax-free amount	50,000	
Amount of insurance subject to tax	$ 50,000	
Table I cost of $1,000 of insurance per year (12 × $0.40)		4.80
Amount includible in gross income (50 × $4.80)		$240.00

Any amount that X had contributed toward the cost of the insurance would be deducted from $240 in determining the amount includible in her gross income. None of the cost of the insurance would be taxed to her if the policy designated her employer or a charity as beneficiary.

§6.59. Group-Term Life Insurance: Assignment

The irrevocable assignment of group-term insurance is a particularly attractive estate-planning tool because it permits a prospectively large item to be eliminated from the insured's gross estate at little or no present gift tax cost. In general group-term insurance is subject to the same gift and estate tax rules as other forms of life insurance.

Estate Tax. Some of the special estate questions that arise because of the particular characteristics of group-term insurance have been resolved by the IRS largely in the taxpayer's favor. To begin with, in 1968 the IRS ruled that the proceeds of an employer-provided group policy would not be included in the employee's gross estate under §2042 if the employee had irrevocably assigned all of his or her interests in the insurance prior to death. Rev. Rul. 68-334, 1968-1 C.B. 403, *restated and superceded,* Rev. Rul. 69-54, 1969-1 C.B. 221, *modified,* Rev. Rul. 72-307, 1972-1 C.B. 307. Following the issuance of Rev. Rul. 69-54, most states adopted statutes that expressly authorize the assignment of interests in group insurance. Unfortunately, however, some states limit the class of persons to whom such an assignment can be made. *See* Wash. Rev. Code §48.18.375 (1979). Even where assignments are permitted by state law, they may be barred by the terms of the master group policy. Before attempting to make an assignment, the planner should review the master policy. Experience indicates that it is not safe to rely upon the description of the insurance contained in the certificate of insurance given to the insured employee. The certificate constitutes evidence of the insurance coverage, but its terms are subordinate to those of the master policy. Poling v. North America Life & Cas. Co., 593 P.2d 568 (Wyo. 1979); Estate of Max Gorby, 53 T.C. 80 (1969), *acq.,* 1970-1 C.B. xvi. If the master policy prohibits assignments, the employee may ask the employer to lift the prohibition. Employers and insurers commonly cooperate promptly to remove any restrictions on assignments.

Although Rev. Rul. 69-54 helped clear the air regarding the effect of assignments, some nagging doubts remained regarding the effectiveness of an assignment of annually renewable term insurance under §2035. That section requires insurance to be included in the insured's gross estate if the insured dies within 3 years following a transfer of the insurance. *See* §6.21, *supra.* Planners were concerned that the IRS might treat each annual renewal as giving rise to "new" insurance each year. If so, the insurance could not be assigned more than one year prior to death and the proceeds would be includible in the estate of the insured in all cases. That concern was largely alleviated by the Technical Advice Memorandum issued in 1980 by the National Office of the IRS, LR 8034017. The memorandum concluded that the proceeds of an annually renewable group-term policy were *not* includible in the insured's gross estate where the insured assigned the insurance more than 3 years prior to death. In 1982 the IRS ruled that an employer's renewal of a group-term policy by payment of the annual premium did not give the employee any new rights in the insurance. Rev. Rul. 82-13, 1982-1 C.B. — . Accordingly, the insurance was not includible in the estate of an employee who effectively assigned all interests in the insurance more than 3 years prior to death. The result of the ruling hinged on the nature of the policy, which provided for automatic renewal upon payment of the annual premium. Under the changes to §2035 made by the 1981 Act the premiums paid by the insured or the insured's employer within 3 years of death are usually not includible in the insured's estate.

A change of position by the IRS on another issue provides further encouragement for the assignment of group-term insurance. The IRS first ruled that an insured employee could not effectively assign an interest in group insurance that was provided at the time of the employee's death under a policy that was not in effect when the assignment was made. Rev. Rul. 79-231, 1979-2 C.B. 323. It involved an employee, who, in 1971, assigned to his wife all of his interest in any life insurance that might be provided by his employer. The assignment was made more than 3 years prior to his death, during a time when his group insurance was provided under a master policy issued by Company Y. In 1977 the employer terminated the master policy with Company Y and entered into a new master policy with Company Z. However, the terms of the master policies were identical in all relevant respects. Shortly after the master policy with Company Z became effective, the employee assigned all of his interest in it to his wife. As luck would have it, the employee died within 3 years of that assignment. In Rev. Rul. 79-231 the IRS ruled that the assignment that the employee made in 1971 was ineffective to transfer his rights in the insurance that was provided by the master policy subsequently issued by Company Z. According to the IRS, the employee could not make such an "anticipatory assignment" of insurance that was not in effect at the time. Accordingly, it held that the insurance was not assigned until 1977, as a result of which it was includible in the insured's estate under §2035.

Rev. Rul. 79-231 was revoked by the IRS less than a year after it was issued and a contrary ruling issued, Rev. Rul. 80-289, 1980-2 C.B. 270. The later ruling held upon identical facts that "the [second] assignment will not be treated as a transfer under Section 2035 of the code." In it the IRS "maintains the view that the anticipatory assignment was not technically effective as a present transfer of the decedent's rights in the policy issued by Company Z. Nevertheless, the Service believes that the assignment in 1977 to D's spouse, the object of the anticipatory assignment in 1971, should not cause the value of the proceeds to be includible in the gross estate of the decedent under section 2035 where the assignment was necessitated by the change of the employer's master insurance carrier and the new arrangement is identical in all relevant aspects to the previous arrangement with Company Y." Similar problems could arise if, subsequent to an assignment, the group policy is renewed or the amount of insurance is increased, as happens when the amount of coverage is tied to the employee's salary or position. The assignment of interests in existing group policies should attempt to deal with the problem by providing that the assignment covers all interests in the existing group insurance, all interests in group insurance provided by any renewal or replacement, and all changes in the amount of the insurance. Such an explicit assignment, if made more than 3 years prior to the assignor's death, should help insulate the proceeds of the insurance from inclusion in the insured's gross estate.

Gift Tax. The amount of a gift resulting from the assignment of group-term insurance depends upon all of the circumstances, including the length of time for which the premiums have been paid, the extent to which the employer is obligated to make future payments, and the health of the insured. An assignment of group-term insurance may involve a gift composed of one or more of the following components: (1) an amount equivalent to the cost of a term policy for the unexpired portion of the period through which the premium on the group policy had been paid at the time of assignment (a proportionate part of the premium actually paid allocable to the cost of the unexpired period is an acceptable method of valuing this interest (Reg. §25.2512-6(a)), but it may be difficult or impossible to determine, which may justify using the Table I cost for this purpose); (2) the value of any right the assignment may carry with it to require the assignor or another person to make future premium payments; and (3) any additional value the insurance may have because of the insured's poor health. The problem of valuation is also discussed at §6.28, *supra.* Further gifts will occur as later premiums are paid directly or indirectly by the employer or other third party. Thus, where the insured's employer is not obligated to pay future premiums on group-term insurance that the employee has assigned, any future premium payments involve an indirect gift by the employee to the assignee. Rev. Rul. 76-490, 1976-2 C.B. 300. On the other hand, the assignment of a group-term policy on the last day of the premium payment period does not involve a present gift where the employer is not obligated to make further premium payments. *Id.*

Without any analysis Rev. Rul. 76-490 incorrectly concluded that the payment of future premiums on group-term insurance assigned to a trust would qualify for the annual gift tax exclusion. The conclusion is incorrect if, as indicated by the facts, the beneficiary was not entitled to any current benefits in the trust. Apparently the trustee was required to retain the insurance until the death of the insured when the proceeds would be distributed to the beneficiary. A later ruling does hold that an annual exclusion is not available with respect to the employer's payment of premiums where the trustee of the insurance trust will retain the proceeds in trust following the death of the insured. Rev. Rul. 79-47, 1979-1 C.B. 312. The availability of the annual exclusion for transfers of insurance to a trust turns on the extent of the beneficiary's present interests in the trust and not on whether or not the proceeds are immediately distributable by the trustee when the insured dies. When a trustee is required to retain insurance and the beneficiary is not entitled to any current benefits under the trust, the beneficiary does not have a present interest in the insurance or in subsequent premium payments. Commissioner v. Warner, 127 F.2d 913 (9th Cir. 1942); Reg. §25.2503-3(c), Example 2. Of course, the orginal transfer to the trust and the payment of subsequent premiums may qualify for the annual exclusion if the beneficiary has a *Crummey* power to withdraw property as it is added to the trust. *See* §7.36, *infra* and LRs 8006109, 8021058.

Problem 6-7. W, who was born on February 15, 1942, is a computer technician employed by Eduself, Inc. Her marriage was dissolved 5 years ago and her two children, S (13) and D (15), live with her. W's property other than group-term insurance provided by Eduself is worth about $250,000. She also has an expectant interest in her parents' estates, which could bring her another $250,000 on the death of the survivor of them. Her life is insured for an amount equal to 4 times her annual salary (now $25,000) under Eduself's group plan, which meets the requirements of §79. It is not possible to identify the exact amount of premiums paid with respect to the insurance on W's life. W's insurance advisor has suggested that she assign the insurance to an irrevocable trust for the benefit of her children. Under the plan, an independent person would act as trustee. Distributions of income and principal would be made to S and D in the discretion of the trustee until the trust terminated. When the younger living child reaches 25 or upon the death of W, whichever last occurs, the trust would terminate and the principal would be distributed in equal shares to S and D or to the survivor of them.

What would be the income, gift, and estate tax consequences of assigning the insurance to the trust? Should the assignment be drafted to take into account any increases in W's salary or changes in the insurer? Would the gift tax consequences be improved if the trust allowed each beneficiary to withdraw a proportionate part of any property that is added to the trust (including the payment of any premiums on the group insurance) during a limited period following notification of the addition? *See* §7.36, *infra.* Would a beneficiary's failure to exercise the power have any gift or estate tax consequences?

§6.60. *Group-Term Life Insurance: Retired Lives Reserve* (*RLR*)

Retired lives reserve is a specialized type of group-term life insurance that is designed to provide for the continuation of group-term insurance coverage for employees after retirement. It involves a current payment made entirely by the employer of the cost of current group-term insurance and a contribution to a reserve fund or trust that will bear the cost of continuing the group-term insurance after an employee retires. RLR plans are designed so that the contributions to the reserve fund, plus the tax-free income earned by the fund, will be sufficient to pay the cost of providing group-term insurance to the retired employees covered by the plan. For a more detailed description of RLR, *see* Fromberg & Bodnar, Retired Lives Reserve: An Alternative Solution to Retirement Insurance Coverage, 48 J. Tax. 224 (1978). Pending the completion of its review of the subject, the IRS will not issue rulings or determination letters regarding whether life insurance purchased under an RLR plan will be considered group-term insurance. §5.01, Rev. Proc. 80-22, 1980-1 C.B. 654.

The employer's entire payment for RLR insurance is currently deductible, providing it is reasonable in amount and constitutes compensation to the employee (§162); the employer is not the beneficiary of the policy; and the employer does not have any right to recapture contributions to the reserve so long as any active or retired employee remains alive. Rev. Rul. 69-382, 1969-2 C.B. 28. RLR plans assume that the employer's contributions to the reserve fund constitute payment of the cost of post-retirement group-term insurance that is not taxable to employees by reason of §79(b)(1) and that the contributions do not jeopardize the current exclusion of the cost of $50,000 of group-term insurance under §79(a).

An RLR plan is attractive to employees because it assures them of important post-retirement insurance coverage. Under other group-term life insurance plans the insurance commonly terminates upon retirement unless converted by the employee. Many employees do not convert their group-term insurance upon retirement because of the substantial cost of continuing the coverage as permanent insurance or as individual term. An RLR plan is attractive to an employer because it allows the employer to select the class of employees to be covered, provided the selection is based upon factors relating to employment. Ultimately, however, RLR plans may be prohibited from discriminating in favor of officers, directors, or highly compensated employees. Finally, RLR plans are attractive because the full amount of the employer's payment is currently deductible and the earnings on the reserve fund accumulate tax-free.

Insurance provided an employee under an RLR plan is probably assignable to the same extent as regular group-term insurance. *See* §6.59, *supra.* Accordingly, an employee should be able to remove the insurance from the employee's estate by an assignment made more than 3 years prior to death. However, the value of the insurance for gift tax purposes is uncertain. RLR advocates typically argue that the insurance has no greater value than group-term insurance that the employer is not obligated to continue. (*See* Rev. Rul. 76-490, 1976-2 C.B. 300, discussed at §6.59, *supra*). However, the insurance might have a significantly greater value, either at the time of the assignment or when the employee retires and the right to continued coverage provided by the reserve becomes fixed. The IRS might contend that a gift of the insurance included a portion of the reserve fund already paid in and allocable to the insurance on the employee's life. Also, the gift might have a greater value if the employer is obligated to make future premium payments and contributions to the reserve fund. In fact, where the employer is obligated to continue the insurance until the employee retires and to continue contributing to the reserve fund, a transfer of the insurance might be treated as a gift of the right to receive the face amount of the policy when the employee dies. The present value of the right to receive a specified amount upon the death of a person is shown in the actuarial table at Reg. §25.2512-9(f) (column 4). At the least, an employee who assigned his or her RLR insurance will make gifts as future premiums and contributions to the reserve fund are paid by the employer.

§6.61. *Minimum-Deposit Life Insurance Plans*

A minimum-deposit plan involves the systematic borrowing and use of the increase in cash value of a policy to pay the annual premiums. In order to reduce the cash outlay required of the owner in early years of a minimum-deposit plan, some companies offer policies that build up their cash values relatively fast. Where a participating policy is involved, the dividends are usually applied under the fifth dividend option to buy term insurance equal to the amount of the outstanding loan, which maintains the level of protection provided by the policy.

Minimum-deposit plans are generally competitive with term insurance if the interest paid on the outstanding policy loan is deductible for income tax purposes. However, under §264(a)(3) interest paid on loans that are directly or indirectly used to pay premiums on policies issued after August 6, 1963, is deductible only if the payment satisfies one of the exceptions to the general rule. In general the only reliable and useful exception for planning purposes is the "four-in-seven" exception, which requires that at least 4 of the first 7 premiums be paid with funds that are not borrowed. See §264(c)(1), discussed at §6.42, *supra*. Accordingly, most illustrations involving minimum-deposit plans assume that the owner will pay premiums for 4 of the first 7 years without borrowing and that the interest payments are deductible. The most advantageous illustrations assume that premiums are paid without borrowing in the first, fifth, sixth, and seventh years. Hill & McKay, The Flowering of Financed Life Insurance, 118 Tr. & Est. 59, 62 (1979). Of course, in order to preserve their use of funds as long as possible, insurers would generally prefer the owner to pay the first 4 premiums without borrowing.

The owners of existing policies may, of course, take advantage of the benefits of a minimum-deposit plan by borrowing the increase in cash value each year and using it to pay premiums. However, that approach is not generally advanced by insurance agents unless it also involves the sale of additional policies. After all, minimum-deposit plans are advocated principally for the purpose of selling additional cash value policies. Given the structure of the plans, they are promoted more heavily when the market rate of interest does not exceed the loan rate specified in the policy or exceeds it by a small amount. The reason is simple: It is contrary to the insurer's interests to promote low rate policy loans during periods when the insurer can invest the funds more profitably itself.

§6.62. Leased Life Insurance

In the mid-1960s some promoters touted "leased life insurance" plans under which the owner of a policy assigned it to a leasing company in exchange for its cash surrender value, but retained the right to designate the beneficiary. The company then "leased" the policy back to the assignor for a level annual charge in exchange for which the company agreed to pay the annual premiums and to pay the face amount of the policy to the designated beneficiary. The annual charge represented the difference between the increase in the cash surrender value and the premium, plus the sum of the interest expense incurred by the leasing company in borrowing the cash surrender value of the policy, the cost of other expenses, and a profit. Stripped to its bare essentials the plan represented a clever attempt to allow the owner of a policy to claim an interest deduction for the excess of the annual premium over the increase in the cash surrender value. In Murray Kay, 44 T.C. 660 (1965), the Tax Court considered the lessor to be the agent of the lessee and allowed a deduction for the portion of the annual charge that represented interest paid to the insurer. However, Rev. Rul. 66-298, 1966-2 C.B. 48 held that an interest deduction was not allowable where the agreement did not establish an indebtedness on the part of the lessee. Aside from the absence of tax advantages, a leased life insurance plan does not adequately protect the interests of the lessee. Snyder, Leading a Tax-Sheltered Life, N.Y.U. 25th Inst. Fed. Tax. 765, 776-779 (1976).

§6.63. Universal Life Insurance

In 1981 several companies introduced a new policy line, called universal life. At base, this type of policy offers a fixed amount of insurance under a form of ordinary life plan plus an investment medium for voluntary contributions by the policyholder in excess of the cost of the fixed amount of insurance. The policies typically provide for the payment of a death benefit equal to a fixed amount of insurance plus the amount of the policy's cash value at the time of the insured's death. In the case of universal life, the cash value of the policy is made up of the voluntary additional contributions made by the policy owner (less a fee of from 5 to 10% of the amount of each addition) plus the accumulated earnings on the cash value. The return on the cash value is determined by the insurer, usually according to a formula stated in the policy (*e.g.,* the current interest rate on 13-week United States Treasury bills). Of course, the return is only paid on the *net* amount of the contributions to the cash value, after the payment of all fees. Most policies require the payment of a substantial first-year fee similar to the agent's commission on an ordinary life policy. By way of illustration, the fee on a $100,000 policy ranges between $300 and $750. (Some companies do not charge such a fee, but they charge a higher fee on contributions to the cash value.) Importantly, the cash value may be borrowed by the policy owner or withdrawn at any time, which may trigger the payment of an additional small fee. Presumably the availability of the deduction for interest on borrowed funds would be governed by §264. *See* §6.42, *supra.*

Universal life is a more attractive investment if the cash value is not treated as a separate fund and is considered to be the equivalent of the cash value or reserve under a more traditional type of life insurance policy. If so, the cash value will be treated as life insurance for purposes of §101 and the current earnings on the cash value will not be taxed to the policy owner until they are withdrawn. A private letter ruling issued in early 1981 with respect to E.F. Hutton Life reached favorable conclusions on both points. LR 8116073, modified by LR 8121074. However, the conclusions are questionable and may not be adhered to when the IRS issues a revenue ruling concerning universal life. If the current earnings on the cash value of a universal life policy are not sheltered, the net return on the policy owner's investment would not be competitive with the return available on other liquid investments (*e.g.,* money market funds).

§6.64.   *Veterans' Life Insurance*

The government has traditionally made a limited amount of life insurance available to members of the armed forces during active duty at little or no cost. Earlier programs allowed the veterans to continue the insurance after separation from service under a variety of low cost term or cash value policies. The plan adopted by Congress in 1965 allowed members to purchase Servicemen's Group Insurance coverage of up to $15,000 from a large number of participating private insurance companies at a uniform premium cost. 38 U.S.C. §§765 to 776 (1976). However, until 1974 Servicemen's Group Insurance could only be converted into cash value policies that were available through the participating life insurance companies. 38 U.S.C. §768(c), repealed by Pub. L. 93-289 §5(a)(5), 88 Stat. 168. In 1974 Congress increased the maximum to $20,000 and authorized conversion to a new type of insurance, Veterans' Group Life Insurance. 38 U.S.C. §777. However, the only form of Veterans' Group Life Insurance available upon separation from service is a 5-year nonparticipating and nonrenewable term policy. 38 U.S.C. §777(b)(1976).

The proceeds of life insurance policies issued under the World War Veterans' Act of 1924, the National Service Life Insurance Act of 1940, and the Servicemen's Indemnity Act of 1951 are includible in the estate of the deceased serviceperson or veteran. Rev. Rul. 55-622, 1955-2 C.B. 385. The proceeds of Servicemen's Group Life Insurance and Veterans' Group Life Insurance policies are also no doubt subject to inclusion in the gross estate of a deceased serviceperson or veteran. Inclusion of the proceeds of the latter types of policies in the gross estate of the insured under §2042(2) is inevitable because the insured is the only person who may designate a beneficiary and neither the insurance nor any of the benefits under it may be assigned. 38 C.F.R. §§9.16, 9.20 (1975).

Community Property. In Wissner v. Wissner, 338 U.S. 655 (1950), a 5-to-3 decision, the Supreme Court held that the spouse of a member or veteran of the armed services did not acquire an interest in a National Service Life Insurance policy under a state's community property law. It reasoned that Congress intended to provide "a uniform and comprehensive system of life insurance for members and veterans of the armed forces" (338 U.S. at 658) and to give the insured the exclusive right to name the beneficiary. From that the Court concluded that it would frustrate the intent of Congress to recognize that a member's spouse had a community property interest in a government policy. The program was held to be a constitutional exercise of the congressional power over national defense. Because the proceeds of a veteran's policy are not community property they are fully includible in his or her gross estate under §2042(2). Estate of Hugh C. Hutson, 49 T.C. 495 (1968). Consistent with that rule, the proceeds of a veteran's policy were not treated as community property for purposes of calculating the pre-1982 maximum allowable marital deduction. Hunt v. United States, 59-2 U.S.T.C. ¶11, 891, 4 A.F.T.R.2d ¶6051 (E.D. Texas 1959).

§6.65.   Death Benefit Only Plans

Although the Internal Revenue Service has sought to fit the pure death benefit under almost every section of the Internal Revenue Code defining the gross estate for federal estate tax purposes, these attempts have met with only limited success. The exclusion of pure death benefits from the

> employee's estate opens a significant loophole in the Code's transfer tax provisions. The Service has recently attempted to reach these benefits under the gift tax. These efforts, although ingenious, remain stopgap measures. Wolk, The Pure Death Benefit: An Estate and Gift Tax Anomaly, 66 Minn. L. Rev. 229, 229-230 (1982).

Employment contracts sometimes provide for the payment of benefits akin to life insurance. In particular, the employer may be required to make specified payments to members of the employee's family if the employee dies while actively employed. In most litigated cases the value of such benefits has not been included in the employee's gross estate.

The so-called pure death benefit is analogous to the group insurance provided by some employers that is payable to beneficiaries designated by the employer and not the employee. *See* §6.16, *supra*. However, there is an important difference in the income taxation of the payments: Amounts payable under death benefit plans are taxed as income in respect of a decedent to the extent they exceed $5,000 (*see* §§101(b), 691(a)). Accordingly, substantially all of the amounts paid under a death benefit plan are included in the recipient's gross income. Of course, if the payments are included in the deceased employee's gross estate, the recipient is allowed an income tax deduction under §691(c) for the estate tax attributable to the benefits. In contrast, the proceeds of group-term insurance are generally not included in the recipient's gross income. *See* §101(a) and §6.34, *supra*.

Estate Tax. As Professor Bruce Wolk indicates, the courts have rarely required pure death benefits to be included in the employee's gross estate. Inclusion is generally not required by §2039, which only applies to contracts or agreements under which the decedent was, or might become, entitled to receive an annuity or other lifetime benefit. For the purpose of determining whether or not the decedent held such a right, consideration is given to "any combination of arrangements, understandings or plans arising by reason of the decedent's employment." Reg. §20.2039-1(b)(ii). Note, however, that §2039(a) is concerned only with post-retirement benefits. Contractual provisions for payment of a salary or disability benefits generally are not taken into account. Estate of Schelberg v. Commissioner, 612 F.2d 25 (2d Cir. 1979) (disability benefits); Estate of Murray J. Siegel, 74 T.C. 613 (1980) (disability benefits); Estate of Firmin D. Fusz, 46 T.C. 214 (1966), *acq.*, 1967-2 C.B. 2 (salary). More important, the IRS has ruled that benefits accruing under qualified plans are not to be considered together with rights arising under nonqualified plans (*e.g.*, death benefit only plans). Rev. Rul. 76-380, 1976-2 C.B. 270 (qualified retirement plan is not aggregated with nonqualified survivor's income benefit plan for purposes of determining includibility of the value of the survivor's benefits under §2039). Accordingly, insofar as §2039 is concerned, it is "safe" to provide an employee with a death benefit only plan and a qualified retirement plan.

Courts have also generally not required inclusion of pure death benefits under §2033 whether or not the benefits were subject to the unilateral control of the employer (*i.e.*, the benefits were revocable). *See* Wolk, *supra*, at 235-240. In the typical case exclusion is based on the employee's lack of any property interest in the benefits and lack of control over their disposition following his or her death. *E.g.*, Estate of Tully v. United States, 528 F.2d 1401 (Ct. Cl. 1976); Kramer v. United States, 406 F.2d 1363 (Ct. Cl. 1960). Even where the employee has a lifetime interest in the benefits, inclusion under §2033 is precluded because the interest terminates upon the employee's death. *See* Estate of Edward H. Wadewitz, 39 T.C. 925 (1963), *aff'd on other grounds*, 339 F.2d 980 (7th Cir. 1964) (inclusion required under §2039).

Inclusion under one or more of the transfer sections, §§2035 to 2038, is possible if the decedent made the requisite transfer of an interest in the benefits. Several courts have found that the employee's agreement to render future services in exchange for a compensation package that included the death benefit constitutes such a transfer. *E.g.*, Estate of Tully v. United States, 528 F.2d 1401 (Ct. Cl. 1976). The conclusion seems correct, but does not itself require inclusion under any of the transfer sections. Indeed, more often than not the benefits have been excluded from the employee's estate for failure to satisfy other requirements of those sections.

Prior to the adoption of the 1981 Act pure death benefits paid under contracts entered into within 3 years of death were potentially includible in the employee's gross estate under §2035. *See* Estate of Bernard L. Porter, 54 T.C. 1066 (1970), *aff'd*, 442 F.2d 915 (1st Cir. 1971) (death benefits paid under contracts entered into 3 weeks prior to decedent's death with 3 closely held corporations were included under §2035). The changes made by the 1981 Act may preclude such inclusion of such benefits. In particular, pure death benefits do not appear to fall within any of the exceptions enumerated in §2035(d)(2) to the general exclusionary rule of §2035(d)(1).

Pure death benefits are probably not includible in the employee's gross estate under §2036. Section 2036(a)(1) does not apply because the employee cannot possess or enjoy any of the benefits during his or her lifetime — they only arise following death. The power of the employee to affect the beneficial enjoyment of the benefits by changing the terms of the employment agreement with the employer might require inclusion under §2036(a)(2). However, inclusion may not result because §2036(a)(2) "does not include a power over the transferred property itself which does not affect the enjoyment of the income received or earned during the decedent's life." Reg. §20.2036-1(b)(3). *See* Wolk, *supra* at 241.

Inclusion under §2037 is possible if the employee retains a reversionary interest in the benefits, the value of which immediately before the employee's death exceeds 5% of the value of the benefits. §2037(a). For purposes of §2037 a reversionary interest includes a possibility that the property transferred by the decedent will return to the transferor or the transferor's estate. §2037(b)(1). However, the reach of §2037 is avoided by precluding payment of the benefits to the employee's estate (since the right to the benefits only arises upon the employee's death, in no event could they return to the employee).

Section 2038(a)(1) requires inclusion of a pure death benefit if the employee held the power, exercisable alone or in conjunction with any other person, to alter, amend, revoke, or terminate the enjoyment of the benefits. The employee's power to affect the enjoyment of the benefits by a drastic action such as divorcing a spouse, terminating employment, or renegotiating the amount of his or her salary, is probably not such a power. Estate of Tully, 528 F.2d 1401 (Ct. Cl. 1976). That conclusion is consistent with the IRS's concession that the power to cancel employer-provided group insurance by terminating employment is not an incident of ownership for purposes of §2042(2). See §6.16, *supra*. The *Tully* court also found that the mere possibility of bilateral contract modification did not constitute a §2038(a)(1) power. Estate of Tully, 528 F.2d at 1405. *See also* Kramer v. United States, 406 F.2d 1363 (Ct. Cl. 1969). The Tax Court has held that an express retention by the employer and employee of the power to modify the terms of the agreement required inclusion of the death benefit under §2038(a)(1). Estate of Murray J. Siegel, 75 T.C. 613 (1980). The includibility of the benefit should not turn on the question of whether or not the power to modify the contract was expressly reserved by the parties: A contract may generally be modified by the parties although they have not expressly reserved the right to do so.

Gift Tax. Until 1981 the IRS did not attempt to subject death benefit only plans to the gift tax. However, in declining to apply the estate tax to such benefits, some courts suggested that the contract entered into between the decedent and his employer involved a gift. *E.g.*, Estate of Tully v. United States, 528 F.2d 1401, 1404 (Ct. Cl. 1976) ("Tully in substance, if not in form, made a gift of part of his future earnings to his wife.") Of course, the gift tax can only be imposed if the employee made a transfer of value. Moreover, the imposition of the gift tax depends upon the time at which the transfer became complete, the valuation of the interests transferred, and the availability of the annual exclusion. Perhaps because of its lack of success in subjecting pure death benefits to the estate tax, the IRS has ruled that the employee makes a completed gift of the amount of the death benefit at the time of his or her death, when the gift first became susceptible of valuation. Rev. Rul. 81-31, 1981-1 C.B. 475. The ruling also holds that the gift qualifies for the annual exclusion under §2503(b).

Presumably the execution of an employment contract that provides for the payment of a death benefit does involve a transfer of value by the employee. As mentioned above, several courts have reached that conclusion in pure death benefit cases arising under the estate tax. However, the transfer may be incomplete at the time the contract is executed because of the expressly or impliedly reserved power of the employer and employee to change its terms. *See* Reg. §25.2511-2(e). The difficulty of valuing such a gift led the IRS to the questionable conclusion in Rev. Rul. 81-31 that the gift was completed at the time of the employee's death when the amount of the gift first became susceptible of valuation.

As Professor Wolk notes, the protection provided by the death benefit may involve a continuing indirect gift by the employee analogous to the indirect gifts made by an employee each time his or her employer pays the premium on a term insurance policy that is owned by another party. *See* Rev. Rul. 76-490 and §6.59, *supra*. However, such indirect gifts would be difficult to value and subject to dispute in virtually every case. Although the death benefit is somewhat analogous to employer-provided term insurance, it presents a different problem as it does not involve the payment of premiums (or other amounts indicative of its value). Any continuing indirect gifts that are found to take place might qualify for the annual gift tax exclusion, depending on the terms of the employment contract and the manner in which the benefits were payable. By analogy to the term insurance cases the annual exclusion may be available where the benefits are payable outright to an individual or to a trust in which an individual has a sufficient present interest. *See* §6.59, *supra*.

Revenue Ruling 81-31 held that the employee's gift of the death benefit was not completed until the employee died, when, according to the IRS, the amount of the gift first became susceptible of valuation. The approach reaches the IRS objective of subjecting the death benefit to a transfer tax, but it is not consistent with the basic thrust of the gift tax. First, the difficulty of valuing a transfer generally does not cause it to be incomplete. Second, the IRS approach is inconsistent with the fundamental concept that the gift tax only applies to completed inter vivos transfers. That concept is evidenced by Reg. §25.2511-2(f), which states, "The relinquishment or termination of a power to change the beneficiaries of transferred property occurring otherwise than by the death of the donor (the statute being confined to transfers by living donors) is regarded as the event which completes the gift and causes the tax to apply." No doubt the validity of the ruling will be challenged.

Income Tax

The courts have uniformly held that post-death payments to an employee's widow are to be treated as "income in respect of a decedent" despite the fact that under the terms of the employment contract, the employee would never be entitled to actual receipt of the income. Estate of Nilssen v. United States, 322 F. Supp. 260, 265 (D. Minn. 1971).

The income taxation of pure death benefits is relatively simple. A payment under a death benefit only plan is taxable to the recipient as income in respect of a decedent under §691. Such a characterization is appropriate because the payment is solely attributable to the decedent's lifetime services and is not subject to any other contingencies. *See* Rev. Rul. 73-327, 1973-2 C.B. 214. Accordingly, the payment is includible in the recipient's gross income except to the extent of the special $5,000 exclusion allowed under §101(b) for payments made by an employer on account of an employee's death. Of course, a totally voluntary payment to the members of a deceased employee's family may constitute a nontaxable gift under §102. Certainly a voluntary payment would be excludible if it satisfied the test articulated in Commissioner v. Duberstein, 363 U.S. 278 (1960) (*i.e.*, that the gift proceed from detached and disinterested generosity or out of affection, respect, admiration, charity, or like impulses. *Id.* at 285). Presumably the employer would not be entitled to deduct such an excludible payment.

Where a death benefit is paid in periodic installments, it is subject to the rules of §72. In such a case, the $5,000 exclusion is treated as the employee's investment in the contract. If the amount receivable in 3 years is equal to or exceeds the amount of the exclusion, the entire amount of each payment is excluded from the recipient's gross income until the $5,000 has been excluded. Thereafter the full amount of each payment is includible in the recipient's gross income. §72(d); Rev. Rul. 58-153, 1958-1 C.B. 43. If the amount receivable in 3 years is less than $5,000, that amount is amortized over the period the payments will be made. As in other cases the annuitant's life expectancy is determined according to Table I of Reg. §1.72-9, printed at §8.29, *infra.*

The estate tax treatment of the death benefit does not affect the amount includible in the recipient's gross income: Whether or not the death benefit is included in the employee's gross estate, its basis is not adjusted under §1014 because of the limitation imposed by §1014(c). ("This section shall not apply to property which constitutes a right to receive an item of income in respect of a decedent under §691.") However, where the death benefit is included in the employee's gross estate, the recipient is entitled to an income tax deduction for the additional estate tax imposed because of the inclusion of the death benefit. §691(c). In brief, the estate tax applicable to the employee's estate is computed with and without the inclusion of all items of income in respect of a decedent. The additional tax arising by reason of the inclusion of those items, for which the income tax deduction is allowed, is apportioned between them according to their respective estate tax values. Finally, a §691(c) deduction is allowable to the recipient of an item of income in respect of a decedent proportionately as the income from the item is reported as income by the recipient.

Problem 6-8. In 1981 Ada, an unmarried woman, joined A,B&C, Inc. as an executive. Ada signed A,B&C's standard employment agreement, which provides that the employer will make a lump sum payment of an amount equal to double her annual salary to her surviving spouse or children if she dies during the contractual period. If she does not leave a surviving spouse or children, a lump sum amount equal to her annual salary will be paid to the beneficiary she designates, otherwise to her personal representative. Ada did not designate a beneficiary in the agreement. Ada's current salary is $50,000, which she expects will continue to increase by annual increments at least equal to the yearly increases in the consumer price index. A,B&C also provides its employees with health insurance, a group-term life insurance plan that meets the requirements of §79 (Ada's life is insured for $50,000), and a qualified retirement plan. It does not provide any nonqualified post-retirement benefits to Ada or the other employees. Last week Ada married Fred, a longtime friend who owns 10% of the outstanding stock of A,B&C and is a director and chairman of the executive committee of its board of directors. However, Fred is not an employee of A,B&C. Ada has asked you to explain the manner in which the lump sum death benefit is likely to be treated for income, gift, and estate tax purposes.

§6.66. Gifts of Life Insurance under the Uniform Gifts to Minors Act

Most states have adopted the 1966 revision of the Uniform Gifts to Minors Act under which life insurance policies or annuity contracts on the life of a minor or a member of the minor's family may be given to the minor by registering it "in the name of the donor, another adult [an adult member of the minor's family, a guardian of the minor] or a trust company, followed, in substance, by the words: 'as custodian for ___(name of minor)___ under the [name of enacting state] Uniform Gifts to Minors Act.'" Act §2(a)(4), 8 U.L.A. 199 (1972).

The federal tax consequences that generally flow from the transfer of property to a custodian for a minor also apply in the case of life insurance. *See* §7.36, *infra.* In addition, the proceeds of a policy may be includible in the estate of the insured under §§2038 or 2042(2) if the insured is acting as custodian at the time of his or her death. The broad powers a custodian has to invest and reinvest the custodial property probably constitute incidents of ownership for purposes of §2042. Inclusion under §2042 might occur whether or not the policy had been given to the minor by the insured-custodian. See the discussion of incidents of ownership held in a fiduciary capacity, §6.18, *supra*. In contrast, §2038 would apply to the insurance only if the insured had transferred it to himself or herself as custodian for the minor.

The income from custodianship property is taxed to the minor except to the extent it is used to discharge the legal obligation of another person to support the minor. Presumably the income will be taxed to the minor although it is used to pay premiums on a policy that insures the life of the donor or the donor's spouse. Of course, if a trust were involved the income would be taxed to the grantor to the extent the income is or may be applied by the grantor alone, or without the consent of an adverse party, to payment of premiums on policies of insurance on the life of the grantor or the grantor's spouse. *See* §677(a)(3), §6.39 *supra,* and §10.32, *infra*.

§6.67. *Life Insurance and the Uniform Simultaneous Death Act*

The Uniform Simultaneous Death Act, 8 U.L.A. 608 (1972), is in effect in almost all states. Under the basic rule of §1 of the Act, where devolution depends upon the priority of death of two persons and there is no sufficient evidence that they died otherwise than simultaneously, the property of each is disposed of as if he or she had survived the other. Thus, if a husband and wife die simultaneously, the husband's property is distributed as if he survived his wife and the wife's property is distributed as if she survived him. The parties may prescribe a different rule in the governing instrument, which will control over the provisions of the Act.

Section 5 of the Act provides a special rule for distribution of life or accident insurance where the insured and the beneficiary die simultaneously. Under it the proceeds of the policy are distributed as if the insured had survived the beneficiary. In such event the proceeds are paid to any contingent beneficiary or beneficiaries who survive the insured. Of course, if no beneficiary survives the insured, the proceeds will be paid in accordance with the terms of the policy, which usually call for payment either to the estate of the insured or to the owner of the policy. Payment to the estate of the insured is generally undesirable because it may unnecessarily subject the proceeds to federal and state death taxes. *E.g.,* §2042(2); Ill. Ann. Stat. Ch. 120, §375 (Smith-Hurd 1980 Supp.). Payment to the insured's estate may also subject the proceeds to claims of creditors against the insured. Accordingly, insurance should generally name both primary and contingent beneficiaries.

The estate tax advantage of naming a contingent beneficiary is illustrated by the cases where the husband's life was insured under a policy owned by his wife that named her a primary beneficiary and their children as contingent beneficiaries. Estate of Meltzer v. Commissioner, 439 F.2d 798 (4th Cir. 1971); Estate of Wein v. Commissioner, 441 F.2d 32 (5th Cir. 1971); Old Kent Bank & Trust Co. v. United States, 430 F.2d 392 (6th Cir. 1970); Estate of Chown v. Commissioner, 428 F.2d 1395 (9th Cir. 1970). Under these decisions neither the policy nor its proceeds was includible in the gross estate of the insured. Moreover, none of the proceeds was includible in the wife's gross estate because she was deemed to have predeceased the insured. Only the interpolated terminal reserve value of the policy was includible in the wife's gross estate under §2033. As a result, the proceeds passed to the insured's children free of estate taxation except for the value of the policy included in the wife's estate.

Community Property. A special problem may arise when a husband and wife die simultaneously owning community property insurance on the life of one of them that names the other as beneficiary. If no contingent beneficiary is named, the proceeds of the policy will be paid in accordance with the terms of the policy as if the insured had survived (*i.e.,* either in equal shares to the estates of the husband and wife as owners of the policy or entirely to the husband's estate as the insured under the policy). In California and Washington, and perhaps Idaho and Nevada, the presumption that the insured survived the beneficiary will persist through the distribution of the proceeds by their estates. Estates of Saunders, 317 P.2d 528 (Wash 1957); Wedemeyer's Estate, 240 P.2d 8 (Cal. App. 1952). Under that approach the entire proceeds may be distributed to the beneficiaries named in the insured's will or to the intestate successors of the insured.

Example 6-26. H and W died simultaneously and intestate owning a community property policy on H's life that named W as sole beneficiary. H was survived by his father, F, and W was survived by her mother, M. Under the terms of the policy the proceeds were payable to the owner of the policy if no beneficiary survived the insured. Because the insured (H) is deemed to have survived the beneficiary (W), the proceeds will be paid in equal shares to the estates of H and W. Then W's one-half share will be distributed to H's estate because he is deemed to have survived her. For the same reason H's one-half share of the proceeds will not be distributed to W. Finally, the entire proceeds will be distributed as an asset of H's estate (*i.e.,* to F), as W did not survive H. As a result the entire proceeds of the community property policy will be paid to the relatives of the insured to the total exclusion of the relatives of the noninsured spouse. Of course, H and W could have controlled by will the distribution of the proceeds from their estates and could have directed that a different presumption of survivorship should govern the disposition of their estates.

This problem will not arise if the policy names a contingent beneficiary who survives the insured. It will also not arise in Arizona, New Mexico, and Texas, which have adopted the substance of the amendment to §5 of the Act proposed by the Uniform Commissioners in 1953. The amendment provides that "if the policy is community property of the insured and his spouse, and there is no alternative beneficiary except the estate or personal representatives of the insured, the proceeds shall be distributed as community property under Section 4." 8 U.L.A. 621 (1972). Under §4 one-half of the community property is distributed as if the husband had survived and one-half as if the wife had survived. By way of illustration, §4 would require the proceeds of the policy described in Example 6-26 to be distributed one-half to F (H's intestate successor) and one-half to M (W's intestate successor). Consistent with that result one-half of the proceeds would be included in the gross estate of each spouse. Rev. Rul. 79-303, 1979-2 C.B. 332 (Texas law).

F. PLANNING WITH LIFE INSURANCE

§6.68. Introduction

Planning for the ownership, premium payments, and beneficiary designations of life insurance is a critical but often neglected aspect of estate planning. The overall objective is to integrate life insurance fully into the client's estate plan, which requires that it be coordinated with the client's will and other elements of the plan. As always, the federal tax considerations are important, but they should not dominate the planning.

Life insurance is a uniquely valuable estate-planning tool for clients with large estates. Its current value is often a small fraction of the amount of the death benefits, which are generally not subject to the income tax. Through proper planning a large amount of insurance can be excluded from the client's estate, at little or no gift tax cost, without necessarily divesting the client of any items of substantial current value. The insurance is often made available for the support of the surviving spouse through a QTIP trust, only part of which may be included in her gross estate. The nominal value and low cost of group-term insurance generally makes it the most economical type to transfer or to acquire for a trust or a person other than the insured. Split-dollar insurance is also popular for essentially the same reason.

§6.69.   *Life Insurance Planning for the Average Client*

The insurance plan for a married couple whose combined gross estates are within the amount of the credit equivalent can be quite simple. Because no estate tax will be due on the death of either spouse it is unnecessary to eliminate the insurance proceeds from their gross estates. Instead, the principal question is how best to settle the insurance proceeds for the benefit of the insured's spouse and children.

Where the insured's spouse has little property, he or she is usually named as primary beneficiary and their children as contingent beneficiaries. The lawyer may only need to verify that the beneficiary designations are consistent with the plan. Policies frequently do not designate contingent beneficiaries, which makes it necessary to add the children or others as contingent beneficiaries. In most cases the noninsured spouse's interest in the policies on the insured's life will pass to the insured under the residuary clause of the noninsured spouse's will. This may be satisfactory for the average client. However, when the estates are large enough for estate taxes to be a concern, the noninsured spouse should consider disposing of his or her interest in the policies in a way that will not cause it to be included in the insured's gross estate.

Where the insured's spouse has a substantial amount of property, he or she could be named as beneficiary. However, such action could cause some unnecessary estate tax to be imposed when the noninsured spouse dies. Inclusion of the proceeds in the noninsured spouse's gross estate is avoided if he or she is given only a limited interest in the proceeds, either under a settlement option selected by the insured or under an inter vivos or testamentary bypass trust established by the insured. *See* §6.73, *infra.* As indicated previously, where an option is selected by the insured the proceeds are not includible in the beneficiary's gross estate, but where the option is selected by the beneficiary they are includible. *See* §6.24, *supra.* The cost of making the proceeds payable to the surviving spouse outright is illustrated by the following example:

> **Example 6-27.** H died in 1982 leaving an estate of $225,000, including $100,000 in insurance, all of which passed outright to his surviving spouse, W. No estate tax was payable by H's estate because the gifts to W qualified for the marital deduction. Of course, no tax would be due from H's estate in any case because of the unified credit available to his estate. Whatever remains of the $225,000 is includible in W's estate when she dies. If it and her other property amount to $500,000 some estate tax would be due if she dies prior to 1986. On the other hand no tax would be due from W's estate if she dies after 1982 and only $275,000 is subject to tax. For example, H could leave the proceeds to a trust for W's benefit or elect a settlement option under which she was a ben-

eficiary, neither of which would require the proceeds to be included in her estate.

Some clients will prefer to permit the proceeds to be subject to taxation upon the death of the surviving spouse in order to give him or her more freedom and greater control over the proceeds. After all, they reason, the surviving spouse may consume the proceeds for support or may substantially eliminate them from his or her estate by making annual exclusion gifts prior to death. Of course, the lawyer should discuss with the client the tax and nontax consequences of settling the proceeds in various ways consistent with his or her basic objectives.

Protecting Minor Children. The insured's spouse will no doubt provide for their minor children, if he or she survives the insured and receives the proceeds outright. If the insured's spouse does not survive, the proceeds should not be made payable to the minor children outright, which might necessitate the appointment of a guardian to collect and manage the proceeds. Instead, the proceeds should either be left with the insurer under a settlement option or be made payable to the trustee of a contingent trust for the children. A trust is generally preferable because it is more flexible and can provide greater protection for the children in the event of emergency. Also, a trust may produce a greater current yield than is received under settlement options. Overall, the family is generally best protected if the assets are concentrated in one trust for the benefit of the children, rather than being held in 2 or more trusts.

The Use of Trusts. The preparation of an inter vivos insurance trust or a will containing a trust will cost more than a nontrust will. However, a trust generally better meets the needs of the family. In addition, a trust may save some estate administration expenses and possibly some income, inheritance, and estate taxes.

If the plan calls for establishing a trust for the benefit of the insured's surviving spouse and children, either a funded or unfunded revocable trust or a testamentary trust might suffice. Before making a recommendation, however, the lawyer must determine whether or not the local law authorizes the designation of the trustee of an unfunded revocable trust or a testamentary trust as beneficiary of life insurance policies. Either designation might be challenged if it is not authorized by statute or judicial decision. Fortunately, a growing number of states have adopted statutes that permit the designation of the trustee of an unfunded trust as beneficiary. *E.g.,* Ind. Code Ann. §27-1-12-16 (Burns 1975); N.Y. EPTL §13-3.3(a)(1) (McKinney 1980 Supp.); Wash. Rev. Code §48.18.450 (1979). A larger number of states specifically authorize the designation of the trustee named or to be named in the insured's will as beneficiary. *E.g.*, Cal. Prob. Code §§175 to 183 (West 1981 Supp.); Ill. Ann. Stats. Ch. 110½ §4-5 (Smith-Hurd 1978); Ind. Code Ann. §27-1-12-16(C) (Burns 1975); N.Y. EPTL §13-3.3(a)(2) (McKinney 1980 Supp.); Wash. Rev. Code §48.18.452 (1979). On the other hand, the designation of the trustee of a funded revocable trust is probably valid in all states.

Plan Based upon a Revocable Trust. A plan based upon a revocable trust involves the preparation and execution of a trust agreement and the designation of the trustee as beneficiary of the insurance. Typically, the insured retains ownership of the policies rather than assigning them to the trust and the insured continues to pay the premiums on the policies. However the trust may be funded by transferring some other assets to the trust. If that is done, the trust is not vulnerable to challenge as a "dry" trust. Some lawyers believe that a token fund of, say $10, is sufficient for this purpose, while others believe a significant amount of assets should be transferred to the trustee. Funding the trust, of course, makes it a bit more cumbersome to deal with the assets and may require the preparation of fiduciary income tax returns. If the trustee charges a substantial minimum annual fee for a funded trust it may not be economical to create a trust with a nominal fund. On the other hand, where the trust is unfunded, trustees typically charge only a nominal acceptance or review fee for executing the trust agreement and agreeing to serve following the death of the insured. Often, no other fee is charged until after the insured's death. The use of a trust is attractive in part because of the discretionary powers that can be conferred upon the trustee. If the trustee is given those powers, a beneficiary of the trust cannot act as trustee without substantial risk that the assets over which the beneficiary holds the powers will be included in the beneficiary's gross estate.

An inter vivos trust can be the vehicle used to consolidate the insured's assets and to provide for their unified management following his or her death. This can be accomplished by "pouring over" the client's residuary estate into the trust. The pour over technique is validated by the Uniform Testamentary Additions to Trust Act, 8 U.L.A. 629 (1972), which is in effect in almost all states. Under a common plan the client's residence and tangible personal property are left to the surviving spouse by will and the life insurance and residuary estate pass into the trust. A chart of the plan looks like Chart 6-1, below. *See* §10.8, *infra*, for a more detailed discussion of pour over provisions.

Plan Based upon a Testamentary Trust. Where the plan is based upon a testamentary trust, the life insurance proceeds are made payable to the trustee of the trust established by the will of the insured. The beneficiary designation is valid in states such as California, Illinois, Indiana, New York, and Washington, which have adopted statutes that specifically au-

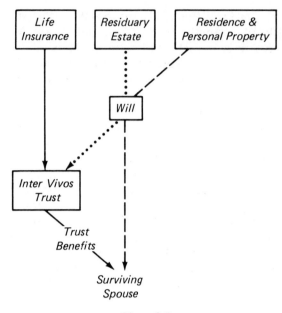

Chart 6-1

thorize it. In some states the designation may be vulnerable to challenge as a testamentary transfer because the trustee cannot be ascertained and appointed until after the death of the insured. An old Massachusetts decision, Frost v. Frost, 88 N.E. 446 (Mass. 1909) invalidated an assignment to the trustees named in the will because it was considered to be a testamentary disposition that failed to comply with the requirements of the wills act. Although most courts would probably strain to uphold the designation of a testamentary trustee as beneficiary, prudence suggests adopting a more reliable approach in states that don't specifically authorize such a designation. The chart for a plan based upon a testamentary trust would be practically identical to Chart 6-1. The trusts are essentially the same except for the time of creation and that a testamentary trust would be a "court" trust subject to continuing supervision by the probate court.

Where the local law permits the designation of the trustee of an unfunded inter vivos trust or the trustee of a testamentary trust as beneficiary of life insurance, the choice between them is a close one. In either case, the surviving spouse or other beneficiary can be given substantial interests in the trust and extensive powers over the trust property without causing it to be included in his or her gross estate.

The preparation of an inter vivos trust and a complementary will may cost more than a will with a testamentary trust. However, the testamentary trust may generate higher costs of administration because of local law requirements regarding the reports and accounts the trustee must file. The trustee of an inter vivos trust is generally not required to file reports and accounts with the court. The testamentary trust has the edge when it comes to having ready access to the court for instructions — there is often no mechanism available to the trustee of an inter vivos trust by which to obtain such instructions.

A testamentary trust generally lacks the secrecy of an inter vivos trust because it is contained in a will, which is accessible to the public after the testator's death. Also, the actual operation of a testamentary trust may be deferred for some time until the trustees are appointed and qualify to serve. Finally, the designation of a testamentary trustee as a beneficiary of life insurance could jeopardize the extent to which the proceeds are exempt from creditor's claims and the local death tax. Those risks do not arise in states that preserve the exemption for insurance paid to the trustees named in a will. *E.g.*, Ill. Ann. Stats. Ch. 110½ §4-5 (Smith-Hurd 1978); Ind. Code Ann. §27-1-12-16(E) (Burns 1975); N.Y. EPTL §13-3.3 (McKinney 1980 Supp.).

§6.70. *Life Insurance Planning for Wealthier Clients*

Estate plans for wealthier clients of course seek to insulate the insurance proceeds from the imposition of any estate tax on the death of the insured. Implementation of the plan may involve the exclusion of the insurance from the estate of the insured, as would occur if the insured neither held any incidents of ownership in the insurance nor transferred it within 3 years of his or her death. *See* §6.71, *infra.* Essentially the same result is produced if the insurance is made payable to or for the benefit of the surviving spouse in a way that qualifies for the marital deduction. *See* §6.72, *infra.* Of course, the availability of the deduction does not eliminate the insurance from the insured's estate for purposes of determining whether his or her estate satisfies the requirements of §§303, 2032A, and 6166. For purposes of those sections a better result is produced if the insurance in excluded from the insured's estate. More sophisticated plans may involve the transfer of the insurance to an irrevocable trust, which may insulate the proceeds from inclusion in the estates of both spouses. *See* §6.73, *infra.* Irrevocable insurance trusts can, of course, be created for beneficiaries other than the insured's spouse.

§6.71. *Life Insurance Planning for the Wealthier Client: Ownership by a Person Other Than the Insured*

Insurance originally acquired by a person other than the insured or assigned by the insured more than 3 years prior to death generally is not included in the insured's estate. However, the proceeds are includible in the estate of a beneficiary who survives the insured. In effect this plan allows the tax on the proceeds to be deferred until the death of the beneficiary.

Prior to the adoption of the unlimited marital deduction a married couple's insurance plan often involved the "cross ownership" of insurance in order to take advantage of this approach. That is, each spouse owned the insurance on the life of the other. If the noninsured spouse were to die first, the plan usually also called for him or her to leave the insurance on the surviving spouse's life in a way that would not require it to be included in the estate of the insured spouse. Thus, the wife's will might leave all of her interests in insurance on the life of her husband to their children or to a trust for the benefit of their children.

Applications and Assignments. Where the noninsured spouse originally applies for the insurance, the application and policy should clearly indicate that both spouses intend the applicant to own all interests in the insurance. The lawyer should review the application and the policy to be sure that the insured will not have any incidents of ownership in the policy. Similar precautions must be taken where the insured assigns his or her interest in the insurance to another person.

Community Property. Particular attention must be given to ownership problems in community property states, where the presumption favoring community property may cause insurance acquired during marriage to be treated as community property unless there is clear evidence to the contrary. An oral agreement that the insurance is the separate property of the noninsured spouse may overcome the presumption in some states (Kroloff v. United States, 487 F.2d 334 (9th Cir. 1973) (Arizona law)), but not in others, some of which require the agreement to be evidenced by a writing apart from the policy (Kern v. United States, 491 F.2d 436 (9th Cir. 1974) (Washington law)). The seriousness of this problem is reduced by the availability of the unlimited marital deduction. However, characterizing the insurance as community property may still carry disadvantages with it.

Premium Payments. The insured makes a gift to the owner to the extent he or she pays a premium directly or indirectly. Reg. §25.2503-3(c), Example (6); Rev. Rul. 76-490, 1976-2 C.B. 300 (an indirect gift is made by the employee when the employer pays a premium on a group-term insurance the employee had assigned to a trust). The premium payment is a gift of a present interest, which qualifies for the annual exclusion where the insurance is owned by another individual. Reg. §25.2503-3(c), Example (6); *see also* §6.31, *supra.* It also qualifies for the marital deduction where the owner is the payor's spouse.

Beneficiary Designations. The noninsured owner is usually designated as the primary beneficiary of the insurance. The owner may need the proceeds for support or it may be necessary to make the proceeds available to the insured's estate to meet taxes, debts, or expenses of administration. Of course, where the proceeds are payable to an independent trustee there is more of an assurance that the proceeds will be made available to the insured's estate. The trustee should be authorized to loan the proceeds to the executor of the insured's estate or to use them to buy assets from his or her estate. Where the owner survives the insured, payment of the proceeds to anyone else involves a gift by the owner to the payee. *See* §6.32, *supra.* In any case, a contingent beneficiary should be designated in each policy to prevent payment of the proceeds to the estate of the insured, which might unnecessarily increase the insured's gross estate and eliminate any otherwise applicable state death tax exemptions.

Successive Ownership. As noted above, the plan should also provide for disposition of the owner's interest in the insurance if the owner predeceases the insured. Generally speaking, the insurance should pass under the owner's will and not by the designation of a successive owner in the insurance itself, which could be overlooked when later changes are made in the owner's estate plan. To avoid subsequent inclusion in the estate of the insured, the insurance should not be left to the insured, nor should the insured be given any incidents of ownership in it. Instead, the owner should consider bequeathing the insurance to adult children or to the trustees of a trust for the benefit of minor children. If the insured is named as executor of the noninsured owner's will, the insured's power over the policy should be limited in order to avoid inclusion of the insurance in the insured's estate should the insured die during administration of the owner's estate. Also, if a policy is left in trust, the insured should not hold any incidents of ownership in the policy in any capacity. *See* §6.18, *supra.* Because of the possibility that inclusion might result if the insured holds an incident of ownership in other fiduciary capacities, a policy should not be given to the insured as custodian for a minor child. For the same reason, the insured should not serve as guardian for an incompetent person who owns a policy on his or her life.

§6.72.   *Life Insurance Planning for the Wealthier Client: Using Marital Deduction Gifts*

The optimum tax result may be produced by designating the noninsured spouse or a suitable trust as beneficiary. Such an approach has the advantage of not requiring the transfer of existing policies and preserves control over the insurance to the insured until his or her death. Under this plan the surviving spouse can make insurance proceeds directly available to meet estate obligations without estate tax disadvantage — the proceeds are already includible in the estate of the insured. Of course, the amount included in the insured's estate is offset by the marital deduction where the insurance is payable outright to the surviving spouse. Where the insurance is payable to a trust that meets the requirements of §2056(b)(7) the insured's executor may elect to claim the marital deduction with respect to all or part of the insurance. *See* §5.18, *supra*.

Community Property. The same plan is now also used in community property states. Prior to the adoption of the unlimited marital deduction a different plan was commonly used in community property states. Under it the proceeds were typically paid in a form that would not subject them to taxation upon the surviving spouse's death. In that way the insured's one-half interest, for which no marital deduction was allowable under the pre-1982 law in any case, would not be taxed again on the surviving spouse's death. The plan was usually built around a bypass trust for the survivor's benefit. However, the same tax effect was produced if the insured left his or her one-half interest with the insurer under a settlement option.

Beneficiary Designations. Under this plan, the insured's spouse may be designated as primary beneficiary and their children as contingent beneficiaries. However, from the tax perspective the plan has greater flexibility if the insurance is payable to a trust that meets the requirements of §2056(b)(7). It is less desirable to leave the proceeds on a settlement option with the company. The one-half interest of the noninsured spouse is generally paid to him or her outright, although it could be left to the trust or left with the company under a settlement option.

Premium Payments. The payment of premiums does not involve a gift because the insured owns the insurance. There is a gift to the insured, however, where a premium is paid by another person. There is no gift where community property funds are used to pay the premiums on a community property policy. *See* §6.31, *supra*.

Successive Ownership. Where the insured owns the entire interest in a policy there is no need to provide for disposition of the policy upon death — the policy matures at that time. In the case of a community property policy, the interest of the noninsured spouse should be left in a way that does not increase the insured's gross estate if the noninsured spouse dies first. As mentioned above, this usually involves leaving the noninsured spouse's interest to adult children or to the trustees of a trust for the benefit of minor children. In such a case, if the noninsured spouse dies first, the ownership interests of the insured spouse and the recipients of the noninsured spouse's interest in the policy will remain the same if they contribute equally to premium payments following his or her death. If one of the owners pays more than one-half share of subsequent premiums without intending to make a gift to the other owner, the payor's interest in the policy will increase proportionately in the states that follow the apportionment rule. Scott v. Commissioner, 374 F.2d 154 (9th Cir. 1967). The ownership interests probably also remain equal in inception-of-title states, with a party who paid more than his or her share of the premiums having a right of reimbursement for the excess he or she paid.

> **Example 6-28.** H's life was insured under a $100,000 nonparticipating cash value policy that was issued 20 years ago and was owned by H and W as their community property until W's death 10 years ago. W bequeathed her interest in the policy to their children, A and B, who made all subsequent premium payments on the policy without intending to make a gift to H. One-half of the value of the policy, determined under Reg. §20.2031-8, was includible in W's gross estate. When H died this year the proceeds were paid outright to A and B. In states that follow the apportionment rule, H's gross estate includes only the one-half interest in the $25,000 that is attributable to his share of the premiums that were paid on the policy up to the time of W's death. The other $75,000 is attributable to A and B's ownership interest in the policy, derived from premium payments made by them ($50,000) and W ($25,000). One-half of the proceeds is probably includible in H's estate in an inception-of-title state, subject to a claim by A and B for one-half of the premiums they paid following W's death.

§6.73.   Insurance Planning for the Wealthier Client: Irrevocable Life Insurance Trusts

In many cases the optimum tax result consistent with a client's overall plan is produced when insurance on the client's life is owned by an irrevocable trust. For example, the insurance may be owned by a trust that makes the proceeds available to a surviving spouse without requiring the proceeds to be included in the estate of the insured or the surviving spouse. Of course, the reach of §§2035 and 2042 must be avoided in order for the insurance to avoid inclusion in the insured's estate. Generally §2042 does not cause any unusual planning or drafting problems, but transfers within 3 years of death are trapped by §2035(d). Inclusion in the estate of the noninsured spouse is avoided by following the general format of a bypass trust. It is often much more difficult to devise a plan that also avoids subjecting the insured to any gift or income tax costs.

Group-term insurance and split-dollar insurance are particularly attractive candidates for transfer to an irrevocable life insurance trust. The assignment of either type usually involves little or no gift tax liability and does not deprive the insured of the use or control of an asset with substantial current value, which the insured might later need. Also there is little current economic loss if the insured's employer or other financing party ceases making premium payments. However, if others ceased making premium payments, the continuation of the insurance could impose a substantial burden on the insured. Where group-term insurance is assigned to the trust, the assignment should include any replacement or renewal insurance and any increase in the amount of coverage. *See* §6.59, *supra.*

Estate Tax Considerations. A trust agreement should be carefully drawn to prevent the insured from holding any incident of ownership in the insurance in any capacity. This requires that all interests in preexisting policies of insurance must be completely and effectively assigned to the trustee and that the insured must not have any control over any other insurance the trustee may acquire on his or her life. To avoid a dispute with the IRS regarding the effect of holding incidents of ownership in a fiduciary capacity, the insured should not have any control over the insurance. Perhaps the most comprehensive protection is provided if the trust instrument prohibits the insured from acting as trustee or successor trustee. Also, to guard against inclusion in the insured's gross estate under §2036, the trust should not permit the assets to be applied in satisfaction of the insured's obligations including the support of dependents. Finally, the agreement should completely dispose of all interests in the insurance so the insured will not have any reversionary interests in it. Although the following discussion focuses on an irrevocable trust created in part for the benefit of the insured's spouse, many of the points are equally applicable to trusts of which other persons are the beneficiaries.

The trust may safely give the trustee discretion to loan the proceeds to the insured's executor, or use them to purchase assets of the insured's estate. A broad form of authorization is useful to free the proceeds to be used to meet the cash requirements of the insured's estate. The provision should be carefully drafted because the proceeds are includible in the insured's estate to the extent they "are subject to an obligation, legally binding . . . to pay taxes, debts, or other charges enforceable against the estate." Reg. §20.2042-1(b).

More aggressive planners may authorize an independent trustee to pay such of the debts, expenses, taxes, and other obligations of the insured's estate as may be requested by the insured's executor. Such a use of the proceeds should not cause them to be included in the insured's gross estate. In particular, the proceeds should not be includible under §2042(1) ("receivable by the executor"). *See* §6.14, *supra*. Nor should the power affect the deductibility of the items for estate tax purposes. The power is, in effect, a special power to appoint the proceeds to the persons whose interests in the probate estate are augmented by payment of the expenses by the trust. The power might constitute a general power of appointment if it were held by a person who would benefit from its exercise. Accordingly, part or all of the proceeds could be included in the gross estate of the power holder.

If the trust is structured to meet the requirements of §2056(b)(7), the insured's executor will have the power to elect to claim a marital deduction with respect to any of the insurance that is included in the insured's estate. Such a trust is ordinarily includible in the surviving spouse's estate only to the extent a marital deduction was claimed in the estate of the deceased spouse. *See* §2044. The survivor may be given the income from the trust and a special testamentary power to appoint the trust property to and among a limited class, such as their issue. The surviving spouse should not be given an unlimited power of withdrawal, a general power of appointment, or any other control that would cause trust assets to be included in her gross estate under §2041. Although the surviving spouse could act as trustee, it is preferable to have an independent trustee, or at least an independent cotrustee. One important reason for using an independent trustee is the broad range of discretionary powers that can safely be given to an independent trustee, but not to a beneficiary who is also a trustee. A cotrustee may also provide important continuity if the surviving spouse resigns or ceases to act as trustee because of death or incompetence.

If existing policies are to be included in the trust, they must be assigned to the trustee. In order to eliminate any possibility that the insured retained any control over the insurance, the policies themselves should be held by the trustee. Similarly, the trustee should have possession of any policies that are subsequently issued or assigned to the trustee. Also, the trustee must be designated as primary beneficiary under the policies.

The trust assets are includible in the estate of the noninsured spouse under §§2036 or 2038 to the extent he or she is treated as a grantor of the trust and is entitled to its income or holds a power over the disposition of its income or corpus. *See* §6.24, *supra*. Accordingly, the noninsured spouse should not have any interest in the policies that are transferred to the trust. In the ideal case the policies are acquired by the trustee with funds initially contributed by a person other than the insured or the insured's spouse.

The noninsured spouse is treated as a grantor of the trust to the extent he or she pays premiums on the insurance or otherwise contributes property to the trust. *See* §2036(a)(1). A noninsured spouse who pays any premiums may be treated as having transferred a proportionate part of the insurance to the trust and not merely the amount of the premiums. To avoid inclusion in the noninsured spouse's estate, the premiums should be paid with funds in which the noninsured spouse does not have any interest. The insured might pay the premiums from his or her own property, recognizing that the payments constitute gifts. In this connection remember that premium payments made by the insured's employer are treated as having been made by the employee. Rev. Rul. 76-490, 1976-2 C.B. 300. Of course, if the trust is funded, the premium payments may be made by the trustee. Funding requires that someone make more substantial gifts to the trust. Also, if the insured provides the funds, the income of the trust will be taxed to the insured under §677(a) to the extent the income could be used without the consent of an adverse party to pay the cost of insurance on the insured's life or that of the insured's spouse. In some cases a family member other than the noninsured spouse may pay the premiums, which involves gifts by that person but does not increase the risk that the proceeds will be included in the estate of the noninsured spouse.

Some of the rigidity of an irrevocable trust can be ameliorated if the trustee has given the power to distribute the trust assets, including insurance policies, to the designated beneficiaries at any time the trustee believes it would be in their best interests so to do. Of course, the power should not be held by the insured, because that would cause the proceeds to be includible in his or her estate under §2038. *See also* §2042(2). Cautious advisors also counsel against giving such a power to the spouse of the insured. Unfortunately, the tax effects of such a "safety valve" are not well established. If the safety valve is controlled by an independent party, presumably the trust assets would not be included in the gross estate of either spouse. However, the trust assets might be included in the insured's estate if the trustee were subservient to the insured and the insured treated as holding the power. If the fortunes of the insured change, or it is otherwise desirable to terminate the trust, the trustee holding such a power could do so. If the trustee is given any powers to make discretionary distributions, the planner must be alert to the generation-skipping tax problems that might arise under §2613.

Community Property. The noninsured spouse's interest in community property insurance held in a trust is particularly vulnerable to inclusion in his or her estate under §2036. Where the noninsured spouse has a life income interest in the trust the effect of inclusion may be ameliorated by claiming a consideration offset for the actuarial value of that interest. As in the widow's election cases (*see* §9.27, *infra*), the noninsured spouse is considered to have exchanged a remainder interest in his or her community share of the proceeds for a life income interest in the other share of the proceeds. A form of the community property widow's election trust may produce very favorable tax results. *See* Price, The Uses and Abuses of Irrevocable Life Insurance Trusts, U. Miami 14th Inst. Est. Plan. ¶1116.3 (1980); *see also* §6.24, *supra*.

Gifts to the insured. Some optimistic insurance advisors suggest that inclusion in the noninsured spouse's estate can be avoided if the noninsured spouse gives his or her interest in the insurance to the insured, who in turn transfers it to the trust. Unfortunately, this two-step process is not likely to satisfy the IRS, who will probably insist that actually the noninsured spouse transferred his or her interest in the policy to the trust. The IRS would argue that the noninsured spouse is the transferor and the intermediate transfer to the insured spouse served no purpose apart from attempting to avoid the estate tax upon the noninsured spouse's death. Their argument is buttressed by the fact that the courts are committed to determining the tax consequences of transactions according to their substance and not their form: "The substance of a transaction rather than its form must ultimately determine the tax liabilities of individuals. . . . When one overall transaction transferring property is carried out through a series of closely related steps, courts have looked to the essential nature of the transaction rather than to each separate step to determine tax consequences of the transfer." Johnson v. Commissioner, 495 F.2d 1079, 1082 (6th Cir.), *cert. denied*, 419 U.S. 1040 (1974). The gift approach will have a greater chance of success if the gift and the transfer to the trust are separated in time and are not related. Note that the full amount of the insurance will be includible in the insured's estate under §2035 if the insured dies after receiving the noninsured spouse's interest in the insurance and within 3 years of transferring the entire interest in the insurance to the trust.

Sale of policies to the insured. There is perhaps a greater possibility of avoiding inclusion in the noninsured spouse's estate if the noninsured spouse's interest in the insurance is sold to the insured. Of course, in order to produce the desired result, the insured must make the purchase with noncommunity funds, which the insured may already have or which may be generated by partitioning some community property funds into equal units separately owned by the husband and wife. Again, there is some risk that the sale will be ignored unless the taxpayers can establish an independent (*i.e.*, nontax) purpose for it. Otherwise the IRS may argue that in substance the noninsured spouse has transferred his or her interest to the trust, reserving a life interest in the proceeds. Here also the risk of inclusion in the noninsured spouse's estate is lower where the sale and transfer are separated in time and are not directly related. If the insured dies within 3 years of the transfer, the insurance is all includible in his or her estate. Of course, inclusion in the insured's estate is not a serious present problem if the insurance qualifies for the marital deduction.

> **Example 6-29.** H purchased W's one-half community property interest in a policy on his life with separate funds that resulted from the equal partition of community assets. Subsequently H transferred the policy to an irrevocable trust of which W was the life income beneficiary. If H dies within 3 years of making the transfer the entire proceeds will be included in his gross estate. However, if the trust is properly drawn, the insured's executor may elect to claim a marital deduction with respect to part or all of the proceeds. Of course, if such an election is made, a proportionate part of the trust would be included in W's estate under §2044.

If H lived more than 3 years following the transfer of the policy to the trust in Example 6-29, none of the proceeds would be included in his gross estate and possibly none of the trust property attributable to the proceeds would be included in W's estate.

Sale of policies to the trustee. A sale of the noninsured spouse's community property interest to the trustee is generally not feasible for 2 reasons. First, the trust is usually not funded with enough assets to support the purchase. Second, and more important, the sale could result in a transfer of the policy for value, which could cause the proceeds to be subject to the income tax when they are paid. *See* §6.35, *supra.* Because of the transfer for value rule it is generally undesirable to sell a policy to the trustee.

Aggressive clients may be willing to take the risks involved in giving or selling the noninsured spouse's interest in policies to the insured spouse for addition to the trust. The decision is theirs, but the lawyer should be sure they understand the risks and appreciate the irrevocable nature of the trust. Because the trust is irrevocable its provisions cannot be changed after it is established.

§6.74. *Other Types of Life Insurance Trusts*

The inherent flexibility of the trust device challenges planners to adapt it to meet the specialized needs of particular clients. Within the limits imposed by the insurance and tax laws, there is a vast range of circumstances in which an insurance trust may be crafted to help a client. Some of them are appropriate only for clients who are willing to assume the risks that the arrangement may be challenged by the IRS and possibly fail to be sustained by the courts.

Business Uses. Insurance trusts have a wide range of applications where closely held businesses are involved. For example, the insurance proceeds paid to the trustee can be used to buy the insured's stock from the insured's executor and thereby give a child who is active in the business voting control over those shares. This plan has the advantage of allowing the insured's other children to share in the equitable ownership of the stock through their beneficial interest in the trust without involving them directly in the management of the company.

Charitable Uses. An irrevocable life insurance trust can also be used as a vehicle for making charitable contributions. If the trust is properly drawn, current premium payments are deductible for income and gift tax purposes. Depending on the terms of the trust the insurance proceeds might be includible in the insured's gross estate. Inclusion would result, for example, if the insured retained the right to designate the charities that would receive the proceeds. *See* §2038. The insured's estate would be entitled to an offsetting charitable deduction. However, the inclusion of the proceeds in the insured's estate could make it more difficult for it to satisfy the percentage tests of §§303, 2032A, and 6166.

Problem 6-9. H, who is now 55, has a gross estate of about $750,000 excluding $400,000 face amount of insurance policies that H owns on his life. The policies have been in effect for several years and have a cash surrender value and an interpolated terminal reserve of $55,000. H's wife, W, is 50 and in good health. Their two children, S and D, are 23 and 21 respectively. W, who is a successful free lance author, has an estate of about $250,000. H and W currently have wills that leave their estates in trust for the survivor of them for life, remainder to their children. The trusts would have independent trustees and meet the requirements of §2056(b)(7). H and W have asked you to advise them regarding the gift and estate tax consequences of (1) assigning the insurance policies to W; (2) making the insurance proceeds payable to the trustee under H's will; and (3) assigning the insurance policies to a separate irrevocable trust for the benefit of W, S, and D that also meets the requirements of §2056(b)(7) if H dies first. Under each plan H would continue to pay the annual premiums of about $20,000.

Estimate the tax consequences for them under the existing law assuming that H dies first. For purposes of the estimates assume that the values of the properties remain constant; H's executor elects under §2056(b)(7) to take a marital deduction with respect to the trust property to the extent it exceeds the credit equivalent available to his estate; no other deductions are available to either estate; and only the unified credit is available to each estate. In each instance, assume that H dies this year shortly after the plan is put into effect, survived by W, who dies unmarried 4 years later survived by S and D. Next, assume that H lives for 4 years following the implementation of the plan, survived by W, who dies 4 years later survived by S and D.

BIBLIOGRAPHY

I.   General surveys of insurance and insurance law:

       Chapman, Life Insurance as a Planning Tool — The Life Insurance Policy, N.Y.U. 33d Inst. Fed. Tax. 723 (1975)

       The Consumers Union Report on Life Insurance: A Guide to Planning and Buying the Protection You Need (rev. ed. 1977)

       Wren, The Role of Life Insurance in Estate Planning, 41 St. John's L. Rev. 6 (1966)

       Wright, Life Insurance and Its Use in Estate Planning, 23 Okla. L. Rev. 125 (1970)

II. General surveys of taxation and insurance:

       Berall, Use of Life Insurance in Estate Planning — Recent Developments, N.Y.U. 31st Inst. Fed. Tax. 1053 (1973)

       Eliasberg, The Estate Taxation of Life Insurance: A Survey of Recent Developments, 26 U. So. Cal. 26th Tax Inst. 1 (1974)

       Gordon, Life Insurance as a Planning Tool, N.Y.U. 33d Inst. on Fed. Tax. 793 (1975)

       Rice, R. S. & Rice, T. R., Family Tax Planning, Ch. 19 (rev. 1978)

       Schlesinger, How to Use Insurance Trusts in Estate Planning, in J. K. Lasser, Estate Tax Techniques 797 (perm. ed. rev. 1978)

       Simmons, S. P., Federal Taxation of Life Insurance (1966)

III. Specific topics:

Assignments:

    Kahn & Waggoner, Federal Taxation of the Assignment of Life Insurance, 1977 Duke L.J. 941

Death benefit only plans:

    Wolk, The Pure Death Benefit: An Estate and Gift Tax Anomaly, 66 Minn. L. Rev. 229 (1982)

Financed life insurance (minimum deposit):

    Hill & McKay, The Flowering of Financed Life Insurance, 118 Tr. & Est. 59 (1979)

    Hutchings, Financed Life Insurance: Obtaining Interest Deductions under Minimum Deposit Plans, 24 Tax Law. 101 (1970)

Generation-skipping tax:
  Note, Application of the New Generation-Skipping Tax to Life Insurance Proceeds: A Headache for Everyone Involved, 30 U. Fla. L. Rev. 586 (1978)

Group insurance:
  Roberts, J. E., Federal Income Estate and Gift Taxation of Group Life Insurance (1976)
  Roberts & Martin, How to Cope with the New Regulations Under Internal Revenue Code Section 79, 57 Taxes 635 (1979)

Income taxation:
  Dopheide, The Federal Income Taxation of Life Insurance, U. Miami 6th Inst. Est. Plan. Ch. 19 (1972)

Insurance trusts:
  Keydel, Irrevocable Insurance Trusts: The Current Scene, U. Miami 10th Inst. Est. Plan., Ch. 5 (1976)
  Oshins, Planning with Irrevocable Life Insurance Trusts in Community Property Jurisdictions, 5 Comm. Prop. J. 97 (1978)
  Price, The Uses and Abuses of Irrevocable Life Insurance Trusts, U. Miami 14th Inst. Est. Plan., Ch. 11 (1980)
  Simmons, Irrevocable Life Insurance Trusts, U. So. Cal. 28th Tax Inst. 23 (1976)

Retired lives reserve:
  Fromberg & Bodnar, Retired Lives Reserve: An Alternative Solution to Retirement Insurance, 48 J. Tax. 224 (1978)
  Powell, Income and Estate Tax Aspects of Retired Lives Reserve, 118 Tr. & Est. 26 (1979)

Split dollar:
  Comment, Two Worlds of Split-Dollar Life Insurance, 1976 Det. Coll. L. Rev. 123
  Dopheide, Split- and Unsplit-Dollar for the Controlling Shareholder, U. Miami 15th Inst. Est. Plan., ch. 8 (1981)
  Morgan, Split Dollar Insurance — New Developments Suggest Planning Techniques That Save Taxes, 58 Taxes 75 (1980)

CHAPTER 7

Planning Lifetime Noncharitable Gifts

Perhaps to assuage the feelings and to aid the understanding of affected taxpayers, Congress might use different symbols to describe the taxable conduct in the several statutes, calling it a "gift" in the gift tax law, a "gaft" in the income tax law, and a "geft" in the estate tax law. Commissioner v. Beck's Estate, 129 F.2d 243, 246 (2d Cir. 1942).

A. INTRODUCTION

§7.1. Scope

Lifetime gifts continue to play a major role in estate planning. The unification of the federal gift and estate taxes in 1976 eliminated some, but not all, of the tax advantages of noncharitable inter vivos gifts. Gifts still can be used to shift income from the donor to other family members, to remove further appreciation in value from the donor's estate, to enable the donor's estate to qualify for some special tax elections, and to minimize the overall state and federal transfer tax burdens. *See* §§7.7 to 7.11, *infra*.

This chapter first reviews some of the main nontax considerations involved in counselling clients about gifts. After that it discusses the major tax objectives of gifts, the tax factors involved in selecting property to give, and the various methods of making gifts. The part dealing with methods of making gifts focuses on the various ways of making gifts to minors because of their importance and their illustrative value. Some references are made in the text to state gift tax laws that are in effect in a small but important minority of states including California, Minnesota, New York, North Carolina, Virginia, and Wisconsin.

§7.2 Nontax Considerations

Ingratitude, thou marble-hearted fiend,
More hideous when thou showest thee in a child
Than the sea-monster!
* * *
How sharper than a serpent's tooth it is
To have a thankless child!

King Lear, Act 1, scene 4

Inter vivos gifts generally do not precipitate a family tragedy as they did in King Lear's case. However, before a client adopts a gift program, careful consideration should be given to the financial, family, and emotional circumstances of the client and the prospective donee. In some cases those factors will suggest that the client, the intended donee, or both of them might suffer if a substantial gift were made.

Despite tax advantages, gifts should only be made if they are consistent with the client's overall estate plan. The ultimate decision of whether or not to make a gift must be made by the client, but it is appropriate for the lawyer to make recommendations regarding gifts and other components of the estate plan. For example, a review of the client's affairs may lead the lawyer to recommend that the client make some noncharitable gifts as a part of the client's lifetime estate planning. Otherwise the client's annual exclusions may go unused and the estate tax payable upon the client's death may be unnecessarily high. The lawyer must be prepared for some rejections, however. Although all of the circumstances known to the lawyer may support the adoption of a gift program, the client may reject the idea because of other factual, emotional, or financial considerations. For example, a client may have philosophical convictions that are inconsistent with substantial lifetime gifts, or may be reluctant to make gifts because of memories of the Great Depression of the 1930s and a fear of becoming economically dependent on others.

Economic Position. The economic position of the client is one of the most important factors in evaluating the desirability of a gift program. The factor involves a consideration of the client's net wealth, in view of his or her income, age, health, family obligations, and the extent to which future security is provided by employee benefit plans, medical and disability insurance, etc. Relatively small gifts or gifts for the support or education of a family member often have little adverse impact on the donor's economic position and are easily justifiable in many cases. However, a client should be discouraged from making substantial gifts if they may jeopardize his or her economic independence or standard of living. A client must understand the irrevocable nature of a gift, which generally means that the property cannot be counted on for the client's use or support.

Age and Health. The age and health of a client are also particularly significant factors. In general, an older client is in a better position to make substantial gifts than a younger client of equivalent wealth. A younger client faces a longer time during which he or she may become disabled, suffer economic losses, or have substantial increases in family obligations. For example, an elderly widow or widower with grown, independent children is generally in a better position to make substantial gifts than a young married person of equivalent wealth who has dependent children. On the other hand, a young parent with a modest-sized estate may prudently make gifts within the amount of the annual gift tax exclusion to a child under the Uniform Gifts to Minors Act, or to a trust for the child, in order to gain the benefits of income splitting within the family and to accumulate an educational fund for the child at the lowest tax cost. (*See* §§7.27 to 7.38, *infra,* which discuss the major alternative methods of making gifts to minors.) Sound planning may also call for a younger person to transfer life insurance that has little or no current economic value, such as group-term insurance or an employee's interest under a split-dollar plan, to a family member or to a family trust. In that way the size of the client's estate may be controlled without giving up an asset of substantial current value. (*See* §§6.66 to 6.72, *supra,* for a discussion of the basic plans for disposing of life insurance.)

Emotional and Family Circumstances. The emotional and family circumstances of the client and the client's family must also be considered in planning a gift program. The emotional attachment or identification that a client feels with respect to particular property, such as a collection of coins, stamps, paintings, or antiques, may make it difficult for the client to give it to another person without feeling some anxiety or pain. Similarly, a client who has built up a successful business may be reluctant to give up its management or any significant ownership interest in it. Giving up the challenge and the responsibility of owning and operating a business could have a morbid effect on the client, which the client may consciously or unconsciously view as a partial death. There are other circumstances in which the lawyer must be sensitive to the feelings of the client and the client's family. For example, in some circumstances tax benefits will be obtained if gifts are made by or to a dying person, but the family might take offense unless the topic is raised most tactfully.

The age, abilities, feelings, and financial circumstances of prospective donees and other family members must also be taken into account in formulating a gift program. For example, it may be unwise to make a substantial outright gift to a minor or a very elderly person. In either case the donee may be unable to make an effective sale or other transfer of the property without the appointment of a guardian. Along with some other problems, this may be overcome by making the gift in trust rather than outright. (See §§7.34 to 7.38, *infra* for a discussion of trusts for minors and Chapter 10 for a general discussion of trusts.) Care should be exercised in making substantial outright gifts to persons who have little or no financial or investment experience. Also family discord may arise if a large gift is made to one child but not to others, or if disproportionate gifts are made to children or other donees who are equally related to the client. Disproportionate gifts may be justified, however, where the needs of the donees are different and some face greater educational, medical, or other expenses than the others. Finally, a client may choose to pay some outstanding debts of a spendthrift, to whom the client may be reluctant to make a large outright gift.

Substantial gifts are most effective when they are coordinated with the donee's estate plan. In particular, a gift should generally be structured so that the gifted property will not return to the donor if the donee predeceases the donor. This problem is aggravated in the case of an outright gift to a minor or gift under the Uniform Gifts to Minors Act because minors generally lack the capacity to make a will. This is a serious disadvantage because such gifts would be subject to distribution as intestate property if the donee dies prior to attaining his or her majority. A minor donee's intestate property would usually pass to his or her surviving parent or parents. Of course, the probability that a minor will die prior to attaining majority is quite small. This problem is avoided entirely by making the gift to a trust under which the trust property will be distributed to persons other than the donor if the donee dies before the trust terminates. The annual exclusion is available for transfers to a trust insofar as the trust meets the requirements of §2503(b) or (c). See §§7.34 to 7.38, *infra*. An annual exclusion is also available to the extent the donee holds a *Crummey* power under which he or she can withdraw property that is transferred to the trust. *See* §7.36, *infra.* If the trust contains a properly drafted *Crummey* power, the annual exclusion is available although the trust is a discretionary one (*i.e.,* the beneficiary does not have any fixed right to receive distributions of income or principal).

B. LOCAL PROPERTY LAW

§7.3. Significance of Local Law

In order to constitute a gift for federal gift tax purposes a transfer must be effective under local law to pass an interest in the property to the donee. The federal law describes the types of transfers that constitute taxable gifts, but the question of whether or not there has been an effective gift is decided under local law. "The sole criterion, for the purpose of the gift tax, is whether the particular conveyance is effective under the local law to transfer an interest in the property to a donee." Rev. Rul. 57-315, 1957-2 C.B. 624.

§7.4. Inter Vivos Gifts and Gifts Causa Mortis

Two general types of gifts are recognized for property law purposes — inter vivos gifts and gifts causa mortis. This chapter is concerned only with inter vivos gifts, which are usually immediately effective and irrevocable. In contrast, gifts causa mortis are made in contemplation of death and remain revocable until the death of the donor.

Gifts causa mortis are not used in estate planning because of their revocable nature, which deprives them of any income, gift, or estate tax significance (*i.e.,* the donor remains taxable on the income (§676)), the gift is incomplete (Reg. §25.2511-2(c)), and the property is includible in the donor's gross estate (§2038). In addition, gifts causa mortis are generally not favored by the courts because of their similarity to oral wills, which lack the formality and evidentiary reliability of written wills.

§7.5. Elements of Inter Vivos Gifts

A valid gift requires donative intent on the part of the donor, delivery to the donee or donee's agent, and some form of acceptance. In contrast, donative intent on the part of the transferor is not required in order to subject a transfer to federal gift taxation. Reg. §25.2511-1(g)(1). The local law may require a written instrument in order to transfer some interests in personal property and a deed is usually required to transfer interests in real property. Federal law governs the transfer of some types of property, such as United States Savings Bonds. United States v. Chandler, 410 U.S. 257 (1973).

The donor must be competent and not acting under fraud, duress, or undue influence. However, under the substitution of judgment doctrine, the guardian, conservator, or committee of an incompetent may make gifts of the ward's property. *See* Substitution of Judgment Doctrine and Making of Gifts from an Incompetent's Estate, 7 Real Prop., Prob. & Tr. J. 479 (1972), which surveys the law of American states. Under this doctrine the court may authorize the fiduciary to make inter vivos gifts to the ward's relatives in order to reduce the overall transfer tax burden where it is consistent with the ward's estate plan and the property will not be needed for the ward's care and support. *See, e.g.,* In re Morris, 281 A.2d 156 (N.H. 1971); In re duPont, 194 A.2d 309 (Del. Ch. 1963).

Delivery. The type of delivery that is required depends upon the nature and location of the property involved and the circumstances of the parties. Actual physical delivery of tangible personal property or of a stock certificate or other physical evidence of a chose in action is preferred, but other forms of delivery may suffice. For example, tangible personal property contained in a locked receptacle may be delivered constructively by giving the donee the key to the receptacle. Broadly speaking, tangible or intangible personalty may also be effectively delivered if the donee is given a writing evidencing the gift (a deed of gift in the case of tangible personalty or an assignment in the case of a chose in action).

Effective delivery may also be made through a third party. In general delivery to a third party is immediately effective if the third party represents the donee, but it is not effective until ultimate delivery to the donee where the third party represents the donor. This analysis is reflected in the gift tax regulations: "If a donor delivers a properly indorsed stock certificate to the donee or the donee's agent, the gift is completed for gift tax purposes on the date of delivery. If the donor delivers the certificate to his bank or broker as his agent, or to the issuing corporation or its transfer agent, for transfer into the name of the donee, the gift is completed on the date the stock is transferred on the books of the corporation." Reg. §25.2511-2(h).

Acceptance. Acceptance by the donee is also a necessary element of a gift. However, the significance of this requirement is diminished by a presumption of acceptance by the donee. The presumption, which applies to all donees including minors and incompetents, facilitates the completion of gifts where delivery is made to the third party.

§7.6. Gifts of Community Property

All of the community property states limit the power of one spouse, acting alone, to give community property to a third person. *See* §3.24, *supra.* Some do not allow gifts to be made without the express or implied consent of the other. Cal. Civ. Code §5125(b) (West 1981 Supp.); Wash. Rev. Code §26.16.030(2) (1979). The other states generally permit one spouse to make a gift of community property to a third party so long as the gift is not unfair or "constructively fraudulent." The question of whether or not a gift of community property to a third party is constructively fraudulent requires the court to consider a number of factors, including "the size of the gift in relation to the size of the community estate, the adequacy of the estate remaining to support the wife in spite of the gift, and the relationship of the donor to the donee." Horlock v. Horlock, 533 S.W.2d 52, 55 (Tex. Civ. App. 1975). The court in *Horlock* upheld the deceased husband's gift of over 13% of total estate to his teenage daughters where the community estate was large and the gifts resulted in tax savings. Gifts that are capricious, excessive, and arbitrary are constructively fraudulent although the donees are the children of the donor. Logan v. Barge, 568 S.W.2d 863 (Tex. Civ. App. 1978).

C. TAX OBJECTIVES OF GIFTS

§7.7. General

The main tax objectives of inter vivos gifts are discussed in this part. The objectives are largely independent, but some are inconsistent with others. For example, shifting ordinary income or capital gains from donor to donees (§7.9) may not be consistent with making gifts of nonbusiness assets in order to qualify for the benefits of §§303, 2032A, or 6166 (§7.10). It is important to have the objectives in mind when it comes to helping the client choose the property to give (§§7.12 to 7.17). The objectives also help to identify which method should be used to make gifts to minors (§§7.27 to 7.38).

§7.8. Eliminate Further Appreciation in Value from the Donor's Estate

One of the common reasons for making an inter vivos gift is to remove from the donor's tax base any further appreciation in the value of the gifted property. In effect, a gift freezes the amount that will be taxed to the donor at the value of the property on the date of the gift less the amount of the allowable gift tax exclusion. Note that where the donor dies after December 31, 1981, outright gifts made within 3 years of death generally are not includible in the donor's estate under §2035.

Inter vivos gifts are particularly attractive to the extent they qualify for the annual gift tax exclusion. Gifts in excess of the allowable exclusions are often useful, at least where the amount of the tax is offset by the donor's unified credit. Even when some gift tax must be paid by the donor, a gift program may save a substantial amount of transfer taxes. This result is clear where the property appreciates in value following the gift. A saving may also result because the gift tax paid by the donor is not subject to the gift or estate tax unless the donor dies within 3 years and the amount of the gift tax is grossed up under §2035(c). In calculating the benefit of an inter vivos gift upon which a gift tax is paid some consideration must be given to the effect of losing the use of the amount paid in tax. For a mathematical model that permits a comparison of the adjusted estate tax cost of retaining the property with the adjusted gift tax cost of making a present gift of it, see Officer & Banks, Estates vs. Gifts in a Period of Inflation, 58 Taxes 68 (1980).

In planning inter vivos gifts it is important to bear in mind that the donor's basis generally carries over to the donee. §1015. The basis of gifted property is stepped up (or stepped down) when the donor dies only if it is included in his or her gross estate. §1014. The carryover of basis may be a negative factor where the donee is expected to sell the property after the donor's death; it is largely irrelevant if the donee is not expected to do so. Even if the donee sells the property the capital gains tax payable on a sale may be less than the additional estate tax that would be payable by the donor's estate if the gift were not made. Also, the donee's basis in the property is increased by the amount of any gift tax paid with respect to the appreciation element of the gift (the excess of the fair market value of the property at the time of the gift over the donor's adjusted basis). §1015(d)(6).

Example 7-1. An unmarried donor, D, had made taxable gifts in prior years that absorbed the full amount of D's unified credit, but did not require any gift tax to be paid. Earlier this year D gave a relative, B, $10,000 in cash. Before the end of the year D gave B 100 shares of stock that had an adjusted basis of $10 per share and a current market value of $100 per share. D must pay a gift tax by reason of the $10,000 gift of stock to B, of which 90% is attributable to the excess of the value of the shares over the donor's basis. B has a basis in the shares equal to D's basis of $1,000, plus the gift tax paid by D with respect to the $9,000 of unrealized appreciation.

§7.9. Shift Income from Donor to Donee

"Income splitting" within the family is another of the major purposes of making inter vivos gifts. The total family income tax burden may be substantially reduced if income-producing assets are distributed among several family members rather than being concentrated in the hands of one or both parents. The potential income tax savings of transferring income-producing property to children is limited by §63(e), which in effect denies the benefit of the zero bracket amount to children who are under 19 or are full-time students if they have unearned income for the year and may be claimed as dependents by their parents. However, some income tax savings will ordinarily result in any case because of the steeply progressive nature of the income tax.

The capital gains tax on the sale of an appreciated asset may be reduced by transferring it to a donee in a lower income tax bracket prior to sale. Of course, the tax is computed at the rates applicable to the donor where the asset is transferred to a trust that sells it within 2 years. §644.

A gift is also useful where the property will be sold and the gain on a sale would be ordinary income to the donor, but capital gain to the donee. Of course, the gift tax consequences of the transfer must be taken into account in deciding whether to make the gift. The combined gift and capital gains taxes may be less than the income tax that the donor would pay on the gain if it were all taxed to the donor as ordinary income.

> **Example 7-2.** A married donor, D, who is involved in real estate development and sales gave his married, adult son, S, and his spouse a parcel of undeveloped real property that had an adjusted basis of $1,000 and a current value of $40,000. The entire value of the gift to S and his spouse is sheltered by the available annual exclusions if it is split between D and his spouse. The donor's basis in the property ($1,000) carries over to the donees under §1015(a) as does the donor's holding period. See §1223(2) and Reg. §1.1223-1(b). Ordinarily the real property will be a capital asset in the hands of the donees and any gain they realize will be capital gain. However, if the sale was prearranged by D, the donees may be treated as D's agents and the gain may be taxed to D as ordinary income. See Salvatore v. Commissioner, 434 F.2d 600 (2d Cir. 1970).

§7.10. Reduce Nonbusiness Holdings of Donor in Order to Qualify for Benefits of §§303, 2032A, and 6166

Gifts of nonbusiness assets may enable the donor's estate to meet the percentage tests of §303 (redemption of stock included in decedent's gross estate treated as payment in exchange for stock and not dividend); §2032A (special use valuation of farm or business assets); and §6166 (deferral and installment payment of estate tax attributable to closely held business). The percentage requirements of those sections and their basic limits are summarized in Table 7-1. For a more detailed discussion of them, *see* Chapters 11 and 12, *infra*.

Table 7-1
Summary of Requirements

Code Section	Percentage Requirement	Nature of Benefit
303	Stock included in gross estate must exceed 35% of excess of gross estate over deductions allowable under §§2053 and 2054. §303(b)(2)(A). Stock of 2 or more corporations may be aggregated if 20% or more of the value of the outstanding stock of each is included in decedent's gross estate. §303(b)(2)(B).	Redemption of stock treated as sale and not dividend to extent of total death taxes plus funeral and administration expenses allowable as deductions under §2053. §303(a).
2032A	Adjusted value of qualified real and personal property must exceed 50% of adjusted value of gross estate *and* adjusted value of qualified real property must exceed 25% of adjusted value of gross estate, which must pass to a qualified heir. §2032A(b)(1).	Value of qualified real property for estate tax purposes may be reduced by up to $600,000 for decedents dying in 1981 ($700,000 in 1982 and $750,000 in 1983 and thereafter) based upon its valuation for farming or closely held business purposes. §2032A(a)(2), (e).
6166	Closely held business must constitute more than 35% of value of gross estate reduced by deductions allowable under §§2053 and 2054. §6166(a)(1). Two or more businesses may be aggregated for this purpose, if 20% or more of total value of each is included in decedent's gross estate. §6166(c). [Same tests as for §303.]	Proportion of estate tax attributable to closely held business may be deferred for 5 years and paid in installments over following 10 years. §6166(a). Interest on the tax imposed on the first $1,000,000 in value of the closely held business is subject to a 4% annual rate; the remainder is subject to a variable interest rate established annually under §6621. §6601(j).

§7.11. Minimize State Transfer Tax Costs

Inter vivos gifts are also encouraged by the fact that a minority of states impose gift taxes while all states other than Nevada impose some form of death tax. Thus, in a majority of states the imposition of any state transfer tax may be avoided by making inter vivos gifts. Of course, gifts made within 2 or 3 years of death are often subject to state death taxation. A growing number of states impose only a death tax equal to the maximum credit allowable under §2011 for state death taxes (a so-called pick up tax).

A state transfer tax saving often results from inter vivos gifts even in the states that have gift tax laws. First, the laws of most states provide an annual exclusion, or a similar exemption, which shelters modest-sized annual gifts from the tax. Many also allow gift splitting, which permits a couple to transfer up to double the annual exclusion amount to each donee annually without incurring any gift tax liability. Second, the amount of state gift tax payable on a transfer is generally not included in the tax base in computing the gift tax (*i.e.,* it is not "grossed up"). Of course, the amount of the tax may be "grossed up" at death for state death tax purposes if the donative property is subject to the death tax and a credit is allowed for the gift tax. Third, most state transfer tax systems are not unified, which permits donors to take full advantage of the 2 sets of exemptions and low initial rates that are characteristic of dual transfer tax systems.

Any amount paid in state gift taxes on transfers made within 3 years of death is not grossed up and included in the donor's gross estate under §2035(c). That provision requires inclusion of only the federal gift tax paid by the decedent or the decedent's estate on gifts made by the decedent or his or her spouse within 3 years of death.

For several years the IRS contended that §2033 required inclusion of the state gift tax paid on an inter vivos gift where the property transferred was later included in the donor's inheritance tax base and a credit was allowed for the gift tax previously paid. Rev. Rul. 75-63, 1975-1 C.B. 294. In essence the IRS viewed the gift tax in such a case as a prepayment of the donor's inheritance tax liability, which is not deductible under §2053. An earlier ruling denied a deduction for state gift taxes unpaid at death to the extent a credit was allowable for them against the state death tax. Rev. Rul. 71-355, 1971-2 C.B. 334. However, the rulings recognized that such indirect payments of state death taxes did qualify for the credit under §2011 for state death taxes. The IRS contentions were consistently rejected by the courts. For example, in Estate of George E. P. Gamble, 69 T.C. 942 (1978), *acq.,* 1981-2 C.B. — , the Tax Court pointed out, "Because the decedent's lifetime payment of his State gift tax liability resulted in nothing that was capable of passing from him at the time of his death, respondent's reliance upon section 2033 to increase the value of his gross estate is misplaced." *Id.* at 950. In Estate of

Lang v. Commissioner, 613 F.2d 770 (9th Cir. 1980), *aff'g in part and rev'g in part*, 64 T.C. 404 (1975), *acq.*, 1981-2 C.B. — , the court held that a state gift tax paid after death remains a gift tax and is therefore deductible under §2053. In late 1981 the IRS reversed itself and revoked Rev. Ruls. 71-355 and 75-63. Rev. Rul. 81-302, 1981-2 C.B. — . The most recent ruling concedes that state gift taxes on property that is later included in the donor's inheritance tax base are not assets of the estate where they were paid prior to death; that they are deductible where they were not paid prior to death; and that they accordingly do not qualify for the state death tax credit under §2011.

The transfer of property into a joint tenancy with another person can save state transfer taxes in states that treat joint tenancies favorably for tax purposes on the death of a joint tenant. In some states none of the joint tenancy property is taxed when a joint tenant dies; in others only the decedent's proportional interest is subject to tax. The overall saving will, of course, be less if the creation of the joint tenancy requires the payment of gift tax. However, in many cases there are strong tax and nontax reasons for not transferring assets into coownership with a spouse or others. For a more complete discussion of cotenancies, *see* Chapter Three, *supra*.

D.   TAX FACTORS INVOLVED IN SELECTING PROPERTY TO GIVE

§7.12.   *Give Appreciated Property?*

Where the donees are in lower income tax brackets than the donor it may be advantageous to give them property with more, rather than less, built-in gain. As indicated below, a larger basis adjustment is allowable under §1015(d)(6) for gift tax paid on a gift of highly appreciated property than on a transfer of less appreciated property. The transfer of highly appreciated property is often desirable where the donees are expected to sell the property within a short time. Also, the capital gain to the donor on the sale of retained property will be smaller if the donor retains assets that have appreciated less in value. On the other hand, where the donor is very elderly or in failing health, highly appreciated property might be retained in order to take full advantage of the tax-free step up in basis at death that is available under §1014 for property that is included in the donor's gross estate.

If the gifts to a particular donee during the year will be large enough to require payment of some gift tax, they should be arranged to take maximum benefit of the adjustment that is available under §1015(d)(6). Under it the basis of the donee is increased by the portion of the gift tax that is attributable to the appreciation element. The amount of the adjustment will be higher if the donor transfers more highly appreciated property to the donee. The allocation formula provided by the Code is:

$$\frac{\text{Net appreciation in value of gift}}{\text{(fair market value less adjusted basis)}} \times \text{Gift tax paid}$$
$$\text{Fair market value of the gift}$$

Where a donor plans to give the same person cash (or unappreciated property) and appreciated property during the same year, a larger adjustment is usually allowable if the donor transfers the cash or unappreciated property first. The annual exclusion applies to the first gift made to a donee during the year (Reg. §1.1015-5(b)(2)), as a result of which any gift tax paid on gifts made to the same donee is allocable to later gifts.

> **Example 7-3.** Donor, D, whose unified credit was used up by prior gifts, gave his son, S, $10,000 in cash on January 1, 1982, and 100 shares of XYZ, Inc. on December 30, 1982. The XYZ shares had an adjusted basis of $10 per share and a fair market value of $100 per share. The annual exclusion was applied to offset the gift of cash so the full amount of tax ($3,200) was imposed with respect to the gift of XYZ, Inc. stock. The donee's basis is $38.80 per share (the donor's basis of $10 per share plus the portion of the gift tax allocable to the appreciation element of each share, $28.80):
>
> $$\frac{\$9,000}{\$10,000} \times \$3,200 = \$2,880$$
>
> If the XYZ stock had been transferred first and the cash second, no tax would have been payable with respect to the gift of stock and there would have been no adjustment to basis under §1015(d). In that case the taxable gift would be limited to the amount of the cash gift. No adjustment would be allowable for 2 reasons. First, cash has no appreciation element. Second, cash has a carryover basis equal to its fair market value (face amount), which cannot be increased.

§7.13. Do Not Give Property Subject to an Encumbrance in Excess of Its Basis

In order to raise funds with which to pay the gift tax, a donor may borrow against appreciated property prior to making a gift of it. However, as explained in §7.25, *infra,* the income tax consequences are neither entirely favorable nor entirely settled. A transfer of encumbered property will probably be treated as an exchange to the extent of the indebtedness, which will require the donor to realize gain if the indebtedness exceeds the donor's basis. Johnson v. Commissioner, 495 F.2d 1079 (6th Cir.), *cert. denied,* 419 U.S. 1040 (1974). A gift to charity of property subject to an encumbrance in excess of its basis is also treated as a sale or exchange — a part gift and part sale in most instances. *See* §8.28, *infra.*

A taxpayer contemplating a gift of encumbered property should consider other strategies, including a net gift of the property (*see* §7.24, *infra*), a sale of it on the installment basis (*see* §§9.3 to 9.7, *infra*), or an exchange of it for a private annuity (*see* §9.8 to 9.14, *infra*). For a comparative analysis of several methods, *see* Note, Part Gift-Part Sale, Net Gift and Gift of Encumbered Property — Specialized Strategies for Gifts of Unique Property, 50 Notre Dame Law. 880 (1975).

§7.14. Do Not Give Property with a Basis That Exceeds Its Current Fair Market Value

Under §1015(a) the donor's basis in an asset carries over to the donee, except that for the purpose of determining loss the basis cannot exceed the fair market value on the date of the gift. Thus, in the case of a gift of an asset that has an adjusted basis of $10,000 and a fair market value of $5,000, the donee's basis is limited to $5,000 for the purpose of determining loss. In such a case the donee's basis cannot be increased by any amount of the gift tax. None of the tax was imposed with respect to net appreciation — there wasn't any. *See* §1015(d)(6). A donor should not make a gift that involves losing the tax benefit of a loss. Instead, a donor should sell the depreciated property, take advantage of the loss, and make a gift of the proceeds or of other property.

A terminally ill taxpayer may choose to sell assets that have declined in value in order to make use of the loss for income tax purposes. If depreciated assets are retained until death their bases are stepped down and no one will be entitled to claim a loss. §1014. Of course, §267 bars a deduction for the loss on a sale to certain related taxpayers.

§7.15. Do Not Give Property with Positive Tax Characteristics

A high bracket taxpayer should retain assets that generate tax exempt income or that shelter other income. Thus, the donor should avoid making gifts of tax exempt municipal bonds, depreciable property, or other property that generates deductions in excess of income. Instead, a donor should generally make gifts of appreciated property that produces ordinary income.

§7.16. Give Property That Reduces the Value of Assets Retained by the Donor

A gift may be used to reduce the donor's ownership interest in a closely held business to the point at which it may be valued at a discount for estate tax purposes. For example, if a donor who owns 60% of the stock of a closely held business gives 11% of the stock to others, the donor has retained a minority interest (49%) that may qualify for a discount. If the donor wants to preserve the benefits of §§303, 2032A, or 6166, it may be necessary to limit gifts of stock. *See* §7.10, *supra.* Also, a fractional interest in real property may be valued at less than a proportionate part of the total value, at least when a discount is supported by expert opinion.

The IRS will not allow a minority discount for shares owned by one person where his or her family retains a controlling interest in the corporation (interests included under §2035 were aggregated with decedent's other interests for purposes of evaluation). Rev. Rul 81-253, 1981-2 C.B. — . *See also* Rev. Rul 79-7, 1979-1 C.B. 294. However, gifts to several donees are generally not aggregated for purposes of valuation. Rushton v. Commissioner, 498 F.2d 88 (5th Cir. 1974) (blockage discount denied for gifts to several donees on the same day); Mathilde B. Hooper, 41 B.T.A. 114 (1940) (estate tax discount allowed for minority interest in family corporation), *acq. on valuation issue,* 1940-1 C.B. 3; *contra,* Driver v. United States, 38 A.F.T.R.2d 76-6315 (W.D. Wisc. 1976) (gifts made within 3 days of each other were aggregated, no minority discount allowed).

§7.17. Do Not Make a Gift That Will Have Adverse Income Tax Consequences for the Donor

Most property can be transferred by gift without causing the donor to realize any income. However, gain will be realized when a gift is made of some special types of assets. For example, the gift of an installment obligation constitutes a disposition of the obligation under §453B, which requires the donor to realize gain or loss measured by the difference between its fair market value at the time of transfer and its basis. *See* Reg. §1.453-9. The transfer of an installment obligation does not constitute a disposition if the transferor continues to be treated as its owner for income tax purposes. *See* Rev. Rul. 74-613, 1974-2 C.B. 153 (transfer to revocable trust is not a disposition, grantor treated as owner under §§671 to 677).

A disposition of section 38 (investment credit) property prior to the end of the useful life that was taken into account in computing the §38 credit requires a recapture of any excess credit. §47(a). "Disposition" is defined to include a transfer by gift (Reg. §1.47-2(a)(1)), but does not include a transfer by reason of death (§47(b)(1)). Accordingly, a donor should generally not make a gift of investment recapture property, at least not before the end of its useful life.

Gifts of some other types of recapture property do not have the same negative tax consequences. A gift of §1245 property (depreciable personal property) or §1250 property (depreciable real property) does not trigger recapture of depreciation. Instead, the potential for depreciation recapture carries over to the donee. Similarly, a gift of farm recapture property does not cause the recapture of excess deductions. §1251(d). Instead, the donor's excess deductions account carries over to the donee in certain cases. §1251(b)(5). If a taxpayer plans to sell one of these types of recapture property, the taxpayer should consider giving it to one or more family members who are in lower income tax brackets prior to finalizing the sale. Spreading the income among several taxpayers can substantially reduce the capital gain tax on the sale.

Problem 7-1. Owner, O, is a single taxpayer whose marginal income is subject to the maximum income tax rate. Earlier this year O gave each of her children, S and D, $10,000 in cash. Before the end of the year O plans to give each of them an additional $25,000 in property. O has made prior taxable gifts of $700,000 on which the gift tax has been paid. The following assets are available to give to S and D:

Item	Basis	Fair Market Value
Cash	$ 75,000	$ 75,000
$150,000 6% municipal bonds	150,000	100,000
500 shs. IBM	50,000	60,000
600 shs. Midas Mfg.	18,000	72,000

The bonds and the IBM and Midas shares had been held by O for more than a year. IBM pays a relatively small cash dividend and Midas pays none at all. Which assets should O give to S and D? How much gift tax will be due? What basis will S and D have in the assets?

E. SPECIALIZED GIFT TECHNIQUES

"Transactions within a family group are subject to special scrutiny in order to determine if they are in economic reality what they appear to be on their face." . . . The presumption is that a transfer between closely related parties is a gift. Estate of Pearl G. Reynolds, 55 T.C. 172, 201 (1970).

§7.18.   Introduction

Several specialized techniques of making gifts have evolved to meet the estate-planning needs of wealthy clients. Among them are some arrangements that may not be treated as gifts for gift tax purposes: the interest-free demand loan; the payment by one spouse of the entire joint income or gift tax liability; and arrangements by which the donor performs services for others gratuitously or allows them the free use of property. In addition, there are a variety of ways in which gifts can be structured to deal with particular types of property. They include the transfer of the donor's residence to a family member, the installment gift, the "net" gift, the gift of encumbered property, and the part gift and part sale. Wealthy individuals may also provide valuable assistance to family members in other ways that are not treated as gifts, but which help them to increase their estates. For example, a wealthy parent may tell children about investment opportunities rather than acting upon them himself or herself. Similarly, a wealthy individual may assist the investment program of other family members directly or by guaranteeing loans made to them by others. In short, there are many ways by which one person may help another increase his or her wealth without incurring any gift tax liability.

The taxation of a family's wealth can also be controlled by various types of intrafamily transfers for consideration that have donative overtones. See Chapter 9, infra. Some of them, such as the sale of property on the installment method, can be used to "freeze" the value of the seller's estate. Others, such as the family annuity, seek broader tax benefits, including a reduction in the size of the seller's estate. In some circumstances a transfer for consideration may meet the client's needs better than a gift, with little or no reduction in the overall tax benefits.

§7.19.   Nongifts: Interest-Free Demand Loans

According to the IRS an interest-free loan involves a taxable gift. Rev. Rul. 73-61, 1973-1 C.B. 408. In its view a loan for a fixed period involves a gift equal to the value of the right to use the money for the period of the loan, which can be actuarially determined. If the loan is repayable on demand, the IRS recognizes that the amount of the gift can only be calculated at the end of each year. Although the IRS position is supported by logic and tax policy it has been rejected in 3 cases involving intrafamily interest-free demand loans. However, courts have recognized that a gift in the full amount of the loan occurs if the statute of limitations runs on the right of the lender to enforce a note. Estate of Grace E. Lang, 64 T.C. 404 (1975), aff'd, 613 F.2d 770 (9th Cir. 1980).

In a case that antedated Rev. Rul. 73-61 a federal district court held that interest-free demand loans made by parents to their children did not constitute taxable gifts. Johnson v. United States, 254 F. Supp. 73 (N.D. Tex. 1966). The court reasoned that the parents had no duty either to invest their funds or to charge interest on funds they loaned to their children. The same result was reached in split decisions by the Tax Court and the Court of Appeals for the Seventh Circuit in a later case that involved interest-free demand loans of $18 million that 3 partners made to various family trusts. Lester Crown, 67 T.C. 1060 (1977), aff'd, 585 F.2d 234 (1978); accord, Esther C. Dickman, 41 T.C.M. 620 (1980).

Despite the broad language in the Crown opinions, a taxable gift may occur when a low-interest or no-interest loan is made for a fixed period. In such cases it is possible to determine actuarially the value of the note. If the value of the property transferred exceeds the value of the note, the transaction involves a gift. That result is supported by a Tax Court decision that held that a taxable gift occurred when a parent sold a building she owned to her children for a note, payable over a fixed period, at a below-market rate of interest. Gertrude H. Blackburn, 20 T.C. 204 (1953). The gift tax law clearly applies where the value of the property transferred exceeds the value of the consideration received in the exchange. §2512(b). However, the Tax Court has held that an interest-free intrafamily loan for a 10-year term did not constitute a taxable gift. Esther C. Dickman, 41 T.C.M. 620 (1980). "Congress must act if these types of loans are to become taxable events." Id at 624.

The income tax consequences of low-interest or no-interest loans are not entirely clear. Beginning with J. Simpson Dean, 35 T.C. 1083 (1961), nonacq., 1973-2 C.B. 4, the courts have held that the income of the borrower is not increased by an interest-free loan. Interest was generally not imputed because the borrower would have been entitled to an offsetting interest deduction. However, later cases, including Max Zager, 72 T.C. 1009 (1979), indicate that income may be realized by the borrower if the borrower would not be entitled to an offsetting interest deduction. For example, a borrower might realize interest income if the borrowed funds were invested in tax exempt securities, with respect to which an interest deduction is barred by §265. In Crown the Court of Appeals was careful not to express any view regarding the Commissioner's contention that the interest-free loans gave rise to constructive income to the lenders. 585 F.2d at 236, n.3.

The cancellation of interest due on a note does constitute a gift for gift tax purposes. Republic Petroleum Corp. v. United States, 397 F. Supp. 900, 917 (E.D. La. 1975), mod. on other issues, 613 F.2d 518 (5th Cir. 1980). Again, the overall income tax consequences are not clear. In such a case the lender might also be required to realize income under the constructive receipt doctrine. If so, the borrower should be entitled to deduct the same amount. Of course, deductions under §163 are generally allowable only for interest that is actually paid.

Previously the irrevocable short-term trust was the only effective way for a donor to shift income to a donee and to retain a reversionary interest in the property. *See* §7.38, *infra*. The interest-free demand loan is more attractive, assuming it works, because (1) no gift tax is payable by the donor, (2) capital gains realized by the donee are taxable to the donee and not the donor, and (3) the donor can recover the property at any time in contrast to the 10-year wait that is required in the case of the short-term trust. If an interest-free demand loan is made to a trust, §676(a) might require the lender to be treated as owner of the trust to the extent of the amount of the loan. *See* §10.31, *infra*. In such a case the IRS may argue that the lender has the power to revoke the trust and recapture the trust property to the extent of the loan.

Clients should not expect the IRS to concede any tax benefits arising in connection with interest-free loans. For example, where parents made an interest-free loan to a child and borrowed the funds back at a market rate of interest the IRS denied the parents a deduction for interest payments made to the child on the ground that no true debtor-creditor relationship existed. Rev. Rul. 82-94, 1982-1 C.B. — .

Problem 7-2. W, who has previously made taxable gifts of $400,000, plans to make interest-free demand loans of $200,000 each to her adult children, S and D. W expects S and D to invest the funds in highly liquid debt obligations that yield 14% annual interest. The interest income will probably be used by S and D to pay some of their living expenses that W has been paying from her after-tax income. What are the best income, gift, and estate tax consequences that W could expect? What are the worst? Will W have suffered any tax disadvantages if the worst case occurs?

§7.20. Nongifts: Payment by One Spouse of Entire Income or Gift Tax Liability

The payment by one spouse of the entire joint income tax liability for the year is not treated as a gift for gift tax purposes. Reg. §25.2511-1(d). Under that regulation the same rule applies to the payment of the federal gift tax applicable to gifts that are split under §2513. Prior to 1982 these exceptions to the gift tax allowed a wealthy spouse to make modest indirect transfers to his or her spouse free of tax. In years after 1981 the exceptions have little significance because of the unlimited marital deduction.

Example 7-4. H and W, who are both employed and have substantial incomes, filed a joint income tax return for 1980. W, who is the wealthier spouse, paid their entire income tax liability. In addition, W paid all of the gift taxes that were due on gifts she made in 1980, which were split with H under §2513. Neither the payment of the income tax nor the gift taxes involved a gift from W to H.

§7.21. Nongifts: Free Services and Free Use of Property

As yet the IRS has not sought to apply the gift tax to the free performance by one person of services for another. This position is consistent with dictum in Commissioner v. Hogle, 165 F.2d 352 (10th Cir. 1947), to the effect that the gratuitous performance of services does not constitute a taxable gift. It is also consistent with Rev. Rul. 66-167, 1966-1 C.B. 20, which held that a fiduciary's waiver of the right to receive statutory compensation did not constitute a gift where the fiduciary decided to serve gratuitously within a reasonable time after assuming office and the fiduciary thereafter took no action inconsistent with that position. However, a gift does take place where one person (the donor) pays another person to perform services for a third person (the donee).

Allowing another person the free use of property is more vulnerable to treatment as a gift. Perhaps because of the valuation problems and other administrative difficulties the IRS has not sought to impose the gift tax on those transactions. Providing another person with the free use of property no doubt confers a benefit upon the user, but defining the rules under which an arrangement of that type would be taxed would be exceptionally difficult. The difficulty is illustrated by the complex, yet somewhat inadequate, law on "free loans" adopted by the United Kingdom. Finance Act 1976, §§115 to 117.

> **Problem 7-3.** H has been making annual cash gifts to his daughter, D, equal to the maximum allowable annual exclusion. In addition, this year H wants to provide D with a car that will cost about $10,000. H is willing to give D the money with which to buy the car, to buy it and retain title in his name, or to buy it and transfer title to D at a later time. In any case H will pay the $800 annual cost of insurance on the car. D and H live in the same city, but D plans to keep the car at her apartment. D would make the car available to H if he needed it and would ask him to use it occasionally during any extended period that she might be away. What would be the gift tax consequences of the various alternatives under consideration by H, including his payment of the insurance premiums each year?

§7.22. Gift of a Residence with Continued Occupancy by Donor

The gift of a residence to a family member is usually intended to remove any further appreciation in its value from the donor's estate. That goal may be achieved although the donor continues to occupy it until the time of death. However, the value of achieving that goal must be balanced against the tax and nontax risks the gift involves. Often the potential saving in taxes is outweighed by the risks.

A basic problem with this technique is that the value of the residence will be included in the donor's gross estate if the donor continues to use or occupy it pursuant to an express or implied understanding or agreement. Guynn v. United States, 437 F.2d 1148 (4th Cir. 1971); Rev. Rul. 70-155, 1970-1 C.B. 189. For purposes of §2036 it is not necessary that the retained interest be expressed in the instrument of transfer or that the donor have a legally enforceable right to possession or enjoyment. Estate of Emil Linderme, Sr., 52 T.C. 305 (1969). Continued co-occupancy of the residence by the donor and the donee-spouse does not of itself support an inference of an understanding or agreement regarding the retained use or enjoyment by the donor. Estate of Allen D. Gutchess, 46 T.C. 554 (1966). In contrast, exclusive occupancy of the residence by the donor is a very important factor in determining whether there was an understanding or agreement. Estate of Adrian K. Rapelje, 73 T.C. 82 (1979); Estate of Emil Linderme, Sr., *supra.* As indicated by Rev. Rul. 78-409, 1978-2 C.B. 234, the IRS has a very expansive view of what constitutes an "understanding or agreement."

The case for exclusion of the residence from the donor's estate is improved where the gift is reported on a timely filed gift tax return and the donee pays the real estate taxes, insurance, and other costs of owning the residence. If the donor and the donee are married and both occupy the residence, it is not necessary for the donor to pay any rent for the donor's continued use of it. In other cases the donor should pay a fair rental. It is helpful if there is a written rental agreement that establishes the terms under which the donor occupies the premises.

The gift of a residence usually involves some other tax consequences that should also be taken into account. First, if the gift succeeds and the residence is not included in the donor's estate, the donee will take a carryover basis in the property determined under §1015 instead of an estate tax value determined under §1014. This factor is less significant if the donee does not intend to sell the residence. Second, as a result of the gift it may no longer be possible to exclude a substantial part of the gain under §121 if it is sold at a gain. That section allows a one-time exclusion of up to $125,000 of the gain realized on the sale of a principal residence by a person 55 or older. Third, the residence may no longer qualify for the preferential property tax treatment that may be available for residential property owned and occupied by senior citizens.

On the nontax side there is always the risk that the donee might deprive the donor of any use of the property. Also, at some point the donor may no longer be able to pay the fair rental value of the property, which could jeopardize exclusion of the property from the donor's estate if the donor continued to occupy it. Perhaps more important, the gift makes the residence subject to disposition by the donee inter vivos and at death and reachable by the donee's creditors. Where a gift is made, the donee's will should be checked to be sure that the property will be disposed of in an acceptable manner should the donee predecease the donor.

§7.23. Installment Gifts: Periodic Forgiveness of Transferee's Notes

Various techniques are used to keep the value of a gift within the amount of the allowable annual exclusions. Thus, a donor may limit the amount of the gift made in a particular year by transferring a partial interest in an asset to the donee. However, under this approach the value of the interests retained by the donor may continue to appreciate in value. That risk can be avoided by transferring all of the donor's interests in a particular item of property in exchange for the donee's notes that have a value equal to the excess of the value of the transferred property over the amount of the allowable annual exclusions for the current year. In successive years the donor may forgive an amount of the notes equal to the annual exclusion. Of course, the forgiveness of the notes may trigger recognition of gain by the donor under the installment sales rules. *See* §9.6, *infra.*

The amount of a gift is the value of the property transferred reduced by the value of notes or consideration received in exchange by the donor. §2512(b). "If a donor transfers by gift less than his entire interest in property, the gift tax is applicable to the interest transferred. The tax is applicable, for example, to the transfer of an undivided half interest in property, or to the transfer of a life estate when the grantor retains the remainder interest, or vice versa." Reg. §25.2511-1(e). Of course, for income tax purposes the transfer of property in exchange for a note would be treated as a sale to the extent of the consideration received, which could be very undesirable from the donor's point of view. In some cases the valuation of the transferee's note is a troublesome issue. For example, the IRS has indicated that a low-interest note, due when the borrower's home is sold, has no ascertainable value. LR 8103130. Accordingly, the full amount of the loan may be treated as a gift.

A promissory note given to the transferor by the donee may not be recognized by the IRS as consideration if it is systematically forgiven in annual increments equal to the annual gift tax exclusion. In such cases the IRS may argue that the notes must be disregarded and the transfer treated as a gift of the entire value of the property. That result must follow, according to the IRS, if the transferor intended from the outset to forgive the notes that he or she received. Rev. Rul. 77-299,

1977-2 C.B. 343. The issue has been most frequently litigated in the Tax Court, which has generally recognized valid, enforceable notes as consideration, particularly when they were secured. "This Court has held that when property is transferred in exchange for a valid, enforceable and secured legal obligation, there is no gift for Federal tax purposes." Estate of J. W. Kelley, 63 T.C. 321, 324 (1974), *nonacq.*, 1977-2 C.B. 2. *See also* Selsor R. Haygood, 42 T.C. 936 (1964), *acq. in result*, 1965-1 C.B. 4, *withdrawn and nonacq. substituted*, 1977-2 C.B. 2, and Nelson Story III, 38 T.C. 936 (1962). The IRS succeeded in Minnie E. Deal, 29 T.C. 730 (1958), where the Tax Court found that the notes executed by the transferee-daughters "were not intended to be enforced and were not intended as consideration for the transfer by the petitioner, and that, in substance, the transfer of the property was by gift." *Id.* at 736. A gift may occur where the notes have a value less than their face amounts because the interest rate provided for in the notes is less than the market rate (Gertrude H. Blackburn, 20 T.C. 204 (1953)) or because of other factors (*e.g.*, Estate of Pearl Gibbons Reynolds, 55 T.C. 172 (1970)).

Notes are frequently used to insulate transfers of cash from the gift tax, such as in the case of interest-free demand loans. *See* §7.19, *supra.* Under the approach generally taken by the Tax Court such notes can be written down at an annual rate equal to the allowable annual exclusions without jeopardizing their status.

§7.24. *Net Gifts*

A "net gift" is a gift that is conditioned upon the donee's payment of the gift tax on the transfer. It is a useful planning technique, particularly where it is desirable for the donee to sell the property in order to generate funds with which to pay the tax. For example, the donor may not have sufficient funds to pay the tax and the tax on the gain would be less if the property were sold by the donee. On the gift tax side the IRS has been cooperative — it recognizes that where a gift is made subject to a condition that the donee pay the gift tax, the donor receives consideration equal to the amount of the gift tax the donee is obligated to pay. Rev. Rul. 75-72, 1975-1 C.B. 310 (including formula for computation of deduction); Rev. Rul. 76-49, 1976-1 C.B. 294 (including formula for computation of deduction where donee will pay both the federal and state gift taxes). In such cases the donor makes a gift of an amount equal to the value of the property less the amount of tax payable on the transfer.

> **Example 7-5.** Donor, D, made a gift of property worth $103,000 to his son, S, in 1981 on condition that S pay the federal gift tax on the transfer. In prior years D had made taxable gifts of $250,000. The

deduction is $25,373.13 based on the formula:

$$\frac{\text{Tentative Tax}}{\text{1 Plus Rate of Tax}} = \text{Tax Due}$$

First, the tax is calculated without regard to the condition, which indicates a tax of $34,000 (the "tentative tax"). Next, the formula calculation is made:

$$\text{Tax Due} = \frac{\$34,000}{\text{1 Plus .34}} = \$25,373.13$$

Finally, the calculation is proved by using the "true tax" to calculate D's gift tax liability for the quarter in the ordinary way:

Gross transfer for year	$103,000.00
Less: Gift tax on transfer	25,373.13
Net transfer	$ 77,626.87
Less: Annual exclusion	3,000.00
Taxable gift for year	$ 74,626.87
Prior gifts by donor	250,000.00
Total taxable gifts	$324,626.87
Tax on total gifts	96,173.13
Less: Tax on prior gifts	70,800.00
Tax on gift for year	$ 25,373.13

Even in the case of a net gift, the donor's unified credit is used in computing the amount of the gift tax. Rev. Rul. 79-398, 1979-2 C.B. 338. The policy was explained in an earlier private letter ruling, LR 7842068, as follows: "The unified credit must be used in computing the gift tax. The credit relates to the gift tax of the donor and consequently can only be used against the tax imposed upon the donor's transfers. The fact that a donee is going to satisfy the donor's primary obligation to pay the gift tax does not make the tax a tax on the donees [sic] transfers. Therefore, the unified credit to be used is the donor's credit." In the view of the IRS, no consideration flows from the donee to the donor for the amount of tax equal to the donor's available unified credit. Rev. Rul. 81-223, 1981-2 C.B. — .

Income Tax. A net gift generally does not have an adverse income tax consequence where the donor's basis in the property is equal to or greater than the gift tax to be paid by the donee. Where the donor's basis is less than the tax, the income tax consequences of a net gift were uncertain until the Supreme Court decision in Diedrich v. Commissioner, — U.S. — (1982). Under *Diedrich* it is clear that the donor realizes a gain in such a case. All along the IRS contended that this type of transaction involved a part gift and part sale in which the gift tax paid by the donee was an amount realized by the donor, LR 7752001. Under that approach the donor had a capital gain to the extent that the amount of the gift tax paid by the donee exceeds the donor's adjusted basis in the property. In *Diedrich* the Supreme Court accepted the IRS argument because the donor is statutorily liable for payment of the gift tax §2502(d). Earlier cases had reached inconsistent outcomes.

Initially, the courts held that a net gift transaction did not have any income tax consequences to the donor; the Tax Court found it difficult to see that the donor received anything as a result of the gift. Richard H. Turner, 49 T.C. 356 (1968), *aff'd per curiam,* 410 F.2d 752 (6th Cir. 1969), *nonacq.,* 1971-2 C.B. 4. The Sixth Circuit later purported to limit *Turner* to its peculiar facts in Johnson v. Commissioner, 495 F.2d 752 (6th Cir.), *cert. denied,* 419 U.S. 1040 (1974), which involved the transfer of encumbered property (*see* §7.25, *infra*). In addition, *Turner* was followed in several other net gift cases: Estate of Kenneth W. Davis, 30 T.C.M. 1363 (1971), *aff'd per curiam,* 469 F.2d 694 (5th Cir. 1972); Estate of Douglas Henry, 69 T.C. 665 (1978); Victor W. Krause, 56 T.C. 1242 (1971).

The Tax Court recognized that the IRS argument had a great deal of force, but asserted that "[t]hings have gone too far by now to wipe the slate clean and start all over again." Edna Bennett Hirst, 63 T.C. 307, 315 (1974), *aff'd,* 572 F.2d 427 (4th Cir. 1978). The IRS continued to litigate the issue, but was generally met consistently with memorandum decisions citing *Turner* and *Hirst* as conclusive and refusing to reconsider the issue. *See, e.g.,* John T. Benson, 37 T.C.M. 989 (1978); Estate of Norman D. Weeden, 39 T.C.M. 699 (1979).

The Eighth Circuit decision in the *Diedrich* case rejected the *Turner-Hirst* line of cases and held that when a donor transfers appreciated property in exchange for the donee's promise to pay the resulting gift taxes, the donor realizes a gain to the extent that the gift taxes paid exceed the donor's adjusted basis in the property. Diedrich v. Commissioner, 643 F.2d 499 (8th Cir. 1981), *reversing* Victor P. Diedrich, 39 T.C.M. 433 (1979), and Frances D. Grant, 39 T.C.M. 1088 (1980). In addition, other courts of appeals, when urged to extend the *Turner-Hirst* rationale to other factual settings, refused to do so and strongly criticized the rationale itself. *See* Estate of Levine v. Commissioner, 634 F.2d 12 (2d Cir. 1980) and Evangelista v. Commissioner, 629 F.2d 1218 (7th Cir. 1980).

The holding period of the donee in net gift cases is unclear. Citizens' National Bank of Waco v. United States, 417 F.2d 675 (5th Cir. 1969) concluded that "tacking" of the donor's and donee's holding periods is allowable under §1223(2) because the donor's basis carried over to the donee under §1015. Thus, if a donee sells the property at a gain within a year of the transfer, the donor's holding period can be taken into account in determining whether or not the gain was long term. As noted below, where the gift is made to a trust, the gain on a sale made within 2 years of the transfer will be characterized as if the donor had made the sale and taxed to the trust at the donor's rates. Aside from §644 the IRS argues that the issue is governed by Reg. §1.1015-4(a)(1) where the transfer involves a part gift and part sale. Under it the donee's basis is the greater of the amount paid for the property *or* the donor's adjusted basis for the property, *plus* an adjustment under §1015(d)(6) for gift tax paid with respect to the transfer. (In the case of a net gift the donee's basis apparently includes both the amount paid by the donee [the amount of the gift tax] plus an increase in basis under §1015(b)(6) on account of the gift tax paid with respect to the appreciation element.) Accordingly, the IRS will deny tacking under §1223(2) where the price paid by the donee exceeds the donor's basis. LR 7752001.

Where the gift is made in trust the gain on a sale made by the trustee within the following 2 years will be taxed under §644 as if the sale had been made by the donor. *See* §10.2, *infra.* By its terms §644 applies to a sale made within 2 years, whether the transfer is characterized as a net gift or a part gift and part sale, if the fair market value of the property on the date of the transfer exceeds its adjusted basis in the hands of the trustee. In characterizing the proceeds of a sale the holding period of the grantor should be taken into account (§644(c)), which could be important if tacking is not allowed.

A gift to a trust may also generate adverse income tax consequences where the trust income is used to pay the donor's gift tax. In such cases the courts have rejected the part gift and part sale analysis and have held that the trust income was taxable to the donor as ordinary income under the *Clifford* doctrine. Estate of A. E. Staley, Sr., 47 B.T.A. 260 (1942), *aff'd*, 136 F.2d 368 (5th Cir. 1943), *cert. denied*, 320 U.S. 786 (1945). The income may be taxed to the grantor under §677 to the extent it is, or in the discretion of a nonadverse party may be, used to pay the donor's gift tax liability. Estate of Craig R. Shaeffer, 37 T.C. 99 (1961), *aff'd*, 313 F.2d 738 (8th Cir.), *cert. denied*, 375 U.S. 818 (1963). However, the income of the trust is not taxable to the grantor on that theory after the donor's obligation is discharged by payment of the tax. Thus, where the trustee borrows the funds to pay the tax the trust's subsequent income is not taxed to the donor even when it is used to repay the loan. Repayment of the loan discharges the trust's obligation and not that of the donor. Estate of Annette S. Morgan, 37 T.C. 981 (1962), *aff'd*, 316 F.2d 238 (6th Cir.), *cert. denied*, 375 U.S. 825 (1963); Victor W. Krause, 56 T.C. 1242 (1971). In general §677 does not apply if an encumbrance is paid with funds other than trust income. *See* Comment,

Tax Consequences of Funding Trusts with Encumbered Property: The
Demise of Section 677, 28 U. Fla. L. Rev. 708, 710 (1976).

The possibility that a net gift may result in some income tax liability to
the donor should not deter most clients from using the net gift. First of
all, the net gift may reduce the total amount of gift tax that the donor
must pay. *See* Example 7-5, *supra*. Thus, even though the donor might
incur some income tax liability, the gift tax cost is reduced. Second, the
recognition of gain by the donor may not result in a much larger income
tax liability than if the donee sold the property. Where the gain will be
taxed as long-term capital gain the maximum rate applicable to the
donor (or the donee) is relatively low. Overall, the decision of whether to
use a net gift should be made in light of the marginal income tax rates of
the donor and the donee, the client's financial resources, the availability
of income averaging, and the other tax and nontax factors that are involved in deciding whether to make a gift.

> **Problem 7-4.** Donor, D, made a gift of securities that had a basis of
> $25,000 and a fair market value of $210,000 to her niece, N, on
> condition that N pay any federal gift tax due on the transfer. As-
> suming that D had previously made taxable gifts of $500,000, but
> made no other gifts during the year, how much gift tax must be
> paid by N and what is her basis in the property? How much gain,
> if any, will D have on the transaction?

§7.25.   Gifts of Encumbered Property

Where a donor makes a gift of encumbered property, only the excess of
the value of the property over the amount of the encumbrance is generally subject to the gift tax. D. S. Jackman, 44 B.T.A. 704 (1941). This
result is logical and consistent with the treatment of net gifts (§7.24,
supra). However, if the donee can require the donor to satisfy the encumbrance out of other property, the value of the gift is not reduced by the
amount of the encumbrance. Estate of D. Byrd Gwinn, 25 T.C. 31
(1955).

The income tax consequences for the donor of this type of gift also
should be considered in advance. If the donor's basis exceeds the amount
of the encumbrance they are simple enough — the donor will not realize
any gain as a result of the gift. However, since 1971 the courts have recognized that the donor will realize gain under the *Crane* doctrine (Crane v.
Commissioner, 331 U.S. 1 (1947)) where the amount of the encumbrance
exceeds the donor's basis. The trend began with Malone v. United States,
326 F. Supp. 106 (N.D. Miss. 1971), *aff'd per curiam*, 455 F.2d 502
(5th Cir. 1972). In *Malone* the donee, a trustee, formally assumed the

donor's personal obligation for the mortgage indebtedness on the encumbered real property that was transferred to the trust. Because the indebtedness was assumed, the court readily concluded that the gift resulted in an economic benefit to the donor equal to the excess of the indebtedness over the donor's basis in the property. The concept was significantly extended in Johnson v. Commissioner, 495 F.2d 1079 (6th Cir.), *cert. denied*, 419 U.S. 1040 (1974), which held that the donor received an economic benefit when encumbered stock was given to a trustee although the donor was not personally liable for the indebtedness and it was not assumed by the trustee. The taxpayer in *Johnson* borrowed $200,000 on a nonrecourse basis against stock that he gave to a trustee 3 days later. The stock had a basis of about $11,000 and a value of $500,000 at the time of the gift. Under those circumstances the donor realized a gain of $189,000 when the gift was made. The rule established in *Johnson* is logical, fair, and consistent with Reg. §1.1011-2(a)(3), which requires that the amount of an indebtedness be treated as an amount received for purposes of applying the bargain sale rules whether or not the transferee agrees to pay the debt.

Johnson was followed in Estate of Aaron Levine, 634 F.2d 12 (2d Cir. 1980), *affirming* 72 T.C. 780 (1979), where the donor gave a trustee real property that was subject to encumbrances that had been entered into over a long period of years, the total amount of which exceeded his basis. Although the timing of the loans in *Levine* did not evidence a plan to bail out the mortgage proceeds from the start, the donor nonetheless "reaped a tangible economic benefit from this transaction and such economic benefit is subject to tax under the rationale of Crane v. Commissioner, *supra*." 72 T.C. at 792.

> **Example 7-6.** D owns 1,000 shares of XYZ, Inc. stock, which has a basis of $1 per share and a current value of $100 per share. If D sells the stock for $100 per share D will realize a capital gain of $99 per share or a total of $99,000. If D borrows $99,000 against the stock D will not realize any gain until D disposes of the stock. However, under *Johnson* and *Levine* if D borrows on the stock and later makes a gift of it D will realize a gain at the time of the gift.

Where there is a gift of encumbered property the donee's basis will reflect both the gain realized by the donor and the portion of any gift tax paid that is attributable to the appreciation element of the gift. As the court explained in *Johnson*, Congress authorized increases in a donee's basis by both the amount of gain recognized in connection with gifts to trusts and the amount of gift tax paid, although that may superficially appear to be redundant.

Until the *Johnson* decision was handed down in 1974 a taxpayer might have borrowed against an appreciated asset, then given it away without ever being required to pay any income tax on the amount by which the loan exceeded his or her basis. If the transaction were carefully structured the obligation could be satisfied by the donee without any income tax liability to the donor. In the pre-*Johnson* era the grantor might be taxed on the income under §677 in the case of a gift to a trust. Even in the case of a trust, the reach of §677 was avoided if (1) the trustee assumed liability for the obligation (Edwards v. Greenwald, 217 F.2d 632 (5th Cir. 1954) or (2) the obligation was satisfied with funds other than trust income (Estate of Annette S. Morgan, 37 T.C. 981 (1962), *aff'd*, 316 F.2d 238 (6th Cir.), *cert. denied*, 375 U.S. 825 (1963)).

§7.26.   *Part Gift and Part Sale*

Under another approach the donor may sell part of the property to the intended donee in order to generate funds with which to pay the gift tax on a gift of the balance of the property. The plan may be implemented in either of 2 ways, which have substantially different income tax consequences. Under the first, the donor gives part of the property to the donee, who uses it as security to borrow funds with which to purchase the remainder of the property. In this case the gift and the sale relate to separate interests, which are respected for gift and income tax purposes. Under the second method all of the property is transferred to the donee for less than adequate and full consideration in money or money's worth (*i.e.*, it is a bargain sale). The owner's gift tax liability is the same under both approaches. However, under the first method the gain is computed separately for the property sold, while in the second gain is determined by reference to the transferor's basis in the entire property.

> **Example 7-7.** O plans to transfer 1,000 shares of XYZ, Inc. stock to his daughter, D, in exchange for $15,000 which O will use to pay the taxes that will be due as a result of the transfer. The stock has a basis of $10 per share and a value of $50 per share. Whichever method is used, the transfer will involve a gift to D of property worth $35,000 for gift tax purposes.
>
> Under the first method O would give D 700 shares outright, which involves a gift of $35,000 ($50 × 700). The gift would not cause O to recognize any gain unless the shares were encumbered. D's basis in those shares would be O's basis ($10) plus any gift tax paid with respect to the net appreciation in value of the shares. *See* §1015. Also, the time O held these shares could be taken into account in determining D's holding period. *See* §1223(2). If O sells the remaining 300 shares to D for $50 each, O would have a capital

gain of $12,000 ($50 × 300 − ($10 × 300)). D's basis in those 300 shares would be their cost of $50 each (§1012), the holding period of which would begin with the date of purchase. Thus, if no gift tax were paid with respect to the gift of 700 shares, D would have a total basis of $22,000 in the 1,000 shares (700 × $10) + (300 × $50).

O's gain would be much smaller under the second method (*i.e.,* if O makes a part gift and part sale of the 1,000 shares to D for $15,000). In case of a part gift and part sale, "the transferor has a gain to the extent that the amount realized by him exceeds his adjusted basis in the property." Reg. §1.1001-1(e)(1). Here the amount realized ($15,000) exceeds his basis ($10,000) by only $5,000. However, in this case D's basis will be limited to the price paid ($15,000) plus the portion of the gift tax paid with respect to the net appreciation. *See* Reg. §1.1015-4(a). Accordingly, the IRS might argue that the time O held the shares could not be taken into account for holding period purposes. *See* LR 7752001.

As Example 7-7 indicates, income and gift tax consequences must be taken into account in choosing which method to use in effectuating a part gift and part sale. The outcomes should also be compared with the results produced by other techniques, such as the net gift. *See* §7.24, *supra.* In this connection it is important to note that bargain sales to charity are subject to different rules. *See* §1011(b) and §8.28, *infra.*

Problem 7-5. A widow, W, owns a parcel of unimproved waterfront property near her home that she wants to give to her son, S. The lot, which W purchased in 1970 for $20,000, is now worth $100,000. The note W gave when she purchased the property, which is secured by a first mortgage, has been paid down to $10,000. W has made taxable gifts of $400,000 in prior years. She understands that a transfer of the lot would be subject to some gift tax, but she is unwilling to dip into her savings to pay it herself. S would be glad to pay any federal taxes that W might incur in connection with the transfer.

Calculate the gift tax consequences assuming (a) W transfers the lot to S conditioned upon his payment of the gift tax (*i.e.,* a net gift); (b) W sells the lot to him for approximately the amount of the gift tax liability she would incur as a result of the transfer, $21,000; and (c) W makes the transfer and the gift tax is voluntarily paid by S. What would be the income tax consequences of each of those 3 methods of structuring the transaction? In particular, would W recognize gain, what basis would S have in the property, and what would be his holding period for the property?

F.   GIFTS TO MINORS

§7.27.   Importance of Gifts to Minors

Gifts to minors have always been important in estate planning, but recent changes in the income, gift, and estate tax laws have made them even more important. First, the unification of the gift and estate tax laws increased the tax savings that result from making gifts that are within the annual exclusion and are not included in the donor's tax base at any time. Many clients are able to take advantage of that opportunity by making annual regular gifts to their minor children or grandchildren in forms that qualify for the annual exclusion. However, they need help in selecting the property to give and type of transfer to make. Second, the Tax Reform Act of 1976 made trusts for minors more attractive from the income tax perspective by excluding income accumulated before the beneficiary's birth or attainment of age 21 from the reach of the throwback rules. §665(b). Third, the use of trusts is also made more attractive by the availability of annual exclusion for transfers to trusts that give the beneficiary a properly drafted *Crummey* power (*see* §7.36, *infra*). The principal methods of transferring property to minors are discussed in the following sections, including outright gifts, Series E bonds, various forms of multiparty bank accounts, gifts under the Uniform Gifts to Minors Act, and gifts in trust. The discussion points out the wide differences in tax and nontax consequences that flow from different methods of making gifts to minors. For example, some transfers constitute completed gifts for gift tax purposes while others do not. Also, in the case of some gifts the subsequent income is taxed to the donor, while under others it is taxed to the donee or to a trust for the donee's benefit. Finally, in some cases the property is includible in the donor's gross estate, while in others it is not.

§7.28.   Outright Gifts

The transfer of property directly into the name of a minor is generally unadvisable because of its nontax consequences. There is some risk that the minor donee might dissipate the property instead of saving it, which is usually what the donor has in mind. On the other hand, it may be necessary to obtain the appointment of a guardian in order to sell, exchange, lease, or otherwise deal with property that stands in the name of a minor. Also, if the donee dies prior to attaining the age of majority the property may return to the donor under the intestate succession law instead of passing to the donee's siblings or other relatives. Finally, even if a guardian is appointed, the donee will gain full control over the property when he or she attains the age of majority, which many clients consider to be far too soon.

If a minor owns stock, the transfer agent may require that assignments and other documents pertaining to the stock be signed by a duly appointed and acting agent. F. Christy, Transfer of Stock §218 (5th ed. 1975). Transactions involving life insurance, real property, or other assets may also require the participation of a guardian. Local law and practice regarding the deposit and withdrawal of funds from accounts standing in the name of minors vary widely. Some institutions permit a minor to make small withdrawals if the minor is capable of writing his or her name and seems to understand the transaction, while others do not. As indicated below there is a simplified procedure for redemption of Series E bonds that stand in the name of a minor.

Gift Tax. The transfer of property into a minor's name is subject to state and federal gift taxes. However, the annual gift tax exclusion is available with respect to bona fide transfers except where the gift consists of a future interest in property.

Income Tax. The income from property that is transferred into the name of a minor is taxed to the minor if it belongs to the minor and cannot be used to satisfy the donor's legal obligation of support. *See* Rev. Rul. 58-65, 1958-1 C.B. 13. Thus, dividends paid on stock given to a minor are taxed to the minor where they are reinvested for the minor's benefit and are not borrowed or otherwise used by the donors in any way. Sandifur v. United States, 64-2 U.S.T.C. ¶9817, 14 A.F.T.R.2d 5082 (E.D. Wash. 1964). However, the income is taxed to the donor where the donor continues to exercise control over the property and the income it generates. Little v. United States, 191 F. Supp. 12 (E.D. Tex. 1960); Henry D. Duarte, 44 T.C. 193 (1965). In sum, the income is taxed according to the economic reality of the situation and not necessarily according to the way title is held.

Estate Tax. Property that is given to a minor is includible in the minor's gross estate under §2033 and is not generally includible in the donor's gross estate under §2035. However, the property is includible in the donor's gross estate under §2036 if the donor continues to use and control the property or expends it to satisfy a legal obligation to support the donee.

Overall, it is generally better to make small gifts under the Uniform Gifts to Minors Act and larger ones under a carefully planned and drafted trust. Those methods do not involve the problems of management that may arise where an outright gift is made to a minor. However, gifts made under the Uniform Act do suffer from some of the same nontax disadvantages as outright gifts.

Where an outright gift is made to a minor, a guardian may be appointed to participate in transactions affecting the property. However, a guardian cannot legitimately "undo" the gift and return the property to the donor or to a custodian under the Uniform Gifts to Minors Act. Once the gift has been made, little can generally be done to relieve the situation.

§7.29. Series E Bonds

Funds are often invested for minors in Series E bonds because of their security and ease of purchase. The applicable federal regulations require that "[t]he registration must express the actual ownership of, and interest in, the bond. The registration is conclusive of such ownership except [to correct an error in registration]." 31 C.F.R. §315.5 (1980). Under them bonds owned by natural persons may be registered only in the name of 1 person as sole owner ("X"); 2 persons as coowners ("X or Y"); or 2 persons as owner and beneficiary ("X payable on death to Y" or "X P.O.D. Y"). 31 C.F.R. §315.7(b)(1980). However, bonds owned by a minor may be registered in the name of the minor's guardian or in the name of a custodian under the Uniform Gifts to Minors Act.

Minor as Sole Owner. The purchase of a bond in the name of a minor has the same tax consequences as any other outright transfer of property to a minor. As indicated in Rev. Rul. 68-269, 1968-1 C.B. 399, *Situation 3*, the purchase constitutes a completed gift from the purchaser to the donee regardless of when the bond is actually delivered to the minor. Accordingly, it qualifies for the annual exclusion under §2503(b). The regulations permit a minor to redeem a bond that is registered in the minor's name if the minor understands the nature of the transaction.

If the minor dies owning the bond, it is includible in the minor's gross estate under §2033. Under ordinary circumstances the bond is not includible in the donor's estate.

The interest on a savings bond is ordinarily reported by a cash basis taxpayer when the bond is redeemed or reaches final maturity. Under §454(a), a taxpayer may elect to report the yearly increase in redemption value on the bond and all other appreciation-type securities. Taxpayers seldom elect to report the annual increase as it accrues because the election applies to all appreciation-type obligations and binds the taxpayer for all subsequent taxable years. Also, once the election is made, it can be changed only with the permission of the IRS.

Minor as Coowner. Bonds purchased with the funds of a minor must be registered in the name of the minor without a coowner or beneficiary. However, bonds purchased with funds not belonging to a minor may be registered in the name of the minor as owner or coowner. 31 C.F.R. §315.6(c)(1980).

The purchase of a bond in the name of the purchaser and another individual in coownership form ("X or Y") does not constitute a completed gift. A completed gift does take place when a bond purchased by X is reissued in Y's name alone (Rev. Rul. 55-278, 1955-1 C.B. 471) or when Y surrenders the bond for redemption without any duty to account to X for the disposition of the proceeds. Reg. §25.2511-1(h)(4); Rev. Rul. 68-269, 1968-1 C.B. 399, *Situation* 5. Where X provides the entire purchase price of the bond, none of the bond is includible in Y's gross estate if Y predeceases X. Of course, if X dies first, the bond is includible in X's estate under §2040 (*i.e.,* one-half the value of the bond is included if X and Y are husband and wife, otherwise the full value is included). Generally, when either coowner dies, the bond belongs entirely to the survivor. 31 C.F.R. §315.70(b) (1980).

While both coowners are living, either of them may redeem the bond by separate request. 31 C.F.R. §315.37 (1980). In contrast, the bond may be reissued only upon the request of both owners. A gift from one coowner to the other is effective only if the bond is reissued in the name of the donee — mere physical delivery to the intended donee is insufficient. United States v. Chandler, 410 U.S. 257 (1973). As the Supreme Court explained in *Chandler,* "the regulations thus made the jointly issued bond nontransferable in itself and permitted a change in ownership, so long as both co-owners were alive, only through reissuance at the request of both co-owners." *Id.* at 260.

For income tax purposes the unreported increase in value of a bond is ordinarily not taxed until redemption or maturity. Where one of the coowners obtains payment on the bond, presumably the increase is taxed to that person alone. If the ownership of a bond is changed by reissue, the prior owner is liable for the income tax on the increase in value up to the date of reissue. *See* Rev. Rul. 54-327, 1954-2 C.B. 50. However, income is not realized where a bond is reissued at the request of the sole owner in his or her name and the name of another person as coowners. Rev. Rul. 70-428, 1970-2 C.B. 5. A change in ownership resulting from the death of an owner is also not a taxable event. Instead, the unreported increase in value to the date of death constitutes income in respect of a decedent that is subject to taxation under §691 when received by the owner. Rev. Rul. 64-104, 1964-1 C.B. 223.

Minor as Beneficiary. The registration of a bond in the name of "X, payable on death to Y" or "X P.O.D. Y" has the same tax consequences as registration in the coownership form ("X or Y"). Specifically, this type of registration does not involve a gift from X to Y and the bond is fully includible in the estate of X if X predeceases Y. Where X and Y are not husband and wife and Y did not contribute to the purchase of the bond nothing is includible in Y's estate if he or she predeceases X. (Where X and Y are husband and wife presumably one-half of the value of the bond is includible under §2040(b) in the estate of the spouse first to die.) Also, the annual increase in redemption value of the bond is ordinarily not taxed on a current basis for income tax purposes. Income would be realized, however, when the bond is redeemed, finally matures, or is reissued in the name of an owner other than X (the original purchaser). The payable-on-death form of registration is an effective will substitute insofar as Series E bonds are concerned.

Because of their relatively low yield Series E bonds are not a particularly attractive way to invest a substantial amount for a minor. However, they are safe and are easily purchased and redeemed. If a client intends to invest a small amount in Series E bonds for a minor, consideration should be given to making the gift under the Uniform Gifts to Minors Act.

§7.30.   Payable on Death (P.O.D.) Bank Accounts

The P.O.D. form of multiparty account is recognized as nontestamentary in Article 6 of the UPC. However, the P.O.D. form must be used with more care in non-UPC states, which sometimes treat P.O.D. accounts as testamentary transfers that are invalid unless they are executed in the manner required of wills. *E.g.,* Truax v. Southwestern College Oklahoma City, Oklahoma, 522 P.2d 412 (Kan. 1974) (P.O.D. account invalid); Blais v. Colebrook Guaranty Savings Bank, 220 A.2d 763 (N.H. 1966) (P.O.D. account invalid); Estate of Tonsik, 235 N.E.2d 239 (Ohio App. 1968) (P.O.D. account upheld on basis of local statute).

Where X deposits funds in an account that stands in the name of "X payable on death to Y," the deposit does not have any significant federal tax impact: The interest on the account is taxable to X; the deposit does not constitute a gift because the funds may be freely withdrawn by X; and the account is includible in X's gross estate. If Y predeceases X nothing should be included in Y's gross estate.

§7.31.   The Savings Account or Tentative Trust

A tentative trust is created when X opens an account in the name of "X as trustee for Y." Under this arrangement X has the right to withdraw and use funds from the account without any duty to account to Y. Y is entitled to the balance of the account if X dies first. In contrast, the tentative trust is terminated if Y predeceases X. Fundamentally, the tentative trust is a simple form of will substitute that does not involve a present completed gift to the named beneficiary. A trust of this type is also recognized in Article 6 of the UPC as a valid form of multiparty nontestamentary transfer. A tentative trust is sometimes called a Totten trust, after the case in which it was held valid by the New York Court of Appeals, Matter of Totten, 71 N.E. 748 (N.Y. 1904).

A tentative trust does not have any present income, gift, or estate tax impact. The income is taxed to the depositor-trustee because the arrangement is completely revocable. §674. For the same reason there is not a completed gift to the donee when the trustee deposits funds in the account. Reg. §25.2511-2(c). If another party deposits funds in the account, presumably the deposit constitutes a gift to the trustee and not a gift to the trust beneficiary. Such a deposit qualifies for the annual exclusion because of the trustee's right to use the account for his or her own benefit. Any balance on hand when the trustee dies is includible in the trustee's gross estate under §§2036 and 2038 to the extent the trustee funded the account. Estate of Sulovich v. Commissioner, 587 F.2d 845 (6th Cir. 1978). The portion of the account funded by others is includible in the trustee's estate under §2041 if the trustee had the power to withdraw and use the funds without restrictions. Of course, if the beneficiary survives the trustee, the account becomes the beneficiary's property and is includible in the beneficiary's gross estate at death. If the beneficiary predeceases the trustee the account is not includible in the beneficiary's estate. Instead, in such a case, the trust terminates and the balance is includible in the former trustee's estate as owned property under §2033.

The tentative trust is generally an unsatisfactory way to hold funds for a minor. Because of its revocable nature the tax consequences are not favorable. Overall, it is preferable to make a gift to the minor under the Uniform Gifts to Minors Act or to a trust for the minor's benefit. Unfortunately, the personnel who handle new accounts at some financial institutions may push customers into tentative trusts because they aren't sufficiently familiar with the Uniform Gifts to Minors Act and other forms in which accounts might be opened.

§7.32. Joint Accounts

The deposit of funds by one person in a joint account with another ("X or Y") may give the other person a present interest in the account. However, it is not possible to generalize about joint accounts because the state laws regarding them vary substantially.

The joint account is often intended only to serve as a will substitute. This is recognized in Article 6 of the UPC, under which the deposit of funds in a joint account ("X or Y") does not alone give Y a present interest in any of the funds represented by the deposit. In particular, UPC §6-103(a) provides that "[a] joint account belongs, during the lifetime of all parties, to the parties in proportion to the net contributions by each to the sums on deposit, unless there is clear and convincing evidence of a different intent." When a party to a joint account dies the funds on deposit belong to the surviving party or parties unless there is clear and convincing evidence of another intent. UPC §6-104(a).

For gift tax purposes the deposit of funds in a joint account does not constitute a completed gift if the depositor retained the power to withdraw all of the funds. In such a case a gift takes place when the donee withdraws funds from the account without any duty to account to the depositor. Reg. §25.2511-1(h)(4). Here, again, the income from the account is taxable to the depositor and the account is includible in the depositor's gross estate except to the extent it is traceable to funds contributed by others. A gift occurs at the time the deposit is made where the state law restricts the depositor's right to withdraw the funds for his or her own use.

§7.33. Gifts under the Uniform Gifts to Minors Act

All states have adopted the Act in its original or revised form in order to facilitate gifts to minors. The Act authorizes gifts of certain types of property, which vary somewhat from state to state, to be made to a minor under its provisions. The basic form of the Act permits gifts of securities, life insurance policies, annuity contracts, or money to be made under it. Some states have expanded the types of assets that may be transferred to include other types of personal property and interests in real property. In general a gift is made under the Act by registering the asset, or depositing the fund, in the name of the donor, another adult, or a trust company "as custodian for (name of minor) under the   (name of state)   Uniform Gifts to Minors Act." §2(a)(2), 8 U.L.A. 198 (1972). By complying with the statutory procedure the donor makes an irrevocable gift to the minor that incorporates the existing provisions of the Act. The custodian is a fiduciary whose investment and reinvestment of the property is governed by the "prudent man" standard. However, unlike property held in trust, the title to the property held by a custodian is vested in the minor and not the trustee. Liberty National Life Ins. Co. v. First National Bank, 151 So. 2d 225, 227-228 (Ala. 1963). The Act authorizes the custodian to pay over or apply any or all of the property for the support, maintenance, education, and benefit of the minor. Property in the hands of the custodian must be distributed to the donee when he or she reaches the age specified in the statute, which varies from 17 to 21. If the minor dies prior to attaining that age, the property must be paid to the minor's estate.

Gift Tax. A gift under the Act constitutes a completed gift that qualifies for the annual gift tax exclusion. Rev. Rul. 59-357, 1959-2 C.B. 212.

The resignation of a custodian or the termination of the custodianship does not involve a further gift. Of course, a gift of separate property may be split between the donor and the donor's spouse under §2513. When community property is given, each spouse is the donor of one-half of the property.

Income Tax. The income from the custodial property is taxed to the minor currently whether or not it is actually distributed or expended for his or her benefit. However, the IRS contends that to the extent the income is applied to discharge the legal support obligation of *any* person, the income must be taxed to that person. Rev. Rul. 56-484, 1956-2 C.B. 23, approved in Rev. Rul. 59-357, 1959-2 C.B. 212. It is clear that the income is taxable to the donor to the extent it is used to satisfy the donor's obligations. For example, if the donor has assumed responsibility for paying the minor's private school tuition, the custodial income will be taxed to the donor to the extent it is used to meet that expense. Morrill v. United States, 228 F. Supp. 734 (D. Me. 1964) (irrevocable trust).

The existence and extent of a parent's legal obligation to support a minor depends upon local law, which is often far from clear. Although children may be emancipated at 18, some parental obligations may persist, at least in the case of incompetent or dependent children. However, the income of a custodianship may be safely accumulated for the minor or expended for items of "super support" that parents are clearly not obligated to provide under the local law (*e.g.*, travel, private music or dance lessons).

A custodian may not execute a valid Subchapter S election. Rev. Rul. 66-116, 1966-1 C.B. 198. However, a guardian may do so and the IRS will recognize an election signed by a custodian if the same person is also the minor's guardian. Rev. Rul. 68-227, 1968-1 C.B. 381.

One additional risk should be taken into account where appreciated property is transferred under the Act and sold within 2 years. The IRS may contend that the sale is subject to §644 and the gain must be taxed to the minor as if the donor had sold the property. The contention should be rejected, however, because §644 only applies to sales or exchanges by a trust. Although the Act may be viewed as providing for a statutory trust, a custodianship is not treated as a trust for property law purposes or for other income tax purposes. A trustee holds legal title to trust assets whereas the minor holds "indefeasibly vested legal title" to property given to the minor under the Act.

Estate Tax. The custodial property is includible in the donor's gross estate if the donor is acting as custodian at the time of his or her death. Rev. Rul. 59-357, 1959-2 C.B. 212. In such a case the property is includible under §2038 because of the custodian's power to distribute the custodial property and, in effect, to terminate the custodial arrangement. Stuit v. Commissioner, 452 F.2d 190 (7th Cir. 1971). The same result follows if another person was the original custodian, but the donor was acting in that capacity at the time of his or her death. Rev. Rul. 70-348, 1970-2 C.B. 193. The custodial property is not includible in the estate of the donor's spouse, although he or she elected to be treated as the donor of one-half of it under §2513 and was acting as custodian at the time of his or her death. Rev. Rul. 74-556, 1974-2 C.B. 300. That result is clearly correct under §§2036 and 2038 — the consenting spouse did not actually own or transfer any part of the property of which she was acting as custodian at the time of her death. Of course, one-half of the property would be includible in the custodian's estate if the gift had consisted of community property. Also, if the consenting spouse has the power as custodian to apply the property to discharge a legal obligation to support the minor, there is some risk that the property would be included in the consenting spouse's estate under §2041.

The reciprocal trust doctrine (*see* §6.20, *supra*) applies where donors make related gifts under the Uniform Gifts to Minors Act and appoint each other as custodian. Thus, the deceased custodian's estate included the gifts nominally made by his spouse where they had made identical contemporaneous gifts to their minor children and named each other as custodian. Exchange Bank & Trust Co. v. United States, 49 A.F.T.R.2d — (Ct. Cl. Tr. Div. 1981).

The Act provides an efficient and economical method of transferring limited amounts of certain types of property to minors. However, most clients are reluctant to make substantial gifts under the Act because the property must be paid over to the donee at an early age. Also, if the minor dies prior to attaining the age of majority, the property must be paid over to the donee's estate. Because a minor cannot make a will, the property would pass under the intestate succession law, which may be inconsistent with the donor's estate plan. Most often the donor is a parent, who makes the gift to remove the property from his or her estate. Of course, the parent may disclaim succession to the deceased child's intestate property under §2045, but that might further frustrate the donor's estate plan. These disadvantages are avoided, however, if the gift is made to a properly drawn trust. *See* §§7.34 to 7.38, *infra*.

Problem 7-6. H deposited $25,000 of his separate property cash in an account in the name of his wife, W, as custodian for their daughter, D, under the Uniform Gifts to Minors Act. W opened an account in the name of "W as trustee for D" and deposited $25,000 of her separate property cash in the account. Assuming that neither H nor W made any other gifts during the year and that both H and W have exhausted their unified credits through prior gifts, what are the income, gift, and estate tax consequences of the deposits? How would your answers be different if the funds deposited in the accounts were community property?

§7.34. Gifts in Trust: General Comments

Trusts are frequently used as vehicles for making gifts to minors because of their great flexibility. In order to maximize the tax savings that result from transfers in trusts, the trusts are usually drafted to qualify for the annual gift tax exclusion. That is particularly important because gifts within the annual exclusion are generally not included in the donor's transfer tax base at any time. Until recently the most common method of qualifying for the annual exclusion was to draft the trust so that it met the requirements of §2503(c). The use of §2503(c) trusts is discussed in the next section, §7.35, *infra*. Now, however, it is more common to use trusts that (1) continue past the donee's minority, (2) provide only for discretionary distributions to the donee, and (3) qualify for the annual exclusion by giving the minor a limited, noncumulative power to withdraw assets as they are added to the trust. Such a power of withdrawal is often called a *Crummey* power after Crummey v. Commissioner, 397 F.2d 82 (9th Cir. 1968), which allowed an annual gift tax exclusion for assets transferred to a discretionary trust for a minor. *See* §7.36, *infra*. Some trusts require the trustee to distribute the income to the minor currently, the actuarially determined value of which constitutes a present interest under §2503(b). *See* §7.37, *infra*. Minors are also sometimes the beneficiaries of short-term trusts, which are discussed at §7.38, *infra*.

§7.35. Gifts in Trust: §2503(c) Trusts

Under §2503(c) a transfer for the benefit of a donee under the age of 21 is not a future interest if the following requirements are met:

1. The property and the income may be expended by or for the benefit of the donee before the donee attains 21;
2. Any portion of the property not expended for the donee's benefit will pass to the donee when the donee attains 21; and
3. The property and its income will be payable to the donee's estate or as the donee may appoint under a general power of appointment if the donee dies prior to 21.

Property or Income. The section literally requires both the property *and* its income to be expended or distributed in the prescribed manner. However, the IRS has acquiesced in decisions that allow an exclusion to the extent that either the income *or* the principal interest meets those requirements. Arlean I. Herr, 35 T.C. 732 (1961), *nonacq.*, 1962-2 C.B. 6, *withdrawn and acq. substituted*, 1968-2 C.B. 2, *aff'd*, 303 F.2d 780 (3d Cir. 1962); Rev. Rul. 68-670, 1968-2 C.B. 413.

Example 7-8. X transferred property to T as trustee of a trust for the benefit of B, a minor. The trustee was authorized to expend income, but not principal, for the support, comfort, and general welfare of B until B reached 21 or sooner died. At that time any accumulated income was payable to B if B was then living, otherwise to B's estate. After B attained 21 the income was payable to B in the discretion of the trustee. The principal of the trust and any income accumulated after B attained 21 was payable to B at age 35. An exclusion under §2503(c) is available with respect to the actuarily determined value of the right to receive the income until B attains 21.

No Substantial Restrictions. The requirement that the income or principal may be expended by or for the benefit of the donee prior to attaining 21 is met only if the trustee's discretion to expend funds is not subject to any "substantial restrictions." Reg. §25.2503-4(b)(1). Rev. Rul. 67-270, 1967-2 C.B. 349, holds that this requirement is met if the trust property may be expended during the donee's minority "for purposes which have no objective limitations (*i.e.,* 'welfare,' 'happiness' and 'convenience') and which provisions when read as a whole approximate the scope of the term 'benefit,' as used in section 2503(c) of the Code." In contrast, no annual exclusion is allowable if the trustee's power to make distributions is limited. Thus, no exclusion is allowable where the trustee can make distributions to the donee only if the donee's needs are not met by the donee's parents or from the donee's own resources. Rev. Rul. 69-345, 1969-1 C.B. 226.

A trust that provides for the discretionary use of income for a minor until 21, at which time all the accumulated income is distributable to the beneficiary and all of the income is payable to the beneficiary thereafter, qualifies under §2503(c) only to the extent of the income interest for the beneficiary's minority. The right to receive the income after 21 is a future interest that cannot be combined with the pre-21 income interest for the purpose of the annual exclusion. The possible accumulation of the income prior to age 21 prevents the post-21 income interest from being a present interest for purposes of the annual exclusion. Levine v. Commissioner, 526 F.2d 717 (2d Cir. 1975).

Payable to the Donee at 21. Under the second requirement the interest must pass to the donee when the donee attains 21. In Rev. Rul. 73-287, 1973-2 C.B. 321, the IRS held that an annual exclusion was available under §2503(c) for a transfer under a version of the Uniform Gifts to Minors Act that provided for distribution to the donee at age 18 instead of 21. It reasoned that §2503(c) set the maximum restrictions that may be attached to gifts to minors. "Therefore, a provision that the custodial property be paid to the minor donee when he attains the age of

18 years will meet the requirement that the property pass to the donee at least by his attainment of age 21, and, hence, will satisfy the greater age requirement of section 2503(c) of the Code." Accordingly, an annual exclusion should be available for a gift to a trust that requires the necessary distributions be made to the donee before he or she becomes 21.

This requirement may be satisfied although the trust does not automatically terminate when the donee reaches 21. It is sufficient if the donee has the power to compel distribution upon reaching the age of 21, whether the power is a continuing one or is exercisable only for a limited period. Rev. Rul. 74-43, 1974-1 C.B. 285. However, the failure to exercise the power may cause the donee to be treated as the transferor of any interest that others have in the trust to the extent the amount that could be withdrawn exceeds the greater of $5,000 or 5% of the value of the property subject to the power. *See* §§2041 and 2514. Whether the lapse of the power constitutes a taxable gift depends upon several factors including the extent to which the donee retains any power over disposition of the property.

Payable to the Donee's Estate or as the Donee Appoints. If the donee dies prior to 21, any remaining interest must be payable to the donee's estate or as the donee appoints under a general power of appointment. Apparently this requirement was imposed "to insure inclusion of the property, which had the benefit of a gift tax exclusion, in the gross estate of the beneficiary for estate tax purposes in the event that he dies prior to reaching age 21." Cornelius A. Ross, 71 T.C. 897, 900 (1979), *aff'd,* 652 F.2d 1365 (9th Cir. 1981). In *Ross* no annual exclusion was allowed under §2503(c) for a trust that provided for distribution of the property to the donee's "heirs at law" if he died prior to 21. The problem is, of course, that a distribution to the minor's "heirs at law" is not the equivalent of a distribution to the minor's estate. The requirement is satisfied if the donee is given a general testamentary power of appointment although the donee is unable to exercise the power under the local law because of his or her minority. Reg. §25.2503-4(b). The possession of a general power of appointment is sufficient to cause the property to be included in the gross estate of the power holder although he or she lacks the capacity to exercise it. §2041; Rev. Rul. 75-351, 1975-2 C.B. 368. This is consistent with the position that the IRS has taken in connection with the allowance of a marital deduction under §2056(b)(5). *See* §5.17, *supra.* If the trust otherwise qualifies, a marital deduction is allowable although the surviving spouse is incapable of exercising the power of appointment because of legal incapacity. *See, e.g.,* Rev. Rul. 75-350, 1975-2 C.B. 366.

The annual exclusion is not available under §2503(c) if the trust itself imposes any restrictions on the exercise of the power. Thus, in Gall v.

United States, 521 F.2d 878 (5th Cir. 1975), *cert. denied,* 425 U.S. 972 (1976), the exclusion was denied where the donee was required to be 19 in order to exercise the power and state law allowed persons of 19 years of age *and* younger married persons to execute wills.

Income Tax. The income of a §2503(c) trust is taxed to the minor if it is distributed to the minor or used for the minor's benefit except to the extent the income is taxed to the grantor under §§671 to 677. *See* §§10.26 to 10.32, *infra.* In other cases the income is taxed to the trust. The grantor may act as trustee of a §2503(c) trust without causing the income to be taxed to him or her. In particular, under §674(b)(5)-(7) any person may hold discretionary powers to distribute or accumulate income during a beneficiary's minority or to distribute corpus to the income beneficiary of a trust so long as any distribution of corpus is charged to the beneficiary's proportionate interest in the principal of the trust. Income that is accumulated before the beneficiary reaches 21 is not subject to the throwback rules when it is distributed. §665(b). This allows considerable flexibility in income tax planning. Again, under §644, the gain on appreciated property that is sold within 2 years following its transfer to the trust is taxed as if the donor had made the sale.

Estate Tax. The trust property is includible in the donee's gross estate if it is payable to the donee's estate or if the donee holds a general power of appointment over it. It is also includible if the donee does not exercise a power to compel distribution of the trust property when he or she attains 21 and he or she remains a beneficiary of the trust until death. Under §2041(a)(2) the failure to exercise the power of withdrawal constitutes a release and the property is includible in the donee's gross estate if the release results in a disposition "of such nature that if it were a transfer of property owned by the decedent, such property would be includible in the decedent's gross estate under sections 2035-2038, inclusive." The failure to exercise the power might also involve a gift of an interest in the trust to other parties, such as contingent remaindermen who will be entitled to the property if the donee does not survive to a specified age or event.

Example 7-9. Parent, P, transferred property to a trust under which the principal and income could be expended by the trustee for the benefit of P's daughter, D, until she reached 21. Under the trust D had the power to withdraw all of the trust assets by written notice delivered to the trustee within 60 days following her twenty-first birthday. The income from any property that is not withdrawn is payable to D annually and the principal is distributable to her when she reaches 45. If D dies prior to 21 the trust property is payable to her estate, but if she dies after reaching 21 and prior to 45, the trust property is payable to P's then living descendants per stirpes.

The trust meets the requirements of §2503(c). Accordingly, an annual exclusion is available to P for property he transferred to the trust during D's minority. D's power to withdraw the property of the trust constitutes a general power of appointment under §2041. If she allows the power to lapse, or otherwise releases it, she has probably made a taxable gift of the contingent remainder interest. *See* Reg. §25.2514-3(c). However, under §2514(e) a lapse of a general power of appointment is subject to gift tax only to the extent that the property that could have been appointed by the donee of the power exceeds the greater of (i) $5,000 or (ii) 5% of the total value of the assets out of which the exercise of the lapsed power could have been satisfied. If the power lapses and D dies prior to attaining 45, a similar proportion of the trust assets is includible in her estate under §2041(a)(2). *See* Reg. §20.2041-3(d)(3), (4).

The trust property is subject to inclusion in the donor's estate under §2036(a)(2) or §2038(a)(1) if the trustee has the power to make discretionary distributions to the beneficiary and the donor is acting as trustee at the time of the donor's death. *See* Lober v. United States, 346 U.S. 335 (1953). The property might also be includible in the donor's estate under §2036(a) if the trust provides the beneficiary with types of support that the donor is obligated to provide under the local law. On the other hand, one leading decision holds that the property is not includible in the parent-donor's estate where there is an independent trustee and none of the property is ever used for the support of the child-donee. Estate of Jack F. Chrysler, 44 T.C. 55 (1965), *acq.,* 1970-2 C.B. xix, *rev'd on other issues,* 361 F.2d 508 (2d Cir. 1966).

Evaluation. A custom-made §2503(c) trust may better meet the needs of a client who wishes to make modest gifts to a minor than a gift under the Uniform Gifts to Minors Act. For example, the trust can be drafted to prevent the property from returning to a donor-parent if the donee dies prior to 21. That is achieved by providing for payment of the trust property to another person or to a trust for another person if the donee dies prior to 21 without validly exercising a general testamentary power of appointment. Both from the tax and nontax perspectives, the main shortcoming of a §2503(c) trust is the requirement that the interest pass to the donee upon attaining age 21. Most clients would be happier if the property were neither payable to the donee at 21 nor all subject to the donee's power of withdrawal. As indicated above, the power of withdrawal can cause gift and estate tax problems for the donee. For those reasons if a client wants the trust to continue after the donee attains 21, it is usually better to create a discretionary trust that gives the donee a

Crummey power to withdraw assets for a limited time after they are transferred to the trust. As explained in the next section, neither the property nor the income of a *Crummey* trust is required to pass to the donee upon his or her attaining age 21.

§7.36.   Gifts in Trust: Discretionary Trust with **Crummey** Powers

A trust that gives the trustee discretion to make distributions of income and principal before and after the donee attains his or her majority is an excellent way to provide for the flexible management and distribution of family wealth. It can also have 2 significant tax advantages. First, the annual exclusion is available for transfers to the trust if the beneficiary is given a *Crummey* power. Second, the throwback rules do not apply to income that is accumulated prior to the beneficiary's birth or the attainment of age 21. If the trust is properly drafted, the trust assets are not includible in the grantor's estate except to the extent they are subject to §2035. The trust may be drafted to terminate when the beneficiary attains a certain age or to continue after the beneficiary's death for the benefit of the beneficiary's children or others. Importantly, the trust may be drafted to qualify for the $250,000 grandchild exclusion under the generation-skipping tax. §2613(a)(4)(A), (b)(5)(A).

Gift Tax. The transfer of property to a discretionary trust usually constitutes a completed gift for gift tax purposes. The more important question is whether or not the transfer qualifies for the annual exclusion.

Annual Exclusion. Property that is transferred to a discretionary trust does not ordinarily qualify for the annual exclusion because the donee does not have a present interest in it. However, in late 1973 the IRS conceded that a gift to a discretionary trust for a minor qualifies for the annual exclusion if the donee has the present right to demand distribution of the property. Rev. Rul. 73-405, 1973-2 C.B. 321. The ruling recognizes that "it is not the actual use, possession, or enjoyment by the donee which marks the dividing line between a present and a future interest, but rather the right conferred upon the donee by the trust instrument to such use, possession, or enjoyment." Accordingly, the annual exclusion is available where a minor donee is given the power to withdraw property transferred to the trust if there is no impediment under the trust or the local law to the appointment of a guardian who could exercise the power for the minor. For gift tax purposes the transfer of property to a trust that contains a properly drafted *Crummey* power is treated as if the property had been transferred outright to the donee.

The content of a *Crummey* clause will vary somewhat, depending upon the other provisions of the trust and the circumstances of the parties. For example, the form may differ if (1) there are multiple rather than single beneficiaries; (2) gifts may be made to the trust by more than one donor each year; or (3) the trust principal will be distributed to the donee at some point instead of remaining in trust for the donee's lifetime. In particular, the lawyer should consider the points that are raised in the following paragraphs.

Limit the Amount? Under a typical *Crummey* clause the donee is given a limited noncumulative power exercisable within a specified period following notice, to withdraw property that is transferred to the trust. Considering the nature and purpose of the trust it is generally undesirable to give the donee a broader power to make withdrawals, at least during the donee's minority. However, it is also necessary to consider whether the trust should limit the dollar value of property that can be withdrawn each year. A limit is imposed in many instruments in order to prevent the lapse of the power from resulting in adverse gift or estate tax consequences for the donee. The 2 most common limits on the amount that can be withdrawn by the donee each year are (1)$10,000 per donor and (2) $5,000 or 5% of the principal value of the trust. Sometimes the former limit is stated "not to exceed $10,000 per donor, or $20,000 per donor if the donor is married at the time the property is transferred to the trust." Such a provision assumes that the donor's spouse will consent to split the gift. The amount that can be withdrawn should not be made to depend upon whether the gift is split — which will not be determined until after the gift is made (*i.e.,* when a gift tax return is filed). To the extent a transfer is subject to such a qualification the gift constitutes a future interest for which no annual exclusion is available.

It is generally preferable to limit the amount that can be withdrawn to the amount of the annual exclusion allowable to each donor, which protects the availability of the annual exclusion for all donors. (Such a restriction also limits to some extent the gift and estate tax consequences of a failure to exercise the power in a year when the transfers to the trust exceed the statutorily sheltered $5,000 or 5% amount.) The limit may be expressed as a fixed dollar amount or by reference to "the annual exclusion allowable under IRC section 2503(b)." The 1981 Act increased the annual exclusion from $3,000 to $10,000. However, under a transitional rule, the increase does not generally apply to powers created under instruments executed prior to September 13, 1981. Act §441(c)(1).

If a $5,000 or 5% limit is used, the failure to exercise the power does not constitute a gift. §2514(e); LR 8003152. The lapse of such a power will not cause any of the trust to be included in the donee's gross estate. §2041(b)(2). However, when a $5,000 or 5% limit is used, the full amount of the annual exclusion is not available to a donor who transfers a larger amount to the trust.

Problem 7-7. B is the beneficiary of a trust that gives B the power to withdraw property that is added to the trust by giving the trustee written notice of exercise of the power within 60 days after receiving notice of its addition to the trust. The income of the trust is distributable to B in the discretion of the independent trustee. Principal is distributable to B at age 30. If B dies before age 30, the principal is distributable to such of B's issue as B may by will appoint. However, the amount that can be withdrawn each year is limited to the greater of $5,000 or 5% of the principal value of the trust. This year X, Y, and Z successively gave $10,000 each to the trust, which increased the value of its assets to $100,000. What are the gift tax consequences of the transfers to the trust? If B allows the power to lapse with respect to those additions, what are the estate, gift, and income tax consequences?

Where the client wants to preserve the annual exclusion for all transfers to the trust and the client is not concerned about the gift and estate tax consequences of a lapse of the power, the power can be drawn to allow the beneficiary to withdraw an unlimited amount of the property added to the trust during the year. (Of course the client should also recognize that the beneficiary might exercise such a power — which could discomfit the donor.) The lapse of the power with respect to any particular addition will not result in any gift tax liability if the donee also holds a special testamentary power of appointment that prevents the lapse from constituting a complete gift. *See* Reg. §25.2511-2(b).

Should Each Beneficiary Be Given the Power? The power of withdrawal may be given to any number of beneficiaries, including incompetent persons. Where there are multiple beneficiaries, each of them is usually given a power to withdraw a pro rata portion of property that is added to the trust each year, subject to an aggregate annual limit. The number of annual exclusions that may be claimed is maximized if each beneficiary is given the power. If the donor is willing to settle for fewer annual exclusions, the power may be given to one or more of the beneficiaries, but not to the others. It is theoretically possible to qualify transfers to the trust for a large number of annual exclusions by giving the power to persons who have no other beneficial interest in the trust (*e.g.,* all of the lawyers in the draftsman's office). However, it is difficult to imagine a case where it would be appropriate to do so. There is a high probability that the IRS would disregard such a power on the ground that it lacked substance and was a sham.

Notice to the Beneficiary? In order to qualify for the annual exclusion for property transferred to the trust, it is necessary for the beneficiary to have a reasonable opportunity to exercise the power of withdrawal prior to its lapse. Rev. Rul. 81-7, 1981-1 C.B. 474 (trust funded on December 29, power lapsed on December 31). Letter Ruling 7946007 did not allow an annual exclusion where the adult beneficiary did not receive timely notice. Also, in LR 8006048 the IRS was unwilling to rule that the beneficiary had a present interest in the initial corpus of the trust where the trust instrument did not require the trustee to give the beneficiary notice of the power of withdrawal. In general, it is preferable to include a provision requiring the trustee to give the beneficiary prompt notice of additions to the trust, or notice within a certain number of days, say 7 or 10. Even if the trust does not expressly require the trustee to give notice, the trustee of a *Crummey* trust should give prompt written notice to the beneficiary of any addition to the trust. Giving actual notice of each addition can be a nuisance, however, particularly where frequent additions are made to the trust, as may occur where the employer pays monthly premiums on group-term insurance held by the trustee. Where employer-provided group-term insurance will be held in the trust perhaps the withdrawal clause could be drawn to permit a single annual notice, in advance, of premium payments that will be made during the year.

Some planners are reluctant to include a provision in the trust requiring the trustee to give the beneficiary written notice of the receipt of additional property. They feel it is risky to include such a provision because of the possibility that the trustee might not comply exactly with its provisions, which could jeopardize the availability of the annual exclusion. In their view it is preferable to advise the trustee separately that the trustee should give the beneficiary timely notice. The availability of the annual exclusion should depend upon whether or not the beneficiary receives notice of the transfer of the property to the trust and not upon the inclusion of a provision requiring notice. It may be better to require the trustee to give notice, however, because a direction contained in the trust puts the trustee on notice regarding the requirement and may be taken more seriously than the planner's advice regarding the current requirements of the tax law. Also, the inclusion of the requirement might satisfy an IRS examiner without the donor being required to prove that notice was in fact given to the beneficiary when property was added to the trust.

Must the Trust Have Liquid Assets to Satisfy a Withdrawal? Some lawyers fear that an annual exclusion will not be available unless the trust has sufficient liquid funds to satisfy an exercise of the power of withdrawal. However, the IRS has not asserted such a requirement. Quite to the contrary, several letter rulings have allowed annual exclusions for gifts to *Crummey* trusts of term or group-term policies of insurance on the donor's life. *E.g.*, LRs 7826050, 7935091, 8006048. In fact, the IRS has indicated that where the beneficiary holds a *Crummey* power an

annual exclusion is allowable for the premium payment made by an
employer on a group-term life insurance policy that the employee had
transferred in trust. LR 8006109. Logically the right of withdrawal
should be sufficient to create a present interest in the beneficiary
whether the assets transferred to the trust are cash, securities, insurance,
or tangible personal property. That is, the annual exclusion should be
available whether or not the trustee has liquid assets on hand during the
time the power is exercisable. The power could be satisfied by the transfer of an undivided interest in whatever assets are held in the trust.
Nonetheless, the conservative and safer practice is to fund the trust with
sufficient liquid assets to support a withdrawal by the beneficiaries equal
to the amount of the annual exclusion (*i.e.,* $10,000 each).

How Long Should the Power Be Exercisable? In order to qualify for the
annual exclusion the beneficiary must have a reasonable time within
which to exercise the power of withdrawal. Trusts usually permit the
beneficiary to exercise the power either (1) for a specified number of
days following notice of the transfer, or (2) at any time during the calendar year in which the transfer was made. Private letter rulings have
upheld the allowance of the annual exclusion in cases that allowed withdrawals for 30 days (LR 8004172) or 60 days (LR 7947066) following the
transfer, or at any time during the calendar year (LR 7935006).

Permitting a withdrawal to be made only during the calendar year in
which the property was added to the trust is less desirable for 2 reasons.
First, the IRS may not allow the annual exclusion when the transfer is
made late in December on the ground that the beneficiary did not have a
reasonable time within which to withdraw the property. Of course, in
Crummey an exclusion was allowed where the trust contained such a
provision and the transfer was made 2 weeks before the end of the year.
That threat can be eliminated by providing that the power may be exercised by the beneficiary during a specified minimum period in any case.
For example, the beneficiary could be authorized to withdraw property
at any time during the calendar year in which the property is added to
the trust, or for a period of 30 days following the addition of the property, whichever is longer. Of course, the power to withdraw a gift made
after December 1 in any year would lapse in the following calendar year.
Such a lapse would be aggregated with any others that take place during
the same calendar year for purposes of applying the $5,000 or 5% limits
of §§2041 and 2514. Some planners deal with the problem by prohibiting
any additions from being made to the trust after a specified date, such as
November 30. *See* LR 8006048. However, that approach unduly restricts
the ability of prospective donors to make qualifying gifts to the trust.

Second, the use of a clause that permits the beneficiary to withdraw the
property at any time during the calendar year may increase the liquidity

requirements of the trust. If the power exists throughout the entire year, the beneficiary may be treated as owner of a greater portion of the trust under §678 than if it existed only for a short time. The liquidity problem is particularly severe if the trustee must always have sufficient liquid assets on hand to satisfy all of the withdrawals that could be made at any time. Retaining that degree of liquidity should not be required in order to enable the donors to claim annual exclusions when they add property to the trust. Note also that the liquidity problem is substantially reduced if the power may be exercised only for a limited number of days following notice.

Should the Donor Be Permitted to Designate Whether a Particular Transfer to the Trust May Be Withdrawn? The trust may include a provision that permits the donor to designate whether or not an addition of property made by him or her shall be subject to withdrawal. *See* Keydel, Irrevocable Insurance Trusts: The Current Scene, U. Miami 10th Inst. Est. Plan. ¶508.1 (1976). The provision probably does not cause any federal tax problems apart from the loss of annual exclusions for additions that are not subject to withdrawal. It might also protect subsequent additions from withdrawal by the beneficiary and against the claims of his or her creditors. However, such a provision could be bothersome where additions are frequently made to the trust, such as premium payments made by the insured's employer on group insurance that is held in trust. That problem could be eliminated, however, if the additions — except for those expressly designated by the donor — were subject to withdrawal.

Separate Trusts or One Trust for Multiple Donees? Where there will be multiple donees, it is usually simpler to create a separate trust for each of them than it is to create a single trust with multiple beneficiaries. However, the donor is entitled to an annual exclusion for each trust beneficiary who has the right to withdraw a pro rata portion of the property that the donor transferred to the trust. Rev. Rul. 80-261, 1980-2 C.B. 279. Separate trusts can be easier to administer in some respects and are generally more beneficial from the income tax point of view because each trust is to some extent a separate taxpayer, which allows each trust a $100 exemption and separate use of the progressive rate schedule. When there are separate trusts, some economies of scale can be achieved if the assets of the trusts are managed as a unit, which can be authorized expressly in the trust instrument.

Income Tax. A *Crummey* trust is usually subject to the same income tax rules as a §2503(c) trust. *See* §7.35, *supra.* In addition, however, the beneficiary is treated as the "owner" of the trust under the grantor trust rules to the extent the beneficiary holds a power to withdraw assets of the trust. §678(a)(1). The income is taxed to the beneficiary under §678 although the beneficiary is a minor and lacks the legal capacity to withdraw the property. "[I]t is the existence of a power rather than the capacity to exercise such a power that determines whether a person other than the grantor shall be treated as the owner of any part of the trust." Rev. Rul. 81-6, 1981-1 C.B. 385. *See also* Rev. Rul. 67-241, 1967-2 C.B. 225 (widow holding $5,000 or 5% withdrawal power is treated as partial owner of trust). Accordingly, under §678 a portion of the trust income will be taxed to the beneficiary in a year that property is added to the trust although no income is distributed to, or expended for, the benefit of the beneficiary. Under §678(b), where the grantor trust rules require the income of the trust to be taxed to the grantor, it is not taxed to the beneficiary. For example, the income is taxable to the grantor to the extent it is used to satisfy the grantor's legal obligation to support any person (§677(b)). Again, the trustee must also be aware that the gain on the sale of appreciated property within 2 years after it is added to the trust is taxed as if the grantor had made the sale unless the sale takes place after the grantor's death. *See* §644.

Estate Tax. The estate tax consequences of a *Crummey* trust are generally the same as those of a §2503(c) trust. *See* §7.35, *supra.* Inclusion in the donee's estate is usually limited to the amount in excess of the $5,000 or 5% limit with respect to which the donee's power of withdrawal has lapsed. *See* §2041(b)(2). Insofar as the donor is concerned, none of the trust should be included in the donor's estate unless either the trust income or property is used to discharge the donor's obligations or the donor is acting as trustee at the time of death.

Sample Crummey Clause:

Withdrawal rights. The beneficiary, or her guardian, shall have the right to withdraw from the trust an amount of the assets originally transferred to the trust not to exceed $20,000 in value by giving written notice, within thirty days of her receipt of a copy of this instrument, to the trustee of her intention to exercise such right. [A copy of the trust will be delivered to the beneficiary, or to her guardian, on the date the property is transferred to the trust.]

Trustee shall promptly give written notice to the beneficiary of the receipt of any additional property that is gifted to the trust by any donor. The beneficiary shall have the right to withdraw such property, exercisable by giving written notice to the trustee within thirty days following receipt of the trustee's notice that property has been gifted to the trust. Such right of withdrawal shall apply only to the additional property covered by such notice. The value of the property subject to withdrawal shall not exceed the lesser of

   (a) $10,000 per donor, or $20,000 per donor for each donor
           who is married at the time of the gift to the trust, or
   (b)   the total value of such additional property.
   If the beneficiary is a minor on the date of this instrument or at
the time of any subsequent transfer of property to the trust, or at
any such time otherwise fails in legal capacity, the beneficiary's
guardian may exercise on behalf of the beneficiary any right of
withdrawal provided for in this article. Whether any such right of
withdrawal is exercised by the beneficiary or her guardian, the
property received pursuant to such exercise shall be held for the
use and benefit of the beneficiary.

§7.37.   *Mandatory Distribution of Income Trust (§2503(b))*

Trusts for minors usually do not require the income to be distributed
currently. However, in order to qualify for the annual exclusion, a trust
for a minor may require the income to be distributed currently to the
donee, the donee's guardian, or a custodian for the donee under the
Uniform Gifts to Minors Act. In those cases the annual exclusion is
available for the actuarially determined value of the income interest.
Reg. §25.2512-9. As indicated in Reg. §25.2503-4(c), the remainder interest does not qualify for the annual exclusion: "[A] transfer of
property in trust with income required to be paid annually to a minor
beneficiary and corpus to be distributed to him upon his attaining the
age of 25 is a gift of a present interest with respect to the right to income
but is a gift of a future interest with respect to the right to corpus."

   From the nontax point of view a mandatory distribution trust is generally less desirable than a *Crummey* trust because of the difficulty of
providing for current distribution of income in a satisfactory way. Direct
payment of the income to the beneficiary is generally considered to
involve an unacceptable risk of waste by the beneficiary. The other
methods of distribution also have some disadvantages. Requiring the appointment of a guardian to receive distributions of income involves some
additional complexity in drafting and operating the trust. More important, the conduct of a guardianship proceeding is cumbersome and expensive in most states. Distribution to a custodian is a better choice, but it
does involve a bit of additional complexity in drafting and operating the
trust.

   The mandatory distribution trust involves 2 tax disadvantages. As
indicated above, the full value of the property transferred to the trust
does not qualify for the annual exclusion. Also, the income-splitting
potential of the trust is limited where the distribution must be made to
the minor or a custodian for him or her (income received by the custodian is taxed currently to the minor).

§7.38.   *Irrevocable Short-Term Trusts*

Short-term trusts, which are also called Clifford, 10-year, or grantor trusts, are also sometimes created for minors. For a further discussion of the grantor trust rules, §§671 to 677, see §§10.26 to 10.32, *infra.* Short-term trusts are generally used by a taxpayer in a high income tax bracket to shift income to another family member temporarily, without permanently divesting himself or herself of all interests in the property. Importantly, the grantor may retain a reversionary interest in property transferred to the trust if the reversion will not, or is not reasonably expected to, take effect in possession or enjoyment within 10 years following its transfer to the trust. §673(a). Also, under the specific provisions of §673(c), the grantor is not treated as the owner of any portion of a trust if the reversionary interest will take effect upon the death of the income beneficiary or beneficiaries, regardless of his, her, or their life expectancies. In the absence of special provisions the capital gains realized by a short-term trust are currently taxable to the grantor because of the grantor's reversionary interest in them. §677(a)(2); Rev. Rul. 75-267, 1975-2 C.B. 254.

> **Example 7-10.** Grantor, G, transferred property in trust to pay the income to his daughter, D, for a period of 11 years or until D's earlier death when the trust would terminate. Upon termination of the trust the principal is payable to G, if he is then living, otherwise to the persons G designates under a general testamentary power of appointment. G's retention of a reversionary interest would not cause the income to be taxed to G. *See* Reg. §1.673(a)-1(b). If the reversionary interest were also to take effect upon the grantor's death, the income would be taxable to G if his life expectancy was less than 10 years at the time of transfer to the trust. Reg. §1.673(a)-1(c).

Where a minor is the income beneficiary of a short-term trust, the income may be paid to a custodian for the minor under the Uniform Gifts to Minors Act in order to avoid the necessity of establishing a guardianship for the minor. Such a plan is a bit more complicated, but it qualifies the income interest of the trust for the annual exclusion and facilitates the management of the income during the beneficiary's minority.

In order to avoid having the grantor treated as the owner of the trust and taxable on its income the trust must also satisfy the following general rules:

1.   Neither the grantor nor a nonadverse party may have the power to revoke the trust at any time within the period during which the

      grantor would be treated as owner if a reversion were to become effective (*i.e.*, 10 years) (§676);

2. Neither the grantor nor a nonadverse party may exercise certain controls over the beneficial enjoyment of the principal or income without the consent of an adverse party (§674);

3. Neither the grantor nor a nonadverse party may permit any person to

    (a) deal with the trust corpus or income for less than adequate consideration in money or money's worth (§675(1))

    (b) permit the grantor to borrow from the trust without adequate interest and security (§675(2)) or

    (c) exercise, or permit any person in a nonfiduciary capacity to exercise, certain administrative powers without the consent of a person in a fiduciary capacity (§675(4));

4. The income may not be payable to or for the use of the grantor or the grantor's spouse or accumulated for them without the consent of an adverse party (§677(a)(1)).

The rules are actually much more detailed, as a result of which short-term trusts must be prepared very carefully, particularly if the grantor will serve as trustee. In general, a lawyer should use short-term trust forms that are tried and true instead of preparing the trust from scratch.

    The assets that will be transferred to the trust must also be selected with care. For example, the election of a domestic corporation to be taxed under Subchapter S, §§1371 to 1379, is generally terminated if a trust becomes a shareholder or if a new shareholder fails to consent to the election. However, as explained in §12.7, *infra*, certain trusts may be Subchapter S shareholders if the grantor is treated as the owner of the entire trust under §§671 to 677.

    Gift Tax. The transfer of property to a short-term trust constitutes a taxable gift, which may qualify for the annual exclusion depending upon the particular provisions of the trust. The availability of the annual exclusion depends upon the extent of the beneficiary's current interest in the trust. An exclusion is available for the actuarial value of the beneficiary's income interest if the income must be paid to the beneficiary currently. Based upon the 6% tables of Reg. §25.2512-9, the right to receive an income interest for 10 years is worth 44.16% of the value of the property transferred to the trust. Thus, where a grantor transfers $10,000 to a trust that requires the income to be paid to the beneficiary for a 10-year period the grantor has made a gift to the beneficiary of a present interest worth $4,416. The gift is valued on the basis of a 6% rate of return although the property transferred to the trust actually yields more or less than 6%. Thus, a grantor may transfer property to the trust that generates income of 12%, but only be taxed on the basis of a 6% yield.

The annual exclusion is also available to the extent that the beneficiary holds a *Crummey* power over the property transferred to the trust. Thus, the annual exclusion is allowable where the grantor transfers $10,000 to a *Crummey* trust under which the trustee has the discretion to distribute the income to the beneficiary or accumulate it for distribution to the beneficiary at the end of a 10-year period, when the principal will be returned to the grantor. Here, again, the failure to exercise the *Crummey* power constitutes a gift of a future interest to the extent it exceeds the greater of $5,000 or 5% of the value of the property out of which the exercise of the power might be satisfied. *See* §2514(c).

Finally, the annual exclusion is available to the extent that the trust meets the requirements of §2503(c). Where the beneficiary is 11 or older at the time of the transfer, it is difficult to draft a trust that satisfies both the requirement of §673 that the donor's reversionary interest not take effect within 10 years and the requirement of §2503(c) that the interest involved be distributed to the beneficiary upon his or her reaching age 21. The donor's reversionary interest in the property may not take effect until after the passage of 10 years and the income interest of the beneficiary to age 21 may qualify for the annual exclusion as explained above at §7.38. Of course, if the donor does not retain a reversionary interest, the income will not be taxed to the grantor under §673 although the trust lasts fewer than 10 years. Finally, the income of the trust is taxable to the grantor if it may be accumulated and distributed to the grantor on the death of the beneficiary or termination of the trust. Duffy v. United States, 487 F.2d 282 (6th Cir. 1973), *cert. denied*, 416 U.S. 938 (1974).

Estate Tax. If the beneficiary dies prior to termination of the trust, the trust corpus is not usually includible in the beneficiary's gross estate. However, any accumulated income is includible unless the instrument requires it to be paid over to another person.

The grantor's reversionary interest in the trust is includible in the grantor's estate if the grantor dies prior to termination of the trust. The trust assets are also subject to inclusion in the grantor's estate if the grantor had the power to accumulate or distribute income or make discretionary distributions of corpus. *See* Reg. §20.2038-1(a).

Problem 7-8. G transferred $100,000 to the independent trustee of a 10-year reversionary trust. The income of the trust is payable each year to G to the extent of the lesser of (1) 6% of the original principal of the trust or (2) the actual income of the trust. Any additional income is payable to G's elderly mother, M. The trustee proposes to invest the trust fund in high quality corporate bonds that yield 12%. What are the gift, estate, and income tax consequences of the trust and the proposed invesment?

BIBLIOGRAPHY

I. Gifts in general:

    Cowley & Jones, Estate and Gift Tax Unification: The Concepts and Selected Giving Problems, N.Y.U. 36th Inst. Fed. Tax. 273 (1978)

    Fiore, Ownership Shifting to Realize Family Goals, Including Tax Savings, N.Y.U. 37th Inst. Fed. Tax., Ch. 38 (1979)

    Hodges, Current Strategies for Using Lifetime Gifts to Reduce Total Estate and Gift Taxes, 47 J. Tax 266 (1977)

    Lentz, Lifetime Gifts After '76, 12 Real Prop. Prob. & Tr. J. 339 (1977)

    Turnier, The Role of Gift Giving in Estate Planning, 59 N.C.L. Rev. 377 (1981)

II. Interest-free loans:

    Edwards, What Planning Opportunities Does CA-7's No-Gift-Tax Holding in *Crown* Open Up?, 50 J. Tax. 168 (1979)

    Hull & Kaster, Interest Free Loans Are Not Gifts, But Problems Remain In Their Use, 6 Est. Plan. 66 (1979)

    Livsey, Tax Aspects of Interest Free Loans, U. So. Cal. 31st Tax. Inst. 35 (1979)

III. Net gifts and installment gifts:

    Mintz & Braddock, The Installment Gift Technique: How It Works, the Problems Involved in Its Use, 49 J. Tax. 158 (1978)

    Note, Part Gift-Part Sale, Net Gift and Gift of Encumbered Property — Specialized Strategies for Gifts of Unique Property, 50 Notre Dame Law. 880 (1975)

    Recent Development, Net Gift Doctrine, 63 Cornell L. Rev. 1074 (1978)

IV. Techniques for making gifts to minors and *Crummey* provisions:

    Madden, Restrictive Future Interest Gifts to Minors May Qualify for the Annual Exclusion, 49 J. Tax. 348 (1978) (focuses on §2503(c) trusts)

    Sarno & Amlicke, Current Techniques to Obtain Full Advantages of Making Gifts to Minors, 6 Est. Plan. 334 (1979)

    Simmons, Drafting the *Crummey* Power, U. Miami 15th Inst. Est. Plan., Ch. 16 (1981)

    Ziegler, Gifts to Minors — Three Variations, 24 Tax Law. 297 (1971)

CHAPTER 8

GIFTS TO CHARITABLE ORGANIZATIONS

> [T]he words of such an act as the Income Tax, for example,
> merely dance before my eyes in a meaningless procession:
> cross-reference to cross-reference, exception upon excep-
> tion — couched in abstract terms that offer no handle to seize
> hold of — leave in my mind only a confused sense of some
> vitally important, but successfully concealed, purport, which it
> is my duty to extract, but which is within my power, if at all, only
> after the most inordinate expenditure of time. Learned Hand,
> Thomas Walter Swan, 57 Yale L.J. 167, 169 (1947).

A.   INTRODUCTION

§8.1.   *Background*

Historically, Americans have generously supported charitable causes.
The social value of charitable gifts is recognized in the income, gift, and
estate tax laws, each of which has allowed a deduction for charitable gifts
from an early time in its history. Over the years these deductions are
consistently among the most important to taxpayers, both in terms of
dollars involved and the number of taxpayers who claim them.

  The words Judge Hand wrote about the income tax law in general
apply even more forcefully to the complex provisions that pertain to
many gift transactions, including gifts of appreciated property and gifts
of partial interests to charitable donees ("split gifts"). Fortunately, simple
rules govern the deductibility of simple outright gifts to churches,
schools, and similar charitable organizations. In those cases only the first

sentence of §170(a) is usually significant: "There shall be allowed as a deduction any charitable contribution (as defined in subsection (c)) payment of which is made within the taxable year." Pity the other donors, and their lawyers, who must grapple with the remaining 9 single-spaced pages of §170. The need for simplification is recognized by the Treasury, which has called for abolition of the income tax charitable deduction. Blueprints for Basic Tax Reform 95 (1977). Given the political realities of the situation, the deduction is likely to remain with us, growing more complex year by year.

The charitable deduction provisions of the income tax law (§170), the gift tax law (§2522), and the estate tax law (§2055) are similar in many respects. The principal differences are that the income tax law limits the amount of deductions and requires that adjustments be made when certain types of property are transferred, whereas the gift and estate tax laws neither impose limits nor require adjustments. There are also slight differences in the types of organizations that qualify for the deductions under the 3 statutes. For example, the estate and gift taxes, but not the income tax, allow deductions for gifts to foreign charities. §§2055(a)(2), 2522(a)(2), 170(c)(2)(A). Curiously, gifts to community chests are explicitly recognized as charitable in the income and gift tax laws, but not in the estate tax law. §§170(c)(2), 2522(a)(2), 2055(a)(2). It is not possible to identify any policy that is served by the differences in the language of the 3 statutes.

In the following pages the federal tax consequences of outright gifts to charity are discussed first. The percentage limitations on income tax deductions and various types of charities are developed in the context of that discussion. Gifts of partial interests, gifts in trust, and special types of transfers are explored later in the chapter.

For income tax purposes gifts to qualifying charitable organizations are deductible by individual taxpayers who itemize deductions subject to the percentage limitations and adjustments required by §170. Depending upon the character of the charitable donee, the deduction is limited to either 20% or 50% of the donor's adjusted gross income. Until 1982 a deduction was only allowed to taxpayers who itemized their deductions.

In order to stimulate charitable contributions the 1981 Act changed the law to allow a limited charitable deduction on an experimental basis to taxpayers who do not itemize. Subject to the otherwise applicable percentage limitations, the new provisions allow a taxpayer who does not itemize to deduct 25% of contributions of up to $100 for 1982 and 1983 (a maximum of $25), increasing to 25% of any contributions of up to $300 for 1984 (a maximum of $75), 50% of any contributions for 1985, and 100% of any contributions for 1986. §§63, 170(i). The allowance of the deduction will expire in 1987 unless Congress extends it beyond 1986. The change may cause some increase in the amount of charitable gifts. However, it will reintroduce some of the complexity and administrative problems that were eliminated by the adoption of the zero bracket amount.

The allowance of an income tax deduction for charitable contributions has been criticized by some commentators who contend that the deduction should be replaced by a credit. They argue that a credit would be of equal value to all taxpayers whereas a deduction is of variable value, depending upon the donor's marginal income tax rate. Other commentators contend that the income tax deduction should be unlimited, which would make it conform more closely to the gift and estate tax deductions.

Until the experimental deduction becomes fully effective in 1986, a charitable contribution produces a smaller income tax benefit for a donor who does not itemize. The actual disparity in treatment of taxpayers is often further increased because donors who do not itemize usually make cash contributions from earned income while wealthy donors often contribute appreciated property. Within the limits established by §170, a deduction is usually allowed for the full value of the appreciated property without requiring the donor to recognize any gain.

> **Example 8-1.** D gave a public charity stock D had owned for more than a year. The stock had a basis of $1,000 and a fair market value of $10,000. The gift will reduce D's income tax by $5,000 assuming that D is in the 50% income tax bracket and that the gift is fully deductible. If D had sold the stock for $10,000, D would have paid a tax of $1,800 on the gain (50% × (40% × $9,000)). A contribution of the remaining $8,200 would have reduced D's income tax for the year by $4,100.

Gifts of appreciated property must be carefully planned in view of the donor's contribution base (adjusted gross income), the nature of the property, and the character of the donee organization.

B.   FEDERAL TAX CONSEQUENCES OF OUTRIGHT GIFTS

§8.2.   Qualified Charities (§170(c))

For income tax purposes a charitable deduction is allowed only for gifts made "to or for the use of" an organization listed in §170(c). In the case of contributions by individuals the list includes:

1. A state or federal governmental unit, if the gift is made for exclusively public purposes;
2. A domestic corporation, trust, community chest, fund, or foundation that is organized and operated exclusively for religious, charitable, scientific, literary, or educational purposes, to foster national or international sports competition or for the prevention of cruelty to children or animals;
3. A post or other organization of war veterans;
4. A domestic fraternal organization, operating under the lodge system, but only if the gift is exclusively for religious, charitable, scientific, literary, or educational purposes, or for the prevention of cruelty to children or animals; and
5. A nonprofit cemetery company.

Gifts to or for the use of organizations listed in items 1, 2, and 4, and gifts to organizations listed in item 3 usually qualify for gift and estate tax deductions. *See* §§2055(a), 2522(a). A gift to a cemetery company, item 5, does not qualify for a gift or an estate tax deduction.

Qualified charities are themselves divided into 2 classes: the so-called public charities described in §170(b)(1)(A) (§8.3, *infra*) and all others (§8.4, *infra*). Gifts to public charities qualify for the maximum allowable income tax deduction, which is 30% or 50% of the donor's contribution base depending upon the nature of the property transferred. The term "contribution base" is defined as adjusted gross income, computed without regard to any net operating loss carryback under §172. §170(b)(1)(E). Churches, hospitals, and schools are common examples of public charities. A ceiling of 20% applies to gifts made "*to*" other charities described in §170(c) such as cemetery companies, posts or organizations of war veterans, fraternal lodges, and some nonoperating private foundations. The 20% limit also applies to gifts made "*for the use of*" public charities.

A list of organizations that meet the requirements of §170(c) is published biennially by the IRS. Cumulative List, Organizations Described in Section 170(c) of the Internal Revenue Code of 1954, IRS Publication No. 78. Additions, deletions, and changes are published in cumulative bimonthly supplements. The Cumulative List is available on a subscription basis from: Superintendent of Documents, U.S. Government Printing Office, Washington, D.C. 20402.

A donor has some assurance that a deduction will be allowed for a gift made to an organization named in the Cumulative List. Rev. Proc. 72-39, 1972-2 C.B. 818, provides that where the IRS subsequently revokes a letter ruling or determination letter previously issued to the organization a deduction will generally be allowed for gifts made prior to publication in the Internal Revenue Bulletin of an announcement that gifts to the organization are no longer deductible.

§8.3. Public Charities (§170(b)(1)(A))

As indicated above, a larger income tax deduction is allowed for gifts made to a certain group of preferred charities. In contrast, the estate and gift tax laws do not distinguish between the character of qualified charities.

In 1969 the maximum deduction was increased to 50% for a wide range of public charities described in §170(b)(1)(A)(i)-(viii). The charities that qualify include churches; schools with a regular faculty, curriculum, and student body; organizations that provide medical or hospital care or perform medical research or education; organizations that receive a substantial part of their support from federal and state sources and from the general public and use their funds for educational organizations owned or operated by a state or a state agency; and state or federal governmental units in the case of gifts made exclusively for public purposes. §170(b)(1)(A)(i)-(v). Trusts, funds, or foundations described in §170(c)(2), such as publicly or governmentally supported museums, libraries, community centers, United Funds, and the American Red Cross, also qualify provided they receive a substantial amount of their support from a state or federal governmental unit or from the general public. §170(b)(1)(A)(vi). Three types of private foundations described in §170(b)(1)(D) also qualify for the 50% limitation. They are:

1. A private operating foundation described in §4942(j)(3); Regs. §§53.4942(b)-1, -2;
2. A private nonoperating foundation that distributes all of the contributions it receives to public charities or makes certain other qualifying distributions within 2½ months following the close of its taxable year (Reg. §1.170A-9(g)); and
3. A private foundation that pools contributions in a common fund and allows contributors (or their spouses) to designate the public charities that will receive the annual income and the portion of the fund attributable to their gifts. See Reg. §1.170A-9(h).

Finally, organizations described in §509(a)(2) or (3) are also treated as public charities for purposes of the 50% limit. §170(b)(1)(A)(viii). Section 509(a)(2) describes certain types of organizations that have broad public support, normally receive more than one-third of their support from gifts, grants, contributions, membership fees, etc., and do not receive more than one-third of their support from gross investment income. See Reg. §1.509(a)-3. A §509(a)(3) organization (a "supporting organization") is one organized and operated exclusively to support one or more specified public charities; it must be operated, supervised, or controlled by or in connection with one or more public charities; and it must not be controlled directly or indirectly by the donor or "disqualified" persons. *See* Reg. §1.509(a)-4. The use of supporting organizations as a vehicle for charitable gifts is popular because they are treated as public charities for income tax purposes and they are not subject to the private foundation rules.

§8.4. Nonpublic Charities

The deduction for gifts to private foundations and other charities not described in §170(b)(1)(A) is limited to the lesser of (1) 20% of the donor's contribution base for the year or (2) the excess of 50% of the donor's contribution base over the amount of the donor's gifts to public charities. §170(b)(1)(B). As indicated above, gifts "for the use of" all charities are subject to a 20% limit.

> **Example 8-2.** During a year in which Donor, D, had a contribution base of $25,000 he made cash gifts that totaled $10,000 to churches and schools described in §170(b)(1)(A). D also gave $5,000 in cash to the local post of the war veterans. The gifts of $10,000 to public charities are fully deductible as they do not exceed 50% of D's contribution base. Only $2,500 of the gift made to the war veterans' organization, a nonpublic charity, is deductible. The gift to it did not exceed 20% of D's contribution base, but it did exceed the difference between 50% of his contribution base ($12,500) and the amount of his gifts to public charities ($10,000). The nondeductible portion of a gift to a nonpublic charity cannot be carried over and deducted in a later year. *See* §170(d) and §8.5, *infra*.

> **Gifts "for the Use of" a Charitable Organization.** For the purposes of §170 a gift of an income interest is considered to be a gift "for the use of" the charity, whether or not the gift is made in trust. In contrast, a gift of a remainder interest is a gift "to" the charity, unless the remainder will be held in trust after the termination of the preceding interests, in which case it is a gift "for the use of" the donee. Reg. §1.170A-8(a)(2).

> **Example 8-3.** D transferred Blackacre to the trustee of a charitable remainder annuity trust that meets the requirements of §664(d)(1). The trust provides that an annuity of 5% of the initial fair market value of the property transferred to the trust will be paid to D and, upon the death of D, Blackacre will be distributed to the H Hospital, a public charity that meets the requirements of §170(b)(1)(A). D made a gift of the charitable remainder interest "to" the H Hospital.

§8.5.   Charitable Contributions Carryover (§170(d)(1))

In general, contributions "to" public charities may be carried over for the next 5 taxable years to the extent they exceed the 50% limitation or the special 30% limitation that generally applies to gifts of appreciated capital gain property. §170(d)(1); Reg. §1.170A-10. No carryover is allowed for a gift (1) "for the use of" a public charity, or (2) "to or for the use of" a nonpublic charity (*e.g.,* private foundations).

> **Example 8-4.** H and W, who file joint returns, have a contribution base of $50,000 in year 1 and $40,000 in year 2. In year 1 they made cash gifts of $30,000 to a public charity and $2,000 to a nonpublic charity. In year 2 they gave $18,000 in cash to a public charity. Under §170(d)(1) they are entitled to a deduction of $25,000 for year 1 (50% of their contribution base), which leaves a carryover of $5,000 to year 2. No deduction is allowed with respect to the $2,000 contribution to the nonpublic charity because of the limit of §170(b)(1)(B). *See* §8.4, *supra.* Also, no carryover is allowed for a gift to a nonpublic charity. H and W are entitled to a deduction of $20,000 for year 2 ($18,000 plus $2,000 of the $5,000 carryover from year 1) and a carryover of $3,000 to the next year.

§8.6.   When Is a Gift Made? (Reg. §1.170A-1(b))

The time at which a gift is considered to be made can be of vital importance to the donor. It of course affects the year in which a gift may be deducted and the total amount of gifts made in a particular year.

> Ordinarily, a contribution is made at the time delivery is effected. The unconditional delivery or mailing of a check which subsequently clears in due course will constitute an effective contribution on the date of delivery or mailing. If a taxpayer unconditionally delivers or mails a properly endorsed stock certificate to a charitable donee or the donee's agent, the gift is completed on the date of delivery or, if such certificate is received in the ordinary course of the mails, on the date of mailing. If the donor delivers the stock certificate to his bank or broker as the donor's agent, or to the issuing corporation or its agent, for transfer into the name of the donee, the gift is completed on the date the stock is transferred on the books of the corporation. Reg. §1.170A-1(b).

A note given to a charity by its maker is a mere promise to pay, which is not deductible until it is paid. Rev. Rul. 68-174, 1968-1 C.B. 81. Similarly, a pledge made to a charity is deductible when it is paid, not at the time it is made. Mann v. Commissioner, 35 F.2d 873 (D.C. Cir. 1929); *cf.,* Rev. Rul. 78-129, 1978-1 C.B. 67. On the other hand, a gift made to a charity by charging an amount against the donor's bank credit card is deductible in the year the charge is made even though the bank is not paid until the following year. Rev. Rul. 78-38, 1978-1 C.B. 67.

§8.7.   Valuation of Gifts (Reg. §1.170A-1(c))

The amount of a gift of property other than money is the fair market value of the property at the time of the gift. Of course, where the property has a value in excess of its basis, the amount of the gift that is deductible for income tax purposes must be reduced in some cases. *See* §8.9 to 8.12, *infra*. Reg. §1.170A-1(c). The donor must provide detailed information regarding gifts of property other than money that exceed $200 in value. Reg. §1.170A-1(a)(2)(ii). A gift of encumbered property qualifies for the charitable deduction only to the extent the fair market value of the property exceeds the amount of the encumbrances. Winston F.C. Guest, 77 T.C. 9 (1981). Because the valuation of art objects is uncertain in many cases, since the 1960s a panel of art experts has advised the IRS regarding valuation of art.

§8.8.   Gifts of Depreciated Property

As a general rule, property with a basis in excess of its fair market value (depreciated property) should not be given to charity. The reason is simple: Property given to charity is valued at its fair market value for purposes of the charitable deduction. Reg. §1.170A-1(c). Also, no loss deduction is allowable under §165 where depreciated property is given to a charity. Lavar Withers, 69 T.C. 900 (1978).

Two rules prevent taking a loss deduction when depreciated property is given to charity. First, noncasualty losses of an individual are deductible only if they are incurred in a trade or business or in a transaction entered into for profit although not connected with a trade or business. §165(c)(1), (2). Charitable gifts are not made in either of those contexts. Second, a deduction is allowed only when a loss is "sustained," which requires that the loss be recognized for income tax purposes. Although a loss may be "realized" as a result of a gift to charity, no loss is "recognized." As *Withers* points out, a gift to charity constitutes a "sale or other disposition," which may cause a loss to be realized, but it does not constitute the "sale or exchange" that must occur for a loss to be "recognized." *See also* §1001(a), (c) and Reg. §1.1001-1(a).

§8.9.   Gifts of Ordinary Income Property (§170(e)(1)(A))

A special rule applies to gifts of "ordinary income property" (*i.e.*, property that would not generate long-term capital gain if it were sold for its fair market value on the date of the transfer). Thus, it includes capital assets held for less than one year, property held for sale in the ordinary course of business, works of art and manuscripts created by the donor, depreciable tangible personal property or real property, §306 stock, and §341 stock of a collapsible corporation. *See* Reg. §1.170A-4 (b)(1). When ordinary income property is given to a charity, the amount of the contribution is reduced to the extent the gain would not have been long-term capital gain had the property been sold by the donor at its fair market value on the date of the gift. *See* Rev. Rul. 80-33, 1980-1 C.B. 69 (contribution of §306 stock).

In effect this rule puts the donor in the same position he or she would have been in had the property been sold for its fair market value and the proceeds contributed to charity.

> **Example 8-5.** D gave a charity ordinary income property that had a basis of $5,000 and a fair market value of $10,000. The contribution is reduced by $5,000, the amount of the gain that would not have been capital gain had D sold the property. Thus, D is treated as having made a gift of $5,000. The outcome would be the same if D had sold the property for $10,000 and given the proceeds to charity. In that case D's income would have been $5,000 greater, but the amount of his contribution would be $10,000, unreduced under §170(e)(1)(A). Of course, in the latter case, D might not be entitled to deduct the full amount of the gift, depending upon the particular character of the donee and the size of the donor's contribution base.

Under §170(e) the deduction allowed to an artist who contributes to charity a work he created is limited to the donor's basis in the work — the cost of materials. Maniscalco v. Commissioner, 632 F.2d 6 (6th Cir. 1980).

§8.10.   Gifts of Capital Gain Property: General (§170(b)(1)(C))

Special rules also apply to gifts of property that would have produced long-term capital gain had it been sold for its fair market value on the date of the gift, including property used in a trade or business as defined in §1231(b). §170(b)(1)(C)(iv). In general, the charitable deduction for a gift of such "capital gain property" cannot exceed 30% of the donor's contribution base. This 30% ceiling applies in addition to the percentage limitations that are based upon the nature of the donee organization. Thus, a donor's gift of capital gain property to a public charity is generally subject to an overall 30% limit instead of the basic 50% limit. However, the 50% limit applies if the donor elects to reduce the amount of the gift by 40% of the capital gain. *See* §8.11, *infra*. Gifts of capital gain property to nonpublic charities remain subject to a 20% limit. A contribution of 30% property is taken into account *after* gifts of other property: "For purposes of applying the 50-percent and 20-percent limitations described in paragraphs (b) and (c) of this section, charitable contributions of 30-percent capital gain property paid during the taxable year . . . shall be taken into account after all other charitable contributions paid during the taxable year." Reg. §1.170A-8(d)(1).

> **Example 8-6.** Last year when D had a contribution base of $20,000, D made gifts of $10,000 in cash and $6,000 in capital gain property to public charities. D's charitable deduction for the year is limited to $10,000 (50% × $20,000). D is entitled to carry over the $6,000 gift of capital gain property to the next year. If the entire $16,000 in contributions were 30% capital gain property, D could deduct $6,000 for last year and carry over the balance for the following 5 years. §170(d)(1) and Reg. §1.170A-10(c)(1)(ii).

§8.11. Gifts of Capital Gain Property: Election to Reduce Amount of Gift (§§170(b)(1)(C)(iii), 170(e))

A donor may elect to have the 50% limit apply to all gifts of capital gain property made to public charities during the year. §170(b)(1)(C)(iii). However, if the election is made, the amount of the gifts must be reduced by 40% of the gain that would have been realized had the property been sold. §170(e)(1). The election can be used to increase the amount of the current deduction in a wide range of circumstances. In some cases it may increase both the amount that is deductible in the current year and that deductible during the carryover period. That may occur where the gifts during the year far exceed the amount that could be deducted in that year and during the carryover period.

> **Example 8-7.** D expects to have an adjusted gross income of about $25,000 in this year and each of the following 5 years. Earlier this year D gave a parcel of real property that D had held for more than a year to a public charity. The property had a basis of $20,000 and a fair market value of $200,000. Without the election D's deduction is limited to $7,500 per year (30% × $25,000) or a total of $45,000 over the 6-year period during which the deductions could be claimed. If D elects to reduce the amount of the gift by 40% of the gain component, D's contribution deduction will be subject to the 50% limitation. By reducing the amount of the gift by $72,000 (40% of the gain of $180,000), D could deduct $5,000 more each year. The deduction would be $12,500, which is 50% of D's contri-

bution base. Thus, by making the election, D could deduct a total of $75,000 instead of only $45,000.

It may also be useful to elect under §170(b)(1)(C) where a gift to a public charity exceeds 30% of the donor's contribution base, but the gain component is relatively small. Here again, if the donor reduces the amount of the gift by 40% of the gain, the limit on the amount of the deduction is increased from 30% to 50%.

> **Example 8-8.** D had a contribution base of $50,000 in a year during which she made a gift of securities worth $25,000 to a public charity. The securities, which D had held for more than a year, had a basis of $24,000. Unless the election is made D could only deduct $15,000 for the year of the gift (30% × $50,000). The remaining $10,000 would be carried over to the next year. If D elects to reduce the amount of her gift by $400 (40% × $1,000), she could deduct $24,600 this year, but would have no carryover to next year. The return earned on the tax saved by the additional $9,600 deduction this year will more than offset the $400 reduction in the amount of the contribution.

Finally, the election may increase the amount of the deduction that could be taken on a decedent's final income tax return or by a terminally ill donor. The election could produce a saving because a decedent's excess contributions cannot be carried over to his or her successors. See §691(b). Of course, the unused portion of an excess contribution that is attributable to the surviving spouse may be carried over and used by the surviving spouse in a later year. See Reg. §1.170A-10(d)(4)(iii).

If the donor elects to have §170(e)(1) apply to gifts of capital gain property, the amount of the gift is reduced for all purposes. Thus, the amount of the gift is reduced for the purpose of determining the amount of any carryover deductions. Also, where an election is made for a year subsequent to the gift (i.e., a carryover year), the amount of the carryover must be recomputed. In some cases an election totally eliminates the carryover.

> **Example 8-9.** D gave a public charity stock he had owned for more than a year, which had a fair market value of $90,000 and a basis of $10,000. In the following year D gave the charity an additional $30,000 of stock he had also owned for more than a year and that had a basis of $6,000. In each year D had a contribution base of $200,000 and made no other charitable gifts. Ordinarily D would be entitled to deduct $60,000 each year (30% × $200,000). Half of the deduction for the second year would be attributable to the carryover from the first year ($30,000). If D elects to subject the first

gift to §170(e)(1), the gifts for the first year would be reduced to $58,000, all of which could be deducted in the first year but there would be no carryover. Specifically, under §170(e)(1) the $90,000 gift would be reduced by $32,000 (40% × $80,000 gain). If D instead makes the election in the second year, the amount of the first-year gift would be recomputed under §170(e)(1) to determine whether there would be any carryover to the second year. In this case there would not be any carryover because the deduction claimed in the first year ($60,000) exceeded the amount of the gift ($58,000) as recomputed. The amount of the deduction for the first year would not be reduced, but the carryover would be eliminated. *See* Reg. §1.170A-4(d), *Example* (4).

Where a gift of capital gain property is planned or made, the lawyer should be alert to the consequences of making an election. The examples amply demonstrate the need to study the consequences of an election carefully before it is made. Ideally, the planning will precede the gift; however, the election is important to consider in all cases.

§8.12.   *Gifts of Capital Gain Property: Tangible Personal Property (§170(e)(1)(B)(i))*

The amount of a gift of tangible personal property is not reduced (*i.e.,* it is equal to the fair market value of the property on the date of the gift) where the donee's use of the property is related to its exempt functions. However, the amount of a gift of tangible personal property must be reduced by 40% of the gain component where the donee's use of the property is unrelated to the purpose for which its tax exemption was granted under §501(c). This rule applies independently of the overall 20% and 50% limitations on the amount of a donor's charitable deduction. The application of the rule is illustrated in the following passage: "For example, if a painting contributed to an educational institution is used by that organization for educational purposes by being placed in its library for display and study by art students, the use is not an unrelated use; but if the painting is sold and the proceeds used by the organization for educational purposes, the use of the property is an unrelated use." Reg. §1.170A-4(b)(3). Applying this rule the amount of the contribution was reduced where the donor gave an antique automobile to a college and could not show that the car would not be put to an unrelated use. LR 8009027.

A gift or estate tax deduction is available for the value of tangible personal property that is transferred outright to a charity. A gift of a work of art that is given to a charity whose use of the property is related to its exempt purpose is subject to a special rule added by the 1981 Act.

See §§2055(e)(4), 2522(c)(3). Under it, the work of art and the copyright on the work of art are treated as separate properties. Thus, a charitable contribution deduction is allowable for the value of a work of art although the donor retains the copyright or transfers it to a noncharity (and vice versa).

§8.13. Gifts of Future Interests in Tangible Personal Property (§170(a)(3), Reg. §1.170A-5)

A present charitable deduction is not generally allowable for the transfer of a future interest in tangible personal property. Under §170(a)(3) a gift of a future interest in tangible personal property is treated as made only when all intervening interests in the property (1) have expired or (2) are held by persons other than the taxpayer or those standing in a relationship to the taxpayer described in §267.

> **Example 8-10.** Last year Donor, D, transferred a painting to a museum by deed of gift, reserving a life (or term) interest in it. For purposes of §170 the gift was not complete at the time of the transfer. A gift of the painting will take place if D relinquishes all interest in the painting and transfers present possession of it to the museum.

As indicated above in §8.12 the amount of a contribution of appreciated tangible personal property must be reduced as provided in §170(e)(1)(B) where the donee's use of the property is unrelated to the purpose or function for which its exemption was granted under §501(c).

Gift and Estate Tax. No deduction is usually allowable for gifts of future interests in tangible personal property unless the interest is a remainder interest in a charitable remainder annuity trust or a charitable remainder unitrust. *See* Part D, *infra*. However, a marital deduction could be claimed with respect to the full value of tangible personal property in which the donor's spouse is given a qualifying income interest for life. *See* §2056(b)(7). Of course, in such a case the property is includible in the donee spouse's estate under §2044. If the property passes to charitable remaindermen on the death of the donee spouse a charitable deduction should be allowed to the donee spouse's estate under §2055.

> **Example 8-11.** D transferred a collection of antique dolls to a local museum by deed of gift, but retained the possession of them for life. The transfer does not qualify for an income tax deduction until D's interest terminates. The transfer of a future interest in the

dolls constitutes a completed gift for gift tax purposes. However, no gift tax deduction is allowable. §2522(c)(2). The value of the dolls is includible in D's estate if D retains possession of them until his death, §2036, but D's estate would be entitled to an equivalent deduction as an outright gift to the qualified charity. §2055(a).

Problem 8-1. Client, C, will have a contribution base of about $50,000 this year. Before the year ends C intends to make cash gifts of $5,000 to a local church, $10,000 to the Metropolitan Foundation, a nonprofit charitable trust that receives contributions from the public generally and distributes the property each year for charitable purposes, and $5,000 to the local Veterans of Foreign Wars (VFW) post. What will be the maximum deduction allowable to C if all of the planned contributions are made? How would your answer differ if C made gifts of the same amounts by transferring to the donees appreciated securities held for more than one year that had bases equal to one-half of their fair market values? In that case should C elect to have the gifts treated as if they were subject to §170(e)(1)(B)?

Problem 8-2. Donor, D, expects to have an adjusted gross income of about $100,000 this year and next year. D plans to make gifts of $10,000 each to 5 public charities, including the local public art museum, the state law school, a local church, the American Red Cross, and the American Society for the Prevention of Cruelty to Animals. D would prefer to make the gifts from noncash assets, but would consider any reasonable alternative that might improve D's overall income and tax position. The assets that are available to transfer to the charities include the following, each of which has been held for more than a year unless otherwise noted:

　　1,000 shares of Argo, Inc. (basis of $10,000, current value of $30,000)

　　$25,000 face value of municipal bonds (basis of $25,000, present value of $20,000)

　　1,000 shares of Beta Co. (basis of $10,000, present value of $5,000)

　　Blackacre (unimproved land that D bought within the last year for $5,000, present value of $10,000), and

　　a Ben Shahn signed print (basis of $1,000, present value of $10,000)

How would you recommend that D carry out the gift program? Specifically, what assets should D transfer, and to which charities? Would it be advisable for D to sell any assets and transfer the proceeds to the charities?

C.   GIFTS OF PARTIAL INTERESTS

§8.14.   General

The Tax Reform Act of 1969 strictly limited the availability of income, gift, and estate tax deductions for gifts of partial interests to charities. In general, charitable gifts of less than the donor's entire interest in property do not qualify for a charitable deduction unless they are made to a charitable remainder trust, a pooled income fund, or a charitable lead trust. *See* Part D, *infra*, §§8.19 to 8.27. Two major exceptions to this rule allow deductions for gifts of partial interests that are not made in one of the special forms. The exceptions apply to a gift not in trust of a remainder interest in a personal residence or a farm (§8.15, *infra*) or of an undivided portion of the donor's entire interest in property (§8.16, *infra*). A deduction is allowable for a gift of the donor's entire interest in property, even though it is a partial interest in the property. §8.17, *infra*. However, no deduction is allowable for an interest that may be defeated by the occurrence of an act or event unless the possibility that the act or event will occur is so remote as to be negligible. §8.18, *infra*.

§8.15.   Remainder Interest in Personal Residence or Farm

A gift of a remainder interest in a personal residence or farm qualifies for the income, gift, and estate tax deductions. §§170(f)(3)(B)(i), 2055(e), 2522(c)(2). The IRS has restricted the deductions to *nontrust* gifts of remainder interests, although the availability of the deductions is not so limited by the statutes. Regs. §§1.170A-7(b), 20.2055-2(e), 25.2522(c)-3(c)(2); Ellis First National Bank of Bradenton v. United States, 550 F.2d 9 (Ct. Cl. 1977); Rev. Rul. 76-357, 1976-2 C.B. 285. The restriction is unwise because the interests of a remainderman are better protected when a trust is used. It also discourages the use of a trust to make a residence or farm available to an improvident or incompetent individual for life. The gift of a legal life interest to such a person is unwise and may necessitate the appointment of a guardian. Unfortunately, guardianships are frequently cumbersome and expensive. As long as the IRS adheres to its present view, charitable gifts of such remainder interests should not be made in trust.

For purposes of the deductions, "personal residence" means any property used by the donor as a personal residence, even though it is not the donor's principal residence. Thus, a vacation home qualifies as a personal residence. The donor's stock in a cooperative housing corporation also qualifies as a personal residence if the donor used the unit as a personal residence. Regs. §§1.170A-7(b)(3), 20.2055-2(e)(2)(ii);

25.2522(c)-3(c)(2)(ii). "Farm" is defined as "any land used by the taxpayer or his tenant for the production of crops, fruits, or other agricultural products or for the sustenance of livestock." Regs. §§1.170A-7(b)(4); 20.2055-2(e)(2)(iii), 25.2522(c)-3(c)(2)(iii). A house, barn, or other improvements located on a farm are included in the term.

The exception applies when the charity will receive the donor's entire interest in the personal residence or in a part of a farm upon termination of the particular estate. Thus, a gift of a residence to one individual for life and, upon the life tenant's death, in equal shares to another individual and a charity as cotenants does not qualify. Rev. Rul. 76-544, 1976-2 C.B. 288 (estate tax). However, a gift of a remainder in a specified portion of the donor's farm acreage does qualify. Rev. Rul. 78-303, 1978-2 C.B. 122. That result follows because "farm" is defined in the regulations as "any land" used for agricultural purposes. Accordingly, a gift of any portion that is so used meets the requirements of this exception. The IRS has contended that no deduction is available where under the terms of the gift the personal residence or farm is to be sold upon the termination of the life estate. Rev. Rul. 77-169, 1977-1 C.B. 286. However, that position was rejected by the Tax Court in Estate of Eliza W. Blackford, 77 T.C. 1246 (1981). Also, the IRS has ruled that a deduction was allowable in a similar case where the state law gave the charitable remainderman the right to take the real property rather than the proceeds of sale. LR 8141037.

Depreciation and Depletion. For income tax purposes the value of a remainder interest in real property must take into account depreciation and depletion of the property. §170(f)(4). Under Reg. §1.170A-12(a)(1), depreciation is calculated on the straight line method and depletion is determined by the cost recovery method. Where a remainder consists of both depreciable and nondepreciable property, the depreciation or depletion is based only upon the fair market value of the depreciable or depletable interests. Thus, the fair market value of a residence must be allocated between the improvements, which are depreciable, and the land, which is not depreciable. The expected value of the property at the end of its life is also considered to be nondepreciable for this purpose. Reg. §1.170A-12(a)(2). The regulations provide the formulae that are used to calculate the value of remainder interests following a single life (§1.170A-12(b)), a term of years (§1.170A-12(c)), and more than one life or a term of years concurrent with one or more lives (§1.170A-12(e)). The method of valuation is illustrated by the following example:

Example 8-12. W, a 60-year-old widow, gave the remainder interest in her residence to a public charity. At that time, the residence was worth $75,000, of which $25,000 was allocable to the land and $50,000 to the improvements. The improvements have a useful life of 45 years at the end of which they will be worth $5,000. For purposes of §170 the gift consists of $45,000 in depreciable property (the value of the house ($50,000) less the expected value of its improvements at the end of 45 years ($5,000)) and $30,000 in nondepreciable property (the value of the land ($25,000) plus the expected value of the improvements at the end of 45 years ($5,000)). The value of the remainder interest in the nondepreciable property is discounted to present value under the 6% actuarial tables of Reg. §25.2512-9 by applying the remainder factor for a 60-year-old female (.36774) to the nondepreciable property (.36774 × $30,000 = $11,032). The value of the remainder interest in the depreciable property is calculated in the same manner, but first the remainder factor must be reduced by a factor determined in the manner described in Reg. §1.170A-12(b)(2). The adjustment involves dividing (1) the difference between the R-factor for a female aged 60 from column 2 of Table C(2) of Reg. §1.170A-12 less the R-factor for her terminal age (either 110 or the sum of the age of the life tenant and the estimated useful life of the depreciable property) by (2) the product of multiplying (a) the useful life of the property by (b) the D-factor for a female aged 60 from column 3 of Table C(2). The R-factors for ages 60 and 105 are 13969.4983 and .04650173 respectively and the D-factor is 2559.440.

$$\frac{13969.4983 - .04650173}{45 \times 2559.440} = .12123$$

The value of the interest in the depreciable property is $11,093 ($45,000 × (.36774 − .12123)). The total charitable deduction is $22,125 ($11,032 + $11,093).

§8.16. Undivided Portion of Donor's Entire Interest

An exception to the partial interest rule is also made for a gift of an undivided portion of the donor's entire interest in property. §§170(f)(3)(B)(ii), 2055(e)(2), 2522(c)(2). According to the IRS a gift of an undivided interest made in trust does not fall within the exception although the statutes do not expressly impose that requirement. Regs. §§1.170A-7(b)(1), 20.2055-2(e)(2)(i), 25.2522(c)-3(c)(2)(i). The IRS position is illustrated by a ruling that denied an estate tax deduction where the decedent gave his residuary estate to a trust under which the income was payable in equal shares to his surviving spouse and a charity for the spouse's lifetime and, upon her death, the principal was distributable one-half to the charity and one-half to the decedent's heirs. Rev. Rul. 77-97, 1977-1 C.B. 285. The ruling noted that a deduction would have been allowed if the decedent had created 2 separate trusts, one for charitable purposes and one for private purposes. The IRS could just have easily have recognized that the charity's right to a specified share of the income and principal is a sufficiently distinct portion to justify treatment as a separate trust. See Reg. §20.2056(b)-5(c), which deals with the somewhat related problem of what constitutes a specific portion in the context of the marital deduction.

In order to qualify under this exception, the regulations require that an undivided interest consist of a fraction or percentage of every substantial interest or right that the donor owns in the property, which must extend over the entire term of the donor's interest. Reg. §170A-7(b)(1)(i). Thus, where an individual has a remainder interest in a trust created by another person, a gift to charity of a fractional interest in the remainder would qualify as an undivided interest. Interestingly, the same regulation treats a gift of the possession and control of property for a specified portion of each year as a gift of an undivided interest.

Qualified Conservation Contribution. Section 170(h) allows a deduction for the value of certain partial interests in real property given exclusively for conservation purposes to qualified charitable organizations. The amount of the gift of such an interest is equal to the amount by which it reduces the value of the property retained by the donor. *See* Rev. Rul. 76-376, 1976-2 C.B. 53. Such a gift may generate a substantial income tax deduction and reduce the value of the donor's retained interests for real property tax purposes without interfering with the donor's use of the property. However, gifts for conservation purposes should be carefully planned in light of the provisions of §170(h) and the deleterious effect that perpetual restrictions could have on the property retained by the donor and on the broader community.

The partial interests for which a deduction may be claimed are defined in §170(h)(2) to include:

1. The entire interest of the donor other than his or her interest in subsurface oil, gas, or other minerals and the right of access to such minerals;
2. A remainder interest; and
3. A restriction (granted in perpetuity) on the use that may be made of the real property.

The last category covers easements and other interests in real property that have similar attributes under local law (*e.g.*, restrictive covenants). For purposes of §170(h) conservation purposes include 4 objectives. In order to satisfy the requirements of the subsection, it is only necessary to satisfy one of them. Under §170(h)(4)(A) they are limited to

1. The preservation of land for outdoor recreation by the general public or for the education of the general public;
2. The protection of a relatively natural fish, wildlife, or plant habitat, or similar ecosystem;
3. The preservation of open space (including farmland and forest

land) where the preservation is for the scenic enjoyment of the
general public and will yield a significant public benefit or is pursuant to a clearly defined federal, state, or local government conservation policy and will yield a significant public benefit; and

4. The preservation of an historically important land area or a certified historic structure.

The qualified organizations to which contributions may be made are
limited to governmental units and publicly supported charitable organizations.

§8.17. Donor's Entire Interest in Property

A deduction is allowed for a gift of the donor's entire interest in property, although it is only a partial interest. "Thus, if securities are given to
A for life, with the remainder over to B, and B makes a charitable
contribution of his remainder interest to an organization described in
section 170(c), a deduction is allowed under section 170 for the present
value of B's remainder interest in the securities." Reg. §170A-7(a)(2)(i);
Rev. Rul. 79-295, 1979-2 C.B. 349 (gift tax deduction allowable). A deduction is not allowed, however, where the partial interest results from a
division of the property that was made by the donor in order to avoid the
restrictions imposed by §170(f)(3)(A). For example, a deduction is not
allowed where the donor transfers a remainder interest in property to a
private donee and immediately thereafter transfers the reserved life
estate to a qualified charity. *Id.* A deduction is allowed, however, where
the donor contributes all of the interests in a property to charities. Reg.
§1.170A-7(a)(2)(ii). For example, a deduction for the full value of the
property is allowed where the donor gives an income interest in property
to one charity and at the same time gives the remainder to another
charity.

§8.18. Transfers Subject to a Condition or Power

A deduction is not allowed for a gift to a charity that may be defeated by
the subsequent performance of some act or the happening of some
event, unless the possibility of occurrence of the act or event is so remote
as to be negligible. Regs. §§1.170A-1(e), 1.170A-7(a)(3). Thus, a deduction is allowable for a gift of land to a qualified charity for so long as it is
used for park purposes only if the possibility that the land would be used
for other purposes appears on the date of the gift to be so remote as to
be negligible. Reg. §1.170A-1(e). However, because the test is essentially
a factual one, which may be questioned by the IRS, it is generally not
desirable to give a defeasible fee interest to a charity. A gift of a defeasi-

ble fee is also undesirable because it may restrict the use of the property for generations, involve subsequent litigation, and require a substantial expenditure to trace the donor's successors. See, *e.g.*, the discussion of Brown v. Independent Baptist Church of Woburn, 91 N.E.2d 922 (Mass. 1950) in W. Leach & J. Logan, Future Interests and Estate Planning 44 (1961).

D. GIFTS IN TRUST

§8.19. General Limitations

In general, deductions are allowed for a gift of a remainder interest in trust made after 1969 only if the trust is a charitable remainder annuity trust, a charitable remainder unitrust, or a pooled income fund. *See* §170(f)(2)(A). Charitable remainder trusts and pooled income funds are discussed in §§8.20 to 8.23, *infra*. Estate and gift tax charitable deductions are allowed for a gift of an income interest only if the charitable interest is in the form of a guaranteed annuity or a unitrust interest. No income tax deduction is allowed to the donor for a gift of such an income interest unless the donor is treated as the owner of the trust under the grantor trust rules. *See* §170(f)(2)(B). Otherwise the transfer of property to a trust of which there is a charitable income beneficiary and private remaindermen does not qualify for any present charitable deduction. However, it is possible to structure the trust so that the transfer does not constitute a completed gift and that deductions will be available for income and gift tax purposes for the annual income distributions to charity. §8.26, *infra*. Note that a transfer of a legal life estate to a spouse with remainder to a charity may qualify for the unlimited gift and estate tax marital deductions. §§2056(a), (b)(7), 2523(f). On the death of the spouse the property is includible in his or her estate and an offsetting charitable deduction should be allowable under §2055.

§8.20. Charitable Remainder Trusts (§664(d))

A trust qualifies as a charitable remainder trust only if it satisfies the requirements of §664(d), which are designed to assure that the charitable remaindermen will receive the full benefit of the remainder interest. The requirements, which are elaborated extensively in the regulations, severely restrict the nature and extent of the permissible noncharitable interests. Because of the complexity of the requirements and the hyper-technical positions taken by the IRS, charitable remainder trusts should be drafted very carefully — preferably with the supervision of an expert. The task was eased somewhat in 1972 when the IRS published sample trust provisions that satisfy the statutory requirements. Rev. Rul. 72-395, 1972-2 C.B. 340. However, the IRS interpretation of the requirements changes from time to time as indicated by a 1980 revenue ruling, which made mandatory two of the previously optional provisions that appeared in Rev. Rul. 72-395. Rev. Rul. 80-123, 1980-1 C.B. 205. In order to qualify for an estate tax charitable deduction, Rev. Rul. 80-123 requires a charitable remainder trust to provide that the obligation to pay the noncharitable beneficiary begins on the date of the decedent's death. Recognizing that the proper amount of the payments will not be finally established until a much later time in most cases, the governing instrument must also require corrective payments to be made in the case of an overpayment or underpayment to the beneficiary.

The propensity of the IRS to disqualify trusts on picayune grounds is illustrated by LR 7942073, which held that a testamentary trust did not qualify because the will included an in terrorem clause (*i.e.*, one under which a beneficiary who contested the will would lose all rights in the trust). In the ruling the IRS adhered strictly to the rule that payments must be made either for the life or lives of person(s) living at the time of the transfer to the trust or for a term not to exceed 20 years. Reg. §1.664-3(a)(5). According to the IRS a trust does not qualify if the noncharitable interest may terminate prematurely because of the occurrence or nonoccurrence of a specified event. *See, e.g.,* Rev. Rul. 76-291, 1976-2 C.B. 284 (termination of distributions to individual upon remarriage). It seems unreasonable to disqualify the trust because the noncharitable interest may terminate early, which can only increase the value of the charitable interest.

CRAT. Charitable remainder trusts must make specified annual distributions to one or more beneficiaries, at least one of whom is a noncharity. Of course, a charity must have an irrevocable remainder interest in the trust. The amount of the annual distributions is strictly limited by the Code and regulations. A charitable remainder annuity trust (CRAT) must provide for an annual payout of a certain sum, which is not less than 5% of the initial net fair market value of the trust property. The amount may be expressed as a specified dollar amount or as a percentage or fraction of the initial fair market value of the trust assets. In the latter case the trust must provide for appropriate adjustments to be made if the initial value of the trust is incorrectly determined. Reg. §1.664-2(a)(1)(iii). Because the amount of the payments is fixed at the outset, the payout may not vary from year to year and no additional property may be transferred to the trust.

Example 8-13. Donor, D, transferred securities worth §200,000 to a charitable remainder annuity trust from which D is entitled to an annual payment of $10,000 for life. The trust provides for the minimum 5% annual annuity payment allowed under §664(d)(1). The trust could have called for a larger annual payment, but not a smaller one.

CRUT. A charitable remainder unitrust (CRUT) must provide for a payout each year of a fixed percentage of at least 5% of the annually determined net fair market value of its assets. Thus, the amount of the annual payment made from a unitrust will vary from year to year according to the value of the trust corpus. Property may be added to a unitrust if it contains provisions that require appropriate adjustments in the amount of the payout.

Income Only Unitrust. An exception made by §664(d)(3) recognizes an "income only" unitrust as an authorized form of charitable remainder trust. To qualify under this exception, the unitrust must provide for payment to the noncharitable beneficiary of (1) the net income of the trust in the years that it does not exceed a specified unitrust percentage of at least 5% and (2) the net income for the year in excess of the unitrust percentage to the extent that the payments for prior years were less than the specified unitrust amount for those years. Under this alternative, if the net income of the trust for the first year were $4,000 and the unitrust amount were $5,000, the trustee would be required to distribute $4,000. If the income of the trust in the second year were $6,000 and the unitrust amount were again $5,000, the trustee would be required to distribute the full $6,000 in order to make up for the $1,000 deficiency in the first year. Such a trust may be appropriate where the current beneficiary will not need a stable flow of funds for support and the property contributed to the trust may generate little or no income in some years, particularly the early ones. It has been used by some planners, for example, in connection with gifts of appreciated real property that generate little, if any, current income.

Basic Income Taxation of Charitable Remainder Trusts. The income taxation of charitable remainder trusts and their beneficiaries is governed by §664. To begin with, the trusts themselves are ordinarily exempt from taxation. §664(c). Amounts distributed to the beneficiaries are characterized as ordinary income to the extent of the trust's ordinary income for the current year and undistributed ordinary income for prior years. §664(b)(1) Next, the distributions are considered to be composed of capital gain to the extent the trust has capital gain for the year and undistributed gain for prior years. §664(b)(2). Finally distributions are constituted of other income (*e.g.*, tax exempt income) to the extent the trust has any for the current year and undistributed other income for prior years. §664(b)(3). Any remaining amount of a current distribution is considered to be composed of principal. §664(b)(4).

The transfer of property to a charitable remainder trust does not usually involve the realization of any gain or loss. Accordingly, a donor can achieve a degree of tax-free diversification by transferring appreciated assets to a charitable remainder trust, which sells them and invests in a broader range of assets.

Restrictions on Distributions. Trust distributions to the noncharitable beneficiaries must be limited to the specified annuity or unitrust amounts. §§664(d)(1)(B), (2)(B). Thus, a trust will not qualify as a charitable remainder trust if it permits any other use or application of trust assets for the benefit of noncharities. The inability to distribute additional amounts in case of accident, illness, or other emergency is a major drawback, which deters some individuals from establishing charitable remainder trusts.

Restrictions on Investments. Under Reg. §1.664-1(a)(3), a charitable remainder trust cannot "include a provision which restricts the trustee from investing the trust assets in a manner which could result in the annual realization of a reasonable amount of income or gain from the sale or disposition of trust assets." Accordingly, a trust generally should not direct the trustee to retain any particular asset or assets or impose any limits on the trustee's power to sell or dispose of trust assets.

Charitable remainder trusts may invest in tax exempt securities, but pooled income funds may not. *See* §8.23, *infra.* However, if there were an understanding or agreement that the trustee would sell the property transferred to a charitable remainder trust and invest in tax exempt securities, the donor might be taxed on the gain. See Rev. Rul. 60-370, 1960-2 C.B. 203, dealing with the so-called Pomona College Plan.

Valuing the Charitable Remainder in a CRAT. For purposes of the income, gift, and estate tax charitable deductions, the fair market value of a remainder interest in a CRAT following one life or a term of years is determined under the basic estate tax actuarial tables contained in Reg. §20.2031-10. Reg. §1.664-2(c). For example, if the donor in Example 8-13 above were a woman aged 50, the factor for an annuity payable at the end of each year is 12.5793. Thus, D's annuity would be worth $125,793 and her charitable gift would be worth $74,207, subject to any adjustments that might be required by §170 for income tax purposes. The amount includible in a transferor-annuitant's estate under §2036 is the amount necessary at the 6% rate specified in Reg. §20.2031-10 to yield the guaranteed annual payment. Rev. Rul. 82-105, 1982-1 C.B. — .

Problem 8-3. Donor, D, transferred securities that had a basis of $10,000 and a fair market value of $200,000 to a CRAT of which her church was the remainderman. The trust provided for an annual payment to D of $10,000 per year for life. D is a 65-year-old woman who has an adjusted taxable income of $40,000 each year. The trustee immediately sold the securities for $200,000 and purchased tax exempt municipal bonds that generate exactly $10,000 of income each year. What are the income, gift, and estate tax consequences of D's gift to the CRAT? How will the annual $10,000 distributions be taxed to D?

Valuing the Charitable Remainder in a CRUT. The value of the remainder interest in a CRUT after one life or a term of years is calculated according to Reg. §1.664-4, which involves the use of some special factors set forth in the regulation. The IRS will, upon request, furnish a factor for the value of remainder interests in a CRUT that cannot be calculated from the tables contained in Reg. §1.664-4.

Example 8-14. On January 1, a woman aged 50, W, transferred securities worth $200,000 to a charitable remainder unitrust. The trust called for the payment to W on December 31 of each year of an amount equal to 5% of the fair market value of the trust as determined at the beginning of each tax year of the trust. The adjusted payout rate for the trust is determined by multiplying the 5% basic payout rate by the factor specified in Table F of Reg. §1.664-4 for use when the first valuation date precedes the first payout date by 12 months (.943396). In this case the adjusted payout rate is 4.717%, the product of 5% × .943396. The factor to be used to value the remainder for a trust having this adjusted payout rate is interpolated from the factors published in Table E-2 for females aged 50.

Factor for woman aged 50, 4.6% payout	.31046
Factor for woman aged 50, 4.8% payout	.29664
Difference	.01382

$$\frac{4.717\% - 4.6\%}{0.2\%} = \frac{X}{.01382} = .00808$$

Factor for woman aged 50, 4.6% payout	.31046
Less value of X	.00808
Interpolated factor	.30238
Present value of remainder in $200,000 =	$60,476

Where a remainder interest in a CRAT or CRUT is dependent upon the continuation or termination of more than one life, the value of the remainder is determined in accordance with IRS Publication No. 723, Valuation of Last Survivor Charitable Remainders.

Chance That Charitable Interest in a CRAT Will Not Become Effective Must Be Negligible. (Reg. §§20.2055-2(b), 25.2522(a)-2(b)). No charitable deduction is allowed where the probability that the noncharitable beneficiary will survive the exhaustion of a fund in which a charity has a remainder interest exceeds 5%. Rev. Rul 77-374, 1977-2 C.B. 329. The determination of whether the fund of an annuity trust will be exhausted prior to the life beneficiary's death is based upon an assumed 6% rate of return and the beneficiary's life expectancy under Table LN of Reg. §20.2031-10. In Rev. Rul. 77-374, the computations indicated that the annual payments of $40,000 per year for life from a fund of $400,000 to a 61-year-old female would completely exhaust the fund in less than 16 years. No deduction was allowed because Table LN indicates that there is a greater than 63% probability that a female aged 61 would survive to age 77. The probability (.63174) is determined by dividing the number of females surviving to age 77 out of the original cohort of 100,000 (52,693) by the number living at age 61 (83,409).

Private Foundation Rules. Charitable remainder trusts are "split interest" trusts, the governing instruments of which must comply with the requirements of §508(e). §4947(a)(2). Accordingly, the instruments must prohibit the trustee from self-dealing (§4941(d)) and making taxable expenditures (§4945(d)). In addition, the instruments must ban any jeopardy investments (§4944) and excess business holdings (§4943) during any period that any annuity or unitrust amount is payable to a charity. *See* §§508(e), 4947(b)(3)(B), and Reg. §53.4947-2(b)(1). Most states have adopted legislation under which charitable trusts are deemed to include the required provisions. However, it is prudent to include the prohibitions in the trust instruments themselves, if only to alert the trustees to their existence.

Requests for Rulings. If the provisions of a charitable remainder trust are at all unusual, the lawyer should consider requesting a private letter ruling from the IRS regarding its qualification for income and gift tax purposes. The National Office will rule on prospective income and gift tax matters and on completed transactions before a return is filed, but not on matters relating to the application of the estate tax to the estate of a living person. Sec. 5.01, 5.02, Rev. Proc. 80-20, 1980-1 C.B. 633. A request should comply with the procedures outlined in Rev. Proc. 80-20 and should be addressed to:

> Assistant Commissioner (Technical)
> Internal Revenue Service
> 1111 Constitution Avenue, N.W.
> Washington, D.C. 20224

A request for a ruling must contain a full statement of all facts relating to the transaction and copies of all documents involved. The request must also include an explanation of the grounds that support the applicant's views and a statement of relevant authorities. Secs. 9.05, 9.08, Rev. Proc. 80-20, 1980-1 C.B. 633.

§8.21.   Advantages of Charitable Remainder Trusts

A lifetime gift to a charitable remainder trust or pooled income fund is attractive mainly because it supports current income and gift tax charitable deductions although the charity will not have the beneficial use of the property until the expiration of the private interests. In the meantime the donor, or other noncharitable beneficiaries, may receive payments from the trust. Because charitable remainder trusts are not subject to taxation (§664(c)), the trustee may sell the property that is transferred to it without incurring any income tax on the gain. Thus, the transfer of property to a trust may facilitate its sale and, in effect, the receipt of a higher net yield by the donor.

> **Example 8-15.** Donor, D, transferred highly appreciated securities that produced a low current yield to a qualifying charitable remainder trust in which D retained a current interest. The trustee may sell the securities and reinvest the proceeds without subjecting the gain to taxation. For income tax purposes distributions received by D will be characterized successively as ordinary income to the extent of the trust's ordinary income for the year and the undistributed income for prior years, then as capital gain to the extent of the trust's capital gain, then as other (*i.e.*, tax exempt) income, and, finally, as a tax-free distribution of corpus. *See* §664(b).

§8.22.   Comparison of CRATs and CRUTs

CRATs and CRUTs are similar in many respects; however, there are some important distinctions. Often a client's choice between them is based upon the client's judgment regarding the desirability of having a fixed payout (CRAT) or one that depends upon the annual value of the trust assets (CRUT). The payout of a CRAT is stable — it neither increases if the value of the trust assets increases in an inflationary period nor decreases if the value of the assets falls during an economic downturn. A CRUT is generally considered to protect the beneficiary better against the ravages of inflation if the assets of the trust increase in value, which is not always the case. Where the payout rate is 6% or less, a client may favor a CRAT because the value of the charitable remainder is greater. In such a case the remainder is slightly larger in the case of a CRAT because the excess of the assumed 6% rate of return over the payout is attributed to the remainder that passes to charity. In contrast, the payout of a CRUT is assumed to increase each year by the specified percentage of the annual increase in principal (the excess of the assumed 6% rate of return over the payout rate). The annual valuation of assets, which is required in the case of a CRUT, may also be difficult and involve additional costs. The fact that a CRUT may provide for the subsequent transfer of additional assets, but a CRAT cannot, is usually not an important consideration.

§8.23. Pooled Income Fund (§642(c)(5))

Income, gift, and estate tax deductions are also available where property is transferred to a pooled income fund, which is defined in §642(c)(5) as a trust:

(A) to which each donor transfers property, contributing an irrevocable remainder interest in such property to or for the use of [a public charity], and retaining an income interest for the life of one or more beneficiaries (living at the time of the transfer);

(B) in which the property transferred by each donor is commingled with property transferred by other donors who have made or make similar transfers;

(C) which cannot have investments in securities which are exempt from the taxes imposed by this subtitle

(D) which includes only amounts received from transfers that meet the requirements of this paragraph;

(E) which is maintained by the organization to which the remainder interest is contributed and of which no donor or beneficiary of an income interest is a trustee; and

(F) from which each beneficiary of an income interest receives income, for each year for which he is entitled to receive the income interest referred to in subparagraph (A), determined by the rate of return earned by the trust for such a year.

When property is transferred to a pooled income fund, participation units in the fund are allocated to the holder of the life interest. As in the case of a common trust fund, the number of units depends upon the value of the property transferred to the fund and the value of the fund's other assets. The regulations contain detailed rules for the valuation of assets of the fund and allocation of units. *See* Regs. §1.642(c)-5, -6. Sample provisions for inclusion in the governing instruments of pooled income funds were published by the IRS in Rev. Rul. 82-38, 1982-1 C.B. —. Because of the complexity of the rules regarding pooled income funds, a donor should be hesitant to transfer property to a fund unless the charity has obtained a ruling from the IRS verifying that the fund meets the requirements of §642(c)(5), etc.

The amount of the charitable contribution for property transferred to a pooled income fund depends upon the age of the income beneficiaries and the rate of return earned by the fund over the preceding 3 years. Under §642(c)(5) the life income interests are valued according to the highest rate of return earned by the fund in the preceding 3 years. If the fund has been in existence for less than 3 years, a 6% rate of return is used for this purpose. In recent years funds have generally earned more than a 6% rate of return. Accordingly, a contribution to a fund that has been in existence for less than 3 years will usually generate a larger income tax charitable deduction (and gift tax deduction) than a contribution to a more mature fund.

The present value of a remainder interest dependent upon the termination of one life is determined according to actuarial tables G-1 and G-2 of Reg. §1.642(c)-6(d). When a life income interest terminates, the corresponding charitable remainder interest must be severed from the fund and paid over to or retained for the benefit of the designated public charity. Reg. §1.642(c)-5(b)(8).

No gain or loss is incurred by the donor when property is transferred to a qualified pooled income fund. However, gain may be realized if the donor either receives any property from the fund in addition to the income interest or transfers encumbered property to the fund. Reg. §1.642(c)-5(a)(3). The fund and the beneficiaries are generally taxed according to the rules applicable to a noncharitable trust, except that the grantor trust rules do not apply (Reg. §1.642(c)-(5)(a)(2)) and the fund is not taxed on its long-term capital gains. §642(c)(3).

Overall, a pooled income fund offers an attractive way for a donor to make a charitable gift that wouldn't justify the expense of establishing and operating a separate charitable remainder trust. The opportunity to achieve tax-free diversification of investments is another important advantage of a fund. However, unlike charitable remainder trusts, a fund cannot invest in tax exempt securities (§642(c)(5)(C), Reg. §1.642(c)-5(b)(4)). Accordingly none of the income received from the fund will ordinarily be tax exempt. Also, the statute bars a donor or beneficiary from serving as a trustee of the fund. §642(c)(5)(E). However, "[t]he fact that a donor of property to the fund, or a beneficiary of the fund is a trustee, officer, director or other officer of the public charity to or for the use of which the remainder interest is contributed ordinarily will not prevent the fund from meeting the requirements of section 642(c)(5) and this paragraph." Reg. §1.642(c)-5(b)(6).

§8.24.   Gifts to Trusts Other Than Charitable Remainder Trusts and Pooled Income Funds (§§170(f)(2)(B), 2055(e)(2)(B), 2522(c)(2)(B))

Deductions are also allowed for a gift in trust of a current charitable interest in the form of a guaranteed annuity or unitrust interest. For this purpose a guaranteed annuity is a determinable amount, payable at least annually for a specified term or for the life or lives of designated persons who are living at the time of the transfer. Reg. §1.170A-6(c)(2)(i)(A). A unitrust is a fixed percentage of the fair market value of the property determined yearly. A trust that provides for such current payments to charity is usually called a charitable lead trust. A gift of a guaranteed annuity or unitrust interest is deductible for income tax purposes only if the income of the trust will be taxed to the donor under the grantor trust rules. §170(f)(2)(B).

Subject to the other limitations imposed by §170, a donor is entitled to a present deduction for the full value of a guaranteed annuity or unitrust interest given during the year to a qualified charity if the donor is treated as the owner of the trust for income tax purposes. A gift of a guaranteed annuity or unitrust amount also qualifies for a gift tax deduction. Such a gift may appeal to a client whose income will be subject to the maximum rate in the year of the gift but will be subject to lower rates in subsequent years. The rules prevent a donor from taking a large deduction at the outset and avoiding taxation on the trust income in later years by relinquishing the interests or controls that caused the donor to be treated as its owner under the grantor trust rules. If the donor ceases being treated as owner of the trust, he or she is considered to have received income equal to the excess of the amount of any deduction received for the gift, over the discounted value of the income that was taxed to the donor under the grantor trust rules. §170(f)(2)(B). The amount must be included in the donor's final income tax return if the donor ceases to be treated as owner of the trust by reason of death. Reg. §1.170A-6(c)(5), *Example* (3).

§8.25.   Guaranteed Annuity Interests and Unitrust Interests

Income, gift, and estate tax deductions are allowed for a gift of a guaranteed annuity interest to a charity. For this purpose a guaranteed annuity interest is an irrevocable right, pursuant to the trust, to receive an amount each year that is determinable on the date of the gift for a fixed term or for the life or lives of individuals who are living on the date of the gift. Reg. §1.170A-6(c)(2)(i). An interest does not qualify unless it is a guaranteed annuity interest in all respects. Thus, the right to receive payments under an income only unitrust (the lesser of a fixed amount or the actual income of the trust) does not qualify. Rev. Rul. 77-300, 1977-2 C.B. 352 (gift tax). Similarly, an interest does not qualify if a payment may be made from the trust for a private purpose prior to the expiration of the charitable annuity interest, unless the payments must be made from assets that are devoted exclusively to private purposes. Any income in excess of the annuity amount may also be payable to a charity, but it will not increase the amount of the allowable deduction.

A unitrust interest is an irrevocable right to receive payment each year of a fixed percentage of the net fair market value of the trust assets, determined annually. The value may be determined either on one date each year or by taking the average value on more than one date, provided that the same method is used each year. Reg. §1.170A-6(c)(2)(ii)(A). In general, the other rules applicable to a guaranteed annuity also apply to a unitrust interest.

> **Example 8-16.** Donor, D, transferred $100,000 in trust to pay $5,000 a year for the first 5 years and $7,500 for the next 5 years to a qualified charity, C. At the end of the 10-year period the trust property will be distributed to D's then living issue, per stirpes. The interest given to C is a guaranteed annuity (Reg. §1.170A-6(c)(2)(i)(B)) but it is not deductible by D for income tax purposes unless D is treated as the owner of the trust under the grantor trust rules. Gift and estate tax deductions are available for the gift to C in any case. The interest would qualify as a unitrust interest if it were expressed as a fixed percentage (*e.g.*, 8%) of the fair market value of the trust assets determined on a specified date each year (*e.g.*, January 15). Of course, no annual exclusion is available for the remainder interest in the trust.

§8.26. *Gifts of Income Interests*

An ordinary income interest in a trust does not qualify for the income, gift, or estate tax charitable deductions. However, the disallowance of the income tax deduction may be circumvented to some extent if the income is not taxed to the donor under the grantor trust rules.

> **Example 8-17.** Donor, D, created a trust this year that provided for the net income to be paid to a qualified charity, C, for 10 years at the end of which the trust property will be returned to D if D is then living, otherwise to D's then living issue. The transfer to the trust does not qualify for an income tax deduction under §170. However, the income of the trust will not be taxed to D unless D is treated as the owner of the trust under the grantor trust rules. Importantly, the trust is entitled to a deduction for the amount

distributed to charity each year. §642(c). Note that the transfer does not qualify for the gift tax charitable deduction because it is not in the form of a guaranteed annuity or fixed percentage of the fair market value of the property distributed annually. §2522(c)(2)(B). As explained below the gift tax disadvantage would be eliminated if the gift of the income were incomplete when the trust was created. The gift would be incomplete if, for example, D retained the power each year to appoint the accumulated income to and among a class of charities.

A less satisfactory result follows where the donor is treated as the owner of the trust, as the donor would be if the reversionary interest will take effect within 10 years following the transfer. In that case the donor is required to include, in computing income, "the items of income, deductions, and credits against tax of the trust." §671; Reg. §1.673(a)-1. A donor who is required to report the income of the trust should be entitled to a deduction for the amount paid to charity, subject to the limits and other provisions of §170. However, the transfer to the trust would not qualify for the gift tax deduction.

The gift tax detriment of transferring property to a trust of which the income is payable to charity is avoided if the gift to the charity is not completed until the income is ready for distribution to the charity. See, e.g., LR 8017058. For example, the gift is incomplete at the time of the initial transfer if the donor retains the right to designate the charity that will receive the net income earned by the trust during each year. See Rev. Rul. 77-275, 1977-2 C.B. 346. The grantor is not taxed on the income of a trust under the grantor trust rules merely because the grantor retains the power to allocate income or principal among charities. §674(b)(4); see §10.29, infra. Importantly, the retention of such a power renders the gift incomplete until the power is exercised. Reg. §25.2511-2(c). When the donor designates the charity to receive the accumulated income, the gift is completed. The gift consists of the entire interest in the trust's accumulated income, which is not a split interest and for which an offsetting gift tax deduction is allowable under §2522(a). LR 8144051. Note that a gift tax deduction is not allowable where the donor designates the charity in advance of the receipt of the income. Rev. Rul. 77-275, supra. In such a case the designation gives the charity an income interest that does not qualify for the gift tax deduction. "No deduction is allowable under section 2522 of the Code with respect to such a completed gift due to [the donor's] retained right to reversion of the trust property upon termination and because the income right is not in the form prescribed by section 2522(c)(2)." The grantor of such a trust should instead retain the power to choose the charities to receive the net income for each year after the income is in hand. The payment to the charities is deductible under §642(c)(1) for income tax purposes even though it is paid after the close of the trust's taxable year. LR 8152078. Under that section, "[i]f a charitable contribution is paid after the close of [the] taxable year and on or before the last day of the year following the close of such taxable year, then the trustee or administrator may elect to treat such contribution as paid during such taxable year."

The slight differences between the charities described in §170(c) and those described in §§2055(a) and 2522(a) can also cause tax problems for the donor. For example, a gift tax deduction is not allowable where a trust permits the grantor, or another person, to designate the charitable recipient from among charitable organizations described in §170(c). In order to assure that a gift tax charitable deduction is also available, the selection must also be limited to charities that are described in §2522(a). The point is elaborated in LR 8017058 with respect to an irrevocable short-term trust. In most instances the authority to make distributions of trust property to undesignated charities should be limited to ones that meet the requirements of §§170(c), 2055(a), *and* 2522(a).

§8.27. *Payments to Charity from a Trust upon Death of Grantor*

For a variety of purposes it is important to distinguish between gifts made "in trust" and "not in trust." The distinction should be drawn in projecting the tax consequences that flow from the transfer of property to a trust from which payments will be made to charity following the grantor's death. The transfer of property to a revocable trust does not generally have any significant present income or gift tax consequences because of its revocable character. The grantor may safely provide for a distribution to be made to charity upon the grantor's death. Rev. Rul. 75-414, 1975-2 C.B. 371, pointed out that a trust may be used as a conduit to make *outright* distributions of a specified percentage of the trust corpus to a charity upon the grantor's death. The ruling allowed an estate tax deduction for a specified percentage of the trust property, augmented by a pour over from the grantor's estate, that was payable to charity upon the grantor's death. A deduction was allowed because the gift constituted an outright transfer of an undivided interest in the trust property. An estate tax deduction is also allowable where a trust provides for payment of a specified sum to charity upon the grantor's death. In that case the gift would constitute the grantor's entire interest in that particular sum. Of course, a charitable deduction is allowable only to the extent that the property given to charity is included in the decedent's gross estate. §2055(d).

The transfer of property to an irrevocable trust that provides for a later distribution to charity may have very different consequences. For example, the transfer usually constitutes a completed gift for gift tax purposes. However, a charitable gift tax deduction is not allowed unless the charitable interest is in the form of a CRAT, CRUT, guaranteed annuity, or unitrust amount. Thus, some gift tax liability could be incurred at the time of the transfer in respect of the charitable interest. The transfer to the trust also would not qualify for an income tax deduction unless it took one of those forms. Presumably the grantor's estate would be entitled to an estate tax charitable deduction for the value of the payment made from the trust at the time of the grantor's death. Recall that the marital deduction is available on an elective basis with respect to the full value of the property transferred to a trust in which the surviving spouse has a qualifying income interest for life. §§2056(b)(7), 2523(f). The value of the property is includible in the donee-spouse's estate under §2044. As noted above, if the remainder passes to charity upon the donee-spouse's death, the donee-spouse's estate should be entitled to an offsetting charitable deduction under §2055.

E. SPECIAL TYPES OF TRANSFERS

§8.28. Bargain Sales to Charity (§1011(b))

A "bargain sale" (or part gift and part sale) occurs when property is sold to a charity for less than its fair market value. It may be an appropriate technique where a donor wants to recover part or all of his or her investment in an asset. For example, a client who does not want to make an outright gift of property to a charity may be willing to transfer it to the charity for an amount equal to its cost. The excess of the fair market value of the property over the consideration received by the donor (the "gift" portion) usually qualifies as a charitable contribution subject to the provisions of §170.

Under a provision that was added by the Tax Reform Act of 1969, §1011(b), a portion of the seller's adjusted basis is disregarded for the purpose of determining gain on the sale. That subsection provides: "If a deduction is allowable under section 170 (relating to a charitable contribution) by reason of a sale, then the adjusted basis for determining the gain from such sale shall be that portion of the adjusted basis which bears the same ratio to the adjusted basis as the amount realized bears to the fair market value of the property." Thus, the following formula should be used to calculate the donor's adjusted basis under §1011(b):

$$\frac{\text{Amount realized}}{\substack{\text{Fair market value of} \\ \text{property transferred}}} \times \text{Adjusted basis} = \substack{\text{Adjusted basis} \\ \text{to compute gain}}$$

Problem 8-4. An unmarried seller, S, owns 100 shares of common stock that were purchased more than a year ago for $10 per share or a total of $1,000. Recently, when the stock was worth $100 per share, or a total of $10,000, S sold it to a public charity for $1,000. Assume that S will make no other charitable gifts during the year and that S will have a contribution base of $30,000 for the year. What amount would S ordinarily be entitled to claim as a charitable contribution deduction? How would your answer differ if S died during the year? Compute the gain that S would be required to report on the transaction. Would the income tax consequences to S be any different if S instead sold 10 shares of the stock to the charity for $1,000 and made a gift of the other 90 shares?

In the case of a bargain sale the donor realizes the same amount of gain that would have been realized if he or she sold a separate portion of the property to the charity for its full value and made a gift of the remainder.

For purposes of §1011(b), if property is transferred subject to an indebtedness, the amount of the indebtedness is treated as an amount realized by the seller even though the transferee does not agree to assume or pay the indebtedness. Reg. §1.1011-2(a)(3). The principles of Crane v. Commissioner, 331 U.S. 1 (1947), apply to such a case, with the result that the donor may realize income as a consequence of making the gift. Winston F.C. Guest, 77 T.C. 9 (1981). The income tax consequences of a bargain sale of encumbered property are also illustrated in Rev. Rul. 81-163, 1981-1 C.B. 433.

Under the pre-1970 law, if property were sold to a charity in a bargain sale, the proceeds were not taxable to the extent of the seller's entire adjusted basis in the property. In addition, the seller was entitled to a charitable deduction for the excess of the fair market value of the property over the sale price. Thus, when property was sold for an amount equal to the seller's basis, the entire appreciation in value of the property was allowable as a charitable deduction and the seller did not realize any gain. Of course, gain was realized by a seller who received an amount that exceeded his or her basis. Under the pre-1970 rules the seller was not required to allocate any part of his or her basis to the gift portion of the transaction.

Gift and Estate Tax. In the case of an outright transfer in connection with a bargain sale, the donor is entitled to a gift tax deduction in the amount of the gift portion. Similarly, the donor's estate is entitled to an estate tax charitable deduction if the property is included in the donor's gross estate. Where the donor makes a bargain sale of a partial interest in property, such as a remainder interest, a deduction is not allowed unless the interest falls within one of the exceptions to the split-interest rules. *See* §§8.14 to 8.18, *supra.*

§8.29. *Charitable Gift Annuities*

Charitable deductions are also allowable when property is transferred to a charity in exchange for an annuity. In such cases the donor is treated as having made a charitable gift of the amount by which the value of the transferred property exceeds the value of the annuity contract. For this

Table 8-1
Ordinary Life Annuities—One Life—Expected Return Multiples

Ages			Ages			Ages		
Male	*Female*	*Multiples*	*Male*	*Female*	*Multiples*	*Male*	*Female*	*Multiples*
6	11	65.0	41	46	33.0	76	81	9.1
7	12	64.1	42	47	32.1	77	82	8.7
8	13	63.2	43	48	31.2	78	83	8.3
9	14	62.3	44	49	30.4	79	84	7.8
10	15	61.4	45	50	29.6	80	85	7.5
11	16	60.4	46	51	28.7	81	86	7.1
12	17	59.5	47	52	27.9	82	87	6.7
13	18	58.6	48	53	27.1	83	88	6.3
14	19	57.7	49	54	26.3	84	89	6.0
15	20	56.7	50	55	25.5	85	90	5.7
16	21	55.8	51	56	24.7	86	91	5.4
17	22	54.9	52	57	24.0	87	92	5.1
18	23	53.9	53	58	23.2	88	93	4.8
19	24	53.0	54	59	22.4	89	94	4.5
20	25	52.1	53	60	21.7	90	95	4.2
21	26	51.1	56	61	21.0	91	96	4.0
22	27	50.2	57	62	20.3	92	97	3.7
23	28	49.3	58	63	19.6	93	98	3.5
24	29	48.3	59	64	18.9	94	99	3.3
25	30	47.4	60	65	18.2	95	100	3.1
26	31	46.5	61	66	17.5	96	101	2.9
27	32	45.6	62	67	16.9	97	102	2.7
28	33	44.6	63	68	16.2	98	103	2.5
29	34	43.7	64	69	15.6	99	104	2.3
30	35	42.8	65	70	15.0	100	105	2.1
31	36	41.9	66	71	14.4	101	106	1.9
32	37	41.0	67	72	13.8	102	107	1.7
33	38	40.0	68	73	13.2	103	108	1.5
34	39	39.1	69	74	12.6	104	109	1.3
35	40	38.2	70	75	12.1	105	110	1.2
36	41	37.3	71	76	11.6	106	111	1.0
37	42	36.5	72	77	11.0	107	112	.8
38	43	35.6	73	78	10.5	108	113	.7
39	44	34.7	74	79	10.1	109	114	.6
40	45	33.8	75	80	9.6	110	115	.5
						111	116	0

purpose the annuity is valued according to the tables set forth in Rev. Rul. 72-438, 1972-2 C.B. 38.

Example 8-18. A 65-year-old male, M, transferred securities with a basis of $20,000 and a current value of $100,000 to a public charity, C, in exchange for its nonassignable promise to pay him $5,000 each year in monthly installments for life. The value of the right to receive payments of $5,000 per year for the life of a 65-year-old male is $51,630. That figure is determined by multiplying the amount of the annual payment ($5,000) by the factor for a 65-year-old male from Table A of Rev. Rul. 72-438 ($10.104) as increased for the monthly payment mode ($0.222). M made a gift to C of the $48,370, the amount by which the value of the property transferred ($100,000) exceeded the value of the annuity ($51,630). M realized gain on the transfer, which is determined under the bargain sale rules and is usually reported over the life expectancy of the annuitant in the manner described below.

The bargain sale rules apply to charitable gift annuity transactions that give rise to a charitable deduction under §170. Reg. §1.1011-2; LR 8117045. Accordingly, a donor will realize some gain when appreciated property is transferred to a charity in exchange for an annuity. In this respect a gift annuity has less favorable income tax consequences than a gift to a charitable remainder trust or a pooled income fund. However, where the annuity contract is not assignable and the donor is one of the annuitants, the gain is not reported immediately. Instead, a portion of each payment is reported as gain over the period of the annuitant's life expectancy. Reg. §1.1011-2(a)(4)(iii). The portion treated as gain is determined by dividing the gain by the annuitant's life expectancy according to Table I of Reg. §1.72-9 (Table 8-1). However, the gain is reported only from the portion of the annual payment that represents the return on the donor's investment in the contract as determined under §72. Even if the annuitant lives longer than expected, none of the portion attributable to the annuitant's investment in the contract is taxed. The application of these rules is illustrated by the following example, which is a slightly changed and updated version of Reg. §1.1011-2(c), *Example* (8):

Example 8-19. A woman 65 years of age, W, transferred securities which were worth $100,000 and had a basis of $20,000 to a public charity, C, in exchange for its nonassignable promise to pay her $5,000 per year in monthly installments for life. The present value of the annuity, calculated from Table A of Rev. Rul. 72-438, is $57,060 ($5,000 × ($11.190 + $0.222)). Thus, W made a gift to C of $42,940. Under the bargain sale rules W's adjusted basis in the securities was $11,412:

$$\frac{\$57,060}{\$100,000} \times \$20,000$$

Accordingly, W realized a gain on the transfer of $45,648 ($57,060 − $11,412), which will be reported over the 18.2 year period the payments are expected to be made according to Table I of Reg. §1.72-9. W must report a gain of $2,508.13 each year out of the portion of the payment attributable to her investment in the contract. The portion of each payment that is attributable to her investment in the contract is determined by dividing her investment ($57,060) by the expected return on the contract ($91,000). The expected return is simply the amount of the annual payment ($5,000) multiplied by W's life expectancy of 18.2 years determined under Table I of Reg. §1.72-9. W's investment in the contract is $57,060, the present value of the annuity, divided by the expected return ($91,000) or 62.7%. The annual payment of $5,000 is multiplied by the exclusion ratio (62.7%) to determine the amount that is excludible each year from W's income ($3,135). However, the gain of $2,508.13 must be reported out of that portion of each payment until the full gain ($45,648) has been taxed. Thereafter, the full $3,135 is received tax free. The gain is the excess of W's investment in the contract ($57,060) over her adjusted basis in the sale portion ($11,412). Each year W must report as ordinary income the amount ($1,865) by which the annuity payment ($5,000) exceeds the exclusion portion ($3,135).

A gift tax charitable deduction is allowable under §2522 for the excess of the value of the property transferred to the charity over the value of the annuity determined according to Rev. Rul. 72-438, 1972-2 C.B. 38. The deduction is allowable although the gift did not take the form of a charitable remainder trust or pooled income fund because the donor did not retain an interest in the *same* property that was transferred to the charity. Rev. Rul. 80-281, 1980-2 C.B. 282. As is the case with other annuities, nothing is ordinarily includible in the donor-annuitant's gross estate at death. Some value would be included under §2039 if the annuity is payable to another person following the donor's death.

Problem 8-5. A client, X, whose annual adjusted gross income is about $75,000 each year, plans to make a gift to a local hospital foundation. Presently X is thinking of transferring securities with a basis of $50,000 and a value of $100,000 to the trustee of a trust of which X's 80-year-old mother would be entitled to receive the net income each year for life and the hospital foundation would be the remainderman. What are the income, gift, and estate tax consequences of making the gift in that form? Would the outcome be any different if X transferred a vacation residence to the trust, assuming that it also had a basis of $50,000 and a fair market value of $100,000? Would any deductions be available if X gave the foundation the exclusive right to use, occupy, and control X's summer residence for 6 months each year? If X wishes to make a split-interest gift of the type under consideration, what device would you recommend that X use in lieu of the trust described above?

Problem 8-6. Owner, O, sold stock worth $25,000 to a public charity for a cash payment equal to O's basis of $5,000. What are the income and gift tax consequences of the sale assuming that O had held the stock for more than a year? Is the overall result the same as if O had sold a portion of the stock on an exchange of $25,000 and had made a gift of the $20,000 cash to the charity? If O were terminally ill, would it be better to make such a gift during O's lifetime or by will?

Problem 8-7. What are the main considerations that might lead a client to prefer a charitable remainder unitrust over a charitable remainder annuity trust (and vice versa)? Along the same lines, why might a client choose to make a gift to a pooled income fund instead of establishing a charitable remainder trust? How do those devices compare with a bargain sale of property to a charity on the installment method?

§8.30. Gift and Redemption of Appreciated Stock

An outright gift of closely held stock to a charity, followed by a redemption of the stock, can be an effective way of making a charitable gift without reducing the shareholder's after-tax income. The use of this technique can leave a shareholder who is in the 50% marginal income tax bracket with the same net income as an equivalent increase in salary or dividend distribution. The anticipated redemption of the shares would prevent the shares from being purchased from the charity by anyone else. Also, the redemption might increase the proportionate interests of the other shareholders without the imposition of a gift tax. The valuation of the shares for income and gift tax purposes may require an appraisal by an expert. However, the amount paid in redemption of the shares is some evidence of their value. In order to avoid problems with the IRS or ethical problems, the amount claimed as a deduction should not exceed the amount for which the stock is redeemed.

The redemption of the shares is not taxed to the donor if the gift placed the shares beyond the donor's control and the donee was not obligated to surrender the shares for redemption. Carrington v. Commissioner, 476 F.2d 704 (5th Cir. 1973); Rev. Rul. 78-197, 1978-1 C.B. 83. The donor and donee may discuss the possible redemption of the shares prior to the consummation of the gift, but the donee cannot be obligated to redeem them.

Example 8-20. X owned a majority interest in Zero, Inc. Any dividends paid to X would be subject to an income tax rate of 50%. Thus, a $10,000 increase in dividends would leave X with about $5,000 net. If X instead contributed stock worth $10,000 to a public charity, the resulting charitable deduction would reduce X's income tax liability by $5,000 (50% × $10,000). The gift would give X the same amount of after-tax income as a dividend distribution, but would not require payments to the other shareholders. A redemption of the stock by Zero, Inc. for $10,000 would require the same cash outlay as a $10,000 increase in X's salary and less than the payment of a dividend to all shareholders.

BIBLIOGRAPHY

Ashby, The Uses of Charitable Income Interests in Estate Planning, 115 Tr. & Est. 12 (1976)

Burke, Charitable Giving and Estate Planning, 28 Tax Law. 289 (1975)

Comment, Charitable Remainder Trusts, Pooled Income Funds and the 1976 Tax Reform Act, 46 U.M.K.C. L. Rev. 357 (1978)

Moore, Estate Planning Under the Tax Reform Act of 1969: The Uses of Charity, 56 Va. L. Rev. 565 (1970)

Moore, Role of Charitable Dispositions in Estate Planning, U. Miami 13th Inst. Est. Plan, Ch. 6 (1979)

Muchin, Lubelchek & Grass, Charitable Lead Trusts Can Provide Substantial Estate Planning Benefits, 49 J. Tax. 2 (1978)

Note, Taxation of Charitable Gift Annuities: Valuation and Policy Considerations, 67 Va. L. Rev. 1523 (1981)

Report of Committee on Charitable Giving, Trusts and Foundations. Model Charitable Remainder Unitrust, 10 Real Prop., Prob. and Tr. J. 535 (1975)

Report of Committee on Tax Estate Planning — Pre-Death. Planning Considerations for Charitable Contributions, 13 Real Prop., Prob. & Tr. J. 581 (1978)

Weithorn, S., Tax Techniques for Foundations and Other Exempt Organizations (1964) (5 volumes with annual supplements)

CHAPTER 9

Intrafamily Transfers for Consideration

501

First, inquiries into subjective intent, especially in intrafamily transfers, are particularly perilous. The present case illustrates that it is, practically speaking, impossible to determine after the death of the parties what they had in mind in creating trusts over 30 years earlier. Second, there is a high probability that such a trust arrangement was indeed created for tax-avoidance purposes. And, even if there was no estate-tax-avoidance motive, the settlor in a very real and objective sense did retain an economic interest while purporting to give away his property. Finally, it is unrealistic to assume that the settlors of the trusts, usually members of one family unit, will have created their trusts as a bargained-for exchange for the other trust. "Consideration," in the traditional legal sense, simply does not normally enter into such intrafamily transfers. United States v. Estate of Grace, 395 U.S. 316, 323-324 (1969).

A. INTRODUCTION

§9.1. *Overview*

This chapter deals with 4 devices that have developed as important alternatives to the traditional methods of transferring family wealth. They are, in order of consideration: the installment sale, the private annuity, the gift or sale and leaseback, and the widow's election. Each of them has significant nontax advantages and disadvantages. However, they are used primarily to reduce the parties' overall federal tax burdens.

Each of the devices has attributes that make it more suitable for use in some cases than in others. Of the 4 discussed here, the installment sale and the private annuity resemble each other the most. They are both frequently used to "cap" a client's estate by transferring appreciated property to a younger family member at little or no gift tax cost. Their appeal does not generally lie in the income tax area. In contrast, the gift and leaseback is used primarily to improve the family's income tax position by shifting income from the donor-lessee to the donee-lessor. However, the income tax savings may be offset to some extent by increased transfer tax costs — at least where the donor retains a reversionary interest in the property. The widow's election is primarily a testamentary device, which distinguishes it from the others. It may produce gift and estate tax savings, but the possibility of achieving an overall income tax saving is unlikely.

§9.2. *Legal Ethics*

A lawyer should be sensitive to the conflict-of-interest problems that are inherent in advising both parties to an intrafamily transfer for consideration. In some respects the conflicts are worse in a family setting, where both parties to a transaction may be less alert than they would be in dealing with an unrelated party. It is perfectly acceptable for the same lawyer to represent both parents and children regarding more or less independent estate-planning matters; it is less certain that the same lawyer can adequately represent them when their interests conflict. The parties may be content to have the same lawyer represent them at the time a transaction is planned and they contemplate no difficulties. However, future events could easily cause dissatisfaction. For example, in a private annuity transaction the transferee may complain if the annuitant "lives too long" and the transferee winds up paying more for the property than if it had been purchased in an installment sale. On the other hand, the transferor may complain if the transferee is unable to make annuity payments and the transferor has no security interest in the property. At a minimum the lawyer should point out the existence of the conflicts and the lawyer's inability to represent all parties zealously. Everyone, including the lawyer, is better protected if each party is represented by a separate competent lawyer.

B. THE INSTALLMENT SALE

[T]he term "installment method" means a method under which the income recognized for any taxable year from a disposition is that proportion of the payments received in that year which the gross profit (realized or to be realized when payment is completed) bears to the total contract price. §453(c).

§9.3. General

The installment sale is a very useful device that allows owners of appreciated property to achieve a variety of planning goals. On the nontax side, an installment sale may help retain a unique asset within the family. It is also attractive because the gain on a sale is deferred and taxed ratably as payments are received (or as the purchaser's notes are cancelled) unless the seller elects not to use the installment method of reporting. *See* §453(d). However, recognition of gain by the seller is accelerated in some cases where a related purchaser resells the property or an installment obligation is cancelled or otherwise terminated. *See* §§9.6 to 9.7, *infra*. When property is sold for full and adequate consideration, only the value of the installment obligation is included in the seller's estate — any further appreciation in value of the property is excluded. Thus, an installment sale can effectively freeze the value of the seller's estate. Although the same goals may be achieved through use of a private annuity (Part C, *infra*), the installment sale is superior in several respects. The most important differences between the 2 devices are:

1. The overall cost of the property and the duration of payments are known in the case of an installment sale, but not where the property is exchanged for a private annuity;
2. The seller may retain a security interest in the property in the case of an installment sale, whereas the retention of a security interest will cause a private annuity to be taxed as a closed transaction (*i.e.*, all of the gain will be taxed at the time of sale); and
3. The purchaser may deduct interest payments made in connection with an installment sale, but no part of the payments made under a private annuity is deductible.

The terms of §453 are broad enough to support taxing a private annuity transaction as an installment sale: "For purposes of this section — (1) In general. The term 'installment sale' means a disposition of property where at least 1 payment is to be received after the close of the taxable year in which the disposition occurs." §453(b). The potential application of the installment sales rules to private annuities is also indicated by the extension of the rules to apply to sales where the sales price or the payment period is indefinite. *See* §453(i). However, private annuities may continue to be treated differently. The House Ways and Means Committee Report on the Installment Sales Revision Act of 1980 noted that private annuities were also used to make intrafamily sales of appreciated property. It continued to say that "[t]he bill does not deal directly with this type of arrangement." H.R. Rep. No. 1042, 96th Cong., 2d Sess. n.12 (1980).

The tax consequences of an installment sale should also be compared with those of an inter vivos gift or a disposition at the owner's death. Of course, not all clients are able to make substantial inter vivos gifts, which deprives them of the current use of the property and may require payment of state and federal gift taxes as well. The gift tax cost of transferring an asset is not necessarily reduced by making the gifts over a number of years. The value of the interests retained by the donor may continue to increase in value until they are finally disposed of or the donor dies.

> **Example 9-1.** An unmarried taxpayer, T, owns property worth $100,000, which is appreciating at an annual rate of 10%. A gift of the entire interest to a single donee would result in a taxable gift of $90,000. Instead, T could transfer undivided one-fifth interests to the donee each year for 5 years. Assuming that no discount would be available for a gift of a fractional interest, the taxable gift in the first year would be $10,000 ($20,000 − $10,000). However, the 80% retained by T would be worth $88,000 at the end of the year (80% × $110,000). The next gift would have a value of $22,000 ($\frac{1}{5}$ × $110,000) and so on.

Also, in the case of a gift, the donee usually takes only a carryover basis in the property. In contrast, a person who acquires property from a decedent will have a stepped-up basis determined under §1014. Where the property is retained by the owner until death, the unrealized appreciation in its value will never be taxed for income tax purposes. In general, the gain on an installment sale *will* be taxed at some point. Gain will be taxed upon virtually any disposition of the obligation, whether or not any consideration is received by the seller. Thus, the inter vivos cancellation of an installment obligation and the bequest of an obligation to the obligor are both taxable dispositions. *See* §§453B(f) and 691(a)(5) and §9.6, *infra.* The gain is also taxed if the obligation otherwise becomes unenforceable, as it might if the seller allows the statute of limitations to run with respect to its payment. In that case the seller would also have made a gift. *See* §9.4, *infra.*

§9.4.   Gift Tax Consequences

Where property is transferred for less than adequate and full consideration, then the amount by which the value of the property exceeds the value of the consideration is a gift, except where the sale is made in the ordinary course of business. §2512(b); Reg. §25.2512-8. Accordingly, where the valuation of the property is subject to dispute, the sale price should be based upon a competent appraisal in order to reduce the risk that the transaction involves a gift. Also, the obligation should carry a reasonable rate of interest. An installment obligation with a fixed payment schedule is worth less than its face value if it carries a below-market rate of interest. Gertrude H. Blackburn, 20 T.C. 204 (1953) (gift tax case involving sale of real property to children for notes carrying $2\frac{1}{4}\%$ interest when market rate on similar notes was 4%). A demand note is probably worth its face amount regardless of the rate of interest it bears. *See* Crown v. Commissioner, 585 F.2d 234 (7th Cir. 1978), discussed at §7.23, *supra.* Under §453(f)(4) a demand note is treated as a payment received in the year of sale, which would require the gain to be recognized at that time.

A transfer nominally structured as a sale may be disregarded by the IRS and treated as a gift where it lacks substance. The IRS has frequently asserted that an intrafamily transfer of property in exchange for notes of the transferee is taxable as a gift where the transferor does not intend to enforce the notes. *E.g.,* Rev. Rul. 77-299, 1977-2 C.B. 343 and *see* §7.23, *supra.* It is questionable whether the gift tax outcome should turn upon a subjective matter such as the transferor's intent to forgive the notes in the future. The courts have generally disregarded the transferor's intent and characterized the transfer as a sale where valid, enforceable, interest-bearing notes are given in exchange for property. *See, e.g.,* Estate of J.W. Kelley, 63 T.C. 321 (1974), *nonacq.,* 1977-2 C.B. 2; Selsor R. Haygood, 42 T.C. 936 (1964), *acq. in result,* 1965-1 C.B. 4, *acq. withdrawn and nonacq. substituted,* 1977-2 C.B. 2. The initial transfer of a remainder interest in unimproved, nonincome-producing real property was held to be a gift where the transferor took back noninterest-bearing, unsecured demand notes that she subsequently forgave at the rate of $3,000 per year. Minnie E. Deal, 29 T.C. 730 (1958). Aside from the *Deal* case the IRS has generally been unsuccessful in the courts.

A gift also occurs if the transferor gratuitously transfers the obligation or cancels or forgives it. For this purpose allowing the statute of limitations to run is treated as a forgiveness. Estate of Lang v. Commissioner, 613 F.2d 770 (9th Cir. 1980). Of course, any such disposition of an installment obligation would also trigger recognition of gain by the transferor. *See* §9.6, *infra.* Cancellation of accrued interest alone involves a gift of the interest. Republic Petroleum Corp. v. United States, 397 F. Supp. 900, 917 (E.D. La. 1975), *mod. on other issues,* 613 F.2d 518 (5th Cir. 1980).

§9.5. *Estate Tax Consequences*

Where an installment sale is made for full consideration, the property transferred is not includible in the transferor's estate. Instead, under §2033 the transferor's estate includes the proceeds that were received, which include the fair market value of the installment obligation. For estate tax purposes the value of the obligation may be discounted if it carries a below-market rate of interest. Estate of G.R. Robinson, 69 T.C. 222 (1977) ($1,120,000 unpaid balance of note for installment sale of stock carried 4% interest discounted by stipulation to yield 8½%, or $930,100); *see also* Reg. §20.2031-4.

Neither the value of the transferred property nor the value of the unpaid balance of the purchaser's obligation may be included in the seller's estate where the obligation terminates on the death of the seller. At least 2 cases have reached that result where the sale was bona fide and for full and adequate consideration and the provision for cancellation was bargained for by the parties. Estate of John A. Moss, 74 T.C. 1239 (1980), *acq.,* 1981-1 C.B. 2 (note given in connection with redemption of decedent's stock by corporation, the other stock in which was owned by unrelated employees of the corporation); Ruby Louise Cain, 37 T.C. 185 (1961) (note given in connection with redemption of decedent's stock by corporation, the other stock in which was owned by decedent's son and daughter-in-law). In some respects such a transaction resembles a private annuity. However, unlike an annuity, the termination of the obligation would probably cause the seller's estate to be taxed on the unreported portion of the gain. *See* §9.6, *infra.* Note that the sale of the stock might be treated as a distribution in the nature of a dividend unless it qualifies under one of the exceptions of §302(b). *See* §11.15, *infra.*

If the transferor receives less than full and adequate consideration, the value of the property at the time of the transferor's death may be included in the transferor's estate under §§2035 to 2038. Because of the possibility that the consideration may not equal the value of the property, the transferor should not retain any interests or controls that could cause inclusion under those sections. This rules out sales to trusts over which the transferor retains discretionary powers of distribution. However, in such a case the amount includible is limited to the excess of the value of the property on the appropriate estate tax valuation date over the consideration received by the transferor. §2043(a).

Example 9-2. T sold Blackacre, which was worth $100,000, to a relative, X, for $75,000, of which $25,000 was paid at the time of transfer and $50,000 was represented by a note with a reasonable rate of interest that was payable at the rate of $5,000 annually. The sale involved a gift of $25,000. T died within 3 years of the sale. Blackacre had a value of $150,000 on the valuation date applicable to T's estate. If T had died before 1982, $75,000 of Blackacre's value would be included in T's gross estate under the former provisions of §2035 ($150,000 − $75,000). Where T dies after 1982, none of the post-gift appreciation in the value of Blackacre is includible unless he or she retained an interest sufficient to cause inclusion under §§2036 to 2038. *See* §2035(d)(2). In any case, the value of the cash and note given by X are includible in T's gross estate.

Estate of Transferee. If the transferee's estate is liable for the indebtedness, the value of the property is includible in his or her estate, which is entitled to a deduction under §2053 for the amount of the obligation, including interest accrued to the date of death. Reg. §20.2053-7. However, where only a portion of the property is included in the decedent's estate, only a corresponding portion of the obligation is usually deductible. Estate of Horace K. Fawcett, 64 T.C. 889 (1975), *acq.*, 1978-2 C.B. 2. In most cases the full value of the property is includible in the transferee's gross estate and a deduction is allowable for the balance of the obligation.

If the transferee's estate is not liable for the indebtedness, only the value of the property less the amount of the indebtedness is includible in his or her estate. Reg. §20.2053-7. Thus, only the net value of the property is includible in the transferee's estate where the purchase was financed with a nonrecourse note.

> **Example 9-3.** D purchased Blackacre from X for $100,000, of which D paid $10,000 down and gave a note for $90,000. D and D's estate were personally liable on the note. When D died Blackacre was worth $150,000 and the note had been paid down to $40,000. Under Reg. §20.2053-7 the full value of Blackacre must be included in D's estate, which is entitled to claim a deduction for $40,000. If D's estate were not liable on the note, only the value of Blackacre net of the note would be reported on Schedule A of D's estate tax return.

The ability to enforce the indebtedness against the transferee's estate is important, particularly in the case of nonresidents who are not citizens of the United States. If the loan is without recourse and can be collected only from the property and not from the debtor's estate as a whole, the estate may claim the full amount of the indebtedness as a deduction. Estate of Harcourt Johnstone, 19 T.C. 44 (1952), *acq.*, 1953-1 C.B. 5. Otherwise, the estate may deduct only that proportion of the indebtedness (and other §§2053 and 2054 items) "which the value of that part of the decedent's gross estate situated in the United States at the time of his death bears to the value of the decedent's entire gross estate wherever situated." Reg. §20.2106-2(a)(2).

§9.6. *Income Tax Consequences*

The income tax rules applicable to installment sales were substantially simplified and liberalized by the Installment Sales Revision Act of 1980 (the "1980 Act"). The most significant estate-planning features of the installment sales rules are discussed in the following pages. For a valuable, comprehensive analysis of the rules, *see* Emory & Hjorth, An Analysis of the Changes Made by the Installment Sales Revision Act of 1980, 54 J. Tax. 66, 130 (1981).

The installment sales rules are intended to allow the gain on the sale of real property or a casual sale of personal property to be reported as payments are received. Gain on an installment sale is reported on the installment method unless the transferor makes a timely election not to use that method. §453(d). A taxpayer might elect not to use the method where he or she has current losses that would offset the gain on the sale. The method does not affect the character of gain as capital gain or ordinary income. It also does not affect the way in which losses are reported—the installment method is totally inapplicable to losses.

In general, the installment method applies to any disposition of property where one or more payments will be received in future years. §453(b)(1). However, it does not apply to a sale of depreciable property between the taxpayer and the taxpayer's spouse, the taxpayer and an 80%-owned entity, or two 80%-owned entities. §453(g)(1); §1239(b). By reason of §1239 the gain recognized on a sale of depreciable property to a spouse or a controlled corporation is ordinary income. Similarly, the gain on the sale of a noncapital asset to a controlled partnership is treated as ordinary income. §707(b)(2).

Under the installment method, the gain recognized for a tax year is "that proportion of the payments received in that year that the gross profit (realized or to be realized when payment is completed) bears to the total contract price." §453(c). Sometimes that proportion is called the gross profit ratio, which can also be expressed as a percentage. For purposes of the ratio, gross profit is calculated by reducing the gross selling price by the transferor's adjusted basis and the expenses of sale. For example, if property having a basis of $10,000 is sold for $50,000, the transferor's gross profit is $40,000. The total contract price is the amount the transferor will ultimately receive as a result of the sale, including cash, notes, and other property received, but not encumbrances on the property except to the extent they exceed the transferor's adjusted basis. Except where the property is sold subject to an encumbrance in excess of the transferor's basis, the total contract price is essentially the sale price of the property.

> **Example 9-4.** T sold property to X that had a basis of $50,000, subject to a $20,000 mortgage. The purchase price was $100,000, of which $10,000 was paid in the year of sale and the balance of $70,000 was due in equal annual installments with a reasonable rate of interest over the following 7 years. X gave T a nonnegotiable promissory note for the balance. For purposes of the installment

sale rules, T's gross profit was $50,000 (the $100,000 selling price less T's basis of $50,000). The total contract price is $80,000, which is the total amount T will receive disregarding the mortgage that is within the amount of T's basis. Accordingly, 62.5% of each payment ($50,000 ÷ $80,000) must be recognized as gain.

Payments Received. In general, gain is recognized only as payments are received by the seller, or when the obligation is sold, exchanged, or otherwise disposed of by him or her. For purposes of the installment sale rules "payment" has a broad and somewhat undefined meaning. The planner must be alert to the circumstances under which the seller may be treated as having received payment without having actually received any cash or other property.

The receipt of an evidence of indebtedness of the purchaser is not ordinarily treated as payment. §453(f)(3). However, the receipt of an obligation that is payable on demand does constitute payment. §453(f)(4)(A). The receipt of a readily tradeable obligation issued by a corporation or government or political subdivision thereof is also treated as payment. §453(f)(4)(B). The following paragraph reviews some other situations that have been found to involve the receipt of payment by the seller.

Security Interests and Escrow Accounts. The transferor's retention of a security interest in the property does not constitute a payment or otherwise jeopardize the application of the installment sale method. However, funds deposited in an escrow account for future distribution to the transferor are considered to be a payment unless there is a substantial restriction, other than the passage of time, upon the transferor's right to receive the sale proceeds. Rev. Rul. 73-451, 1973-2 C.B. 158. Thus, "the substitution of the escrow deposit for the deed of trust as collateral for the installment sale obligation represents payment of the remaining unpaid balance of the obligation." Rev. Rul. 77-294, 1977-2 C.B. 173, 174. In order to qualify as a substantial restriction upon the transferor's right to the proceeds, the provision "must serve a bona fide purpose of the purchaser, that is, a real and definite restriction placed on the seller or a specific economic benefit conferred on the purchaser. In [Rebecca J. Murray, 28 B.T.A. 624 (1933), *acq.*, XII-2 C.B. 10 (1933)], for example, receipt of the payments from the escrow account was contingent on the sellers refraining from entering a competing business for a period of five years." Rev. Rul. 79-91, 1979-1 C.B. 179.

Property Subject to Encumbrance. Where an existing mortgage is assumed by the purchaser, the mortgage is treated as a payment received only to the extent it exceeds the transferor's basis. That treatment is consistent with the recognition of gain when the owner makes a gift of property that is subject to encumbrances in excess of its basis. *See* §7.13, *supra*. Along the same line, the IRS has ruled that in the case of a casual sale of personal property, the buyer's assumption and payment of secured and general unsecured liabilities is not considered to be a payment received by the seller if the liabilities were incurred in the ordinary course of business and not to avoid the pre-1980 Act requirement that the initial payment not exceed 30% of the selling price. Rev. Rul. 73-555, 1973-2 C.B. 159.

Where the mortgage assumed by the buyer exceeds the seller's basis, the payment of commissions and other expenses of sale may affect the amount of payments received in the year of sale. Under the regulations, those items reduce the gross profit but not the amount of payments received by the seller. Reg. §§1.453-1(b), -4(c). However, in the Ninth Circuit selling expenses are added to the seller's basis. Kirschenmann v. Commissioner, 488 F.2d 270 (9th Cir. 1973). An increase in the seller's basis reduces the amount of the payments received in one year of sale by reducing the amount by which the mortgage assumed by the buyer exceeds the seller's basis. The IRS has announced that it will not follow the *Kirschenmann* case. Rev. Rul. 74-384, 1974-2 C.B. 152.

Inter Vivos Disposition of Obligation. Gain or loss is usually recognized whenever the seller sells, exchanges, or otherwise disposes of the installment obligation. §453B. However, the IRS does concede that the transfer of an obligation to the trustee of a trust is not a disposition if the income of the trust is taxable to the transferor under the grantor trust rules. Rev. Rul. 74-613, 1974-2 C.B. 153. Accordingly, the installment sale rules should not deter the holder of an installment obligation from creating a revocable trust.

For estate-planning purposes perhaps the most important rule is one that treats the cancellation of an installment obligation as a taxable disposition. §453B(f). When a note is cancelled or otherwise becomes unenforceable, the seller is treated as having received the full face amount of the obligation where the obligor is a related person. §453B(f)(2). The term "related person" is discussed in the next section. §9.7, *infra.* This provision reverses Miller v. Usry, 160 F. Supp. 368 (W.D. La. 1958), which held that a father's forgiveness of his son's installment note did not constitute a disposition of the note for income tax purposes. Where the obligor is not a related party, gain or loss is limited to the difference between the seller's basis and the fair market value of the obligation. §453B(a), (f)(1).

Example 9-5. T sold Blackacre, which had a basis of $10,000, to X for $100,000, represented by an interest-bearing note on which no principal payments were due until 5 years following the sale. T gave the note to X before any principal payments had been made. If X is a related party, T will recognize a gain of $90,000 in the year the note becomes unenforceable by reason of the gift. If X is not a related party, T will recognize gain in an amount equal to the excess of the fair market value of the note over his or her basis in it.

Disposition at Death. In general, the rules regarding the inter vivos disposition of an installment obligation do not apply to the transmission of an installment obligation at death. §453B(c). Instead, the unreported gain attributable to an installment obligation is treated as an item of income in respect of a decedent. §691(a)(4). As such the gain component is barred by §1014(c) from acquiring a new basis by reason of the holder's death. For that reason the person who receives an installment obligation from a decedent is taxed on payments in the same manner the decedent would have been. §691(a)(1)(B). However, for income tax purposes, the seller's successor is allowed a deduction for the portion of the federal and state death taxes paid by the seller's estate with respect to the unreported gain. §691(c). For purposes of computing the 60% long-term capital gains deduction (§1202), the amount of the gain is first reduced by the amount of the deduction allowable for federal and state death taxes. §691(c)(4). The application of these rules is illustrated in the following example.

> **Example 9-6.** T bequeathed an installment note of an unrelated party to a child, C. The note had a value in T's estate equal to its face amount, $20,000, of which $10,000 was attributable to the unreported long-term capital gain. T's estate paid $4,000 in estate tax with respect to the unreported gain. If C receives payment of the entire amount due on the note in one year, $20,000, C must include the full $10,000 gain in gross income. However, C is entitled to a $4,000 deduction for the estate tax paid with respect to the gain. The 60% long-term capital gain deduction is based upon the $6,000 excess of the gain over the death taxes. Thus, only $2,400 of the gain is ultimately subject to tax.

The rules cannot be avoided by bequeathing the obligation to the obligor or providing in the seller's will for cancellation of the obligation. Under the 1980 Act, any cancellation of the obligation or its transmission to the obligor triggers the recognition of gain "by the estate of the decedent (or, if held by a person other than the decedent before the death of the decedent, by such person)." §691(a)(5). Where the decedent and the obligor are related parties, the obligation is treated as having a value that is not less than its face amount.

> **Example 9-7.** T sold capital gain property to a related party, P, in exchange for P's note that was payable at the end of 10 years. T died prior to the payment of the note, which T bequeathed to P.

Under §691(a) the bequest of the note to P, a related obligor, requires T's estate to recognize all of the unreported gain on the sale. The same result would follow if the obligation were cancelled by T's will. Of course, no gain would be recognized by T's estate if the note were bequeathed to a person other than the obligor.

Because of this rule it is particularly important to plan carefully for the transmission of the installment obligation of family members. For example, the obligation might be bequeathed to the obligor's children or to a trust for their benefit instead of being left to the obligor. Even where the obligations will pass to the obligors, the tax cost can be reduced by cancelling or distributing them during a year in which the estate either has capital losses or other deductions to offset the gain or has little or no other income.

Imputed Interest (§483). Intrafamily installment sale transactions must be planned with the imputed interest rules of §483 in mind. In general, those rules are designed to prevent the parties from converting the portion of deferred payments that would otherwise constitute interest into capital gain by increasing the purchase price and eliminating any provision for payment of interest. Thus a seller cannot treat the full amount of deferred payments as the proceeds of sale and none of it as interest.

Deferred payments made with respect to contracts entered into on or after July 1, 1981, are considered to include unstated interest of 10% simple interest compounded semiannually unless they provide for at least 9% simple interest. Reg. §§1.483-1(c)(2)(ii)(C), (d)(1)(ii)(C). From July 24, 1975, until September 29, 1980, the rates were 7 and 6% respectively. Reg. §1.483-1(c)(2)(ii)(B), (d)(1)(ii)(B). The regulations also include discount tables that are used both to determine whether the requisite test is satisfied and to calculate the amount of each payment that constitutes imputed interest. Under a special provision added by the 1981 Act, imputed interest on $500,000 of the proceeds of a sale by an individual to a member of his or her family is limited to 7% compounded semiannually. §483(g). For this purpose the term "family" has the same meaning it does in §267(c)(4). However, the limit does not apply to the extent the sales price for such sale (or sales) between the same individuals exceeds $500,000 for the calendar year.

Section 483 only applies to payments that are due more than 6 months after a sale or exchange of property, one or more of which is due more than one year after the transaction. §483(c)(1)(A). Accordingly, no interest is imputed if all payments are due within one year of the sale. Reg. §1.483-1(b). Also, insofar as the seller is concerned, the rules do not apply if all of the gain would be ordinary income. §483(f)(3). However, the interest may be imputed whether the sale results in a gain or a loss.

That is, interest may be imputed on deferred payments when a sale results in a loss just as it would in the case of a sale at a gain.

§9.7.   Resale by Related Person

Prior to 1980 the installment sale was often used to transfer appreciated property to a family member or to the trustee of a trust established by the transferor, who would promptly sell the property for its full market value. In most cases neither the original transferor nor the related buyer was required to recognize any gain at the time of the resale. *See, e.g.,* Rushing v. Commissioner, 441 F.2d 593 (5th Cir. 1971); William D. Pityo, 70 T.C. 225 (1978). If the resale did not involve a payment to the original seller, the resale usually did not require him or her to recognize any gain. The related seller usually had no gain on the resale because his or her basis in the property was fixed by the installment sale. In effect, the installment sale technique allowed a family group to realize the gain without subjecting it to current taxation.

The 1980 Act does not directly prohibit the use of the installment method of reporting gain on sales to related parties. Instead, it provides that the disposition of the property by a related purchase triggers recognition of gain by the original transferor. §453(e). In general, recognition is not triggered where the resale of property other than marketable securities occurs more than 2 years after the installment sale. Where the resale rule applies, gain is recognized by the original transferor only to the extent the amount realized on the resale exceeds the payments made on the original transaction. To that extent the gain flows through and is taxed to the original transferor as if the original transferor received the proceeds of the resale. If the original transferor is required to recognize gain because of a resale, any later payments received by the original transferor are not taxed until they equal the amount realized from the resale that triggered the acceleration of gain. §453(e)(5).

"Related Person." For purposes of §453 the term "related person" means one whose stock would be attributed to the original transferor under §318(a), excluding paragraph (4). §453(f)(1). Accordingly, the term extends to spouses, children, grandchildren, and parents, but not brothers and sisters. The term also includes certain entities in which the transferor has an interest. The House Ways and Means Committee Report states that "the principles of the general corporate stock ownership attribution rules (Code sec. 318) will apply in determining the related party status of partnerships, trusts, and estates." H.R. Rep. No. 1042, 96th Cong., 2d Sess. 14 (1980). Under those rules the trustee of a trust would be treated as a related party if the original transferor's spouse, children, granchildren, or parents were beneficiaries.

What Dispositions Constitute Resales? In general, the resale rule applies to voluntary dispositions made by the related party unless it is established to the satisfaction of the IRS that none of the dispositions had the avoidance of federal income tax as one of its principal purposes. §453(e)(7). Thus, the recognition of gain by the original transferor normally will be accelerated if the resale violates the basic rules. However, an exception insulates a corporation's sale of stock that it had purchased in an installment sale. §453(e)(6)(A). Also, a disposition following the death of the original transferor or the related party is not treated as a resale. §453(e)(6)(C).

Unfortunately, the 1980 Act does not provide any guidance regarding the application of the nonavoidance exception to other voluntary transfers. According to the House Ways and Means Committee Report the regulations will provide definitive rules concerning its application. From the Report it appears that most gifts and transfers to controlled corporations or partnerships will not constitute resales:

> In appropriate cases, it is anticipated that the regulations and rulings under the nontax avoidance exception will deal with certain tax-free transfers which normally would not be treated as a second disposition of the property, e.g., charitable transfers, gift transfers, and transfers to a controlled corporation or a partnership. H.R. Rep. No. 1042, 96th Cong., 2d Sess. 14 (1980).

However, a related party should be very cautious about making any gift of the property until the IRS position is established. A related party should also be slow to make an installment sale of the property, which the Report indicates will be treated as a resale if it "would permit significant deferral of recognition of gain from the initial sale when proceeds from the resale are being collected sooner." *Id.* at 14.

Involuntary Transfers. The 1980 Act specifically exempts gain arising from an involuntary conversion if the original transfer occurred before the threat or imminence of the conversion. §453(e)(6)(B). The Report also indicates that other involuntary conversions will fall within the nonavoidance exception, including foreclosure by a creditor of the related party and bankruptcy of the related party. *Id.* at 14.

Two-Year Rule. The resale rule does not apply to dispositions made more than 2 years following the original transfer except in the case of marketable securities. §453(e)(2)(A). Under §453(f)(2), "the term 'marketable securities' means any security for which, as of the date of disposition, there was a market on an established securities market or otherwise." The running of the 2-year period is suspended for any period during which the related person's risk of loss is substantially diminished by holding a "put" with respect to the property, by a short sale, or by any other transaction. §453(e)(2)(B). In the case of marketable securities the resale rule applies until the installment obligation is satisfied or one of the parties to the original transfer dies.

Example 9-8. T sold marketable securities with a basis of $20,000 and a fair market value of $100,000 to his son, S, in exchange for a $100,000 nonnegotiable promissory note that carried a reasonable rate of interest. Under the terms of the note no principal payments were due for 10 years. S sold the securities for $100,000 cash immediately after he received them from T. Under the resale rule T must recognize the full $80,000 gain in the year in which S, a related party, sold them. S realized no gain on the sale because his cost basis in the securities was $100,000. Any subsequent payments received by T are tax free since all of the gain has been taxed to him already under the resale rule. If the original transfer had involved property other than marketable securities, T would not have been required to recognize any gain on a resale made more than two years after the original transfer.

Problem 9-1. X sold a parcel of unimproved land, Blackacre, to his daughter, D, for $100,000. D paid $10,000 at the time of closing and gave X 9 $10,000 notes, one of which was due in each of the following 9 years and which included a reasonable rate of interest. The notes were secured by a mortgage on Blackacre and were worth their face amounts. X had a basis of $40,000 in Blackacre, which he had inherited several years before the sale to D.

(1) How much gain, if any, must X report in the year of the sale?

(2) What are the income, gift, and estate tax consequences if X gave all 9 of the notes (a) to D outright; (b) to D in his will; (c) to the H Hospital; or (d) to his son, S?

(3) Is the gain accelerated if X transfers the notes to a trust of which he is treated as the owner under §673?

(4) What are the income tax consequences for X and D if (a) D sells Blackacre for $100,000 cash within a year following her purchase of Blackacre from X; (b) D gives Blackacre to the State Park Department immediately following the purchase; or (c) D dies a year after the purchase and Blackacre is sold by her executor for $100,000 cash?

Problem 9-2. W owns a ranch, Happy Acres, which has a basis of $100,000 and a current value of $1,500,000. Prior to September 29, 1980, W gave State University an option to purchase Happy Acres from W for $100,000 down and a payment of $100,000 in each year for the following 19 years. Under Reg. §1.483-1(g), Table

VI, the deferred payments have a present value of about $1,000,000 — the $900,000 balance that W will receive constitutes imputed interest at 7%.

(1) What is the total amount of gain realized by W on the sale under the bargain sale rules? *See* §8.28, *supra.*

(2) What is the total charitable contribution made by W in the year of sale?

(3) How much of the first $100,000 payment that W will receive at the time of sale must be reported as gain?

(4) How much of the later payments will consist of return of capital, gain, and imputed interest?

C. THE PRIVATE ANNUITY

It is also well established that the substance of a transaction rather than its form determines the tax consequences of a transaction unless the statute indicates that form is to govern. . . . "This principle is peculiarly applicable to annuities and trusts because they are easily susceptible of manipulation so as to create illusion." . . . Indeed, we have frequently viewed a series of related transactions as a whole and found that what was in form a transfer of property to a trust in exchange for an annuity was in substance a trust of which the "annuitant" was a grantor-owner or beneficiary. Esther La Fargue, 73 T.C. 40, 53 (1979).

§9.8. *General*

A private annuity is usually entered into between family members in order to achieve gift and estate tax savings. It may be used instead of the installment sale to lower the tax cost of retaining a unique asset within the family. However, the tax and nontax risks of using a private annuity are formidable enough to deter most planners and clients. As indicated above, the new installment sale rules may be extended to apply to private annuities. Such an extension might improve some aspects of the transaction (*e.g.*, perhaps the seller-annuitant could retain a security interest in the property without disadvantage).

In its simplest terms a private annuity involves the transfer of property from one person to another in return for a promise to pay the transferor a specified periodic sum for an agreed period. Samuel v. Commissioner, 306 F.2d 682 (1st Cir. 1962). If the transaction is properly structured, the initial transfer does not give rise to any current income or gift tax liabilities and no part of the property is includible in the transferor's estate. Usually appreciated property is transferred by an older to a younger family member. Unfortunately, the income tax rules applicable to such a transfer are not entirely clear.

Where the transfer is made to the trustee of a trust created by the transferor, the income, gift, and estate tax goals may not be achieved. The quotation at the beginning of this section fairly indicates the risk that the IRS and the courts will treat the transaction as a trust in which the grantor has retained a life interest and not as an annuity. If the transaction is treated as a trust, the income is taxable to the grantor under §677(a) (Esther La Fargue, 73 T.C. 40 (1979)); the transfer of the remainder in the trust is taxable as a gift (Lazarus v. Commissioner, 513 F.2d 824 (9th Cir. 1975)); and the trust principal is includible in the grantor's estate (§2036). The use of the transferred property as the source of annuity payments was apparently considered the most significant factor by the courts in *Lazarus* and *La Fargue*. Indeed, in *La Fargue* the Tax Court stated that "we have serious doubts whether section 72 rather than the grantor trust provisions of sections 671 through 677 would apply to any situation where the assets transferred to the trust are *the* engine designed to fuel the so-called annuity payments." 73 T.C. at 58. An asserted private annuity transaction was also treated as a transfer to a trust with a retained life interest in Sidney B. Stern, 77 T.C. 614 (1981).

§9.9. *Nontax Considerations*

As mentioned above, a private annuity may help preserve a farm, a business enterprise, or other unique asset within the family and free the transferor from the burdens and risks of management. A forced sale of the property to an outsider may be avoided if the family member-transferee can afford to make the necessary payments. However, the overall tax savings may be diminished if the transferee must sell the property in order to make payments or to meet other expenses.

The uncertain duration of the payments may be a source of financial problems as well as family discord. Where a parent and one child are parties to a private annuity, the arrangements may cause some resentment on the part of the other children — particularly if the parent does not survive as long as expected according to the mortality tables that were used to calculate the amount of the annuity payments. In that case the child-purchaser enjoys a windfall of sorts. On the other hand, the child-purchaser may become resentful if the annuitant "lives too long." Before entering into a private annuity, the parties should consider very carefully both the financial and the emotional aspects of the transaction. Significant risks also exist because the transferee's promise must be unsecured in order to defer the taxation of the gain element. First, the property may be entirely expended during the annuitant's lifetime and the transferee will be unable to make the required payments. Expenditure could be caused by tort claims, business reverses, or other events. Second, continuation of the payments may be threatened if the transferee predeceases the annuitant. The obligation to continue the payments could deplete the transferee's estate, particularly if the annuitant lives longer than expected. However, these problems can be relieved to some degree by insuring the transferee's life. Third, the planned retention of the property within the family could be threatened by dissolution of the transferee's marriage. For example, the divorce court may allocate the property between the transferee and the transferee's spouse. *See, e.g.,* Stanger v. Stanger, 571 P.2d 1126 (Idaho 1977) (ranch received by husband in exchange for annuity is community property).

Substantial legal costs and other expenses may be incurred in connection with a private annuity. Because of the complex and evolving nature of the tax rules, it is almost always necessary for the planner to do some legal research. Additional time is also required to project the tax consequences and to prepare the necessary documents. The uncertainty of the tax rules and the overall complexity of the transaction may cause the fees to be greater in the case of a private annuity than for an inter vivos trust or an installment sale. As noted above, independent representation of the transferor and transferee is generally desirable because of the inherent conflict in their economic interests. It may also be desirable to obtain a professional appraisal of any property for which there is not a ready market.

§9.10. *Income Tax Consequences of Transfer*

No gain or loss arises at the time of the initial transaction (*i.e.,* when the property is transferred for an unsecured private annuity). According to the courts the transferee's obligation cannot be valued: "Where both the annuitant's life span and the obligor's ability to pay are uncertain no fair market value should be ascribed to the contract or obligation." Commissioner v. Kann's Estate, 174 F.2d 357, 359 (3d Cir. 1949). Ordinarily gain or loss in a private annuity transaction is reported by the annuitant as annuity payments are received. *See* §9.11, *infra.*

The same rules apply in the case of an annuity issued by a corporation which writes annuity contracts infrequently. *See* 212 Corp., 70 T.C. 788, 799 (1978). In contrast, gain is recognized immediately by the transferor where appreciated property is transferred to a corporation, trust, or other organization that, from time to time, issues annuity contracts. Rev. Rul. 62-136, 1962-2 C.B. 12. In Dix v. Commissioner, 392 F.2d 313 (4th Cir. 1968) the court held that the ruling only applied to corporations that wrote enough annuity contracts to get a good spread of the actuarial risk.

In 2 cases a bare majority of the Tax Court held that the gain on a private annuity must be reported in the year of the transfer if the annuity is adequately secured. 212 Corp., 70 T.C. 788, 802-803 (1978); Estate of Lloyd G. Bell, 60 T.C. 469 (1973). According to those cases, where appreciated property is transferred for an annuity that has an actuarially determinable value in excess of the transferor's basis, "the exchange represents a 'closed transaction' and the resulting gain is taxable in the year of exchange." 212 Corp., *supra* at 803. Presumably this approach would also apply where the transfer results in a loss. That is, where property with a fair market value below its adjusted basis is transferred in exchange for a secured annuity the loss would be deductible in the year of the exchange, subject to the other provisions of the Code, particularly §267. In the long run it seems likely that the Tax Court rule will be rejected in favor of one that allows the annuitant to report a pro rata part of each payment as gain. That approach was suggested by the dissenting judges in *Bell* and 212 Corp., who pointed out that the regulations provide for proration where appreciated property is transferred to a charitable organization in exchange for an annuity. *See* §8.29, *supra.* The mere fact that the annuity is secured should not cause such a radically different tax result.

Where the annuity is secured, it is unclear whether the transferor could invoke the revised installment sale rules to avoid reporting all of the gain in the year of transfer. As mentioned above, Congress apparently did not intend that private annuity transactions should be subject to the installment sales rules. *See* §9.3, *supra.*

§9.11.   Income Taxation of Annuitant

The tax treatment of annuity payments is simple enough where no gain results from the transfer of property in exchange for an annuity. That will occur, for example, when cash or property with a basis equal to its fair market value is transferred in exchange for an annuity. Since no gain results from the transfer, each annuity payment will consist of only 2 elements — a nontaxable recovery of capital, and a fully taxable annuity element. The amount allocated to each element depends upon the exclusion ratio, which is simply the investment in the contract divided by the expected return. In these "no gain" cases, the investment in the contract is the amount of cash or the value of the property transferred. The expected return is the amount of the annual payment multiplied by the life expectancy of the annuitant as determined under the first table in Reg. §1.72-9. *See* §8.28, *supra.*

> **Example 9-9.** A 65-year-old female, F, transferred cash of $100,000 to her daughter, D, in exchange for D's unsecured promise to make a payment of $10,752.11 to F each year for life.

The transaction does not involve any gift because the annuity has a value of exactly $100,000 under Table A(2), Reg. §20.2031-10. Therefore, the investment in the contract is $100,000. According to Table I, Reg. §1.72-9, F's life expectancy is 18.2 years. Thus, the expected return is $195,688.40 ($10,752.11 × 18.2). The exclusion ratio applicable to each payment is 51.1% ($100,000 ÷ $195,688.40). W is entitled to exclude $5,494.50 of each payment as a return of capital for however long she lives. The other $5,257.61 is taxed as ordinary income.

The transaction described in Example 9-9 would involve a gift from F to D if the value of the property transferred exceeded the value of the annuity. In that case, F might incur some gift tax liability. *See* §9.13, *infra*. Also, D's basis in the gift portion of the property would be determined under §1015. *See also* Rev. Rul. 55-119, 1955-1 C.B. 352.

The proper income treatment of annuity payments is less clear where appreciated property is transferred to a noncharity in exchange for an unsecured annuity. In this case the annuitant is also entitled to exclude a portion of each payment based upon the exclusion ratio. However, the IRS has ruled that the investment in the contract is limited to the transferor's adjusted basis in the property transferred in exchange for the annuity and not its fair market value. Rev. Rul. 69-74, 1969-1 C.B. 43. It reasoned that "[s]ince the amount of the gain is not taxed in full at the time of the transaction, such amount does not represent a part of the 'premiums or other consideration' paid for the annuity contract." According to the IRS, each payment is initially composed of 3 elements: a tax-free return of capital, a capital gain element, and a fully taxable ordinary income element. The tax-free element is determined by dividing the investment in the contract (the adjusted basis in the property transferred) by the expected return. The capital gain element is calculated by dividing the gain (the value of the annuity determined under §20.2031-10 less the adjusted basis in the property) by the life expectancy of the annuitant according to Table I, Reg. §1.72-9. All of the gain is taxed if the annuitant survives as long as expected under the mortality table. According to Rev. Rul. 69-74 the second element of any further payments is taxed as ordinary income. Finally, the remainder of each payment is taxed as ordinary income (total payment − (return of capital + capital gain)).

Example 9-10. The facts are the same as those of Example 9-9, except that F transferred securities with a basis of $10,000 and a fair market value of $100,000 in exchange for the annuity payments of $10,752.11 each year. Under the approach taken in Rev. Rul. 69-74, the exclusion ratio would be 5.11%, which would allow F to exclude $549.43 of each $10,752.11 annual payment as a return of capital. F would be required to report 45.99% of each payment ($4,945.05) as capital gain until the full $90,000 gain is reported. Thereafter that portion of each payment would be reported as ordinary income. Throughout her life F must report the third element of each payment ($5,257.63) as ordinary income. The ordinary income element is the amount by which each payment exceeds the return of capital and capital gain elements ($10,752.11 − ($549.43 + $4,945.05)).

Rev. Rul. 69-74 conflicts with the 1939 Code rules as set forth in Rev. Rul. 239, 1953-2 C.B. 53. Perhaps more important, it also conflicts with the present manner of taxing payments received under a gift annuity issued by a charitable organization. Reg. §1.1011-2(c), *Example* (8). See §8.29, *supra,* for a discussion of the gift annuity rules. The exclusion ratio for gift annuities is higher because it is calculated by dividing the fair market value of the property transferred by the expected return. A ratable part of the gain realized on the transaction is reported out of each payment received throughout the annuitant's life expectancy. After all of the gain has been reported on a gift annuity the full amount of the annual exclusion portion is nontaxable. This contrasts sharply with Rev. Rul. 69-74, which taxes the gain portion of each payment as ordinary income after all of the gain has been reported.

A transfer of appreciated property involves a gift from the transferor to the transferee-obligor where the value of the property transferred exceeds the value of the annuity. Unless the exchange was an ordinary business transaction Rev. Rul. 69-74 requires the excess to be disregarded in determining the income tax consequences to the transferor. The gift portion is significant when it comes to determining the transferee's basis for purposes of determining gain or loss or computing depreciation. *See* Rev. Rul. 55-119, 1955-1 C.B. 352 and §9.12, *infra.*

§9.12. Income Taxation of Transferee

The transferee is not allowed any income tax deduction for payments made to the annuitant even though the annuitant must report part of each payment as income. Given the existing background, it is doubtful that a deduction would be allowed, even if the parties designated part of each payment as "interest." "Most courts hold that the entire amount of each annuity payment constitutes a payment of the purchase price of the assets received in exchange for the promise to pay the annuity. Thus the payments constitute capital expenditures, no part of which is excludable [deductible] as 'interest on indebtedness.'" Dix v. Commissioner, 392 F.2d 313, 318 (4th Cir. 1968). The denial of a deduction is consistent with the method for determining the transferee's basis in the assets, which takes into account the total amount of payments made by the transferee. In contrast, in the case of an installment sale, the actual or imputed interest is deductible by the purchaser.

The general rules for calculating depreciation and gain or loss are set out in Rev. Rul. 55-119, 1955-1 C.B. 352, which was issued under the 1939 Code. However, its rules also apply to transactions arising under the 1954 Code. Rev. Rul. 72-81, 1972-1 C.B. 98.

Depreciation. Initially, the allowance for depreciation is based upon the value of the annuity contract, determined under Reg. §20.2031-10. Any annuity payments made in excess of that value are added to the basis of the property for the purpose of determining future depreciation. Once the annuitant dies, the depreciation allowance is fixed by the total amount of annuity payments made reduced by the amount of depreciation deductions previously allowed.

Example 9-11. A 70-year-old female, F, transferred nondepreciable property worth $20,000 and depreciable property that was worth $80,000 and had a useful life of 50 years and a salvage value of $10,000 to her daughter, D, in exchange for D's promise to pay her an annuity of $12,700 per year. Using Table A(2) from Reg. §20.2031-10, the value of the annuity is $100,627.18. D is entitled to claim a depreciation allowance of $1,450.03 per year for the first 7 years or until F earlier dies, calculated as follows:

$$\frac{\frac{\$80,000}{\$100,000} \times \$100,627.18 - \$10,000}{50} = \$1,450.03$$

If F died after 5 years, the future depreciation allowance would be $745.55 per year, determined as follows:

$$\frac{\frac{\$80,000}{\$100,000} \times \$63,500 - (\$10,000 + \$7,250.15)}{45} = \$745.55$$

In the latter calculation the figure of $63,500 is the total amount of payments actually made to F and $7,250.15 is the total amount of depreciation deductions allowed for the period prior to F's death.

Gain or Loss. Where the property is disposed of by the obligor after the annuitant's death, for the purpose of determining gain or loss its basis is the total of the payments made under the contract, less the total amount of depreciation allowable to the transferor. Thus, in example 9-11, if D sold the property for $100,000 one year after F's death, her gain would be $44,495.70:

Sale price		$100,000.00
Less:		
Payments to F	$63,500.00	
Minus depreciation	7,995.70	55,504.30
Gain		$ 44,495.70

The computation of gain or loss is more complicated where the property is disposed of prior to the annuitant's death. For the purpose of determining gain the transferee's basis is the total of payments made under the contract (reduced by the total amount of allowable depreciation) plus the value of future payments due under the contract determined in accordance with Reg. §20.2031-10. *See, e.g.,* LR 8102029. When it comes to calculating the amount of a loss, the basis is limited to the total amount of payments made to the time of sale reduced by the total amount of depreciation allowable. Additional gain or loss may be recognized by the transferee depending upon how many future payments are made by the time of the annuitant's death. For example, further gain is recognized if the annuitant dies before receiving payments equal to the amount of the basis used for purposes of computing gain. In the case of a disposition that gives rise to a recognized loss, any subsequent payments made to the annuitant give rise to losses in the year or years made.

§9.13. Gift Tax Consequences

Where the value of the property transferred exceeds the actuarially determined value of the annuity, the transfer involves a gift unless it is an ordinary business transaction. Rev. Rul. 69-74, 1969-1 C.B. 43. In most circumstances any gift to the transferee will qualify for the annual exclusion. *See* §2503(b). Of course, the transferor makes a gift to the annuitant where the annuity is payable to a person other than the transferor. Such a gift qualifies for the annual exclusion where the commencement of the annuity payments is not deferred. *See* Reg. §25.2503-3(b). The transaction will result in a gift by the transferee if the value of the annuity exceeds the value of the property transferred. Here again, the annual exclusion should be available if the annuity is payable currently.

Private annuity transactions are usually planned to avoid any gift element and to avoid inclusion in the transferor's estate. Accordingly, the property to be transferred should be valued carefully and the amount of the annuity determined in accordance with the proper table of Reg. §20.2031-10. Of course, the economic realities of the transaction must be considered, including the impact of income taxes on the transferor and transferee.

§9.14. Estate Tax Consequences

Significant estate tax problems are likely to arise in 2 situations: (1) where the value of the property transferred exceeds the value of the annuity and (2) where the annuity is payable to another person after the death of the transferor. In other situations the threat of inclusion in the transferor's estate is virtually eliminated because of the adequacy of the consideration received in exchange for the property transferred (*i.e.*, the value of the annuity equals or exceeds the value of the property transferred). Thus, inclusion under §§2035 and 2036 is not much of a threat in most cases. Even where the value of the property transferred exceeds the value of the annuity, the amount includible is reduced by the value of the annuity at the time of transfer. §2043(a).

Where the annuity is payable to another person after the transferor's death, the amount includible in the transferor's estate is determined under §2039. The annuity is first valued under Reg. §20.2031-10. Next, the portion of the annuity value includible in the decedent's estate is determined by the proportion of the purchase price that he or she contributed. §2031(a), (b). Thus, if the decedent had paid one-half of the cost of the annuity, only one-half of its value would be included in his or her gross estate.

The property transferred to the obligor is includible in the obligor's estate. Of course, if the obligor predeceases the annuitant, the obligor's estate is entitled to a deduction for the actuarial value of the payments it is required to make to the annuitants. Estate of Charles H. Hart, 1 T.C. 989 (1943). However, where the annuitant dies prior to the time the obligor's estate tax return is filed, the deduction may be limited to the amount of the payments actually made. Estate of Chesterton v. United States, 551 F.2d 278 (Ct. Cl.), *cert. denied*, 434 U.S. 835 (1977).

> **Problem 9-3.** A 70-year-old widow, W, proposes to transfer the farm she owns to her daughter, D, in exchange for an unsecured private annuity. The farm has a basis of $200,000 and a fair market value of $600,000. How much would the annual payments have to be in order for the transaction to involve no gift element? Assuming that Rev. Rul. 69-74 will apply, what would be the income, gift, and estate tax consequences of W's transfer of the farm to D in exchange for an annuity of that amount? If the farm generates an annual net pretax income equal to 5% of its value, will the income from the farm be sufficient to support the annual payments that D

must make to W? What other nontax factors should D and W consider before entering into the proposed transaction? How would the income tax treatment of the transaction differ if it were taxed as under the installment sale rules?

D.   THE GIFT OR SALE AND LEASEBACK

§9.15.   General

The transfer and leaseback of business property is a popular way for individuals with large personal service incomes, such as doctors or dentists, to attempt to shift income to lower bracket family members. The typical plan involves the transfer of property that is used in the transferor's business to the trustee of a short-term trust, who leases the property back to the transferor. If the plan succeeds, the rental payments are deductible by the transferor and are taxed at low rates to the trust or its beneficiaries. The main problem is the potential of a challenge by the IRS, which continues to oppose the deductibility of payments made to short-term trusts. The deductibility of the payments has appeared on the IRS's National List of Prime Issues. *See* CCH 1980 Stand. Fed. Tax Rep., Index ¶195

The initial transfer may be structured as a gift or a sale, depending on the particular circumstances of the parties. It usually takes the form of a gift to a short-term trust in order to allow the transferor to retain a reversionary interest in the property. However, the chance that the IRS and the courts will permit the rental payments to be deducted is vastly greater where the lessee does not serve as trustee and does not retain any interest in the property. For example, in one case the IRS denied a deduction for rental payments made while the lessee held a reversionary interest in the property, but allowed a deduction for rental payments made after the lessee relinquished his reversionary interest. C. James Mathews, 61 T.C. 12 (1973), 15, *rev'd*, 520 F.2d 323 (5th Cir. 1975), *cert. denied*, 424 U.S. 967 (1976). In some instances the IRS has challenged the deduction although there was an independent trustee and the transferor did not retain a reversionary interest. *E.g.*, Skemp v. Commissioner, 168 F.2d 598 (7th Cir. 1948).

Deductions were also challenged, but allowed, in one case where the transferees were minors and the transferor acted as their guardian. Brooke v. United States, 468 F.2d 1155 (9th Cir. 1972). The probability that deductions will not be allowed is also greater where the property is sold to a trust or another family member. Of course, the gift tax cost of an outright transfer and the economic effects of not retaining an interest in the property must also be considered.

An installment sale and leaseback is a variation on the theme that involves little or no gift tax cost. However, a sale transaction is ordinarily more complicated and could require the transferor to report a gain on the transaction. The gain would be taxable as ordinary income to the extent it involved depreciation recapture under §§1245 and 1250. An installment sale and leaseback transaction may also involve annual forgiveness of the installment notes, as in Hudspeth v. Commissioner, 509 F.2d 1224 (9th Cir. 1975). In *Hudspeth* the parents avoided the 160-acre limit on the quantity of federally irrigated land that may be owned by one person (320 acres by a husband and wife) by making installment sales of the excess acreage to their children. The children in turn leased the purchased property to their parents. Installment payments were made by the children in part with rental payments from the parents and the balance with cash gifts from the parents. The Tax Court held that the original transfers to the children were not bona fide sales and, therefore, constituted gifts of the entire interest in the property. On appeal the Ninth Circuit reversed — holding that the transfers were sales and not gifts. "The parents were under no obligation to continue to make annual gifts to the children although they expected to do it. The children's obligation to make the annual payments continued regardless of whether the parents made these gifts." *Id.* at 1227.

On the negative side, an outright gift or sale of the property involves some of the same nontax risks as a private annuity. For example, the property is subject to disposition by the transferee and to the claims of the transferee's creditors. However, in the case of a sale the transferor could retain a security interest without significantly jeopardizing the outcome. The seller's interests might also be protected to some degree by the terms of the lease.

§9.16. Overall Consequences

The savings that may arise in a gift and leaseback transaction are primarily traceable to the difference between the income tax rates applicable to the transferor and the transferee. Viewed most simply, the transaction will increase the income tax deductions available to the transferor by the excess of the annual rental over the otherwise allowable depreciation deduction. The taxes and interest paid by the transferor may also be deductible where he or she retains an interest in the property and is personally liable for them. Walther v. Commissioner, 316 F.2d 708 (7th Cir. 1963) (Indiana law; grantor is liable for and may deduct mortgage interest payments on property transferred to short-term trust).

Trust. The depreciation deduction for property held in trust is generally allocated between the beneficiaries and the trustee on the basis of the trust income allocable to each. §167(h). Where the income must be computed and distributed without regard to depreciation, the entire amount of the deduction is allowed to the beneficiary. In contrast, where local law or the instrument requires the establishment of a depreciation reserve, the deduction is allowed to the trustee and not to the beneficiary. Reg. §1.167(h)-1(b). The beneficiaries' cash flow position is enhanced if the deduction is available to them. A trust instrument should contain an appropriate provision dealing with this issue. The original Uniform Principal and Income Act, 7A U.L.A. 461 (1978), does not authorize a depreciation reserve. However, §13(a)(2) of the Revised Uniform Act, 7A U.L.A. 455 (1978), requires that a charge be made against income for depreciation where it is called for by generally accepted accounting principles.

Annuity. The gift tax consequences of the transaction should also be taken into account, particularly where a current payment would be required. Because the transferor's retained reversionary interest is includible in the transferor's gross estate, one cannot assume that an annuity transaction will reduce the size of the transferor's gross estate. *See* §9.20, *infra.*

Sale. Where the transaction takes the form of a sale, the savings are reduced to the extent the transferor must pay taxes on the gain. However, a sale does increase the basis against which the transferee may compute depreciation. A sale for the full market value of the property eliminates any present gift tax and will prevent the property from being included in the transferor's gross estate if the rental is fair and the transaction is properly planned. *See* §9.20, *infra.*

In evaluating the transaction, the lawyer and client must also consider the professional fees and other costs of carrying out the transaction. When those costs are aggregated with the offsetting tax considerations, the potential savings may be slight. The evaluation is incomplete unless the client also takes into account the nontax consequences of the transaction. For some, the loss of the ability to deal directly with the property is significant. Aggressive clients may savor the opportunity to duel with the IRS, while more cautious ones would prefer to avoid the anxiety of an audit and confrontation with the IRS.

§9.17. *Income Tax Consequences of Transfer*

A gift of business property to a trust or other beneficiary does not ordinarily require the transferor or the transferee to report any income.

There are exceptions to the rule for special types of property. Thus, an early disposition of section 38 property requires investment credit recapture. *See* §47(a). In the case of a gift the transferor's basis in the property carries over to the transferee as provided in §1015 for purposes of depreciation and otherwise.

Where the transfer is made by sale, gain may be recognized by the transferor, which can be reported on the installment basis in appropriate cases. *See* Part B, *supra.* A sale at the market price of the property would avoid the imposition of any gift tax on the transaction and should avoid any threat of inclusion in the transferor's estate. *See* §§9.4 to 9.5, *supra.* However, a sale may involve depreciation recapture where §1245 (personal) property or §1250 (real) property is transferred. The rules of those sections apply to sale and leaseback transactions. Reg. §1.1245-1(a)(3).

> **Example 9-12.** Last year T sold equipment to an irrevocable trust for $8,000. T paid $10,000 for the equipment and had taken depreciation deductions of $4,000 during the time T owned it. T's gain on the sale was $2,000 — the difference between the $8,000 sale price and the $6,000 basis. The entire amount of the gain is ordinary income under §1245(a) and not gain realized from the sale of §1231 property. *See* Reg. §1.1245-1(b).

The gain would also be ordinary income where the sale is made between husband and wife or between an individual and a controlled corporation. *See* §1239. Of course, under §267 losses on transfers to related taxpayers are not deductible.

§9.18. *Income Tax Consequences of Rental Payments*

The IRS has taken a very narrow view of the circumstances in which rental payments are deductible in leaseback cases. Section 162(a)(3) allows a deduction as an ordinary and necessary business expense for

> (3) rentals or other payments required to be made as a condition to the continued use or possession, for purposes of the trade or business, of property to which the taxpayer has not taken or is not taking title or in which he has no equity.

Where there is a prearranged plan of transfer and leaseback, the IRS has argued that no deduction is allowable because the overall transaction lacks any valid business purpose. Thus, the rental payments made by the lessee are not ordinary and necessary expenses for which a deduction is allowable. Where the lessee retains a reversionary interest the IRS has sometimes also denied the deduction because the taxpayer had an equity interest in the property. *See* §162(a)(3).

Another view of the business purpose requirement has been taken by most courts:

> [W]e think that where, as here, a grantor gives business property to a valid irrevocable trust over which he retains no control and then leases it back, it is not necessary for us to inquire as to whether there was a business reason for making the gift. Admittedly there was none. Under such circumstances the test of business necessity should be made by viewing the situation as it exists after the gift is made. At that point, since Alden Oakes needed a building for practicing medicine, he agreed to rent the property from the trustee for a reasonable amount. Consequently, we believe there is a sound basis for holding that the rent paid by Oakes was, in terms of section 162, both "ordinary and necessary" and "required to be made as a condition to continued use * * * of property." Alden B. Oakes, 44 T.C. 524, 532 (1965).

The Tax Court and most appellate courts have rejected the IRS position, concluding instead that it is sufficient if the lease itself serves a valid business purpose. As the court observed in Quinlivan v. Commissioner, 599 F.2d 269, 273 (8th Cir.), *cert. denied,* 444 U.S. 996 (1979), "Congress has specified that the business purpose test is concerned with the 'continued use or possession' of the property. There is no justification for adding an inquiry into the origin of the lessor's title in applying this requirement." *See also* Brown v. Commissioner, 180 F.2d 926 (3d Cir. 1950), *cert. denied,* 340 U.S. 814 (1950); Skemp v. Commissioner, 168 F.2d 598 (7th Cir. 1948). On the other hand, the Fourth Circuit will not bifurcate the transfer and leaseback — it insists that the overall transaction have a valid business purpose. Perry v. United States, 520 F.2d 235 (4th Cir. 1975), *cert. denied,* 423 U.S. 1052 (1976).

The Fifth Circuit once championed the business purpose test. Van Zandt v. Commissioner, 341 F.2d 440 (5th Cir.), *cert. denied,* 382 U.S. 814 (1965). However, more recently that court has indicated that it is not enough to "conjure up some reason why a businessman would enter into this sort of arrangement." Mathews v. Commissioner, 520 F.2d 323, 325 (5th Cir. 1975), *cert. denied,* 424 U.S. 967 (1976). In *Mathews* the court focused on the substance of the overall transaction and held that no deduction is allowable unless it has some economic reality. Although "economic reality" is a term that had been used before in the leaseback cases, Brooke v. United States, 468 F.2d 1155 (9th Cir. 1972), its meaning is by no means clear. The *Mathews* opinion does state that economic reality is not present where there is a prearranged agreement to lease the property back to the transferor. According to the court, the prearrangement assures that the transferor will continue to have control over the property regardless of the independence of the trustee. The economic reality test could be very difficult to satisfy, particularly if the taxpayer must establish the absence of an express or implied prearrangement in the context of a family transaction. An analogous problem arises where a transferor continues to occupy a residence given to another family member. *See* §7.22, *supra*.

No Equity Interest. In order to be deductible as rent, the statute requires that the taxpayer have no equity in the rental property. §162(a)(3). In several cases the IRS has argued that the statute bars a deduction where the lessee holds a reversionary interest in the property. The argument has been rejected by most courts. However, it was accepted in 2 cases — Chace v. United States, 303 F. Supp. 513 (M.D. Fla. 1969), *aff'd per curiam*, 422 F.2d 292 (5th Cir. 1970), and Hall v. United States, 208 F. Supp. 584 (N.D.N.Y. 1962). The pertinent part of §162(a)(3) is ambiguous, but most courts agree that the requirement is intended to prevent taxpayers from converting a capital expenditure (purchase of asset) into a currently deductible expense (rent). For example, in C. James Mathews, 61 T.C. 12, 23 (1973), *rev'd on other grounds*, 520 F.2d 323 (5th Cir. 1975), *cert. denied*, 424 U.S. 967 (1976), the Tax Court said, "section 162(a)(3) should not be read to cause rental payments to become nondeductible merely by virtue of a lessee's property rights in an asset, which rights are not derived from the lessor or under the lease, and which will become possessory only after the lease expires." *See also* Quinlivan v. United States, 599 F.2d 269 (8th Cir.), *cert. denied*, 444 U.S. 996 (1979). This ban on deductions should not pose any problem for most gift and leaseback transactions.

Tax Court Requirements. The Tax Court has established specific requirements that must be met in order to sustain the deductibility of rental payments in leaseback cases. *See* Hobart A. Lerner, M.D., P.C., 71 T.C. 290 (1978); C. James Mathews, 61 T.C. at 18-19; and Richard R. Quinlivan, 37 T.C.M. 346 (1978). The requirements were also adopted by the Eighth Circuit in the appellate opinion in *Quinlivan*, 599 F.2d at 273:

1. The grantor must not retain "substantially the same control over the property that he had before" he made the gift;
2. The leaseback should normally be in writing and must require the payment of a reasonable rental;
3. The leaseback (as distinguished from the gift) must have a bona fide business purpose; and
4. The taxpayer must not possess a disqualifying equity interest in the property.

The first requirement implies the necessity of having an independent trustee, which has been stated explicitly in some cases. *E.g.*, Brooke v. United States, 468 F.2d 1155 (9th Cir. 1972) (involving a guardianship and not a trust); Alden B. Oakes, 44 T.C. 524, 529 (1965). In Lewis H. V. May, 76 T.C. 7 (1981), the Tax Court left open the question of whether there must be an independent trustee in all cases. Although some courts are willing to treat the lessee's lawyer or accountant as an independent party for this purpose, it is safer to use a corporate trustee.

Suggested Approach. A leaseback from a family member or a trustee is subject to challenge by the IRS in any case. The threat is greatest where the transaction involves a short-term trust and the lessee holds a reversionary interest in the property. Even in those cases a deduction for rental payments will be upheld by most courts if the transaction has these characteristics:

1. The trustee is independent (preferably a corporate trustee);
2. The lease is written and enforceable under the local law;
3. The lease terms, including its duration and rental, are negotiated after the initial transfer;
4. The rental is reasonable — neither inadequate nor excessive;
5. The lease of the property serves a legitimate business purpose of the lessee; and
6. The lessor and lessee respect and enforce the terms of the lease.

The taxpayer's cause is helped immeasurably if there are valid nontax business purposes for the overall transaction. It is relatively simple to identify some plausible nontax motives where the initial transfer involves an outright gift or sale. For example, in Brooke v. United States, 468 F.2d 1155 (9th Cir. 1972), the nontax motives for a gift to minor children and leaseback from their guardian were found to be "abundant and grounded in economic reality." They included a desire: to provide for the health and education of the minors; to avoid friction with medical partners; to withdraw assets from the threat of malpractice suits; and to diminish the ethical conflict arising from ownership of a medical practice and an adjoining pharmacy.

Grantor Trust Rules. The benefit of the deduction is lost if the income of the trust is taxable to the transferor under §§671 to 677. For example, the income of a short-term trust is taxable to the transferor under §677(a) where an independent trustee has discretion to accumulate trust income for distribution to the transferor upon termination of the trust. Duffy v. United States, 487 F.2d 282 (6th Cir. 1973), *cert. denied*, 416 U.S. 938 (1974). From the income tax point of view the *Duffy* transaction' should result in a wash — the taxpayer is allowed a deduction for the rental paid to the trust, but the income of the trust is taxed to him under the grantor trust rules. Of course, such a taxpayer suffers some overall loss because of the costs incurred in creating the trust and the imposition of a gift tax on the transfer to the trust. The grantor trust rules are examined in detail in Part D of Chapter 10, §§10.26 to 10.32, *infra*.

§9.19. Gift Tax Consequences

The initial transfer of property to the trust involves a gift unless the transferor receives full and adequate consideration. The significance of inter vivos gifts is increased by the unified transfer tax structure, particularly where the principal may ultimately be included in the transferor's gross estate, as in the case of all short-term trusts in which the transferor retains a reversionary interest. This makes it particularly important that the transfer qualify for the maximum number of annual gift tax exclusions. Where a trust is involved an exclusion is usually available only if the income is distributable currently, or the trust satisfies the requirements of §2503(c). *See* §§7.33 to 7.38, *supra*. In appropriate cases the transfer could be structured to qualify for the marital or charitable gift and estate tax deductions. For example, the initial transfer might be made outright to a charity or to a charitable remainder trust or charitable lead trust. Great caution is required in planning a transfer to a charitable trust because of the complexity of the tax rules. *See* §§8.19 to 8.27, *supra*.

The amount of the gift is determined under the usual gift tax rules. Accordingly, term or other limited interests are valued by reference to the actuarial tables of Reg. §25.2512-9. However, where the rental is fixed at the time of the initial transfer, the value of the gift is "measured by the present worth of the right to receive the net rentals from the property during the term of the trust, provided the right to such rentals is under the terms of the transfer and applicable State law fixed or vested." Rev. Rul. 57-315, 1957-2 C.B. 624. The ruling also points out that the gift of the rentals is complete at the time of transfer although the rentals are not deductible by the lessee for income tax purposes.

Where the gift is valued by reference to the actuarial tables, the transaction may result in a partially nontaxable transfer. This phenomenon will occur if the reasonable rental payments under the lease exceed the 6% rate of return on which the actuarial tables are based.

> **Example 9-13.** T transferred a building worth $100,000 to the independent trustee of a 10-year trust, the income of which was distributable annually to T's 3 children. For gift tax purposes T is considered to have made a gift of income interests worth a total of $44,160.50. To the extent the rental payments (or other income of the trust) exceed $6,000 per year T will, in effect, make tax-free gifts to the children. However, note that excessive rental payments by T would probably involve further gifts to the beneficiaries of the trust.

A nontaxable gift of this type is not unusual. In fact, the value of a term interest in a trust is "understated" in any case where the assets that are transferred to the trust or acquired by the trustee yield more than 6%.

§9.20. Estate Tax Consequences

Where the initial transfer is made to a short-term trust, the value of the transferor's reversionary interest is includible in his or her estate under §2033 if the transferor dies during the term of the trust. The full value of the property may be included in the transferor's estate under §2036(a) if the lease was prearranged or the rental is not adequate. *See* Estate of William du Pont, Jr., 63 T.C. 746 (1975) (inclusion where property transferred outright and leased back at inadequate rental); Estate of Roy D. Barlow, 55 T.C. 666 (1971), *acq.,* 1972-2 C.B. 1, 3 (no inclusion where property transferred outright more than 3 years prior to death and decedent paid fair rental under written leases). Apart from the tax-free shift to the transferee of income in excess of 6%, a gift and leaseback transaction entered into with a short-term reversionary trust does not reduce the size of the transferor's estate. The reason is simple: At the end of the trust term the appreciated assets are returned to the grantor.

> **Example 9-14.** Five years ago O transferred a new building worth $200,000 to the independent trustee of a 10-year trust, the income of which was payable annually in equal shares to O's 4 children. At the end of 10 years the trust will end and the building will revert to O. After the transfer O leased the building at a reasonable rental for a 10-year term. When the building was transferred to the trust O made gifts to the children of interests worth $88,321 according to Table B, Reg. §25.2512-9 (factor .441605 × $200,000). The gifts qualified for the annual gift tax exclusion because the income is distributable currently. Assuming that the annual gift tax exclusion was $10,000 at the time of the transfer, it resulted in taxable gifts of $48,321. If O were to die now, the reversionary interest would be includible in O's estate. Assuming that the present fair market value of the building is $300,000, the reversionary interest would be worth $224,177, Table B, *supra* (factor .747258 × $300,000). Including the taxable gifts of $48,321, a total of $272,498 is taken into account in determining the tentative tax on O's estate. Any value attributable to the remaining 5 years of the lease would also be includible in O's estate. Of course, the full value of the property would be includible in O's gross estate if O survived the term of the lease and owned the property outright at the time of O's death. Again, the taxable gifts of $48,321 would be taken into account in calculating the estate tax on O's estate. The transfer does cause the income from the lease to be taxed to the children and to be excluded from O's estate.

Outright Gift and Leaseback. Where the transfer is made by outright gift all of the property may escape inclusion in the donor's estate if he or she pays a reasonable rental. The available annual exclusions may substantially eliminate the tax cost of removing the value of the property from the donor's tax base. The gift and estate tax consequences of adopting this approach are illustrated by the following example, which should be compared with Example 9-14, *supra*.

> **Example 9-15.** O transferred a new office building worth $200,000 to the independent trustee of an irrevocable trust of which O's 4 children were the life income beneficiaries and their issue were the remaindermen. O did not retain any interest in the property and held no control over the trust. After the transfer O leased the building from the trustee on reasonable terms. At the time of the transfer to the trust O made gifts of the entire value of the property. Assuming that 4 $10,000 annual exclusions were available, the transfer resulted in taxable gifts of $160,000. If O had not previously made any taxable gifts, the gift tax on the transfer would be offset by O's unified credit. Only the amount of the taxable gifts ($160,000) should be taken into account in calculating the tentative tax on O's estate. However, the full value of the property could be included in O's estate if he or she in effect retained the use of the property by paying an unreasonably low rental or if the transaction otherwise ran afoul of §§2036 to 2038.

Sale and Leaseback. Where the initial transfer takes the form of a bona fide sale for the full value of the property, none of it is includible in the seller's estate. In this case the consideration received by the seller is includible in lieu of the property itself. The value of an installment note or other obligation received as consideration would depend upon a variety of factors, including the interest rate, security, and collectibility. *See* Reg. §20.2031-4. If the sale price is inadequate the property may be included in the seller's estate under §§2035 to 2038. However, in such a case the estate would be entitled to an offset under §2043(a) for the consideration received.

> **Problem 9-4.** T's income from a medical practice is subject to a 50% marginal income tax rate. T proposes to relocate in a building he recently purchased for $150,000. At the time of the purchase T paid $30,000 down and executed a note for the $120,000 balance. T is required to pay 12% interest for 10 years, at the end of which all of the principal is due. T is personally liable on the note, which is secured by a mortgage on the property. Based on an assumed useful life of 15 years, under the straight line method, T could deduct depreciation of $10,000 each year.
>   T proposes to transfer the property to the independent trustee of an irrevocable trust. The trust will have a term of 10 years and 1 day, during which the income will be paid in equal shares to T's 4

adult children A, B, C, and D, whose marginal income tax rates are about 30%. Under the proposed arrangement, the trustee will lease the building to T, who will pay real property taxes of $2,000 on the property and continue to make payments of principal and interest on the note. In addition, the lease will require T to pay a rental of $1,500 per month. Under the terms of the trust income will be calculated without regard to depreciation, which will be available to the beneficiaries under §167(h). What are the income, gift, and estate tax implications of the proposed trust?

E.   THE WIDOW'S ELECTION IN COMMUNITY PROPERTY AND COMMON LAW STATES

§9.21.   *General*

Life or other limited interests in property may be transferred for consideration in a wide variety of settings. However, thus far most of the litigated cases have involved the community property widow's election, which serves as the primary focus of this part. The tax consequences of the transfers are determined according to more or less universal rules, which apply regardless of slight variations in the settings or relationships of the parties. For example, the purchaser of a life interest in a trust is entitled to amortize its cost whether it was purchased from a decedent's estate in connection with a widow's election (Estate of Christ v. Commissioner, 480 F.2d 171 (9th Cir. 1973)) or from the settlor of the trust (Manufacturer's Hanover Trust Co. v. Commissioner, 431 F.2d 664 (2d Cir. 1970)). Also, the same estate tax rules apply whether the interest is acquired in the context of a will contest (United States v. Righter, 400 F.2d 344 (8th Cir. 1968)) or a widow's election (Estate of Vardell v. Commissioner, 307 F.2d 688 (5th Cir. 1962)). It is important to have a basic grasp of the tax rules and to be alert for circumstances in which they may apply — the rules can be very helpful in planning some transactions.

The planning device under discussion was labelled the "widow's election" long ago. While it is equally available to spouses of either sex, the wife most often survives her husband. Consequently, this part generally refers to the first spouse to die as the "husband" and to the surviving spouse as the "widow." No suggestion of marital or sexual inequality is intended by this choice of language. The convention is adopted in the interest of brevity and clarity.

§9.22.   *Testamentary Elections*

A transfer for consideration may take place because a testamentary election is required expressly or impliedly by a decedent's will. For example, a testamentary gift may be conditioned upon the beneficiary transferring an asset he or she owns to another person. In other cases the necessity of making an election may be implied rather than expressed directly in the will. Thus, T may make a gift to X and purport to give Y an item of property that is actually owned by X. In such a case X may elect either to accept the gift from T and transfer the item of his or her property to Y, or to reject the gift from T and not transfer any of his or her own property to Y. An election may also be required where the testator and the beneficiary of a testamentary gift are joint tenants in other property that the testator's will gives to a third party. *E.g.,* Estate of Waters, 100 Cal. Rptr. 775, 778 (Cal. App. 1972).

> **Example 9-16.** T owned the entire interest in Blackacre, which T's will devised to X. Although T and X owned Whiteacre as joint tenants with right of survivorship, T's will purported to devise Whiteacre to Y. The devise of Blackacre to X may be conditioned upon X transferring Whiteacre to Y.

Widow's Election. The term "widow's election" has quite different meanings in common law and community property states. In common law property states, the term usually refers to the statutory right of a surviving spouse to elect to receive a specified share of the deceased spouse's estate (a so-called nonbarrable share) in lieu of taking under the decedent's will. *See, e.g.,* UPC §2-201. The concept is an important one that may have significant tax consequences in some instances, such as cases involving the marital deduction.

In community property states the term usually refers to a plan under which the widow is given an interest in the deceased husband's share of the community property, conditioned upon her making a specified disposition of her share of the community property. The widow is forced to make an election because the husband could not effectively dispose of more than his one-half of the community property. *See* §3.24, *supra.* As explained below, the tax cases generally treat the widow as having purchased the preferred interest in the husband's share of the community property by making the required transfer of her share of the community property.

The basic concept of the community property widow's election can be adapted for use in common law property states. For example, if each spouse owns a substantial amount of separate property, the husband's will may make a gift of an appropriate part of his property to a trust of which his wife is the life income beneficiary. However, the gift to the widow of the income interest in the trust may be conditioned upon the transfer by her of a specified amount of her property to the trust, or to a similar, separate trust. Some commentators have suggested that a modified form of widow's election could be used where the wife does not have a substantial estate. They suggest that the husband's will could create a life estate-general power of appointment marital deduction trust and a residuary trust. Then, the wife could be given the power to draw down the principal of the marital deduction trust and exchange it for a life income interest in the residuary trust. If she makes the exchange, presumably she would be treated as a purchaser of the income interest in the residuary trust. As such she might be entitled to the same tax benefits as the widow-beneficiary of a community property widow's election trust. However, the tax consequences of this approach are not established. In addition, it is subject to the same uncertainty as the community property widow's election regarding the application of §1001(e) to the sale by the residuary trust of a life interest to the widow *See* §9.25, *infra.*

The substantive law regarding the community property widow's election has evolved largely from cases that arose prior to the advent of significant income, gift, or estate taxes. *E.g.,* In re Smith's Estate, 40 P. 1037 (Cal. 1895). The cases usually involved a husband's will that attempted to dispose of all of the community property, yet made some provision for his widow. Although a will is generally presumed to dispose of only the testator's property, where it was clear that he had attempted to dispose of all of the community property, the courts held that the widow was required to elect whether to accept the provisions of the will and allow her share of the community property to pass under the will or to reject the will and retain her share of the community property. *E.g.,* Herrick v. Miller, 125 P. 974 (Wash. 1912). Litigation was frequently required in order to determine whether an election was required and whether the widow had made an election by accepting benefits under the will or by acquiescing in the distribution of some property in accordance with the terms of the will. These problems are generally avoided in modern wills, which usually require the election to be made in a particular way and within a specified time following the testator's death. Modern wills also generally make a conditional gift to the widow of an interest in the trust funded with the husband's share of the property rather than attempting also to dispose directly of her interest in community property. However, some commentators still write of the election as if the husband were disposing directly of the entire interest in the community property.

Typical Widow's Election Plan. Under a typical widow's election plan, the husband's will leaves his share of the community property to a trust, all of the income of which is distributable to his widow if she also transfers her share of the community property to the same trust, or to a separate trust that is subject to essentially the same terms. Their children are usually the remaindermen of the trust or trusts. The widow will receive no benefit from the trust of the husband's share of the community property unless she transfers her share to the trust. In any event the widow is usually entitled to receive specific bequests and a family allowance from the husband's estate.

The widow's election can be adapted for use in connection with an inter vivos trust or in connection with gifts to persons other than a spouse. *See, e.g.,* United States v. Righter, 400 F.2d 344 (8th Cir. 1968) (estate tax approach of widow's election cases applied to trust created by decedent and others in settlement of will contest). However, the following discussion generally focuses on testamentary widow's election plans involving married persons. The nontax considerations are discussed first, after which the tax consequences are developed in some detail. The tax concepts are discussed at some length because they may be applied in other contexts in community and common law states.

Inter Vivos or Post-Mortem Election? The testator's spouse may agree during the testator's lifetime to accept the benefit of the plan and be bound by the terms of the will. *E.g.,* In re Wyss' Estate, 297 P. 100 (Cal. App. 1931); Rev. Rul. 69-346, 1969-1 C.B. 227. Use of a binding inter vivos election is generally unwise because it deprives the widow of the opportunity to evaluate the suitability of the plan after her husband's death. One of the attractive features of the traditional widow's election is the "second look" it gives the widow.

Where a plan involves an inter vivos election, the lawyer should seriously consider suggesting that each spouse be advised by independent counsel:

> There may be many cases where a single attorney is consulted and no question exists about the fairness or reasonableness of the agreement to both parties. The presence of advice from independent counsel is a desirable cautionary step, however, where there is a possibility that the fairness or reasonableness of the agreement will be subject to later attack. Whitney v. Seattle-First National Bank, 579 P.2d 937, 940 (Wash. 1978).

Ideally, the surviving spouse should also be advised by independent counsel where the election is made following the testator's death. In that way the draftsman of the will, who generally serves as counsel to the executor, will not be subject to a conflict of interest.

Where the plan contemplates a post-mortem election, the husband's will should specify the period during which the widow may elect under the will. It is important that the widow be given ample time to consider the tax and nontax effects of an election before it must be made. For example, she might be permitted to elect at any time prior to final distribution of the testator's estate. The will should also specify whether the election may be made on the widow's behalf by her guardian (or her personal representative if she survives her husband, but dies before making an election). Even apart from such a provision, some states permit the widow's personal representative to make the election. Estate of Murphy, 544 P.2d 956 (Cal. 1976). In contrast, the UPC does not permit an election to take a nonbarrable share to be made by the survivor's personal representative. UPC §2-203.

The *"Voluntary" Widow's Election.* Some couples reject the use of a "forced" election of the type described above, in favor of a plan that permits the widow to add some or all of her property to the trust created under her husband's will. Under this plan the widow is not required to transfer any of her property to the trust in order to receive the income from her husband's share of the property. Instead, any property the widow transfers to the trust is typically held in a separate fund, which may be withdrawn by her at any time. Such a plan facilitates unified management of the community property, yet provides the surviving spouse with a high degree of flexibility. The husband's share of the community property is usually left to a trust that meets the requirements of a qualified terminable interest property trust under §2056(b)(7). Of course, the property of the trust is includible in the widow's estate under §2044 to the extent the husband's executor claims a marital deduction with respect to the trust. However, the plan does not produce any of the income or estate tax benefits that are sought through the use of the forced widow's election. Specifically, the widow is not entitled to any amortization deduction and the amount included in her estate will not be reduced by a consideration offset under §2043(a). See §9.30, *infra.*

§9.23.   Nontax Consequences of a Forced Election

Some clients are attracted to a widow's election by its nontax advantages. "Such wills offer the greatest protection to the estate, and at the same time give to the widow as nearly an assured income as possible without any of the responsibility or hazard of caring for the property." Falknor, Liability of the Entire Community Estate for the Payment of State Inheritance Tax Where Husband Undertakes to Dispose of Entire Community Estate by Will and Wife Elects to Take Under the Will, 5 Wash. L. Rev. 55 (1930). The plan offers unified management of community assets, which is particularly helpful in the case of closely held business interests. There is also an advantage to having the entire community property managed by a professional trustee where the wife does not have any business experience or does not want to manage her share of it.

The plan also assures that the community property, or at least the husband's share, will pass to their children or the other remaindermen named in his will. Furthermore, the property held in trust is not subject to an estate administration upon the widow's death and cannot be diverted by her to other persons. Of course, many of these advantages are available under other plans, such as a voluntary widow's election.

A forced election plan is more complex than the ordinary plan for disposing of the community property. As a result it may be more difficult for clients to understand and more costly to implement. In addition, there is a substantial risk that some of the tax advantages sought by the parties will be challenged. Overall, the forced widow's election is not suitable for most clients. A widow's election plan should be used only if it is understood by the husband and wife and is completely acceptable to them. Otherwise there is too great a risk that the widow will resent the plan and feel that she was not treated fairly by her husband or his planner. In short, the plan should be consensual and not imposed on a wife who does not understand it or has some objection to it.

The nontax considerations are thoughtfully reviewed in a short article by Kahn and Gallo, The Widow's Election: A Return to Fundamentals, 24 Stan. L. Rev. 531 (1972). In general the authors favor a voluntary widow's election over a forced one.

§9.24. Gift Tax Consequences

In the typical widow's election, the widow is considered to have transferred a remainder interest in her share of the property in exchange for a life interest in the decedent's share. Commissioner v. Siegel, 250 F.2d 339 (9th Cir. 1957); Zillah Mae Turman, 35 T.C. 1123 (1961), acq., 1964-2 C.B. 7. Under this approach the widow does not make a gift where the actuarially determined value of the life interest she receives is equal to or greater than the value of the remainder in the property she transfers.

> **Example 9-17.** H's executor transferred his net share of the community property, worth $300,000, to a typical widow's election trust, the H trust. The decedent's 67-year-old widow, W, elected to transfer her share of the community property, worth $375,000, to an identical trust, the W trust, in order to receive the income from both trusts for life. Upon her death the trust property is distributable to their then living descendants, by right of representation. Under Table A(2), Reg. §25.2512-9, the factor for the life estate of a 67-year-old female is .52583 and the factor for the remainder is .47417. Here, W transferred a remainder worth $177,814 ($375,000 × .47417) in exchange for a life estate worth $157,749.

Accordingly, W made a gift of $20,065. The gift is a future interest
that does not qualify for the annual exclusion.

An election to take under the husband's will does not result in a gift
where the widow retains a power of appointment over the property she
transferred to the trust. Reg. §25.2511-2(b). Thus, the IRS recognized in
LR 7746044 that the widow's gift was not complete at the time of her
election where she retained a special power of appointment over the
property she transferred to the trust. However, the ruling concluded
that under Estate of Sanford v. Commissioner, 308 U.S. 39 (1939), the
gift became complete when she subsequently released the power of appointment. At that time she made a gift of the entire remainder value of
the trust attributable to the property she transferred to the trustee. The
widow's gift in LR 7746044 was not reduced by the value of the life
interest she received in her husband's share of the property. She had
already received that interest, which was not affected by her release. The
gift was larger because it took place later, which increased the value of
the remainder interest, and because the widow received no consideration
for the transfer. The analysis of LR 7746044 was followed by the Tax
Court in Myra B. Robinson, 75 T.C. 346 (1980).

The widow's retention of any power of appointment over the property
she transfers threatens the treatment of the election as a transfer for
value. As Professor Stanley Johanson has pointed out, where a power is
retained the transaction more closely resembles a gratuitous transfer
than a transfer for value. Revocable Trusts, Widow's Election Wills,
and Community Property: The Tax Problems, 47 Tex. L. Rev. 1247,
1309-1311 (1969). That is a serious problem because the principal tax
advantages of the widow's election are lost if the transaction is not
characterized as a transfer for value: (1) The widow will be unable to
amortize the "cost" of the life estate in her husband's share of the property, and (2) the widow's estate will be unable to claim a consideration
offset under §2043(a) for the value of the life estate she received. The
Tax Court has held that the widow's estate is not entitled to a consideration offset where she held a general power of appointment over the
property. Estate of Bluma Steinman, 69 T.C. 804 (1978). Given the
uncertainty regarding this issue, either the widow should not retain any
power, or the power should be limited to a testamentary special power to
appoint the corpus to and among their descendants (or some other limited class).

Voluntary Election. Where the election is a voluntary one, the widow
receives no consideration in exchange for her transfer. Instead, she
makes a gift of the full value of the remainder interest in her property.
However, no completed gift occurs where she retains a general or special
power of appointment over the property. Here the retention of a power
of appointment can add flexibility to the plan at no tax cost. Of course,

where a voluntary election is involved the widow is not entitled to an amortization deduction and her estate will not be entitled to a consideration offset under §2043(a).

> **Problem 9-5.** H died this year leaving a will that gave property worth $400,000 to a typical widow's election trust, the H trust, the income of which was payable to his 70-year-old widow, W, if she transferred her share of the community property to an identical, separate trust, the W trust. W was entitled to receive the income from both trusts if she made the required transfer. Otherwise she was not entitled to any benefit from the H trust. Upon W's death the property of the H and W trusts is distributable to the then living issue of H and W, by right of representation. W elected to take under the will and transferred her share of the community property, worth $450,000, to the W trust. What are the gift tax consequences of the transfer? How would they vary if W retained a special testamentary power of appointment over the W trust? If she had retained a special testamentary power of appointment, would you advise her to release it? What would be the gift tax consequences if W was entitled to the income from the H trust in all events, and she transferred her share of the property to the W trust without retaining any power over it?

§9.25. *Income Tax Consequences: Background*

The holder of a life or other term interest acquired by gift, bequest, or inheritance cannot deduct any amount because of shrinkage in value of the interest due to the passage of time. §273. On the other hand, a life interest in a testamentary trust is treated as a capital asset for purposes of characterizing the gain realized on a sale or exchange of the interest. McAllister v. Commissioner, 157 F.2d 235 (2d Cir. 1946), *cert. denied*, 330 U.S. 826 (1947); Rev. Rul. 72-243, 1972-1 C.B. 233. Equally as important, the purchaser of a life or other term interest is allowed to amortize its cost over its life, thereby reducing or eliminating the tax on income received from it. Commissioner v. Fry, 283 F.2d 869 (6th Cir. 1960), *affirming*, 31 T.C. 522 (1958); Bell v. Harrison, 212 F.2d 253 (7th Cir. 1954); Rev. Rul. 62-132, 1962-2 C.B. 73.

Prior to the Tax Reform Act of 1969, where a life estate or other term interest was sold, the seller's basis was determined by multiplying his or her entire basis in the property by the appropriate factor from Table I, Reg. §20.2031-7. Rev. Rul. 72-243, 1972-1 C.B. 233. Under this rule the seller seldom realized any gain on the sale. Moreover, under the *McAllister* line of authority any gain would be capital gain and not ordinary income.

The Tax Reform Act of 1969 added §1001(e), under which the

seller's basis is disregarded to the extent it arises under §§1014 or 1015. As a result of this change, the full amount received by the seller of a term interest acquired by gift or bequest is gain where the sale takes place after October 9, 1969. The legislation only disadvantages the seller of a life or other term interest — it does not prevent the purchaser from amortizing the cost of the life interest.

> **Example 9-18.** T's will left $100,000 in trust to pay the income to a 65-year-old male, M, for life. Upon M's death the corpus is distributable to X. The income of the trust is taxable to M, who is barred by §273 from claiming any amortization deduction. M's interest constitutes a capital asset for purposes of characterizing the gain realized on any sale or other disposition. If M sold his interest prior to October 10, 1969, his basis would be determined under §1014 by multiplying the value of the trust corpus by the appropriate factor specified in Table I of Reg. §20.2031-7 for a person of M's age. Reg. §1.1014-5(a). Thus, the interest had a basis of $33,420 under that table, which assumes only a 3½% rate of return ($100,000 × factor .33420). If the sale took place after October 9, 1969, M's basis would be zero pursuant to §1001(e).

The legislative history of §1001(e) does not indicate whether or not Congress considered the possibility of applying the provision in the widow's election context. In the early 1970s it was rumored that the IRS would issue a ruling to the effect that §1001(e) would not apply to a widow's election unless a distribution from the estate was made in satisfaction of the widow's right to receive a specific dollar amount or a specific item of property. Estate Planning Through Family Bargaining, 8 Real Prop., Prob. & Tr. J. 223, 265 (1973). However, the ruling was never issued and the probability that §1001(e) will apply to the widow's election is sufficient to deter most planners from recommending that a client use a forced widow's election plan. Neither the Code nor any identifiable considerations of tax policy would prevent the application of §1001(e). Freeland, Lind & Stephens, What Are the Income Tax Effects of an Estate's Sale of a Life Interest?, 34 J. Tax. 376 (1971); Wilson, The Widow's Election Viewed in the Light of the 1976 Tax Reform Act and the 1975 California Probate Code Revision, 28 Hastings L.J. 1435, 1442 (1977).

§9.26. *Income Tax Consequences: The Trustee*

> In a situation involving a widow's election where the taxpayer exchanges the remainder interest in her community property for a life interest in her husband's community property, what actually occurs can be characterized

as part gratuitous disposition-part sale or exchange. Where the wife received property worth more than the value of the property she transfers, the property received in excess should be viewed as a "bequest" from the husband which is not amortizable. But where the wife transfers property worth more than the value of that which she receives, she purchases property equivalent to the value of the "received" property and is deemed to have made a gift to the beneficiaries of the estate of, and should pay a gift tax on, the excess. Kuhn v. United States, 392 F. Supp. 1229, 1239-1240 (S.D. Tex. 1975).

In the case of a forced widow's election trust the trust may realize a substantial gain if the plan is carried out and the widow transfers her share of the community property to the trust in exchange for a life interest in the decedent's share. The gain will occur if § 1001(e) applies to the transaction and the trust's basis in the life interest transferred to the widow is disregarded to the extent it is determined under § 1014. In most circumstances the full amount realized by the trust will constitute capital gain. The amount realized is equal to the actuarially determined value of the remainder interest the widow transferred to the trust. However, where the value of the remainder interest exceeds the actuarially determined value of the life interest transferred to the widow, the amount realized by the trust is probably limited to the value of the latter (the life interest). Lane, Widow's Election as a Private Annuity: Boon or Bane for Estate Planners, 44 S. Cal. L. Rev. 74, 93 (1971). In determining the amount realized by the trust, this analysis properly ignores the gift element of the transaction. Such an approach is consistent with the cases that impose a similar limit on the amount amortizable by the widow for income tax purposes. Estate of Christ v. Commissioner, 480 F.2d 171 (9th Cir. 1973).

Example 9-19. H's executor transferred property worth $350,000 to a typical widow's election trust, the H trust. His 70-year-old widow, W, transferred property worth $400,000 to an identical trust, the W trust, as required by H's will. According to Table A(2), Reg. § 20.2031-10, the remainder W transferred in the W trust had a value of $209,840 ($400,000 × .52460) and the life estate she received in the H trust had a value of $166,390 ($350,000 × .47540). The trust realized only the value of the life estate, $166,390, on the exchange and not the full value of the remainder interest transferred by W. The excess constituted a gift from W to the remaindermen of the W trust.

If § 1001(e) does not apply to a widow's election, the trust's basis will be determined under § 1014. Accordingly, the trust will usually have little or no gain to report. Assuming that the amount realized by the trust is limited in the manner described above, the trust will seldom realize an amount greater than the trust's basis in the interest transferred. Under Reg. §1.1014-5 the trust's basis in the life interest transferred to the widow is determined by multiplying the adjusted basis of the decedent's share of the property by the factor for the widow's life estate provided by Table A(2), Reg. §20.2031-10. The widow's life interest will have an equivalent value if the assets held in the trust are valued for federal estate tax purposes on the date of the husband's death and the widow's election is effective on that date. Because of fluctuations in the value of the assets held by the trust, the life interest will have a different value if the valuation date and the date of the election are not the same.

Example 9-20. H's executor transferred assets to a typical widow's election trust, the H trust, which had a total basis of $350,000 and a fair market value of $400,000 on the date they became subject to the trust. His 70-year-old widow, W, transferred property to an identical trust, the W trust, which had a fair market value of $450,000 on that date. The remainder W transferred in the W trust had an actuarial value of $236,070 ($450,000 × .52460) and the life estate she received in the H trust had a value of $190,160 ($400,000 × .47540). However, the trustee's basis in the life interest in the H trust is only $166,390 ($350,000 × .47540). Presumably the trustee realized a gain of $23,770 ($190,160 − $166,390).

The trust does not realize gain in the case of a voluntary widow's election because the widow's transfer of property to the trust is entirely gratuitous and does not involve any exchange or transfer for consideration.

Character of the Gain. The gain realized by the trust will probably be characterized as capital gain rather than ordinary income. Some commentators have suggested that the transaction might be treated as an assignment of income by the trust, in which case the gain would be ordinary income. *See* Freeland, Lind & Stephens, What Are the Income Tax Effects of an Estate's Sale of a Life Interest?, 34 J. Tax. 376 (1971); and Lane, Widow's Election as a Private Annuity: Boon or Bane for Estate Planners, 44 S. Cal. L. Rev. 74, 93-95 (1971). However, the existing appellate court decisions support treating the gain as capital gain. They include a closely analogous case that involved the sale of a legal life estate that the seller carved out of a fee interest that he owned (Estate of Johnson N. Camden, 47 B.T.A. 926 (1942), *nonacq.*, 1943 C.B. 28, *aff'd per curiam*, 139 F.2d 697 (6th Cir. 1944), *nonacq.*, 1944 C.B. 34). Capital gain status was also recognized where the taxpayer sold a remainder interest in her ranch and retained a life estate. Eileen M. Hunter, 44 T.C. 109 (1965). Of course, any tax cost incurred as a result of the sale may be more than offset by the amortization deduction that is allowable to the widow as the purchaser of the life interest in the trust. *See* §9.28, *infra*.

§9.27. *Income Tax Consequences: The Widow*

[W]here the value of the rights surrendered [by the widow] exceeds the value of the rights received, only a portion of what is surrendered is allocated to the "purchase price" of the rights received and the rest is presumed to be a gift to the remaindermen. Estate of Christ v. Commissioner, 480 F.2d 171, 172 (9th Cir. 1973).

The widow may also realize a gain if she elects to transfer her share of the community property to the trust. In broad terms she is viewed as exchanging a remainder interest in her share of the community property for a life interest in her deceased husband's net share of the property. As a result of the exchange, she realizes an amount that can not exceed the actuarially determined value of the life interest she receives. If the value of the life interest the widow receives exceeds the value of the remainder she transfers, the amount realized is probably limited to the value of the remainder. In such a case the amount by which the value of the life estate exceeds the value of the remainder is properly characterized as a testamentary gift to the widow.

The amount of the widow's gain, if any, depends upon her basis in the property she transferred, which can only be determined after identifying the nature of the interest she transferred. Based upon the approach taken in the amortization cases and reflected in the quotation above, the widow will be treated as having transferred a remainder interest in her share of the community property, but only to the extent its value did not exceed the value of the life interest she received. Both of those values are determined by reference to the fair market value of the underlying assets and not their bases. She is considered to have made a gift to the remaindermen to the extent the remainder may have a greater value than the life interest.

Under §1014(b)(6) the widow is considered to have acquired her share of the community property from her deceased husband. Accordingly, the federal estate tax value of her husband's interest in the community property becomes the basis of her interest. When she transfers her share of the community property to the trust, the total basis should be allocated between her life estate and the remainder according to the respective actuarial factor for each. Such a method is applied to determine the bases of life estates and remainder interest in property acquired from a decedent. Reg. §1.1014-5. "Neither the Code nor the regulations prescribe a method for allocating a lump-sum basis when the

owner of a fee simple interest conveys, inter vivos, a less-than-fee estate."
Eileen M. Hunter, 44 T.C. 109, 115 (1965). Although *Hunter* involved a
slightly different method of allocation, the Court seemed to approve the
approach taken in Reg. §1.1014-5, which had also been applied in an
earlier case, Estate of Johnson N. Camden, 47 B.T.A. 926 (1942),
nonacq., 1943 C.B. 28, *aff'd per curiam*, 139 F.2d 697 (6th Cir. 1944),
nonacq., 1944 C.B. 34.

> **Example 9-21.** H's executor transferred property worth $650,000
> to a typical widow's election trust, the H trust. His 60-year-old
> widow, W, transferred property with a basis and a value of
> $800,000 to an identical trust, the W trust, as required by H's will.
> According to Table A(2), Reg. §20.2031-10, the factor for W's life
> estate is .63226 and for the remainder is .36774. Thus, the life
> estate in the H trust is worth $410,969 ($650,000 × .63226) and the
> remainder in the W trust has a basis and a value of $294,192
> ($800,000 × .36774). W should not realize a gain on the transaction
> although the value of the life estate she received in the H trust
> exceeded the basis of the remainder in the property she trans-
> ferred to the W trust. The excess constituted a testamentary gift
> from H to W. W might have a gain, however, if H's executor elected
> to use the alternate valuation date when the property had a lower
> value than on the date of distribution. Thus, W would have a gain
> in this example if her share of the community property had a value
> of $800,000 on the date it became subject to the trust and a basis of
> $700,000 (its value on the alternate valuation date). The value of
> the remainder transferred by W, which would limit the amount
> realized by her, would remain $294,192 but the basis allocable to
> the remainder would be reduced to $257,418. Presumably the
> $36,774 difference would constitute gain to W.

Character of the Gain. Any gain realized by the widow should be
capital gain, just as it would be if realized by the trust. *See* §9.26, *supra.*

> **Problem 9-6.** T's will devised Blackacre to X provided that X trans-
> fer 1,000 shares of DEF, Inc. stock to Y. X elected to receive Black-
> acre and transfer the stock to Y. Blackacre was valued to $200,000
> for estate tax purposes, which was also its fair market value at the
> time of X's election. X had an adjusted basis of $50,000 in the DEF,
> Inc. stock which was worth $100,000 at the time of his election.
> What are the income tax consequences of X's election? Would it
> make any difference if X were required to transfer the stock to a
> qualified public charity instead of another individual? If 2 parcels
> of income-producing real property were involved in the exchange,
> would it be nontaxable under §1031?

Problem 9-7. H's will left property with a basis and a fair market value of $400,000 to a typical widow's election trust, the H trust. His 63-year-old widow, W, accepted the plan and transferred property with a basis and a fair market value of $450,000 to an identical, separate trust, the W trust, as required by H's will. If §1001(e) applies to the transaction, what are the income tax consequences of W's election? How would they differ if §1001(e) does not apply? What basis will the trustee have in the assets of the 2 trusts? What would be the income tax consequences if W promptly sold her life interest in the H trust to her brother, B, for $265,000? Would the results be any different if W sold the life interest she retained in the W trust?

§9.28. Income Tax Consequences of Trust Distributions

For income tax purposes the trust is recognized as a separate taxpaying entity. Under the basic trust income tax rules, the income distributed to the beneficiaries is taxed to them and not to the trust, and the income retained by the trust is taxed to it. *See* §10.2, *infra*. However, capital gains are taxed to the trust and not to the beneficiaries if they are allocated to corpus and are not paid, credited, or required to be distributed during the taxable year. *See* §643(a)(3) and Reg. §1.643(a)-3(a). Presumably distributions to the widow are taxed in accordance with those rules even though she is treated as a purchaser of the life interest in the decedent's share of the trust property.

Amortization Deduction. The widow is entitled to an amortization deduction under §167 for the cost of the life interest she purchased in her deceased husband's share of the trust. Estate of Daisy F. Christ, 54 T.C. 493 (1970), *aff'd*, 480 F.2d 171 (9th Cir. 1973); Gist v. United States, 296 F. Supp. 526 (S.D. Cal. 1969), *aff'd*, 423 F.2d 1118 (9th Cir. 1970); Kuhn v. United States, 392 F. Supp. 1229 (S.D. Tex. 1975). As yet no court has accepted the IRS counter argument that the widow's life interest was acquired gratuitously and, hence, no deduction was allowable because of §273. "Interpreting §273 to prohibit amortization in a case such as this one could only occur by permitting form to conquer substance. The instant taxpayer does not receive income from the subject life estate as a result of a 'gift, bequest or inheritance.' She has acquired the life estate after exchanging valuable property, the right to which was undisputedly hers at the time of the exchange. She therefore will be permitted to amortize the cost basis of life estate payments received and reduce her taxable income by ratable annual deductions, pursuant to 26 U.S.C. §167(h)." Kuhn v. United States, 329 F. Supp. at 1240.

No amortization deduction is allowable to a widow who accepts the income interest in a trust established by her husband's will in lieu of a statutory share of his property. Helvering v. Butterworth, 290 U.S. 365 (1933). In that case the Court reasoned that by electing to accept the provisions of his will the widow waived her statutory rights instead of exchanging them for a life interest in the trust. The courts have thus far refused to follow the *Butterworth* approach in cases involving community property.

The amount of the amortization deduction is determined by dividing the cost of the life interest the widow acquired by her life expectancy according to Table I, Reg. §1.72-9, §8.29, *supra.* Gist v. United States, *supra.* For this purpose the cost is the lesser of the actuarially determined values of (1) the remainder interest she transferred or (2) the life estate she received.

> **Example 9-22.** H's executor transferred property worth $200,000 to a typical widow's election trust established under H's will, the H trust. H's 70-year-old widow, W, transferred property worth $300,000 to an identical trust, the W trust, as required by H's will. According to Table A(2), Reg. §20.2031-10(f), W's life estate in the H trust is worth $95,080 and the remainder she transferred in the W trust is worth $157,380. Under Table I, Reg. §1.72-9, W's life expectancy is 15 years. W may deduct $6,338.67 each year ($95,080 ÷ 15).

The purchaser of a life interest is entitled to amortize its cost although it generates tax exempt income. Section 265 denies deductions that are otherwise allowable under §212 for expenses of producing tax exempt income. It does not affect amortization deductions, which are allowable under §167. Manufacturer's Hanover Trust Co. v. Commissioner, 431 F.2d 664 (2d Cir. 1970). Accordingly, a widow is entitled to amortize the full cost of the life interest although it generates tax exempt income.

Voluntary Widow's Election. No amortization deduction is allowable in the case of a voluntary election. The deduction is allowable only where the life interest was acquired for consideration.

> **Problem 9-8.** H's will left property with a basis and a fair market value of $500,000 to a typical widow's election trust, the H trust. His widow, W, elected to take under his will and transferred property with a basis and value of $650,000 to an identical, separate trust, the W trust. As a result of the election, W is entitled to the income from both trusts for life. Upon W's death the trust property will pass to their issue. What amortization deduction is W entitled to take each year assuming she is 50 years old? How much would the deduction be if she were 60, or 70? If W dies before she reaches her

life expectancy, could her executor deduct any "loss" on her investment? On the other hand, if W lives beyond her life expectancy, could she continue to deduct amortization? Would the amortization deduction be affected if the trustee purchased tax exempt bonds for one or both trusts?

§9.29.   Estate Tax Consequences: The Husband's Estate

The use of a forced widow's election does not affect the amount of property included in the husband's gross estate on his death. Only his share of the community property is includible whether or not his widow elects to transfer her property in accordance with his plan. If the widow elects to accept an interest in the testamentary trust created by his will and to transfer her share of the community property to the trust, it does not augment his estate in any way. Instead, the widow's share passes directly from her to the trustee and does not become part of his estate. Coffman-Dobson Bank & Trust Co., 20 B.T.A. 890 (1930), *acq.* X-1 C.B. 13 (1931). The same rule applies where the transfer is made pursuant to an inter vivos election. Pacific National Bank, 40 B.T.A. 128 (1939), *acq.*, 1939-2 C.B. 28. If the widow elects to take under the husband's will, she receives a life income interest in the trust. No marital deduction is allowable to the husband's estate to the extent of the value of the remainder interest the widow was required to transfer. §2056(b)(4); United States v. Stapf, 375 U.S. 118 (1963). It is unclear whether or not a deduction would be allowable under §2056(b)(7) for the balance. *See* §5.18, *supra.* A deduction should be allowable if the widow's interest constitutes a qualifying income interest for life in a sufficiently separate portion of the property transferred to the trust by the decedent.

§9.30.   Estate Tax Consequences: The Widow's Estate

The widow should not hold any control over the property her husband transferred to the trust that might cause it to be included in her estate under §2041. Of course, any portion of the trust with respect to which a marital deduction was allowed to the husband's estate under §2056(b)(7) is includible in the widow's estate under §2044. Apart from those concerns, the main issue is the extent to which the trust may be included in the widow's estate under §2036(a)(1). Of course, none of the property she transferred to the trust is includible in her estate under §§2035 to 2038 if she received full and adequate consideration in exchange for it. The adequacy of the consideration requires a comparison of the value of the interests she transferred with the value of the interests she received. If the widow did not receive full consideration, the property she transferred must be included in her estate, valued on the date of her death, less the value of the interests she received in exchange. §2043(a). Under the "frozen dollar" approach of §2043(a), the consideration she received is limited to its actuarial value on the date of her election. United States v. Past, 347 F.2d 7 (9th Cir. 1965). The consideration offset is not based on the actual amount of income she received. The portion of the value of the trust that is includible in her estate under §2036(a) is fixed by her percentage contribution to the corpus of the trust. In contrast, the consideration offset is fixed and not proportional. Also, the value of the offset is determined by the actuarial tables in effect on the date of the election, which were used to determine the gift tax consequences of the transfer, and not on subsequently adopted tables that assume a higher yield. Estate of Elfrida G. Simmie, 69 T.C. 890 (1978), *aff'd*, 632 F.2d 93 (9th Cir. 1980).

In determining the adequacy of the consideration, the courts seem to consider that the widow transferred the entire interest in her property in exchange for a life interest in the net amount of property her husband transferred to the trust. United States v. Righter, 400 F.2d 344 (8th Cir. 1968); United States v. Past, 347 F.2d 7 (9th Cir. 1965); Estate of Lillian B. Gregory, 39 T.C. 1012 (1963) (dicta). That approach totally ignores the value of the life estate the widow retained in her share of the property. It would be logical, and consistent with the gift tax treatment, to consider that the widow transferred only a remainder interest in her property in exchange for a life interest in the decedent's property, or that she transferred the entire interest in her property but is credited with receiving a life estate in all of the property transferred to the trust. The significance of the difference is illustrated in the following example:

> **Example 9-23.** The community property estate of H and W had a total value of $1,200,000 when H died. Under H's will his net share of the property, $450,000, passed to the trustee of a widow's election trust, the H trust. All of the net income of the H trust was payable to his widow, W, for her life, if she survived him and transferred her share of the community property to an identical trust, the W trust. Upon W's death the remainder interests in both trusts were distributable to their children. If W did not transfer her share of the community property to the W trust, she would have received no benefit from the H trust. W was 65 years of age when she elected to transfer her share of the community property, $550,000, to the W trust. According to Table A(2) the factor for the life estate of a 65-year-old female is .55803 and the factor for the remainder following her life is .44197. Thus, W's life interest in H's share of the property is worth $251,114 and the remainder is worth $198,886. W's life interest in her share of the property is worth $306,917 and the remainder is worth $243,083.

Under the approach apparently taken by the courts, W received only a life estate in H's property, worth $251,114, in exchange for the full value of her share of the property, $550,000. (This ignores the value of the life interest W retained in her share of the property, which, at 6%, should yield her income of $306,917 over her lifetime.) W's estate must include the value of the W trust on the estate tax valuation date applicable to her estate less the consideration she received, valued in accordance with §2043(a) at the time of her election. This "frozen dollar" approach limits the consideration offset to $251,114 regardless of any increase in the size of the trust corpus. *See* United States v. Past, 347 F.2d 7 (9th Cir. 1965).

Under the alternative theory nothing is includible in W's gross estate under §§2035 to 2038; W transferred an interest worth $243,083 for which she received an interest worth slightly more, $251,114.

Voluntary Election. No offset is allowable in the case of a voluntary election because the widow does not receive any additional interests by reason of the election and transfer.

Problem 9-9. When H died earlier this year H and W owned community property worth a total of $1,000,000. H left his net share of the property, $400,000, to a typical widow's election trust, the H trust. His 60-year-old widow, W, accepted the plan and transferred her share of the property, worth $500,000, to an identical trust, the W trust. Does W's election result in any gift tax liability assuming that she had not previously made any taxable gifts? If the value of the property remains the same, will the estate tax due from her estate be more or less than if she had elected against the will and retained outright ownership of her interest in the community property ($500,000)?

§9.31.   Alternative Widow's Election Plans: Measured Elections

Planners have shown considerable ingenuity in devising variations on the basic widow's election plan. Some plans, such as the voluntary measured election developed by Miller and Martin, are primarily concerned with reducing or eliminating the estate tax on the widow's share of the property. Voluntary Widow's Election: Nation-Wide Planning for the Million Dollar Estate, 1 Cal. W.L. Rev. 63 (1965). Under it the widow receives a life interest in the husband's net share of the property if she transfers property with an exactly equivalent value to their children or to a trust for the benefit of their children. The object of the plan is to assure that the life interest the widow receives will constitute full and adequate consideration for the property she transfers. As a result, her transfer does not involve a gift and none of it will be included in her gross estate under §2036. *See* §9.30, *supra*. However, the exchange will involve the same income tax consequences as the traditional election. Thus, the trustee may realize a substantial gain under §1001(e). The widow might also realize a small gain, but she will be entitled to amortize the cost of her interest.

> **Example 9-24.** H left his residuary estate to the trustee of a testamentary trust who was authorized to sell a life interest in the trust to W in exchange for the transfer by W of property with a value equal to the actuarial value of the life interest to the trustee of a separate trust for the benefit of their adult children. Under H's will the life estate was required to be valued by multiplying the fair market value of the trust assets by the appropriate life interest factor from Table A(2), Reg. §20.2031-10. Thus, if W was 60 years old at the time and the trust assets had a value of $500,000, she would be required to transfer property to the trustee with a value of $316,130. Under those assumptions, W's life estate in H's trust is worth $316,130 ($500,000 × .63226). Because of §1001(e) the trustee would probably realize a gain of the same amount as a result of the exchange. However, W would be entitled to an amortization deduction of $14,568.20 based upon a life expectancy of 21.7 years. Table I, Reg. §1.72-9. §8.29, *supra*. W might also realize a gain on the transaction, but it would probably be quite small because the basis in the property she transferred is adjusted to its estate tax value in H's estate under §1014. Because W made the transfer for full and adequate consideration, it does not involve a gift. For the same reason, no part of the property is includible in her gross estate.

§9.32.   *Alternative Widow's Election Plans: Annuity Trust-Accumulation Trust Plans*

Another approach, dubbed the "annuity" widow's election by some commentators, takes a different tack. The concept is developed in more detail in Professor Norman Lane's article, The Widow's Election as a Private Annuity: Boon or Bane for Estate Planners, 44 So. Cal. L. Rev. 74, 132-138 (1971). It is also discussed in H. Weinstock, Planning an Estate: A Guidebook of Principles and Techniques §§5.25 to 5.29 (1977). Under this plan the husband's share of the property is transferred to a discretionary bypass trust in which the widow does not have any fixed rights. However, the trustee of the trust is authorized to make distributions of principal and income to the widow after the separate trust funded with her share of the property is exhausted. The "annuity" aspect is a feature of the trust funded with the widow's share of the community property. If the widow follows through with the plan, she transfers her share of the community property to a separate trust in which she retains the life income interest and the right to receive an annual fixed payment of principal.

The overall objective of the annuity plan is to reduce the amount of property that is subject to inclusion in the widow's estate. That is accomplished by requiring her trust to be exhausted before she is entitled to any distribution from the husband's trust. The transfer to the widow's trust will involve at least a small gift, equal to the value of the property transferred less the value of the widow's right to income and principal distributions. Whatever amount remains in the widow's trust at her death is fully includible in her gross estate. No consideration offset is available under §2043(a) because she did not receive any fixed consideration in exchange for the transfer of her property to the trust. Since the plan does not involve a sale or exchange, no gain or loss is realized on the transfer of the widow's property to the trust. For the same reason the widow is not entitled to any amortization deduction.

The plan assumes that the widow will consume a substantial part of her share of the community property during her lifetime. The result is essentially the same as if she used her share of the community property to purchase an annuity. Indeed, such an approach has been suggested by other commentators. *See, e.g.,* Cohen, Recent Developments in the Taxation of Private Annuities, U. So. Cal. 16th Tax Inst. 491 (1964). Backup support for the widow is provided by a discretionary trust which, incidentally, would not qualify for a marital deduction under §2056(b)(7) in the husband's estate. The plan could generate some estate tax savings. However, the widow may feel a bit insecure if her future security depends upon the trustee's exercise of discretion.

§9.33. *State Tax Consequences*

The state income and transfer tax consequences of a widow's election should not be ignored at any stage. A widow's election plan may have an important impact on the state death tax when the husband dies. For example, the election may be taxed as if the deceased husband transferred his share of the community property to the remainderman of the widow's election trust. In re Estate of Brubaker, 98 Cal. Rptr. 762 (Cal. App. 1971) (former California inheritance tax law). The transfer may also result in a taxable gift from the widow to the remainderman. Finally, when the widow dies, some of the property she transferred to the trust will probably be subject to the death tax. Some states that impose inheritance taxes may not allow the widow's share of the property to be reduced by any consideration she received from her husband. *E.g.,* In re Estate of Patten, 419 P.2d 157 (Wash. 1966) (former Washington inheritance tax law). Such states reason that a consideration analysis is inappropriate where the state tax is based upon the value of the property received by the transferee and not upon the value of the property to the decedent or to his or her estate.

§9.34. Conclusion

The forced widow's election is probably not suitable for most clients. Although the widow can be given the benefit of a second look at the plan after her husband's death, her options are very limited. In order for the election to qualify as a bargained-for exchange the plan must be relatively inflexible and the widow must, in effect, be disinherited if she elects against the will. The tax consequences remain generally favorable, except for the probability that the trust will realize a large gain if the widow elects to take under the will. That consideration alone is sufficient to deter many planners from recommending a forced widow's election plan.

A voluntary widow's election plan may be more consistent with the overall planning goals of most clients. The attractiveness of the plan is enhanced by the 1981 Act, which made a marital deduction available under §2056(b)(7) for the property the husband leaves to the trust. Unfortunately such a trust cannot allow any distributions to be made to any other person during the widow's lifetime. Flexibility can be added to the plan by transferring an amount equal to the amount sheltered by the unified credit in the husband's estate to a discretionary trust from which distributions could be made to other family members. In addition, the widow could be given a special testamentary power to appoint the assets of one or both trusts. As noted above some commentators have encouraged the use of a voluntary widow's election instead of a forced one. *See, e.g.,* Kahn & Gallo, The Widow's Election: A Return to Fundamentals, 24 Stan. L. Rev. 531 (1972).

BIBLIOGRAPHY

I.   General discussions of family transfers for value:

 Croft & Hipple, Planning Lifetime Property Transfers: Private Annuities, Installment Sales and Gift-Leasebacks, 11 Real Prop., Prob. & Tr. J. 253 (1976)

 Fiore, Estate and Value Opportunity Shifting Through Installment Sales, Private Annuities and Interest Free Loans, U. Miami 14th Inst. Est. Plan., Ch. 7 (1980)

 Report of Committee on Tax and Estate Planning — Predeath Estate Planning Through Family Bargaining, 8 Real Prop., Prob. & Tr. J. 223 (1973)

II. Installment sales:

　　Emory & Hjorth, An Analysis of the Changes Made by the Installment Sales Revision Act of 1980, 54 J. Tax. 66, 130 (1981)

　　Ginsburg, Taxing the Sale for Future Payment, 30 Tax. L. Rev. 471, 532 (1975)

　　Goldstein, Installment Obligations and the Estate Plan, U. Miami 8th Inst. Est. Plan., Ch. 14 (1974)

　　Joint Report on H.R. 3899: Simplification of Installment Sale Reporting, 33 Tax Law. 349 (1980)

III. Private annuities:

　　Ekman, Private Annuities Revisited, U. Miami 8th Inst. Est. Plan., Ch. 11 (1974)

　　Johnson, The Lazarus Complex: Estate Planning for Intrafamily Transfers Through the Use of Private Annuities and Installment Sales, 16 Idaho L. Rev. 7 (1979)

　　Malloy & Bufkin, Critical Tax and Financial Factors that Must Be Considered When Planning a Private Annuity, 3 Est. Plan. 2 (1975)

　　O'Sullivan, The Private Annuity: A New Look at an Old Estate Planning Tool, 17 Washburn L.J. 466 (1978)

IV. Gift or sale and leaseback:

　　Aitken, Coping with the Tough New Court Tests for Deductions in Leaseback Situations, 44 J. Tax. 47 (1976)

　　Elder, Gifts and Leasebacks: The Current Scene, U. Miami 11th Inst. Est. Plan., Ch. 14 (1977)

　　Rental Payments Under "Clifford" Trust and Leaseback or Similar Arrangements as Deductible "Ordinary and Necessary Business Expenses" Under §162 of Internal Revenue Code of 1954 (26 USC §162(a)(3)), 44 A.L.R. Fed. 195 (1979)

V. Widow's election — transfer of life or term interests for consideration:

　　Freeland, Lind & Stephens, What Are the Income Tax Consequences of an Estate's Sale of a Life Interest? 34 J. Tax. 376 (1971)

　　Johanson, Revocable Trusts, Widow's Election Wills and Community Property: The Tax Problem, 47 Texas L. Rev. 1247 (1969)

　　Lane, Widow's Election as a Private Annuity: Boon or Bane for Estate Planners, 44 S. Cal. L. Rev. 74 (1971)

　　Miller & Martin, Voluntary Widow's Election: Nation-Wide Planning for the Million Dollar Estate, 1 Cal. W.L. Rev. 63 (1965)

CHAPTER 10

TRUSTS

The purposes for which trusts can be created are as unlimited as the imagination of lawyers. There are no technical rules restricting the creation of trusts. The trust can be and has been applied as a device for accomplishing many different purposes. One of the most important is and has always been the making of family settlements. Through the trust it is possible to separate the benefits of ownership from the burdens of ownership. The whole responsibility for the management of the property is thrown upon the trustee. It is possible to create successive interests which could not be effectively created by giving successive legal interests. It is possible to make the extent of the interests of the beneficiaries dependent upon the discretion of the trustee. It is possible, to a certain extent at least, to protect the beneficiaries in the enjoyment of their interests by making those interests inalienable and putting them beyond the reach of creditors. 1 Scott, Trusts §1 at p. 4 (3d ed. 1967).

A.   INTRODUCTION

§10.1.   Scope

The most important and most common types of trusts are considered in this chapter, including the revocable trust (§§10.5 to 10.15), the irrevocable permanent trust, and the irrevocable short-term trust (§§10.16 to 10.32). Some features of specialized types of trusts are reviewed in other chapters (*e.g.*, marital deduction trusts are discussed in Chapter 5; insurance trusts in Chapter 6; trusts for minors in Chapter 7; charitable remainder trusts in Chapter 8; and widow's election trusts in Chapter 9).

The opening sections of this chapter summarize the basic income, gift, and estate tax consequences of establishing a trust. Included here is a review of the basic income tax rules applicable to trusts. Because the trust is widely used as a probate avoidance device, some comparisons are drawn between the tax treatment given trusts on the one hand and estates on the other. Some of the same tax points recur at later places in the chapter, particularly in the review of the grantor trust rules in §§10.27 to 10.32, *infra*.

The second part, Part B, takes a long look at the revocable trust, which is probably the most common form of trust. It includes a review of some of the substantive law regarding the use of the trust, proceeds to a discussion of the advantages and disadvantages of the trust, and concludes with a summary of the principal tax consequences of using that form of trust.

Planning the powers and interests of a beneficiary in an irrevocable trust is the subject of Part C. It extends from a consideration of the use of multiple trusts through the nature and transferability of the beneficiary's interest to the conferral of powers of appointment and the appointment of the beneficiary as fiduciary. Part D is a companion piece, which is concerned with planning the grantor's interests in an irrevocable trust. Those parts also include a consideration of the grantor trust rules and the use of the short-term irrevocable trust. Since definitive income tax rules were added in 1954 the short-term irrevocable trust has become a popular way to shift income from the grantor to others. The trust is attractive to many clients because it allows the grantor to retain a reversionary interest in the property — so long as the reversion is not expected to take effect within 10 years. Despite the unification of the transfer tax structure in 1976 the short-term trust remains a profitable estate-planning tool for taxpayers with excess current income.

The concluding part of this chapter, Part E, briefly discusses the choice of trustee and the selection of property to transfer to the trustee. Although this book does not give detailed attention to trust administration, which is itself a substantial and complicated subject, Part E does discuss 2 matters about which trusts often should include additional directions: the investment of trust funds and the allocation of receipts and disbursements between income and principal. A planner must be concerned about a host of other matters regarding administration of the trust, of which these 2 serve as good illustrations. The part concludes with a discussion of the use of perpetuities savings clauses.

A Perspective on Planning. A carefully planned and drafted trust is a valuable planning tool. Particular care is required in the case of an irrevocable trust because the inflexibility of the arrangement necessarily limits its ability to meet the beneficiaries' long-term needs. In general, the planner is challenged to make the trust as flexible as possible without giving up any of the potential tax savings. The dual objectives of flexibility and tax savings are often met by giving the trustee some discretion to make distributions to a class of beneficiaries and by giving some beneficiaries special power of appointment over the trust property. The ultimate balance between flexibility and tax savings should be struck by the client after receiving an adequate explanation from the planner. Above all, a client should not be permitted to create a trust unless he or she understands its terms and effect.

Shams. The planner and client should be wary of trust plans that are held out to generate substantial tax savings, but seem to lack economic reality or substance. In recent years many gullible taxpayers, particularly medical professionals and others with large personal service incomes, have bought expensive trust packages they hoped would insulate their income from taxation. Instead, they have often been denied a deduction under §212 for the cost of the trust package (Rev. Rul. 79-324, 1979-2 C.B. 119), taxed on the income of the trust, and held liable for a 5% penalty for "negligence or intentional disregard of rules and regulations." *E.g.,* Richard L. Wesenberg, 69 T.C. 1005 (1978) (physician); Louis Markosian, 73 T.C. 1235 (1980) (dentist).

Trusts of the type involved in the *Wesenberg* and *Markosian* cases have been marketed under a variety of names. In any case the arrangement generally calls for the taxpayer to transfer all of his or her property and future services to a trust in which the taxpayer has a substantial interest and over which the taxpayer and other nonadverse parties have substantial controls. Through this miraculous medium the income received by the trust is supposed to escape taxation. Quite to the contrary, because of the taxpayer's retained interests and controls the income of the trust is taxed to the grantor under §§671 to 677, Rev. Rul. 75-257, 1975-2 C.B. 251. For the same reason, the transfer of property to the trust is not a completed gift (Rev. Rul. 75-260, 1975-2 C.B. 376) and the property transferred to the trust is fully includible in the transferor's estate. Rev. Rul. 75-259, 1975-2 C.B. 361.

Another expensive but ineffective package involves the transfer of property to a "foreign tax haven double trust." Rev. Rul. 80-74, 1980-1 C.B. 137. The promoter of the "double trust" involved in Rev. Rul. 80-74 represented that the trust would radically reduce or eliminate the taxpayer's income tax liability, avoid probate, eliminate estate and gift tax liabilities, and avoid state and local taxes. The plan involves the creation of a trust in a foreign country by an agent of the promoter to which the taxpayer transfers income-producing property. The income of the trust is distributed to a second foreign trust that makes distributions to the taxpayer and his family as directed by the taxpayer as trustee. Not surprisingly, Rev. Rul. 80-74 concludes that the creation of the trusts is a sham and will not be recognized for tax purposes. Instead, all of the income will be taxed to the grantor, who is not entitled to a deduction under §212 for the expenses incurred in connection with the establishment of the "double trust."

§10.2. *Income Tax Summary*

A trust is generally treated as a separate entity, subject to the same basic tax rules that apply to individuals. Thus, a trust reports the same items of income and is usually entitled to the same types of deductions and credits as individuals. In addition, a trust is allowed a deduction for amounts paid, credited, or required to be distributed to beneficiaries during the year. §§651(a), 661(a). The deduction is limited, however, to the distributable net income (DNI) of the trust, which is the taxable income of the trust adjusted as provided in §643(a). The beneficiaries are required to report an amount equal to the distribution deduction in their returns. §§652(a), 662(a).

A trust does not receive the benefit of the zero bracket amount and is not subject to the tax on self employment income. Limited personal exemptions are allowable to trusts: A trust that is required to distribute all of its income currently, has no charitable beneficiaries, and makes no distributions of principal during the year (a "simple" trust) is entitled to a $300 exemption; all other trusts ("complex" trusts) are entitled to $100 exemptions. (Estates are generally subject to the rules applicable to complex trusts, but are entitled to a $600 personal exemption.) Where capital gains of a trust are not distributed, a trust is entitled to the 60% long-term capital gains deduction under §1202. A trust is subject to the same tax rate that applies to married persons who file separate returns (§1(e)). The tax may be offset by some credits, but not the §41 credit for political contributions (§642(a)(2)).

The separate existence of a trust is largely disregarded to the extent the grantor or any other person is treated as owner of the trust under Subpart E, §§671 to 678. The rules of Subpart E establish the exclusive means by which the income of a trust is includible in the income of a grantor or other person solely by reason of his or her dominion and control over the trust. Reg. §1.671-1(c). However, the rules do not govern the outcome of cases involving the assignment of income, whether or not the assignment is to a trust. "[F]or example, a person who assigns his right to future income under an employment contract may be taxed on that income even though the assignment is to a trust over which the assignor has retained none of the controls specified in sections 671 through 677." *Id.* Under §§671 to 677 the grantor is treated as the owner of a trust to the extent he or she retains any of the interests or controls proscribed by §§673 to 677 (*e.g.*, a reversionary interest that will take effect within 10 years (§673), controls over the beneficial enjoyment of the trust (§674), extensive administrative controls (§675), or a power to revoke the trust (§676)). *See* §§10.26 to 10.32, *infra*.

A person other than the grantor of a trust is treated as its owner to the extent he or she has the power, acting alone, to vest the corpus or income of the trust in himself or herself. §678(a). *See* §10.20, *infra*. However, a person other than the grantor is not treated as the owner of any part of the trust of which the grantor is treated as the owner under §§671 to 677 (*i.e.*, the provisions of §§673 to 677 prevail over those of §678). Where the grantor or another person is treated as the owner of the entire trust, a fiduciary income tax return (Form 1041) should not be filed for the trust. "Instead, all items of income, deductions, and credit from the trust should be reported on the individual's Form 1040 in accordance with its accompanying instructions." Reg. §1.671-4(b). In other cases, the income, deductions, and credits attributable to the part of a trust of which the grantor or another person is treated as the owner are not reported by the trust on its Form 1041, but should be shown on a separate statement attached to that form. Reg. §1.671-4(a).

As noted above, the beneficiaries of a trust are generally required to report the amount of distributions they receive to the extent the trust was allowed a distribution deduction. §§652(a), 662(a). However, tracking the provisions of §102, a trust is not allowed to deduct, and the beneficiaries are not required to report, a distribution made in satisfaction of a specific gift of money or other property that is payable all at once or in not more than 3 installments. §663(a). Reflecting the conduit principle, a distribution has the same character in the hands of a beneficiary as it had in the hands of the trustee. §§652(a), 662(b). Specifically, a distribution is considered to consist of the same proportion of each class of items entering into the computation of the trust's DNI as the total of each class bears to the total DNI of the trust, unless the trust instrument or local law specifically allocates different classes of income to different beneficiaries. Trusts generally do not attempt to allocate specific classes of income to particular beneficiaries. However, some trusts attempt to do so, particularly where there is a wide disparity in the income tax rates applicable to the beneficiaries or where there is a charitable beneficiary. Examples of provisions the IRS will recognize as specific allocations of income to different beneficiaries are set forth in Reg. §1.652(b)-2(b). The general allocation principles are described in Regs. §§1.652(b)-1; 1.662(b)-1, -2.

Where the trust and a beneficiary have different taxable years, the amount the beneficiary is required to include in his or her income is based on the income of the trust for the year (or years) that end within the beneficiary's taxable year. The trustee should have this rule in mind when he or she chooses a taxable year for a testamentary trust or an inter vivos trust that has become irrevocable by reason of the grantor's death.

Example 10-1. A testamentary trust reports its income on the basis of a fiscal year ending on June 30. The beneficiaries are cash basis taxpayers who file calendar year returns. The amount of distributions reported by the beneficiaries in their returns for calendar 1983 are determined by the trust's return for the year beginning on July 1, 1982, and ending on June 30, 1983. The same rule applies where the first year of the trust is a short one (*e.g.*, if the testamentary trust were established after July 1, 1982) (*e.g.*, February 15, 1983). *See* Regs. §§1.652(c)-1, 1.662(c)-1.

However, the fiduciary of a trust may elect under §663(b) to treat any amount that is properly paid or credited to a beneficiary within the first 65 days following the close of the taxable year as an amount properly paid or distributed on the last day of such taxable year. This 65-day rule allows trustees to avoid the unintentional accumulation of income, which might otherwise be subject to the throwback rules of §§665 to 668. By way of illustration, the trustee in Example 10-1 could elect to treat amounts properly paid or credited within 65 days following June 30, 1983, as if they had been distributed prior to that date. The election, of course, has an impact on the distribution deduction of the trust and the amounts reportable as income by the beneficiaries.

A trust that does not distribute all of its income currently (a complex trust) initially bears the tax on any ordinary income it accumulates. As explained below, ordinary income that has already been taxed to the trust may be subject to an additional tax under the throwback rules of §§665 to 667 when it is distributed. The rules are designed to prevent trusts from being used to defeat the progressive character of the income tax, which would otherwise be possible if accumulated income could be distributed tax free to higher bracket beneficiaries. Importantly, the throwback rules do not apply to capital gains or to any distributions made by estates. Accumulation distributions are taxed to the distributees under a special form of income averaging. The amount of an accumulation distribution includes any income tax paid by the trust with respect to the distribution (*i.e.*, the tax paid by the trust is "grossed up"). A distributee is allowed a credit for the taxes paid by the trust and treated as distributed to him or her. However, the credit can only be applied against the distributee's additional tax computed under the throwback rules — it cannot give rise to a refund or be used as a credit against the distributee's other tax liability. §666(e).

Distributable Net Income (§643(a))

The term "distributable net income" has no application except in the taxation of estates and trusts and their beneficiaries. It limits the deductions allowable to estates and trusts for amounts paid, credited, or required to be distributed to beneficiaries and is used to determine how much of an amount paid, credited, or required to be distributed to a beneficiary will be includible in his gross income. It is also used to determine the character of distributions to the beneficiaries. Distributable net income means for any taxable year, the taxable income (as defined in section 63) of the estate or trust, computed with the modifications set forth in §§1.643(a)-1 through 1.643(a)-7. Reg. §1.643(a)-0.

As indicated in the regulation, the taxable income of the trust is the starting point from which DNI is computed. Naturally, no deductions are taken into account for the distributions to beneficiaries or for the personal exemption otherwise allowable under §642(b). §§643(a)(1), (2). Capital gains are excluded unless they are allocated to income or are paid, credited, or required to be distributed to a beneficiary during the taxable year. However, capital gains paid, permanently set aside, or to be used for charitable purposes are taken into account to the extent a charitable deduction under §642(c) was allowed with respect to the gains. §643(a)(3), Reg. §1.643(a)-3(a)(3). Losses from the sale or exchange of capital assets are excluded except to the extent they enter into the determination of any capital gains that are paid, credited, or required to be distributed to any beneficiary during the year. The treatment of capital gains and losses accords with normal trust accounting rules under which they do not enter into the computation of net income. (Importantly, capital gains are not subject to the throwback rules — once they are taxed to the trust they will not attract a tax upon distribution.) Gains and losses are taken into account in computing the DNI of a trust in some circumstances, such as the year in which the trust terminates or makes partial distributions. *See* Reg. §1.643(a)-3(d), *Example* (4). The deduction under §1202 for 60% of the amount of long-term capital gains is disregarded, except to the extent it is allocable to capital gains that are paid, permanently set aside, or to be used for charitable purposes. §643(a)(3). Reg. §1.643(a)-3(c). Where capital gains are included in DNI, the distributee will be entitled to the §1202 deduction. In other cases the trust will take the §1202 deduction in computing its tax.

Under §643(a)(4) in the case of a simple trust extraordinary dividends and taxable stock dividends are excluded to the extent the trustee in good faith does not pay or credit them to any beneficiary and they are allocated to corpus. Conversely, extraordinary dividends and stock dividends are included in computing DNI in the case of a complex trust, or where the dividends are not allocated to corpus for trust accounting purposes. Here again the distinction parallels normal trust accounting rules.

The amount of tax-exempt interest received by the trust is included in computing DNI, reduced by the expenses attributable to it that are not deductible by reason of §265 (which bars the deduction of expenses under §212 to the extent they are incurred in connection with the production of tax-exempt income). §643(a)(5). The amount included is also reduced by a portion of the tax-exempt interest that is considered to be paid, permanently set aside, or to be used for charitable purposes. The latter reduction is required because the full amount of the charitable payments or set asides is already deducted by the trust under §642(c). Similarly, the amount of any dividends or interest excluded from gross income under §116 is included in computing DNI. §643(a)(7). The character of such dividends and interest does carry over to the beneficiaries under the conduit principle. The computation of DNI under §643 is illustrated by the following example from Reg. §1.643(d)-2(a):

> *Example.* (1) Under the terms of the trust instrument, the income of a trust is required to be currently distributed to W during her life. Capital gains are allocable to corpus and all expenses are charges against corpus. During the taxable year the trust has the following items of income and expenses:

Dividends from domestic corporations	$30,000
Extraordinary dividends allocated to corpus by the trustees in good faith	20,000
Taxable interest	10,000
Tax-exempt interest	10,000
Long-term capital gains	10,000
Trustee's commissions and miscellaneous expenses allocable to corpus	5,000

> (2) The "income" of the trust determined under §643(b) which is currently distributable to W is $50,000, consisting of dividends of $30,000, taxable interest of $10,000 and tax-exempt interest of $10,000. The trustee's commissions and miscellaneous expenses allocable to tax-exempt interest amount to $1,000 (10,000/50,000 × $5,000).
> (3) The "distributable net income" determined under section 643(a) amounts to $45,000 computed as follows:

Dividends from domestic corporations		$30,000
Taxable interest		10,000
Nontaxable interest	$10,000	
Less: Expenses allocable thereto	1,000	9,000
Total		49,000
Less: Expenses ($5,000 less $1,000 allocable to tax-exempt interest)		4,000
Distributable net income		45,000

In determining the distributable net income of $45,000, the taxable income of the trust is computed with the following modifications: No deductions are allowed for distributions to W and for personal exemption of the trust (section 643(a)(1) and (2)); capital gains allocable to corpus are excluded and the deduction allowable under section 1202 is not taken into account (section 643(a)(3)); the extraordinary dividends allocated to corpus by the trustee in good faith are excluded (section 643(a)(4)); and the tax-exempt interest (as adjusted for expenses) and the dividend exclusion . . . are included (section 643(a)(5) and (7)). . . .

Rules Applicable to Simple Trusts (§§651, 652). A trust that is required to distribute all of its income currently (which has reference to its income as determined for trust accounting purposes), does not provide for payment of any charitable gifts, and does not make any distribution other than of current income is a "simple" trust. §651, Reg. §1.651(a)-1. All other trusts are "complex" trusts. The classification, which affects the computation of DNI, the personal tax exemptions, etc., is made each year. Accordingly, a trust that requires all income to be distributed currently and authorizes the trustee to make discretionary distributions of principal is a simple trust except for years during which it distributes principal. In contrast, a trust that authorizes the trustee to accumulate income is necessarily a complex trust. Note that a trust is a complex trust in its final year and in the year in which it makes any partial distributions of corpus. Estates are subject to most of the rules applicable to complex trusts.

Under §651(a) a simple trust is entitled to deduct the amount it is required to distribute currently. However, the amount of the deduction cannot exceed the trust's DNI, reduced by the amount of items reflected in DNI, but not included in the trust's income (*e.g.*, life insurance excludible under §101(a) and municipal bond interest exempt under §103). §651(b). It is necessary to make the reduction so the trust will not benefit doubly from the items — once because they are excluded from income and again as the result of a distribution deduction. The point is illustrated in this example from Reg. §1.651(b)-1: "Assume that the distributable net income of a trust as computed under §643(a) amounts to $99,000 but includes nontaxable income of $9,000. Then distributable net income for the purpose of determining the deduction allowable under section 651 is $90,000 ($99,000 less $9,000 nontaxable income)."

The beneficiary of a simple trust includes in his or her income the amount of income required currently to be distributed for such year, whether or not actually distributed. §652(a), Reg. §1.652(a)-1. However, the amount includible in the beneficiary's income cannot exceed the trust's DNI for the year. Where the amount required to be distributed exceeds DNI, each beneficiary includes in his or her income an amount equivalent to his or her proportionate share of DNI. Each item distributed to a beneficiary has the same character in his or her hands that it had in the hands of the trust. "For example, to the extent that the amounts specified in §1.652(a)-1 consist of income exempt from tax under section 103, such amounts are not included in the beneficiary's gross income." Reg. §1.652(b)-1. (This exclusion is consistent with the disallowance of a distribution deduction for items excluded from the trust's income as noted above.)

Amounts included in a beneficiary's gross income are treated as consisting of the same proportion of each class of items entering into DNI as the total of each class bears to DNI unless the terms of the trust specifically allocate different classes of income to different beneficiaries. This point is illustrated by this example from the regulations, Reg. §1.652(b)-2(a):

> Assume that under the terms of the governing instrument beneficiary A is to receive currently one-half of the trust income and beneficiaries B and C are each to receive currently one-quarter, and the distributable net income of the trust (after allocation of expenses) consists of dividends of $10,000, taxable interest of $10,000, and tax-exempt interest of $4,000. A will be deemed to have received $5,000 of dividends, $5,000 of taxable interest, and $2,000 of tax-exempt interest; B and C will each be deemed to have received $2,500 of dividends, $2,500 of taxable interest, and $1,000 of tax-exempt interest. However, if the terms of the trust specifically allocate different classes of income to different beneficiaries, entirely or in part, or if local law requires such an allocation, each beneficiary will be deemed to have received those items of income specifically allocated to him.

In determining the nature of amounts distributed to the beneficiaries and included in their incomes, it is necessary to allocate the deductions of a trust that enter into the computation of DNI. The rules under which the allocations are made are described in Reg. §1.652(b)-3. In brief, the rules provide: First, all deductible items directly attributable to one class of income are allocated to it (with the exception of excludible dividends and interest). Examples include expenses incurred in carrying on a trade or business, and expenses incurred in connection with the rental of property. Second, deductions not directly attributable to a specific class of income may be allocated to any class of income, including capital gains, that is taken into account in computing DNI. Examples of expenses that are not directly attributable to a specific class of income include trustee's commissions, safe deposit box rental, and state income and personal property taxes. Reg. §1.652(b)-3(c).

Example 10-2. The trust had income of $40,000 after direct expenses, consisting of $10,000 of business income, $10,000 of rental income, $10,000 of taxable interest, and $10,000 of tax-exempt income. The trustee's commissions were $4,000. One-fourth of the commissions must be allocated to the nontaxable income. The trustee may allocate the balance of the deductions in his or her discretion among items included in DNI (*e.g.*, business income or rental income). The balance of $3,000 must be used to reduce the amount includible in the beneficiaries' income even though the governing instrument or local law treats a portion of the commissions as attributable to corpus because they relate to capital gains or other items not included in income for trust accounting purposes. Reg. §1.652(b)-3. In effect, charging a portion of the commissions to corpus increases the amount of income received tax free by the beneficiary. "Thus the greater the commissions, legal fees or other expenses charged to corpus, the greater is the spendable income (after taxes) received currently by the beneficiaries, the increase being at the expense of principal." A. Michaelson & J. Blattmachr, Income Taxation of Estates & Trusts 50 (10th ed. 1978).

Third, if any deductions directly attributable to one class of income exceed that class of income, they may be allocated to another class of income. However, excess deductions attributable to nontaxable income may not be allocated to any other class of income.

Rules Applicable to Complex Trusts (§§661, 662). In computing the taxable income of a complex trust, the trust is allowed a deduction under §661(a) of an amount equal to the sum of 2 classes (or "tiers") of distributions. The first tier consists of the amount of income the trust is required to distribute currently, including the amount of an annuity or other item required to be paid currently out of income or corpus to the extent it is paid out of income for the current year). This amount corresponds to the deduction allowable to simple trusts. The second tier consists of any other amounts properly paid or credited or required to be distributed during the taxable year. It includes, for example, an annuity to the extent it is not payable out of current income, distributions of property in kind, and discretionary distributions of corpus. Of course, the distribution deduction cannot exceed the trust's DNI, reduced as in the case of a simple trust, by the amount of nontaxable items included in DNI (*e.g.*, life insurance proceeds excludible under §101(a), municipal bond interest that is tax exempt under §103).

The character of the amounts deducted by the trust and includible in the beneficiaries' income is determined in essentially the same manner as in the case of a simple trust. Thus, the character of each distribution consists of a proportionate amount of each class of income. §§661(b), 662(b). However, adjustments may be required, depending upon the amount of the distributions, the tiers to which they belong, and the amount of the trust's DNI. In brief, first tier distributions are taken from DNI first in determining the consequences of the distributions. Thus, if the first tier distributions absorb the full amount of the trust's DNI, no income is carried out to the second tier beneficiaries. In such a case, each first tier beneficiary is taxed on a proportionate amount of the distribution.

> **Example 10-3.** The trust provided for distribution of all current income in equal shares to A, B, and C. In addition, the trustee was authorized to make discretionary distributions of principal to the income beneficiaries, their spouses, or their children. Last year the trust income was $30,000 and its DNI was $27,000. The trustee distributed $10,000 to each of A, B, and C. He also made a discretionary distribution of $5,000 of principal to B. The trust has a distribution deduction of $27,000, the amount of its DNI for the year. That amount also establishes the maximum amount reportable by A, B, and C. Under the tier system, A, B, and C each report $9,000 of income. The second tier distribution to B is not deductible by the trust or includible in B's income.

Where the distributions to the first tier beneficiaries are less than the trust's DNI, a proportionate amount of the excess is included in the income of the second tier beneficiaries. For example, had the DNI of the trust in Example 10-3 been $32,000, each first tier beneficiary would have included $10,000 in his or her income and the second tier beneficiary, B, would have included the remaining $2,000 in his income. As pointed out by Arthur Michaelson and Jonathan Blattmachr, "The rationale of the tier system is that first-tier distributions are more realistically distributions of income than are other distributions by the trust, and hence should be the first to be taxed as income and thus to absorb distributable net income." Income Taxation of Estates & Trusts 21 (10th ed. 1978).

The separate share rule of §663(c) also applies to complex trusts that have more than one beneficiary with substantially separate and independent shares for the sole purpose of determining the amounts of DNI allocable to them under §§661 and 662. The application of the rule is significant where income is accumulated for one beneficiary and a distribution is made to the other beneficiary in excess of his or her proportionate share of income.

> **Example 10-4.** The trust provided for the income to be divided into equal shares for the benefit of A and B. The trustee was authorized to distribute or accumulate each share and to make such distributions of principal as he believed was in the best interests of the beneficiaries. Last year the trust income and its DNI was $20,000. The trustee accumulated A's share of the income ($10,000), but distributed B's share of the income to him along with principal of $5,000. Each share is treated as a separate trust. Thus, B received a distribution of only the DNI allocable to his share —

he was not required to report any of the DNI allocable to the income accumulated in A's share of the trust. However, the other $5,000 distributed to B might be a taxable accumulation distribution under the throwback rules.

The separate share rule does not permit the separate shares to be treated as separate trusts for any other purpose. Thus, it does not affect the filing of returns, the personal exemptions available, the allocation of excess deductions on termination of the trust, etc. The separate share treatment is mandatory, not elective. Reg. § 1.663(c)-1(d). It is not applicable to estates. Reg. § 1.663(c)-3(f).

Throwback Rules (§§665 to 667). The throwback rules of §§665 to 667 apply to accumulation distributions of ordinary income made by complex trusts. The rules do not apply to income accumulated by estates, which are less susceptible to tax avoidance through the accumulation of income. They also do not apply to accumulated capital gains, which encourages the use of trusts that recognize, are taxed on, and accumulate capital gains. (Note, however, that §644 does discourage the sale of appreciated property by a trust for 2 years following its transfer to the trust.) A further exception exempts income accumulated prior to the beneficiary's birth or his or her attainment of 21 years of age.

The throwback rules may subject an accumulation distribution by a trust that had undistributed net income for a preceding taxable year to an additional tax. The definitions of accumulation distribution and undistributed net income are critical to the application of the rules. Under §665(b) an accumulation distribution occurs where the amount of the second tier distributions (amounts properly paid, credited, or required to be distributed) exceeds the amount of DNI reduced by the amount of first tier distributions (amounts of income required to be distributed currently). A first tier distribution does not constitute an accumulation distribution although it exceeds the trust's DNI. Reg. § 1.665(b)-1A(c)(3). For all practical purposes, income accumulated before the birth of the beneficiary or his or her attainment of 21 is not taken into account in applying the throwback rules.

Undistributed net income is defined in §665(a) as the amount by which the trust's DNI for the year in question exceeds the sum of its first and second tier distributions and the amount of taxes borne by the trust on its DNI. For example, if a trust had DNI of $30,000 for the year, properly made distributions of $10,000 to beneficiaries, and paid a tax of $3,000 on its income, the trust would have an undistributed net income of $17,000 for the year. Distributions made within the first 65 days following the end of a taxable year are taken into account to the extent provided in §663(b) in determining the undistributed net income and accumulation distributions of the trust. *See* Reg. § 1.665(b)-1A(a)

Where a beneficiary receives an accumulation distribution the computation of the special tax requires several steps. First, the accumulation distribution is spread over the years the trust had undistributed net income, beginning with the earliest (but not prior to 1969) and moving forward. Second, the total amount of the accumulation distribution is divided by the number of years determined in step one over which the accumulation had taken place, excluding any year in which the undistributed net income was less than 25% of the average undistributed net income. §667(b)(3). Third, the average accumulation determined in step two is added to taxable income of the distributee for 3 of his or her 5 taxable years immediately preceding the year of the accumulation distribution (the years with the highest and the lowest taxable incomes are eliminated). §667(b)(1). Fourth, the distributee's tax for each of those 3 years is recalculated, with the inclusion of the average accumulation, and the additional amounts are added together and divided by 3. Fifth, the average increase in tax is multiplied by the number of years used as the denominator in step two (the years during which the distribution was deemed to have been accumulated). The excess of that amount over the amount of taxes paid by the trust and deemed distributed to the distributee is the additional amount of tax imposed in connection with the accumulation distribution.

Example 10-5. This year T received an accumulation distribution of $24,000, representing undistributed net income of the trust for the preceding 7 years. The trust had paid $4,000 in income tax on the income represented by the accumulation distribution. The total accumulation distribution is $28,000, which is considered to have been accumulated at the rate of $4,000 for each of the preceding 7 years. The years of T's highest and lowest taxable income during the 5 years immediately preceding the accumulation distribution are excluded and the average distribution of $4,000 is added to T's taxable income for each of the remaining 3 years. The additional income tax attributable to the inclusion of the $4,000 is then calculated. The average increase in tax for the 3 years is determined by adding the amount of the additional income tax for each year and dividing by 3. The resulting amount is multiplied by 7, representing the years during which the income was accumulated. The resulting amount represents T's tax liability, which is reduced by a credit for the $4,000 in tax previously paid by the trust. There would be no throwback had the income all been accumulated prior to T's birth or his or her attainment of 21. There would also be no throwback where accumulated income of an estate is distributed. Of course, a distribution to an estate beneficiary may carry out the current DNI of the estate, which is includible in the beneficiary's income.

The throwback rules discourage the creation of multiple accumulation trusts. First, in computing the special tax under §667(b)(1), the taxable income of a distributee includes the amount deemed distributed to him or her in prior years as a result of earlier accumulation distributions. §§667(b)(4). That is, the computation of the special tax takes prior accumulation distributions into account. Where accumulation distributions are made from more than one trust in the same taxable year the distributions are deemed to have been made consecutively in the order chosen by the distributee. §668(b)(5). Second, under §667(c) a special rule applies where a distributee receives accumulation distributions attributable to his or her same prior taxable year from more than 2 trusts. The accumulation distributions from the third and any additional trusts do not include any portion of the taxes paid by the trusts, nor is the distributee entitled to any credit for such taxes. An accumulation distribution is only taken into account for purposes of this rule where it, together with any other accumulation distributions deemed to have been made for the same year, amounts to $1,000 or more. §667(c)(2). Note that this de minimis rule may be satisfied by accumulation distributions made in more than one year. Similarly, the overall rule may come into play as a result of accumulation distributions made to the beneficiary in more than one of his or her taxable years. Note also that the special exclusion for income only accumulated prior to the distributee's birth or attainment of 21 does not apply to accumulation distributions received from more than 2 trusts with respect to the same prior taxable year of the distributee. §§665(b), 667.

It is possible, and may be profitable, to split income between 1 or 2 discretionary trusts and a beneficiary under 21. In such a case the trustees can optimize the allocation of income among the taxpayers by accumulating or distributing the income of the trusts. For that purpose the trusts could authorize the trustees to make income distributions to a minor beneficiary or to a custodian for the minor under the Uniform Gifts to Minors Act. Such a distribution would enable an adult to retain control over the funds although they are treated as having been distributed to the minor. In any event the income accumulated during the beneficiary's minority will be taxed to them and will not be subject to the throwback rules when an accumulation distribution is made to the beneficiary.

Other Multiple Trust Rules. From time to time the IRS has attempted to consolidate multiple trusts for tax purposes. In that connection it adopted Reg. §1.641(a)-0(c):

(c) Multiple trusts. Multiple trusts that have —
(1)   No substantially independent purposes (such as independent dispositive purposes),

(2) The same grantor and substantially the same beneficiary, and
(3) The avoidance or mitigation of (a) the progressive rates of tax (including mitigation as a result of deferral of tax) or (b) the minimum tax for tax preferences imposed by section 56 as their principal purpose,

shall be consolidated and treated as one trust for the purposes of subchapter J.

However, the IRS has generally not been successful in consolidating multiple trusts for tax purposes where the trustee has respected the separate character of the trusts by administering them separately and maintaining separate records. *See, e.g.,* Estelle Morris Trusts, 51 T.C. 20 (1968), *aff'd per curiam,* 427 F.2d 1361 (9th Cir. 1970) (separate identity of 10 trusts created for each of 2 minor beneficiaries upheld despite grantors' tax avoidance motivation). As the Tax Court pointed out in *Estelle Morris,* multiple trusts have been consolidated by the courts where they were not separately administered, citing Boyce v. United States, 190 F. Supp. 950 (W.D. La.), *aff'd per curiam,* 296 F.2d 731 (5th Cir. 1961) (90 trusts with a total initial corpus of $17,400 were shams), and Sence v. United States, 394 F.2d 842 (Ct. Cl. 1968) (19 trusts).

Problem 10-1. The Smith Family Trust established on January 1, 1979, required one-half of the current income to be distributed to the beneficiary, Sally Smith. The balance of the income could be accumulated or distributed to Sally's siblings, John and Norman. The taxable receipts of the trust, distributions to Sally, and related amounts for 1979 and subsequent years were as follows:

Year	Taxable Receipts	Distributions to Sally	Taxable Income	Tax Paid	Undistributed Income
1979	$40,000	$20,000	$20,000	$4,800	$15,200
1980	30,000	15,000	15,000	3,600	11,400
1981	38,000	19,000	19,000	4,550	14,450
1982	40,000	20,000	20,000	4,600	15,400
1983	35,000	80,000	-0-	-0-	-0-

Assuming that Sally became 21 prior to 1979, what was the amount of the accumulation distribution made to her in 1983? To which prior years is the accumulation distribution allocated? What is the amount of the average accumulation that will be added to Sally's income for 3 of her 5 taxable years immediately preceding 1983 in order to calculate the special tax? Would any accumulation distribution have taken place if Sally had become 21 after 1981? Would there have been an accumulation distribution if the trustee had distributed $17,500 to Sally in 1983 and $17,500 had been distributed to John, who also became 21 prior to 1979? What if a $17,500 distribution were also made to Norman, who was born more than 21 years prior to 1979?

Optimum Tax Results. The optimum income tax results may be attained if a trustee is given discretion to sprinkle income among a class of beneficiaries or accumulate it for later distribution. *See* §10.18, *infra.* Flexibility is increased if the trustee is also given authority to distribute trust principal to the beneficiaries. Such powers should not be held by the grantor or a potential distributee because of the adverse income, gift, and estate tax consequences. An adroit sprinkling of income among beneficiaries may substantially reduce the overall income tax cost of trust distributions. The accumulation of income can result in some overall savings through deferral (*i.e.,* no interest is charged on the additional tax imposed on accumulation distributions). Of course the throwback rules prevent a trust from permanently absorbing the entire tax liability on income that is accumulated after the beneficiary becomes 21.

Sale of Appreciated Property within 2 Years (§644). When the capital gain throwback rule was abolished in 1976, §644 was adopted to deter the transfer of appreciated property in trust in order to shift the gain to the trust, where it would be subject to the trust's lower progressive tax rates. Section 644 applies (1) where property that has a fair market value in excess of its basis is transferred to a trust and (2) the property is sold at a gain by the trust within 2 years of its transfer to the trust. §644(a)(1). In such a case §644(a)(2) subjects the trust to a tax equal to the tax that would have been imposed had the grantor made the sale. The overall income tax result is essentially the same as if the grantor made the sale and transferred the net proceeds to the trust. Whether the gain is taxed as ordinary income or capital gain is also determined by reference to the character of the property in the hands of the grantor. §644(c). The rule does not apply to sales made following the grantor's death or sales made by a charitable remainder trust or pooled income fund. §644(e). Note that no exception applies to sales by charitable lead trusts. The special rules of §§644(d) and (f) prevent circumvention of the tax through making short sales or installment sales.

Recognition of Loss (§267). Section 267 bars a deduction for a loss arising from a sale to a related party. Insofar as trusts are involved, no deduction is allowed where property is sold by the fiduciary of a trust (1) to a beneficiary of the trust (§267(b)(6)), (2) to the fiduciary of another trust created by the same grantor (§267(b)(5)), or (3) to the beneficiary of another trust created by the same grantor (§267(b)(7)). However, loss that is not allowable to the transferor under §267 may be utilized by the original purchaser for purposes of computing gain on a subsequent disposition of the property. §267(d). (Note that the benefit of this rule is only available to the *original* purchaser and not to his or her transferees. Reg. §1.267(d)-1(a)(3).)

> **Example 10-6.** A trustee, T, sold stock with a basis of $1,500 to a beneficiary, X, of the trust for $1,000. T is not allowed to deduct the $500 "loss" on the sale to X. If X later sells the stock for $2,000, X realizes a gain of $1,000, but is required to recognize only $500, which is the excess of the realized gain ($1,000) over the loss ($500) not allowed to T. If T gave the stock to another person, the donee could not make use of the loss to offset any gain he or she realized on a subsequent sale or exchange.

In contrast, an estate is entitled to a deduction for the loss that is incurred when an estate sells property to a trust created by the decedent or to a party who was related to the decedent. Rev. Rul. 77-439, 1977 C.B. 85 (sale of property to executor, who is child of decedent); Rev. Rul. 56-222, 1956-1 C.B. 155 (sale of stock to a trust created by decedent). The same rule applies to losses incurred when an asset is distributed in satisfaction of a pecuniary legacy at a time when it is worth less than its adjusted basis. Estate of Hanna v. Commissioner, 320 F.2d 54 (6th Cir. 1963).

Section 1244 Stock. A limited ordinary loss deduction is allowed under §1244 for loss on the sale or exchange of the stock in a qualifying small business corporation. However, the loss is only allowed to an individual or partner who held the stock continuously from the time of its original issue. In particular, "[a] corporation, trust, or estate is not entitled to ordinary loss treatment under section 1244 regardless of how the stock was acquired." Reg. §1.1244(a)-1(b). Thus, the transfer of otherwise qualifying stock to a trust cuts off any possibility of obtaining an ordinary loss deduction under §1244.

Subchapter S Stock. Beginning in 1976 several amendments were made to §1371 that permit certain trusts to be shareholders in Subchapter S corporations. The trusts are (1) a trust of which the grantor is treated as the owner under §§671 to 677; (2) a voting trust; (3) a testamentary trust, but only for a 60-day period following the transfer of stock to it. §1371(e). In 1978 the rules were liberalized to allow a grantor trust to be an eligible shareholder for 60 days following the death of the person who was treated as owner of the trust under §§671 to 677. §1371(e)(1)(B). However, if the entire corpus of the trust is includible in the grantor's gross estate, the trust is an eligible shareholder for a period of 2 years following the grantor's death. Under §1371(e) the grantor is treated as the shareholder of the stock held in the trust, which may relieve the trustee of the necessity of filing a consent to the election not to be taxed as a corporation.

Changes made by the 1981 Act allow additional types of trusts to be shareholders. In particular, a trust, all of which is treated as owned by an individual other than the grantor under §678, §1371(e)(1)(A) may be a shareholder until 60 days following the individual's death. Also, the individual beneficiary of a "qualified Subchapter S trust" may elect to be a shareholder. Briefly, a qualified Subchapter S trust is one under which all of the income is payable currently to an individual who is a citizen or resident of the United States; the principal of which cannot be distributed during the term of the trust to anyone other than the income beneficiary; and which terminates no later than the death of the income beneficiary. If the trust terminates prior to the death of the income beneficiary, the assets must be distributed to the income beneficiary. §1371(g)(3).

The estate of a deceased shareholder is an eligible shareholder for so long as required to complete the administration of the estate. *See* §12.7, *infra.* The IRS has recognized that an estate may remain an eligible shareholder during the period that payment of the estate tax is deferred under a prior version of §6166. Rev. Rul. 76-23, 1976-1 C.B. 264.

Redemptions under §303. Section 303 applies to distributions in redemption of stock included in a decedent's estate and held by any person at the time of redemption, including the trustee of a trust created by the decedent. Reg. §1.303-2(f). Where the value of the stock included in the decedent's estate constitutes more than 35% of the decedent's adjusted gross estate, the distribution is treated as full payment in exchange for the redeemed stock. However, the amount that may be redeemed is limited to the sum of the death taxes imposed on the decedent's estate and the amount of funeral and administration expenses that are deductible under §2053. §303(b)(2)(A). The 1976 Act added a limitation that limits the rule to instances in which the shareholder is liable for payment of the taxes and administration expenses. Thus, stock that the parties might wish to redeem under §303 should not be transferred to a beneficiary or a trust that is not liable for payment of death taxes and expenses of administration. For a more complete discussion of redemptions under §303, see §§11.14 to 11.21, *infra.*

Payment of Income Tax by Fiduciary. A trust is not quite as favorably situated as an estate when it comes to payment of income taxes. Under §6152(a)(2) an estate, but not a trust, may elect to pay its income tax liability in 4 equal quarterly installments instead of 1 single payment. If an estate elects to make installment payments, the first one-quarter of the tax must be paid when the tax would otherwise be due (*i.e.,* on the fifteenth day of the fourth month following the close of the tax year). Subsequent payments are due 3, 6, and 9 months after the date prescribed for payment of the first installment. Reg. §1.6152-1(b).

§10.3. Gift Tax Summary

The transfer of property to a trust constitutes a gift to the extent of the value of the interests that pass from the grantor's control. Reg. §25.2511-2(a), (b). The gift may be incomplete, however, because of powers retained by the grantor over the beneficial interests in the trust. Of course, there is no completed gift if the grantor retains a power of revocation. The regulations require the grantor to file a gift tax return in such a case, specifying the reasons he or she believes the transfer is not taxable. Reg. §§25.2511-2(j); 25.6019-3(a). In practice returns are very seldom filed with respect to the transfer of property to a revocable trust.

An annual gift tax exclusion is available insofar as a trust beneficiary is entitled to the unrestricted right to "the immediate use, possession, or enjoyment of property or the income from property. . . ." Reg. §25.2503-3(b). In general no exclusion is available with respect to the beneficiary's interests in a discretionary trust. However, transfers to a trust qualify for the annual exclusion to the extent the beneficiary has a *Crummey* power that allows him or her to withdraw the transferred property for his or her own use. For a more complete discussion of the availability of the annual exclusion, *see* §§2.5 and 7.35 to 7.38, *supra*.

For gift tax purposes the gifts provided for in a revocable trust become complete if the power to affect the beneficial enjoyment of the property is released or otherwise terminates during the grantor's lifetime. Estate of Sanford v. Commissioner, 308 U.S. 39 (1939); Reg. §25.2511-2(f). However, the gifts probably do not become complete merely because the grantor becomes incompetent and may no longer exercise the retained power.

> **Example 10-7.** T transferred Blackacre to X as trustee of an irrevocable trust. The income of the trust was payable in the trustee's discretion to T's siblings, A, B, and C. Upon the death of the survivor of A, B, and C, the trust property was distributable to their then living issue. The transfer of Blackacre to the trust constituted a completed gift with respect to which no annual exclusions are available. However, annual exclusions would be available if the beneficiaries were given *Crummey* powers of withdrawal. Also, the gifts would be incomplete to the extent T retained a special power of appointment over the trust. *See* Reg. §25.2511-2(b).

§10.4. Estate Tax Summary

The value of assets held in a trust may be included in the grantor's estate under any of the provisions of §§2035 to 2038. Most commonly the problems of inclusion arise under §§2036 or 2038 with respect to powers the grantor has retained over the disposition of trust property. In this connection it is important to note that the trust is includible in the grantor's estate under §§2036 and 2038 if a proscribed power is exercisable by the grantor alone *or* in conjunction with any other person. Note also that those sections make no exception for powers held by the decedent in a fiduciary capacity (*i.e.,* as trustee). A trust is, of course, includible in the grantor's estate under §2036(a)(1) to the extent he or she has directly or indirectly retained the use or benefit of the property.

Shares of stock in a controlled corporation are includible in the grantor's estate if he or she retained the right to vote the shares. §2036(b). For this purpose a corporation is a controlled corporation if the decedent owned or had voting control of 20% or more of its stock after giving effect to the attribution rules of §318. §2036(b)(2). Thus, stock in a controlled corporation that is transferred to a trust of which the transferor is the trustee and holds the power to vote the stock is includible in the transferor-trustee's gross estate.

Property transferred by another person to a trust that is revocable by the grantor is includible in the grantor's estate under §2041(a)(2) (with the exception of property subject to an unexercised power created before October 22, 1942).

Alternate Valuation Date. Property held in a trust qualifies for alternate valuation just as other assets do that are included in the decedent's gross estate. However, property that is distributed, sold, exchanged, or otherwise disposed of within 6 months after the decedent's death is valued on the date of its distribution, sale, exchange, or other disposition. The provisions of a revocable trust regarding distributions should be drafted with an eye toward §2032 in order to preserve the full benefit of alternate valuation for the trust assets. *See* §12.17, *infra.*

Deduction of Expenses under §2053. Section 2053(a) allows a deduction for administration expenses incurred with respect to property subject to an estate administration proceeding. Since 1954 a comparable deduction has been allowed by §2053(b) for expenses of administration incurred with respect to property includible in the decedent's gross estate, such as property held in a revocable trust, but not subject to the claims of the decedent's creditors. The deduction is allowable to the extent that the costs are paid before expiration of the period of limitations for assessments under §6501 (*i.e.,* within 3 years following the date upon which the estate tax return is due). Deductions are limited to expenses "occasioned by the decedent's death and incurred in settling the decedent's interest in the property or vesting good title to the property in the beneficiaries. Expenses not coming within [this] description . . . but incurred on behalf of the transferees are not deductible." Reg. §20.2053-8(b).

Benefits under Qualified Plans. Interests in a qualified employee benefit plan or an individual retirement arrangement are often made payable to the trustee of an inter vivos or testamentary trust in order to consolidate the employee's assets in one trust for purposes of management and administration. The trust that is designated as beneficiary is typically a bypass trust that will prevent the trust property from being included in the trust beneficiary's estate. The designation of the trust as beneficiary is satisfactory if it does not unintentionally require the interests to be included in the employee's gross estate. The proceeds of insurance policies on the testator's life and the testator's residuary estate are also often made payable to the trustee of an inter vivos trust.

In general, interests in a qualified plan are excludible from a deceased employee's estate to the extent they are attributable to contributions made by the decedent's employer. §2039(c). However, the exclusion does not apply to the extent the interests are receivable by the executor. *Id.* For this purpose interests are receivable by the decedent's executor to the extent they are subject to a legally binding obligation to pay taxes, debts, or other charges enforceable against the estate. *See* Reg. §§20.2039-2(b) and 20.2042-1(b). The exclusion is available where the plan benefits are paid to an inter vivos or testamentary trust that prohibits use of the funds to pay obligations of the estate. Rev. Rul. 73-404, 1973-2 C.B. 319. Also, the trustee may be authorized, but not required, to use the proceeds for the benefit of the estate. Rev. Rul. 77-157, 1977-1 C.B. 279. *See also* Estate of Joseph E. Salsbury, 34 T.C.M. 1441 (1975). Dictum in a 1942 case, Estate of Charles H. Wade, 47 B.T.A. 21 (1942), *acq.* 1944 C.B. 29, suggests that the benefits would be includible if a trustee having such discretionary authority actually used them to discharge estate obligations. It is doubtful that the dictum would be followed, particularly in view of Rev. Rul. 77-157, *supra.* Finally, the exclusion is not jeopardized if the trustee is authorized to purchase assets from the decedent's estate or to loan funds to the decedent's executor. The inclusion of qualified plan benefits in a deceased employee's estate is not particularly hurtful if the benefits pass to the employee's surviving spouse in a way that qualifies for the marital deduction. Of course, they will not qualify to the extent they are subject to a legally binding obligation to pay estate expenses. *See* §2056(b)(4). The elections available with respect to the income and estate tax treatment of lump sum distributions are discussed at §12.20, *infra.*

Life Insurance Proceeds. Insurance on a decedent's life is also often made payable to an inter vivos or testamentary trust. The proceeds, like benefits under a qualified plan, are includible in the insured's estate to the extent they are "receivable by the executor" although the insured had no incidents of ownership in the insurance. §2042(1). *See* §6.14, *supra.* For that reason life insurance proceeds that are otherwise not includible in the insured's estate should not be made subject to a legally binding obligation to pay debts, taxes, and other expenses of the insured's estate. Where they are paid to a trust, the trustee may be given discretionary power to use the proceeds to buy estate assets or make loans to the estate. Some clients, who are willing to risk a confrontation with the IRS, also give the trustee the discretionary power to use the proceeds to satisfy obligations of the estate.

Deferral of Estate Tax. The estate tax attributable to a closely held business interest that is includible in the decedent's estate may be deferred under §6166. The deferral is available whether the business interest is held outright or in a trust. Where the business constitutes more than 35% of the decedent's adjusted gross estate, §6166 allows the tax to be paid in installments over a 10-year period, the first of which is due 5 years after the estate tax return is filed. *See* §§11.26 to 11.32 and 12.40 *infra.* Prior to 1982 the executor could elect to pay the tax attributable to the business interest in 10 annual installments. *See* former §6166A.

Discharge of Executor and Other Fiduciaries from Personal Liability for Estate Tax. Under §§3466 and 3467 of the Revised Statutes, 31 U.S.C. §§191, 192 (1979 Supp.), an executor or other fiduciary is personally liable for debts due the United States, including federal tax liabilities, to the extent the fiduciary disposes of the decedent's property without paying the debts due the United States. *See* §12.42, *infra.* An executor may apply for discharge from personal liability for the estate tax under §2204(a), in which case the government must notify the executor of the amount of the tax within 9 months of the request. The executor is discharged from personal liability upon payment of the amount found to be due and furnishing bond for any amount the payment of which has been deferred under §§6161, 6163, or 6166. Section 2204 was amended in 1970 to extend essentially the same opportunity to fiduciaries other than executors. §2204(b). *See* Price, Recent Tax Legislation — The Excise, Estate and Gift Tax Adjustment Act of 1970, 47 Wash. L. Rev. 237, 273-279 (1972). Accordingly, since 1970 it has been possible for the trustee of a revocable trust to obtain a discharge from personal liability for the decedent's estate tax. The prior inability to obtain such a discharge was a matter of some concern to trustees. The change removed one of the obstacles to the use of a revocable trust as the principal dispositive instrument in an estate plan.

Flower Bonds. Some issues of United States Treasury bonds issued prior to 1971 are redeemable at par, plus accrued interest in payment of the federal estate tax. *See* §12.41, *infra*. Because of the low interest rates the bonds usually carry, ones with several years until maturity typically sell at substantial discounts. For federal estate tax purposes the bonds are valued at par plus accrued interest to the extent they are redeemable. Rev. Rul. 69-489, 1969-2 C.B. 172. However, not all bonds held in trust qualify for redemption. Under the applicable Treasury regulations, 31 C.F.R. §306.28 (1973), bonds held in trust at the time of the decedent's death are redeemable only "(a) if the trust actually terminated in favor of the decedent's estate, or (b) if the trustee is required to pay the decedent's Federal estate tax under the terms of the trust instrument or otherwise, or (c) to the extent the debts of the decedent's estate, including costs of administration, State inheritance and Federal estate taxes, exceed the assets of his estate without regard to the trust estate." 31 C.F.R. §306.28(b)(iii) (1973). Thus, some care must be taken in planning the terms of the grantor's will and trust where the trustee may acquire flower bonds for the purpose of redeeming them on the grantor's death. In particular, the will should not provide for payment of all death taxes from the residuary estate. In appropriate cases, the trust should provide that the trustee shall pay the federal estate tax liability of the decedent's estate. Alternatively, the trustee may be directed to pay so much of the tax as he or she may be asked by the decedent's executor to pay.

Special planning is also called for where the trust is funded with community property. Bonds that are held as community property are redeemable only to the extent of the decedent's one-half interest. This problem can be avoided by giving the trustee authority to partition some of the community property held in trust into equal units of separate property and to use a spouse's share of the property to purchase redeemable Treasury bonds for his or her separate account. Otherwise the trustee would be required to buy twice as many bonds as would be needed to satisfy the tax due on the death of the spouse.

B. THE REVOCABLE TRUST

§10.5. Scope

This part is concerned with the tax and nontax aspects of the revocable trust, which is one of the most important and flexible devices available to the estate planner. Although a revocable trust offers little in the way of present tax advantages, its flexibility and substantial nontax advantages make it a favorite of many planners and their clients. The use of revocable trusts has been encouraged by academics (Casner, Estate Planning — Avoidance of Probate, 60 Colum. L. Rev. 108 (1960)) and by a wide group of nonacademic proponents (*e.g.*, N. Dacey, How to Avoid Probate (1965)).

The opening sections of this part discuss some important matters of substantive law. The next sections deal with the basic advantages and disadvantages of revocable trusts. The last sections summarize the principal income, gift, and estate tax consequences of using a revocable trust in an estate plan.

A revocable trust may be funded or unfunded, but the funded variety receives most of the attention in this part. The principal form of the unfunded revocable trust is the unfunded life insurance trust, which is discussed at §6.71, *supra*.

Perhaps most often a funded revocable trust is established to provide lifetime management of the grantor's property and to avoid probate (*i.e.*, to serve as a will substitute for a substantial part of the client's property). Where the trust has a single grantor, the trust becomes completely irrevocable upon his or her death. The trust may include any of a wide variety of plans for the administration of the property following the grantor's death. A particular client's choice will depend upon the age, experience, and needs of his or her surviving spouse and children. Thus, the assets of the trust may be distributed soon after the grantor's death or held in trust for a substantial period, such as the lifetime of one or more beneficiaries. A trust that will continue following the grantor's death should be planned in view of the general considerations applicable to irrevocable trusts (*see* Parts C and D, *infra*).

The planner and client may intend to transfer all of the client's property to the trust in order to avoid probate completely. Even in that case the client should have a "backup" will to dispose of any property or claims that may not be included in the trust at the time of the client's death. A backup will usually provides for a gift of the grantor's residuary estate to the trustee of the revocable trust (the residuary estate is "poured over" to the trust and is not held in a separate trust under the will). The validity of the pour over will is discussed at §10.8, *infra*. Life insurance proceeds, employee benefits, and other property may also be made payable to the trustee. Such a program is attractive because it facilitates the unified management and administration of the grantor's property and the distribution of the property according to a single plan. A chart of such a plan might look like Chart 10-1, (p. 585).

Pour Back or Reverse Pour Over. The grantor's assets are most frequently unified by a pour over of the type diagrammed in Chart 10-1. However, in some cases the assets of a revocable trust are "poured back" and added to the probate estate for purposes of disposition. A pour back is less common because it reduces or eliminates some of the basic advan-

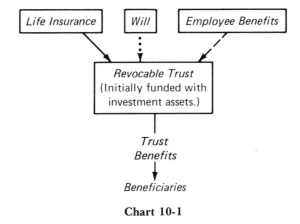

Chart 10-1

tages of a revocable trust (*e.g.*, reducing probate costs; preserving secrecy). It also eliminates any uncertainty regarding the validity of the disposition — which might plague a pour over in some jurisdictions. The use of a pour back also allows the grantor to control the ultimate disposition of the property simply by changing the terms of his or her will, which is ambulatory and can be changed unilaterally. The trustee is not required to concur in such a change and need not know the terms of the grantor's will as it exists from time to time.

§10.6. Reserving the Power to Revoke

Under the law of most states a properly created written trust is irrevocable unless the power to amend or revoke is expressly or impliedly reserved in the trust instrument. Holmes v. Holmes, 118 P. 733 (Wash. 1911); Restatement (Second), Trusts §330 (1959). However, the laws of California, Oklahoma, and Texas provide that a voluntary trust is revocable unless the instrument that creates the trust expressly provides that it is irrevocable. Cal. Civ. Code §2280 (West 1954); Okla. Stat. Ann. Tit. 60, §175.41 (West 1971); Tex. Rev. Civ. Stat. Ann. art. 7425b-41 (Vernon 1960). In any case, a trust instrument should specify whether it is amendable or revocable or not. Otherwise there is some risk that the character of the trust might not be properly established or understood by the grantor. It is important to eliminate as many uncertainties as possible in order to avoid disputes with the client, the client's successors, and the tax authorities. For example, the failure of a Texas trust to provide that the trust was irrevocable caused the corpus of the trust to be included in the grantor's gross estate under §2038. Estate of Alvin Hill, 64 T.C. 867 (1975), *acq.*, 1976-2 C.B. 2, *aff'd by order,* 568 F.2d 1365 (5th Cir. 1978).

A reservation of the power to revoke the trust should include a suitable provision regarding exercise of the power and disposition of the trust property upon revocation. The same paragraph often governs amendments of the trust. The paragraph might provide as follows:

> The grantor reserves the power to amend or revoke this trust in whole or in part by an instrument in writing delivered to the trustee during the grantor's lifetime. However, without the trustee's consent an amendment may not substantially increase the duties or liabilities of the trustee or change the compensation of the trustee. If the trust is completely revoked, the trustee shall promptly deliver all of the trust fund to the grantor or as the grantor may designate. [This power is personal to the grantor and may not be exercised on the grantor's behalf by a guardian, custodian, or other representative. This power may be exercised by an attorney in fact for the grantor acting under a durable power of attorney or by a guardian of the grantor's estate.]

In order to be effective an exercise of the power of revocation must comply with the terms of the trust. Under the foregoing provision, for example, an oral revocation would be ineffective. A written revocation that is not delivered to the trustee during the grantor's lifetime, or otherwise does not comply with the terms of the trust, would also be ineffective. *See, e.g.,* In re Button's Estate, 490 P.2d 731 (Wash. 1971); Restatement (Second) Trusts §330, comment *j* (1959). The bracketed sentences are alternative provisions, one of which should be included regarding the exercise of the power by a representative of the grantor.

Community Property. The community property character of assets transferred to the trust is preserved if the trust satisfies the requirements of Rev. Rul. 66-283, 1966-2 C.B. 297, and the applicable local law. *See* §3.22,*supra.* Rev. Rul. 66-283 requires that the spouses have the power to alter, amend, or revoke the trust as long as both are alive. In addition, the trust must specify that any property withdrawn from the trust will retain its community character. Following the death of one spouse the surviving spouse usually holds the power to amend or revoke the trust with respect to the portion of the trust attributable to the one-half share of community property he or she contributed to the trust. The decedent's share generally is held for the surviving spouse in a bypass trust that he or she cannot amend or revoke.

§10.7.   Nontestamentary Nature of Revocable Trusts

In the past, the validity of revocable trusts was frequently challenged for failure to comply with the formal requirements of the Statute of Wills. Challengers argued that the grantor's retention of a life interest in the trust and an unrestricted power of revocation made the trust testamentary. To them, it was comparable to a customary testamentary disposition, which became operative only upon the death of the maker and did not affect the maker's title until that time. Most courts resolved the issue according to whether or not the establishment of the trust gave another person an interest in the property transferred to the trust. If an interest is created in another person, the trust is nontestamentary even though the grantor reserved a life interest and the power to revoke the trust. Restatement (Second) Trusts §57 (1959). The influential decision in National Shawmut Bank v. Joy, 53 N.E.2d 113, 124 (Mass. 1944), put it this way: "The reservation by the settlor, in addition to an interest for life, of a power to revoke the trust, did not make incomplete or testamentary the gift over to the statutory next of kin." More recent cases, involving declarations of trust provided by mutual fund companies, have generally reached the same result. *E.g.,* Farkas v. Williams, 125 N.E.2d 600 (Ill. 1955). For the purpose of determining the validity of the trust, the interest of the beneficiary other than the grantor suffices if it is a contingent equitable remainder (*i.e.,* the beneficiary must survive the grantor in order to receive the property upon the grantor's death).

§10.8. *Validity of Pour Over to Revocable Trust*

Until the widespread adoption in the 1960s of the Uniform Testamentary Additions to Trust Act, 8 U.L.A. 629 (1972), the validity and effect of a testamentary addition to a revocable trust was uncertain. The Act, which validates pour overs to pre-existing trusts, is included in the UPC as §2-511. In one form or another the Act has been adopted by almost all states and the District of Columbia. 8 U.L.A. 217 (1981 Supp.). Because of local variations in the statute, the governing one should be examined carefully before drafting either a testamentary pour over or an amendment of a trust with respect to which a pour over will has already been executed. Note that the Uniform Act authorizes a pour over to a trust created by the valid will of a person who predeceased the testator, but does not authorize a pour over to a trust provided for in the will of a living person. Also, remember that incorporation by reference or the doctrine of independent significance may be used in some cases to uphold a particular disposition. That is, the Uniform Act should not be considered the exclusive method by which the assets of a probate estate can be made subject to the terms of a previously written trust.

Under UPC §2-511, property poured over to a pre-existing trust will be administered in accordance with the provisions of the trust including any amendments made before the death of the testator, regardless of whether they are made before or after the execution of the testator's will. However, a few states limit the pour over to the trust as it existed when the will was executed (*i.e.*, insofar as the pour over is concerned, no effect is given to subsequent amendments).

The Uniform Act does not purport to have any effect on the validity or effect of the designation of a revocable trust as beneficiary of life insurance or pension benefits. Many states have statutes that validate such designations.

§10.9. Claims of Creditors against Grantor

The grantor's creditors can generally reach any beneficial interest the grantor retains in a trust. This rule applies although the trust includes a spendthrift clause that purports to restrict the voluntary or involuntary transfer of the grantor's interests. Restatement (Second) Trusts §156 (1959).

Power of Revocation. In the absence of statute, most courts have concluded that the grantor's creditors cannot reach the assets of a revocable trust established for others at a time when the grantor was solvent. *E.g.,* Guthrie v. Canty, 53 N.E.2d 1009 (Mass. 1944); Van Stewart v. Townsend, 28 P.2d 999 (Wash. 1934). Of course, the creditors can reach the assets if the grantor revokes the trust and takes possession of them. Several important states have statutes that allow the grantor's creditors to reach the assets of a revocable trust. They include Florida (Fla. Stat. Ann. §726.08 (West 1969)), Indiana (Ind. Code Ann. §30-1-9-14 (Burns 1972)), Kansas (Kan. Stat. Ann. §58-2414 (1976)), and Michigan (Mich. Stat. Ann. §26.155(118) (1974)).

Bankruptcy. Under §70(a)(3) of the former Bankruptcy Act, the trustee in a bankruptcy could exercise any power that the bankrupt could have exercised for his own benefit. The language of the Revised Bankruptcy Act (the "Code"), adopted in 1978 and codified in Title 11, U.S.C., is less explicit on the point, but presumably the rule continues to apply. This conclusion is supported by a negative implication drawn from §541(b) of the Code: "Property of the [debtor's] estate does not include any power that the debtor may only exercise solely for the benefit of an entity other than the debtor." 11 U.S.C. §541(b) (1979 Supp.). Also, the leading treatise states that "[t]he same result would apply under the Code." 4 Collier, Bankruptcy ¶541.21 at 541-81 (King ed. 1980).

General Power of Appointment. In some states creditors are allowed to reach property of a trust over which the grantor retained a general power of appointment. Others limit their reach to trusts in which the grantor also reserved a life interest. Where the grantor reserved an inter vivos power exercisable in his or her own favor, creditors should be able to reach the assets of the trust à la the Bankruptcy Code.

Spouse's Elective Share. The extent to which the property of a revocable trust is subject to a surviving spouse's elective share varies according to the terms of the local law. Under UPC §2-202(1)(ii), property over which the decedent retained a power of revocation is included in the decedent's augmented estate. The New York law is to the same effect. N.Y. EPTL §5-1.1(b)(1)(E) (McKinney 1967). In the absence of statute, the outcome may turn on whether the court determines that a particular transfer in trust is "illusory" or a "fraud on the surviving spouse."

Other Creditors of a Deceased Grantor. The extent to which the grantor's creditors can reach the assets of a revocable trust following the grantor's death is uncertain in most jurisdictions. Unless the grantor retained a beneficial interest in the trust the creditors may be unable to reach the assets. In State Street Bank & Trust Co. v. Reiser, 389 N.E.2d 768 (Mass. App. 1979), the court held that "where a person places property in trust and reserves the right to amend and revoke, or to direct disposition of principal and income, the settlor's creditors may, following the death of the settlor, reach in satisfaction of the settlor's debts to them, to the extent not satisfied by the settlor's estate, those assets owned by the trust over which the settlor had such control at the time of his death as would have enabled the settlor to use the trust assets for his own benefit."

Also, a relatively recent New York decision held that the assets of a revocable trust are subject to claims of the deceased grantor's creditors. In re Matter of Granwell, 228 N.E.2d 779 (N.Y. 1967). The decision was based on New York law, under which the grantor of a revocable trust is considered to have retained ownership of the trust assets until death insofar as creditors are concerned. The possibility that the assets of a revocable trust cannot be reached by the grantor's creditors following the grantor's death is cited by some planners as an additional advantage of establishing a revocable trust. The advantage may be illusory, and costly if the trustee is required to engage in litigation after the grantor's death.

Problem 10-2. On January 1 T established a revocable trust with X Bank, to which T promptly transferred some stocks and bonds. Under the terms of the trust, T was entitled to receive the income for life and the principal would be distributed to C Church upon T's death. The will T also executed on January 1 gave his residuary estate to "the trustee acting at the time of my death of the revocable trust established by me on the date hereof." On February 1 T filed a validly executed beneficiary designation form substituting the trustee for T's mother as beneficiary under a policy of insurance on his life. On March 1 T withdrew all of the assets of the trust in order to finance the purchase of Blackacre. T owned Blackacre, some cash, and miscellaneous property when he died on May 1. Under the law of your state, is T's mother or the C Church entitled to Blackacre? To the insurance on T's life? What could T have done to avoid the uncertainty that resulted when he withdrew the assets of the trust?

§10.10. *Principal Advantages of Revocable Trusts*

Revocable trusts offer a number of nontax advantages both during the grantor's lifetime and thereafter. The principal lifetime advantages arise from the trustee's management of, or availability to manage, the trust property. Even where the grantor starts out as trustee, a successor trustee can assume the responsibility for managing the trust property if the grantor resigns or becomes unable or unwilling to act as trustee. The trust can also serve as an important probate avoidance device for assets located in the state of the grantor's domicile and in other states.

Inexperienced or Absent Grantor. A revocable trust may be suitable to provide for the management of property that belongs to a client who lacks investment experience or confidence. In such a case, the grantor's responsibility for investment of the trust fund can be increased as he or she gains experience. The trustee's professional management of the trust property may also appeal to a client whose work, studies, or other activities will take him or her out of the country or otherwise make him or her unavailable for protracted periods.

Avoiding Guardianships. The establishment of a revocable trust is often especially attractive to older clients because the existence of the trust may obviate the necessity of having a guardian appointed if the grantor becomes incompetent or is otherwise unable or unwilling to manage property. By creating a trust the client can avoid the expense, complications, delays, and publicity of a guardianship proceeding. Also, the grantor is free to choose the trustee who will manage the property and make disbursements for his or her benefit in the event of disability or incompetency.

> The protective trust can be established with someone other than the donor [grantor] as the initial trustee, or can be created as a so-called convertible or standby trust in which the donor initially retains investment and management powers, with these powers passing to the other trustee or trustees at a later date under defined circumstances, as, for example, certification by a qualified physician that the donor is no longer capable. The mechanism should not be a court decree, which would usually subject the trust to then becoming a so-called court trust, defeating some of the purposes. In such a trust, the power of revocation should be reserved to the donor alone, as it would be disadvantageous, should the donor become incompetent, for a conservator or committee to revoke the trust and upset

the donor's estate plan. Report, The Revocable Living Trust as an Estate Planning Tool, 7 Real Prop., Prob. & Tr. J. 223, 224 (1972).

A durable power of attorney can serve as an effective substitute for a guardianship if the power is broad enough and a designated attorney in fact survives the principal. However, a trust offers more comprehensive protection and greater flexibility than a durable power of attorney. The devices can be coupled, however, to provide for the creation of a revocable trust if the principal does become incompetent. Specifically, a durable power can authorize the attorney in fact to transfer the principal's property to the trustee of a revocable trust in the event of the principal's incapacity. Perhaps the surest method is to attach the form of the trust to be used to the durable power of attorney. *See* §4.33, *supra.*

The trust instrument should authorize the trustee to disburse funds to or for the benefit of the grantor at any time, including payment of the cost of providing for the grantor's care and support during any period he or she is disabled or incompetent. The trust may bar any amendment or revocation of the trust while the grantor is incompetent or may allow certain changes to be made by his or her attorney in fact under a durable power of attorney. For this purpose the trust should define what constitutes incompetency in a way that coordinates with any durable power of appointment executed by the grantor (*e.g.*, certification by the grantor's attending physician that he or she is unable to understand and manage financial affairs unassisted).

Maintaining Separate Character of Property Owned by Husband and Wife. A revocable trust can also be used to maintain the separate character of assets owned by each spouse. Preventing the inadvertent commingling of assets and loss of their separate identity is particularly important in community property states (especially so in the case of second or third marriages).

A "Trial Run." A revocable trust allows the grantor to observe the operation of the trust and the conduct of the trustee during the grantor's lifetime. The trust can be left in place if the grantor is satisfied. In appropriate cases the revocable trust can serve as the grantor's principal estate-planning instrument, the grantor's insurance can be made payable to the trustee, and the grantor's other assets can be poured over into the trust. On the other hand, if the grantor is not happy with the operation of the trust or the conduct of the trustee, the grantor can amend or revoke the trust or change the trustee.

Avoiding Probate; Providing Continuity. When the grantor dies there is usually some unavoidable delay in the appointment of a personal representative and the management of the grantor's "owned" property.

That property is subject to an estate administration proceeding, which often entails detailed court supervision, delays, and additional expenses. Property held in a revocable trust is not subject to administration in the grantor's estate and may not be taken into account in calculating the fees of the grantor's personal representative and those of the lawyer for the personal representative. The trustee may continue to invest and manage trust property without interruption following the death of the grantor. Thus, distributions of income and principal can continue to be made to the grantor's family. Subject to the liabilities of the trust for taxes, etc., the trustee may also promptly distribute the assets of the trust. Of course, the trustee might be reluctant to make any large distributions soon after the grantor's death — the distribution of property would fix the alternate valuation date of any assets distributed and could subject the trustee to personal liability for the decedent's unpaid taxes. *See* §§12.17 and 12.42, *infra*. The delays are minimized and the continuity is best if a person other than the grantor is serving as trustee at the time of the grantor's death.

In order to avoid unnecessary delays in filling the office of trustee, the trust should name at least one successor trustee. It is particularly important to do so where an individual is named as the initial trustee. Trusts frequently authorize the individual trustee or the adult beneficiaries of the trust to name a further successor trustee. Of course, the beneficiaries generally should not have the power to become successor trustees because of the potentially adverse income and estate tax consequences. *See* §10.20, *infra*.

Secrecy. A revocable trust may also appeal to a person who does not want the disposition of his or her property to be a matter of public record. A relatively high degree of secrecy can be maintained with respect to the content of an inter vivos trust. However, in some jurisdictions the public has access to the state death tax file for an individual decedent, which will include a copy of any revocable trusts created by the decedent. Also, the trustee may be asked to provide a copy of the trust to a stockbroker or transfer agent in order to transfer securities held in the trust. However, such a request may be satisfied without providing a copy of the trust if the lawyer provides the stockbroker with a letter stating that the trust was validly created, is revocable by the grantors, etc.

Wills and other documents involved in the administration of an estate are matters of public record. The provisions of the wills of prominent individuals are frequently reported by the press. For example, a section in Trusts and Estates magazine highlights "wills of the month."

Avoiding Ancillary Estate Administration Proceedings. In general, an estate administration proceeding must be conducted in each state in which a decedent owned real property. The necessity of conducting multiple proceedings can be avoided by transferring the properties to a revocable trust. The trustee of such a trust is most often an individual because of restrictions on the conduct of business in some states by nonresident corporate trustees.

By using a trust, the grantor has some latitude in choosing the law that will apply to the construction and administration of the trust. The choice of law could have an important effect on the rights of creditors and the extent of a surviving spouse's right to claim an elective share of the grantor's property. *See* §9.22, *supra*.

Avoiding Court Supervision. In many states testamentary trusts are subject to continuing court supervision, which often carries along with it burdensome and expensive requirements to file annual reports and accounts with the court. A revocable trust is a noncourt trust, which is generally not subject to those requirements either during or after the grantor's lifetime. In some circumstances it is beneficial for a trust to be treated as a "court trust" with prompt access to the court for instructions and settlement of disputes. However, the advantage of court trusts in this regard is slight. The court's jurisdiction over the parties concerned with a noncourt trust can usually be invoked through an action brought under the appropriate state's general declaratory judgments act, by another civil action, or by a judicial accounting proceeding.

Not all of the advantages apply in every case. Nonetheless, a revocable trust often provides a client with the most satisfactory way of organizing his or her property.

§10.11. *Principal Disadvantages of Revocable Trusts*

As a general rule the legal costs of preparing a revocable trust (with a suitable pour over will) are higher than those for preparing a will that includes a comparable trust. The difference is traceable in part to the greater complexity of the revocable trust. However, it has been suggested that the difference is also due to the fact that "the charges of the profession for will drafting have notoriously lagged behind the actual cost and value of the service, in hopes of future benefit or otherwise." Report, The Revocable Living Trust as an Estate Planning Tool, 7 Real Prop., Prob. & Tr. J. 223, 227 (1972). The trustee's fees can also be a substantial additional cost, at least where there is a professional trustee. These costs are offset somewhat by the fact that the cost of establishing and operating a revocable trust is usually deductible for income tax purposes. On the other hand, the cost of preparing a will is a nondeductible personal expense. *See* §1.17, *supra*.

Tax Returns and Record Keeping. The trustee must obtain a taxpayer identification number for the trust. §6109; Rev. Rul. 63-178, 1963-2 C.B. 609. Also, the trustee will be required to prepare a statement of the income, deductions, and credits of the trust although the income is all taxable to the grantor. *See* §10.2, *supra.*

The assets of the trust should be transferred into the name of the trustee of the particular trust (*i.e.,* "X, as trustee under trust agreement dated March 1, 1982"). In order to handle receipts and disbursements of the trust and to deal efficiently with the trust assets, it is generally necessary to open bank and brokerage accounts in the name of the trustee.

The trustee's fiduciary duties also require the assets of the trust to be segregated from other property and carefully accounted for. Accordingly, the trustee must keep accurate records of transactions affecting the trust. The overall accounting and bookkeeping requirements can be burdensome if performed by a family member as trustee and an unexpected cost if performed by someone hired by the family member. Again, however, the costs are generally deductible under §212. *See* §1.17, *supra.*

Loss of Income Splitting. The opportunity to have post-mortem income taxed to the decedent's estate and not to the beneficiaries is generally lost to the extent that income-producing property is transferred by a revocable trust outside the decedent's estate. With proper planning, the income of an estate can often be permanently taxed to the estate and not to the beneficiaries. *See* §4.4., *supra.* The throwback rules of §§665 to 667 deny such an opportunity in the case of trusts. Under them, virtually any subsequent distribution of property by the trust would be deemed to carry out accumulated income that would be taxed to the distributee as if it had been received by him or her in the year of its accumulation. *See* §10.2, *supra.*

Miscellaneous. The transfer of property to a trust may also involve some other income tax disadvantages. The transfer of §1244 stock to a trust of course prevents a subsequent loss in the stock from qualifying as an ordinary deduction. Also, §267 bars a deduction for a loss on a sale of trust property to a beneficiary. However, the transfer of property to a revocable trust will not trigger recapture of depreciation under §§1245 or 1250 or the recognition of gain on an installment sale under §453B.

§10.12. Summary of Tax Consequences

Creation of a living revocable trust is an estate planning technique taken in general for other than tax reasons. The action has almost no immediate tax consequences, and is generally neutral as to taxes for the long run. The income is taxed to the donor during his lifetime, inasmuch as he has the power to revoke. Nor are any assets transferred to the trust removed from the donor's gross estate for federal estate tax purposes. The power to revoke and also the retained life estate require this result. Finally, there has been no taxable gift, again because of the retained power of revocation, there having been no termination of the donor's dominion and control. While on the donor's death the trust can serve as the vehicle for division into marital and residue trusts, minimizing estate taxes on the estate of the surviving spouse, such a function could be accomplished as well by a testamentary trust, and is not distinctive to the revocable living trust. Report, The Revocable Living Trust as an Estate Planning Tool, 7 Real Prop., Prob. & Tr. J. 223 (1972).

§10.13. Income Tax Considerations

In general the creation of a revocable trust has no significant income tax consequences during the grantor's lifetime. Because the trust is revocable, its income is fully taxed to the grantor under the grantor trust rules regardless of whether it is distributed or accumulated. *See* §676. The transfer of property to a revocable trust generally does not constitute a taxable event or otherwise trigger the realization of gain. For example, the IRS has recognized that the transfer of an installment obligation to a revocable trust is not a "disposition" under §453B. Rev. Rul. 74-613, 1974-2 C.B. 153 (applying the pre-1980 rules of former §453(d)). In contrast, the transfer of an installment obligation to an irrevocable trust of which the grantor is not treated as the "owner" under §§671 to 677 is a disposition that triggers recognition of gain. Rev. Rul. 76-530, 1976-2 C.B. 132.

The legal and accounting costs of establishing and operating the trust and the trustee's fees are usually deductible by the grantor under §212(2). *See* §1.17, *supra.* Of course, the fees are not deductible to the extent they are attributable to tax exempt income. §265.

On the negative side, the grantor's estate is lost as a separate taxpayer to the extent income-producing property is transferred to the trust. *See* §4.4, *supra.*

The transfer of stock to a revocable trust does not impair the ability to redeem the stock under §303. As noted above in §10.2, such a trust is an eligible stockholder of a subchapter S corporation during the grantor's lifetime. §1371(e)(1)(A). It may also be an eligible shareholder following the grantor's death. *See* §1371(e)(1), (g).

The transfer of stock to a trust causes it to lose its character as section 1244 stock. Accordingly, any loss subsequently realized on the stock is not deductible as an ordinary loss.

§10.14.   Gift Tax Considerations

The transfer of property by the grantor to a revocable trust does not have any immediate gift tax consequences. Any gift provided for in the trust is incomplete at the time of transfer. Under Reg. §25.2511-2(c), "A gift is incomplete in every instance in which a donor reserves the power to revest the beneficial title to the property in himself." As noted above, grantors seldom comply with the regulation which requires a gift tax return to be filed specifying the reasons he or she believes the transfer is not taxable. Reg. §§25.2511-2(j); 25.6019-3(a).

The gifts provided for in a revocable trust do become complete if the power to affect the beneficial enjoyment of the property is released or otherwise terminates during the grantor's lifetime. Estate of Sanford v. Commissioner, 308 U.S. 39 (1939); Reg. §25.2511-2(f). However, the gifts probably do not become complete merely because the grantor becomes incompetent and may no longer validly exercise the power. In analogous cases, the tax consequences of a power are generally determined without reference to the legal capacity of its holder. See §5.19, supra, and Rev. Rul. 75-350, 1975-2 C.B. 366. A gift of course takes place when trust property is distributed to a person other than the grantor.

> **Example 10-8.** T transferred Blackacre to the trustee of a revocable trust. The income of the trust was payable to T for life and upon T's death the corpus was distributable to T's children, A, B, and C. The transfer of Blackacre to the trust did not constitute a completed gift. However, any distribution of property from the trust to A, B, or C during T's lifetime would constitute a gift. Also, the gift of the remainder interest to A, B, and C will become complete if T releases the power of revocation and does not retain any other power to affect the beneficial enjoyment of the trust.

§10.15.   Estate Tax Considerations

The transfer of property to a revocable trust is largely unimportant insofar as the grantor's estate tax is concerned. The property of the trust is includible in the grantor's gross estate under §§2036(a)(2) and 2038(a)(1). Note that under both sections the property of the trust is includible in the grantor's estate if the power to revoke is exercisable by the grantor alone *or* in conjunction with any other person. The alternate valuation method is available with respect to property held in a revocable trust. See §2032. For alternate valuation purposes the division of the assets of a formerly revocable trust into separate trusts upon the death of the grantor constitutes a distribution. See Rev. Rul. 73-97, 1973-1 C.B. 404 and §12.17, *infra.*

Deductions are allowable for funeral expenses, debts, claims, and administration expenses actually paid from the property of the trust before the expiration of the period of limitation for assessment provided in §6501 (3 years after the estate tax return is filed). §2053(b). Also, deductions are allowable for qualifying charitable transfers (§2055) and transfers to a surviving spouse (§2056).

C. PLANNING THE BENEFICIARY'S INTERESTS IN AN IRREVOCABLE TRUST

§10.16. Scope

This part is concerned with planning and drafting the powers and interests of a beneficiary of an irrevocable trust. The material is generally applicable to permanent irrevocable trusts, including testamentary trusts and trusts that began life as revocable trusts. Issues regarding impermanent (*e.g.,* 10-year) irrevocable trusts are discussed in more detail in Part D, *infra,* and §7.38, *supra.* Some nontax considerations are mentioned, but this part is primarily concerned with the federal tax consequences of giving the beneficiary certain important interests or powers. The coverage ranges from sections concerning the benefits of multiple trusts and the mandatory or discretionary distribution of income to ones concerning the consequences of giving the beneficiary general or special powers of appointment and the appointment of the beneficiary as trustee.

§10.17. Multiple Trusts

Until recently multiple accumulation trusts were frequently used to decrease a family's income tax liability by proliferating the number of separate taxpayers among whom income is divided for tax purposes. Prior to 1969 the utility of accumulation trusts was based in large measure on rather broad exceptions to the throwback rules. For example, the rules did not apply to capital gains, to income accumulated more than 5 years prior to the current distribution, or where there had not been an addition to the trust for more than 9 years. The advantage of using multiple trusts, of course, depended on recognition of the trusts as separate taxpayers. As noted above in §10.2, trusts that are administered separately have a good chance of being recognized by the courts as separate.

The tax advantages of multiple trusts were diminished by the 1969

Act, which eliminated all of the former exceptions to the application of
the throwback rules and subjected capital gains to the rules. Subsequently the rules were modified to eliminate their application to capital
gains (§643(a)(3)) and to income accumulated prior to the beneficiary's
birth or attainment of 21 years of age (§665(b)). By reason of those
modifications it is often advantageous to establish multiple trusts funded
with appreciated capital assets or created for the benefit of minors. Recall, however, that the gain on a sale of appreciated assets made within 2
years of the time the assets are transferred to the trust is generally taxed
under §644 as if the grantor had made the sale. *See* §10.2, *supra.*

§10.18. *Mandatory or Discretionary Distributions?*

The distributive provisions of each trust must be planned in light of the
wishes of the grantor and the overall circumstances of the beneficiaries.
One of the most important decisions to be made in planning a trust
concerns the extent to which the trustee will have discretion to distribute
income and principal. A trust may prescribe a rigid scheme for the
distribution of income or it may give the trustee discretion to accumulate
income or to "sprinkle" income among several beneficiaries. A mandatory distribution trust may meet the needs of the income beneficiaries
and remaindermen, but it is probably too inflexible to meet their long-
range tax and nontax needs. In particular, the mandatory distribution of
all of the income to one income beneficiary often subjects the income to
unnecessarily high income tax rates. The distributions also swell the
beneficiary's estate, which may cause the imposition of an otherwise
avoidable estate tax bite. The flexibility of the trust is enhanced and
greater tax savings are made possible if the trustee is given discretion to
distribute income among several beneficiaries and to accumulate undistributed income and add it to principal.

Regardless of the provisions of the trust for the distribution of income, the capacity of the trust to meet the needs of the family over time
is enhanced if the trustee is authorized to distribute principal to the
beneficiaries (and, perhaps, to their issue). Of course, the terms of the
trust and distributions must be planned in light of the generation-
skipping tax. *See* §§2.17 to 2.26, *supra.* It must also be borne in mind that
a trust will not qualify for the marital deduction under §2056(b)(7) if it
allows distribution of principal to persons other than the decedent's surviving spouse during the lifetime of the surviving spouse.

From the beneficiary's point of view a discretionary trust may be less
satisfactory because of the uncertainty regarding distributions. However,
the potential for conflict between the beneficiary and trustee is reduced if
the trustee communicates frequently and effectively with the beneficiary
regarding the status of the trust and the trustee's plans for making

distributions. The security of the beneficiary is also enhanced if the beneficiary holds a limited power to withdraw trust assets, such as the noncumulative power to withdraw each year the greater of $5,000 or 5% of the value of the trust property. *See* §10.22, *infra*.

The indefiniteness of the beneficiary's interest in a discretionary trust generally prevents an effective transfer of the interest by the beneficiary. The indefiniteness also precludes the allowance of a credit to the beneficiary's estate under §2013 for the estate tax paid in the grantor's estate. As stated in Rev. Rul. 67-53, 1967-1 C.B. 265:

> Where a trustee possesses the power, in his absolute and uncontrolled discretion, to pay out net income to the income beneficiary of a trust or to accumulate such income, the beneficiary's interest cannot be valued according to recognized valuation principles as of the date of the transferor's death. Therefore, notwithstanding the fact that such income was actually paid to the decedent-transferee, the credit for tax on prior transfers under section 2013 of the Code is not allowable with respect to such an interest.

In contrast, a noncumulative power to withdraw the greater of $5,000 or 5% of the value of the trust property qualifies as property for purposes of the credit for tax on prior transfers to the extent of the value of the power on the date of the first decedent's death. Rev. Rul. 79-211, 1979-2 C.B. 319.

Distribution or Accumulation of Income. The trust may simply authorize the trustee to pay the income to a named beneficiary or accumulate the income for later distribution. The potential for income splitting and tax saving is obvious where the beneficiary is under 21 and the accumulated income will not be subject to the throwback rules. *See* §665(b) and §§7.27, 7.36, *supra*. Savings are also possible where the current income beneficiary is in a high marginal income tax bracket, but the trust is not. In such a case, the accumulation of the income will at least result in the deferred payment of the tax at the higher rate (when an accumulation distribution is made to the beneficiary). More hopefully, the accumulated income will be subject to a lower rate of tax when it is distributed. That may occur if the distribution is made to the beneficiary from whom it was withheld after retirement or during a period of relatively lower income. A saving can also occur if the accumulated income is later distributed to other, low bracket, family members. Such a distribution might be made, for example, following the death of the original beneficiary. *See* Halbach, Discretionary Trusts and Income Tax Avoidance After the 1976 Tax Reform Act, U. Miami 12th Inst. Est. Plan., Ch. 3 (1978).

Sprinkling of Income. More impressive income and estate tax savings are possible where the trustee has discretion to "sprinkle" the income among a group of beneficiaries. In making distributions the trustee can take into account the needs of the beneficiaries and their respective income tax brackets. For example, the trustee of a family bypass trust can be given discretion to distribute income to and among a class of persons including the grantor's surviving spouse and children. In appropriate cases the class might also include the grantor's grandchildren, which would require consideration of generation-skipping tax problems. *See* §§2.19 to 2.26, *supra*. Where the income exceeds the needs of the surviving spouse, or where he or she has no need for the income, the trustee holding such a power could distribute the trust income to children who are in lower income tax brackets. Such distributions also avoid increasing the size of the surviving spouse's estate, which is an important consideration.

Powers Held by Independent Trustees. The trustee or trustees may be given a free hand to distribute income or principal, or both, to the beneficiaries of the trust, provided that the grantor is not a trustee and no more than half of the trustees are "related or subordinate parties who are subservient to the wishes of the grantor." §674(c). The term "related or subordinate party" is defined in §672(c) as a nonadverse party who is

(1) The grantor's spouse if living with the grantor;
(2) Any one of the following: The grantor's father, mother, issue, brother, or sister; an employee of the grantor; a corporation or any employee of a corporation in which the stock holdings of the grantor and the trust are significant from the viewpoint of voting control; a subordinate employee of a corporation in which the grantor is an executive.

The definition of subordinate or related party is very helpful to grantors because of the persons who are not included within it. For example, a wide range of persons who are related to the grantor by affinity or consanguinity are not within its scope (*e.g.*, niece, nephew, son-in-law, mother-in-law, grandparent). Also, the term ordinarily does not include persons who perform professional services for the grantor, such as an accountant or lawyer. Given those definitions, a client can usually find a suitable person to act as trustee who will not be classified as a related or subordinate party.

A related or subordinate party is deemed to be subservient to the grantor in the exercise of the powers held by the subordinate party unless a preponderance of the evidence shows that the subordinate party is not subservient. §672(c).

The §674(c) exception permits an independent trustee to hold powers "(1) to distribute, apportion, or accumulate income to or for a beneficiary or beneficiaries, or to, for, or within a class of beneficiaries; or (2) to pay out corpus to or for a beneficiary or beneficiaries or to or for a class of beneficiaries (whether or not income beneficiaries)." However, the exception does not apply if any person has a power to add beneficiaries who are entitled to receive income or corpus, except where the action is to provide for after-born or after-adopted children. For this purpose the power of the beneficiary of a nonspendthrift trust to assign his or her interest is not considered to be a power to add a beneficiary. Reg. §1.674(d)-2(b).

> **Example 10-9.** T transferred property to a trust under which an independent trustee had the power to determine the amount of income distributed annually to each of the beneficiaries named in the trust. The grantor is not treated as owner of the trust by reason of the independent trustee's power to sprinkle income among the named beneficiaries. A contrary result would be reached if the grantor had the unrestricted power to remove the independent trustee and become trustee. *See* Reg. §1.674(d)-2.

Powers Limited by an Ascertainable Standard Held by a Trustee Other Than the Grantor or the Grantor's Spouse. Section 674(d) establishes an additional exception under which a trustee, other than the grantor or spouse living with the grantor, can hold a power to distribute, apportion, or accumulate income for a beneficiary or beneficiaries or to, for, or within a class of beneficiaries if the power is limited by a reasonably definite external standard set forth in the trust instrument. By the terms of §674(d) a power is within the exception whether or not the conditions of §§674(b)(6) or (7) are satisfied. Thus, the power over income may be exercised by the trustee without regard to the age or competency of the beneficiaries or the ultimate disposition of the income or corpus. The powers permitted by this exception are very helpful where the requirements of §674(c) cannot be met (*e.g.*, the trustee is not independent), or the grantor does not wish to give the trustee broader discretion. The power is particularly appropriate where the trust will last beyond the minority of multiple beneficiaries, some of whom may need more income than others to provide for education, support, medical care, or emergency expenses. Reg. §1.674(b)-1(b)(5) describes powers that are limited by reasonably definite external standards in the following passage:

> It is not required that the standard consist of the needs and circumstances of the beneficiary. A clearly measurable standard under which the holder of a power is legally accountable is deemed a reasonably definite standard for this purpose. For instance, a power to distribute [income] for the education, support, maintenance, or health of the beneficiary; for his reasonable support and comfort; or to enable him to maintain his accustomed standard of living; or to meet an emergency, would be limited by an ascertainable standard. However, a power to distribute [income] for the pleasure, desire, or happiness of a beneficiary is not limited by a reasonably definite standard.

As in the case of §674(c), the exception does not apply if any person has a power to add beneficiaries, except where the power is limited to providing for after-born or after-adopted children.

Grantor as Trustee. Because of the generally adverse income, gift, and estate tax consequences, great care must be exercised if the grantor will have any discretion to make distributions. To begin with, the possession of the power to make discretionary distributions of income or principal may cause the income to be taxed to the grantor under §674. *See* §10.29, *infra*. As mentioned above, the grantor is taxable on the trust's income if a discretionary power of distribution is held by a nonadverse party other than an independent trustee within the exception of §674(c). Finally, where the grantor is trustee it is likely that any discretionary powers of distribution held by the trustee-grantor will cause the trust to be included in the grantor's estate under §§2036 and 2038. Thus, in United States v. O'Malley, 383 U.S. 627 (1966), the irrevocable trusts that the decedent established for his wife and daughters were included in his estate because of his power, as cotrustee, to pay out or accumulate the income of the trusts. Moreover, under §2038 the trust is includible in the grantor's estate where the grantor held the power, as trustee, to distribute the trust property to the beneficiary prior to the time specified for termination of the trust. Lober v. United States, 346 U.S. 335 (1953).

Beneficiary as Trustee. Unless the grantor is treated as the owner of the trust, a beneficiary-trustee is taxable on the income of the trust to the extent the beneficiary has the power, acting alone, to acquire the principal or income. *See* the discussion of §678 at §10.24, *infra*. Thus, all of the income of a trust is taxed to a beneficiary-trustee who holds the power to distribute all of the income or principal to himself or herself. On the estate tax side, a trust over which a beneficiary-trustee holds a discretionary power to make distributions is includible in the beneficiary's estate under §2041. In contrast, the beneficiary could safely hold purely administrative powers. Reg. §20.2041-1(b).

"Absolute" or "Uncontrolled" Discretion. The trust may provide that the trustee's discretion shall be "absolute," "unlimited," or "uncontrolled." Such a provision does not completely insulate the trustee's conduct from court review, but it severely limits the court's supervisory role. According to the Restatement, in such a case the court will not consider whether the trustee acted beyond the bounds of reasonable judgment. Rather, the court will only consider whether the trustee acted in a state of mind contemplated by the trustor. Restatement (Second) Trusts §187, comment *j* (1959). Thus, a court's inquiry might be limited to determining whether the trustee acted arbitrarily or dishonestly. Because of the restricted review and reduced protection for the beneficiaries, it is generally undesirable to give the trustee such broad and unfettered discretion.

Standards to Guide the Exercise of Discretion. It is helpful to the trustee and beneficiaries if the trust includes a statement of standards to guide the trustee in making distributions. *See* Halbach, Problems of Discretion in Discretionary Trusts, 61 Colum. L. Rev. 1425 (1961). A trust might include, for example, a statement of the objective and subjective criteria that the trustee should consider. In addition, the trust should indicate whether priority should be given to one or another of the beneficiaries. When it comes to making distributions of principal, the trustee will also be helped by an indication that the grantor was primarily (or secondarily) concerned with the needs of the current beneficiaries as opposed to the preservation of principal for the remaindermen.

The trust should also indicate the extent to which the resources or income of the beneficiaries should be taken into account in making a decision regarding distributions. The provisions may require the trustee to consider the beneficiary's resources (or income) or merely authorize the trustee to consider them.

Transferability of the Beneficiary's Interest. In the case of a discretionary trust other than a self-settled trust, a transferee or creditor of the beneficiary cannot force the trustee to make any payments of income or principal. Restatement (Second) Trusts §155(1) (1959). However, this rule only applies where the trustee has uncontrolled discretion to pay the income or principal of the trust to the beneficiary. Neither a transferree nor a creditor can require the discretion to be exercised in favor of making a payment. A transferee or creditor is generally entitled to the benefit of any payment the trustee decides to make unless the trust includes a valid restraint on alienation. Restatement (Second) Trusts §155(2) (1959). Thus, "if the trustee does pay over any part of the trust property to the beneficiary with knowledge that he has transferred his interest or after the trustee has been served with process in a proceeding by a creditor of the beneficiary to reach his interest, the trustee is personally liable to the transferee or creditor for the amount so paid, except so far as a valid provision for forfeiture for alienation or restraint on alienation has been imposed. . . ." Restatement (Second) Trusts §155, Comment *h* (1959).

The same general rule applies to the interest of a beneficiary in a trust that gives the trustee the discretion to make payments to a group of beneficiaries. Neither a beneficiary nor a transferee or creditor of a beneficiary can force the trustee to make any payment. However, the trustee may be liable if a payment is made to a beneficiary after the trustee received notice that the interest of the beneficiary had been assigned.

Sample Provisions. A provision authorizing discretionary distributions could be expressed in a variety of ways. The following represents one possible approach to the challenge of drafting the basic provision. The provision could be expanded to cover related matters, such as the extent to which unequal distributions of principal or income are to be taken into account upon a final distribution of the trust.

> Distributions. The trustee shall distribute so much of the income and principal of the trust to or for the benefit of my surviving spouse and issue as my trustee believes is desirable to provide for the comfortable support, maintenance, education, and general welfare of each of them. The trustee is authorized to make distributions to one or more of them in unequal amounts and to the exclusion of one or more of the others of them. In making decisions regarding distributions, I direct the trustee (1) to give primary consideration to the needs of my surviving spouse and secondary consideration to the needs of all others and (2) to give such consideration as the trustee deems appropriate to the resources and income of each beneficiary apart from the beneficiary's interest in this trust.

Support Trusts. According to Restatement (Second) Trusts §154 (1959), "if by the terms of a trust it is provided that the trustee shall pay or apply only so much of the income and principal or either as is necessary for the education or support of the beneficiary, the beneficiary cannot transfer his interest and his creditors cannot reach it." The rule requires that a distinction be drawn between a trust for support and a trust under which part or all of the income is payable to the beneficiary with a statement that the payments are to be used for education or support. Such a statement of purpose does not prevent the transfer of the beneficiary's interest.

§10.19.   *Spendthrift Clauses — Restricting the Transfer of a Beneficiary's Interests*

In the absence of a restriction imposed by the trust, the equitable interests of a beneficiary in the income and principal of an ordinary trust are freely alienable and may be reached by the beneficiary's creditors. As noted above, the beneficiary's interests in a support trust or a discretionary trust are not transferrable because of the limited nature of the beneficiary's interest. Restatement (Second) Trusts §§154, 155(1) (1959). Perhaps more importantly, most states recognize "spendthrift clauses" that restrict the right of a beneficiary to transfer an interest in the income or principal of a trust. Restatement (Second) Trusts §§152, 153 (1959).

> A spendthrift trust is one in which, either because of a direction of the settlor or because of statute, the beneficiary is unable to transfer his right to

future payments of income or capital and his creditors are unable to subject the beneficiary's interest to the payment of their claims. Such a trust
does not involve any restraint on alienability or creditor's rights with respect to property after it is received by the beneficiary from the trustee, but
rather merely a restraint with regard to his rights to future payments
under the trust. G. Bogert, Trusts §40, at 147 (5th ed. 1973).

The planner should advise a prospective grantor regarding the effect
of including or excluding a spendthrift clause. The inclusion of a
spendthrift clause is effective in most states to prevent the beneficiary
from making any gift or sale of an interest in income or principal. For
example, such a clause might prevent an immature beneficiary from
transferring an interest to a religious cult, making an unwise sale of the
interest, or otherwise dissipating the trust fund. A spendthrift clause is
also usually effective to insulate the trust assets from the claims of most
creditors. Many states allow the beneficiary's interests to be reached by
certain preferred creditors. Claimants typically included in that category
are: (1) a former spouse or dependents for alimony support, (2) creditors who provide the beneficiary with the necessities of life, and (3) the
United States or a state for taxes. *See* Restatement (Second) Trusts §157
(1959).

The inclusion of a spendthrift clause reduces the beneficiary's flexibility in dealing with trust interests. Thus, the clause will prevent an income
beneficiary from assigning his or her income interest to another person.
Such a restriction could prevent the family from a beneficial reallocation
of the income within the family in order to reduce the overall income tax
burden. An assignment of income for a period of 10 years or more can
shift the income tax burden to the assignee. *See* Rev. Rul. 55-38, 1955-1
C.B. 389. However, a spendthrift clause generally does not prevent a
beneficiary from disclaiming an interest in the trust. Many disclaimer
statutes specifically provide that a beneficiary may disclaim an interest
whether or not it is subject to a spendthrift provision or similar restriction. *E.g.*, UPC §2-801(e); Wash. Rev. Code §11.86.070 (1979).

Form. A short form of spendthrift clause of the following type is
adequate for most purposes:

> No interest of a beneficiary in the principal or income of this trust may
> be anticipated, assigned or encumbered, or subject to any creditor's claim
> or legal process prior to its actual distribution to the beneficiary.

A more detailed clause may require the trustee to pay the income or
principal directly to or for the benefit of the beneficiary and not upon
any written or oral direction or assignment by the beneficiary. Even if the
trust prohibits the beneficiary from transferring the interest, the beneficiary may validly direct the trustee to distribute the interest in the
trust to another person. In such a case the beneficiary's direction is

recognized as a revocable authorization to pay. Restatement (Second) Trusts, §152, Comment *i* (1959).

Planners should be aware of the extent to which the governing law exempts interests in trusts from the claims of creditors and the extent to which grantors can further restrict the voluntary or involuntary alienation of a beneficiary's interest. Many clients believe that a beneficiary's interest in a trust should be insulated from the beneficiary's own inexperience or imprudence. Their trusts should include provisions that prevent any voluntary or involuntary transfers of the beneficiary's interests in the trust.

Self-Settled Trusts. The owner of property cannot insulate it from the reach of existing or subsequent creditors by transferring it to a trust of which the owner is a beneficiary. On the contrary, the beneficial interest of the owner in such a trust generally is transferrable and reachable by the owner's creditors. Restatement (Second) Trusts §156(1) (1959). Indeed, many states have statutes under which transfers in trust for the use of the transferor are void as to existing or future creditors.

The identity of the grantor and the extent of the grantor's interests are also important for federal gift and estate tax purposes. The reciprocal trust doctrine is sometimes applied to determine the true identity of the grantor of trusts established at the same time by related taxpayers for the benefit of each other. The doctrine is explained at §6.20, *supra.* By applying the doctrine, the trusts are "uncrossed" with the result that the beneficiary of a trust is treated as its grantor. Accordingly, the trust assets are fully includible in the beneficiary's estate under §2036.

The transfer of property to an irrevocable trust nominally for the benefit of others is an incomplete gift if the assets of the trust are subject to the claims of the grantor's creditors whenever the claims arise. *E.g.,* Rev. Rul. 76-103, 1976-1 C.B. 293. That ruling involved a trust that gave the trustee the absolute discretion to distribute income and principal to the grantor. Under the governing state law, the property of the trust was subject to the claims of the grantor's creditors. Accordingly, the transfer to the trust was incomplete for gift tax purposes *and* the trust property is includible in the grantor's estate because of the grantor's "retained power to, in effect, terminate the trust by relegating the grantor's creditors to the entire property of the trust."

§10.20. General Powers of Appointment

"The term 'general power of appointment' means a power which is exercisable in favor of the decedent, his estate, his creditors, or the creditors of his estate. . . ." §2041(b)(1). A general power of appointment is the antithesis of a spendthrift restraint. Powers that might be characterized as general powers of appointment under §§2041 and 2514 should be seldom conferred except as required to qualify for a specific tax benefit. The creation of general powers of appointment should be avoided because of the potentially adverse income, gift, and estate tax consequences for the holder: The income from property subject to a presently exercisable general power is taxable to the holder under §678; the exercise or lapse of a general power is usually treated as a taxable gift by §2514; and property subject to a general power is includible in the holder's estate under §2041. Also, the grantor may not want to confer such a broad power of disposition on another person — a special power of appointment may provide sufficient flexibility.

The statutory definition of a general power of appointment is broad and encompasses "all powers which are in substance and effect powers of appointment regardless of the nomenclature used in creating the power and regardless of local property law connotations." Reg. §20.2041-1(b)(1). Importantly, the definition extends to powers held in a fiduciary capacity and to joint powers (with the exception of joint powers held with either the creator of the power or a party with an interest that would be adversely affected by an exercise of the power, §§2041(b)(1)(C)(i), (ii)). The trustee's power to distribute income among the members of a class that includes the trustee is a general power of appointment over the income. Also, the property of a trust is includible in the beneficiary's estate where the beneficiary and 2 other persons held the power, as trustees, to terminate the trust and distribute the trust property to the beneficiary. Maytag v. United States, 493 F.2d 995 (10th Cir. 1974). Where the trustee has discretion to make distributions to the beneficiary, the beneficiary should not have the power to remove the trustee and become successor trustee, unless the beneficiary is barred from participating in the exercise of the discretionary powers. Under the regulations, a person who has the power to become trustee is treated as having all of the powers of the trustee. Reg. §20.2041-1(b)(1).

In some cases the conferral of a general power of appointment carries tax benefits that outweigh the disadvantages. Thus, the beneficiaries of a permanent irrevocable trust may be given *Crummey* withdrawal powers so the gift tax annual exclusion will be available with respect to property transferred to the trust. See §7.36, *supra.* Also, giving the grantor's grandchildren a general power of appointment is a way of qualifying their interests in a continuing trust for the grandchild exclusion to the generation-skipping tax. See §2.24, *supra.*

§10.21. Special Powers of Appointment

Where it is consistent with the client's plan, a current beneficiary of the trust may be given a special power of appointment over the income or principal. The conferral of an appropriate special power substantially increases the flexibility of the trust at little or no additional gift or estate tax cost. For example, a surviving spouse may be given a testamentary special power to appoint the trust assets to and among the trustor's descendants rather than mandating a fixed method of distribution. In such a case the exercise of the power would not cause the trust to be included in the surviving spouse's estate. In order to avoid inclusion of the trust property in the beneficiary's estate, the power should expressly prohibit an appointment in favor of the beneficiary, "his estate, his creditors, or the creditors of his estate." §2041(b)(1).

A power is more flexible if it is exercisable during the beneficiary's lifetime. However, it is more common to create powers that are only exercisable upon the beneficiary's death (*i.e.,* a testamentary power). Such a limitation helps preserve the trust property during the beneficiary's lifetime and insulates the beneficiary from pressure by permissible appointees to exercise the power currently in their favor. Limiting the power to an exercise at death also eliminates the risk that the power might be characterized as a general power where it is exercisable in favor of persons whom the power holder has a lifetime legal obligation to support. *See* Reg. §20.2041-1(c). On the other hand, giving the beneficiary a currently exercisable power allows greater flexibility in meeting the economic and estate-planning objectives of the family group. Thus, the holder may appoint trust property to family members in lieu of transferring "owned" property to the appointee. The appointment of trust corpus pursuant to a special power of appointment does not constitute a gift of the corpus. §2514(b), (c). However, where the power holder is entitled to receive the income of the trust for life, such an appointment constitutes a gift of a proportionate part of the holder's income interest. Reg. §25.2514-1(b)(2); Rev. Rul. 79-327, 1979-2 C.B. 342; *contra,* Self v. United States, 142 F. Supp. 939 (Ct. Cl. 1956). Also, as professors Douglas Kahn and Lawrence Waggoner have pointed out, an income beneficiary's special power is an invalid power appendant to the extent it purports to divest him or her of the right to the income from the trust. He or she holds that right apart from the purported power. D. Kahn & L. Waggoner, Federal Taxation of Gifts, Trusts and Estates §11-75 (2d ed. 1982). Presumably no gift would occur in case of the exercise of a special power over the corpus if the power holder were only entitled to receive distributions of income in the discretion of another person.

Problem 10-3. X is entitled to receive all of the income of a testamentary trust created by the will of X's brother, B, that has a corpus of $500,000. Under the terms of the trust X may appoint the principal of the trust during X's lifetime to and among B's descendants. In default of exercise of the power the trust property will be distributed to B's descendants per stirpes following the death of X. X exercised the power when she was 70 years of age by appointing property worth $100,000 to her niece, N. Applying the factor from Table A(2) of Reg. §25.2512-9(f), what are the gift tax consequences of the appointment? Does the gift qualify for the annual exclusion? Will the trust property be subject to estate tax when X dies?

The provision creating a power should indicate when and how the power is exercisable; whether the property may be appointed on a further trust; in whose favor it may be exercised; and whether the property may be appointed unequally or to the complete exclusion of some permissible appointees. In addition, the power should specify what will become of the trust property to the extent the power is not validly exercised. Here is a sample provision, creating a testamentary special power of appointment, that answers those questions:

> Upon the death of the beneficiary, the trustee shall distribute the trust property, including the net income then in the hands of the trustee and all income then accrued but uncollected, to and among such of the beneficiary's spouse and issue and charitable organizations as the beneficiary shall appoint by a will executed after the date this trust is created, which states expressly the beneficiary's intention to exercise this power. The beneficiary may appoint the trust property in such shares or interests and upon such terms and conditions as the beneficiary chooses either outright or in trust. In exercising this power the beneficiary is authorized to appoint the trust property to or for the benefit of one or more of the possible appointees to the total exclusion of the other or others of them. However, in no event may this power be exercised in favor of the beneficiary, the beneficiary's creditors, the beneficiary's estate, or the creditors of the beneficiary's estate.
> To the extent the beneficiary does not validly exercise this power, the trustee shall distribute the trust property to those of the beneficiary's issue who survive the beneficiary, such issue to take by right of representation and not per capita. If none of the beneficiary's issue survive the beneficiary, the trustee shall distribute the trust property to _____.

In the case of an inter vivos power, the instrument should also specify how the power could be exercised inter vivos or upon the death of the holder of the power.

§10.22. $5,000 or 5% Power of Withdrawal

Under the basic estate and gift tax rule, the lapse of a post-1942 general power of appointment is treated as a transfer of the property subject to the power. §§2041(a)(2), (b)(2); 2514(b), (e). However, a major exception to that rule allows a beneficiary to hold without substantial disadvantage a noncumulative, inter vivos power to withdraw a limited amount of property from the trust each year. The lapse of general powers of appointment during a calendar year is significant for estate and gift tax purposes only to the extent that the total amount that could have been appointed exceeds the greater of $5,000 or 5% of the aggregate value of the assets out of which, or the proceeds of which, the exercise of the lapsed powers could have been satisfied. §§2041(b)(2), 2514(e). However, property subject to an unlapsed power of withdrawal at the time of the power holder's death is includible in his or her estate although it is limited by the "5 or 5" standard.

Powers of withdrawal, including *Crummey* powers (*see* §7.36, *supra*), are generally tailored so the amount subject to withdrawal each year does not exceed the 5 or 5 limit. Note that the amount sheltered by this exception is apparently limited to a total of $5,000 or 5% annually for all trusts. Accordingly, the planner must proceed with caution where the power holder is, or may be, the beneficiary of more than one trust. However, the lapse of a power to withdraw an amount in excess of the 5 or 5 limit does not have any adverse gift tax consequences if the power holder also has a special power of appointment over the remainder. In such a case Reg. §25.2511-2(b) indicates that the lapse would result in an incomplete gift: "[I]f a donor transfers property to another in trust to pay the income to the donor or accumulate it in the discretion of the trustee, and the donor retains a testamentary power to appoint the remainder among his descendants, no portion of the transfer is a completed gift."

Because of the favorable gift and estate tax treatment of 5 or 5 powers, it is common to give one to the surviving spouse or other life income beneficiary of an irrevocable trust. Giving the power obviously increases the flexibility of the trust and reduces the beneficiary's dependence on the trustee. It also increases the beneficiary's "comfort level," which is particularly important to the establishment and maintenance of a good relationship between the beneficiary and the trustee. Some beneficiaries enjoy withdrawing some amount each year as "mad money" to use as they wish.

If lapses of post-1942 general powers in any calendar year exceed the 5 or 5 limit, the excess is treated as a transfer by the power holder, which may involve a taxable gift. Also, the excess is includible in the power holder's estate under §2041(a)(2) if the lapse is "of such a nature that if it were a transfer of property owned by the decedent, such property would be includible in the decedent's gross estate under sections 2035 to 2038, inclusive."

Example 10-10. B, the life income beneficiary of a trust, had the power to withdraw $50,000 of principal in a specified calendar year. B did not exercise the power, as a result of which it lapsed.

The principal of the trust was worth $800,000 at the end of that calendar year. B is treated as having transferred property worth $10,000 to the trust. That figure represents the excess of amount B could have withdrawn ($50,000) over the greater of $5,000 or 5% of the value of the property subject to the power (5% × $800,000 = $40,000). Accordingly, for estate tax purposes, B is treated as the grantor of 1/80 of the trust principal ($10,000/$800,000). Thus, $15,000 would be includible in B's estate if the trust has a value of $1,200,000 at the time of his or her death. Note also that the lapse of the power might have involved a taxable gift to the remaindermen.

A 5 or 5 power is often given to a surviving spouse who is the beneficiary of a testamentary trust, particularly one that meets the requirements of a qualified terminable interest property trust under §2056(b)(7). In such a case the power provides desirable flexibility to the trust and security to the surviving spouse.

Income Tax. Under §678 the holder of a power of withdrawal is treated as owner of the portion of the trust subject to withdrawal. *See* §7.36, *supra,* and §10.24, *infra.* Of course, the rule does not affect the taxation of trust income where the power holder is entitled to all of the income in any case. However, it does cause the power holder to be taxed on a portion of the income of a trust that is distributable to other beneficiaries. Rev. Rul. 67-241, 1967-2 C.B. 225 (surviving spouse with 5 or 5 power is taxable on proportionate part of income payable to decedent's 2 children).

Sample Provision

In addition, the Beneficiary shall have the power in each calendar year to withdraw from the principal of the trust, an amount not to exceed the greater of $5,000 or five percent of the value of the principal of the trust determined as of the end of the calendar year. This power may be exercised in whole or in part each year by a written notice delivered to the trustee. The power of withdrawal is noncumulative, so that the power of withdrawal with respect to a particular calendar year can only be exercised during the calendar year.

Problem 10-4. B was the income beneficiary of a trust, funded with $100,000. The trust gave B the noncumulative annual right to withdraw $5,000 of the trust principal. The trust was in effect for 5 years prior to the year of B's death, during which time the value of the principal remained the same and B never exercised the power. How much of the value of the trust, if any, is included in B's estate under §2041? How would your answer differ if the amount that could be withdrawn each year was $10,000? What would be the result if B died on June 15 and the power permitted the withdrawal to be made only during the last 3 months of each calendar year?

§10.23.   Power to Withdraw Trust Assets Limited by an Ascertainable Standard

The flexibility of the trust can also be increased somewhat without adverse gift or estate tax consequences by giving the beneficiary a power to withdraw trust property, "which is limited by an ascertainable standard relating to the health, education, support, or maintenance" of the power holder. §§2041(b)(1)(A), 2514(c)(1). Note that the standard must be ascertainable *and* must relate to the power holder's health, education, support, or maintenance to qualify under this exception. Such a power is often most important because of the increased sense of security it gives to the power holder.

A power only falls within the scope of this exception if it is subject to an ascertainable (*i.e.*, objective) standard and not an indefinite (*i.e.*, subjective) standard. State law determines the nature and extent of a right of withdrawal conferred by a trust. However, the regulations contain helpful examples of provisions that are acceptable. They include powers that are exercisable "for the holder's 'support,' 'support in reasonable comfort,' 'maintenance in health and reasonable comfort,' 'support in his accustomed manner of living,' 'education, including college and professional education,' 'health,' and 'medical, dental, hospital and nursing expenses and expenses of invalidism.'" Reg. §20.2041-1(c)(2). The same regulation points out that "[a] power to use property for the comfort, welfare, or happiness of the holder of the power is not limited by the requisite standard."

A power that is intended to escape treatment as a general power because of this exception must be carefully drawn. The safest course is to couch the power in exactly the language of one of the examples set forth in the regulation. Any deviation from the approved language creates a risk the IRS will treat the power as a general power of appointment. Thus, a power that could be exercised "in cases of emergency or illness" has been treated as a general power by the IRS and Tax Court. Under the governing state law a withdrawal might be made for an emergency that was not related to the power holder's health, education, support, or maintenance. Estate of Ida Maude Sowell, 74 T.C. 1001 (1980). Of course, a power that does not seem to be sufficiently objective may be "saved" by a sympathetic application of state law. For example, an uncontrolled right, power, and authority to use and devote such of the corpus of the trust from time to time as the beneficiary in her judgment believed necessary for her maintenance, comfort, and happiness was held to be limited by an ascertainable standard under Massachusetts law. Estate of Brantingham v. United States, 631 F.2d 542 (7th Cir. 1980). The IRS believes that the *Brantingham* case was incorrectly decided and has stated that it will not follow the holding. Rev. Rul. 82-63, 1982-1 C.B. — .

The other 2 types of post-1942 powers of withdrawal that are not treated as general powers are of little use for planning purposes. *See* §§2041(b)(1), 2514(c). The first exception is for a power only exercisable in conjunction with the creator of the power. §§2041(b)(1)(C)(i), 2514(c)(3)(A). The use of such a power is unsatisfactory because the property subject to the power would be includible in the creator's estate under §2038(a)(1) because of the creator's retained power to distribute the property in conjunction with another person. The exception is also unsuitable for planning purposes because it only applies during the lifetime of the creator of the power.

The second exception is for power that is only exercisable in conjunction with a person having a substantial interest in the property adverse to an exercise of the power by the beneficiary. §§2041(b)(1)(C)(ii), 2514(c)(3)(B). As Dean Casner has indicated, "This exception is of little or no use in estate planning because it is highly unlikely that the desired flexibility will be introduced into the estate plan where the decision as to whether a power will be exercised rests with one who will be adversely affected by the exercise." 3 A.J. Casner, Estate Planning 1255-1256 (4th ed. 1980).

§10.24. Beneficiary as Trustee

> [F]iduciary powers in the hands of the wrong persons may constitute dangerous powers for tax purposes either under the grantor rules of the income and estate tax laws or, in the case of a beneficiary serving as trustee, under various rules (especially those relating to general powers of appointment) of the estate, gift and income tax laws. Halbach, Discretionary Trusts and Income Tax Avoidance After the 1976 Tax Reform Act, U. Miami 12th Inst. Est. Plan. ¶308 (1978)

The suitability of appointing a beneficiary as trustee or cotrustee depends primarily on family planning and tax considerations. Insofar as the trust law is concerned, the appointment of a beneficiary as trustee does not impair the validity of the trust so long as the trust has either another trustee or another beneficiary. Put somewhat differently: The sole beneficiary of a trust cannot be the sole trustee. As stated in Restatement (Second) Trusts §99 (1959), Beneficiary as trustee,

> (1) One of several beneficiaries of a trust can be one of several trustees of the trust.

(2)   One of several beneficiaries of a trust can be the sole trustee of the trust.
(3)   The sole beneficiary of a trust can be one of several trustees of the trust.
(4)   If there are several beneficiaries of a trust, the beneficiaries may be the trustees.
(5)   The sole beneficiary of a trust cannot be the sole trustee of the trust.

The planner must recognize and attempt to deal with the potential conflict of interest between the economic interests of the beneficiary and the duties of a beneficiary as trustee. One approach is to attempt to eliminate the sources of potential conflicts through the use of special trustees and the imposition of limits on the powers of the beneficiary-trustee. However, such an approach can cause the trust to be complicated and potentially confusing. (A special trustee is one who holds only limited powers over the trust — usually in order to insulate a beneficiary-trustee from adverse tax consequences that would result if they were held by the beneficiary-trustee.) Another, perhaps more common, approach is to refer to the existence of potential conflicts in the trust and to authorize the trustee to act with regard to those matters regardless of his or her personal interest.

The income, gift, and estate tax ramifications of appointing a beneficiary as trustee are considered in the following paragraphs. Giving the beneficiary power to remove the trustee and appoint a successor is reviewed in the next section.

Income Tax. The appointment of a beneficiary as trustee of an inter vivos trust can cause the income to be taxed to the grantor under the grantor trust rules unless the beneficiary-trustee is an adverse party as defined in §672 (*i.e.,* the holder of a substantial interest that would be adversely affected by the exercise or nonexercise of the power). The risk arises primarily under §674, under which the grantor is generally treated as the owner of a trust to the extent the grantor or a nonadverse party has the power to control the beneficial enjoyment of the income or principal of the trust. However, as noted below, the exceptions of §674(b) permit the grantor or a nonadverse party to hold some limited, but important, powers regarding distributions. *See* §10.29, *infra.*

The appointment of a beneficiary as trustee may cause the income of the trust to be taxed to the beneficiary under §678. In general, §678(a) treats a person other than the grantor as owner of a trust if the person has a power, acting alone, to acquire the corpus or income. However, the rule does not apply to income that is taxable to the grantor under §§671 to 677. §678(b).

Example 10-11. O transferred property to a trust that was revocable by the joint action of O and O's sister, S. The trustee of the trust is O's brother, B, who has the power to distribute income each year to one or more members of a class that includes B. The power held by B is not within any of the exceptions created by §674(b). However, the income is not taxed to O under §674 because B is an adverse party as to the power over income. O is treated as the owner of the entire trust under §676 because of the power of revocation held jointly with S, a nonadverse party. Following the death of O the income of the trust will be taxed to B under §678.

Also, under §678(a) the income of the trust is taxable to a person who holds the power, acting alone, to use the income or corpus of the trust to satisfy his or her own legal obligations. Reg. §1.678(a)-1(b). However, a trustee is not taxed on the income of a trust merely because the trustee holds the power to apply the income to the support or maintenance of a person the trustee is legally obligated to support except to the extent the income is so used. §678(c). The latter rule is analogous to the one applicable to the grantor under §677(b).

Gift Tax. A taxable gift may occur where a beneficiary-trustee distributes the income or principal of the trust to another person. For example, a gift takes place if the beneficiary-trustee appoints income to which he or she is entitled to another person. Reg. §25.2514-3(e), *Example* (1). In such a case, the beneficiary, in effect, exercises a general power of appointment in favor of the other person. The distribution of principal to others may involve a taxable exercise of a general or special power of appointment under §2514. A gift would occur, for example, where the beneficiary-trustee distributes to others principal that he or she was free to distribute to himself or herself. The distribution of principal to others under a special power of appointment may involve a gift where the holder of the power is entitled to receive income distributions from the trust that will be diminished by the appointment. Reg. §25.2514-1(b)(2); Rev. Rul. 79-327, 1979-2 C.B. 342; and §10.21, *supra*.

Estate Tax. The property of the trust is includible in the estate of a beneficiary-trustee who holds a power, exercisable alone or in conjunction with others, to apply the principal of the trust for his or her own benefit. §2041(a)(2). However, as explained above in §10.23, the rule does not apply to powers that are limited by certain ascertainable standards or to certain joint powers.

In order to avoid a contest with the IRS, a person should not be authorized to use principal for the support of persons the power holder is obligated to support (*e.g.*, minor or disabled children). The risk of confrontation arises because of Reg. §20.2041-1(c)(1), which provides, "A power of appointment exercisable for the purpose of discharging a legal obligation of the decedent or for his pecuniary benefit is considered a power of appointment exercisable in favor of the decedent or his creditors." In this connection note that the exception for powers limited by an ascertainable standard only applies to standards "relating to the health, education, support or maintenance of the decedent." §2041(b)(1)(A); *see* §10.23, *supra*.

§10.25.   Removal and Replacement of Trustee

The beneficiary can be given some protection against an indolent or unresponsive trustee by empowering the beneficiary (or another reliable person) to remove the trustee and appoint a person other than himself or herself as successor trustee. This point should be thoroughly explored with the grantor, who may want to limit either the circumstances under which the power might be exercised or the class of successor trustees. For example, the grantor might want to limit the exercise of the power to cases in which all of the adult beneficiaries concur in the action. Where a corporate fiduciary serves as initial trustee, the grantor might also want to limit the successor trustees to a "corporate trustee qualified to carry on trust business in the state of my domicile at the time of my death or in such other state as may be the situs of the trust at the time of such appointment."

Where the holder of the power is a beneficiary, the trust should ordinarily prohibit the holder from becoming successor trustee. Such a restriction is suggested because a person who has an unlimited power to remove a trustee and to become successor trustee is considered to have all of the powers of the trustee. *See* Reg. §20.2041-1(b)(1). In the future the IRS might argue that a similar rule should apply under §678 for income tax purposes.

D.   PLANNING THE GRANTOR'S INTERESTS IN AN IRREVOCABLE TRUST

Technical considerations, niceties of the law of trusts or conveyances, or the legal paraphernalia which inventive genius may construct as a refuge from surtaxes should not obscure the basic issue. That issue is whether the grantor after the trust has been established may still be treated as owner of the corpus. . . . And where the grantor is the trustee and the beneficiaries are members of his family group, special scrutiny of the arrangement is necessary lest what is in reality but one economic unit be multiplied into two or more by devices which, though valid under state law, are not conclusive so far as §22(a) [now §61(a)] is concerned. Helvering v. Clifford, 309 U.S. 331, 334-335 (1940).

§10.26.   Scope

Serious income, gift, and estate tax problems can arise if the grantor retains beneficial interests in a trust or powers over the administration of the trust or the distributions to be made by the trust. The tax consequences that flow from the retention of a power to revoke the trust are considered in §§10.12 to 10.15, *supra*. The following sections examine the income, gift, and estate tax consequences that occur where the grantor retains other common interests or powers over the trust. Considerable attention is given to the so-called short-term trust, which is frequently established to deflect the income from property to other family members for a relatively short period, at the end of which the property will revert to the grantor.

Unfortunately, the criteria for determining the consequences of the retention of interests or powers are not the same for income, gift, and estate tax purposes. In fact, distinctions between the tax rules encourage taxpayers to take advantage of slight differences in the reach of the taxes. An example is the "defective trust," which is a permanent irrevocable trust that is drafted to include a "defect" sufficient to cause the grantor to be treated as the owner for income tax purposes (and presumably entitled to the deductions and credits of the trust), but not sufficient to cause the trust to be included in the grantor's estate. Irrevocable life insurance trusts are sometimes drafted as defective trusts in order to allow the grantor to claim a deduction for interest paid by the trust on loans against policies held in the trust. *See* §6.41, *supra*.

§10.27.   Summary of Tax Consequences

The grantor trust rules of §§671 to 677 establish the rules for determining whether the income of a trust is taxed to the grantor. Viewed differently, the rules specify the requirements that must be met in order to cause the income to be taxed to the trust or its beneficiaries and not to the grantor. Regulation §1.671-1(a) contains this concise statement of the circumstances under which the grantor will be treated as owner and taxed on the income:

> (1) If the grantor has retained a reversionary interest in the trust, within specified time limits (section 673);
> (2) If the grantor or a nonadverse party has certain powers over the beneficial interests under the trust (section 674);
> (3) If certain administrative powers over the trust exist under which the grantor can or does benefit (section 675);
> (4) If the grantor or a nonadverse party has a power to revoke the trust or return the corpus to the grantor (section 676); or
> (5) If the grantor or a nonadverse party has the power to distribute

income to or for the benefit of the grantor or the grantor's spouse (section 677).

Under section 678, income of a trust is taxed to a person other than the grantor to the extent that he has the sole power to vest corpus or income in himself.

The income of a trust is also not taxed to the grantor to the extent it is taxable to the grantor's spouse under §71 (alimony and separate maintenance) or §682 (income of estate or trust payable to spouse in case of divorce or separate maintenance).

The rules of §§671 to 677 are usually referred to in connection with irrevocable short-term trusts in which the grantor holds a reversionary interest. However, *all* irrevocable trusts should be planned and drafted with the grantor trust rules in mind. A failure to satisfy the rules will cause the income of any type of trust to be taxed to the grantor.

To the extent the grantor is treated as owner of the trust, he or she must report the items of income, deduction, and credit attributable to the trust. In such cases, the grantor's income is not limited to the distributable net income of the trust. Under Reg. §1.671-4 the trust does not report the income, deductions, and credits on its fiduciary income tax return (Form 1041): Instead they are shown on a separate statement attached to the trust's return. The trust must obtain a tax identification number and file annual returns even though all of the income is reported by the grantor.

Adverse Party. For purposes of Subchapter J, the term "adverse party" is defined as "any person having a substantial beneficial interest in the trust which would be adversely affected by the exercise or nonexercise of the power which he possesses respecting the trust. A person having a general power of appointment over the trust property shall be deemed to have a beneficial interest in the trust." §672. The regulations point out that a trustee is not an adverse party merely because of his or her interest as trustee. Reg. §1.672(a)-1(a). Powers over the trust are often sanitized if their exercise is subject to the consent of an adverse party.

A beneficiary is ordinarily an adverse party. However, if the beneficiary only has the right to share in part of the income or corpus, the beneficiary may be an adverse party only as to that part. Reg. §1.672(a)-1(b). In addition, a person who is an adverse party with respect to the income interest in a trust, may or may not be adverse with respect to the exercise of a power over corpus. In determining whether or not a person is an adverse party, the critical question involves the effect of the exercise or nonexercise of the power on the powerholder's beneficial interests in the trust — not the effect on the grantor's interests. The last point is illustrated by Reg. §1.672(a)-1(d):

> [I]f the grantor creates a trust which provides for income to be distributed
> to A for 10 years and then for the corpus to go to X if he is then living, a

power exercisable by X to revest the corpus in the grantor is a power exercisable by an adverse party; however, a power exercisable by X to distribute part or all of the ordinary income to the grantor may be a power exercisable by a nonadverse party (which would cause the ordinary income to be taxed to the grantor).

The proper identification of adverse parties is important because an adverse party is allowed to hold broad powers over a trust without causing the grantor to be treated as its owner. In particular, an adverse party can hold powers that (1) affect the beneficial enjoyment of the trust (§674), (2) can cause a revocation of the trust and the return of the trust property to the grantor (§676), and (3) permit the income of the trust to be accumulated or distributed to or for the benefit of the grantor or the grantor's spouse (§677(a)). The existence of such a power does not ordinarily cause any income, gift, or estate tax problems for the grantor. However, the mere existence of the power can have negative tax consequences for the power holder. Specifically, a person other than the grantor who holds the power "to vest the corpus or the income therefrom in himself" is treated as the owner of the trust under §678(a). In addition, the exercise or nonexercise of a power held by an adverse party may involve a gift to the other persons who are beneficially interested in the trust. *See* Reg. §25.2514-1(b)(2).

Example 10-12. G created a 10-year reversionary trust under which a related party, X, has the power to distribute the income to and among the members of a class that includes X. Any income that is not distributed is to be accumulated and paid to G upon termination of the trust. X is an adverse party, as a result of which G is not treated as the owner of the trust under §§674(a) or 677(a) by reason of the power held by X. Instead, all of the income is taxable to X under §678. In addition, the distribution of income to other beneficiaries or the accumulation of income for later distribution to G may involve a gift. An accumulation would, of course, constitute a future interest with respect to which no annual exclusion would be available.

Powers that are jointly exercisable by an adverse party and the grantor (or another person) do not produce such a thoroughly negative result. *See* §§678(a), 2041(b)(1)(C), and 2514(c)(3). To begin with, the holder of a joint power is not treated as the owner of the trust under §678(a); that subsection only applies to powers that are exercisable solely by a person other than the grantor. Also, for gift and estate tax purposes a joint power held by the adverse party and the grantor is not a general power of appointment. *See* §§2041(b)(1)(C)(iv); 2514(c)(3)(A). Accordingly, the exercise or nonexercise of such a joint power should not ordinarily involve a gift of the entire interest by the adverse party. The existence of such a joint power would not cause the grantor to be treated as owner of the trust for income tax purposes. However, the grantor's retention of a joint power would cause the trust property to be included in the grantor's gross estate under §§2036 and 2038.

Gift Tax. The transfer of property to a trust constitutes a gift of the value of the property transferred less the value of the donor's retained interest. Rev. Rul. 58-242, 1958-1 C.B. 251. The actuarial tables of Reg. §25.2512-9 are used to value the income interests given to others under the trust unless their use would "violate reason and fact." Rev. Rul. 77-195, 1977-1 C.B. 295 (tables used to value income interest in stock the trustee was required to retain although it had historically yielded only a 3% return). The entire value of the transferred property may be treated as a gift where the trustee is empowered to distribute the trust principal as income (Rev. Rul. 76-275, 1976-2 C.B. 299) or when capital gains are allocable to income and capital losses to principal (Rev. Rul. 77-99, 1977-1 C.B. 295). The gift includes the amount of any appreciation in the property at the time of the transfer where the trustee may sell the property and distribute the gain to the income beneficiary. Accordingly, a trust ordinarily should not provide for distribution of capital gains to the beneficiary even though the grantor is taxed currently under §677(a)(1) on gains that are accumulated for later distribution to the grantor.

A gift also occurs if the period during which others are entitled to the income of the trust is extended by the grantor. *See* §10.28, *infra.* If an extension is planned properly, the income will continue to be taxed to the beneficiary and not to the grantor. However, the right to receive the income for an additional period is a future interest for which no annual exclusion is allowed. Rev. Rul. 76-179, 1976-1 C.B. 290.

Annual exclusion. A transfer to a trust qualifies for the annual gift tax exclusion under §2503(b) to the extent the beneficiary's interest is a "present interest." Rev. Rul. 58-242, 1958-1 C.B. 251. Thus, the beneficiary's income interest in a short-term trust qualifies for the annual exclusion if it is distributable currently to the beneficiary, to a custodian for a minor beneficiary under the Uniform Gifts to Minors Act, to a guardian for the minor, or to a §2503(c) trust for the benefit of a minor beneficiary. *See* Jacob Konner, 35 T.C. 727 (1961), *nonacq.*, 1963-2 C.B. 6, *withdrawn and acq. sub.,* 1968-2 C.B. 2 (§2503(c) trust). The annual exclusion is allowable for an income interest in a minor's trust that satisfies the requirements of §2503(c). *See* Carl E. Weller, 38 T.C. 790 (1962), *acq.,* 1963-1 C.B. 4, *withdrawn and nonacq. sub.* 1963-2 C.B. 6, *withdrawn and acq. sub.* 1968-2 C.B. 3.

Where the income is currently distributable to a class of beneficiaries, such as the grantor's children, the gifts to the members of the class living at the time of the transfer are present interests. However, exclusions are allowable only to the extent the grantor can show that the present interests have present value. This burden is relieved a little by Rev. Rul. 55-678, 1955-2 C.B. 389, which states that "[i]n such cases it is not necessary that the exact value of the gift of the present interest in property be determinable on the basis of recognized actuarial principles." *See also* Rev. Rul. 55-679, 1955-2 C.B. 390. Nonetheless, in order to qualify for the annual exclusion, a trust with multiple beneficiaries should give each beneficiary a discrete interest in the income.

In any case, the value of the income interest in the trust should qualify for the annual exclusion if the beneficiary is given the noncumulative power to withdraw an amount each year equal to the trust's net income. This is merely a variation on the *Crummey* power to withdraw trust assets that is recognized as conferring a present interest on the beneficiary to the extent the power may be exercised currently. *See* §7.36, *supra*, Crummey v. Commissioner, 397 F.2d 82 (9th Cir. 1968), and Rev. Rul. 73-405, 1973-2 C.B. 321.

Where nonincome-producing property is transferred to the trust, the IRS may contend that the income interest has no value. *See* Rev. Rul. 69-344, 1969-1 C.B. 225 (trustee authorized to invest in life insurance policies that are not considered to be income-producing property). The outcome is most likely when the trustee had no power to dispose of the nonincome-producing assets and invest in income-producing property. Berzon v. Commissioner, 534 F.2d 528 (2d Cir. 1976). However, some courts have denied an annual exclusion for the beneficiary's income interest even though the trustee had the power to dispose of the property and invest the proceeds in income-producing property. Fischer v. Commissioner, 288 F.2d 574 (3d Cir. 1961); Stark v. United States, 477 F.2d 131 (8th Cir.), *cert. denied*, 414 U.S. 975 (1973); Van Den Wymelenberg v. United States, 397 F.2d 443 (7th Cir.), *cert. denied*, 393 U.S. 953 (1968); *contra*, Rosen v. Commissioner, 397 F.2d 245 (4th Cir. 1968). The transfer of nonincome-producing property to a trust invites a challenge by the IRS — particularly where the trustee lacks the power to sell the property.

Charitable Deduction. Caution must be exercised in making a charitable gift of an interest in a short-term trust: Ordinarily a gift tax charitable deduction is not allowable where a simple income interest is given to charity. *See* §2522(c)(2). The deduction is only available for a split interest given to charity when the interest is in the form of a "guaranteed annuity or . . . a fixed percentage distributed yearly of the fair market value of the property (to be distributed yearly)." §2522(c)(2)(B). However, this trap is avoided if the grantor retains the right to select the annual charitable recipient of the income until after it is received, which renders the initial gift incomplete. See §8.26, *supra*, for a more complete description of the device. Of course, the grantor is only entitled to an income tax deduction for an "income" interest to the extent the grantor is treated as the owner of the trust under §671. §170(f)(2)(B). In essence, a present income tax deduction is available at the cost of being taxed on the future income of the trust.

Estate Tax. If the grantor dies prior to termination of the trust, the value of the grantor's reversionary interest is includible in his or her gross estate under §2033. Such a reversionary interest is valued in accordance with Reg. §20.2031-10. Of course, if the grantor survives termination of a short-term trust, the property formerly held in the trust is includible in his or her estate.

> **Example 10-13.** G transferred property worth $100,000 to a trust, the corpus of which would revert to G at the end of 10 years. The income of the trust was payable to G's sister, S, for the term of the trust. If G dies 5 years later and the trust still has a value of $100,000, the reversionary interest, worth $74,725.80, is includible in the grantor's estate. This amount represents the value of the trust principal ($100,000) multiplied by the appropriate factor from Table B, Reg. §20.2031-10 (.747258). Of course, if the reversion took effect upon G's death, the full value of the trust property would be includible in G's gross estate.

The value of the trust may also be included in the grantor's estate under §§2036, 2037, or 2038. Avoiding inclusion under those sections is most important where the grantor does not retain a reversionary interest, or where the interest retained by the grantor has little or no value.

Inclusion under §2036 could occur, for example, where the income of the trust is used to discharge the grantor's legal obligation to support a minor child or to make principal payments on a mortgage. Reg. §20.2036-1(b)(2). Of course, §2036(a)(2) mandates inclusion if the grantor retains the power to control beneficial enjoyment of the property (*e.g.*, to designate which of 2 beneficiaries will receive the income). Inclusion may also result where the decedent is identified as the grantor under the reciprocal trust doctrine and the grantor holds powers sufficient to cause inclusion under §§2036(a)(2) or 2038. *See* §6.20, *supra,* and Estate of Bruno Bischoff, 69 T.C. 32 (1977).

Where the grantor retains a reversionary interest contingent on surviving the income beneficiary, the entire value of the property is includible in the grantor's estate under §2037 if the value of the reversionary interest immediately before the grantor's death exceeds 5% of the value of the property. *E.g.*, Rev. Rul. 76-178, 1976-1 C.B. 273 (real property transferred in trust to pay the income to the trust beneficiary for life, after which the property would be returned to the grantor if living, otherwise to the grantor's children). The threat of inclusion under §2037 can be avoided by drafting the trust to exclude the retention of any reversionary interest by the grantor.

The trust corpus is includible in the grantor's estate under §2038(a) if the grantor at death holds a power to alter, amend, revoke, or terminate the trust, exercisable alone or in conjunction with any other person. Inclusion is also required where such a power is "relinquished during the 3-year period ending on the date of the decedent's death." §2038(a)(1).

> **Example 10-14.** T transferred income-producing property worth $100,000 to an irrevocable trust. The trustee has the discretion to distribute the income each year during the 10-year term of the trust to such of T's children, A, B, and C, as he chooses. However, in no event may any of the income be accumulated and distributed to T. Upon termination of the trust, the trust corpus will be distributed to T. The transfer involves a gift of $44,161 (*see* Table B, Reg. §25.2512-9). No annual exclusion is allowable, however, because none of the beneficiaries has a present interest. If T dies prior to termination of the trust, the value of the reversionary interest is includible in his gross estate. The full value of the trust property would be included in T's gross estate in such a case if he retained the power to remove or discharge the trustee and appoint himself as trustee. Reg. §20.2036-1(b)(2).

Effect of Unification on Short-Term Trusts. Unification requires the amount of post-1976 taxable gifts to be included in the donor's tax base at death (§2001(b)(1)(B)), which may increase the tax due at death by pushing the taxable estate into higher marginal brackets. In the case of a short-term trust, the value of the property is also included in the gross estate if the trust has terminated. If the trust has not terminated, only the value of the reversionary interest is includible. In any case, the value of the income interest, computed under the 6% tables, is includible in the grantor's tax base to the extent it constituted a taxable gift (*i.e.*, to the extent its value exceeded the allowable annual exclusions). Of course, the trust removes from the grantor's estate the actual amount of the income received by the income beneficiary — which could far exceed the value of the income interest computed under the 6% tables. If T in Example 10-14, above, survived termination of the trust, T's tax base would include the value of the property returned to him plus the amount of the taxable gift when the trust was created ($34,161). In this connection note that the number of annual exclusions can be multiplied if the gift is split between the donor and the donor's spouse or if the gift of the property is spread over more than one year.

For example, a 10-year income interest in $100,000 has a value of $44,161 based on the 6% tables. Where there is one donor and one current income beneficiary, a gift of $100,000 involves a taxable gift of

$34,161. Of course, if the gift is split between the donor and his or her spouse under §2513, the transfer qualifies for another annual exclusion, which reduces the total amount of the taxable gifts to $24,161. If such a gift were spread over 2 years, the allowable annual exclusions would be doubled (*e.g.*, transfers of $50,000 in each of 2 years would result in taxable gifts of $24,161 by a single donor or taxable gifts of $2,081 by the donor and his or her spouse in the case the gifts were split). Each transfer must remain in trust for the period prescribed by §673 if the grantor is to avoid being treated as owner of the property. *See* §10.28, *infra*.

Overall, the irrevocable short-term trust is still a valuable estate-planning tool because of its ability to shift income from a high bracket grantor to low bracket family members without requiring the grantor to surrender all of his or her interests in the property. If the trust is properly prepared and administered, the income from the property will be taxed to the beneficiary and not to the grantor. Also, the actual amount of the trust's income will not be included in the grantor's estate. For example, a short-term trust may be used by a parent to shift income to a child who is in a much lower tax bracket. The short-term trust has lost some of its lustre because of the unification of the gift and estate tax laws. In addition, the planner should balance the potential income tax savings against the legal, administrative, and other costs that a trust entails and that would not otherwise be incurred by the client.

§10.28. *Retained Reversionary Interest*

Under §673 the income of a trust is not taxed to the grantor because of a retained reversionary interest if the reversion will not take effect until 10 years or more after the transfer (or until after the death of the income beneficiary). In particular, §673(a) provides that the grantor is treated as the owner of any portion of the trust in which the grantor has a reversionary interest in the corpus or income that will or reasonably may be expected to take effect in possession or enjoyment within 10 years following its transfer in trust. Thus, a grantor who has a reversionary interest in a trust with a fixed term of less than 10 years is taxed on the income of the trust throughout its existence. The grantor is not treated as the owner of a trust where the reversionary interest will take effect on the occurrence of an event that is not reasonably expected to take place within 10 years from the date the property is transferred in trust. Reg. §1.673(a)-1(c). For example, the grantor is not treated as the owner of property transferred to a trust in which the reversionary interest will take effect upon the grantor's death, if the grantor's life expectancy was more than 10 years at the time of the transfer. *Id.*

As indicated above, there is one very important exception to the basic 10-year rule: The grantor is not treated as owner where the reversionary interest will take effect on the death of the income beneficiary, regardless of the life expectancy of the income beneficiary at the time of the transfer. §673(c). The grantor's reversionary interest can take effect upon the death of the income beneficiary or at the end of a term of less than 10 years, whichever occurs *later*. However, "[i]f his reversionary interest is to take effect on or after the death of an income beneficiary or upon the expiration of a specific term of years, whichever is earlier, the grantor is treated as the owner if the specified term of years is less than 10 years (but not if the term is 10 years or longer)." Reg. §1.673(a)-1(b).

Time of Transfer. It is important to recognize that the minimum 10-year period runs from the time an asset is transferred to the trust and not from the time the trust document is signed. Thus, the grantor is treated as the owner of property transferred to the trustee several months after the trust agreement was executed where the trust agreement provided that the property would revert to the grantor 10 years and 1 day after it was executed. C. O. Bibby, 44 T.C. 638 (1965). This problem can be avoided by providing that the grantor's reversionary interest in an asset will not take effect until 10 years and 1 day after the date the asset is transferred to the trust. Where property will only be transferred to the trust at the time the trust is created, the trust agreement may provide that the term of the trust will run from the time the property is transferred to the trustee.

Addition of Property to an Existing Trust. The reversionary interest rule also applies to the addition of property to an existing trust. By the terms of §673(a) the grantor is treated as owner of "any portion" of a trust in which the grantor has a proscribed reversionary interest "as of the inception of that portion of the trust." Thus, the grantor is taxed to the extent the income is attributable to property the grantor adds to the trust within 10 years of the time when his or her reversionary interest will, or can reasonably be expected to, take effect. Rev. Rul. 58-567, 1958-2 C.B. 365. However, the grantor is only treated as the owner of the portion of the trust in which he or she has such a reversionary interest. That is, an addition does not "taint" the entire trust and cause the grantor to be taxed on the income from other portions of it.

Problem 10-5. Five years ago T created an irrevocable trust, the income of which is payable to B. T retained a reversionary interest that would take effect at the end of 14 years. T proposes to transfer additional property to the trust next week, consisting of a life insurance policy on his life that has an interpolated terminal reserve of $5,000, cash of $15,000, and stock worth $30,000 in a closely held family corporation that has traditionally paid annual dividends of 2%. Comment on the probable gift and income tax consequences of the proposed additions. What alternative plan would you suggest to T?

Extension of an Existing Trust. The extension of the term of an existing trust is treated as a new transfer in trust that begins on the date the extension is made and ends with the date the reversionary interest will take effect. §673(d). However, the grantor will not be treated as the owner of any portion of a trust for any taxable year by reason of an extension where the grantor would not be treated as the owner apart from the extension. Reg. §1.673(d)-1, *Example.* Thus, an extension will not affect the taxation of the trust income except during the term of the extension.

> **Example 10-15.** T transferred property to an irrevocable trust in which T held a reversionary interest that would take effect at the end of 12 years. After 5 years had passed T extended the period of the trust for 2 years. T is treated as having made a transfer in trust for a term of 9 years (the 7 years that remained of the original term plus the 2-year extension). However, T is not treated as the owner under §673 for the first 7 years of the extension. T is treated as owner for the 2-year period of the extension. T would not be treated as owner of the trust during the period of the extension if the trust had been extended for a period of at least 3 years. In that case T's reversionary interest under the "new" transfer would not take effect within 10 years. For gift tax purposes the extension involves a gift of a future interest.

Gift Tax. The transfer of the income interest constitutes a gift to the extent of its actuarially determined value. It qualifies for the annual gift tax exclusion where the income is payable currently to the income beneficiary or to a guardian or custodian for the beneficiary. Reg. §25.2503-3(b). In contrast, no annual exclusion is available where the trustee may withhold payments of income from the beneficiary. Reg. §25.2503-3(c), *Example* (1).

Estate Tax. The actuarially determined value of the reversionary interest is includible in the grantor's estate under §2033. Inclusion is required whether the reversion was expressly retained or is deemed to have been retained under the Doctrine of Worthier Title. *See* Beach v. Busey, 156 F.2d 496 (6th Cir. 1946), *cert. denied,* 329 U.S. 802 (1947). Where the Doctrine has not been abolished judicially or legislatively, it exists as a rule of construction that prevents a transferor from creating a remainder in his or her own heirs. For a judicial repudiation of the Doctrine, *see* Hatch v. Riggs National Bank, 361 F.2d 559 (D.C. Cir. 1966). Under the Doctrine the grantor is considered to have retained a reversion where property is transferred in trust with a life estate in the grantor (or others) and a remainder to the heirs of the grantor. *See* Johanson, Reversions, Remainders and the Doctrine of Worthier Title, 45 Texas L. Rev. 1 (1966).

As noted above, property in which the grantor retains a reversionary interest may be included in his or her estate under §2037. However, that section only applies where the possession or enjoyment of the property can, through the ownership of the transferred interest, be obtained only by surviving the grantor and the grantor retained a reversionary interest in the property that had a value immediately before the transferor's death in excess of 5% of the value of the property. It is unusual to create a trust that involves a reversionary interest that would subject it to §2037.

§10.29. *Retained Control of Beneficial Enjoyment*

For income tax purposes the grantor is treated as the owner of a trust if the beneficial enjoyment of the corpus or income is subject to the control of the grantor, a nonadverse party, or both, without the consent of an adverse party. §674(a). Under this very broad rule the grantor is taxed on the income of a trust where the grantor or a nonadverse party holds the right to add or delete beneficiaries, to increase or decrease the shares of the beneficiaries in income or principal, or to determine when distributions will be made. However, the rigor of §674(a) is relaxed by important exceptions for (1) certain powers held by anyone including the grantor (§674(b)), (2) powers held by an independent trustee (§674(c)), and (3) powers limited by an ascertainable standard that are held by a trustee other than the grantor or the grantor's spouse (§674(d)). The exception for powers of distribution held by an independent trustee is reviewed at §10.18, *supra*. In general, the scope of each exception varies directly with the degree of the power holder's independence (*i.e.*, the narrowest exception applies to the grantor or a nonadverse party and the broadest to a totally independent power holder). Some thoughtful commentators have proposed that the exceptions be narrowed, but their proposals have not been accepted. *See, e.g.*, Westfall, Trust Grantors and Section 674: Adventurers in Income Tax Avoidance, 60 Colum. L. Rev. 326 (1960).

Powers That May Be Held by Any Person, Including the Grantor **(§674(b)).** The exceptions carved out by §674(b) allow the grantor or any other person to hold a variety of powers over income and corpus. Accordingly, the trust may permit some degree of flexibility over distributions. For example, the exceptions are broad enough to permit the grantor to act as trustee of a §2503(c) trust of which a dependent child is a beneficiary (the grantor would only be taxed on the income actually applied to discharge his obligation to support the child). Section 2503(c) trusts are discussed in more detail at §7.35, *supra*.

The exceptions of §§674(b)(1) to (4) are of limited general significance in planning irrevocable trusts. Briefly, they permit the grantor or a nonadverse party to hold powers:

1. To apply income to the support of a dependent of the grantor to the extent the grantor would not be taxed under §677(b) (*i.e.*, the grantor is taxable to the extent the income is actually applied to satisfy his or her legally enforceable obligation to provide support);

2. To control the beneficial enjoyment of the trust only after the expiration of 10 years or more (*i.e.*, the period specified in §673) (§674(b)(2));

3. To appoint the principal or income of the trust by will, other than income accumulated in the discretion of the grantor or a nonadverse party (§674(b)(3)); and

4. To allocate the principal or income among charitable beneficiaries (§674(b)(4)).

The exception of §674(b)(1) does allow the grantor or a nonadverse party to hold the power to allocate income to the grantor's dependents without adverse income tax consequences unless the power is actually exercised. Also, the exception of §674(b)(4) allows the creation of a unique form of charitable income trust in which the grantor retains the power to designate each year the recipient of the income earned by the trust. *See* §8.26, *supra*.

The §674(b)(5) exception permits the grantor to hold the power to distribute corpus to a current income beneficiary if the distribution will be charged against the distributee's proportionate share of the trust fund. In addition, (b)(5) permits the grantor to distribute corpus to a beneficiary or a class of beneficiaries provided that the power is limited by a reasonably definite standard set forth in the trust instrument (*e.g.*, to defray costs of education or medical care). Subsection (b)(6) allows the grantor to withhold income temporarily from a beneficiary. However, the income must be distributed to the beneficiary (or his or her appointees) or on termination of the trust to the current beneficiaries of the trust in shares irrevocably specified in the trust instrument. Under §674(b)(7) the grantor may withhold income from a beneficiary during his or her incompetency or minority. According to the regulations, to qualify under this exception it is not necessary that the accumulated income be payable to the beneficiary from whom it was withheld or to his or her estate or appointees. Reg. §1.674(b)-1(b)(7). Thus, income accumulated during the minority of a beneficiary may be added to corpus and ultimately distributed to others. Of course, provision for distribution to others could prevent the income interest from qualifying for the annual exclusion under §2503(c). Finally, §674(b)(8) excepts a power to allocate receipts and disbursements between principal and income, even though expressed in broad language.

The principal exceptions established by §674(b) are succinctly described in the following portion of Reg. §1.674(a)-1(b):

(1) *Miscellaneous powers over either ordinary income or corpus.*

(i)   A power that can only affect the beneficial enjoyment of income (including capital gains) received after a period of time such that the grantor would not be treated as an owner under section 673 if the power were a reversionary interest (section 674(b)(2));

(ii)   A testamentary power held by anyone (other than a testamentary power held by the grantor over accumulated income) (section 674(b)(3));

(iii)   A power to choose between charitable beneficiaries or to affect the manner of their enjoyment of a beneficial interest (section 674(b)(4)) [*see* §8.26, *supra*];

(iv)   A power to allocate receipts and disbursements between income and corpus (section 674(b)(8)).

(2) *Powers of distribution primarily affecting only one beneficiary.*

(i)   A power to distribute corpus to or for a current income beneficiary, if the distribution must be charged against the share of corpus from which the beneficiary may receive income (section 674(b)(5)(B));

(ii)   A power to distribute income to or for a current income beneficiary or to accumulate it either (a) if accumulated income must either be payable to the beneficiary from whom it was withheld or as described in paragraph (b)(6) of §1.674(b)-1 (section 674(b)(6)); (b) if the power is to apply income to the support of a dependent of the grantor, and the income is not so applied (section 674(b)(1)); or (c) if the beneficiary is under 21 or under a legal disability and accumulated income is added to corpus (section 674(b)(7)).

The retention of the maximum powers permitted by §674(b) may have adverse tax consequences for the grantor. For example, if the grantor retains the power to withhold income from the beneficiary, the income interest generally will not qualify for the annual gift tax exclusion unless the trust satisfies the requirements of a minor's trust under §2503(c). *See* §7.35, *supra*. The retention of other powers could also prevent the trust from meeting the requirements of §2503(c). Perhaps more important, the retention of the power to distribute or withhold income or corpus would cause the trust to be included in the grantor's gross estate under §§2036 or 2038. Lober v. United States, 346 U.S. 335 (1953).

Problem 10-6. W proposes to transfer property to H as trustee of an irrevocable trust for the benefit of their children, D and S. The income of the trust is distributable to D and S quarterly in equal shares, provided that until a beneficiary attains the age of 21 the trustee may accumulate the beneficiary's share of income and add it to principal. Principal of the trust is distributable to S or D as the trustee believes is necessary or desirable to provide for his or her health, education, maintenance, and support. The trust will terminate when the younger child attains (or would have attained) 35 years of age. Upon termination the principal is distributable in equal shares to S and D, or all to the survivor of them. If both S and D die prior to that time, the principal will go to the then living issue of W's brother, B. Will the income of the trust be taxed to W under §674(a)? If so, would the outcome be any different if (a) W's lawyer, L, acts as trustee or (b) if a separate trust were created for each beneficiary? If W dies prior to termination of the trust, would the value of the trust property be included in her gross estate? Will the transfer to the trust qualify for the annual gift tax exclusion?

§10.30. Administrative Powers

The grantor is taxed on the income of a trust under §675 if certain powers of administration are held by the grantor or a nonadverse party. In general the powers are ones that indicate the trust may be operated substantially for the benefit of the grantor instead of the beneficiaries. A power may be present either because of the terms of the trust instrument or because of the manner in which the trust is operated. Reg. §1.675-1(a). The powers described in §675 are:

(1) Power to deal for less than adequate and full consideration. A power exercisable by the grantor or a nonadverse party, or both, without the approval or consent of any adverse party [that] enables the grantor or any other person to purchase, exchange, or otherwise deal with or dispose of the corpus or the income therefrom for less than an adequate consideration in money or money's worth.

(2) Power to borrow without adequate interest or security. A power exercisable by the grantor or a nonadverse party, or both, [that] enables the grantor to borrow the corpus or income, directly or indirectly, without adequate interest or without adequate security except where a trustee (other than the grantor) is authorized under a general lending power to make loans to any person without regard to interest or security.

(3) Borrowing of the trust funds. The grantor has directly or indirectly borrowed the corpus or income and has not completely repaid the loan, including any interest, before the beginning of the tax year. The preceding sentence shall not apply to a loan that provides for adequate interest and security, if such loan is made by a trustee other than the grantor and other than a related or subordinate trustee subservient to the grantor.

In addition under §675(4), the grantor is treated as the owner of any part of the trust in respect of which any person in a nonfiduciary capacity has, without the consent of any person in a fiduciary capacity:

(A) a power to vote or direct the voting of stock or other securities of a corporation in which the holdings of the grantor are significant from the viewpoint of voting control;

(B) a power to control the investment of the trust funds either by directing investments or reinvestments, or by vetoing proposed investments or reinvestments, to the extent that the trust funds consist of stocks or securities in corporations in which the holdings of the grantor and the trust are significant from the viewpoint of voting control; or

(C) a power to reacquire the trust corpus by substituting other property of an equivalent value.

Note that the tests under §§675(1) and (2) are whether "the grantor or a nonadverse party, or both" have certain powers over the trust property (or income). The grantor is treated as owner of any portion of the trust over which such a power exists. In contrast, §675(3) focuses on whether the grantor has borrowed the corpus or income of the trust. The grantor may be treated as owner of the *entire* trust if such a borrowing takes place. *See* Larry W. Benson, 76 T.C. 1040 (1981) (grantor borrowed entire income of trusts).

None of the powers proscribed by §675 are necessary for the legitimate administration of most trusts. In fact, the exercise of most of the powers described in §675 would constitute a breach of the trustee's fiduciary duties with respect to investments unless expressly authorized. Accordingly, §675 should cause no problems in the ordinary case. The simplest and most effective way to guard against an inadvertent violation of §675 is to provide in the trust instrument that the trustee may not exercise any of the powers described in the section.

Gift Tax. The retention of purely administrative powers does not render a gift incomplete although it necessarily has some impact on the beneficial enjoyment of interests in the trust. Thus, a gift is not incomplete merely because the grantor retains the power, exercisable in a fiduciary capacity, to control the investment of trust assets or to allocate receipts and disbursements between income and principal. A transfer is incomplete, however, if the grantor retains the power to change beneficial interests in the trust unless the power is a "fiduciary power limited by a fixed or ascertainable standard." Reg. §25.2511-2(c).

Estate Tax

We hold that no aggregation of purely administrative powers [retained by the grantor] can meet the government's amorphous test of "sufficient

dominion and control" so as to be equated with ownership. Old Colony
Trust Co. v. United States, 423 F.2d 601, 603 (1st Cir. 1970).

The rule set forth in the *Old Colony Trust Co.* case is consistent with the
treatment of administrative powers in other contexts under the estate tax
law. For example, administrative powers held in a fiduciary capacity do
not constitute a general power of appointment for purposes of §2041.
See Reg. §20.2041-1(b)(1).

The right to vote publicly traded stock transferred to a trust is usually
an unobjectionable administrative power. However, the situation is different where the grantor retains the right to vote stock in a corporation
in which the grantor and related persons own or have the right to vote
20% or more of the voting stock. In 1967 the IRS ruled that the retention of voting control of a corporation, combined with restrictions on the
disposition of the transferred stock, was equivalent to retaining the right
to control the enjoyment of the income of the trust. *See* Rev. Rul. 67-54,
1967-1 C.B. 269, *revoked,* Rev. Rul. 81-15, 1981-1 C.B. 457 (noting the
control may have an effect on the value of the stock). However, when the
issue was litigated, the Supreme Court rejected the IRS position. United
States v. Byrum, 408 U.S. 125 (1972). In *Byrum* the Court held that the
grantor's retained power "to affect, but not control" trust income was
insufficient to cause the trust property to be included in his gross estate
under §2036. A majority of the Court believed that the grantor's power
to vote a majority of the stock was so constrained by the fiduciary duties
applicable to majority shareholders and directors that it did not warrant
inclusion of the stock in his estate.

Congress responded to the *Byrum* decision by enacting §2036(b) in
1976, which was modified in 1978. Under the so-called Anti-*Byrum*
amendments, stock in a "controlled corporation" is included in the
grantor's estate where the grantor retained the right to vote the stock.
For this purpose, a "controlled corporation" is one in which the grantor
owned or had the right to vote at least 20% of the voting stock at some
time after the transfer of the stock and within 3 years of the grantor's
death. The constructive ownership rules of §318 are applied in determining the ownership of stock in the corporation. §2036(b)(2). The new
provisions are thoroughly reviewed in McCord, The 1978 Anti-Byrum
Amendment: A Cruel Hoax, U. Miami 14th Inst. Est. Plan., Ch. 12
(1980).

Problem 10-7. Anne and her mother, Mary, each owns 50% of the
voting stock in the family's successful business, Family, Inc. Anne
plans to transfer some of her stock to herself as trustee of an irrevocable trust for her adult children, Donna and Samuel. In order
to protect her position in the business, Anne would like to retain
the right to vote the Family, Inc. shares she transfers to the trust.

However, she does not wish to retain any direct control over the beneficial interests of her children in the trust. Comment on the income, gift, and estate tax consequences of Anne's plan, assuming that she will be the sole trustee of the trust. Would it make any difference if there were an independent cotrustee? If Anne does not act as trustee at all? Would her position be improved if she appoints an independent trustee, but retains the right to remove the trustee without cause and appoint a successor other than herself? (In this connection, see the discussion of Rev. Rul. 79-353, 1979-2 C.B. 325, at §§10.31 and 10.34, *infra*.)

§10.31. *Power to Revest Title in Grantor*

Under §676(a) the grantor is treated as the owner of any portion of a trust "where at any time the power to revest in the grantor title to such portion is exercisable by the grantor or a nonadverse party or both." Thus, the grantor will be taxed on the income of the trust that is revocable by (1) the grantor, (2) a nonadverse party, or (3) the grantor and a nonadverse party. Apparently the grantor will not be treated as the owner of a trust where the power to revoke is held by an adverse party or may be exercised only with the consent of an adverse party. Thus, the existence of a power to revoke may be shielded by the involvement of an adverse party. However, a distribution to the grantor under such a power would necessarily involve a gift by the adverse party. It is unclear whether §676 might require the grantor-lender to be taxed on the income generated by an interest-free demand loan to a trust. *See* §7.19, *supra*. The IRS could argue that the loan portion of the trust should be treated as owned by the grantor under §676(a). If so, then perhaps any loan by the grantor with a term of less than 10 years would be vulnerable under §673.

The general rule of §676(a) does not extend to powers that can only affect enjoyment of the income for a period commencing after the end of a period of sufficient duration that the grantor would not be treated as owner under §673 if the power were a reversionary interest. §676(b). Under this exception, the grantor may retain a power to revoke the trust and recover title to the corpus provided that the power only becomes exercisable more than 10 years after the property is transferred to the trust or after the death of the income beneficiary.

In order to remove any question regarding the revocability of a short-term trust, the instrument itself should specify that the trust is irrevocable. This is particularly necessary if the trust might be subject to the laws of California, Oklahoma, or Texas, under which a trust is generally revocable unless otherwise specified in the trust instrument. *See* §10.6, *supra*.

Gift Tax. A gift is, of course, incomplete to the extent it is revocable by the grantor. For this purpose, a grantor is considered to have a power that is exercisable jointly with any person who does not have a substantial adverse interest in the property. Reg. §25.2511-2(e). The fact that a nonadverse party has the sole power to revest title in the grantor does not make the transfer incomplete.

Estate Tax. Under §2038, property transferred to a trust is includible in the grantor's estate if the grantor retained the power, alone or in conjunction with any other person, to amend, revoke, or terminate the trust. The rule of §2038(a)(1) extends to powers held at death or relinquished within 3 years immediately preceding death. *See also* §2035(d)(2). The grantor's estate does not include the property of a trust merely because another person holds a power to amend, revoke, or terminate the trust. Understandably, where "the decedent had the unrestricted power to remove or discharge a trustee at any time and appoint himself trustee, the decedent is considered as having the powers of the trustee." Reg. §20.2038-1(a)(3). Here again, some caution must be exercised even when the trustee must always be a corporation or trust company. The IRS has indicated that it will also treat the grantor as having the powers of the trustee where the trust appoints a corporate trustee and retains the power to remove the corporate trustee and appoint another corporate trustee. Rev. Rul. 79-353, 1979-2 C.B. 325. The position taken in the ruling is of doubtful validity. However, to avoid a confrontation with the IRS, any such power should be given to someone else.

§10.32. Retained Income Interest

A grantor may retain an income interest for valid nontax reasons — there are virtually no tax reasons for doing so. For example, a grantor may seek to protect himself or herself against the unwise expenditure or waste of property by transferring it to an irrevocable trust in which the grantor reserves a right to receive income, but no interest in principal. For income and estate tax purposes such a transfer is largely ignored: The ordinary income of the trust is taxed to the grantor whether or not it is distributed; in addition, the entire value of the trust is includible in the grantor's estate under §2036(a).

The basic income tax rule is a broad one — the grantor is treated as the owner of a trust if, without the consent of an adverse party, the income is, or may be: (1) distributed to the grantor or the grantor's spouse, (2) held or accumulated for later distribution to the grantor or the grantor's spouse, or (3) used to pay premiums on policies of insurance on the life of the grantor or of the grantor's spouse. §677(a). Under this rule, the grantor is taxed on the ordinary income of the trust if the grantor or any nonadverse party, such as an independent trustee, has discretion to accumulate the income for later distribution to the grantor. Duffy v. United States, 487 F.2d 282 (6th Cir. 1973), *cert. denied*, 416 U.S. 938 (1974). Likewise, the grantor is taxed currently on capital gains that are allocable to corpus and will be distributed to the grantor or the grantor's spouse at the end of the trust term. Rev. Rul. 66-161, 1966-1 C.B. 164; Rev. Rul. 75-267, 1975-2 C.B. 254. However, capital gains are not taxed to the grantor where they are allocated to corpus and will *not* be distributed to the grantor or the grantor's spouse. Reg. §1.677(a)-1(g), *Example* (1).

Section 677(a) also extends to the use of trust income to satisfy legal obligations of the grantor or of the grantor's spouse, such as contractual payments due from the grantor (*e.g.,* mortgage installments). Income that may be used to discharge the grantor's obligation to support a beneficiary other than the grantor's spouse is taxed to the grantor only to the extent it is actually used for that purpose. §§674(b)(1), 677(b). Income that is used to pay private school tuition of the grantor's minor child is taxed to the grantor where the grantor is expressly or impliedly obligated to make the payments. That rule applies although the local law does not require the grantor to provide his or her children with a private school education. Morrill v. United States, 228 F. Supp. 734 (D. Me. 1964). However, in another case the Court of Claims held that where the local law did not require the grantor to send his children to a private day school, the income of the trust used to pay their tuition is not taxable to him. Wyche v. United States, 36 A.F.T.R.2d 75-5816 (Ct. Cl. Trial Judge's opinion, 1974) (South Carolina law).

Income that might be used to pay premiums of policies insuring the life of the grantor or the life of the grantor's spouse is taxed to the grantor only if policies actually exist during the tax year, "upon which it would have been physically possible for the trustees to pay premiums." Genevieve F. Moore, 39 B.T.A. 808, 812-813 (1939), *acq.,* 1939-2 C.B. 25; *see* §6.39, *supra.* "There were no existing policies upon which premiums might be paid, and no part of the income of the trust estate was used for that purpose. In this situation we have held that no part of the trust income is taxable to the grantor." Corning v. Commissioner, 104 F.2d 329, 333 (6th Cir. 1939). Where policies do exist, the reach of the statute is not defeated by a nominal requirement that income be distributed to an individual beneficiary or to another trust.

Example 10-16. W transferred income-producing property to Trust A, the income of which was payable in equal shares to her 3 children. At the same time she transferred policies of insurance on her life to Trust B, in which the children will each have a one-third interest. W will be taxed on the income of Trust A if it is paid to Trust B pursuant to the consent of the 3 children who are bene-

ficiaries of Trust A. Rev. Rul. 66-313, 1966-2 C.B. 245. *See also*
L. B. Foster, 8 T.C. 197 (1947), *acq.*, 1947-1 C.B. 2.

Support Obligation. Under §677(b) the income of the trust that may
"in the discretion of another person, the trustee, or the grantor acting as
trustee or co-trustee" be applied "for the support or maintenance of a
beneficiary (other than grantor's spouse) whom the grantor is legally
obligated to support or maintain" is taxed to the grantor only "to the
extent that such income is so applied or distributed." This provision
prescribes the exclusive rule for the taxation of such support payments.
Accordingly, the grantor is not treated as having a reversionary interest,
within the meaning of §673, in a trust from which an independent
trustee has discretion to make distributions for the support of his or her
dependent children. Rev. Rul. 61-223, 1961-2 C.B. 125.

By reason of §§674(b)(1) and 677(b) the income of a trust such as a
§2503(c) minor's trust is not taxed to the grantor merely because the
income could be used to satisfy his or her legally enforceable obligation
to support the beneficiary. Instead, the income is taxed to the grantor
only to the extent it is actually used to discharge his or her support
obligations. For this purpose, the extent of the grantor's obligation is
measured by the applicable local law. Brooke v. United States, 468 F.2d
1155 (9th Cir. 1972); Rev. Rul. 56-484, 1956-2 C.B. 23. For example, the
Brooke court did not require the parent-guardian to report the income
that was used to pay "private school tuition, musical instruments, music,
swimming and public speaking lessons," the cost of an automobile for his
oldest child, or the payment of travel expenses to New Mexico for an
asthmatic child. The uncertain status of a parent's support obligation in
most states and the consequent tax uncertainty would be relieved if a
federal standard were adopted. *See* Nitzburg, The Obligation of Support: A Proposed Federal Standard, 23 Tax L. Rev. 93 (1967).

A short-term trust may profitably be used to provide the cost of items
of "super" support for the grantor's children, such as private school
tuition, music lessons, or the "luxuries" that a parent might otherwise
pay for out of his or her own after-tax dollars. The trustee might also be
prohibited from using the funds to provide any item of support the local
law required the grantor to furnish. However, it is generally preferable
to give the trustee broad discretion to make distributions to the minor.

Gift Tax. For gift tax purposes, the transfer to a trust involves a gift
of the actuarially determined value of any interest the grantor does not
retain. Of course, the gift of a remainder is incomplete and not presently
taxable where the grantor retains the power to change the disposition of
the remainder interest. *See* Reg. §25.2511-2(c). A gift of the remainder is
a gift of a future interest that does not qualify for the annual gift tax
exclusion. §2503(b).

There is some uncertainty regarding the gift tax consequences of the grantor's retention of the discretionary right to receive income. The regulations suggest that the grantor has made a gift of the income interest. Reg. §25.2511-2(b). In Rev. Rul. 77-378, 1977-2 C.B. 347, the IRS ruled that where the grantor's creditors could not reach any interest in the trust property, the grantor made a completed gift of the entire value of the property. However, where the income interest can be reached by the grantor's creditors, the transfer is not considered to involve a completed gift of the income interest. Mary M. Outwin, 76 T.C. 153 (1981); Alice Spaulding Paolozzi, 23 T.C. 182 (1954); Rev. Rul. 76-103, 1976-1 C.B. 293.

Estate Tax. A retained discretionary interest in income does not alone require the trust property to be included in the grantor's estate under §2036(a)(1). However, the property of such a trust is includible in the grantor's estate where the income is regularly distributed to the grantor, apparently by prearrangement. Estate of Skinner v. United States, 316 F.2d 517 (3d Cir. 1963). Property transferred outright more than 3 years prior to the transferor's death is likewise includible where the transferor continued to receive the income from the property by prearrangement. Estate of McNichol v. Commissioner, 265 F.2d 667 (3d Cir.), *cert. denied,* 361 U.S. 329 (1959). A prearrangement is not implied where the income is not regularly paid to the grantor. Estate of Uhl v. Commissioner, 241 F.2d 867 (7th Cir. 1957).

Secondary Life Estate. Different tax results follow where another person is given a life income interest in the trust and the grantor reserves a secondary life interest.

First, the income is not taxed to the grantor merely because of a retained income interest that will not take effect until the death of the income beneficiary. Under §673(b) the grantor is not taxed on the income by reason of the retention of a reversionary interest in the income or principal of the trust where the interest is not to take effect until the death of the income beneficiary. Of course, the income would be taxed to the grantor if it could be accumulated for later distribution to the grantor. *See* §677(a)(1).

Second, the transfer would involve a gift to the beneficiary of the life income interest, which is a present interest that qualifies for the annual exclusion. The transfer of the remainder would constitute a taxable gift of a future interest, so no annual exclusion is allowable. §2503(b).

Third, the amount includible in the grantor's estate depends on whether the holder of the preceding life interest predeceases the grantor. Where that person predeceases the grantor, the full value of the trust property is includible in the grantor's estate. In contrast, where the grantor dies first, "the amount to be included in his gross estate under section 2036 is the value of the entire property, less only the value of an outstanding income interest which is not subject to the decedent's interest or right and which is actually being enjoyed by another person at the time of the decedent's death." Reg. §20.2036-1(a).

> **Problem 10-8.** T, a single parent, currently pays the $10,000 private school tuition of her minor children, S and D, out of after-tax earnings from her medical practice. Those, or similar educational costs, will probably continue for at least 10 years. Would T's income tax position be improved by creating a 10-year reversionary trust, the income of which would be used to pay the educational expenses of S and D? Outline the provisions the trust should include for distribution of income and principal, assuming that T or a nonadverse party will serve as trustee. What are the gift tax consequences of funding the trust with (1) $100,000 in corporate bonds that yield 15% each year and are worth $100,000 or (2) 10,000 shares of Alpha-Zeta, Inc. stock, which earns a $1 per share dividend and is worth $20 per share?

E.   ADDITIONAL ISSUES

§10.33.   Introduction

This part is concerned with several additional matters that the planner and the client should consider. They include: the selection and removal of the trustee (§10.34), the selection of property to transfer to the trust (§10.35), provisions regarding investment of trust funds (§10.36), directions regarding the allocation of receipts and disbursements between principal and income (§10.37), and the use of a perpetuities savings clause (§10.38). The topics discussed do not exhaust the matters that should receive the serious attention of the planner and client. They are, however, fairly illustrative of the breadth of concerns that must be considered from the tax and the nontax points of view.

§10.34.   Selection of Trustee

> Ordinarily, the documents I write name individuals as executors or trustees, with individual alternatives, in a sense like a partnership agreement that permits the beneficiaries to participate in the selection and removal of the fiduciary in the future. Ordinarily, where I consider that a corporate

fiduciary is appropriate, it will be as co-trustee or co-executor, with the individuals having the right to remove the bank and hire another, and with the bank to be controlled by individuals. Avery, Role of the Lawyer as a Fiduciary, 4 Prob. Law. 38 (1977).

Except as limited by law, any individual, association, partnership, or corporation that has the capacity to take and hold property may act as a trustee. Restatement (Second) Trusts §§89, 96-98 (1959). Practically speaking, the choice is generally between an individual, such as the grantor or a beneficiary, and a corporate trustee. The choice may be dictated, however, by economic or family circumstances: In the case of a small trust, the appointment of a corporate trustee may be out of the question where the trust would be subject to a substantial annual fee. On the other hand, there may be no suitable family member or other individual available to serve as trustee. Some jurisdictions, including provinces of Canada, provide a public trustee who may be appointed in such cases. However, the concept has not caught on in the United States. The needs of some clients are best met by using multiple trustees (*e.g.*, an individual and a corporate trustee or 2 or more individual trustees).

A corporate fiduciary may be chosen as trustee or cotrustee because of its financial responsibility, its continuity of life, and its overall administrative capabilities. Those considerations are particularly important in the case of large trusts, which usually require more attention to administrative details, investment decisions, and accounting matters. In choosing a corporate fiduciary, the client should review the investment performance and investment philosophy of the ones under consideration. Corporate fiduciaries usually follow a relatively conservative investment policy — which may or may not coincide with the client's plans.

A long trust term usually requires either the appointment of a corporate trustee or the establishment of a suitable mechanism for the selection of successor individual trustees. Where a corporate trustee is appointed trustee of a long-term trust it is often desirable to give the beneficiaries the power to remove the trustee and appoint a successor corporate fiduciary. (A beneficiary generally should not have the power to remove the trustee and appoint himself or herself as successor trustee. *See* §10.20, *supra*.) In the case of individual trustees, the trust might name several successor individual trustees or cotrustees and authorize the survivor of them (or other responsible persons) to appoint further successors, etc.

The quality of services provided by a corporate fiduciary varies according to the ability and interest of the personnel assigned to the trust. Special provisions can be used where a client wants a particular trust officer to work on the account. For example, a trust may express the grantor's wish that the designated trust officer work on, or supervise, the account and provide that the trust should follow the trust officer if he or she later moves to a different corporate trustee. Of course such a provision introduces a degree of instability and could result in the imposition of additional trustees' fees if the designated trust officer does change employment.

It is generally helpful if the lawyer and client discuss the role of the trustee in some detail before the client chooses a trustee. The client's choice should be made in light of all relevant factors including the purposes of the trust, the extent of the duties imposed on the trustee, the complexity and probable duration of the trust, and the reliability and experience of the beneficiaries and other family members. The lawyer can usually help the client make an appropriate choice by pointing out the advantages and disadvantages of the alternatives. The availability of a convenient local office of the trustee is important to some clients.

Although the lawyer may serve as trustee, it is unwise unless he or she has the necessary expertise and is willing to take the time to apply it for the benefit of the trust. As mentioned in connection with the choice of an executor (§4.25 *supra*), the lawyer should not suggest directly or indirectly that he or she serve as trustee. *See also* EC 5-6. The lawyer should also point out that the trustee will usually require legal representation, which is not included in the fee for the trustee's services. In short, the appointment of the lawyer as trustee may not save any fees.

Grantor as Trustee. It is common for the grantor to serve as trustee or cotrustee of a revocable trust, which generally does not involve any tax disadvantages. *See* §§10.12 to 10.15, *supra*. However, some provision should be made for a successor to serve following the grantor's death or disability. For example, another person might be named to serve as cotrustee with the grantor and as sole trustee following the grantor's death. Under another approach the surviving trustee is given the power to appoint a person to fill the vacancy and serve as cotrustree. A corporate fiduciary may be reluctant to serve following an individual trustee unless its potential liability for acts of its predecessor is eliminated by the terms of the trust, an accounting, or agreement of the beneficiaries.

In the case of an irrevocable trust, the grantor can serve as trustee without tax disadvantage if the grantor's powers are appropriately circumscribed. *See* §§10.18, 10.27, and 10.29, *supra*. Serious tax disadvantages arise, however, if the grantor retains the power, alone or in conjunction with any other person, to make discretionary distributions. *See* §§2036(a)(2), 2038(a)(1). The grantor may be willing to take that risk where the trust is relatively small and will probably terminate during the grantor's lifetime. For example, the grantor may decide to serve as trustee of a §2503(c) trust although it will cause the trust to be included in the grantor's estate if the grantor dies prior to distribution of the trust. A similar decision is sometimes made in connection with a discretionary trust that will terminate when the beneficiary attains a relatively young age. Along the same lines, the grantor may choose to serve as custodian of a gift under the Uniform Gifts to Minors Act.

Beneficiary as Trustee. An individual beneficiary, such as the primary income beneficiary, can serve as trustee. The appointment of a beneficiary is logical because of the beneficiary's obvious interest, but it is generally unwise unless the beneficiary is reliable, has reasonably good judgment, and has a modicum of financial or business experience. Of course, care must be exercised not to give the beneficiary any powers that would cause unwanted income, gift, or estate tax consequences. *See* §10.24, *supra*. The appointment of a beneficiary as trustee can cause additional generation-skipping tax problems, depending on the extent of the powers he or she holds. *See* §§2.19 to 2.26, *supra*. The planner should be particularly careful not to give the beneficiary-trustee a power that might be construed as a general power of appointment under §2041, such as an unlimited power to invade trust principal for the beneficiary's own benefit. A beneficiary-trustee could, however, be given a power to invade the trust principal so long as it is either (a) "limited by an ascertainable standard relating to [his] health, education, support or maintenance" (§2041(b)(1)(A)) or (b) limited to a noncumulative power to withdraw the greater of $5,000 or 5% of the value of the trust corpus (§2041(b)(2)). *See* §10.22, *supra*.

Cotrustees. Cotrustees can be helpful in a variety of ways. For example, a corporate fiduciary might be appointed as cotrustee because of its superior administrative capacity and immortality. On the other hand, an individual might be appointed because of his or her interest in the trust or familiarity with the beneficiaries. In order to reduce the risk of conflict and avoid the threat of a deadlock, each cotrustee can be given exclusive authority over specific activities of the trust. For example, one of the cotrustees might be given exclusive power to make certain decisions (*e.g.*, discretion to make distributions) or to act with respect to certain property where there would be adverse tax consequences if the power were shared with the other trustee (*e.g.*, insurance on the individual trustee's life; *see* §6.18, *supra*). Before appointing cotrustees, some thought should also be given to the rate and manner of their compensation. Depending on the circumstances, each trustee may receive a full fee, a single fee may be divided between them, or the individual trustee may forego receiving any compensation. However, it is generally unwise to set forth a rigid compensation schedule in the trust instrument because of the difficulty in anticipating the services that may be required of the trustee and the difficulty of obtaining approval of any change in such a schedule.

Removal of Trustees. It is virtually impossible to obtain the judicial removal of a trustee unless the trustee has engaged in an egregious breach of trust. Accordingly, as suggested above, a responsible person (or persons) is commonly given the power to remove and replace a corporate trustee. A beneficiary may be given the power to remove the trustee and appoint another. However, the beneficiary ordinarily should not have the power to appoint himself or herself, unless the beneficiary could have acted from the outset without adverse tax consequences. *See* §10.25, *supra.* The law should permit a beneficiary to hold the power to remove and replace a corporate trustee without disadvantage.

In Rev. Rul. 79-353, 1979-2 C.B. 325, the IRS held that "reservation by the settlor of the power to remove the [corporate] trustee at will and appoint another [corporate] trustee is equivalent to a reservation of the trustee's powers." The ruling concluded that the trust property was includible in the grantor's estate under §§2036(a)(2) and 2038(a)(1) because of the trustee's power to distribute income and principal to the beneficiaries. The ruling is not supported by the regulations or any other authorities. When the issue is judicially tested, the IRS position should not prevail. However, until that time caution should be exercised in conferring the power to remove and replace trustees. In a later ruling the IRS held that Rev. Rul. 79-353 applies only to transfers made to irrevocable trusts after the date it was published (October 29, 1979). Rev. Rul. 81-51, 1981-1 C.B. 458.

§10.35.   Selection of Property to Transfer in Trust

The choice of property to transfer to the trustee is very important, especially in the case of an irrevocable inter vivos trust. In general the same factors that must be considered in selecting property to transfer by way of inter vivos gift (§§7.12 to 7.17, *supra*) must be taken into account when it comes to selecting property to transfer in trust. In brief, the grantor should avoid transferring property that will cause the recognition of income (*e.g.,* an installment obligation) or will have other adverse income tax consequences. Thus, a grantor in a high income tax bracket might choose to fund an irrevocable trust with appreciated stock rather than municipal bonds that produce tax exempt income. However, care should be exercised in selling property transferred to the trust. Where appreciated property is sold by the trust within 2 years following its addition to the trust, the gain is taxed as if the sale had been made by the grantor. §644. The grantor should also avoid giving away any business interests that might prevent the grantor's estate from qualifying for the benefits of §§303, 2032A, and 6166. *See* §7.10, *supra.* The grantor should also be aware that the potential availability of some income tax advantages may be lost if stock in a small business corporation is transferred to a trust. In particular, the ordinary loss deduction that is allowed under §1244 for a loss suffered on small business stock is allowed only to the original shareholder — not to a trust or other successor shareholder. *See* Reg. §1.1244 (a)-1(b). Also, a trust is not eligible to be a shareholder in a Subchapter S corporation unless the grantor is treated as its owner under §§671 to 677. *See* §1371(e)(1)(A).

Revocable Trusts. The selection of property to transfer to a revocable trust is usually much less significant because the grantor is still treated as the owner of the property for tax purposes. For example, the transfer of an installment obligation to such a trust is not treated as a disposition that triggers recognition of gain. *See* §9.6, *supra*. Similarly, property held in the trust is included in the grantor's gross estate. Hence it may be used to fund a marital gift, and is counted for purposes of meeting the percentage requirement of §§303, 2032A, and 6166.

§10.36. Provisions Regarding Trust Investments

The trustee should generally be given broad authority to invest and reinvest trust property. Limiting the range of permissible investments can unduly restrict the trustee's ability to respond to changing economic circumstances and can impair the value of the trust. Of course, a court may authorize deviation from an investment restriction where there has been an unanticipated change in circumstances and adherence to the restriction would result in substantial losses to the trust and frustrate accomplishment of trust purposes. *See, e.g.,* In re Trusteeship Under Agreement with Mayo, 105 N.W.2d 900 (Minn. 1960); Restatement (Second) Trusts §167 (1959). Where the trust is intended to qualify for the marital deduction the trustee should not be prevented, directly or indirectly, from investing in income-producing property. In fact, because of the requirements of §§2056(b)(5), (b)(7), and 2523(f), the decedent's (or donor's) spouse should be given the power to compel the trustee to invest in income-producing property. Along the same lines, a charitable remainder trust should not restrict the trustee from making investments that would produce a reasonable amount of income or gain. *See* Reg. §1.664-1(a)(3) and §8.20, *supra*.

The nature of the trust property, the relationship of the parties, or other factors sometimes make it desirable to give the trustee more specific directions or authorization. It is particularly appropriate to do so where the trust will be funded with the stock of a closely held family business. The trustee needs and deserves some specific direction regarding the retention of the stock and the operation of the business and, perhaps, exoneration from liability for retention of the stock. In such a case the planner should also attempt to deal with the conflicts of interest that might arise between the trustee, the beneficiaries, nonbeneficiary shareholders, and other persons who are interested in the business. It may also be necessary to give the trustee some specific directions regarding the allocation of receipts and disbursements between income and principal. *See* §10.37, *infra.*

Prudent Person Standard. A basic trust rule requires the trustee to make the trust property productive within a reasonable time. Restatement (Second) Trusts §181 (1959). However, in the absence of contrary directions, the local law usually imposes some limits on the investments a trustee can legally make. At one time most states limited trustees to specified types of investments (the so-called legal lists). Now, most states allow any form of investment that a prudent person "would make of his own property having in view the preservation of the estate and the amount and regularity of the income to be derived." Restatement (Second) Trusts §227(a) (1959). The so-called prudent person rule does not permit speculative investments and is generally considered to require the trust investments to be diversified. Thus, a trustee should not concentrate trust investments in the stock of a single company. Indeed, traditional investment strategy has called for the trust funds to be balanced between common stocks and bonds of various types.

Trustees with Greater Skill. The prudent person standard represents a minimum standard that may be increased where the trustee has greater skill than a person of ordinary prudence (or holds himself out to possess such skill). Restatement (Second) Trusts §176, comment *a* (1959); Estate of Beach, 542 P.2d 994 (Cal. 1975); In re Estate of Killey, 326 A.2d 372 (Pa. 1974). Of course, the terms of the trust can vary the obligations of the trustee, including duties regarding the investment of trust property. As suggested above, the trust may authorize (or direct) the trustee to retain specific assets and attempt to relieve the trustee from any liability that would otherwise attach for failure to dispose of the assets. Regardless of the terms of such a provision, the trustee cannot be completely relieved of all responsibility for trust investments. Despite a direction to retain particular assets, at some point it may be necessary for the trustee to take steps to dispose of them or face the possibility of a surcharge.

The grantor may authorize or direct the trustee to make otherwise improper investments or may prohibit the trustee from making otherwise lawful investments. Thus, a grantor who does not want a corporate trustee to invest in a common trust fund it operates may prohibit it from doing so. Along the same lines, a grantor may prohibit an individual trustee from investing in mutual funds (which, naturally, pay a management fee to their investment advisor). Such a restriction may be appropriate where the trustee is compensated for serving as trustee and the trust is sufficiently large to permit some diversification. In most cases, however, it makes little sense to hamstring a trustee by imposing special investment restrictions or directions. From a practical point of view, restrictive or unusual investment directions may discourage a professional trustee from accepting a trusteeship or may result in the imposition of higher annual fees than normal. Where an individual family member will serve as trustee, it may be desirable to authorize him or her to obtain investment advice at the expense of the trust, and to rely upon the advice without any duty to inquire regarding the reliability of the information provided by the investment advisor.

Exculpatory Clauses. Where an individual acts as trustee without compensation the grantor may wish to exonerate the individual trustee from liability for loss to the trust except for intentional misconduct or gross negligence. Restatement (Second) Trusts §222, comment *a*, explains, "[I]f by the terms of the trust it is provided that the trustee shall not be liable 'except for his wilful default or gross negligence,' although he is not liable for mere negligence, he is liable if he intentionally does or omits to do an act which he knows to be a breach of trust or if he acts or omits to act with reckless indifference as to the interests of the beneficiary." Exculpatory clauses should be used sparingly and only in exceptional circumstances in the case of professional fiduciaries, of whom a higher standard of performance should be required.

Investment Directions. Where the grantor has particular confidence in the skill of an investment advisor, the trustee may be directed to accept the investment directions given by the advisor. In such a case the trustee is ordinarily required to follow the instructions of the advisor. *See* Restatement (Second) Trusts §185 (1959). Presumably a trustee subject to such directions is substantially relieved of investment responsibilities *and* liabilities. A person who has authority to direct or control the investments of the trust may be treated as a fiduciary. Under a fairly common approach, such a person is "deemed to be a fiduciary and shall be liable to the beneficiaries of said trust and to the designated trustee to the same extent as if he were a designated trustee in relation to the exercise or nonexercise of such a power or authority." Wash. Rev. Code §30.24.130 (1979). Some investment advisors are, understandably, unwilling to act in such a capacity and assume the responsibilities of a trustee.

Conflicts Involving Investments. Conflicts regarding investments can arise where the trust and the trustee are both interested in the same business or other property. The planner must be alert to potential conflicts and should discuss any that can be identified with the grantor and, when possible, with the intended trustee. An instrument may identify a particular conflict and authorize the trustee to act with respect to the matter without liability. The problem might arise, for example, where the real property transferred to the trust is leased to the intended trustee or a business in which he or she is interested. In such a case the trust might specifically authorize the trustee to lease the property from the trust upon the same terms and conditions (or upon such other terms and conditions as the trustee deems appropriate). In the case of a corporate trustee, the trust may authorize it to retain and vote any of its own stock that is originally transferred to the trust. It is generally undesirable to authorize a corporate trustee to acquire more of its shares for the account of the trust.

§10.37. Power to Allocate between Principal and Income

The trustee generally should be given discretion to allocate receipts and disbursements between principal and income. An allocation is necessary because of the bifurcated nature of the beneficial interests in a typical trust — the income and principal beneficiaries generally are not the same. The income of the trust is usually payable to one beneficiary (or group of beneficiaries) upon whose death the principal is distributable to another beneficiary (or group of beneficiaries). Two-thirds of the states have responded to the allocation problem by adopting either the original (1931) Uniform Principal and Income Act, 7A U.L.A. 461 (1978), or the Revised (1962) Uniform Principal and Income Act, 7A U.L.A. 429 (1978). The rules prescribed by the Uniform Acts are generally fair and workable. However, as explained below, they do not satisfactorily resolve all allocation problems.

Discretionary Powers of Allocation

[T]he subject is highly technical in nature and . . . the trustees should have broad discretion for their own protection and for the maximum efficiency of the program. The grant of this discretion is valid, although there may be certain limits on its exercise. J. Farr & J. Wright, An Estate Planner's Handbook, §35 at 219 (4th ed. 1979).

Planners often meet the allocation problem by giving the trustee discretion to allocate receipts and disbursements between income and principal as the trustee believes is fair and equitable under the circumstances. Such a power gives the trustee more flexibility in dealing with the complex problems of principal and income allocations while carrying out the terms of the trust and meeting the needs of the beneficiaries.

Section 2 of the original and revised Uniform Acts recognizes that the trustee may be given discretion to make allocations of principal and income. The revised Uniform Act also recognizes that when the trustee is given discretion, "no inference of imprudence or partiality arises from the fact that the trustee has made an allocation contrary to a provision of this Act." §2(b), 7A U.L.A. 435 (1978). More importantly, such a power exercisable in a fiduciary capacity is not treated as a general power of appointment for federal estate tax purposes: "The mere power of management, investment, custody of assets, or the power to allocate receipts and disbursements as between income and principal, exercisable in a fiduciary capacity, whereby the holder has no power to enlarge or shift any of the beneficial interests therein except as an incidental consequence of the discharge of such fiduciary duties is not a power of appointment." Reg. §20.2041-1(b)(1).

It is often desirable to give the trustee some specific directions (or additional authorization) regarding certain allocation matters. The directions in a particular case may run counter to the basic provisions of the Uniform Act. The following paragraphs discuss some of the matters about which trusts commonly provide additional guidance. They include the treatment of stock splits and stock dividends, the amortization of bond premium and the accumulation of discount, and the handling of depreciation.

Stock Splits and Stock Dividends. The lawyer may find it necessary or desirable to specify a rule regarding allocation of stock splits and stock dividends contrary to the basic rule of the Uniform Acts. Under the Uniform Acts, all stock splits and stock dividends of the issuing corporation are allocated to principal. That rule prejudices current income beneficiaries where the trust includes stock in corporations that regularly issue small stock dividends in lieu of larger cash dividends. This problem can be met by providing that the trustee may allocate stock dividends to income in accordance with a formula such as the New York statutory formula. Under N.Y. EPTL §11-2.1(e)(3) (McKinney 1967), stock distributions of 6% or less are allocated to income whether the distribution is called a stock split or a stock dividend. Such a rule fairly meets the needs of the beneficiaries and those of the trustee.

Amortization of Bond Premium and Accumulation of Discount. Corporate and municipal bonds usually carry a fixed rate of interest that is payable semiannually until redemption at face value upon maturity. Because the market rate of interest fluctuates, the current market price of a bond typically depends on 2 factors: (1) the length of time until the maturity of the bond and (2) the difference between the current market rate of interest and the rate specified in the bond. Thus, a bond that carries a rate of interest above the going rate will sell at a price in excess of its redemption value (*i.e.,* it will sell at a premium). If a bond is purchased at a premium and held until maturity, the principal account will be depleted unless an amount equal to the premium is recovered from income. The problem can be met by allocating a portion of each income payment to principal (*i.e.,* the premium is amortized over the life of the bond). However, the Uniform Act prohibits amortization unless the instrument provides otherwise or the trustee is empowered to make discretionary allocations between principal and income.

> **Example 10-17.** At a time when the going rate of interest was 8%, Trustee paid $5,500 for a $5,000 bond that carried a 15% rate. Under §7(a) of the Uniform Act, the full amount of each semiannual interest payment would be allocated to income. 7A U.L.A. 447 (1978). If the bond were held until maturity the proceeds of $5,000 would be allocated to principal — a "loss" of $500.

Section 7(a) of the Uniform Act also prevents accumulation of discount when a bond is purchased for less than its redemption value. 7A U.L.A. 447 (1978). That is, where the trustee purchases a bond for less than its redemption value and holds it until maturity, none of the appreciation received is allocable to income. In this case the income account is disadvantaged by the purchase of a bond that carried an interest rate below the market rate at the time of purchase.

The rules of the Uniform Act are unduly restrictive. They may prevent the trustee from making otherwise attractive investments or result in unfairness to one class of beneficiaries. However, because interest rates and bond prices fluctuate over time, it may be equally undesirable to require the amortization of premium or the accumulation of discount. Instead, the trust may be drafted to give the trustee discretion to deal with the bonds as required to avoid unfairness to the income beneficiaries or the remaindermen according to overall circumstances.

Depreciation. Under §13(a)(2) of the Revised Uniform Act, the trustee is required to make a reasonable charge against income for depreciation where it is appropriate to do so under generally accepted accounting principles. However, no charge for depreciation is required for the "portion of real property used by a beneficiary as a residence or for . . . any property held by the trustee on the effective date of this Act for which the trustee is not then making an allowance for depreciation." 7A U.L.A. 455 (1978). Of course, if depreciation is charged, a smaller amount of income will be available for distribution to the income beneficiaries.

For income tax purposes, the depreciation deduction is allocated between the trustee and the beneficiaries on the basis of the income allocable to each. §167(h); Reg. §1.167(h)-1(b). However, the depreciation deduction is first allocated to the trustee to the extent the income is set aside for a depreciation reserve. Reg. §167(h)-1(b). Overall, it is preferable to give the trustee discretion regarding the establishment of a depreciation reserve.

Unitrusts. Some commentators have pointed out that a private unitrust may be used to avoid problems of allocating between principal and income. *E.g.*, Lovell, The Unitrust: A New Concept to Meet an Old Problem, 105 Tr. & Est. 215 (1966). A unitrust may also substantially eliminate the clash of interests between current beneficiaries and remaindermen. The total annual amount of distributions to the current beneficiaries of a unitrust would be based on a specified percentage of the annually determined value of the trust assets. Thus, the unitrust would not require any allocation between income and principal and the interests of both the current and ultimate beneficiaries would be served by a growth oriented investment policy. The utilization of a unitrust would probably require the trustee to have authority to make investments without regard to the amount of income they generate (the "probable income" to be derived from an asset is one element of the generally applicable prudent person investment standard). By way of illustration, a unitrust might provide for the payment to the current beneficiary of an amount each year equal to 8% of the total value of the trust assets on the last business day of the preceding calendar year.

Problem 10-9. T died recently leaving her residuary estate to a trust of which the income was payable to her son, S, for life. Upon his death the principal was distributable to his then living issue. T's residuary estate included municipal bonds on which the semiannual interest payment was due 3 months after T's death, Series E bonds that were redeemable at amounts in excess of their cost, but on which T had paid no income tax, and common stock in ABC, Inc., which had declared a regular cash dividend and a 5% stock dividend shortly before T's death, payable to shareholders of record on a date subsequent to T's death. Under the law of your jurisdiction, how should the income on the municipal bonds and Series E bonds be allocated? Who should bear the income tax on the increase in value of the Series E bonds? Finally, how should the cash and stock dividends be allocated?

§10.38. *Perpetuities Savings Clause*

An estate plan should specifically provide that any non-vested interest under the plan that has not vested within 21 years after the death of the survivor of a reasonable number of named individuals who are alive when the period of the rule begins to run shall be eliminated. This means that with respect to such non-vested interest, it can be said on the date the period of the rule begins to run that they will vest, *if they ever vest*, within the period of the rule. Such a provision in the estate plan is a saving clause and such clause should go on to provide what the dispositive plan is if a non-vested interest is eliminated when it does not, in fact, vest in time. The alternative dispositive plan must describe interests that vest at the end of 21 years after the death of the named individuals referred to in the saving clause. A.J. Casner, 3 Estate Planning, 1129-1130 (4th ed. 1980).

Trusts should be planned and drafted with a wary eye on the Rule Against Perpetuities. There is no substitute for having a basic grasp of the Rule, which is made easier to acquire by a number of fine articles, books, and treatises. *E.g.,* Leach, Perpetuities in a Nutshell, 51 Harv. L. Rev. 638 (1938); R. Lynn, The Modern Rule Against Perpetuities (1966); L. Simes, Future Interests 253-296 (2d ed. 1966); L. Waggoner, Future Interests 165-338 (West Nutshell Series 1981). Preventive drafting is an enormous help in avoiding problems under the Rule. As suggested in Professor Leach's article, the planner should view with suspicion any gift that is contingent upon the attainment of an age greater than 21 and avoid making gifts contingent upon the taker being alive when an event in the administration of an estate or trust takes place (*e.g.,* when all debts are paid or the estate is distributed). Protection against the ravages of an inadvertent violation of the Rule Against Perpetuities is provided by including an appropriate perpetuities savings clause. Overall, it is desirable to include a savings clause in most trusts although the rigors of the Rule have been relaxed significantly in a number of states by judicial decisions and statutory modifications of the common law Rule.

A perpetuities savings clause can take a variety of forms. Perhaps the most common form simply calls for the trust to terminate at the end of 21 years following the death of the survivor of a designated group of persons and provides for distribution of the trust assets to a specified class of persons. For example, Dean Casner suggests that a will might include a clause along these lines:

> If this trust has not terminated within 21 years after the death of the survivor of my issue living on my death, such trust shall terminate at the end of such 21-year period, and the trust property shall be distributed outright to my issue then living, such issue to take per stripes. A. J. Casner, 3 Estate Planning 1130 (4th ed. 1980).

The persons who are designated to take the property on termination of the trust could be a different class or could be designated differently (*e.g.,* "in equal shares to the persons then entitled to receive distributions of income from the trust"). Another approach, suggested by Professors Leach and Logan, involves giving a corporate fiduciary authority to reform an interest that offends the Rule in a manner that carries out the grantor's intent. *See* Leach & Logan, Perpetuities: A Standard Saving Clause to Avoid Violations of the Rule, 74 Harv. L. Rev. 1141 (1961). The approach taken by Leach and Logan gives a corporate trustee a cy pres power similar to ones that have been given to the courts by some statutes in recent years and ones that have been exercised by some courts on their own. *E.g.,* In re Estate of Chun Quan Yee Hop, 469 P.2d 183 (Hawaii 1970) (reducing a 30-year contingency to 21 years).

In drafting a savings clause of the first type described above, the planner must recognize the difference in the effective dates of a will and an irrevocable trust. A will is effective only upon the testator's death, but an irrevocable trust is effective from the date the trust is created. Because a revocable trust is subject to change or revocation until the time of the grantor's death, it is treated in the same way as a will. Thus, a savings clause that provides for termination of a trust 21 years after the death of the survivor of a class of persons living at the time of the grantor's death is suitable for inclusion in a will, but is not suitable in the case of an irrevocable inter vivos trust. Instead, the clause used in an irrevocable trust should provide for termination of the trust 21 years after the death of the last survivor of a class of persons living at the time the trust was created or who are designated by name. It is easy to overlook the difference in the effective dates and to include an improper clause in an irrevocable trust.

Problem 10-10. H created an irrevocable trust of which his son, S, was the trustee. The trust authorized the trustee "to pay all or part of the net income to H and the balance to S in accordance with their respective needs, of which the trustee shall be the sole judge." Any income that the trustee did not distribute was to be accumulated. Upon the death of H the trust property was to be distributed as H should appoint by will. In default of appointment the trust property would go to H's then living issue, per stirpes. What are the income, gift, and estate tax consequences of the transfer of property to the trust? For this purpose assume, alternatively, that the term "needs" as used in the trust establishes, and does not establish, an ascertainable standard. On the income tax side give particular consideration to the interrelationship of §§674, 677, and 678. For an analysis of a similar case under the pre-1954 law, *see* Funk v. Commissioner, 185 F.2d 127 (3d Cir. 1950), and Wilfred J. Funk, 3 T.C.M. 100 (1944).

BIBLIOGRAPHY

I. Trusts in general:
> Bogert, G., Trusts (5th ed. 1978)
> Casner, A.J., Estate Planning (4th ed. 1980)
> Gallo, Drafting and Exercising Powers of Appointment, 120 Tr. & Est. 41 (1981)
> Halbach, Trusts in Estate Planning, 2 Prob. Law. 1 (1975)
> Inter Vivos Trusts (Cohan & Hemmerling eds., 1975)
> Michaelson, A. & Blattmachr, J., Income Taxation of Trusts (1978)

Restatement (Second) Trusts (1959)

Scott, A. W., Trusts (3d ed. 1967)

II. Revocable trusts:

Lewis, Powers Retained by the Settlor of a Trust: Their Income, Estate & Gift Tax Treatment, 5 Real Prop., Prob., & Tr. J. 1 (1970)

Report, The Revocable Trust as an Estate Planning Tool, 7 Real Prop., Prob. & Tr. J. 223 (1972)

III. Irrevocable trusts:

Bruce, Traps in Irrevocable Trusts, 27 Tul. Tax Inst. (1977)

Casner, Sample Irrevocable Trusts, 23 Prac. Law. 39 (Oct. 1977)

Halbach, Powers of Distribution, Invasion & Appointment, U. So. Cal. 32d Tax. Inst., Ch. 14 (1980)

Ufford, Income Taxation of Funded Irrevocable Trust After the Death of the Grantor, 30 Tax. Law 37 (1976)

IV. Selecting a trustee:

Barber & McComas, Selecting a Trustee: Income and Estate Tax Considerations, 33 Sw. L.J. 635 (1979)

Nagel, Income and Estate Tax Consequences of Removal and Replacement of Corporate Fiduciaries, N.Y.U. 39th Inst. Fed. Tax., Ch. 52 (1981)

Pennell, Estate Planning: Drafting and Tax Considerations in Employing Individual Trustees, 60 N.C.L. Rev. 799 (1982)

V. Grantor trusts:

Calleton, Dangers in Misuse of Short Term Trust: Guidelines for Employing This Valuable Device, 3 Est. Plan. 200 (1976)

Report, Trust Income Taxation and the Obligation of Support, 1 Real Prop., Prob. & Tr. J. 327 (1966)

Westfall, Trust Grantors and Section 674: Adventures in Income Tax Avoidance, 60 Colum. L. Rev. 326 (1960)

Wiggins, Use of Short Term Trust to Build Up Tax Sheltered Fund for Education of Children, 1 Est. Plan. 246 (1974)

Wren, Estate Planning for the Elderly: Use of the Short Term Trust, 17 Ariz. L. Rev. 413 (1975)

CHAPTER 11

Closely Held Business Interests

A.   INTRODUCTION

§11.1.   General

Planning for the management and disposition of a client's interests in a closely held business is a vital element in the formulation of the client's estate plan. The planning typically involves a closely held business corporation, which is the primary focus of this chapter. However, the planning may involve a sole proprietorship or an interest in a partnership. Regardless of the legal form of the enterprise, the planner is confronted with many of the same tax and nontax problems. Nontax factors regarding the client's family are particularly important in planning for the continuation and disposition of a business. For example, the age, health, interests, and capacities of children or employees may dictate whether it is feasible for the business to be continued after his or her death. It is also extremely important to recognize and deal with the valuation and liquidity problems that may arise on the death of the owner of a substantial interest in a business.

The planning frequently involves the use of buy-sell agreements covering the stock or a partnership interest. *See* §§11.3 to 11.7, *infra.* Less often it involves the recapitalization of the corporation in order to "freeze" the value of a senior family member's interest and enable shareholders to hold different types of ownership interests in the corporation. *See* §§11.8 to 11.13, *infra.* The dual capital partnership is also used with some success to achieve an "estate freeze." *See* §§11.22 to 11.25, *infra.* The planning is also often concerned with the post-mortem redemption of stock under §303 and the deferral of estate taxes under §6166. Of course, the plan may call for the client to dispose of some or all of the business interests by way of inter vivos or testamentary gifts to family members or to charities.

§11.2. *About Corporations*

The corporate form has several important nontax advantages that make it attractive to many clients. The limited liability of the shareholders is a very positive feature of the corporate form, as contrasted with the unlimited liability of a general partner or sole proprietor. Corporate shares are almost always nonassessable, which means that the shareholder is liable only for the initial cost of shares purchased from the corporation.

The free transferability of interests in a corporation is often a very important estate-planning consideration. However, the transfer of shares in a closely held corporation is commonly restricted by the terms of a shareholder agreement or otherwise. More important, the theoretical free transferability of shares may be of very little value in the case of a minority shareholder: From a practical point of view he or she is largely at the mercy of the majority.

Gifts of stock can be used to spread the income and the future growth in value of the stock among the owner's family and trusts. However, note that the transfer of shares may have some negative tax consequences, such as the loss of qualification of the stock under §1244. Under that section the *original* owner might be entitled an ordinary loss deduction for a loss incurred with respect to stock in a small business — successive owners would not be. Finally, the corporation has a potentially indefinite existence, unrelated to the life of any shareholder. Thus, a corporation can continue to function uninterruptedly following the death of a shareholder.

"Double Taxation." Under the income tax law a corporation is taxed as a separate entity at progressive rates. Some double taxation inheres in the system for profitable corporations because dividend distributions are taxed as ordinary income to shareholders, but are not deductible by the corporation. Importantly, the taxable income of the corporation can be substantially reduced if liberal salaries are paid to shareholder-employees. The overall tax cost may also be ameliorated by the wide range of fringe benefits that are deductible by the corporation, but are not currently taxable to the employees. They range from contributions to qualified retirement plans (which is generally the most important benefit) to payment of the cost of health and life insurance coverage and club dues and membership fees.

Subchapter S. Additional flexibility is provided by Subchapter S, §§1371 to 1378, which allows domestic corporations with 15 or fewer shareholders to elect not to be taxed as a corporation. If the shareholders make the Subchapter S election, the income *and* losses of the corporation are passed through to them. Shareholders often choose to make a Subchapter S election in the early years of a corporation's existence in order to give themselves the tax benefit of its losses. In such cases the election could be terminated later when the corporation is profitable and has earnings that the shareholders do not want taxed to them currently. A buy-sell agreement can be used to prevent termination of the election through the addition of too many shareholders or the addition of nonqualifying shareholders (*e.g.*, a trust that is not eligible to be a shareholder). The election terminates if the corporation is recapitalized and a second class of stock is issued.

Trapping Assets in the Corporation. Lawyers and clients must recognize that it is difficult to withdraw assets from a profitable corporation for the benefit of the shareholders during their lives without attracting income tax liabilities (*i.e.*, virtually any distribution is taxable as a dividend). While most assets can be transferred to a corporation tax free under §351, distributions from the corporation to the shareholders are usually treated as dividends, subject to taxation as ordinary income. Paraphrasing a popular epigram: Incorporate in haste; repent at leisure.

B. BUY-SELL AGREEMENTS

§11.3. Background

This part reviews the basic considerations involved in drafting buy-sell agreements that either obligate the corporation to purchase a deceased or retiring shareholder's stock (an "entity purchase" agreement) or obligate the other shareholders to purchase his or her stock (a "cross purchase" agreement). Either form of agreement can serve important tax and nontax needs of shareholders in closely held businesses. A properly drafted agreement can establish the value of a deceased shareholder's stock and fix the liability for the payment of state and federal death taxes.

The interests of all shareholders are protected by an agreement that provides a fair method of valuing a deceased shareholder's stock. In the absence of such an agreement the family of a deceased minority shareholder may lack the bargaining power necessary to negotiate a fair agreement with the corporation or the surviving shareholders. The preparation of an agreement is beneficial also in that it requires the parties to consider the long-term plans for the business and the need to generate funds with which to purchase the stock of a deceased shareholder. As indicated below, funds are typically provided either by insurance on the lives of shareholders or by corporate earnings that are accumulated in another form. In any case, the liquidity crunch is eased somewhat if the agreement permits an installment purchase of a deceased shareholder's stock.

§11.4.   *Valuation*

> Certainly, an owner wants to avoid a situation where, upon his death, his successors are contractually bound to sell the business interest at the Agreement's price, while the tax authorities successfully ignore that price and use a higher value for tax purposes. Gorman, The Buy-Sell Agreement as a Dispositionary Device: Tax and Valuation Problems in Transferring Corporate, Partnership and Real Estate Interests at Death, N.Y.U. 34th Inst. Fed. Tax 1591, 1594 (1976).

Careful consideration must be given to the selection of a method for fixing the value of the shares that are subject to the agreement. Using the current value of the shares is usually not adequate because of changes that will inevitably take place before a sale occurs. When the need to purchase the shares arises, the price set forth in the agreement may be either too high or too low. An agreement that fixes a price should provide for periodic adjustments of the price and include a backup method of valuation should the parties fail to agree upon an adjustment in the future. The agreement may provide for the value of the shares to be fixed by reference to a single factor, such as their book value or the capitalized earnings of the corporation. However, the use of a single factor is also inadequate because it can distort the value of the shares. Some parties are content to leave the valuation to one or more appraisers named in the agreement or later to be designated by the parties. In any case, the parties may provide for arbitration if a dispute arises. Often the best choice is to provide for valuation of the shares under a multi-factor formula that takes into account factors such as the corporation's book value, its average earnings for the most recent 3- to 5-year period, and the price-earnings ratio of publicly traded corporations in the same line of business.

Some guidance is provided by Reg. §20.2031-2(h) regarding the circumstances in which the value established by a buy-sell agreement will be accepted by the IRS for estate tax purposes:

> Another person may hold an option or a contract to purchase securities owned by a decedent at the time of his death. The effect, if any, that is given to the option or contract price in determining the value of the securities for estate tax purposes depends upon the circumstances of the particu-

lar case. Little weight will be accorded a price contained in an option or contract under which the decedent is free to dispose of the underlying securities at any price he chooses during his lifetime. Such is the effect, for example, of an agreement on the part of a shareholder to purchase whatever shares of stock the decedent may own at the time of his death. Even if the decedent is not free to dispose of the underlying securities at other than the option or contract price, such price will be disregarded in determining the value of the securities unless it is determined under the circumstances of the particular case that the agreement represents a bona fide business arrangement and not a device to pass the decedent's shares to the natural objects of his bounty for less than an adequate and full consideration in money or money's worth.

In order to satisfy the IRS the agreement must: (1) fix the price of the shares directly or by way of a formula, (2) obligate the sale of the shares for that price during the decedent's lifetime *and* following his or her death, and (3) be a bona fide business arrangement and not merely a device for passing the shares to the natural objects of his or her bounty for less than an adequate and full consideration. An agreement is effective to fix the value of the shares if it requires the corporation or the other shareholders to purchase the decedent's shares, *or* if it gives the corporation or the other shareholders the option to purchase the shares. Rev. Rul. 157, 1953-2 C.B. 255.

A requirement that all of the decedent's shares be purchased should be used with caution. First, the disposition of all of the shares will accelerate the time for payment of any estate tax deferred under §6166. *See* Part E, *infra.* Because of that problem, it may be desirable to limit the number of shares that must be sold at the outset. The limit might be based upon the maximum number of shares that could be disposed of without triggering an acceleration under §6166 or exceeding the amount redeemable under §303. Where appropriate, the corporation or the other shareholders could be given an option to purchase the remainder of the shares. A contract for the sale of the shares might be drawn in a way that attempts to fix the price of the shares to be sold (commonly at the federal estate tax value in the decedent's estate) without having the contract treated as a disposition of the shares for purposes of §6166. Such a contract should provide for transfer of the stock certificates at the specified future times, prior to which the seller would be entitled to vote the stock, receive the dividends, etc. Second, the number of shares to be redeemed by the corporation might be limited in order to avoid the risk that the redemption of all of a decedent's stock would cause part of the distribution to be taxed as a dividend. Thus, the agreement might limit the mandatory purchase to a number of shares that have a value equal to the maximum amount redeemable under §303 (*i.e.,* equal to the sum of the state and federal death taxes, and the funeral and administration expenses that are deductible under §2053). *See* §11.17, *infra.* As explained below, the redemption of some shares is treated as a sale or exchange where the stock comprises more than 35% of the excess of the value of the decedent's gross estate over the amounts allowable as deductions under §§2053 and 2054. *See* §§11.14 to 11.21, *infra.* Any excess distribution made in redemption of the stock will be taxed as a dividend under §301 unless it qualifies under one or more of the 3 exceptions created by §302(b). It is difficult to fit within one of the exceptions where a family corporation is involved because of the application of the stock attribution rules of §318. The exceptions are discussed further in §11.15, *infra.*

A buy-sell agreement applicable upon the death or retirement of a party is seldom effective to fix the value of the shares for gift tax purposes. The price fixed in the agreement may have an influence on the valuation of the shares. However, it will not be determinative for gift tax purposes unless a transfer of the shares by gift gives the other party or parties the right to purchase the gifted shares. *See* Commissioner v. McCann, 146 F.2d 385 (2d Cir. 1944) (restrictive provision in by-laws); Krauss v. United States, 140 F.2d 510 (5th Cir. 1944) (restrictive provision in charter).

§11.5. *Funding the Purchase*

Insurance on the lives of shareholders is usually used to fund a buy-sell agreement because of its positive characteristics — liquidity, reliability, and general availability. Unfortunately, however, the exact amount required to fund a purchase is usually not known until a shareholder dies and it becomes possible to value his or her shares under the agreement. The problem is more difficult if one or more shareholders are, or become, uninsurable. In some cases the corporation may establish a reserve for the purpose of funding the agreement, which could be invested in liquid assets other than cash value insurance. Earnings accumulated in the year of a shareholder's death or thereafter are exempt from the accumulated earnings tax to the extent needed to redeem the decedent's stock, but not in excess of the maximum amount redeemable under §303. §537.

Maintaining the necessary number of insurance policies is simple enough when an entity purchase agreement is involved and the policies are owned by the corporation. In such a case, the corporation ordinarily acquires and owns one policy on the life of each shareholder. The corporation is not entitled to a deduction for premiums paid on such policies. §264(a). On the other hand, the premium payments are not income to the shareholders and the insurance proceeds received by the corporation are not subject to the income tax. §101(a). The value of the insurance on a shareholder's life is not directly includible in his or her gross estate.

Under Reg. §20.2042-1(c)(6) a corporation's incidents of ownership are not attributed to the sole or controlling shareholder where the proceeds are payable to the corporation. *See* Rev. Rul. 82-85, 1982-1 C.B. — and §6.19, *supra.* The proceeds received by the corporation may be reflected in the value of his or her shares, depending in part upon the terms of the buy-sell agreement. If the insurance is taken into account in valuing the shares, the shares will be worth more, thereby increasing the amount to be received by the decedent's successors.

Where a cross purchase agreement is involved, each shareholder must own a policy on the life of each other shareholder. Thus, an unmanageable number of policies is required if there are many shareholders. For example, 30 policies of insurance are required if there are 6 shareholders (each shareholder must own policies on the lives of the other 5). The problem is exacerbated if the shareholders own unequal amounts of stock, which requires them to own policies of varying amounts. Problems are also encountered in disposing of policies a deceased shareholder owned on the lives of the survivors. A sale of policies to the noninsured survivors constitutes a transfer for value, as a result of which the proceeds of the policies might be subject to taxation under §101(a)(2). *See* §6.36, *supra.* Of course, a shareholder should avoid purchasing a policy on his or her own life, which would subject the proceeds to the estate tax. The payment of premiums on such policies is not deductible by the shareholders for income tax purposes. If the corporation pays the premiums on policies owned by the shareholders, they will be considered to have received a constructive dividend unless they are employees and the premium payments are treated as additional compensation. Where a cross purchase agreement is used, the proceeds of a policy on the life of a deceased shareholder should not be included in the shareholder's gross estate directly or indirectly.

Installment Payment. The immediate cash requirements are less where an agreement provides for payment of the purchase price in installments or a deceased shareholder's successors are willing to sell the decedent's stock on that basis. *See* LR 7941037. The installment payment of the purchasing price could also reduce the tax cost to the redeeming shareholder, which could be very important if the redemption did not qualify as a sale or exchange of the stock (*i.e.,* if the proceeds were taxed as dividends). The circumstances in which an installment sale is feasible depend upon the financial stability of the company and the shareholders, the relationships between the shareholders, and the needs of the decedent's successors. In some cases the sellers may feel it is necessary to obtain some further assurance that payments will be made when due, such as a guarantee by individual shareholders or others. An installment sale must also be planned carefully in light of the tax circumstances of the decedent's estate. Consideration must be given to the fact that an installment sale would ordinarily involve a disposition of the decedent's stock that could accelerate the time for payment of any estate tax deferred under §6166. *See* §§11.26 to 11.32, *infra*. Finally, interest will be imputed on the unpaid balance unless the purchaser pays at least the test rate of simple interest required by §483. *See* §9.6, *supra*.

Distribution of Appreciated Property. In some cases the parties do not take any steps to provide that the required funds will be available upon the death of a shareholder. Instead, they are content to rely upon the availability of borrowed funds or the distribution of appreciated assets in exchange for the shares. However, neither of those methods is sufficiently reliable in most cases. It may be impossible or very expensive to borrow the necessary funds under the circumstances that exist at the time of a shareholder's death. Where a closely held family corporation is involved, the parties may agree to redeem part of the shares on the installment basis. *See, e.g.,* LR 8043030. The distribution by the corporation of appreciated property in redemption of a decedent's stock is attractive because the corporation is often not required to recognize any gain in such a case. *See* §311(d)(2). In particular, no gain is recognized (1) to the extent the redemption qualifies under §303(a) and §311(d)(2)(D), and (2) where the distribution is made in complete redemption of all of the stock of a person who owned at least 10% of the corporation's outstanding stock during the preceding 12 months (§311(d)(2)(A)). However, the parties usually cannot count on the corporation having suitable appreciated property on hand when a shareholder dies.

Accumulated Earnings Tax. The retention of earnings within the corporation for the purpose of funding an entity purchase agreement may be subject to the tax on unreasonable accumulated earnings. *See* §§531 to 537. The risk exists whether or not the earnings are invested in insurance on the lives of the shareholders. *See* Rudolph, Stock Redemptions and the Accumulated Earnings Tax — An Update, 4 J. Corp. Tax. 101 (1977). The tax is imposed at a rate of $27\frac{1}{2}$% on the first $100,000 of accumulated taxable income and $38\frac{1}{2}$% on the balance. §531. However, an operating company may accumulate $150,000 without being subject to the tax. §535(c)(2). Importantly, the tax only applies if the accumulation was made to avoid the income tax with respect to the corporate shareholders. §532(a).

A corporation may accumulate earnings for the purpose of redeeming a decedent's shares under §303, provided the accumulations take place in the year of the shareholder's death or later. §537(b)(1). Unfortunately, accumulations made prior to the shareholder's death may be subject to the tax. In most cases the tax should not apply, however, because an accumulation of earnings for the purpose of funding a buy-sell agreement is within the reasonable needs of the corporation. Also, such accumulations are not generally made in order to permit the share-holders to avoid income taxation.

§11.6.   Entity Purchase or Cross Purchase?

The basic type of agreement to be used in any given case depends upon the preference of the parties and a number of tax and nontax factors. Although it is difficult to generalize, many planners prefer entity pur-chase agreements. Their preference arises in part because the re-demption of stock by the corporation is often simpler and more easily accomplished than the purchase of the decedent's stock by a number of shareholders under a cross purchase agreement. Also, the purchase of insurance or other provision for funding by the corporation is surer and more easily arranged and maintained. It is also often less expensive for the corporation to provide the necessary financing. Of course, there is some risk that at the time of a shareholder's death the corporation will lack sufficient surplus or other funds that the local corporate law allows to be used to redeem stock. It is often more economical for a corporation to purchase insurance than it is for the shareholders to purchase the policies required to fund a cross purchase agreement. Recall in this connection that neither the corporation nor the shareholders may de-duct the cost of the insurance for income tax purposes. The cost of providing the necessary insurance under a cross purchase agreement can vary substantially depending upon whether the funds are derived from distributions to the shareholders that are deductible (*i.e.,* salaries) or ones that are not deductible (*i.e.,* dividends). The overall cost of cross owned insurance is lower if the necessary funds can be distributed in a form of salaries, which are only subject to taxation at the shareholder level, instead of dividends, which are diluted by income taxes at the corporate *and* shareholder levels. In some cases split-dollar insurance that is provided to shareholder-employees as additional compensation produces the same overall result as a salary increase. *See* §§6.50 to 6.53, *supra,* for a discussion of split-dollar insurance.

The type of agreement must be chosen with particular care where the ownership of stock and control of the corporation is balanced between 2 or more groups. In such a case a redemption of a decedent's shares might disrupt the balance more than the purchase of a limited number of shares by the other stockholders. Note that the IRS would probably not accept a valuation made under an agreement that provided for the sale of shares only to a decedent's nuclear family, to the exclusion of other shareholders. Such an agreement would be vulnerable to attack as an effort to shift the stock to the natural objects of the decedent's bounty at a bargain price.

§11.7. *Caveats*

Ethical Considerations. A planner who advises the shareholders regarding the preparation of a buy-sell agreement must recognize the potential for conflicts of interest between the shareholders. Accordingly, the planner should explain to them at the outset the desirability of having independent counsel and the difficulty of representing any of them adequately when their interests conflict. *See* §1.2, *supra*. Independent counsel should also be recommended in connection with a corporate recapitalization of a partnership freeze. *See* §11.22, *infra*.

Community Property Considerations. Some different planning may be called for where the shares are community property. In such a case, the parties may wish to provide for the sale of all of a couple's stock upon the death of the spouse who is active in the business. It is usually inappropriate to require the sale of the community property stock upon the death of a spouse who is not active in the business. Such a sale could deprive the surviving active spouse of important control and equity interests in the business. Of course, the valuation of the inactive spouse's interest is open to question by the IRS unless it is subject to a binding agreement. In addition, the estate of the spouse first to die may face serious liquidity problems unless he or she takes advantage of the unlimited marital deduction. However, the liquidity crunch may be alleviated if some shares of stock are redeemed under §303 (§§11.14 to 11.21, *infra*) and payment of the estate tax is deferred under §6166 (*see* §§11.26 to 11.32, *infra*). Where it is consistent with the couple's overall plans, the will of the inactive spouse should dispose of his or her interest in the stock in a way that will not subject it to estate taxation again upon the death of the active spouse. Such a disposition is most important where their stock taken together represents control of the corporation. For example, the interest of an inactive spouse in the stock may be left to a bypass trust of which the active spouse is the beneficiary and over which the active spouse has some degree of control.

C. RECAPITALIZATIONS

In a typical recapitalization the parents, who have a substantial interest in the family business, retain preferred stock, and perhaps some common stock, transferring the bulk of the common stock, or all of that stock, to their children. As a result, the value of their interest in the corporation will stay static, since preferred stock is much like a mortgage in terms of economics if not in terms of legal theory. The common stock will carry the growth of the business to the children. The transfer of the common stock can either be done by gift or by sale. To the extent the company grows in value faster than the amount of the dividends paid on the preferred, wealth inures to the children or to trusts that have been established for their benefit. Panel Discussion (and Outlines), The Estate Freezing Rage: A Practical Look at Planning Opportunities and Potential Problems, 15 Real Prop. Prob. & Tr. J. 19, 34 (1980) (statement of John Cohan).

§11.8. Background

Since 1921 recapitalizations have been recognized as a permissible form of tax-free corporate reorganization. §368(a)(1)(E) (an "E-type reorganization"). Neither the Code nor the regulations define the term "recapitalization"; however, the regulations do provide some terse examples. For the estate planner the most important example is this one: "A corporation issues preferred stock, previously authorized but unissued, for outstanding common stock." Reg. §1.368-2(e)(3). The Supreme Court has described a recapitalization as a "reshuffling of a capital structure within the framework of an existing corporation." Helvering v. Southwest Consolidated Corp., 315 U.S. 194, 202 (1942). Simply put, a recapitalization involves an exchange of stock or securities of a corporation for other stock or securities of the same corporation. Thus, the controlling shareholder in a closely held corporation is permitted to exchange some or all of his or her common stock for preferred stock without incurring any current tax liability. Such an exchange gives a shareholder greater flexibility in transferring his or her interests inter vivos or at death. Perhaps more important, it allows the value of his or her interests to be "frozen." A freeze in value is possible because the preferred stock will not increase in value although the corporation prospers in the future. Instead, all of the future growth will be reflected in the value of the common stock.

> **Example 11-1.** Cosmos, Inc. had 1,000 shares of voting common stock outstanding, of which 600 shares were owned by X. The remaining shares are held by members of X's family. X wished to turn over more management responsibilities to the other shareholders, who were also employed by Cosmos. In order to encourage their continued participation in the business of Cosmos, the capital structure was reorganized so they would be the primary beneficiaries of any future growth. Specifically, 6,000 shares of voting, 10% nonconvertible, and nonparticipating preferred stock with a $100 par value were issued to X in exchange for X's 600 shares of common. The preferred stock will lose its voting rights upon the

death of X, when the shares become callable by Cosmos. In similar cases the IRS has ruled that the exchange of the preferred stock for common stock was a tax-free recapitalization under §368(a)(1)(E). *See, e.g.,* LR 8044021. The exchange would involve a gift from X to the other shareholders if the value of the preferred stock received by X were less than the value of the common stock that X surrendered.

Business Purpose. In order to qualify as a tax-free recapitalization, the courts require that the change in the corporation's capital structure serve a valid business purpose. This requirement is met if, for example, the recapitalization either shifts control to the persons active in the management of the corporation (LR 8033025) or encourages the shareholders to remain active in the conduct of the company's business. Some courts have found that it is sufficient if the recapitalization serves the business needs of the shareholders as opposed to the needs of the corporation. Estate of Parshelsky v. Commissioner, 303 F.2d 14 (2d Cir. 1962). However, the IRS and most courts require the recapitalization to serve the business needs of the corporation. Rafferty v. Commissioner, 452 F.2d 767 (1st Cir. 1971), *cert. denied,* 408 U.S. 922 (1972); Rev. Rul. 77-321, 1977-2 C.B. 98. The distinction between corporate and personal purposes is highly artificial where closely held businesses are concerned. As the court noted in *Parshelsky,* "It is not only difficult but often purely formalistic to distinguish between corporate and personal benefit." 303 F.2d at 19. In most cases it is simple enough to identify a corporate business purpose that is served by a proposed recapitalization. Prior to May, 1982, if there was any doubt regarding the sufficiency of the business purpose of the recapitalization, the IRS was often asked to rule on the question before the transaction was consummated. Beginning on May 1, 1982, the IRS refused to issue rulings or determination letters concerning the question of whether a transaction constitutes a recapitalization within the meaning of §368(a)(1)(E) except when the recapitalization was an integral part of a larger transaction and it was impossible to determine the tax consequences of the larger transaction without making a determination with regard to the recapitalization. Rev. Proc. 82-30, 1982-1 C.B. — .

Boot. Gain may be recognized in connection with a recapitalization if "boot" is received as a result of the exchange. For example, gain is recognized where securities (*i.e.,* bonds) are issued to a shareholder who surrendered no securities. §354(a)(1). The gain in such a case is ordinary income if the distribution of the securities had the effect of a dividend. §356(a)(2). A similar result occurs if the principal amount of the securities received exceeds the principal amount of the securities surrendered. §354(a).

§11.9. Valuation Problems

Fundamentally, I look at a standard preferred stock as though it were a Christmas tree. The tree is simple. It has straight lines. And it is easy to understand. But then we start to put ornaments on this Christmas tree, all kinds of ornaments. We give it a low dividend rate, or a high dividend rate, or a high call price, or we make it noncumulative, and so on. As a matter of fact, we have so many ornaments that we can't see the tree. . . . But, I warn you, someone has to value the preferred stock. If you insist on putting so many ornaments on this tree that it is not possible to value it, you are exposing your client to a significant risk.

This brings me to the principal point I want to make on preferred stock valuations. No matter how you dress up the preferred stock with ornaments, you just can't get virtually 100 percent of the value of the company into the preferred stock. I know you would like to do that. And I know your clients would like to do that; believe me, I sympathize with the problem. But there is just no way that a valuation expert can substantiate a conclusion that the value of the preferred stock is equal to 100 percent of the value of the company. Panel Discussion (and Outlines), The Estate Freezing Rage: A Practical Look at the Planning Opportunities and Potential Problems, 15 Real Prop., Prob. & Tr. J. 19, 54 (1980) (statement of Robert Meyers).

Recapitalizations confront the planner with serious problems regarding the valuation of the corporation and of the preferred stock issued in connection with the transaction. The valuation of the stock of a closely held corporation is controversial enough, without adding the difficulty of placing a value on preferred stock issued in a recapitalization of the corporation. Of course, the valuation of the stock is a factual matter upon which the IRS will not issue an advance ruling. Private letter rulings that are issued concerning recapitalization routinely include a statement to the effect that "[n]o opinion is expressed as to the tax effect of the amount, if any, by which the distribution of Company [stock] exceeds or is less than the fair market value of the stock redeemed. A determination of the fair market value of the stock is specifically reserved until the federal income tax returns of the taxpayers concerned have been filed for the tax year the transaction is consummated." LR 8032103. In general, recapitalizations should be planned with the advice of a valuation expert, who will be available to testify if the taxpayer's valuations are challenged.

Gift or Additional Compensation. Although a recapitalization qualifies under §368(a)(1)(E), the exchange of stock may have gift, income, or estate tax consequences under other sections of the Code. For example, where the value of the preferred stock received by a shareholder is less than the value of the common stock surrendered by the shareholder, the recapitalization will involve a gift to the other shareholders or the payment of additional compensation to them. Where the other shareholders are unrelated, the transaction may be treated as a bona fide business transaction that does not give rise to any gift tax liability. *See* Reg. §25.2512-8. If the exchanging shareholder is related to the other shareholders, the IRS will almost certainly charge that the recapitalization involved a gift to the others. The opposite result occurs where the value of the preferred stock received by a shareholder exceeds the value of the common stock he or she surrendered: Either the other shareholders made a gift to the exchanging shareholder or additional compensation was paid to him or her. In Rev. Rul. 74-269, 1974-1 C.B. 87 the IRS stated that it would apply that analysis to recapitalizations:

> However, if *A* receives shares of preferred stock having a fair market value in excess of the fair market value of the common stock he surrendered, or surrenders shares of common stock having a fair market value in excess of the fair market value of the preferred stock received, the amount representing such excess will be treated as having been used to make gifts, pay compensation, satisfy obligations of any kind, or for whatever purpose the facts indicate.

If the value of the preferred stock received in a recapitalization exceeds the value of the common stock, the shareholder might be treated as having received a taxable stock dividend under §§305(b) or (c).

If a post-1981 exchange involves an outright gift, presumably none of the value of the common stock is includible in the exchanging shareholder's estate although he or she dies within 3 years of the exchange. Of course, any common stock included in the shareholder's estate under §§2035(d)(2), 2036(b), or other provision of the Code will be valued on the estate tax valuation date applicable to the shareholder's estate. However, the shareholder's estate should be entitled to an offset under §2043 for the value of the stock that the decedent received in exchange. *See* Ehrlich, Corporate Recapitalization as an Estate Planning Business Retention Tool, N.Y.U. 34th Inst. Fed. Tax 1661, 1669-1971 (1976).

Example 11-2. X, the controlling shareholder of Titan, Inc., exchanged 1,000 of the outstanding 1,500 shares of Titan common stock for 10,000 shares of 8% noncumulative voting preferred stock that had a par value of $100. The recapitalization assumed that X's common stock and the preferred stock he received were each worth $1,000,000, which was roughly two-thirds of the total value of Titan ($1,500,000). The exchange qualified as a tax-free recapitalization under §368(a)(1)(E). The other common shareholders in Titan at the time of the exchange were all related to X. The exchange would involve a gift by X if the value of the common stock that he surrendered exceeded the value of the preferred stock he received. In such a case, presumably only the value of the preferred stock would be included in X's estate.

§11.10. Section 306 Stock

By way of background, §306 was added to the Code in 1954 to block the use of the preferred stock bailout as a device for withdrawing funds from the corporation in the form of capital gains rather than ordinary income. Congressional action was hastened when the bailout won judicial approval in Chamberlin v. Commissioner, 207 F.2d 462 (6th Cir. 1953), *cert. denied,* 347 U.S. 918 (1954). A bailout, such as the one involved in *Chamberlin,* typically involved the following steps:

1. The corporation issued redeemable preferred stock as a stock dividend on the outstanding common stock. The receipt of the stock dividend was not taxable by reason of the predecessor of §305.
2. The common shareholders sold the preferred stock for an amount close to its redemption value to third party investors, who expected the corporation to redeem the stock promptly. Prior to the adoption of §306 the gain on the sale was characterized as capital gain, which would almost always be long-term capital gain because the holding period of the common stock also applied to the preferred stock.
3. The corporation redeemed the preferred stock from the third parties, who usually recognized a small gain on the transaction.

Preferred stock issued in connection with a recapitalization is sometimes classified as "§306 stock," which can have adverse income tax consequences for the distributees. The receipt of §306 stock does not have any immediate adverse income tax consequences. Instead, the characterization of the stock carries forward and often causes the shareholder to realize ordinary income when the stock is sold or exchanged. For example, a sale of part of a shareholder's §306 stock would give rise to ordinary income to the extent the amount received would have been treated as a dividend had the corporation distributed cash instead of the preferred stock. The ordinary income element is limited to the amount by which the earnings and profits of the corporation at the time of distribution exceeded the shareholder's allocated basis in the shares that were transferred. Any additional amount the shareholder receives is capital gain. The classification of the proceeds as ordinary income in such a case would also limit the amount allowable as a charitable deduction if the stock were contributed to charity. *See* §170(e)(1)(A), Reg. §1.170A-4(b)(1) and §8.9, *supra.*

What Is §306 Stock? Stock distributed as a tax-free stock dividend is classified as §306 stock except for common stock that is received as a distribution on common stock. §306(c)(1)(A). More important for present purposes, stock distributed in connection with a recapitalization is classified as §306 stock if the effect of the transaction is substantially the same as a stock dividend or is received in exchange for §306 stock. §306(c)(1)(B). In this connection, Reg. §1.306-3(d) provides, "Ordinarily, section 306 stock includes stock which is not common stock received in pursuance of a plan of reorganization (within the meaning of §368(a)) . . . if cash received in lieu of such stock would have been treated as a dividend. . . ." Accordingly, the classification of the preferred stock received in a recapitalization in part turns upon the application of the rules of §302. *See* §11.15, *infra.* Perhaps most important, preferred stock received by a shareholder in exchange for *all* of the shareholder's common stock may not be classified as §306 stock because the distribution of cash in case of such a complete termination would not be treated as a dividend. *See* §302(b)(3) and Rev. Rul. 59-84, 1959-1 C.B. 71. For purposes of testing the distribution under §302, it appears that the IRS will not apply the attribution rules of §318 where a shareholder surrenders all of his or her common stock in exchange for the preferred. This point is noted in Z. Cavitch, Tax Planning for Corporations and Shareholders §8.06[2] (1980):

> Thus, it appears that if the holder of common stock surrenders *all* of his common stock in exchange for preferred stock, the attribution rules will not be applied for ruling purposes. If, however, the holder of common stock retains or receives *any* amount of common stock, the attribution rules will be fully applicable for ruling puposes.

Thus, preferred stock issued to a shareholder in exchange for all of his or her common stock is not to be classified as §306 stock although other family members continue to own common stock in the same corporation. *See, e.g.,* LRs 7730008, 8018068, 8020124.

Dispositions Not Reached by §306. The §306 taint is less significant if the shareholder plans to retain the stock until the time of his or her death, after which the stock will no longer be classified as §306 stock. Reg. §1.303-6(e) recognizes that "[s]ection 306 stock ceases to be so classified if the basis of such stock is determined by reference to its fair market value on the date of the decedent-shareholder's death or the optional valuation date under section 1014." Also, the proceeds of the sale of the shareholder's entire interest to an unrelated party are not taxed as ordinary income. §306(b)(1)(A); Rev. Rul. 77-455, 1977-2 C.B. 93. Liquidations and certain other dispositions are also excepted by §306(b) from treatment as ordinary income. Despite the exceptions the holder of §306 stock is substantially "locked in" by the tax rules applicable to the stock.

Some clients prefer to surrender all of their common stock in a recapitalization in order to avoid the restrictions applicable to §306 stock. In contrast, other clients are willing to accept §306 stock in order to retain a small, but still significant, equity position in the corporation. A decision regarding this issue should be made in light of the overall circumstances and the client's preferences. If the recapitalization is one with respect to which the IRS will issue a ruling or determination letter, any request that is filed should ask for a determination that the preferred stock issued in the recapitalization is not §306 stock.

§11.11. Section 305 Problems

Section 305 governs the income tax treatment of distributions made by a corporation of its own stock, or rights to acquire its stock. Under the general rule of §305(a), a pro rata stock dividend paid to common shareholders is not includible in their gross income. However, a wide range of actual or constructive distributions are taxable as dividends under §§305(b) and (c). For example, a distribution of stock is taxable under §305(b)(1) if it is payable at the election of any shareholder in money or property instead of stock. Also, a distribution is taxable if it has the result of the receipt of cash or other property by some shareholders and an increase in the proportionate interests of other shareholders in the assets or the earnings and profits of the corporation. §305(b)(2). Importantly, virtually any distribution with respect to preferred stock is treated as a dividend. §305(b)(4). Most reorganizations of closely held family corporations will not involve a distribution that will be treated as a dividend under §305. However, a problem may be encountered under §305(b)(4) if the preferred stock is redeemable at a premium after a specified period.

Redemption Premium. Most commonly the preferred stock issued in connection with the recapitalization of a closely held corporation is not callable by the corporation. Special care must be exercised where the preferred stock is redeemable at a premium after a specified period of time. Under Reg. §1.305-5(b) the preferred stock may carry a reasonable redemption premium without giving rise to a distribution in the nature of a dividend. In particular, the regulations provide that "a redemption premium not in excess of 10 percent of the issue price on stock which is not redeemable for 5 years from the date of issue shall be considered reasonable." Reg. §1.305-5(b)(2). Where the redemption premium is excessive, the preferred shareholders will be considered under §305(c) to have received a distribution of additional stock on the preferred stock over the period of time during which the preferred stock could not be called for redemption. Reg. §1.305-5(b)(1).

Example 11-3. Zero Corp. issued preferred stock worth $100 per share in exchange for common stock in a recapitalization. The preferred stock did not provide for the payment of dividends and is redeemable at the end of 5 years for $185 per share, with yearly increases thereafter of $15 per year. Under the circumstances a call premium in excess of $10 cannot be justified. The $75 excess of the call premium ($85) over the amount of a reasonable premium ($10) is considered to have been received on each share of preferred stock in equal portions over the 5-year call period. Each subsequent increase of $15 per year is considered to be an additional distribution on the preferred stock. *See* Reg. §1.305-5(d), *Example* 5.

The redemption premium problem can be avoided by the parties in a variety of ways when the recapitalization is planned. Most simply, the redemption premium could be eliminated entirely or the stock could be made immediately redeemable or never redeemable. *See, e.g.,* LR 8020124. Where the preferred stock is redeemable at a premium after a fixed period of time, the premium is commonly limited to the amount permitted under the regulations (*i.e.,* 10% on stock that is not redeemable for 5 years). The decision made on this point will, of course, affect the gift and estate tax value of the preferred stock.

§11.12. Other Tax Considerations

A recapitalization will deprive the parties of 2 tax advantages otherwise available to small business corporations. Their significance will depend in part on the profitability of the corporation under consideration. First, a corporation is not eligible for Subchapter S treatment if it has more than one class of stock. §1371(a)(4). Thus, a recapitalization will prevent the corporation from electing Subchapter S treatment and will terminate an existing election. Prior to 1982 the loss of the opportunity to have the corporation's income (and operating expenses) allocated directly to its shareholders generally was not important to profitable corporations. The reduction in the maximum individual income tax rate to 50% makes the loss of Subchapter S status more significant. Second, an ordinary loss deduction is available under §1244 only with respect to common stock. §1244(c)(1). Accordingly, a loss suffered on the sale or exchange of preferred stock cannot be claimed as an ordinary loss under §1244 even though the common stock originally qualified under that section. Of course, the disqualification is of limited significance for profitable corporations.

The preferred stock issued in connection with a recapitalization typically carries the right to a large cumulative dividend. It may be impractical or undesirable for the corporation to assume that obligation. Before proceeding with a recapitalization the parties should also understand that the preferred stock dividends are ordinary income to the recipient but are not deductible by the corporation. This consideration often deters clients from adopting recapitalization plans.

§11.13. Summary

A carefully planned recapitalization is a valuable estate-planning tool that can be used to freeze the value of the ownership interests of some shareholders and to shift future growth to others. A recapitalization can also be helpful in order to allocate a fixed interest (preferred stock) to family members who are not active in the business, and equity interests (common stock) to the family members who play an active part in the business. In the latter case, often only the common stock would carry the right to vote. The terms of the recapitalization should be based upon valuations made by a qualified expert. In appropriate cases the planner may recommend that a letter ruling be requested. Although the IRS will not rule on some matters, such as valuation, a ruling can provide protection against some challenges that otherwise might arise in the future.

Problem 11-1. Stellar, Inc. has 1,000 shares of common stock outstanding, 750 of which are owned by its president Judy Star. The remainder of the shares are owned by her 2 children, Robin (125 shares) and Sam (125 shares). Judy would like to limit the amount of the estate tax that will be due upon her death. She would also like to be able to give property of equal value to her children. However, Robin should receive a greater equity interest in Stellar, Inc., because she is active in the business and Sam is not. Judy is anxious to give more of the responsibility for running the business to Robin, but would like to retain voting control so long as she lives. Stellar, Inc. has been very successful and is now worth about $4,000,000 and has substantial annual earnings. Robin and Sam acquired their shares from Sam, Sr., when he died several years ago. Judy has never made any gifts that required a federal gift tax return to be filed, but she may wish to make some large gifts to the local art museum and opera association. Judy owns a residence worth about $150,000 and liquid investments of about $750,000.

How could a recapitalization help Judy attain her estate-planning goals? What main elements would you include in a recapitalization plan for Judy? If the value of Judy's interest in Stellar, Inc. is frozen, how much estate tax will be due upon her death assuming that she dies next year, the value of her other assets remains the same, and no deductions will be available to her estate? How much more estate tax would be due if the value of Stellar, Inc. doubled and there had been no recapitalization?

D. REDEMPTIONS UNDER §303

The key to successful estate planning in general and to successful planning for redemptions in particular is anticipation. From the moment it becomes apparent that an individual owns a substantial block of corporate stock, the practitioner should determine whether a redemption of the shares will be a likely feature in the administration of the individual's estate. A redemption which qualifies for capital gain treatment is almost always desirable for an estate since it offers the decedent's heirs an opportunity to withdraw large amounts of cash from a corporation without dividend treatment. As long as estates receive a basis in stock equal to estate tax value . . . redemptions which avoid dividend treatment provide an unparalleled opportunity for tax-free distribution of corporate cash. Fox, Options Available to a Corporation Acquiring Its Own Stock From Estate of Deceased Shareholder, 7 Est. Plan. 206, 210-211 (1980).

§11.14. *General*

Section 303 eases the income tax problems of withdrawing enough funds from a closely held business to pay the death taxes and administration expenses incurred by a deceased shareholder's estate. Within the limits of §303 the stock may be redeemed even though the decedent's estate is awash with cash and does not need the proceeds of redemptions to pay the taxes and expenses. Without §303 the redemption of a decedent's stock would often be treated as a dividend unless it qualified under one of the exceptions of §302(b). *See* §11.15, *infra.* If the requirements of §303 are met, a distribution in redemption of a limited amount of the decedent's stock is treated as a sale or exchange of the stock, the proceeds of which qualify for capital gains treatment. Little, if any, gain is usually realized upon a redemption because the stock has a basis equal to its estate tax value in the decedent's estate. §1014(a).

In order to qualify under §303 the stock included in the decedent's estate must constitute more than 35% of the decedent's gross estate less items allowable as deductions under §§2053 and 2054. §303(b)(2). Prior to 1982 the stock was required to compose more than 50% of the decedent's gross estate less deductions allowable under §§2053 and 2054. Under the 1981 Act a decedent's estate includes property transferred within 3 years of death for purposes of §§303, 2032A, 6166, and the lien provisions of subchapter C of chapter 64. §§2035(d)(3). The amount redeemable under §303 is limited to the sum of the state and federal death taxes, including penalties and interest and the funeral and administration expenses that are deductible under §2053. §303(a). However, the 1976 Act added a provision under which a redemption qualifies only to the extent that "the interest of the shareholder is reduced directly (or through a binding obligation to contribute) by any payment" of death taxes and funeral and administration expenses. §303(b)(3). Accordingly, shares specifically bequeathed to one party may not be redeemed under §303 where the obligation to pay death taxes and funeral and administration expenses is imposed on another party.

The use of the proceeds of a redemption made within 4 years of the decedent's death is not restricted. §303(b)(1). Most later redemptions qualify under §303 only where the payment of the estate tax has been deferred under §6166 (or former §6166A) and the amount distributed is applied within one year toward payment of the death taxes and funeral and administration expenses. Redemptions made more than 4 years after the decedent's death must be carefully coordinated with payment of the estate tax installments under §6166 (or former §6166A).

Stock subject to the generation-skipping tax by reason of a generation-skipping transfer occurring at or after the death of the deemed transferor may also qualify for redemption under §303. §303(d). For purposes of applying §303 the stock is considered to be included in the gross estate of the deemed transferor; the relationship of the stock to the decedent's estate is measured by reference to the amount of the generation-skipping transfer; the generation-skipping tax and similar taxes are treated as imposed by reason of the deemed transferor's death; and the period within which distribution may be made in redemption of the stock is measured from the date of the generation-skipping transfer. The application of §303 to generation-skipping transfers should be considerably clearer after regulations are issued by the Secretary as contemplated by §303(d).

In planning a redemption program the parties must consider at least 2 important nontax questions. First, will the redemption result in an undesirable shift of corporate control? Second, will the distribution of funds in redemption of the stock unduly hamper corporate operations or growth? If the answer to either question is yes, the parties should consider redeeming fewer shares or adopting an alternative plan for raising funds.

§11.15. Exceptions of §302(b)

A redemption that does not qualify under §303 will be treated as a distribution in the nature of a dividend unless it qualifies under one of the 3 exceptions established by §302(b). The first exception articulates a subjective test under which a redemption is treated as a purchase if it is "not essentially equivalent to a dividend" in light of all of the facts and circumstances. §302(b)(1). Unfortunately, the scope of the exception is difficult to define, as a result of which it cannot be relied upon in planning. The examples in the regulations and the position taken by the IRS in private letter rulings do give some indication of its parameters. The meaning of the provision has also been clarified in several court decisions. In the leading decision, United States v. Davis, 397 U.S. 301 (1970), the Court held that the exception does not apply unless the redemption results in a meaningful reduction in the shareholder's proportionate interest in the corporation. That result is consistent with the regulations, which indicate that a pro rata redemption does not qualify where only one class of stock is outstanding. Reg. §1.302-2(b). However, a pro rata redemption might qualify as a partial liquidation under §346. It is difficult for a family-owned corporation to meet the requirements of this exception because of the application of the family stock attribution rules of §318.

> **Example 11-4.** When Magma, Inc. was incorporated, its 15,000 shares of common stock were issued equally to H (7,500) and W (7,500). Subsequently H and W each sold 2,500 shares to a key employee of Magma, C, who was unrelated to them. When H died, Magma redeemd H's remaining 5,000 shares from his estate in accordance with the terms of a buy-sell agreement that bound all of the shareholders regarding the disposition of their shares. The redemption reduced the estate's actual ownership of Magma stock from one-third to zero and its constructive ownership of stock from two-thirds to one-half. The IRS has ruled that such a redemption is not essentially equivalent to a dividend. LR 8044034. The redemption would not fall within the terms of this exception if C were a beneficiary of H's estate because the estate would be treated as the constructive owner of C's shares as well. *See* §318(a) and Reg. §1.318-3(a).

Substantially Disproportionate Redemptions (§302(b)(2)). The second exception applies if the redemption is "substantially disproportionate with respect to the shareholder." §302(b)(2). In order to qualify under this exception the redemption must satisfy 3 mathematical tests, which is made difficult by the application of the stock attribution rules. §§302(c)(1), 318. In brief, the tests require that immediately after the redemption the shareholder must own *less* than:
1. 50% of the combined voting power of all classes of stock,
2. 80% of the voting stock that the shareholder owned immediately before the redemption, and
3. 80% of the common stock (whether voting or nonvoting) that the shareholder owned immediately before the redemption.

Because of the second of the tests, "Section 302(b)(2) only applies to a redemption of voting stock or to a redemption of both voting stock and other stock. Section 302(b)(2) does not apply to the redemption solely of nonvoting stock (common or preferred)." Reg. §1.302-3(a)(3). Where a redemption is one of a series, the applicability of this exception is determined by the aggregate effect of the redemptions and not the effect of the one redemption alone. Reg. §1.302-3(a)(3). A redemption is not disproportionate if all of the stock of one class is redeemed or if the same percentage of each shareholder's stock is redeemed. It is also significant that §302(b)(2) does not impose any percentage test with respect to nonvoting preferred stock.

> **Example 11-5.** W, X, Y, and Z each owned 100 shares of the 400 outstanding shares of the common stock of Comet Corp. In addition, X and Y each owned 100 shares of the outstanding 200 shares of Comet's nonvoting preferred stock. The shareholders were not related parties within the meaning of the attribution rules of §318(a). Comet Corp. redeemed 60 shares of common stock from W, 25 shares from X, and 15 shares from Y. In order to qualify under §302(b)(2), after the redemption a shareholder must own less than 20% (80% times 25%) of the 300 shares of common stock that remain outstanding. No test is imposed with respect to the nonvoting preferred stock, none of which was redeemed. After the redemption W owned 40 shares (13.33%); X owned 75 shares (25%); and Y owned 85 shares (28.33%). Accordingly, the redemption is disproportionate only with respect to W. See the example in Reg. §1.302-3(b).

Complete Termination of Interest (§302(b)(3)). Finally, §302(b)(3) treats a redemption of the entire interest of a shareholder as an exchange. This exception is superficially easy to satisfy, but it is complicated by the application of the stock attribution rules. However, the family attribution rules (§318(a)(1)) can be waived if the requirements of §302(c)(2) are met. Section 302(c)(2) requires that after the redemption the former shareholder have no interest in the corporation other than as a creditor; that the former shareholder acquire no interest in the corporation for a period of 10 years other than by bequest or inheritance; and that he or she agree to inform the Treasury of the acquisition of any interest in the corporation within that period. Reg. §1.302-4(a). The attribution rules are not waived if any of the redeemed stock was acquired by the shareholder within 10 years before the date of the distribution from a member of his or her family or if any member of the shareholder's family acquired stock from him or her during that period and tax avoidance was a primary purpose of either acquisition. *See* Reg. §1.302-4(g).

Under the view taken by the IRS it is virtually impossible to qualify under this exception where stock in a family corporation is owned by a trust or estate. Specifically, the IRS takes the position that §302(c)(2) applies only to redemptions from individuals and that redemptions from trusts or estates are not protected by it. Accordingly, in its view where shares are redeemed from a trust or estate the attribution rules cannot be waived.

The position of the IRS has not been accepted by the Tax Court. In Lillian M. Crawford, 59 T.C. 830 (1973), *nonacq.*, 1974-2 C.B. 5, *app. dismissed* (9th Cir. 1973), the Tax Court held that the redemption of all of the shares owned by the deceased shareholder's estate and by his widow, who was its sole beneficiary, constituted a complete termination although his children continued to own the remainder of the shares. Specifically, the court found that the waiver agreement filed by the decedent's estate was effective to bar the attribution of the children's stock to the widow and, through her, to the estate. It was concerned that the IRS position "merely put a premium on tax planning and set a trap for the unwary." *Id.* at 837. *See also* Rodgers P. Johnson Trust, 71 T.C. 941 (1979), which permitted a trust to waive the family attribution rules. The IRS position seems to be clearly wrong as a matter of policy and of law. The qualification of a redemption under §302(b)(3) should not turn on whether the decedent's shares are redeemed from the estate or from its sole shareholder.

Both the IRS and the Tax Court agree that only family attribution can be waived; their dispute is over who can make the waiver. Under no circumstances can the entity attribution rules of §§318(a)(2), (3) be waived. David Metzger Trust, 76 T.C. 42 (1981). In a poorly reasoned and much criticized opinion, the Fifth Circuit held that entity attribution may also be waived. Rickey v. United States, 592 F.2d 1251 (5th Cir. 1979); *see also* Fassler, Waiver of Entity Attribution — The Rickey, Jr. Case, 57 Taxes 658 (1979). In light of the provisions of §302(c)(2)(A) that permit waiver of family attribution, the Fifth Circuit's view seems wholly untenable.

Example 11-6. The estate of H and his surviving daughter, D, were the only shareholders in Alpha Corp. H's widow, W, was the sole beneficiary under H's will. H's interest in Alpha Corp. did not constitute a sufficient portion of his estate to qualify for the redemption under §303. The parties wished to redeem all of the Alpha Corp. shares that were formerly owned by H if the redemption would qualify under one of the exceptions to §302. In the view of the IRS, a redemption from the estate could not qualify because the application of the attribution rules of §§318(a)(2) and (3) could not be waived (*i.e.*, D's stock would be attributed to W and from her to H's estate). *See* Rev. Ruls. 59-233, 1959-2 C.B. 106, and 68-388, 1968-2 C.B. 122. The Tax Court would reach a different conclusion based on the *Crawford* case. It would allow H's estate to waive family attribution of D's shares to W under §318(a)(1) so that there would be no shares to attribute from W to the estate. In any case a redemption of all of the shares formerly owned by H would qualify as a complete termination under §302(b)(3) if the shares were first distributed by H's estate to W and if W complied with the requirements of §302(c)(2). In such a case the family attribution rules would not apply (*i.e.,* D's stock would not be attributed to W), and even the IRS would treat the redemption as a complete termination of W's interest. Rev. Rul. 79-67, 1979-1 C.B. 128.

§11.16.   Thirty-five Percent Requirement

Stock included in a decedent's gross estate qualifies for redemption under §303 only if its federal estate tax value exceeds 35% of the decedent's gross estate less the amount of deductions allowable under §§2053 and 2054. §303(b)(2)(A). For purposes of this computation the amounts deducted under §§2053 and 2054 (*i.e.,* debts, funeral and administration expenses, and casualty losses) are taken into account whether or not they are claimed as deductions for federal estate tax purposes. *See* Rev. Rul. 56-449, 1956-2 C.B. 180 (declared obsolete by Rev. Rul. 80-387, 1980-2 C.B. 386) and §303(b)(2)(a)(ii). Note that the amount of the charitable and marital deductions do not figure into the computation.

> **Example 11-7.** T's gross estate was $1,000,000 including stock in corporation A that had an estate tax value of $475,000. The deductions allowable to T's estate under §§2053 and 2054 amounted to $80,000. The 35% requirement is met in this case because the value of the stock included in T's gross estate ($475,000) comprised more of T's estate than was required by §303(b)(2)(A) ($475,000 ÷ ($1,000,000 − $80,000) = 51.63%).

The personal representative must recognize that the valuation of the stock and other assets may determine whether or not the 35% test is satisfied. The outcome may also be affected by decisions that determine whether other items are included in the gross estate. For example, the exclusion of qualified plan benefits payable in a lump sum will turn on whether the recipient will forego the generally favorable 10-year income averaging under §402. *See* §§2039(c), (f) and §12.21, *infra.*

Stock in 2 or More Corporations. Stock of 2 or more corporations may be combined for purposes of satisfying the 35% requirement if at least 20% in value of the outstanding stock of each corporation is included in the decedent's gross estate. §303(b)(2)(B). In order to qualify for aggregation, the decedent's estate must include at least 20% of the total value of all issues of each corporation's stock. That is, the test does not require that the decedent's estate include 20% of each issue of stock. Thus, the stock in corporations A and B is considered to be the stock of a single corporation for purposes of the 35% requirement if the decedent's estate includes common or preferred stock of each corporation that has a value of more than 20% of all of its stock.

Example 11-8. T's gross estate had a federal estate tax value of $900,000, including 30% of the outstanding stock of corporation A and 25% of the outstanding stock of corporation B. A total of $100,000 was allowable to T's estate as deductions under §§2053 and 2054. T's stock in corporation A was worth $200,000 of its total value of $950,000, and T's stock in corporation B was worth $100,000 of its total value of $450,000. Thus, more than 20% in value of the stock of both corporations was included in T's gross estate. The total value of the stock in the 2 corporations included in T's estate ($300,000) exceeds 35% of the value of T's gross estate reduced by amounts allowable as deductions under §§2053 and 2054 ($900,000 − $100,000). Accordingly, the 35% requirement of §303(b)(2) is satisfied.

The surviving spouse's community property interest in stock cannot be counted for purposes of satisfying the basic 35% test. However, for purposes of the 20% test, the surviving spouse's interest in stock held by the decedent and the surviving spouse as community property, joint tenants, tenants by the entirety, or as tenants in common is considered to be included in the decedent's gross estate. §303(b)(2)(B); cf., Rev. Rul. 61-91, 1961-1 C.B. 714 (comparable issue under former §6166A).

§11.17. Maximum Amount Redeemable

Under §303(a) the maximum amount that can be received in redemption of qualifying stock is fixed by the sum of the death taxes imposed by reason of the decedent's death and the amount of funeral and administration expenses deductible under §2053. As indicated above, the funeral and administration expenses are included in the computation whether they are taken as estate tax or income tax deductions. Note, however, that the amount of debts and casualty losses is not included in determining the ceiling.

Care must be exercised in planning the sequence of distributions in redemption of a decedent's stock. Where more than one distribution takes place, the distributions are applied against the total amount that is redeemable under §303 in the order in which the distributions are made. Reg. §1.303-2(g)(1).

Example 11-9. A maximum of $500,000 of stock was redeemable from corporation X by reason of T's death last year. On January 15 of this year corporation X distributed $400,000 to A's son, S, in redemption of shares T had transferred to a trust and that were included in T's estate under §2036. In February Corporation X redeemed $200,000 shares held by the executor of T's will. The first $500,000 received in redemption of the estate's shares qualifies under §303. One-half of the distribution received by T's executor ($100,000) does not qualify under §303.

§11.18. Time Limit on Redemptions

Under the basic limitation of §303(b)(1) a redemption must take place within 3 years and 90 days after the date the federal estate tax return is filed. §303(b)(1)(A). The proceeds of a redemption made within that period may be used for any purpose. If a petition for redetermination of estate tax by the Tax Court is timely filed, a redemption may be made at any time within 60 days after the Tax Court decision becomes final. §303(b)(1)(B). Also, where the payment of the estate tax is deferred under §6166, a redemption may be made with the time determined under that section for payment of the estate tax in installments. §303(b)(1)(C). A redemption made more than 4 years after the decedent's death qualifies only to the extent it does not exceed the lesser of (1) the amount of death taxes and funeral and administration expenses that remained unpaid immediately before the distribution and (2) the amount paid toward those expenses within one year following the date of the distribution. Of necessity the latter amount is always the lesser. In planning a redemption program the parties should consider the restrictions imposed on the use of the proceeds of redemptions made more than 4 years after the decedent's death. It is particularly important to do so where payment of the estate tax has been deferred under §6166 because of the acceleration provision of that section. See §§11.31, infra.

§11.19. What May Be Distributed

Virtually any property may be distributed in redemption of shares under §303. Although cash is normally distributed, there may be an overall tax benefit if the corporation distributes appreciated property instead of cash. A benefit may occur because the corporation does not recognize gain when it distributes appreciated property in a §303 redemption. §311(d)(2)(D). Thus, a corporation may distribute appreciated securities or other property in redemption of stock without realizing any gain. The distribution of appreciated property does not disadvantage the distributee, who takes a basis in the property equal to its value on the date of distribution. Accordingly, the distributee is usually free to sell the distributed property without realizing any gain. In effect the distribution of appreciated property permits the parties to avoid subjecting the appreciation to taxation. The property that is distributed must be selected carefully to avoid distributions that do have adverse tax consequences.

For example, the distribution of §§1245 or 1250 property triggers depreciation recapture.

§11.20. Inter Vivos Planning for Redemptions under §303

The shareholder and the corporation should ordinarily both do some careful advance planning where the shareholder's stock holdings may meet the requirements of §303. To begin with, the shareholder should avoid making any inter vivos gifts or other dispositions of the stock that might reduce the value of his or her holdings below the required 35%. Instead, steps might be taken to increase the value of the stock relative to the value of the shareholder's other assets. For example, assets that the shareholder owns outright might be transferred to the corporation, tax free, in exchange for additional shares of stock. Such a transfer does double duty by reducing the value of assets outside the business and increasing the amount of stock the shareholder holds. A change in the beneficiary designation of corporate owned life insurance may also boost the value of the shareholder's stock. Where the shareholder has control of a majority of the corporation's stock, its incidents of ownership are attributed to the shareholder and the proceeds are includible in the shareholder's estate under §2042 if the proceeds are payable to a beneficiary other than the corporation. *See* Reg. §20.2042-1(c)(6). In contrast, the proceeds are taken into account in valuing the shareholder's stock where the proceeds are payable to the corporation. *Id.*, Rev. Rul. 82-85, 1982-1 C.B. — .

Special care must be exercised when the shareholder owns stock in several corporations, the holdings in none of which are by themselves sufficient to satisfy the 35% test. Of course, the stock of 2 or more corporations can be aggregated for this purpose where more than 20% in value of each corporation is included in the shareholder's estate. §303(b)(2)(B). *See* §11.16, *supra.* More sophisticated planning may be called for where the client's stock holdings in any one corporation are not large enough to satisfy the 35% requirement and aggregation is prevented because the shareholder owns less than 20% of the stock of each corporation. The effect of aggregation could be approximated, however, if the corporations in which the shareholder owned stock are merged or consolidated prior to the shareholder's death. As a result, the value of the stock in the surviving corporation might be more than adequate to satisfy the 35% test. Stock in 2 or more corporations could, of course, be transferred to a holding company in exchange for some of its stock. While such a step might solve the §303 problem, the estate tax attributable to the holding company might not qualify for deferral under §6166, which is generally available only in the case of an active trade or business. *See* §11.27, *infra.*

The planner should also consider whether it is necessary or desirable to obtain a commitment from the corporation to redeem the stock through an entity purchase agreement or similar arrangement. *See* §§11.3 to 11.7, *supra.* The potential for future problems may be reduced if all shareholders are informed of the plans and approve of them. Some consideration must also be given to the availability of liquid assets to the corporation for the purpose of financing the redemption. A redemption may be adequately financed if, for example, retained earnings are used to purchase insurance on the shareholder's life or to invest in some other relatively liquid form. In any case, the corporation should avoid the imposition of the accumulated earnings tax under §§531 to 537. As noted above, §537 permits a corporation to accumulate funds in the year of a shareholder's death or later, for the purpose of funding a redemption under §303. The planner should also inquire into any restrictions that may be imposed on redemptions by the local law or by the corporation's financing arrangements. Some states restrict redemptions to the amount of the corporation's earned surplus. However, a redemption may be made under §66 of the Model Business Corporation Act so long as the corporation is not insolvent, the redemption does not render the corporation insolvent, and the net assets of the corporation are not reduced below the amount payable to the holders of shares who would have prior or equal rights to the assets of the corporation if it were liquidated.

As mentioned in §11.14, *supra,* the stock to be redeemed should only be given to a person whose interest in the stock will be chargeable for death taxes and funeral and administration expenses allowable under §2053. The stock qualifies under §303 only if the interest of the shareholder is reduced by payment of the death taxes and other expenses. §303(b)(3).

§11.21. Worksheet for §303

In the planning process it is important to determine whether a particular shareholder's stock meets the requirements of §303 and, if so, how much might be redeemed. It is safer and more efficient if the planner uses a worksheet of the following type to make the necessary calculations:

Section 303 Worksheet
(For decedents dying after December 31, 1981)

Part I. Qualifications
   1. Adjusted Gross Estate
         Gross estate (estimate or enter
           from Form 706, page 1, line
           1; include property trans-
           ferred within 3 years of
           death per §2035(d)(3))   _____

> *Less:* Deductions allowable
> under §§2053 and 2054   −_____
>
> Adjusted Gross Estate (item 1)   _____

2. Value of closely held business (the
    value of 2 or more businesses
    may be aggregated under
    §303(b)(2)) (item 2)   _____

3. Divide item 2 by item 1. (If the
    closely held business, item 2, has
    a value of more than 35% of the
    adjusted gross estate, item 1, the
    requirements of §303 are met.)   _____

Part II. Limitation on Redemption
4. Death taxes, including interest and
    penalties, paid by reason of dece-
    dent's death, §303(a)(1):
    a. Federal estate tax (estimate or
        enter from Form 706, page 1,
        line 19)   _____
    b. State death tax   +_____

    Total (item 4)   _____

5. Funeral and administrative ex-
    penses allowable as deductions
    under §2053, whether or not
    claimed on Form 706 (§303(a)(2))
    (item 5)   +_____

6. Total amount redeemable (item 4
    plus item 5)   _____

Caveat. See §303(b)(1) regarding the time within which the redemptions
must be accomplished.

Problem 11-2. Frank Bliss established the Bliss Diaper Service
Company and the Bliss Laundry and Dry Cleaning Service, Ltd.
prior to his marriage to Myra in 1975. Frank now owns 60 of the
100 outstanding shares of common stock in Bliss Diaper Company
and owns 180 of the 240 outstanding shares of common stock in
the Bliss Laundry and Dry Cleaning Service, Ltd. The other shares
are held in trusts for his children by a prior marriage. Both corporations have only issued common stock. All of Frank's assets are
noncommunity property. At present Frank's estate consists of the
following assets:

Cash, notes, and securities	$295,000
Residence	150,000
Life insurance (face amount)	250,000
(present value is $25,000)	

Automobiles and other tangible	
personal property	75,000
60 shares Bliss Diaper Service Company	
(total value of corporation is $300,000)	180,000
180 shares Bliss Laundry and	
Dry Cleaning Service, Ltd.	
(total value of corporation is $400,000)	300,000

Frank and Myra have made no taxable gifts and live in a state that imposes only a pick up tax equal to the amount of the estate tax credit allowable under §2011. Under Frank's present estate plan Myra will receive the tangible personal property, the residence, and the insurance outright. The remainder of Frank's assets will pass to the trust for his children after the payment of all expenses and taxes incurred by reason of his death. If Frank dies this year, how much of Frank's stock could be redeemed under §303 if the only expenses incurred upon his death were funeral and administration expenses of $50,000 allowable as deductions under §2053? What changes in the ownership and organization of Frank's property could be made in order to increase the probability that the stock would qualify for redemption under §303? What change could be made that would permit Frank to give additional stock to the trust without giving up the right to redeem stock under §303? How would your answers differ if the stock and other assets listed above were the community property of Frank and Myra?

E.   PARTNERSHIP FREEZES

A partnership capital freeze, simply stated, is nothing more than the creation of a new partnership, or a restructuring of an existing partnership, that results in at least two classes of partnership interest. A "regular partnership interest" is similar to that well understood by those dealing with a normal type of partnership in its typical structure, i.e., a pro rata sharing of income (including loss and capital) or any other allowable allocation and derivation thereof. A "frozen partnership interest," on the other hand, is substantially different in that it will have a fixed liquidation value and will carry a preferred income distribution position. In many respects the "frozen partnership interest" is comparable to the senior position of preferred stock in corporate equity ownership. Abbin, The Partnership Capital Freeze — An Alternative to Corporate Recapitalization, U. Miami 13th Inst. Est. Plan. §1801.1 (1979).

§11.22.   *General*

Partnerships with more than one type of capital interest (multi-class partnerships), such as limited partnerships, are used for a wide variety of business purposes and have figured prominently in tax shelter programs. Interest has grown in recent years in achieving an estate freeze through the use of a multi-class partnership instead of a corporation with more than one class of stock. Partnership freezes and recapitalizations are generally designed to cap the value of the senior family member's estate, to assure him or her of a steady flow of income, and to shift some of the income from the business to other family members. The senior family member may be entitled to a fixed basic payment and a participation in additional profits, which provides some protection against inflation. A partnership freeze or a recapitalization often involves a substantial gift to other family members. However, the transaction is better insulated from adverse estate tax consequences if there is no gift element. In either case the senior family member whose interest is being frozen can retain effective control of the business, but the estate tax risk of doing so is somewhat greater in the case of family partnerships. Overall, partnerships are often considered to be more attractive because of their greater flexibility and freedom from some of the income tax complications that plague corporations.

Suitable Assets. A multi-class partnership is a useful vehicle for the management and disposition of interests in assets that are likely to appreciate substantially in value (*e.g.,* improved real property or a family farm). As a rule the assets should generate sufficient income to support the fixed payout on the frozen interest. A partnership is less suitable for some other types of assets. For example, the overall limited liability of the corporate form may be critically important where the business involves risks that could exceed insurance limits (*e.g.,* manufacture or transportation of toxic substances).

Advantages. Some planners and clients are attracted to the partnership form because of its perceived income tax advantages over corporations. The advantages are largely traceable to the fact that a partnership, unlike a corporation, is not a taxpaying entity. Instead, a partnership is a conduit through which the income flows to the partners currently. §701. Accordingly, there is no risk of the double taxation of income that may occur in the case of a corporation unless a Subchapter S election is in effect. Note in this connection that a Subchapter S election cannot be made with respect to a corporation with more than one class of stock. On the other hand, as a result of the flow-through characteristic of a partnership, the taxpayers have less control over the time the partnership's income is taxed to them. Also, a partnership is not subject to the special taxes on personal holding company income (§§541 to 547) and on the unreasonable accumulation of earnings (§531 to 537). Finally, partnership interests are not subject to the taint that attaches to some corporate stock by reason of §§305 and 306.

Tax Uncertainties. On the negative side, the use of a family partnership freeze involves some tax risks because of the lack of certainty regarding the application of some income, gift, and estate tax rules. A multi-class partnership might be treated as an association taxable as a corporation under Reg. §301.7701-2, but the risk is slight and can be virtually eliminated by carefully drafting the partnership agreement. *See* Phillip G. Larson, 66 T.C. 159 (1976), *acq.*, 1979-1 C.B. 1; Zuckman v. United States, 524 F.2d 729 (Ct. Cl. 1975). (Under the cited regulation a business is treated as an association taxable as a corporation if it possesses a majority of these 4 characteristics: (1) continuity of life, (2) centralization of management, (3) limited liability, and (4) free transferability of interest.) There is also some uncertainty regarding the application of the family partnership rules of §704(e) to a multi-class partnership.

The uncertainty regarding the application of §§2036 and 2038 to the senior family member's estate is particularly troubling. For example, under what circumstances will the income rights of the frozen interest be treated as a retained income interest in the contributed property under §2036(a)(1)? It is also unclear the extent to which controls held by the senior family member over the affairs of the partnership might subject the transferred property to inclusion in his or her estate under §§2036(a)(2) or 2038. However, the estate tax risks are reduced if the interests are properly valued at the time the partnership is formed (or restructured), the partnership agreement is carefully planned and drafted, and the terms of the agreement are followed by the parties.

Valuation Problems and Costs. The proper valuation of the assets contributed to the partnership and of the frozen interest is essential to the success of the plan, particularly if the formation of the partnership (or its restructuring) is intended to avoid gifts by the senior family members. If no gifts are involved, the potential estate tax problems under §§2035 to 2038 are eliminated. As in the case of a recapitalization, the services of an expert appraiser in fixing values are indispensible. However, the cost of an expert in addition to the lawyer's fees and other expenses of a partnership freeze may be too much for the client: "But professional appraisors are expensive so the cost of achieving success is high. Often the size of the transaction or the antipathy of the client will preclude the services of the professional, and the valuation (and the planner's ability to prove it) are left in doubt." Scheifly, Partnership Recapitalization: Achieving a Capital Freeze, U. So. Cal. 32d Tax Inst. §511.8 (1980).

Ethical Considerations. The interests of the parties to a partnership freeze are sufficiently divergent that a single planner should not represent all of them. The planner who represents the party who initiates the plan, usually the senior family member, should recommend that the other parties retain independent counsel. The use of independent counsel relieves the conflict-of-interest problem and the potential for future disputes and litigation. While additional counsel may increase the initial cost, they provide valuable protection and may also make valuable contributions to the development of plans for the partnership.

Scrutiny by the IRS. Family partnerships are subject to close scrutiny by the IRS for income and transfer tax purposes because of their potential for abuse. The concern of the IRS is reflected in the following passage from the income tax regulations dealing with the reality of a family member's partnership interest (Reg. §1.704-1(e)(iii)):

> A donee or purchaser of a capital interest in a partnership is not recognized as a partner under the principles of section 704(e)(1) unless such interest is acquired in a bona fide transaction, not a mere sham for tax avoidance or evasion purposes, and the donee or purchaser is the real owner of such interest. To be recognized, a transfer must vest dominion and control of the partnership interest in the transferee. The existence of such dominion and control in the donee is to be determined from all the facts and circumstances. A transfer is not recognized if the transferor retains such incidents of ownership that the transferee has not acquired full and complete ownership of the partnership interest. Transactions between members of a family will be closely scrutinized, and the circumstances, not only at the time of the purported transfer but also during the periods preceding and following it will be taken into consideration in determining the bona fides of the purported gift or sale.

§11.23. Creation of Multi-Class Partnership Is Not a Taxable Event

A multi-class partnership can usually be formed or an existing partnership restructured without the imposition of any income tax liability. The contribution of property to a partnership in exchange for a partnership interest is not a taxable event. §721. Instead, the partner has a basis in the partnership interest equal to the amount of money and the basis of other property that he or she contributed to the partnership. §722. Consistently, the partnership takes a carryover basis in the contributed property. §723. The distinction between a partner's basis in his or her partnership interest and the partnership's basis in the property it owns is particularly important in post-mortem planning. Upon the death of a partner the value of his or her partnership interest is adjusted under §1014, but the basis of the partnership property is unaffected unless a timely election is made under §754. *See* §12.7, *infra.*

An existing partnership may be restructured to create preferred and regular capital interests without the imposition of any tax. In LR 7948063 the IRS held that:

> The conversion of the general partnership into a limited partnership will not constitute a sale or exchange of a partnership interest by any of the partners. No gain or loss will be recognized in connection with the conversion except to the extent that any decrease in a partner's share of the liabilities of the partnership, or any decrease in a partner's individual liabilities by reason of assumption by the partnership of such liabilities, exceeds the adjusted basis of the partner's interest in the partnership.

Thus, some partners may exchange their general interests for limited interests, while other partners retain their general interests.

Under some circumstances the exchange of an interest in one partnership for an interest in another partnership is not a taxable event. The Tax Court has held that a general interest in one partnership may be exchanged tax free under §1031 for a general interest in another partnership where the underlying assets of the partnerships are of like kind. Arthur E. Long, 77 T.C. 1045 (1981); *contra,* Rev. Rul. 78-135, 1978-1 C.B. 256. In contrast, a general interest in one partnership cannot be exchanged tax free for a limited partnership interest in another partnership (*i.e.,* the 2 interests are not of like kind as required by §1031). Estate of Rollin E. Meyer, Sr., 58 T.C. 311 (1972), *nonacq.,* 1975-1 C.B. 3, *aff'd per curiam,* 503 F.2d 556 (9th Cir. 1974).

§11.24. *Family Partnership Rules*

The family partnership rules of §704(e) should be borne in mind in structuring a family partnership freeze. The basic rules are relatively simple, but some uncertainties remain regarding their application.

Since 1951 the income tax law has provided for the recognition of family partnerships in which capital is a material income-producing factor. §704(e)(1). Prior to that time the law was quite confused and family partnerships were often disregarded as mere assignments of income. If capital is not a material income-producing factor, the partnership may be disregarded and the "income taxed to the person who earns it through his own labor and skill and the utilization of his own capital." Reg. §1.704-1(e)(1)(i).

> **Example 11-10.** X, who receives substantial fees for lecturing on inner peace and self-fulfillment, formed a partnership with his 2

minor children, A and B. X contributed a nominal amount of capital to the partnership on behalf of A and B. In exchange A, B, and X each received an equal one-third interest in the partnership. The interests of A and B are held by an independent guardian. The partnership assumed the responsibility of booking X's lectures, received the lecture fees, paid X a fixed amount (usually one-half of the total fee), and divided the balance of the income equally between A, B, and X. Under the circumstances capital is not a material income-producing factor for the partnership. Accordingly, the partnership would be disregarded under §704(e)(1) and all of the income would be taxed to X, whose personal services generated all of the income.

Capital as a Material Income-Producing Factor. Under the current regulations capital constitutes a material income-producing factor if "a substantial portion of the gross income of the business is attributable to the employment of capital in the business conducted by the partnership. In general, capital is not a material income-producing factor where the income of the business consists principally of fees, commissions, or other compensation for personal services performed by members or employees of the partnership." Reg. §1.704-1(e)(1)(iv). Of course, even where capital is a material income-producing factor, a family member is not recognized as a partner "unless such interest is acquired in a bona fide transaction, not a mere sham for tax avoidance or evasion purposes, and the donee or purchaser is the real owner of such interest." Reg. §1.704-1(e)(1)(iii).

Trustees and Minors as Partners. A trustee who is unrelated to and independent of the grantor is usually recognized as legal owner of the partnership interests that are held in trust. Reg. §1.704-1(e)(2)(vii). Where the grantor is trustee or the trustee is amenable to the will of the grantor, all of the circumstances will be taken into account in determining whether or not to recognize the trustee as legal owner of the interest. In such a case the trustee will be recognized as a partner only if the trustee actively represents the interests of the beneficiaries in accordance with the obligations of a fiduciary and does not subordinate their interests to those of the grantor. Overall, it is most desirable to have an independent trustee, such as a bank or trust company.

A minor child who is competent to manage his or her own property will be recognized as a partner. Under the regulations a minor is competent if he or she has "sufficient maturity and experience to be treated by disinterested persons as competent to enter business dealings and otherwise to conduct his [or her] affairs on a basis of equality with adult persons, nonwithstanding legal disabilities of the minor under State Law." Reg. §1.704-1(e)(2)(viii). If the minor does not satisfy that test, he or she generally will not be recognized as a partner unless the partnership interest is controlled by another person as fiduciary for the sole benefit of the minor, subject to judicial supervision. An independent guardian would suffice for this purpose. All things considered, a trust is preferable to a guardianship.

Allocation of Income. The allocation of income made in the partnership agreement generally controls for income tax purposes. However, where a partnership interest is acquired by gift the allocation is respected only where the donor partner is allocated reasonable compensation for services he or she renders to the partnership and the share of the income allocated to the donated capital of the donee is not proportionately greater than the share of the income allocated to the donor's capital. §704(e)(2). For purposes of this rule, an interest purchased from a family member is treated as having been acquired by gift. §704(e)(3). An individual's family includes "his spouse, ancestors, and lineal descendants, and any trusts for the primary benefit of such persons." *Id.* Thus, the income allocation cannot initially be structured in a way that unduly favors a partner who is a family member. However, the regulations permit the allocation to take into account the fact that "a general partner, unlike a limited partner risks his credit in the partnership business." Reg. §1.704-1(e)(3)(C). In light of the recognition of the differences in their interests, presumably the income share of the donee general partners can be allowed to grow if the partnership prospers without any increase in the share of the senior limited partner. Note also that the income tax rules of §704(e) do not bar the allocation of future appreciation in value of the partnership property to a donee partner. Such an allocation is, of course, the raison d'être of the partnership freeze.

Retained Control by Donor. The family partnership rules allow the donor to retain controls over the business that are "common in ordinary business relationships" provided the donee "is free to liquidate his interest at his discretion without financial detriment." Reg. §1.704-1(e)(2)(ii)(d). However, the donor may not retain undue control over the distribution of income. In addition, the donor may not retain control over assets that are essential to the business. Thus, the donor may not retain assets that are required for the conduct of the business and lease them to the partnership. The regulations also point out that consideration will be given to the existence of controls that may be exercised indirectly through a separate business organization, estate, trust, individual, or other partnership. Reg. §1.704-1(e)(2)(iii). The estate tax problems generated under §§2036(a)(2) and 2038 by the retention of control over the partnership are discussed in the next section.

§11.25. Planning the Frozen Partnership Interest

The creation of a multi-class family partnership requires decisions regarding the structuring of capital interests, rights to income, and management of the partnership. The allocation of capital in large measure determines the extent to which the creation of the partnership involves gifts to the junior members. For example, a gift obviously occurs if the senior family member contributes $500,000 to the partnership, of which $300,000 is allocated to his or her capital account and $100,000 is allocated to the capital account of each of his or her children. In such a case presumably the interests given to the children would qualify for the annual exclusion if they are individually transferable or are entitled to current income distributions. If the interests are not transferable and do not receive any current income, perhaps no annual exclusion is allowable. In this connection see Berzon v. Commissioner, 534 F.2d 528 (2d Cir. 1976), which did not allow an annual exclusion for gift of stock in trust where the trustee could not freely dispose of the stock and it had paid no dividends for 5 years. Some planners have suggested that the creation of the partnership would be "cleaner" if the gifts to the junior family members preceded the formation of the partnership. Others have questioned what the outcome would be if the capital contribution of the junior family members were financed by an interest-free loan from the senior. Fiore, Dual Capital Partnerships as an Estate Planning Device, N.Y.U. 39th Inst. Fed. Tax. ¶54.05[1] (1981).

Liquidation Preference. The value of the senior's interest and the presence or absence of a gift are also affected by the extent of his or her right to a liquidation preference upon withdrawal from, or termination of, the partnership. The amount of the liquidation preference and, hence, its "frozen" value, is usually equal to or less than the amount of the capital allocated to the senior. The value of the frozen interest is also affected by the extent to which it is protected by the net worth of the partnership assets in excess of the amount of the preference. In order to function properly the interest should be frozen regardless of the gains or losses of the business. As one commentator pointed out, "If the segregated interest bears its share of losses and depreciation, but is restricted from sharing in gain and appreciation, there has likely been no 'freeze,' but merely an assignment of income (not losses) as such income is realized." Scheifly, Partnership Recapitalization: Achieving a Capital Freeze, U. So. Cal. 32d Tax. Inst. ¶503.3 (1980).

Income Interest. The provisions of the agreement regarding the payment of income also affect the valuation of the frozen interest. A frozen interest is usually entitled either to a fixed annual paynᴛent regardless of the income of the partnership (a guaranteed payment) or to a fixed annual payment out of the profits of the partnership. Under §707(c) a guaranteed payment is ordinary income to the payee and is deductible by the payor partners. A payment to be made only out of the profits of the partnership may be cumulative or noncumulative, which will also have an impact on the valuation of the frozen interest. In deciding between the 2 approaches the parties must consider the sufficiency of the income and other resources of the partnership to support the payments and expenses of operating the partnership.

The creation of the multi-class partnership may involve a gift if the frozen interest is not entitled to a sufficient portion of the partnership's income. A gift may occur, for example, where the income currently generated by the property contributed to the partnership by the senior family member exceeds the income allocable to his or her frozen interest. In such a case the value of the frozen interest may not be established by its liquidation preference alone. On the other hand, a serious retained income problem may arise under §2036(a)(1) if the frozen interest is entitled to all or substantially all of the income from the contributed property. For example, where the decedent was entitled to substantially all of the income from the farm under an agreement with the limited partners, who received their interests from the decedent by gift, the IRS ruled that the entire value of the farm was includible in the decedent's estate under §2036. LR 7824005.

The frozen interest should also carry the right to participate in some partnership income in addition to the fixed amount. This approach is suggested because one of the indicia of a partnership is the sharing of profits. There is some risk that a person who is only entitled to a fixed amount each year regardless of the amount of the partnership's profits or losses (*i.e.*, there is no sharing of profits) would not be recognized as a partner. W. McKee, W. Nelson & R. Whitmire, Federal Taxation of Partnerships & Partners §3.02[5] (1978). The transfer of property to the partnership by such person in exchange for interests in the partnership's income and capital might constitute a taxable event. Nelson, The Partnership Capital Freeze: A Precis, 15 Real Prop., Prob. & Tr. J. 99, 104 (1980).

Management and Control. The retention of control by the senior family member must be carefully considered in light of tax and nontax considerations. The senior typically wishes to participate in the business as a limited partner in order to enjoy limited liability. However, under §7 of the Uniform Limited Partnership Act the limited liability is lost by a partner who participates in control of the business. 6 U.L.A. 582 (1969). Section 303 of the Revised Limited Partnership Act is to the same effect, but enumerates some specific actions that a limited partner can take without losing that status. 6 U.L.A. 160-161 (1981 Supp.). Because of the unlimited liability of a regular partner the senior may not wish to hold a regular interest, however slight.

In order to avoid adverse income tax consequences the donor's retained controls should be drafted in light of the family partnership rules. *See* §11.24, *supra*.

Where the formation of the partnership involves a gift, consideration must also be given to the potential inclusion of the gifted interests under §§2036(a)(2) and 2038. In light of United States v. Byrum, 408 U.S. 125 (1972), the retention of controls consistent with ordinary business practices should not require inclusion of the partnership interests held by others. On the other hand, inclusion may result where the donor retains controls over the donee's use and enjoyment of the interest. "[I]f the donor's power (either as a sole general partner or as one of several general partners) goes beyond these normal business powers, and extends to such matters as the power to restrict withdrawal of profits in excess of those reinvested, it seems clear that the donee's interest will be includible in the donor's estate, and the entire plan will have failed." Scheifly, Partnership Recapitalization: Achieving a Capital Freeze, U. So. Cal. 32d Tax Inst. ¶510.2 (1980).

F.   DEFERRAL OF ESTATE TAX UNDER §6166

§11.26.   *Overview*

Congress is sensitive to the problems of generating funds to pay estate settlement costs where an interest in a closely held trade or business is the principal asset of the estate. Until 1977 the ability to defer payment of the estate tax attributable to an interest in a closely held business was governed by §6166. The 1976 Act amended that section slightly, redesignated it §6166A, and added more favorable deferral rules under a new §6166, which imposed stricter tests. In 1981 Congress repealed §6166A (the original §6166) and liberalized the rules of the "new" §6166. Accordingly, §6166 is now the only section that applies in such cases.

While it was in effect, §6166A allowed an executor to elect to pay the estate tax attributable to an interest in a farm or other closely held business interest in equal annual installments over a period of not more than 10 years. Interest on the entire amount of the deferred tax is determined under the floating rate provided for in §6621. However, deferral under §6166A was available only if the value of the business interest exceeded 35% of the value of the decedent's gross estate or 50%

of the value of his or her taxable estate. §6166A(a). For this purpose, a closely held business included a proprietorship and certain partnership and corporate interests.

As noted above, the 1976 Act added §6166, which permitted a 15-year extension of the time within which to pay the tax attributable to a closely held business interest where it amounted to more than 65% of the decedent's gross estate less the deductions allowable under §§2053 and 2054 (expenses of administration, debts, and losses). §6166(a). It allowed an executor to elect to postpone making any payment on the principal amount of the tax for 5 years from the due date of the estate tax return, after which the estate tax was payable in equal annual installments over a period of not more than 10 years. However, annual interest payments were required under §6166 beginning the first year after the return is filed. Deferral under this provision was particularly attractive because interest is charged at only 4% on the tax imposed on the first $1 million in value of the decedent's interest in the business. §6601(j); see §11.30, infra. The balance is subject to the rate that is adjusted annually as provided in §6621.

Extensions under §§6166 and 6166A terminated and the time for payment of the tax may be accelerated if an installment was not paid when due. See §11.31, infra. Prior to 1982 acceleration would have taken place if withdrawals from the business equaled or exceeded one-third (one-half under §6166A), or when there was a disposition of one-third or more, of the decedent's interest in the business (one-half under §6166A). A limited acceleration also occurred if the estate has undistributed net income in any year after the first principal payment is due (§6166) or in any year after its fourth taxable year (§6166A).

Funds with which to pay the deferred tax were often generated by redemptions of the stock that was included in the decedent's estate. However, prior to 1982, planning the redemptions was unnecessarily complicated because the provisions of the deferral sections and of §303 were not coordinated. The pre-1982 alternatives are well described and explained in Fleming, Funding Estate Tax Installment Payments With Section 303 Redemptions After the 1976 Tax Reform Act, 4 J. Corp. Tax. 22 (1977).

Planning was greatly simplified by the 1981 Act that repealed §6166A and liberalized and coordinated the provisions of §§303 and 6166. Most significant, the 1981 Act reduced the percentage tests of §§303 and 6166 to the same amount, 35% of the decedent's gross estate less deductions allowable under §§2053 and 2054. §6166(a). In addition, both §§303 and 6166 were amended to allow the decedent's stock in 2 or more corporations to be aggregated for the purpose of satisfying the percentage test if his or her estate includes 20% or more of the value of each corporation. See §11.16, supra. Under the prior rule aggregation was allowed only if the decedent's stock amounted to *more* than 20% of the value of each corporation. Finally, the Act liberalized several of the acceleration provisions of §6166(g). Most important was the increase from one-third to one-half in the amount of stock that could be disposed of, or the amount that could be withdrawn from the business, without accelerating the time for payment of the tax. *See* §11.31, *infra.*

§11.27. *Closely Held Business*

The definition of the term "closely held business" is the same under §6166 and former §6166A except for differences in the maximum number of partners and shareholders. The interest of a proprietor in a trade or business carried on as a proprietorship qualifies. §§6166(b)(1)(A), 6166A(c)(1). A partner's interest also qualifies if 20% or more of the capital interest in the partnership is included in the decedent's gross estate or there is a limited number of partners (15 for purposes of §6166 and 10 for purposes of former §6166A). §§6166(b)(1)(B), 6166A(c)(2). Similarly, stock in a corporation engaged in a trade or business qualifies if 20% or more of the voting interest in the corporation is included in the decedent's gross estate or there is a limited number of shareholders (15 for purposes of §6166 and 10 for purposes of §6166A). §§6166(b)(1)(C), 6166A(c)(3). Under both sections the determinations are made as of the time immediately before the decedent's death. The limits should be borne in mind in planning the capital structure of a new enterprise or changes in existing ones (*e.g.,* mergers, recapitalizations, and the restructuring of partnerships).

Who Is Counted as a Partner or Shareholder. Stock or partnership interests held by a husband and wife as community property or as co-tenants (joint tenants, tenants in common, or tenants by the entirety) is considered to be owned by only one person. §6166(b)(2)(B). The provision of §6166 regarding interests coowned by a husband and wife seems superfluous. Under a separate, broader provision, "All stock and all partnership interests held by the decedent or by any member of his family (within the meaning of section 267(c)(4)) shall be treated as owned by the decedent." §6166(b)(2)(D). As a result of this provision presumably none of the decedent's spouse, siblings, ancestors, or descendants would be counted as separate shareholders or partners.

Under §6166(b)(2)(C) each person who holds an interest in a corporation, partnership, trust, or estate is considered to own a proportionate interest in the property it owns. Thus, the number of partners or shareholders is not reduced by transferring interests to a trust or other entity.

Example 11-11. W and her husband, H, hold stock in XYZ, Inc., as joint tenants. There are 14 other unrelated shareholders, including a trust of which there are 5 current income beneficiaries. For purposes of §6166 H and W are considered to be one shareholder;

however, each of the beneficiaries of the trust is considered to be a shareholder. Thus, XYZ, Inc. has 20 shareholders.

According to the staff report this provision was included to prevent avoidance of the shareholder and partner limits by the use of partnerships, trusts, and tiers of corporations. General Explanation of the 1976 Act 548.

Trade or Business. Deferral is available only for interests of a proprietor, partner, or stockholder in a "trade or business." §§6166(b)(1). Several Revenue Rulings that were issued regarding §6166A during the time it was designated as §6166 indicate that the trade or business must be an active one in order to qualify for deferral. By way of illustration, a farming, manufacturing, or service enterprise is a trade or business for this purpose, but a collection of investment assets (as in a holding company) is not. "[S]ection 6166 was intended to apply only with regard to a business such as a manufacturing, mercantile, or service enterprise, as distinguished from management of investment assets." Rev. Rul. 75-365, 1975-2 C.B. 471. However, farm real estate constitutes a trade or business where it is operated by tenant farmers under rental agreements whereby the decedent receives a portion of the rental and bears a portion of the expenses and participates in management decisions. Rev. Rul. 75-366, 1975-2 C.B. 472. Real estate development and sales also qualify as a trade or business. Rev. Rul. 75-367, 1975-2 C.B. 472. *See also* Rev. Rul. 61-55, 1961-1 C.B. 713 (ownership, exploration, development, and operation of oil and gas properties was a trade or business, but mere ownership of royalty interests was not). However, the rental of real estate to children in exchange for their agreement to pay taxes and other expenses of the property does not qualify as a trade or business. LR 8020101.

The qualification of an interest in a holding company is uncertain. On the one hand, the holding company itself is probably not engaged in an active trade or business. However, the interest might qualify as a trade or business under §6166 if the companies in which the holding company owned interests were operating companies. That is, the rule of §6166(b)(2)(C), which treats the property of a corporation as being owned proportionately by its shareholders, might be applicable here too. Thus, if the decedent owned 50% of the stock of a holding company, perhaps the decedent would be treated as owning one-half of its assets, including its interests in the active trades or businesses.

§11.28.   Qualification under §6166

Deferral may be made under §6166 only where the value of the closely held interest exceeds 35% of the decedent's adjusted gross estate. In this context the term "adjusted gross estate" means the gross estate reduced by the deductions allowable under §§2053 and 2054 (funeral and administration expenses, debts, and losses). §6166(b)(6). The amount of those items is taken into account whether or not they are claimed as deductions on the federal estate tax return.

The estate's ability to meet the 35% requirement is, of course, affected by the inclusion of assets in the estate and the estate tax valuation of assets. §6166(b)(4). Accordingly, the executor must carefully consider decisions that affect the inclusion of assets (*e.g.,* §2039(f)) and the valuation of assets, including the use of the alternate valuation and special use valuation methods. The latter method allows the value of "qualified real property" to be reduced by as much as $700,000 for decedents dying in 1982 and $750,000 for decedents dying in 1983 or thereafter. In general an election may be made to value qualified real property under §2032A where the real and personal property used in the business constitute 50% or more of the adjusted value of the gross estate and the qualified real property constitutes 25% or more of the adjusted value of the gross estate. Because of the requirements of §6166 an executor should not make an election under §2032A without first determining whether it will prevent the estate from satisfying the 35% test.

As noted above, interests held by the decedent in 2 or more businesses may be aggregated if 20% or more in value of each is included in his or her gross estate. §6166(c). For this purpose the surviving spouse's interest in property held as community property, joint tenants, tenants by the entirety, or as tenants in common is treated as included in the decedent's gross estate.

> **Example 11-12.** H's gross estate had a value of $2,000,000 including his interest in the stock of Corporations One and Two. The funeral and administration expenses, debts, and other deductions allowable under §§2053 and 2054 came to a total of $100,000. H and W owned 25% of the stock of Corporation One as joint tenants, which was worth $900,000 of the corporation's total value of $4,000,000. H and W also owned 30% of Corporation Two as joint tenants, which was worth $600,000 of the corporation's total value of $2,800,000. The stocks constituted qualified joint interests under §2040(b), as a result of which only one-half of their value was includible in H's gross estate. The entire percentage interest of H and W in the stock of both corporations is considered to be owned by H for purposes of satisfying the 20% limit. As a result, the value of H's one-half interests in Corporation One ($450,000) and Corporation Two ($300,000) may be aggregated. Because their total value ($750,000) exceeds 35% of H's adjusted gross estate ($1,900,000), the tax attributable to H's interest in the 2 corporations may be deferred under §6166.

§11.29.   Making a §6166 Election

The election must be made no later than the time the estate tax return is required to be filed, taking into account any extensions of time that are granted for filing the return. §6166(d). Under Reg. §20.6166-1(a), "If it is made at the time the estate tax return is filed, the election is applicable both to the tax originally determined to be due and to certain deficiencies. If no election is made when the estate tax return is filed, up to the full amount of certain later deficiencies (but not any tax originally determined to be due) may be paid in installments." The election must contain (1) the decedent's name and taxpayer identification number; (2) the amount of tax to be paid in installments; (3) the date for payment of the first installment; (4) the number of installments in which the tax is to be paid; (5) the properties shown on the estate tax return that constitute the closely held business; and (6) the facts that form the basis of the executor's conclusion that the estate qualifies for payment of the tax in installments. Reg. §20.6166-1(b).

Although an estate does not appear to satisfy the requirements of §6166 when the return is filed, the executor may file a protective election to defer payment of any portion of the tax remaining unpaid at the time values are finally determined and any deficiencies that are attributable to the closely held business. "A protective election is made by filing a notice of election with a timely filed estate tax return stating that the election is being made." Reg. §20.6166-1(d). Under the pre-1982 law, the executor could also file a protective election under §6166A against the possibility that the requirements of §6166 might not be met when the values were finally determined.

§11.30.   Installment Payments under §6166

Under §6166(a)(2), the maximum amount of the estate tax that can be paid in installments is determined by the ratio of the value of the closely held business to the adjusted gross estate. Again, for purposes of §6166 the term "adjusted gross estate" means the gross estate reduced by the amount of deductions allowable under §§2053 and 2054. §6166(b)(6). The tax may be paid in from 2 to 10 equal annual installments, the first of which is due 5 years after the date on which the federal estate tax was due to be paid. §6166(a)(3).

If the executor elects to take advantage of the maximum deferral, only interest is paid for 4 years following the date on which the estate tax was due to be paid. §6166(f)(1). Interest and principal payments are due in each of the following years until all of the installment payments have been made. A preferential 4% interest rate applies to the tax on the first

$1 million of the value of the business ($345,800) less the amount of the unified credit applicable to the decedent's estate. §6601(j). The balance is subject to the floating rate that is adjusted each year in accordance with §6621. Each principal payment reduces proportionally the amounts that are subject to the 2 interest rates. Specifically, each principal payment reduces the portion of the tax that is subject to the 4% rate by an amount that bears the same ratio to the amount of the principal payment as the original amount of the 4% portion bears to the total amount of tax deferred under §6166. A formula puts it more concisely:

$$\begin{array}{c} \text{Amount of} \\ \text{installment payment} \\ \text{of tax} \end{array} \times \frac{\begin{array}{c}\text{Amount subject} \\ \text{to 4\% rate}\end{array}}{\begin{array}{c}\text{Total amount of} \\ \text{tax deferred}\end{array}} = \begin{array}{c} \text{Annual reduction} \\ \text{in 4\%} \\ \text{portion} \end{array}$$

§11.31. Acceleration under §6166(g)

The deferral election is terminated and the date for payment of the tax is accelerated under the circumstances enumerated in §6166(g). Acceleration occurs if one-half or more in value of the decedent's interest in the business is redeemed, sold, exchanged, or otherwise disposed of. Thus, the sale of a decedent's interest in a closely held business pursuant to a buy-sell agreement would accelerate the time for payment of the tax. However, acceleration does not occur as a result of certain dispositions. Corporate reorganizations and tax-free exchanges are exempted by §6166(g)(1)(C). A liquidation under §331 after which the same business is continued by a partnership in which the estate and other parties will have the same proportionate interest as before does not constitute a disposition or withdrawal of assets. LR 8103066. A transfer of property to a person entitled to receive it by reason of the decedent's will, the law of intestate succession, or a trust created by the decedent is also exempt. §6166(g)(1)(D). Finally, a transfer by reason of the subsequent death of a person who received the property from the decedent (or a transferee of such person) is also exempt, provided that each transferee is a family member (within the meaning of §267(c)(4)) of the transferor. Id.

The time for payment of the tax is also accelerated if withdrawals of money and other property from the business equal or exceed one-half of its value. In either case, a redemption that qualifies under §303 is not counted for purposes of the one-half rule if an amount equal to the redemption distribution is paid on the remaining balance of the estate tax within one year of the distribution. Instead, the amount of the redemption reduces the base against which the one-half is calculated.

Example 11-13. D's adjusted gross estate had a value of $3,100,000 upon which a net estate tax of $1,000,000 was due after giving effect to all allowable credits. D's interest in a closely held corporation was worth $2,100,000 or about 67.75% of D's adjusted gross estate. Pursuant to an election made by D's executor, the time for payment of $677,500 of the tax was deferred under §6166. Under §6166(g) time for payment of the tax would be accelerated if one-half or more in value of the stock were redeemed, sold, exchanged, or otherwise disposed of. Thus, the estate could not redeem or dispose of $1,050,000 of D's stock unless some payments were made on the estate tax liability. However, amounts received in a distribution that met the requirements of §303 are not counted if they are applied in payment of the tax. Thus, if $300,000 of D's stock were redeemed under §303 and the proceeds were applied in payment of the tax, the amount of the redemption would not be counted toward the one-half limit. Instead, the base for computing the one-half limit would be reduced from $2,100,000 to $1,800,000. In effect the withdrawal and application of funds in payment of the principal amount of the tax only causes a one-half reduction in the amount that can be withdrawn without restriction as to its use.

If the estate has undistributed net income for a taxable year ending on or after the date for payment of the first installment, the estate must pay an amount equal to the undistributed income toward the tax on or before the date the income tax return must be filed for the year. §6166(g)(2). Also, if any payment of principal or interest is not made on time, the unpaid portion of the tax must be paid upon notice and demand from the Secretary. §6166(g)(3). However, if the delinquent amount is paid within 6 months of the time it was due, acceleration does not occur. Instead, the preferential 4% rate does not apply to the payment and a penalty is imposed of 5% of the amount of the payment for each month the payment was late. §6166(g)(3)(B).

§11.32.   Worksheet for Making §6166 Calculations

Section 6166 Worksheet
(Fifteen-year deferral)
(For decedents dying after December 31, 1981)

Part I.   Qualifications
    1.   Gross estate (estimate or enter from
       Form 706, page 1, line 1, including
       the value of property transferred

within 3 years of death per
§2035(d)(3)) (item 1)   _____

2. *Less:* Deductions allowable under
   §§2053 and 2054, whether or not
   claimed on Form 706:
   a.   Debts, funeral and administrative
        expenses (allowable under §2053)   _____

   b.   Casualty losses (allowable under
        §2054)   _____

   Total (item 2)   − _____

3. Adjusted gross estate (item 1 less item 2)
   (item 3)   _____

4. Value of closely held business (a proprietorship, partnership, or corporation
   carrying on a trade or business in
   which decedent was one of 15 or
   fewer owners or in which decedent
   owned 20% or more of the capital
   interest. §6166(b). Two or more businesses may be aggregated if at least
   20% of the total value of each business is included in the shareholder's
   estate. §6166(c)). (item 4)   _____

5. Divide item 4 by item 3. (If the closely
   held business represents more than
   35% of the adjusted gross estate, item
   3, the requirements of §6166 are
   met.) (item 5)   _____

Part II.   Amount to be deferred
6. Net federal estate tax (estimate or enter
   from Form 706, line 19) (item 6)   _____

7. Enter percentage from item 5 above
   (item 7)   _____

8. Maximum deferrable amount (item 6 ×
   item 7) (item 8)   _____

9. Years over which payments to be made
   (2–10) (item 9)   _____

(The executor may elect to pay part or all of the amount of tax shown at item 9
in 2-10 equal installments, the first of which is due no more than 5 years after
the date prescribed for payment of the tax (9 months after death). Each succeeding installment is due one year after the preceding installment. §6166(a)(3).)

10.   Amount of annual principal install-
      ments (divide item 8 by item 9)
      (item 10)   _____

Part III.   Interest rates
    11.   Amount of tax deferred (item 8 above)
        (item 11)   _____

    12.   Amount subject to special 4% interest
        rate (not to exceed the larger of the
        amount of tax deferred under §6166,
        or $345,800 reduced by the amount
        of the unified credit). §6601(j)(2).
        (item 12)   _____

    13.   Amount subject to floating rate
        (item 13)   _____

Part IV.   Amount of payments years 1-4
    14.   Annual interest payments years 1-4:
           Item 12 × 4%   _____

           Item 13 × the floating rate   _____   _____

    15.   Total payments years 1-4 (item 14 × 4)   _____

Part V.   Payments in years 5-14
        Unless payments are accelerated voluntarily or involuntarily, the
        same amount of principal will be payable each year. (item 10) In
        addition, interest must be paid on the amount that remains de-
        ferred. Each principal payment reduces the amount subject to each
        interest rate by a proportionate amount. *See* §6601(j)(3).

Problem 11-3. The facts are the same as stated in Problem 11-2,
§11.21, *supra.* In addition, you have learned that each of the Bliss
corporations has 12 shareholders, including the employees and the
beneficiaries of the trust for Frank's children. Myra Bliss, the
executor of Frank's will and the trustee of the trust, has asked you
to tell her whether she can elect to pay some of the estate tax on
Frank's estate in installments. If so, she wants to know the maximum amount of tax that could be deferred, how long it could be
deferred, and the approximate amount of each installment payment. She would also like to know whether any of the funds derived from a §303 redemption of the estate's stock in Bliss Laundry
and Dry Cleaning Service, Ltd. must be used to pay the federal
estate tax. You should also tell her whether or not a redemption of
the maximum amount allowable under §303 would accelerate the
time for payment of the estate tax.

BIBLIOGRAPHY

I.   General discussions of planning for closely held corporations:
        Abbin, The Value-Capping Cafeteria — Selecting the Appro-
          priate Freeze Technique, U. Miami 15th Inst. Est. Plan., Ch.
          20 (1981)

Redemptions with Estate Tax Deferral, 53 J. Tax. 236 (1980)

Fleming, Funding Estate Tax Installment Payments with Section 303 Redemptions After the 1976 Tax Reform Act, 4 J. Corp. Tax. 22 (1977)

Fox, Options Available to a Corporation Acquiring Its Own Stock from Estate of Deceased Shareholder, 7 Est. Plan. 206 (1980)

Liebovitz, Sections 303, 6166 and 6166A: Liquidity Problems in the Payment of Death Taxes, N.Y.U. 38th Inst. Fed. Tax., Ch. 43 (1980)

Pinney, The Busy New Executors Under TRA-1976; Selected Problems Under I.R.C. Section 6166, U. So. Cal. 31st Tax Inst. 971 (1979)

CHAPTER 12

POST-MORTEM PLANNING

A. INTRODUCTION

§12.1. Scope and Organization

Post-mortem estate planning offers the lawyer challenging opportunities to minimize the overall tax costs incurred by reason of the decedent's death and to preserve the maximum amount of property for his or her beneficiaries. The plan adopted during a client's lifetime fixes the basic pattern for the disposition of his or her property at death. However, the tax consequences of the plan can vary substantially depending upon the post-mortem elections made, and other actions taken, by the executor. The executor may make elections regarding matters that range from the treatment of medical expense deductions on the decedent's final income tax return to the payment or deferral of the federal estate tax. Importantly, the distribution of property may be rearranged to a certain degree through the use of disclaimers and applications for family awards and allowances. A checklist of post-mortem matters is included at the end of the chapter (§12.43).

The chapter first reviews the opportunities that arise by reason of the executor's obligation to file a final income tax return for the decedent. §§12.3 to 12.6. Where the decedent leaves a surviving spouse, one of the most important matters to consider is whether the decedent's final income tax return should be a joint one filed with the surviving spouse. Other elections concern the use of medical expense deductions and the accrual of interest income. The decisions made regarding the decedent's final income tax return also have an impact on the income tax planning for his or her estate. That planning includes decisions that are very important to the estate and the beneficiaries, especially the choice of the estate's taxable year and the elections regarding expenses that may be claimed as deductions on the estate's income tax return, the estate tax return, or on both. §§12.7 to 12.16.

Decisions that directly affect the value of property includible in the estate are discussed in Part D, including the use of the alternate valuation method (§12.17) and the special use valuation of real property used in a farm or closely held business (§12.18). That part also covers the election that is available with respect to the treatment of qualified plan benefits (§12.21) and the effect of life insurance settlement options (§12.22).

Part E deals with devices by which the distribution of property may be reordered and reviews the use of family awards and allowances and the so-called widow's election (§§12.23 to 12.25). It concludes with a discussion of the law regarding disclaimers, including a section on planning for the use of disclaimers (§§12.26 to 12.29). The importance of disclaimers has grown substantially since the federal estate and gift tax treatment of disclaimers was clarified by the enactment of §2518 as a part of the 1976 Act.

The planning and income tax consequences of estate distributions are reviewed in Part F, §§12.30 to 12.34. If the distributions are carefully planned, the overall income tax burdens can often be lightened considerably. The part includes a discussion of the use of in kind distributions, which can be used to spread the estate's income among several taxpayers. In some cases an in kind distribution can be made in a way that gives the distributee an increased basis in property at no additional tax cost. The consequences of non-pro rata distributions of community property are also discussed in this part.

The final part is concerned with the payment of the federal estate tax, including the general rules regarding the allocation of the obligation to pay the tax. The various opportunities for deferring the tax are reviewed in §§12.37 to 12.40. The chapter concludes with sections that deal with the payment of the estate tax with "flower bonds" (§12.41), the

release of personal representatives from liability for federal taxes
(§12.42), and the checklist of post-mortem matters (§12.43).

§12.2.   Getting Off to a Good Start

It is very important to establish a good rapport with the personal representative and persons who are beneficially interested in the estate. The
lawyer's relationship with them is likely to be better if he or she provides
them with an adequate explanation of the steps that will be involved in
settling the estate and communicates with them regularly throughout
the administration of the estate. At the outset the lawyer should give the
personal representative a memorandum that outlines his or her duties,
reviews the important steps in the estate proceeding, and estimates the
state and federal death taxes that will be due. In appropriate cases
the memorandum should mention the possible use of disclaimers by the
beneficiaries of the estate. The memorandum or a contemporaneous
letter should outline the legal services that will be performed and repeat
the terms of their agreement regarding the amount and payment of the
lawyer's compensation.

At an early stage the lawyer should also prepare a projection of the
estate's cash needs and the time at which funds will be required for
payment of taxes, administration expenses, legacies, and other purposes.
The amount of some items such as cash legacies will be known, but
others, such as the amount of taxes, can only be estimated. If the decedent had an accountant or other financial advisor, the information and
the help he or she can provide should not be overlooked. In many cases
it is helpful if the personal representative retains the same person to
keep the books for the estate and to prepare or assist in preparing the
estate's fiduciary income tax returns and the estate tax return. His or her
help is useful even when the lawyer's office will keep the books and use its
computer to produce the necessary cash projections and accountings.
Once the cash projection is prepared, the personal representative, the
accountant, and the lawyer must consider the steps that should be taken
to raise the funds. In that connection they must take into account the tax
and nontax impact that each step will have on the estate and the beneficiaries. For example, the respective income tax brackets of the estate
and the beneficiaries should be taken into account in planning the tax
year the estate will use, how long the estate will remain open, and the
policies that should be adopted regarding sales and distributions. The
projection provides the factual base upon which many decisions are
made. Accordingly, it should be prepared with care and updated as
circumstances require. The parties should all recognize that it is only a
projection, which is only as reliable as the assumptions upon which it is
based (*e.g.*, amount of taxes, value of assets).

The lawyer should also counsel the personal representative regarding the filing of a notice of fiduciary relationship. Under §6903, a personal representative must file a notice of appointment as fiduciary. If the notice is filed, the IRS must communicate directly with the fiduciary regarding the tax liabilities of the decedent. In contrast, if the notice is not filed, the fiduciary may not receive direct notice of a deficiency assessed against the decedent. Many lawyers advise against filing the notice because it may trigger an audit of the decedent's income and gift tax returns and no penalty is imposed if the notice is not filed. Nevertheless, it is generally advisable to file the notice if the personal representative and the lawyer are not too familiar with the decedent's business affairs. The personal representative is also required to file a notice of qualification as fiduciary (§6036), which is satisfied by filing Form 56. Under the regulations a notice filed under §6036 constitutes a sufficient notice of fiduciary relationship under §6903. Reg. §301.6036-1(c). If a notice of qualification as fiduciary is filed, the lawyer should see that a notice of termination of fiduciary capacity is filed when the estate proceedings are concluded.

B. INCOME TAX

§12.3. The Decedent's Final Income Tax Return: General

A final income tax return must be filed for the period beginning with the first day of the decedent's taxable year and ending on the day of his or her death. §443(a)(2). The same rates and personal exemption apply although the final year is a short one (*i.e.*, less than 12 full months). The return for the final year must be made by the decedent's "executor, administrator, or other person charged with [his] property." §6012(b)(1). The due date for the final return is the same as if the decedent had lived through the entire taxable year. §6072(a); Reg. §1.6072-1(b). Thus, the final return for a calendar year taxpayer is due on April 15. In all other cases, the final return is due on the fifteenth day of the fourth month following the close of the decedent's regular taxable year. The return is filed with the district director, or the service center, for the district in which the personal representative resides or has his or her principal place of business. §6091(b)(1)(A); Reg. §1.6091-2(a)(1).

If the decedent died early in the year, it may be necessary for the personal representative to file an income tax return for the preceding year.

Example 12-1. X died on February 20, prior to filing an income tax return for the preceding calendar year. The return for that year must be filed by X's personal representative on or before April 15. The return for X's final, short taxable year (January 1–February 20) must be filed on or before April 15 of the following year.

The tax due with respect to a decedent's return must be paid when the return is due. However, the time for payment of the tax may be extended where payment would result in "undue hardship." §6161(a)(1). In contrast, a personal representative may elect to pay the income tax due with respect to an estate's return in 4 equal quarterly installments instead of a single payment, without the imposition of any penalty or interest. §6152(b)(1); Reg. §1.6152-1(b). *See* §12.8, *infra*.

§12.4.   The Decedent's Final Income Tax Return: Election to File a Joint Return

Under §6013(a)(2) a joint return may be filed for the decedent and his or her surviving spouse if the surviving spouse does not remarry before the end of the year and the length of the tax year of either has not been shortened by reason of a change of accounting period under §443(a)(1). A joint return for a decedent and his or her surviving spouse includes the income of the decedent through the date of death and the income of the surviving spouse for the entire taxable year. Reg. §1.6013-1(d)(1). Where a personal representative is appointed prior to the last day for filing the return, the joint return must be made by both the surviving spouse and the personal representative. §6013(a)(3). If no return has been filed for the decedent and no personal representative has been appointed, the surviving spouse may file a joint return. However, if the surviving spouse files such a joint return, a later-appointed personal representative for the decedent may disaffirm it within one year of the last day for filing the return. *Id.*

Advantages of a Joint Return. The principal tax advantage of filing a joint return is traceable to the favorable "split" rates that apply to joint returns. Of course, a surviving spouse may take advantage of those rates for 2 years following the decedent's death if the surviving spouse is supporting a dependent child or stepchild. The overall income tax liability will be reduced if a joint return is filed where the decedent received a large amount of income prior to death and the survivor received little or no income for the taxable year. A similar tax saving is available in the converse case (*i.e.*, where the decedent had little or no income, but the survivor received a large amount of income).

A joint return often allows the parties to make better use of the income tax deductions attributable to a decedent's final taxable year. In some cases the deductions, which cannot be carried over to the decedent's estate, would be wasted if a joint return weren't filed. For example, a decedent may have made charitable contributions prior to death that exceed the amount that is deductible when measured by the decedent's contribution base alone. If a joint return were filed, a larger charitable deduction would be allowable because the percentage limitations would be applied to a contribution base that includes the combined income of the decedent and the surviving spouse. If a joint return weren't filed, the excess charitable contribution would be wasted because it cannot be carried over and used by a deceased donor's estate. *See* Reg. §1.170A-10(d)(4)(iii). A like advantage of filing a joint return exists where the decedent realized a net capital loss in his or her final taxable year. The excess capital loss cannot be carried over to the decedent's estate, but if a joint return were filed, it could offset any capital gains realized by the surviving spouse during the taxable year, before or after the decedent's death. If the surviving spouse's income would not otherwise be sufficient to absorb the full amount of the deductions, the surviving spouse's income might be augmented by making distributions to the surviving spouse from the decedent's estate. Such distribution would carry out some of the estate's distributable net income to the surviving spouse. Of course, the distributions would be of assistance in this regard only if the estate's taxable year ended within the taxable year of the surviving spouse for which a joint return is being filed.

Problem 12-1. H died on January 31 of this year survived by his wife, W. Prior to H's death he suffered a deductible casualty loss of $100,000 and a long-term capital loss of $50,000. H did not realize any capital gains during the month he lived this year, but he did receive ordinary income of about $10,000. W expects to have an income of about $50,000 this year, apart from any income she will receive from H's estate. W has owned some securities for more than a year that have a current value of $40,000 over their bases. H's executor expects that H's estate will receive $60,000 or more of ordinary income by the end of November. Evaluate the desirability and consequences of filing a joint return for the decedent's final taxable year.

Disadvantages of Filing a Joint Return. The principal disadvantage of filing a joint return is the joint and several liability that attaches to the estate and the surviving spouse for the amount of taxes, interest, and penalties. §6013(d)(3). Thus, if a joint return is filed, the assets of the estate are liable for deficiencies and penalties attributable to the survivor's negligence or misconduct. This disadvantage is, of course, not present where the surviving spouse is the personal representative and the principal beneficiary of the decedent's estate. Under the "innocent spouse" provisions, the estate is not liable where it was unaware that the surviving spouse failed to report income that amounted to more than 25% of the amount of gross income reported on the joint return. §6013(e)(1).

§12.5.   The Decedent's Final Income Tax Return: Deduction of Medical Expenses

Under §213(a) individuals are allowed a deduction for income tax purposes of uncompensated medical expenses paid during the year to the extent that the expenses exceed 3% of the taxpayer's adjusted gross income. A remedial provision that was added in 1958 permits medical expenses that are paid within a year following the decedent's death to be treated as if they had been paid when they were incurred. §213(d)(1). As a result, expenses paid within that period may be deducted on the decedent's income tax return for the appropriate taxable year or years. So long as there is no duplication of the deductions claimed, a portion of the medical expenses may be claimed for estate tax purposes and the remainder for income tax purposes. In order to be entitled to claim the expenses as income tax deductions, the estate must file both a statement that the "amount paid" has not been allowed as a deduction for estate tax purposes under §2053 and a waiver of any right to claim it as a deduction under §2053. §213(d)(2). In any case, no refund or credit will be allowed for any taxable year for which the statutory period for filing a claim has expired. Reg. §1.213-1(d)(1).

According to the IRS, where the expenses are claimed as deductions for income tax purposes, the amount that does not exceed 3% of the decedent's adjusted gross income is not deductible for income or estate tax purposes. The portion of the expenses for which no income tax deduction was allowable might be allowable as a deduction for estate tax purposes. Cf. Rev. Rul. 59-32, 1959-1 C.B. 245 (the portion of expenses attributable to tax exempt income, which is not deductible for income tax purposes, may be deducted by the estate tax return). However, the IRS rejected such a contention in a 1977 ruling. Rev. Rul. 77-357, 1977-2 C.B. 328. It concluded that the statement and waiver must recite that the "amount paid" has not been nor will be at any time allowed as a deduction under §2053.

> **Example 12-2.** T died last December, after a 6-month illness during which medical expenses of $20,000 were incurred. The expenses were paid by T's executor early in this year. T's executor claimed an estate tax deduction for $5,000 of the expenses under §2053. The necessary statement and waiver were filed with regard to the other $15,000 in expenses that were claimed on the decedent's final income tax return, which showed an adjusted gross

income of $100,000. Under these circumstances, an estate tax deduction of $5,000 is allowable together with an income tax deduction of $12,000. The latter amount represents the excess of the expenses claimed for income tax purposes ($15,000) over 3% of the decedent's adjusted gross income for the period ($3,000). According to the IRS, no deduction is allowable for the amount within the 3% floor.

§12.6. The Decedent's Final Income Tax Return: Election to Report Accrued Interest as Income

The periodic increase in value of a Series E savings bond, or similar obligation, does not constitute income to a cash basis taxpayer. However, a cash basis taxpayer may elect to report the increase in redemption value as income for the period in which it accrues. §454(a). If the election is made, the taxpayer must report all of the accrued increase in value of all such bonds as income for the year in which the election is made. Thereafter an electing taxpayer must report the amount that accrues each year as income. *Id.*

In the case of obligations owned by a decedent, the accrued interest may be reported on the decedent's final return, a return filed for the estate, or on a return filed by the distributee of the bonds. The IRS recognizes that the person who is obligated to file the decedent's final income tax return may elect to report all of the accrued increase in value as income on that return. Rev. Rul. 68-145, 1968-1 C.B. 203. Such an election does not bind the decedent's estate or the ultimate recipient of the bonds who are separate taxpayers. The election would increase the income tax due on the decedent's final return, which is deductible for estate tax purposes. *See* Reg. §20.2053-6(f). The IRS has allowed an executor to make the election although the decedent had transferred the bonds to a revocable trust. Rev. Rul. 79-409, 1979-2 C.B. 208. It considered that because the grantor could have made the election regarding bonds in the trust (the interest on which was taxed to him under §676), the fiduciary required to file his or her final income tax return "assumed the powers and duties of [the decedent] for this purpose, including the right to make an election under section 454(a) of the Code."

The unreported increment in value reflected in the redemption value of Series E bonds as of the date of the decedent's death constitutes income in respect of a decedent. Rev. Rul. 64-104, 1964-1 C.B. 223. As such the taxpayer who must include it in his or her income is entitled to a deduction under §691(c) for the state and federal death taxes that are attributable to it. The decedent's personal representative, or the distributee of the bonds, may elect under §454(a) to report as income the amount that accrued during the decedent's lifetime. If the election is made, the taxpayer must report as current income the increment in value that accrues in each subsequent year. If no election is made the entire amount of accrued interest is reported in the year in which the bonds are disposed of, redeemed, or reach final maturity. Rev. Rul. 64-104, 1964-1 C.B. 223.

The election is typically used in a way that will cause the accrued interest to be reported on a return that has little or no other income. Depending upon the circumstances that return might be the decedent's final return, the estate's first or last return, a return for a testamentary trust, or a return for an individual distributee. The key is to be aware of the options and to make the necessary decisions in a timely fashion.

§12.7. Subchapter S and Partnership Elections

Two important elections may effect the estate's interests in small business corporations and partnerships. Sections 1371 to 1378 permit certain domestic small business corporations to elect that their income should be taxed directly to their shareholders rather than to themselves. In general, an electing corporation may not have more than one class of stock (§1371(a)(4)) or more than 25 shareholders (§1371(a)(1)), all of whom must be individuals, estates, or trusts described in §1371(e).

An estate may be a shareholder of an electing corporation whether the election is made before or after the decedent's death. Where the election is made after the decedent's death, the estate and all other shareholders must give their consent. §1372(a). The death of a shareholder does not affect an election that was previously made. However, the decedent's personal representative may terminate an election by "affirmatively refusing to consent" to the election. §1372(e)(1)(A). The time within which the refusal may be made expires on the earlier of (1) the sixtieth day following the qualification of the decedent's personal representative or (2) the sixtieth day following the last day of the taxable year of the corporation in which the decedent died. §1372(e)(1)(B). Of course, the election may be terminated at any time if all of the shareholders consent to its revocation. §1372(e)(2).

An estate may continue as a shareholder of a Subchapter S corporation for the entire administration of the estate. The IRS has recognized, for example, that an estate may remain a shareholder during the period that payment of the estate tax is deferred under the predecessor of §6166. Rev. Rul. 76-23, 1976-1 C.B. 264. Certain trusts may also be shareholders during and following the grantor's death. See §10.2, supra.

Partnership Elections. A deceased partner's interest in a partnership is includible in his or her gross estate and takes a basis equal to its federal estate tax value under §1014. However, in the absence of an election under §754, or a distribution and election under §732(d), the death of a partner does not affect the basis of the assets held in the partnership at the time of the partner's death. Accordingly, as a general rule, a deceased partner's estate or successors will have a stepped up basis in the decedent's partnership interest, but the basis of the partnership assets remains unchanged. As a result, the sale of an appreciated partnership asset may require the partnership and, derivatively, the surviving partners and the deceased partner's estate or successors, to recognize gain on the sale. Of course, if a deceased partner's interest is completely liquidated, the decedent's estate or successors take a basis in the distributed assets equal to their basis in the partnership, reduced by the amount of any cash received. §732(b).

The general rule does not provide any current tax advantages where a deceased partner's estate or successors remain in the partnership. In particular, their bases in the partnership assets are not adjusted for purposes of computing gain or loss, depreciation or depletion, etc. §743(a). However, if a partner dies, the partnership may elect under §754 to adjust the basis of partnership property. A similar election can be made if a partnership interest is transferred or partnership property is distributed. Under Reg. §1.754-1(b) the election must be made in a written statement filed with the partnership return for the taxable year in which the partnership interest is transferred (*i.e.,* the year of the partner's death). If such an election is in effect, on the death of a partner the basis of the partner's estate or successors in partnership property is increased or decreased in order to reflect the federal estate tax value of the deceased partner's interest in the partnership. The adjustment also extends to a surviving spouse's interest in a community property partnership interest. Rev. Rul. 79-124, 1979-1 C.B. 225. The regulations make it clear that the adjustment is only made with respect to the interests of the estate or successors of a deceased partner: "The amount of the increase or decrease constitutes an adjustment affecting the basis of partnership property with respect to the transferee partner only. Thus, for purposes of depreciation, depletion, gain or loss, and distributions, the transferee partner will have a special basis for those partnership properties which are adjusted under section 743(b). . . ." Reg. §1.743-1(b).

> **Example 12-3.** X's one-third interest in the XYZ partnership was valued at $100,000 in X's estate. The partnership owned 3 parcels of real property, each of which had a basis of $10,000 and a fair market value of $100,000. If no election is made under §754, the sale of Parcel One for $100,000 would result in a gain of $30,000 to each partner. On the other hand, if the partnership makes a timely

election under §754, the basis of X's estate or successors in Parcel One would be increased to $33,333. Accordingly, the estate (or successors) would realize no gain as a result of the sale.

A properly drawn partnership agreement should specify whether or not the partnership is obligated to make a §754 election if a partnership interest is sold or exchanged or a partner dies. The failure to make such an election can subject the estate to the imposition of a substantial income tax liability. *See* Estate of Ernest D. Skaggs, 75 T.C. 191 (1980).

§12.8. Declaration and Payment of Estimated Tax

Neither an estate nor a trust is required to file a declaration of estimated tax. §6015(h). Moreover, no payments of estimated tax need be made on account of a decedent following the date of the decedent's death. Reg. §1.6153-1(a)(4). However, a surviving spouse remains liable for the payments shown on a joint declaration of estimated tax, unless he or she files an amended declaration. Reg. §1.6015(b)-1(c)(2). Where payments of estimated tax were made on a joint declaration, the surviving spouse and the decedent's personal representative are free to allocate the payments between the surviving spouse and the decedent. If they cannot agree on an allocation, the surviving spouse shall be allocated an amount that bears the same relation to the total payments as the amount of income tax that would be due on the surviving spouse's separate income tax return bears to the total amount of income tax due on the surviving spouse's separate return and the final return of the decedent. Reg. §1.6015(b)-1(c)(2). If a sufficient amount of the payments are allocated to the surviving spouse and the surviving spouse files an amended declaration, it may be unnecessary for the surviving spouse to make any further payments of estimated tax for the year.

§12.9. Selection of a Taxable Year for an Estate or Trust

The estate of a decedent is treated as a separate taxpayer for federal income tax purposes. An income tax return must be filed for each taxable year in which the estate has gross income of $600 or more. §6012(a)(3).

As a new taxpayer, the personal representative may choose a taxable year for the estate. The estate's income may be reported on a calendar year basis, or on the basis of a fiscal year ending on the last day of any month within 12 months of the decedent's death. §441(b).

An estate's fiduciary income tax return (Form 1041) must be filed on or before the fifteenth day of the fourth month following the close of the taxable year. §6072(a). The election of a taxable year is made by timely filing a return for the taxable year on the basis of which the return was prepared. For example, if the decedent died on April 15, the personal representative could elect to report the estate's income on the basis of a calendar year or on the basis of a fiscal year ending on the last day of any month from April through March. The personal representative could elect to use the calendar year by filing a return on or before the following April 15, reporting the income of the estate for the period from April 15 through December 31. Of necessity the first taxable year of the estate will ordinarily consist of less than 12 months. §443(a)(2). However, succeeding taxable years must consist of 12 months, except for the last taxable year of the estate, which ends on the day the administration of the estate is completed. Reg. §1.441-1(b)(4).

The selection of a taxable year for the estate should be based upon the overall circumstances of the estate and its beneficiaries. In particular, the personal representative should project the receipt of income by the estate, the length of time the estate will remain open, the number of deductions that may be claimed as income tax deductions, and the time at which distributions will be made. The planning should also take into account the circumstances and tax brackets of the beneficiaries, which will affect policy decisions that are made regarding distributions, deduction of expenses, etc.

The personal representative will usually try to divide the estate's income into as many taxable years as possible. This gives the estate the full benefit of the progressive rate structure that applies to estates and trusts. §1(e). It also gives the estate the full benefit of the maximum number of $600 exemptions that are available each year the estate is in existence. §642(b).

Example 12-4. T died on February 20 and the executor received a large payment on March 15 that constituted income in respect of a decedent. The estate is expected to remain open for 18 months. If no distributions of income-producing property are made, the gross income of T's estate is expected to remain relatively constant over the period the estate is open. The executor should adopt a tax year that ends soon after receiving the March 15 payment in order to minimize the other income that the estate will report for the period. Thus, the executor might adopt a fiscal year ending on March 31. Such an election would spread the estate's income over 3 taxable years instead of 2, such as would occur if the executor adopted a calendar year. Based upon a fiscal year ending March 31, the 3 taxable years would be:
    Year One: Date of death through March 31.
    Year Two: April 1 through March 31.
    Year Three: April 1 through August 20.

In selecting the taxable year and planning distributions, the personal representative may also seek to defer the income taxation of income that is carried out to the beneficiaries as a result of making distributions to them. The opportunity to defer exists if the selection of a taxable year and distributions are carefully planned. The governing rule requires a beneficiary to report income that is carried out by an estate distribution in the year that includes the end of the estate's taxable year during which the distribution was made. §662(c). The rule sounds complicated, but it is really rather simple, as indicated by this example:

> **Example 12-5.** T died on January 10, 1982. T's personal representative elected to file income tax returns for the estate on the basis of a fiscal year ending on February 28. Any income that was carried out by distributions made to a beneficiary during the estate's first taxable year (January 10-February 28, 1982) would be included in the income of the beneficiary for that year. Income carried out by distributions made during the remainder of that calendar year (March 1 through December 31, 1982) would not be included in the beneficiary's 1982 return. Instead, that income would be reported in the beneficiary's 1983 return. Thus, a calendar year beneficiary who received a distribution on March 15, 1982, would report income arising from the distribution in the beneficiary's return for 1983 unless the estate terminated prior to January 1, 1983. If the estate did not terminate during 1982, its taxable year for the period during which the distribution was made would end on February 28, 1983. In that case the tax on the distribution would not have to be paid until April 15, 1984, more than 2 years after the distribution was made.

The rules described in this paragraph also apply to the reporting of distributions from trusts.

The personal representative may plan for a short final taxable year for the estate in which a large portion of the estate administration expenses will be paid in order to maximize the amount of the estate's nonbusiness deductions that can be carried out to the beneficiaries under §642(h). *See* §12.12, *infra*.

The same general principles apply to trusts. During the lifetime of the grantor of a revocable trust, the income is taxed to the grantor as it is received, regardless of the taxable year selected by the trust. *See* William Scheft, 59 T.C. 428 (1972). However, when the trust becomes irrevocable upon the death of the trustor, the trust is treated as a new taxpayer. As such the trustee may adopt a fiscal year without the approval of the Commissioner. Rev. Rul. 57-51, 1957-1 C.B. 171.

Estates and trusts are generally taxed as individuals, but as noted in §12.8, *supra,* they are not required to file declarations of estimated tax.

§6015, Reg. §1.6015(h)-1. In addition, an estate may pay its income tax in 4 equal quarterly installments following the close of the taxable year. §6152(a)(2). The privilege of making such installment payments does not extend to trusts. The income taxation of trusts is summarized at §10.2, *supra*.

§12.10. *Waiver of Fees*

At an early stage of the proceedings the lawyer should discuss with the personal representative the question of whether he or she will accept or waive the right to receive fees for serving as personal representative. A family member who serves as personal representative often waives the right to receive a fee either to avoid conflict with other beneficiaries or to optimize the tax results. A personal representative who is receiving social security payments may choose to waive part or all of the fee in order not to exceed the amount of earned income that may be received without reducing the amount of social security payments. The right to receive compensation may be waived without risk of adverse gift or income tax consequences provided the waiver is made at a sufficiently early stage.

Amounts paid to a personal representative for serving as personal representative are earned income and are generally deductible by the estate for either income or estate tax purposes. *See* §12.15, *infra.* The tax impact of accepting compensation for serving as personal representative can be ameliorated by having the fee paid in installments over 2 or more tax years. Of course, if no fees are paid, the personal representative is usually not required to report any amount as compensation and the estate is not entitled to any deduction. Under Rev. Rul. 56-472, 1956-2 C.B. 21, a fiduciary may waive all or a portion of the fees he or she is entitled to receive.

A waiver should be executed promptly if the personal representative decides to forego receiving his or her fee. Otherwise the personal representative could face a costly tax conflict with the IRS. In Rev. Rul. 66-167, 1966-1 C.B. 20, the IRS ruled that:

> The crucial test of whether the executor of an estate or any other fiduciary in a similar situation may waive his right to receive statutory commissions without thereby incurring any income or gift tax liability is whether the waiver involved will at least primarily constitute evidence of an intent to render a gratuitous service. If the timing, purpose, and effect of the waiver make it serve any other important objective, it may then be proper to conclude that the fiduciary has thereby enjoyed a realization of income by means of controlling the disposition thereof, and at the same time, has also effected a taxable gift by means of any resulting transfer to a third party of his contingent beneficial interest in a part of the assets under his fiduciary control.

The ruling concludes that the requisite intent to serve gratuitously will be deemed to have been established if the fiduciary, within 6 months of his or her initial appointment, delivers a formal waiver of the right to any compensation to one or more of the estate's primary beneficiaries. The ruling also indicates that an intent to serve gratuitously may be implied where the fiduciary fails to claim fees or commissions at the time of filing the tax returns and accounts and if all of the other facts and circumstances evidence a fixed and continuing intent to serve gratuitously. For this purpose the claiming of fees as a deduction on one or more of the estate's tax returns is considered to be inconsistent with a fixed and definite intent to serve without compensation.

In George M. Breidert, 50 T.C. 844 (1968), *acq.,* 1969-2 C.B. xxiv, the Tax Court refused to follow the test set out in Rev. Rul 66-167 and held that the taxpayer had not realized any income despite an ineffective waiver of executor's fees and despite an actual award of fees by the probate court. The taxpayer did not, in fact, receive the fees and the court found sufficient intent to waive the fees so as to avoid subjecting them to tax.

> **Problem 12-2.** Uncle, U, died last year, leaving all of his property in equal shares to his unmarried nephew, N, and his cousin, C. N is the executor of U's will for which he is entitled to receive a fee this year of $10,000. U's gross estate has a value of $750,000 against which the estate may claim deductions of $25,000 apart from any executor's fee paid to N. N expects to have a taxable income of $60,000 this year excluding any fee he receives from U's estate. Assuming that N could still make a timely waiver of the fee he is entitled to receive, what would be the estate, gift, and income tax consequences of doing so?

C. ESTATE TAX AND INCOME TAX DEDUCTIONS

§12.11. General

This part is concerned with the deductibility of various costs, expenses, and losses for estate tax and income tax purposes. One class of deductions, called deductions in respect of a decedent, can be claimed for both estate and income tax purposes. §12.12, *infra.* However, from the planning perspective the most important are the items that may be deducted on either but not both returns. Such alternatively deductible items give the planner an opportunity to achieve substantial tax savings by carefully allocating the deductions on the estate's tax returns. Where the deductions are claimed for income tax purposes, it is sometimes necessary to make an equitable adjustment of accounts between beneficiaries. *See* §12.16, *infra.* Such adjustments are designed to relieve the residuary beneficiaries of the increase in the estate tax that resulted from claiming alternatively deductible items as income tax deductions.

§12.12. Deductions in Respect of a Decedent

Both income and estate tax deductions are allowed for taxes, interest, business expenses, and some other items for which the decedent was liable, but which were not properly allowable as deductions on his or her final income tax return. The dual deductibility of deductions in respect of a decedent is recognized in Reg. §1.642(g)-2, which provides that deductions accrued at the date of the decedent's death "are allowable as a deduction under section 2053(a)(3) for estate tax purposes as claims against the estate, and are also allowable under section 691(b) as deductions in respect of a decedent for income tax purposes. However, section 642(g) [denial of double deductions] is applicable to deductions for interest, business expenses, and other items not accrued at the date of the decedent's death so that they are allowable as deductions for estate tax purposes only as administration expenses under section 2053(a)(2)." The estate is usually entitled to the income tax deduction. §691(b)(1)(A). However, if the estate is not liable to discharge an obligation, the deduction is allowed to the person who succeeds to the decedent's property subject to the obligation. §691(b)(1)(B).

§12.13. Deductions Allowed Only for Estate Tax Purposes

Some expenses are deductible for estate tax purposes, but not for income tax purposes. This category includes funeral expenses, gift taxes, federal income taxes, and the debts and obligations of the decedent. Also, because of the limitation imposed by §265, administration expenses attributable to tax exempt income are not deductible for income tax purposes. Rev. Rul. 59-32, 1959-1 C.B. 245. However, such expenses are deductible for estate tax purposes. Of course, an item is deductible on the estate tax return only to the extent the requirements of §2053 are satisfied. In general, an expense must be: (1) actually paid, (2) reasonable in amount, and (3) properly allowable under the local law. The last requirement is one that frequently causes a deduction to be denied. For example, no deduction is allowable for funeral expenses imposed on and paid by the surviving spouse in accordance with local law. Rev. Rul. 76-369, 1976-2 C.B. 281. Similarly, only one-half of the amount of the funeral expenses is deductible in community property states that impose the liability for payment of the expenses upon the entire community. Because of that rule Texas and California amended their laws to relieve the surviving spouse from any obligation to pay the funeral expenses of a deceased spouse, as a result of which an estate tax deduction is allowable for the full amount. Rev. Rul. 71-168, 1971-1 C.B. 271 (California); Rev. Rul. 69-193, 1969-1 C.B. 222 (Texas).

§12.14. *Deductions Allowed Only for Income Tax Purposes*

Some expenses incurred after death are deductible for income tax purposes, but not for estate tax purposes. They include income taxes on the estate's post-mortem income, real estate taxes that accrue after death, and interest that accrues after death to the extent it is not allowable as an expense of administration under local law. Note, however, that interest accrued after death may be deductible under §2053(a)(2) where it is allowable as an expense of administration. *See* §12.15, *infra.* The IRS has generally resisted allowing a deduction for post-mortem interest on loans outstanding at the time of the decedent's death. *See* Rev. Rul. 77-461, 1977-2 C.B. 324. However, the Tax Court has allowed a deduction in such instances where the interest was paid to extend debts incurred by the decedent. Estate of William M. Wheless, 72 T.C. 470 (1979), *nonacq.,* 1982-1 C.B. — ; Estate of Jane deP. Webster, 65 T.C. 968 (1976), *acq. and nonacq.,* 1977-2 C.B. 2. According to the Tax Court in the *Wheless* case, "the expenses sought to be deducted as administration expenses must be actually and necessarily incurred in the administration of the estate and they must be allowable administration expenses under local law." 72 T.C. at 479. Similarly, an interest deduction is allowable for interest actually paid with respect to the amount of estate tax that is deferred under §6166 or that was deferred under §6166A. Rev. Rul. 78-125, 1978-1 C.B. 292.

§12.15. *Deductions Allowable Either for Income or Estate Tax Purposes*

Administration expenses and casualty losses are deductible either for income tax or estate tax purposes, but not both. The administration expenses include the fees of the personal representative and of the attorney, which together often account for the bulk of an estate's deductions. For that reason, the executor's election regarding the use of the deductions is very important. Under §642(g) an income tax deduction is allowable only if a statement is filed in duplicate to the effect that the items have not been allowed as deductions from the gross estate of the decedent under §§2053 or 2054 and that all rights to claim the items as deductions under those sections are waived. Reg. §1.642(g)-1. That regulation permits the statement to be filed at any time before the expiration of the limitations period for the taxable year for which the deduction is sought. However, an income tax deduction is not allowable if an estate tax deduction has been finally allowed. *Id.* Filing the statement prevents the executor from changing the plan and claiming the items instead as estate tax deductions. Accordingly, some commentators suggest that the statement and waiver should not be filed because it limits the executor's future flexibility. They reason that the executor can file the statement at any time until the expiration of the limitations period after which the IRS could not disallow the deductions in any case.

The regulations permit alternatively deductible items to be claimed wholly on either return or partly on one return and partly on the other. "One deduction or portion of a deduction may be allowed for income tax purposes if the appropriate statement is filed, while another deduction or portion is allowed for estate tax purposes." Reg. §1.642(g)-2. Of course, a cash basis taxpayer may only deduct the expenses for income tax purposes on the return for the year in which they were paid.

Selling Expenses. Under the pre-1977 law, the expenses of selling property of an estate were allowable both as an offset against the selling price for the purpose of determining gain or loss and as a deductible expense of administration for estate tax purposes. Rev. Rul. 71-173, 1971-1 C.B. 204, following Estate of Viola E. Bray, 46 T.C. 577 (1966), *aff'd,* 396 F.2d 452 (6th Cir. 1968). The 1976 Act amended §642(g) to provide that for tax years ending after October 4, 1976, an item may not be used to offset the sales price for income tax purposes if it is deducted for estate tax purposes. Accordingly, an executor must choose whether to claim the item as an offset to the capital gain or as an estate tax deduction. Where the estate will pay any estate tax it is generally preferable to claim it as an estate tax deduction.

Planning Considerations. The planner should make a decision regarding the return on which the administration expenses and casualty losses will be taken as deductions only after considering carefully the impact on the estate and the beneficiaries. In particular, the planner should compare the marginal estate tax and income tax rates that will apply. Where the rates are essentially the same, the benefit of the deductions may be maximized by splitting them between the two returns. In other cases, it may be beneficial to claim the deductions all on one return or the other.

The planning should also take into account the possibility of carrying out to the estate's beneficiaries the estate's excess income tax deductions in its final taxable year. *See* §642(h). The benefit of the carryover of the deductions is usually maximized if the estate's final taxable year is a short one, during which it has little income. As noted above, expenses are deductible by the estate for income tax purposes only in the year they are paid.

In some cases the combined income tax liability of the estate and the beneficiaries will be reduced if excess deductions arise in the estate's final taxable year and are carried out to the estate's beneficiaries. §642(h). Excess deductions may arise where, for example, substantially all of the lawyer's and executor's fees are paid in the estate's final, short taxable year. In order to plan most effectively for the payment of the fees and closure of the estate the lawyer must be aware of the income tax position of the beneficiaries. Where it will assist the beneficiaries, the lawyer may agree to defer payment of his or her fee until the estate's final taxable year. The deferral, of course, conflicts with the lawyer's interest in being paid currently. A lawyer may be willing to defer payment of a fee where it produces a significant tax saving. However, the possibility that payment of the fee might be deferred should be discussed with the executor at the outset along with other matters relating to the lawyer's compensation. They might provide for the payment of interest on any portion of the fee that is unpaid for more than a specified period after it is earned and billed. However, it may be inappropriate to do so, particularly where the local law prescribes a statutory fee which is customarily not paid until termination of the estate. Charging interest might be questionable unless the lawyer charges interest on the unpaid balance of fees owed by other clients. In any case, the lawyer should be cautious in dealing with the matter because of conflict-of-interest problems. Whether or not there is a technical conflict of interest, the beneficiaries are interested parties, whose interests and concerns should be taken into account. Overall, however, it seems doubtful that the lawyer would be required to forego payment of the fee for a protracted period in order to give the beneficiaries a tax advantage.

§12.16.   *Equitable Adjustments*

> Equitable adjustment is a form of equitable apportionment, the doctrine that requires fiduciaries, in order to deal with beneficiaries fairly, to reallocate or reapportion benefits or burdens received in an initially unfair form under standard accounting rules. Dobris, Equitable Adjustments in Postmortem Income Tax Planning: An Unremitting Diet of *Warms*, 65 Iowa L. Rev. 103, 148 (1979).

In some cases an election made by an executor gives some beneficiaries an economic benefit while it causes others to suffer an economic loss. Where the election involves claiming administration expenses as an income tax deduction some states require an equitable adjustment to be made in the absence of contrary direction in the will. In contrast, claims for adjustment are generally not enforced where they are based on losses allegedly suffered as a result of the executor's election regarding the use of the alternate valuation date or the distribution of property in kind in satisfaction of bequests. For example, income beneficiaries may benefit from an executor's election to use the valuation date that produces the higher valuation and higher bases for estate assets, although the election results in a higher estate tax payment borne by others. Many wills and trusts avoid the problem by waiving the necessity of making any adjustments, by waiving any obligation that the executor do so, or by giving him or her discretion to make an appropriate adjustment. However, it may be unwise to give the executor discretion in the matter where it would subject him or her to a serious conflict of interest (*e.g.*, when the executor is also a beneficiary).

Most of the cases have involved an executor's election to claim administration expenses as a deduction on the estate's income tax return instead of on the estate tax return. Such a use of the deductions is proper where it will result in an overall tax saving (*i.e.*, where the income tax liability will be reduced by a larger amount than the resulting increase in the estate tax liability). The claim for an adjustment arises where the beneficiaries whose share of the estate bears the cost of the administration expenses and the additional estate tax that results from claiming the expenses on the income tax return do not benefit from the income tax saving.

> **Example 12-6.** X died leaving a will that gave income-producing securities to his widow, W, and gave the residue of his estate to his child, C. Under the local law W was entitled to the income from the securities, reduced only by the income taxes and other expenses directly attributable to them. The local law also required the administration expenses and the estate tax to be paid out of the residuary estate. C will have a claim for an equitable adjustment to the extent the estate tax is increased by deducting the administration expenses on the estate's income tax return in a way that only benefits W.

In cases similar to Example 12-6, the courts have required the residuary beneficiaries to be reimbursed from estate income in an amount equal to the increase in the estate tax that resulted from claiming the expenses as income tax deductions. The leading cases are Estate of Bixby, 295 P.2d 68 (Cal. App. 1956), and Estate of Warms, 140 N.Y.S.2d 169 (Surr. Ct. N.Y. Cty. 1955). Statutes in some states require a similar adjustment. *See* Md. Est. & Trusts Code Ann. §11-106(a) (1974); N.Y. EPTL §11-1.2(A) (McKinney 1980 Supp.). Under such an approach the income beneficiaries do enjoy the *net* saving in taxes.

It is not necessary to make any adjustment where the administration

expenses are claimed as a deduction on the estate tax return. In that case
the deduction benefits the beneficiaries whose share of the estate bore
the expenses that generated the deduction. Of course, the executor may
be subject to criticism if a greater overall tax saving would result if the
expenses had been claimed as a deduction on the estate's income tax
return.

D.   ESTATE TAX

§12.17.   *Alternate Valuation Method*

Until 1935 the gross estate was valued on the date of death and the
federal estate tax was due one year later. As a result of the steep decline
in property values that took place during the Great Depression of the
1930s the tax often claimed a disproportionately large portion of the
estate on the payment date. The alternate valuation method was added
to the Code in 1935 in order to prevent the virtual confiscation of estates
when there was a sudden decline in market values. Revenue Act of 1935,
§202, 49 Stat. 1022. It permitted the assets of the estate to be valued on
the date of death or as of a date one year after death. In order to permit
an estate to take full advantage of the alternate valuation date, the date
for payment of the tax was extended from one year after death to 15
months after death. S. Rep. No. 1240, 74th Cong., 1st Sess (1935), reprinted at 1939-1 C.B. 651. Effective January 1, 1971, the alternate
valuation date and the date for payment of the tax were both advanced
by 6 months as a part of a plan to accelerate tax collections. *See* Price,
Recent Tax Legislation — The Excise, Estate and Gift Tax Adjustment
Act of 1970, 47 Wash. L. Rev. 237 (1972).

Under the present provisions of §2032, property included in the gross
estate is valued as of the time of the decedent's death unless the executor
makes a timely election to value it according to the alternate valuation
method. If the alternate valuation method is elected, all items are valued
as follows:

1. Property distributed, sold, exchanged, or otherwise disposed of
    within 6 months of the decedent's death is valued as of the date of
    distribution, sale, exchange, or other disposition.
2. Property not distributed, sold, exchanged, or otherwise disposed
    of within 6 months after the decedent's death is valued as of the
    date 6 months after the decedent's death.
3. Items that are affected by the mere lapse of time are included at
    their values as of the time of death (instead of the later date),
    adjusted for any differences in value that are not due to the mere
    lapse of time. §2032(a).

An election is not effective for any purpose, however, unless the decedent's gross estate is sufficiently large to require a federal estate tax return to be filed. Reg. §20.2032-1(b)(1). The exercise of the election fixes the valuation of assets for estate tax purposes, which affects the amount of the gross estate and, derivatively, the amount of the credit for state death taxes and the amount of the federal estate tax itself. It may also determine whether the estate meets the percentage requirement of §§303, 2032A, or 6166. See §§11.14 to 11.21, and §§11.26 to 11.32, supra, and §12.18, infra. As the estate tax valuation of assets also establishes their bases for income tax purposes, the election may also affect the income tax liability of estates and distributees.

If the alternate valuation method is not used, all assets are valued on the date of the decedent's death. Those values establish the bases for determining gain or loss on a subsequent sale or exchange of the assets. In general, the gain or loss realized on the sale of property acquired from the decedent is long term. Under §1223(11), such property is considered to have been held for more than one year if the seller's basis is determined under §1014. On the other hand, if the alternate valuation method is used, all assets that are sold, exchanged, distributed, or otherwise disposed of within 6 months immediately following the decedent's death are valued at their respective values on the date or dates of their disposition. Thus, where the alternate valuation method is elected, the estate will not recognize any gain or loss on bona fide sales or exchanges that are made within 6 months following death. Where the election is made, all assets that are not sold or otherwise disposed of during the 6 months immediately following death are valued according to their respective fair market values at the end of that period.

Example 12-7. T died last year leaving a gross estate that consisted of the following items, each of which is followed by its date of death and alternate date values:

Asset	Date of Death Value	Alternate Date Value
Cash	$ 50,000	$ 50,000
Life insurance	300,000	300,000
Residence	125,000	150,000
Blackacre	100,000	75,000
ABC Co. stock	50,000	75,000
XYZ, Inc. stock	75,000	100,000
Total	$700,000	$750,000

Within 6 months of T's death the ABC stock was sold for $75,000 and the residence was distributed at a time when it was worth $150,000. If the date of death values are used in valuing the estate, the estate will realize a gain of $25,000 on the sale of the stock. No gain or loss would be realized on the distribution of the residence unless it was distributed in satisfaction of a pecuniary bequest. Instead, the estate tax valuation would generally carry over and become the basis of the devisee in the residence. If the alternate valuation date is elected, the gross estate will be $750,000. However, the estate will not realize any gain on the sale of stock or on any distribution of the residence. In addition, the devisee would have a $150,000 basis in the residence.

Property Affected by Alternate Valuation. Property that forms a part of the decedent's gross estate at the time of death is "included property" that is subject to alternate valuation under §2032. Such property remains included even though it may change form during the alternate valuation period. On the other hand, property earned or accrued after the date of death is generally "excluded property," which is not taken into account for purposes of §2032. Thus, interest or rent accrued to the date of death is included property, but interest or rent accrued after death is excluded property. Likewise, dividends declared and payable to stockholders of record prior to the decedent's death are included property, but dividends declared to shareholders of record after the decedent's death are excluded property. In either case the item would constitute income to the recipient. However, an included item might constitute income in respect of a decedent for which the recipient would be entitled to a deduction under §691(c) for the estate tax attributable to it.

Items Affected by the Passage of Time. The statute and the regulations provide some guidance for the alternate valuation of items whose value changes merely due to the lapse of time. An item, such as a patent, life estate, remainder or term of years, is included in the decedent's gross estate at its value on his or her date of death, adjusted as required for any difference in value not due to the mere lapse of time. §2032(a)(3). The nature of the adjustment is illustrated by the following example, based on Reg. §20.2032-1(f)(1):

Example 12-8. O left a life estate in Blackacre to his daughter, D, and the vested remainder to his son, S. S died survived by D, who was then 40 years old. On the date of S's death Blackacre was worth $100,000 and on the alternate valuation date it was worth $50,000. Under Reg. §20.2031-10(f), the factor for S's remainder interest following the life of a 40-year-old female is .15719. Thus, on the date of S's death his remainder had a value of $15,719 (.15719 × $100,000). For purposes of the alternate valuation the change in value of Blackacre is taken into account, but the same factor is used. Thus, the remainder interest had a value of $7,859.50 (.15719 × $50,000) on the alternate valuation date.

A mortgage or similar obligation included in the decedent's estate is returned at its value on the alternate valuation date where the executor elects to use the alternate valuation method. However, the estate must also include any principal payments received between the date of death and the alternate valuation date. Rev. Rul. 58-576, 1958-2 C.B. 625. Special rules are applied in the case of other assets such as livestock and crops (Rev. Rul. 58-436, 1958-2 C.B. 366, *modified,* Rev. Rul. 64-289, 1964-2 C.B. 173) and mineral interests (Rev. Rul. 71-317, 1971-2 C.B. 328).

Election. An election to value the decedent's assets according to the alternate valuation method is valid only if it is made on an estate tax return filed within 9 months of the decedent's death or within the period of any extension of time allowed by the district director under §6018. §2032(c); Reg. §20.2032-1(b). The last-cited regulation provides that "[i]n no case may the election be exercised, or a previous election changed, after the expiration of such time. If the election is made, it applies to all the property included in the gross estate, and cannot be applied to only a portion of the property." Reg. §20.2032-1(b)(2).

"Distributed, Sold, Exchanged, or Otherwise Disposed Of." In general, the phrase "distributed, sold, exchanged, or otherwise disposed of" describes all possible ways by which property ceases to form a part of the gross estate. Reg. §20.2031-1(c). However, the term does not extend to transactions that are mere changes in form. Thus, it does not apply to a tax-free exchange of stock in a corporation for stock in the same corporation or in another corporation such as in a merger, reorganization, or other transaction described in §§355 or 368(a), with respect to which no gain or loss is recognized for income tax purposes under §§354 or 355. The existing authorities have evolved a test that turns on whether the assets have been placed beyond the dominion and control of the fiduciary or surviving cotenant, or have been the subject of a decree that shifts the economic benefit of the property to a successor. *See* Hertsche v. United States, 244 F. Supp. 347 (D. Ore. 1965), *aff'd per curiam,* 366 F.2d 93 (9th Cir. 1966).

The economic benefit analysis of *Hertsche* was followed in Rev. Rul. 78-378, 1978-2 C.B. 229, which was concerned with whether the passage of property by operation of law to a decedent's devisee constituted a distribution of the property where it remained subject to claims against the estate until a final court order. Under the ruling,

> The delivery of property to the distributee that is subject to a subsequent court decree is not a delivery within the meaning of section 20.2032-1(c)(2)(iii) of the regulations. Under these circumstances, there is not a shifting of economic benefits until the court decree.

For purposes of §2032 property may be sold, exchanged, or otherwise disposed of by the executor, a trustee, or other donee to whom the decedent transferred the property inter vivos; an heir or devisee to whom the property passes directly under local law; a surviving joint tenant; or any other person. Reg. §20.2032-1(c)(3). Entering into a binding contract for the sale, exchange, or other disposition of property constitutes a sale, exchange, or other disposition of the property on the effective date of the contract where the contract is subsequently carried out substantially in accordance with its terms. For example, property that is sold by a trustee or surviving joint tenant within 6 months of the decedent's death will be valued on the date of sale if the executor elects to use the alternate valuation date. On the other hand, the transfer of property by a surviving joint tenant to a revocable trust is not considered to be a sale, exchange, or other disposition because for tax purposes the surviving joint tenant is not considered to have relinquished any authority or power of ownership over the property. Rev. Rul. 59-213, 1959-1 C.B. 244.

The IRS has ruled that the division of the corpus of a revocable trust into 2 equal parts upon the grantor's death in order to facilitate the payment of income to 2 income beneficaries did not constitute a distribution. Rev. Rul. 57-495, 1957-2 C.B. 616. A contrary result was reached in Rev. Rul. 73-97, 1973-1 C.B. 404, where the corpus of the original trust was divided into 2 separate trusts upon the grantor's death. Under the latter ruling, "when the trustee divided the corpus of the original trust into separate trusts, he effectuated a 'distribution' within the meaning of section 2032 of the Code." Rev. Rul. 73-97 indicates that the difference in the outcome of the 2 rulings resulted because the original trust involved in Rev. Rul. 57-495 continued after the division of the corpus into shares whereas the trust involved in Rev. Rul. 73-97 ceased to exist when its corpus was divided and transferred to the trustee of the successor trusts. The distinction is consistent with an earlier ruling that held that the bookkeeping division of estate assets into 3 separate accounts, which corresponded to 3 separate trusts created by the decedent's will, did not constitute a distribution within the meaning of §2032 where the executor retained control over the property held in the accounts. Rev. Rul. 71-396, 1971-2 C.B. 328. Under Rev. Rul. 78-431, 1978-2 C.B. 230, a division of community property into 2 shares, followed by the transfer of the surviving spouse's share into a separate trust, does not constitute a distribution for purposes of §2032. That result is reached because the share of the community property that was included in the decedent's estate remained in the original trust, subject to the control of the original trustee.

Generation-Skipping Tax. Under §2602(d) the trustee of a generation-skipping trust may elect to use the alternate valuation method described in §2032 to value the property that is involved in a taxable termination that occurs at the same time as the death of the deemed transferor. Where 2 or more members of the same generation have present interests in the same trust, a taxable termination generally does not occur until the last of the interests terminates. *See* §2.21, *supra.* In that case the alternate valuation date may be used to value all of the trust assets when the final interest terminates.

> **Example 12-9.** T's will transferred property to a trust that permitted discretionary distributions to be made to his children A, B, and C. Upon the death of the last survivor of A, B, and C, the trust property is to be distributed to T's then living great-grandchildren. Under §2613(b)(2) a taxable termination does not take place until the death of the survivor of A, B, and C. At that time the trustee may elect to value all of the trust property according to the alternate valuation method.

The exercise of the election for generation-skipping tax purposes has no effect on the valuation of the estate of the deemed transferor for estate tax purposes.

Planning Considerations. Before making an election regarding the alternate valuation date, the planner should project the estate and income tax consequences of the action. A projection should be made because the valuation that produces the lower estate tax value may result in higher overall tax liabilities. That is particularly true where the marital deduction will shield all or a large part of the estate from taxation or the tax will be substantially offset by the decedent's unified credit. In such a case there is little or no cost associated with electing to use the higher values. Of course, a surviving spouse's basis in community property is affected by the election.

The electing fiduciary should also consider the effect that the election will have on all of the beneficiaries because of his or her duty of impartiality toward the beneficiaries. The election will affect the amount of the estate tax, which is usually borne by the residuary beneficiaries, as well as the basis of the estate's property in the hands of the decedent's successors. The fiduciary may act more freely where the governing instrument authorizes the exercise of this and other elections without regard to the impact on the beneficiaries of the estate.

§12.18. *Special Use Valuation*

> The Act provides that, if certain conditions are met, the executor may elect to value real property included in the decedent's estate which is devoted to farming or closely held business use on the basis of that property's value as

a farm or in the closely held business, rather than its fair market value determined on the basis of its highest and best use. General Explanation of the 1976 Act 537.

In 1976 Congress added a complex section, §2032A, which permits the executor to elect to value real property that was used as a farm or in connection with a closely held business ("qualified real property") according to its actual use rather than its highest and best use. Ordinarily the value of property included in the gross estate is based upon its fair market value, which takes into account the highest and best use to which the property can be put. Congress was concerned that such a valuation of real property used for farming or other closely held business purposes could result in unreasonably high estate taxes and make "continuation of farming, or the closely held business activities, not feasible because the income potential from these activities is insufficient to service extended tax payments or loans obtained to pay the taxes. Thus, the heirs may be forced to sell the land for development purposes." General Explanation of the 1976 Act 537.

Election. An election to value qualified real property under the special use method must be made on the decedent's estate tax return. §2032A. In addition, the executor must file an agreement to the election that is binding under the local law and is signed by all parties having an interest in the property. Originally the election could only be made on a timely filed estate tax return. However, an amendment made by the 1981 Act allows the election to be made on a late return, if it is the first estate tax return filed by the executor. An election once made is irrevocable.

Maximum Reduction in Value of Property. Under §2032A(a)(2) the use of the special use valuation method could not reduce the value of the qualified real property by more than $500,000. The 1981 Act increased the limit to $600,000 for decedents dying in 1981, $700,000 in 1982, and $750,000 in 1983 or thereafter. In the case of community property, the limits are probably reduced by one-half on account of the community property interest of the surviving spouse. §2032A(e)(10), *see also* LR 8023027. The special use value establishes the basis of the qualified real property for income tax purposes. However, if a recapture tax is imposed because of disposition of the qualified real property or cessation of the qualified use, the basis of the qualified real property may be increased to its fair market value on the estate tax valuation date applicable to the decedent's estate. §1016(c). If the qualified heir elects this basis adjustment, interest must be paid at the annually adjusted floating rate of §6621 on the amount of the recapture tax from a date 9 months after the decedent's death until the due date of the recapture tax. §1016(c)(5)(B).

Basic Requirements. The valuation requirements of §2032A are relatively simple. Real property used in a farm or other business qualifies for
special use valuation if the adjusted value of the real *and* personal property used in connection with the farm or business accounts for a least
50% of the value of the adjusted value of the gross estate. In addition,
the adjusted value of the real property must amount to at least 25% of
the value of the adjusted gross estate. §2032A(b)(1)(B). (The election to
value property under the special use method may be made with respect
to a portion of the decedent's real property, "but sufficient property to
satisfy the [25%] threshold requirements of section 2032A(b)(1)(B) must
be specially valued under the section." Reg. §20.2032A-8(a)(2).) Some
other relatively simple requirements are also imposed by §2032A. Thus,
the decedent must have been a citizen or resident of the United States
(§2032A(a)(1)(A)) and the real property must be located in the United
States (§2032A(b)(1)). The real property must also pass to a member of
the decedent's family, including the decedent's spouse, lineal descendants, parents, grandparents, and aunts or uncles of the decedent and
their descendants (a "qualified heir"). §2032(e)(1), (2).

More complex requirements relate to the ownership, use, and material participation in the management of the property. Unfortunately the
liberalizing amendments made by the 1981 Act added to the already
staggering complexity of §2032A. On the date of the decedent's death
the real property must have been in use by the decedent or a family
member as a farm or for other business purposes. In addition, for at
least 5 of the last 8 years preceding the decedent's death, the decedent or
family member must have (1) owned the real property and (2) used the
real property for farming or other business purposes. §2032A(b)(1)(C).
The decedent or a family member must also have materially participated
in the operation of the farm or other business for at least 5 of the last 8
years preceding the decedent's date of death, disability, or commencement of social security retirement benefits. §2032A(b)(1)(C), (4). Importantly, real property owned indirectly through the ownership of an
interest in a partnership, corporation, or trust qualifies for special use
valuation to the extent it would qualify if it were owned directly.
§2032A(g).

Valuation of Property. Section 2032A provides 3 methods for valuing
real property for special use purposes. Where comparable land is located
in the same locality, from which the average gross cash rental can be
calculated, the executor may value the real property by dividing (1) the
excess of the average annual gross cash rental for comparable land over
the average annual state and local taxes by (2) the average annual effective interest rate for all new Federal Land Bank loans. §2032A(e)(7)(A).
Under a provision added by the 1981 Act, if there is no comparable land
from which the average cash rentals may be calculated, the value may be

based on the average net share rentals received by the lessors of comparable land in the same locality. §2032A(e)(7)(B). Finally, if there is no comparable land in the same locality from which the average cash or net share rentals can be calculated, the real property will be valued according to a multi-factor formula. §2032A(e)(8). It is based upon the following factors:

1. Capitalization of income
2. Capitalization of fair rental value for special use purposes
3. Assessed land values in states that provide a differential or use value assessment law
4. Comparable sales of other farm or closely held business property in the same area and
5. Any other factor that fairly values the farm or closely held business use of the property.

Recapture. The tax benefit of the special use valuation is recaptured if the qualified heir disposes of the real property or ceases to use it for the qualified use within 10 years following the decedent's death and before the death of the qualified heir. §2032A(c)(1). The recapture period was originally 15 years, with a declining percentage subject to recapture in the final 5 years. Cessation of the qualified use may occur if the qualified heir and members of his or her family fail to participate materially in the management of the real property for more than 3 years of any 8-year period ending after the date of the decedent's death. §2023A(c)(6). The amount subject to recapture is the excess of the estate tax liability that would have been incurred had the special use valuation method not been used over the estate tax liability based upon special use valuation. This amount is called the "additional tax." §2032A(c)(2).

Involuntary Conversions and Like Kind Exchanges. An involuntary conversion of the qualified real property during the recapture period does not trigger recapture of the tax where the proceeds are completely reinvested in qualified replacement property. §2032A(h). In general, the replacement property must meet the requirements of §1033(a) and be used for the qualified use under which the special use valuation was allowable for the converted property. §2032A(h)(3)(B). The recapture period is extended by any period beyond the 2-year period referred to in §1033(a)(2)(B)(i) during which the qualified heir was permitted to replace the converted property. §2032A(h)(2)(A)(i). Like kind exchanges of qualified real property also do not trigger the recapture tax except to the extent that property is received in the exchange other than real property that is used for the same qualified use as the original property. §2032A(i).

Personal Liability. A qualified heir is personally liable for the amount of the tax that is subject to recapture with respect to the qualified heir's interest in the property. §2032A(c)(6). The personal liability terminates when the qualified heir dies or the recapture period passes. Also, the personal liability of a qualified heir terminates if he or she provides a bond in an amount equal to the maximum amount attributable to his or her interest that might be recaptured. *See* §2032A(e)(11). A qualified heir may request that the IRS advise him or her of the maximum amount of additional tax attributable to his or her interest. The IRS must notify the heir of that amount within one year of the request. In determining the maximum amount the IRS may not consider any interest on the amount for which the heir might be personally liable.

Special Lien. Code section 6324B provides for a special lien in the amount of the maximum additional tax if special use valuation is used.

Evaluation. The special use valuation provides some estate tax relief for estates that are composed largely of qualified real property. However, many planners are reluctant to advise a client to elect to use the method because of its complexity, the potential for recapture, the personal liability of the qualified heir, and the special lien. Where there are multiple qualified heirs there is also the risk that they may disagree regarding the use or disposition of the property.

Special consideration must be given to the interrelationship between special use valuation and the unlimited marital deduction. As a general rule it appears that the executor and other parties should not elect to make use of special use valuation (with the consequent limitation on basis) where the real property passes to a surviving spouse in a way that qualifies for the unlimited marital deduction. Of course, use of the special use valuation method would increase the amount of property that could be sheltered by the decedent's unified credit from inclusion in the surviving spouse's estate. Their decision will depend in part on the size of the decedent's and surviving spouse's estates, the amount of qualified real property included in the estates, and the survivor's plans for use of the property.

§12.19. Marital Deduction Election re QTIP

The 1981 Act added §2056(b)(7), which makes the marital deduction available on an elective basis for the value of property in which a surviving spouse is given a "qualifying income interest for life." *See* §5.18, *supra.* A qualifying income interest for life is defined as one in which (1) the surviving spouse is entitled to all of the income for life, payable at least annually, and (2) no person has a power to appoint any of the property to a person other than the surviving spouse so long as he or she lives. §2056(b)(7)(B)(iii). The House Report notes that "income interests granted for a term of years or life estates subject to termination upon remarriage or the occurrence of a specified event will not qualify under the committee bill. The bill does not limit qualifying income interests to those placed in trust. However, a qualifying life income interest in any other property must provide the spouse with rights to income that are sufficient to satisfy the rules applicable to marital deduction trusts under present law. (Treas. Reg. §202.2056(b)(f))." H.R. Rep. No. 97-201, 97th Cong., 1st Sess. 161 (1981).

Apparently the election can be made with respect to all or any separate property in which the surviving spouse has a qualifying income interest for life. This follows under §2056(b)(7)(B)(iv), which recognizes that "a specific portion of property shall be treated as separate property." Until regulations are issued under §2056(b)(7), some guidance regarding the meaning of "separate property" may be gleaned from the existing regulations under §2056(b)(5). In particular, the regulations treat a fractional or percentage interest in property as a "specific portion." Reg. §20.2056(b)-5(b),(c). Presumably the election could run to specific portions of the trust (*e.g.*, one-third) or to specific property transferred to the trust (*e.g.*, 100 shares of MNO, Inc. common stock). *See* Reg. §20.2056(b)-5(c), *Example* 2. However, such an interpretation is not entirely consistent with the proposed disclaimer regulations under §2518. In this connection it is important to note that the opportunity to disclaim property exists in addition to the election allowed by §2056(b)(7).

Under §2056(b)(7)(B)(v), the election is made by the executor on the federal estate tax return. Here, note that the election is made by the decedent's executor, not the decedent's surviving spouse. Considerable care should be exercised in planning the election because, once made, the election is irrevocable. §2056(b)(7)(B)(v). Presumably the decedent's will could direct his or her executor to exercise the election in a particular way.

As a general rule an executor should plan the election in a manner that preserves the full benefit of the decedent's unified credit. An "over election" will cause an unnecessarily large portion of the property to be included in the surviving spouse's estate. Thus, where the decedent's surviving spouse receives a qualifying income interest for life in the decedent's entire estate, the executor should not elect to claim a deduction with respect to all of the property. Instead, the executor's decision should preserve the benefit of the decedent's unified credit. The executor should, of course, take into account all relevant considerations including the size of the surviving spouse's estate, the age and health of the surviving spouse, and the advantages of equalizing the sizes of the spouses' taxable estates.

Example 12-10. H died in 1982 leaving his entire $500,000 estate to a trust that satisfies the requirements of §2056(b)(7). W, who is in good health, has an estate of similar size. H's executor should not treat more than $275,000 as qualifying terminable interest property. In that way the full amount sheltered by H's unified credit ($225,000) will not be included in W's estate under §2044.

Problem 12-3. H died in 1982 survived by W and their 2 adult children, D and S. H's will left property worth $250,000 outright to W and the balance of his estate to a trust in which W had a qualifying income interest for life. If W survives until 1987, what would be the estate tax impact of an election by H's executor to treat the property that H left to the trust as qualified terminable interest property, with the exception of an amount equal to the credit equivalent in 1982? For purposes of this problem assume that neither H nor W has made any taxable gifts, that each estate will have expenses allowable as deductions under §2053 equal to 5% of the gross estate, that no separate state death tax applies to their estates, and that the value of the property remains constant. Prepare your tax estimates under the following assumptions regarding the size of the estates of H and W. Also, note the marginal estate tax rates that would apply to the estates of H and W if the election is not made by H's executor.
    (a)   H's estate is $500,000 and W's is $100,000.
    (b)   H's estate is $500,000 and W's is $500,000.
    (c)   H's estate is $1,000,000 and W's is $100,000.
    (d)   H's estate is $5,000,000 and W's is $1,000,000.

§12.20. Consent to Split Gifts

A decedent's surviving spouse and the decedent's personal representative may elect under §2513 to split gifts made during the decedent's lifetime. Reg. §25.2513-2(c). The election can only apply to gifts that were completed prior to the decedent's death. Rev. Rul. 55-506, 1955-2 C.B. 609 (1939 Code). The surviving spouse may execute the consent on behalf of the decedent where the decedent did not leave an estate subject to administration and no personal represenative was appointed. Where the gifts are split the surviving spouse and the decedent's estate are jointly liable for the tax.
    A consent may be signified at any time following the close of the year

in which the gift was made, except a consent may not be given after either spouse has received a notice of deficiency with respect to the gift tax for the year or after April 15th of the year following the year in which the gift was made if a return was filed by either spouse before that date. §2513(b)(2). A consent may be revoked by filing duplicate signed statements of revocation before April 15th of the year following the one in which the gift was made. §2513(c). There is no right to revoke a consent that is filed after April 15. §2513(c)(2).

Deceased Spouse Was the Donor. The surviving spouse may consent to split gifts made by the decedent prior to his or her death in order to reduce the estate tax payable by the decedent's estate. In effect, the surviving spouse may assume the responsibility for payment of the transfer tax attributable to one-half the amount of the decedent's gifts. That result follows because a splitting of the gifts would reduce the amount of the decedent's adjusted taxable gifts otherwise includible in the decedent's tax base under §2001(b) in computing the estate tax on the decedent's estate. Of course, the tax attributable to such a gift is not shifted to the surviving spouse if the gift is entirely drawn back into the decedent's estate under §2035. However, by reason of the changes made by the 1981 Act outright gifts of property other than life insurance made within 3 years of the donor's death are not includible in the donor's estate.

Where the surviving spouse is treated as the donor of one-half of the decedent's gifts, the decedent's estate is given the benefit of any gift tax the surviving spouse paid with respect to gifts that are included in the decedent's estate. *See* §2001(b)(2). Under the statute, the total amount of the gift taxes paid by both spouses with respect to such gifts is deducted from the tentative tax in determining the amount of estate tax on the donor's estate.

Example 12-11. T made outright gifts of $210,000 to each of his 3 children shortly before his death. Previously neither T nor his wife, W, had made any taxable gifts. Apart from the gifts, T's taxable estate is $1,400,000. If the gifts are not split with W, the tentative tax on T's estate would be based on the total amount of adjusted taxable gifts ($600,000) plus the amount of any gift tax paid by T with respect to the gifts ($0) and the amount of T's taxable estate ($1,400,000). The gross tax on T's estate would be $780,800, which would be reduced by the unified credit and the appropriate state death tax credit. On the other hand, if W consented to split the gifts, she would be treated as having made gifts of $285,000 in the year of his death (($630,000 ÷ 2) − $30,000). In such a case, T's tax base would be reduced by the amount of one-half of the gifts ($315,000) to $1,685,000, which would be subject to a gross tax of

$639,050. Thus, the election could reduce the tax payable by T's estate by about $140,000. Of course, by making the election W would be treated as having made taxable gifts of $285,000. A taxable gift of that size made prior to 1984 would require the payment of some gift tax.

Upon the death of the consenting spouse an adjustment is made where a split gift is included in the donor's estate by reason of §2035. In particular, under §2001(e) the amount of such gifts is not included as an adjusted taxable gift in computing the tentative tax on the consenting spouse's estate. Correlatively, the amount of gift tax paid by the consenting spouse is not allowed as an offset in calculating the estate tax on his or her estate. The amount of gift tax paid by the consenting spouse is includible in the gross estate of a consenting spouse who dies within 3 years of the date of the gifts. §2035(c).

By splitting gifts a surviving spouse may increase the amount of property that passes to the beneficiaries of the deceased donor's estate where the splitting would require the surviving spouse to pay some gift tax. This occurs because the tax paid by the survivor reduces the amount of estate tax payable by the donor's estate which, in turn, increases the amount that passes to the donor's beneficiaries. Here, again, the survivor's payment of the tax on the split gift does not appear to constitute a gift. *See* Reg. §25.2511-1(d).

Surviving Spouse Was the Donor. In some cases, an overall tax saving will result if a decedent's personal representative consents to being treated as the donor of one-half of the gifts that were made by the surviving spouse prior to the decedent's death. Such a consent will not reduce the amount of the donor's gross estate because the amount of any gift tax paid by the decedent's estate with respect to gifts made by the decedent or the decedent's spouse within 3 years of death is includible in the decedent's gross estate. §2035(c). However, splitting gifts produces an advantage where the decedent's estate would not otherwise fully utilize the decedent's unified credit.

Example 12-12. T made a gift of $100,000 to his daughter, D. Shortly thereafter T's wife, W, died. W, who had not made any taxable gifts during her lifetime, left her entire gross estate of $100,000 to D. W's personal representative may consent to split the gift made by T. If the consent is given, W will be treated as the donor of one-half of the gift ($50,000), but the estate tax on her estate will still be within the amount of her unified credit. In addition, giving the consent would preserve some of T's unified credit, which could be used later.

A tax saving may also result where the consent would increase the estate tax payable by the decedent's estate by a smaller amount than the corresponding decrease in the gift tax payable by the donor. However, the personal representative should be reluctant to subject the decedent's estate to a greater transfer tax liability unless the donor is also the person who bears the burden of the increase in the estate tax. Needless to say, a serious conflict of interest arises where the donor spouse serves as the deceased spouse's personal representative and the estate tax burden is borne by others.

§12.21. Qualified Plan Benefits

Under the basic rules of §2039 an annuity or other payment under a qualified plan is excludible from the decedent's estate to the extent it is attributable to the employer's contributions or the deductible contributions of a self-employed person to a Keogh plan. §2039(c). However, the exclusion does not apply if the benefits are payable to the decedent's estate or are legally obligated to be used to satisfy estate debts, expenses, or taxes. The exclusion also does not apply if the payment is received in a lump sum unless the recipient irrevocably elects to forego the generally favorable 10-year averaging provisions of §402(e) and the long-term capital gains treatment under §402(a)(2). §2039(f). For this purpose a lump sum distribution is one made "within one taxable year of the receipt" of the employee's entire interest in the plan. §402(e)(4)(A).

An annuity payable under an IRA is also not includible in a decedent's estate if the benefits are payable for a period extending at least 36 months after the decedent's death. §2039(e).

Lump Sum Distribution to a Surviving Spouse. The availability of the unlimited marital deduction makes it unnecessary for a surviving spouse who receives a lump sum distribution to make the §2039(f) election in order to avoid the imposition of an estate tax on the payment. The §2039(c) exclusion applies to a lump sum distribution from a qualified plan that is rolled over to an IRA by the surviving spouse. LR 8119067. However, a surviving spouse must decide whether to defer income taxation of the distribution by rolling it over to an IRA under §402(a)(7) or to permit the distribution to be taxed presently, subject to 10-year averaging and long-term capital gains treatment. In order to defer the income taxation of the distribution, the roll over to an IRA must be made within 60 days following receipt of the distribution. In making the decision the surviving spouse will take into account the fact that the income of an IRA accumulates free of income tax until it is distributed and that a contributor may retain investment direction over property held in an IRA. Note, however, that after 1981 an individually directed account cannot invest in "collectibles" such as works of art, rugs, antiques, metals, gems, stamps, coins, and alcoholic beverages. §408(n).

Lump Sum Distributions to Persons Other Than a Surviving Spouse. As a rule, the §2039(f) election should only be made after preparing estimates of the income and estate tax consequences because of the complex interrelationship between the income and estate tax provisions. *See* Nasuti, How to Coordinate Income and Estate Tax Planning for Qualified Plan Distributions, 49 J. Tax. 194 (1978). Where the estate is small and inclusion of a lump sum distribution in the decedent's estate would result in little or no estate tax liability, the distribution generally should be included in the gross estate under §2039 (*i.e.*, the recipient should not give up the right to use 10-year averaging for income tax purposes). In other cases the potential estate tax saving must be balanced against the income tax advantages of 10-year averaging.

Income Taxation of Lump Sum Distributions. A lump sum distribution will consist of one or more of the following 3 parts: (1) a part attributable to the employee's previously taxed contributions, which is not taxable; (2) a part attributable to the employer's pre-1974 contributions, which is taxed as capital gain unless the distributee elects to treat it as ordinary income; and (3) a part attributable to the employer's post-1973 contributions, which is taxed as ordinary income. Under §402(e)(4) the distributee may elect to tax the ordinary income component under a special 10-year averaging method. A distribution would be taxed in the following way assuming that the election is made to use 10-year averaging and the distribution does not include a capital gain component:

1. The amount of the distribution that is taxable is calculated.
2. A minimum distribution allowance is deducted from the taxable portion of the payment. The allowance is the lesser of $10,000 or one-half of the distribution, less 20% of the amount by which the taxable distribution exceeds $20,000. Thus, there is no allowance where the taxable distribution is $70,000 or more.
3. The portion of the estate tax attributable to the remaining value is deducted at this point. *See* §691(c).
4. The balance is subject to a specially computed tax unless barred by a §2039(f) election. The tax is equal to 10 times the tax that would be imposed on one-tenth of the balance had it been received by a single taxpayer who had no other income except an amount equal to the zero bracket amount. In essence the tax is imposed at the lowest rates applicable to an individual taxpayer if the distribution were received in 10 equal annual installments. §402(e)(2). (If 10-year averaging is not available the balance is taxed as ordinary income in the year of the distribution.)

Because of the wide differences in the circumstances of estates and beneficiaries, it is difficult to generalize regarding the desirability of making an election under §2039(f).

§12.22. Life Insurance Proceeds

A beneficiary of a life insurance policy may accept the benefits under the policy or disclaim the right to receive them. *See* Prop. Reg. §25.2518-4(a), which recognizes the right of a beneficiary to disclaim insurance benefits. Also, a beneficiary is usually free to receive the proceeds outright or to leave them with the insurer under a settlement option. A beneficiary who elects a settlement option is treated as having received the proceeds outright and having transferred them back to the insurer in exchange for its commitment to make payments under the option. The estate and income tax consequences of electing an optional settlement mode are described at §§6.24 and 6.35, *supra.*

> **Example 12-13.** H's life was insured under a policy that designated his wife, W, as the beneficiary. Following H's death W elected to receive the policy proceeds in monthly installment payments over a 20-year period. If W died prior to the end of the 20-year period, the commuted value of any remaining payments would be made to her surviving children.
>
> W's election was not a disclaimer. Instead, W will be treated as if she had received the proceeds outright and transferred them to the insurer in exchange for its commitment to make payments to her for a 20-year period. The interest element of each payment will be taxed to W, subject to the exclusion of up to $1,000 each year under §101(d). *See* §6.35, *supra.* If W dies prior to the end of the 20-year period, the amount that will be paid to her children is includible in her gross estate under §2036. *See* §6.24, *supra.*

The settlement options are usually based upon a low guaranteed rate of interest. Some options do provide for the interest payments to be augmented at the election of the insurer. However, a beneficiary will generally receive a higher net return by taking the proceeds outright and investing them in secure, higher yielding, relatively liquid investments (*e.g.*, certificates of deposit, corporate or municipal bonds). The surviving spouse may find that a settlement option will provide an acceptable after-tax yield because of the annual $1,000 interest exclusion that is available to him or her under §101(d). An optional settlement may also be attractive to a surviving spouse, assuming the insurer is financially sound, because it will not require any further supervision or any payment of fees or commissions.

E. REORDERING THE DISTRIBUTION OF PROPERTY

§12.23. General

This part deals with several important devices by which the distribution of property is reordered after a decedent's death. The family awards and allowances available to a surviving spouse or to minor children are discussed first. The awards and allowances are usually quite limited in amount, but can provide important economic protection for the survivors. Next the focus shifts to the option that most states give a surviving spouse to receive a statutory share of the decedent's property in lieu of the provisions made for him or her in the decedent's will. The concluding sections review the law regarding disclaimers and the circumstances in which they may be used to advantage.

§12.24. Family Awards and Allowances

The share of a decedent's estate that passes to the decedent's surviving spouse or minor children can be increased by taking advantage of the family awards and allowances that are allowed by local law. The family awards generally include a limited probate homestead allowance and a limited allocation of exempt property. *See* UPC §§2-401, 2-402. They usually prevail over any contrary testamentary disposition made by the decedent. However, a surviving spouse may be barred from claiming the awards if the right to them was waived in connection with a property settlement agreement. The awards are sometimes of special value because they are usually exempt from creditors' claims.

Most states permit a surviving spouse or minor or dependent children to claim a homestead or award in lieu of homestead and an allocation of exempt property. However, the awards are usually limited to pitiful amounts. By way of illustration, the UPC suggests a homestead award of $5,000 (§2-401) and an exempt property allocation of $3,500 (§2-402). In addition, the spouse and children are usually entitled to claim a reasonable allowance in money out of the estate for their support during the period of administration. *E.g.*, UPC §2-403. However, some states limit the duration or amount, or both the duration and amount, of family allowance payments. A family allowance is typically payable to the surviving spouse for his or her support and the support of the minor or dependent children. If the decedent did not leave a surviving spouse, it is payable to the children or to the persons who have the care and custody of them. The family allowance is also generally exempt from all claims of the decedent's creditors. Where the decedent left a small estate the protection from creditors can be very important to the family.

The awards and allowances are generally allowable in addition to any property the survivors are entitled to receive by will, intestate succession, or otherwise. However, a testamentary gift to a survivor may be conditioned upon the survivor not claiming a family award or allowance. If so, the beneficiary may not be entitled to receive the gift if he or she makes such a claim. Also, a surviving spouse might be barred from claiming an award or allowance by reason of the provisions of an antenuptial or post-nuptial agreement with the decedent.

Estate Tax. Homestead and exempt property awards of the type provided for in the UPC vest in the survivors upon the decedent's death and qualify as deductible interests for purposes of the estate tax marital deduction. *See* §5.10, *supra.* Use of the awards could play a role in deferring some of the taxes that would otherwise be payable by reason of the decedent's death. In contrast, the family support allowances are usually terminable interests that do not qualify for the marital deduction.

Income Tax. A homestead or exempt property award should be treated as an inheritance that is not subject to taxation by reason of §102(a) and that does not constitute a distribution for purposes of §§661 and 662. Accordingly, such an award does not entitle the estate to a deduction or require the recipient to report any income. A different rule applies in the case of family support allowances. Under Reg. §1.661(a)-2(e) the estate is entitled to a deduction for family allowance payments made from income or principal. A recipient is, of course, required to report family allowance payments in income to the extent of the recipient's share of the estate's distributable net income. Reg. §1.662(a)-2(c). The income tax consequences of family allowance payments must be taken into account in selecting the estate's tax year, making distributions, etc. The lawyer should explain the income tax impact of the payments to the surviving spouse in order to facilitate planning for any income tax liability that may result from them.

§12.25. Widow's Election

Under the law of practically all of the noncommunity property states a surviving spouse may elect to receive a specified share of the decedent's property outright in lieu of the property he or she is entitled to receive under the decedent's will. *See* §9.21, *supra.* The size of the elective share, the property from which it is payable, and the election procedure all vary from state to state. Perhaps the most extensive protection is provided the surviving spouse by the UPC, which greatly expands the property base that is used for computing the elective share. Under the UPC the surviving spouse is entitled to claim one-third of the decedent's "augmented estate," which roughly corresponds to the decedent's gross estate reduced by §2053 deductions. *See* UPC §2-202. However, the share the survivor is entitled to receive is reduced by the value of property he or she received from the decedent during lifetime or at death. The augmented estate concept serves both to prevent a person from transferring property to others in a way that would defeat a spouse's right to a share in the property and to prevent a surviving spouse from claiming a share in the probate estate where he or she had already received a substantial amount of property from the decedent.

Estate Tax. The interests in a decedent's property that a surviving spouse receives pursuant to an election against the decedent's will are considered to pass to the surviving spouse from the decedent for marital deduction purposes. Reg. §20.2056(e)-2(c). Where the surviving spouse receives outright interests in property as a result of the election, the interests normally qualify for the marital deduction. Prior to 1982 an uncommuted common law dower interest in property was treated as a nondeductible terminable interest. In the case of decedent's dying after 1982 the surviving spouse might have a qualifying income interest for life in the property subject to his or her dower interest. If so, the value of the property would be deductible under §2056(b)(7) at the executor's election. *See* §§5.18, 12.19, *supra*. The commuted value of a survivor's dower interest, if requested and paid in accordance with state law, is a deductible nonterminable interest. Rev. Rul. 72-7, 1972-1 C.B. 308. From the estate-planning perspective, a decision regarding the exercise of the spouse's election should only be made after projecting the overall tax and nontax consequences. In some cases the election may help salvage the estate from the ravages of an unwise or ineffective estate plan.

§12.26.   Disclaimers: General

A disclaimer (or renunciation as it is sometimes called) is an unequivocal refusal to accept a power or interest in property to which one is otherwise entitled by gift, will, or operation of law. Disclaimers are a part of the common law of many states. However, an increasing number of states have recently adopted more or less comprehensive statutes on the subject. A disclaimed interest generally passes as if the disclaimant had predeceased the attempt to transfer the property to him or her. Because a disclaimed interest usually passes along to another person, a disclaimer can be used to decrease the amount of property passing to a named beneficiary and to increase the amount passing to others (*e.g.*, the disclaimant's children, the decedent's surviving spouse, a charity). The opportunity to reorder the distribution of property free of tax is one of the most important tools available to the estate planner.

The state laws generally require a disclaimer to be made without consideration and within a reasonable time. The acceptance of any benefit from a transfer generally precludes a valid disclaimer. The underlying theory is that an individual should be relatively free to accept or reject an interest that others attempt to transfer to him or her. However, in order to protect creditors, some states prohibit insolvent persons from disclaiming interests in property.

The federal gift and estate tax consequences of a disclaimer are determined by federal law, which was clarified considerably by the adoption of §2518 in 1976. The 1981 Act went further and, in effect, established a national standard for disclaimers, independent of state law. *See* §2518(c)(3). Prior to 1977 the tax consequences of disclaimers were determined according to a scattered and uncoordinated group of statutes and regulations, augmented by a few judicial decisions. In general, a disclaimer was considered to be effective if it was valid under the governing state law and was made within a reasonable time after the disclaimant learned of the attempted transfer to him or her. Because of the wide differences in state law, identical refusals to accept property made in different states sometimes had different federal gift and estate tax consequences.

A disclaimer must be distinguished from a release, which involves the relinquishment of a power or interest that had been accepted. The difference in concept is recognized by Prop. Reg. §20.2041-3(d)(6)(i):

> A disclaimer or renunciation of a general power of appointment created after December 31, 1976, in the person disclaiming is not considered a release of the power if the disclaimer or renunciation is a qualified disclaimer as described in section 2518 and the corresponding regulations. If the disclaimer or renunciation is not a qualified disclaimer, it is considered a release of the power by the disclaimant.

Although a disclaimed power ordinarily does not pass to another person powers can be validly disclaimed under §2518.

The planner must be alert to the effect other state laws may have on the effectiveness and consequences of a disclaimer. For example, a disclaimer is not recognized as a qualified disclaimer if the property involved can be reached by the disclaimant's creditors under local law. Prop. Reg. §25.2518-1(c)(2). Also, the consequences of a disclaimer may be affected by the local antilapse statute.

Example 12-14. T died leaving the residue of his estate to his 2 daughters, with the request that they provide for his widow. The daughters disclaimed the gift with the intent that the property left to them would pass to their mother under the local intestate succession law. Instead the residuary estate passed to the daughter's minor children by reason of the local antilapse statute. Under the local law a bequest to a beneficiary who was related to the testator passes to the beneficiary's descendants by right of representation if the beneficiary predeceases the testator. *See* LR 7833008.

§12.27. *Disclaimers: Qualified Disclaimer*

Section 2518 added the term "qualified disclaimer" to the estate planner's vocabulary. In brief a disclaimer that meets the requirements of §2518(b) is a "qualified disclaimer," which will be recognized as effective for gift and estate tax purposes. Under §2518(a) if a person makes a qualified disclaimer with respect to an interest in property, the gift and estate tax laws apply as if the interest had never been transferred to the disclaimant. The provisions of §2518 apply to transfers creating an interest in the disclaiming party made after December 31, 1976. Interests created by pre-1977 transfers are subject to the prior law.

A disclaimer of an interest created under a pre-1977 transfer will be respected if (1) it is made effective under state law and (2) it is made within a reasonable time after knowledge of the transfer. Reg. §25.2511-1(c). The "transfer" referred to in the regulations occurs when the interest is created and not later when it vests or becomes possessory. Jewett v. Commissioner, — U.S. — (1982).

In order to constitute a qualified disclaimer under §2518, Prop. Reg. §25.2518-2(a) requires that:

(1) The disclaimer must be irrevocable and unqualified;
(2) The disclaimer must be in writing;
(3) The writing must be received by [the transferor or his legal representative] not later than the date that is 9 months after the later of —
   (i) The date on which the transfer creating the interest in the disclaimant is made, or
   (ii) The day on which the disclaimant attains age 21;
(4) The disclaimant must not have accepted the interest disclaimed or any of its benefits; and
(5) The interest disclaimed must pass either to the spouse of the decedent or to a person other than the disclaimant without any direction on the part of the person making the disclaimer.

Each of the requirements is considered briefly in the following paragraphs.

The requirement that the disclaimer be irrevocable and unqualified will ordinarily not create any problem for the planner. In order to avoid any question on this point, a disclaimer should state that it is irrevocable and is not subject to any qualifications or conditions. The requirement that the disclaimer be in writing is unlikely to cause any serious problems. However, the planner should be sure that the disclaimer also satisfies the local law regarding formalities of execution. For example, some state laws require that disclaimers be acknowledged, witnessed, or recorded. A failure to satisfy the local law with respect to the disclaimer of an interest transferred prior to 1982 meant that the disclaimer was ineffective for federal purposes as well. Prop. Reg. §25.2518-1(c). A disclaimer of a post-1981 transfer will be recognized as a qualified disclaimer if it satisfies the federal law. *See* §2518(c)(3).

Under §2518(b)(2) the disclaimer must be received by the transferor within 9 months after the date on which the transfer was made. A disclaimer can be drafted to provide evidence of the date on which it was received by the transferor. For example, the disclaimer could include a form of receipt to be signed by the transferor:

Receipt of this disclaimer on _____ 198__, is acknowledged.

_____
        [Transferor]

Under the regulations the time limit is generally computed separately with respect to each taxable transfer. Prop. Reg. §25.2518-2(c)(2). In general, a taxable transfer occurs when there is a completed transfer for federal gift or estate tax purposes. However, a disclaimer that is executed within 9 months of a taxable transfer will not be effective if the disclaimant previously accepted an interest in the property.

A qualified disclaimer cannot be made if the disclaimant accepted the interest or any of its benefits, expressly or impliedly, prior to making the disclaimer. For this purpose, a disclaimant is treated as having accepted a benefit from the property if the disclaimant receives any consideration in exchange for the disclaimer, including the agreement of another party to dispose of the property in a way specified by the disclaimant. *See* Prop. Reg. §25.2518-2(d)(1)(i). However, actions taken by the disclaimant in a fiduciary capacity to preserve or protect the property do not constitute an acceptance of benefits. For example, an executor may direct the harvesting of a crop or the general maintenance of a building. Prop. Reg. §25.2518-2(d)(1)(ii). A disclaimant is not treated as having accepted property merely because the title to the property vests in the disclaimant under the local law immediately upon the owner's death.

The requirement that the property pass to the decedent's surviving spouse or to a person other than the disclaimant without any direction on the disclaimant's part can be troublesome, particularly where trusts are involved. A disclaimant may have to disclaim the right to receive a particular interest by more than one method in order to satisfy this requirement. For example, the disclaimer of a residuary beneficiary's right to receive a decedent's estate would not be a qualified disclaimer if the disclaimant would be entitled to receive the property under the intestate succession law. Prop. Reg. §25.2518-2(e)(5), *Example* (3). The disclaimer of a surviving spouse may not be qualified if he or she retains the right to direct the future beneficial enjoyment of the property in a transfer that will not be subject to the federal gift or estate tax. A surviving spouse can validly disclaim an outright bequest if the property will pass to a trust over which the spouse holds no power of appointment. However, such a disclaimer would not be effective if the spouse retained a special power of appointment over the trust. Prop. Reg. §25.2518-2(e)(5), *Example* (5). In such a case, the surviving spouse should also disclaim the power.

Prior to 1982, a disclaimer was recognized as effective for federal tax purposes only if it was effective under local law. Prop. Reg. §25.2518-1(c).

> **Example 12-15.** T died in 1980 leaving a will that made a pecuniary bequest of $10,000 to B and gave the residue of his estate to X. The local law required disclaimers of testamentary gifts to be made within 6 months of the testator's death. B executed a "disclaimer" of any right to the bequest 7 months after T's death. The disclaimer was not effective as a disclaimer under the local law and was, therefore, not a qualified disclaimer for federal tax purposes. B was treated as making a gift of $10,000 to X if the "disclaimer" caused the property to pass to X under the residuary clause. After 1981 the attempted disclaimer would be recognized as a qualified disclaimer under §2518(c)(3).

Under the 1981 Act a written transfer that does not qualify as a disclaimer under local law will be recognized as a qualified disclaimer if it meets the requirements of §§2518(b)(2) and (3) and the transferred property passes to the persons who would have received the property had the transferor made a qualified disclaimer. The statute requires that such a transfer be timely (*i.e.*, made within 9 months after the transfer to the present transferor) (§2518(b)(2)) and that the transferor not accept the interest or any of its benefits (§2518(b)(3)).

Finally, partial disclaimers are allowed under the federal law, but the interests that may be partially disclaimed are limited. *See* §12.28, *infra*.

Disclaimer of Joint Tenancy Interests. The tax position of the survivors would often be improved if a joint tenancy interest could be validly disclaimed. Unfortunately, the state laws are often unclear regarding the ability of a surviving joint tenant to disclaim an interest in the property. The common law generally did not permit joint tenancy interests to be disclaimed because the survivor's title was acquired by operation of law and not by transfer from the decedent at his death. However, under some disclaimer statutes joint tenancy interests may be disclaimed. Even where a joint tenancy interest cannot be disclaimed under local law, it may be if the requirements of §2518(c)(3) are met.

Under Prop. Reg. §25.2518-2(d)(3) the disclaimer of a joint tenancy interest other than a revocable joint tenancy, (*e.g.,* a revocable joint bank account) must be made within 9 months of the creation of the tenancy. This is consistent with the recognition that the creation of a joint tenancy bank account does not constitute a taxable transfer for gift tax purposes. *See* §3.13, *supra*.

> **Example 12-16.** H and W both signed a joint and survivor signa-
> ture card in connection with the establishment of a savings account
> in a financial institution. H deposited $10,000 in the account. Six
> months prior to H's death he received a distribution of $10,000
> from the estate of his father, F, which he deposited in the account.
> W could make a qualified disclaimer of part or all of the interests
> in the account within 9 months following H's death.

Under the circumstances of Example 12-16, the survivor should have the right to disclaim the entire $20,000 where she did not accept any benefit from any part of the account. The disclaimer of the original amount in the account should not be barred by Prop. Reg. §25.2518-3(d)(3)(i), which requires the "entire interest" in the property to be disclaimed.

The disclaimer of a joint tenancy interest must, of course, be made prior to the acceptance of the interest or any benefit from it. In some cases, the IRS seems to have taken the position that the participation in the creation of certain types of joint tenancy accounts in financial institutions involves the acceptance of a benefit. That approach is indicated in the following passage from a ruling that held that a survivor's disclaimer of an interest in a jointly held certificate of deposit was not a qualified disclaimer: "She had an affirmative duty to accept or reject the transfers at their inception. Her failure to refuse to accept the property or, more precisely, her acquiescence in the initial establishment of the joint tenancies, is an acceptance of the interests that cannot be eliminated except by transfer. There can be no disclaimer or renunciation of ownership of property after its acceptance." LR 7911005; *see also* LR 7829008. Perhaps the difference in outcome is premised on a distinction between a joint tenancy bank account and a joint tenancy certificate of deposit. The IRS position is understandable but it seems to strain to find an acceptance of benefits where there probably was none.

§12.28. *Disclaimer of Partial Interests*

Special care must also be exercised in disclaiming partial interests in property, particularly where a trust is involved. On the federal side, §2518(c)(1) permits the disclaimer of an "undivided portion" of an interest. *See* Prop. Reg. §§25.2518-3(b) and (c). The position taken by the IRS on this issue has important implications for marital planning, including the use of the election under §2518(b)(7) to claim a deduction with respect to part of the property in which the surviving spouse has the requisite life interest. *See* §5.18, *supra.*

The regulations recognize that an entire interest in property can be validly disclaimed even though the disclaimant has another interest in the same property. For example, where an income interest in property is bequeathed to A for life, then to B for life, remainder to A's estate, A may disclaim either the income interest, or the remainder interest, or an undivided portion of either. Prop. Reg. §25.2518-3(a)(1)(i). However, as indicated below, where the property is bequeathed to A outright, A cannot disclaim it yet reserve a life interest. The regulations also permit the disclaimer of severable property, such as part of a pecuniary bequest or a portion of the shares of stock bequeathed to the disclaimant. Prop. Reg. §25.2518-3(a)(1)(ii).

More complex rules apply where a trust is involved. A beneficiary may disclaim the "entire interest in income, corpus, or both or . . . an undivided portion of such interests." Prop. Reg. §25.2518-3(a)(2). In general, a beneficiary cannot disclaim either the income interest or the remainder interest in a particular trust asset. However, where property is transferred to the trust at different times, a qualified disclaimer can be made with respect to each transfer.

The regulations also permit the disclaimer of undivided portions of property. However, in such a case the disclaimer must extend to a fraction or percentage of *all* interests the disclaimant holds in the property. In addition, the disclaimer must cover the entire term of the disclaimant's interest in the property. Prop. Reg. §25.2518-3(b). Thus, a disclaimer is not effective if the disclaimant disclaims the fee interest in a parcel of real property, but retains a life estate.

> **Example 12-17.** T devised Whiteacre and Blackacre in trust, to pay the income to X for life, remainder to Y. According to the IRS X may disclaim all or a part of the income interest in the trust, but X may not disclaim the right to receive the income from either Whiteacre or Blackacre. Similarly, Y could disclaim a partial interest in the remainder.

§12.29. Disclaimer Planning

A disclaimer can be used effectively in a wide variety of circumstances. Some common opportunities that involve federal tax benefits include:

1. Skipping a Generation. A financially secure child may disclaim the right to receive an outright bequest, as a result of which the

property will pass to the disclaimant's children outright or to a
trust for their benefit;

2. Decreasing (or Increasing) Gifts to a Surviving Spouse. A surviv-
    ing spouse may disclaim the right to receive property that would
    be sheltered from federal taxation by the decedent's unified
    credit. A disclaimer in such a case will help control (*i.e.*, limit)
    the size of the surviving spouse's gross estate. Prop. Reg.
    §20.2056(d)-2;

3. Perfecting or Increasing Charitable Gifts. A wealthy child may
    disclaim a life interest in a trust, as a result of which the property
    will pass outright to the designated charitable remainderman in
    a way that will qualify for the charitable deduction under §2055.
    Of course, outright gifts may also be disclaimed in favor of char-
    itable alternate takers; and

4. Eliminating a Generation-Skipping Transfer. Finally, a younger
    generation beneficiary of a trust may disclaim an interest in a
    trust in order to prevent a generation-skipping transfer from
    taking place upon the disclaimant's death.

A planner can provide valuable help to clients by alerting them to the
possibilities offered by disclaimers. However, the clients should also be
made aware of the uncertainties and limitations regarding the use of
disclaimers.

The planner should also watch for situations in which it may be advantageous to use a disclaimer even though it will not produce any federal tax benefits. For example, differences between the state and federal
transfer tax laws may cause a disclaimer to result in a state tax saving
although no federal tax is saved. Finally, it may be desirable to use a
disclaimer to help rearrange property ownership even where it will not
save any taxes. For example, a disclaimer could be made by a guardian
ad litem to deflect property from a beneficiary to a trust for the disclaimant's benefit where an outright transfer would subject the property to an
expensive and cumbersome guardianship. Of course, such a disclaimer
can be made only where authorized by local law and often only with
court approval.

F. PLANNING ESTATE DISTRIBUTIONS

The 1954 Code policy adverted to can be both a serious trap for the
unwary and an important post-mortem tax planning tool in the hands of
the sophisticated fiduciary; a tax trap in that the unwary estate practitioner
familiar only with fiduciary accounting principles may suddenly find that
the distribution of a family automobile results in income to the recipient.

On the other hand, the sophisticated use of distributions in creating multiple entities such as testamentary trusts, has significant tax saving possibilities. . . . Estate of Holloway, 327 N.Y.S.2d 865, 866 (Sur. Ct. Nassau Cty. 1972).

§12.30. General

Estate distributions have important estate and income tax consequences. For estate tax purposes distributions have a particularly important impact on the alternate valuation of assets. *See* §12.17, *supra.* However, the income tax consequences of distributions are usually much greater for both the estate and the beneficiaries. Indeed, the proper planning of estate distributions is at the very heart of post-mortem income tax planning.

The opportunities for creative post-mortem income tax planning arise primarily because the estate is recognized as a separate taxpayer and generally acts as a conduit for estate income. In brief, an estate is taxed on any income that is neither currently distributed nor required to be distributed to its beneficiaries. As a result, all of the income received by an estate during a taxable year is taxed to the estate if it does not make any nonspecific distributions during the year. Because the so-called throwback rules of §§665 to 667 do not apply to estates, the executor has considerable flexibility in "splitting" the estate's income between the estate and its beneficiaries. Generally speaking, once an item of income is taxed to the estate the item has no significance in determining the income tax consequences of future distributions to the beneficiaries.

> **Example 12-18.** The estate was taxed on ordinary income of $25,000 in its second taxable year, during which it made no distributions. The estate closed early in the following year and distributed all of its property before it received any income. The distribution of the estate's assets, including the $25,000 of accumulated income, is not taxed to the distributees. Happily, under §642(h), the estate's beneficiaries are entitled to the benefit of the estate's deductions for its final taxable year in excess of its gross income and the estate's net operating loss and capital loss carryovers.

Basic Rule. An estate is allowed deductions for income required to be distributed currently and for "other amounts" properly paid, credited, or required to be distributed during the taxable year. §661(a). Rounding out the picture, the amounts that are deductible by the estate must be reported as income by the beneficiaries. §662(a). Each item distributed retains its particular character in the hands of the beneficiaries (*e.g.*, dividends and tax exempt interest). In general, each distribution is considered to consist of a proportionate part of each item. §662(b); Reg. §1.662(b)-1.

Distributable Net Income (DNI). The amount deductible by the estate and reportable by the beneficiaries is limited to the distributable net income of the estate, a concept that is significant mainly for that purpose. DNI is basically the taxable income of the estate, computed without regard to the distribution deduction and adjusted for capital gains that are added to principal and for certain other items. *See* §643 and §10.2, *supra.*

Tier System. Under the so-called tier system, DNI is allocated first to beneficiaries who are entitled as a matter of right to receive distributions of income. §662(a)(1). DNI is allocated to the first tier beneficiaries in the same proportion that the income required to be distributed currently to each bears to the total amount required to be distributed currently to all beneficiaries. *See* Reg. §1.662(a)-2(b). Where DNI exceeds the amount distributable currently to all beneficiaries, the excess is allocated to the second tier beneficiaries in proportion to the distribution each of them receives. *See* §10.2, *supra.* Under this method of allocation a distribution of principal may require the distributee to report a portion of the estate's income, depending upon whether DNI is completely absorbed by "first tier" distributions.

> **Example 12-19.** X and Y are each entitled to receive $10,000 of current income from the estate each year. X and another beneficiary, Z, are entitled to receive equal shares of the corpus of the estate. During a year in which estate's DNI was $20,000, the executor distributed $20,000 to X, $10,000 to Y, and $10,000 to Z. X and Y are each taxable on $10,000. Apart from the statute the income might be taxed in proportion to the value of each distribution (*i.e.*, 50% to X, 25% to Y, and 25% to Z). As it is, the $10,000 of the amount distributed to X and the $10,000 distributed to Z are not taken into account because the estate's DNI was exchausted by the distributions of income that were required to be made to X and Y. Had the estate's DNI been $30,000, then X would be taxed on a total of $15,000, Y on $10,000, and Z on $5,000. In that event, the additional $10,000 of DNI would be taxed to the second tier beneficiaries, X and Z, in proportion to the amount of corpus distributed to each of them.

Specific Gifts. Distributions in satisfaction of gifts of specific sums of money or of specific items of property that are paid all at once or in 3 or fewer installments are neither deductible by the estate nor includible in the distributee's income. *See* §663(a) and §12.31, *infra.* In order to qualify under this provision, the amount of money or the identity of specific property must be ascertainable under the terms of the will on the date of the testator's death. Reg. §1.663(a)-1(b).

> **Example 12-20.** T's will left $10,000 to X, 1,000 shares of ABC stock to Y, and the residue of his estate to Z. The estate had income of $25,000 during the year, which was accumulated and added to corpus for estate-accounting purposes. During the year the executor distributed $10,000 to X, 1,000 shares of ABC stock to Y, and nothing to Z. The distributions to X and Y are neither deductible by the estate nor includible in the income of X or Y. However, any distribution of residue made to Z during the year would have carried out the estate's DNI to him or her.

Combined with the opportunity to select a fiscal year for the estate and the election regarding the use of the alternate valuation date, carefully planned distributions can help to minimize the overall income tax burden of the estate and the beneficiaries. The timing of distributions has an important impact on the taxation of the estate and the beneficiaries. For example, nonspecific distributions can often be accelerated or deferred to generate the most desirable tax results for the estate and the beneficiaries (*e.g.*, distributions that will carry out DNI might be made during a year in which the estate will have little or no income). The composition and timing of distributions to trusts are also important, particularly where a distribution can be used to carry out DNI to a trust, where it will be "trapped" and not taxed to the trust beneficiaries. (Trapping distributions is discussed in §12.34, *infra*.) In some cases an in kind distribution of appreciated property can be used to effect a tax-free increase in the basis of the property. §12.32, *infra*. In kind distributions can also be used to advantage in other cases. However, non-pro rata distributions to residuary beneficiaries can involve a taxable exchange between the distributees. §12.33, *infra*. In kind distributions require the estate to recognize gain where appreciated property is distributed in satisfaction of a pecuniary gift. §12.32, *infra*.

§12.31. Distributions That Do Not Carry Out DNI

Distributions can be made in satisfaction of most specific gifts without affecting the income taxation of the estate or of the distributees. Specifically, under §663(a)(1) a distribution in satisfaction of a gift of a specific sum of money or of specific property does not carry out the estate's DNI if it is paid or credited all at once or in not more than 3 installments. This exclusion is traceable to the basic rule of §102 that gross income does not include gifts, bequests, and inheritances. In order to come within the ambit of this rule, the specific sum of money or the specific property must be ascertainable under the terms of the decedent's will at the date of death. Reg. §1.663(a)-1(1)(b). Thus, gifts of $10,000 or of 100 shares of XYZ, Inc. stock both qualify as specific gifts, but a gift of one-half of the residue of the estate would not qualify.

A pecuniary formula marital deduction gift of the type that was common prior to the 1981 Act was not treated as a specific bequest for purposes of §663 because the amount of the gift depended upon the exercise of the executor's discretion regarding a number of matters including the valuation of estate assets and the return upon which administration expenses would be claimed. *See* Reg. §1.663(a)-1(b)(1). Accordingly, any distribution made in satisfaction of such a pecuniary gift is subject to the ordinary distribution rules of §§661 and 662 (*i.e.*, it would carry out the estate's DNI to the distributee).

The regulations also provide that the specific gift rule does not apply to annuities or other amounts that are payable only from the income of an estate. Reg. §1.663(a)-1(b)(2). The regulations illustrate the application of this rule by the following example:

> *Example* (3). Under the terms of a trust instrument, income is to be accumulated during the minority of A. Upon A's reaching the age of 21, $10,000 is to be distributed to B out of income or corpus. Also, at that time, $10,000 is to be distributed to C out of the accumulated income and the remainder of the accumulations are to be paid to A. A is then to receive all the income until he is 25, when the trust is to terminate. Only the distribution to B would qualify for the exclusion under section 663(a)(1).

In this example the distribution to B qualifies for the exclusion because it could be satisfied out of income or principal. In contrast, no exclusion is available for the distribution to C, which was payable solely out of accumulated income.

Under the regulations specifically devised real property that passes directly to the devisee under local law is not taken into account for purposes of applying the rules of §§661 and 662. Reg. §§1.661(a)-2(e), 1.663(a)-1(c)(1)(ii). In such a case the real property does not form a part of the Subchapter J estate and is not paid, credited, or required to be distributed by the estate. Accordingly, the devisee and not the estate is required to report the income, deductions, and credits attributable to the real property from the time of the decedent's death. Presumably the same rule applies to any property that passes directly from the decedent to another person under local law. *See* Rev. Rul. 68-49, 1968-1 C.B. 304.

The rules of §663(a)(1) should be borne carefully in mind at all stages. Proper drafting can give the estate plan valuable, additional flexibility. Also, the income tax consequences of various types of distributions must be taken into account in the post-mortem phase when it comes to planning and making distributions from the estate.

§12.32. Distributions in Kind

A distribution in kind carries out the estate's DNI up to the fair market value of the property unless the distribution is classified as one made in satisfaction of a right to receive the specific property distributed. *See* §12.31, *supra.* In the case of a distribution that carries out DNI, the distributee takes a basis in the property equal to its fair market value on the date of distribution. However, the basis cannot exceed the amount included in the distributee's gross income. Reg. §1.661(a)-2(f)(3). Under this rule the unrealized appreciation in estate assets can be eliminated if the estate's distributions are carefully planned. A distributee who needs cash can sell the property promptly without realizing any gain.

> **Example 12-21.** This year T's estate will have a taxable DNI of $50,000. The executor plans to distribute property worth $25,000 to a residuary beneficiary, B. The distribution will give B some needed cash and will carry out one-half of the estate's income to B. Thus, the distribution would effectively split the estate's income between the estate and B. The executor might distribute cash of $25,000 or 1,000 shares of XYZ, Inc. stock, which has an estate tax value of $10,000 and a present value of $25,000. The stock should be distributed because it will have a basis in B's hands equal to its value on the date of distribution ($25,000). B could sell the stock immediately without realizing any gain. On the other hand, a distribution of cash would leave the stock with its original basis of $10,000, which could generate some unnecessary future capital gains.

Of course, if the estate has no taxable DNI for the year, then the value of property distributed to a beneficiary is not included in the distributee's income. In that case, the beneficiary's basis in the property is determined under §1014 (*i.e.*, it is equal to its estate tax value). Thus, in Example 12-21 B would have a basis of $10,000 in the stock if the distribution were made to him or her in a year during which the estate had no taxable DNI.

Where the taxable DNI carried out to the beneficiary as a result of the distribution is less than the value of the property distributed, the beneficiary's basis is determined proportionately under §§661 and 1014. Rev. Rul. 64-314, 1964-2 C.B. 167. Thus, the beneficiary's basis is a composite of the estate's basis and the value of the distributed property. Rev. Rul. 64-314 begins by allocating the estate's basis to the beneficiary. That amount is increased or decreased by a portion of the unrealized appreciation or depreciation in the value of the asset. The amount of the adjustment is determined by "multiplying the unrealized appreciation or depreciation in value of such item (measured from the uniform basis (adjusted to date of distribution)) by a fraction of which the amount (other than cash) includible in the gross income of the beneficiary is the numerator, and the total fair market value of the total property distributed to the beneficiary within the taxable year is the denominator." *Id.*

Example 12-22. T's estate had a taxable DNI of $10,000 last year during which it distributed property to B that had a basis of $25,000 and a fair market value of $50,000. The distribution carried out the entire amount of the estate's DNI to B. However, the basis of the property distributed to B could not be increased to its full fair market value on the date of distribution. Instead it has a basis of $30,000 in B's hands, reflecting the estate's basis of $25,000, increased by $5,000 of its unrealized appreciation determined as follows:

$$\frac{\$10,000}{\$50,000} \times \$25,000 = \$5,000$$

Sale or Exchange. Gain or loss may be recognized by the estate where property is distributed in kind in satisfaction of a pecuniary gift. Thus, an estate will recognize gain where appreciated property is distributed in satisfaction of a cash legacy. Similarly, the estate will recognize gain where appreciated property is distributed in satisfaction of a pecuniary marital deduction gift. The gain is limited to the difference between the estate's basis in the property, determined under §1014, and the fair market value of the property at the time of distribution.

Example 12-23. T's will made a bequest of $10,000 to a friend, F. T's executor plans to satisfy the gift to F by distributing property that has an estate tax value of $5,000 and a current fair market value of $10,000. The estate will recognize a gain of $5,000 if the property is distributed to F in satisfaction of the gift. Of course, under §1223(11) the gain on the sale would be long term. F would have a basis of $10,000 in the property.

Problem 12-4. For this taxable year the estate of T will have a taxable DNI of about $50,000. T's will made cash gifts of $10,000 to X and $5,000 to Y; in addition it gave 100 shares of MNO, Inc. stock to Y and the residue in equal shares to A and B. The will authorized the executor to satisfy the cash gifts by distributing property in kind to the legatees. The executor is planning to make distributions this year in satisfaction of the cash gifts and the bequest of stock to Y. In addition the executor would like to distribute property worth about $10,000 to A and B. The estate will close early next year, during which time it will have little or no income.

What recommendation would you make to the executor regarding the composition of the distributions if the following assets were available for distribution:

Asset	Estate Tax Value	Current Value
Cash	$15,000	$15,000
200 shares MNO, Inc. stock	$100 per share	$150 per share
10 carats loose diamonds	$15,000 per carat	$25,000 per carat
$25,000 municipal bonds	$20,000	$18,000

If the beneficiaries are all in the 50% income tax bracket, would you encourage the executor to defer making some distributions until the estate's final taxable year? If so, which ones would you recommend that he or she defer?

§12.33. Non-Pro Rata Distributions

A personal representative should be cautious about making non-pro rata distributions to the residuary beneficiaries unless such distributions are authorized either by the decedent's will or by the governing state law. In the absence of such authorization a non-pro rata distribution may involve a taxable exchange between the residuary beneficiaries and possibly a violation of the personal representative's fiduciary duty of impartiality. In a letter ruling the IRS has held that an equal but non-pro rata distribution to 3 estate beneficiaries did not result in any gain where the decedent's will authorized such a distribution. LR 8119040.

A non-pro rata distribution may be treated as a taxable exchange where it is made pursuant to the agreement of the residuary beneficiaries and not by reason of the executor's authority. The problem arises because each residuary beneficiary is generally entitled to a proportionate interest in each asset of the residuary estate. The nature of the problem is illustrated in the following example:

Example 12-24. T's will gave his residuary estate "in equal shares to those of my children who survive me." T was survived by 2 children, D and S. T's residuary estate consists of $10,000 and 100 shares of XYZ, Inc. stock, which was worth $5,000 on the estate tax valuation date and $10,000 on the date of distribution. Under the local law D and S are each entitled to receive $5,000 and 50 shares of XYZ, Inc. stock. If the executor distributes $10,000 to S and 100 shares of stock to D pursuant to their agreement, the distribution may be taxed as if S sold "his" 50 shares of stock to D for "her" $5,000. If so, S would be required to report a gain of $2,500 on the transaction ($5,000 sale proceeds, less $2,500 basis under §1014). The gain would be long term under §1223(11). As purchaser, D would have a basis of $5,000 in the 50 shares she purchased from S and a basis of $2,500 in the other 50 shares. No loss could result from such an exchange between related taxpayers because of the provisions of §267.

In Rev. Rul. 69-486, 1969-2 C.B. 159, the IRS held that a non-pro rata in kind distribution to the 2 beneficiaries of a trust involved a taxable exchange between the beneficiaries where the distribution was made pursuant to their agreement and was not authorized by the trust:

> Since the trustee was not authorized to make a non-pro rata distribution of property in kind but did so as a result of the mutual agreement between C and X, the non-pro rata distribution by the trustee to C and X is equivalent to a distribution to C and X of the notes and common stock pro rata by the trustee, followed by an exchange between C and X of C's pro rata share of common stock for X's pro rata shares of notes.

Presumably no taxable exchange would have been involved if the trust or the local law had authorized the trustee to make a non-pro rata in kind distribution.

An unauthorized non-pro rata distribution may violate the fiduciary's duty of impartiality toward the beneficiaries. A violation would certainly occur if each person who was entitled to receive an equal distribution did not receive assets of equal value on the date of distribution. The fiduciary might not be required to take the income tax bases of the assets into account in making a distribution. However, the fiduciary should take the bases into account in planning sales and distributions.

Community Property. Following the death of a spouse, the surviving spouse generally continues to own a one-half interest in the assets they had owned as community property. In general a husband or wife may only dispose by will of his or her interest in the community property. An attempt to dispose of a greater interest in the property may involve the rules applicable to widow's election arrangements. *See* §§9.21 to 9.33, *supra.*

Under the item theory of community property, each spouse owns and is entitled to dispose by will of an equal interest in each community property asset. *See* Estate of Patton, 494 P.2d 238 (Wash. App. 1972). Where the item theory applies, the surviving spouse and other persons who are beneficiaries under the will of the deceased spouse will hold the former community property as tenants in common. A non-pro rata distribution of the former community property to the surviving spouse and the beneficiaries under the will of the deceased spouse might be treated as a taxable exchange under Rev. Rul. 69-486, *supra*.

Example 12-25. H and W owned Blackacre and Whiteacre as their community property. When H died, he devised his one-half interest in Blackacre and Whiteacre to their daughter, D, and left the residue of his estate to W. W, of course, would continue to own a one-half interest in each parcel. After the death of H, Blackacre and Whiteacre would be owned by D and W as tenants in common. A taxable exchange might take place if, pursuant to an agreement between D and W, a fee interest in Blackacre were distributed to D and the fee interest in Whiteacre were distributed to W (or vice versa).

In letter rulings the IRS has indicated that a taxable exchange does not occur if the surviving spouse and the successors of the deceased spouse receive non-pro rata distributions of assets equal in value. LRs 8037124, 8016050. If the letter rulings are followed, no gain would result from the distribution described in Example 12-25. The rulings are based largely upon Rev. Rul. 76-83, 1976-1 C.B. 213, which held that an equal division of the fair market value of community property between spouses made in the context of a separation or divorce was not a taxable event. The extension of the holding of Rev. Rul. 76-83 to dispositions at death is desirable because of the flexibility it gives the parties, its fairness, and its simplicity of administration. The case for not taxing such a distribution is strengthened if the executor of a deceased spouse has the power to administer all of the community property and is given authority to make non-pro rata distributions of community property assets. Perhaps the best protection is provided if the spouses enter into an inter vivos agreement under which the executor of the spouse first to die may be given the power to make non-pro rata distributions of the entire interest in community property in satisfaction of residuary bequests. However, such an agreement might cause the estate of a deceased spouse to lose its claim to a discount in the value of the decedent's one-half community property share in closely held stock if the agreement required the decedent's interest to be valued at one-half of the entire community property interest. That is, the agreement might overcome the favorable holdings of Estate of Bright, 658 F.2d 999 (5th Cir. 1981), and Estate of Elizabeth Lee, 69 T.C. 860 (1978), *nonacq.* 1980-1 C.B. 2; *see* §6.19, *supra*.

A non-pro rata distribution in which the surviving spouse and the successors of the deceased spouse each receive assets of equal value would not involve a taxable exchange if the aggregate theory of community property is followed. Under it, the spouses do not each have a fixed and equal interest in each community property asset. Instead, each of them is merely entitled to receive assets that have a value equal to one-half of the total value of all of the community property. For an application of this theory in the gift tax context, *see* Kaufman v. United States, 462 F.2d 439 (5th Cir. 1972), discussed at §6.32, *supra*.

§12.34. *Trapping Distributions*

A "trapping distribution" is a distribution from an estate to a trust that carries out DNI to the trust, where the income is "trapped" and taxed to the trust. Cornfeld, Trapping Distributions, U. Miami 14th Inst. Est. Plan., Ch. 14 (1980); Income Tax Opportunities and Pitfalls in Estate Distributions, 13 Real Prop., Prob. & Tr. J. 835, 868-871 (1978). The typical case involves a distribution of property from the estate that is characterized as principal under the local law and that is not distributable to the trust beneficiaries as income. As explained below, the income carried out in a trapping distribution is taxed to the trust permanently or temporarily depending on the provisions of the trust regarding distributions. Carefully planned trapping distributions permit an estate's income to be split among the maximum number of taxpayers: the estate, individual distributees of the estate, the trust, and the beneficiaries of the trust.

The ultimate tax consequences of a trapping distribution depend to a large extent on whether the distributee trust is a simple trust or a complex trust. The difference arises because the throwback rules do not apply to simple trusts (*i.e.*, ones required to distribute all of their income currently and to make no distribution of principal during the year). *See* Cohan & Frimmer, Trapping Distributions — The Trap That Pays, 112 Tr. & Est. 766 (1973). Accordingly, a trapping distribution is generally effective to trap the distributed income permanently in a simple trust. The distribution of the principal of a simple trust upon termination will not involve a throwback of the trapped income except to the extent it consists of income in respect of a decedent (IRD) or unrealized accounts receivable. *See* Reg. §1.665(e)-1A(b), especially *Example* (1). Consequently, the executor should avoid distributing IRD to a trust where the intent is to achieve a permanent trap. In the case of a complex trust, the trapped income will be taxed to the beneficiaries when the trust makes an accumulation distribution to them. Of course, the throwback rules do not apply to income accumulated prior to the beneficiary's birth or prior to his or her becoming 21. *See* §10.2, *supra*. Those exceptions permit the trapped income to escape taxation under the throwback rules where the trapping distribution by the estate was made prior to the beneficiary's birth or during the beneficiary's minority. Trapped income is subject to taxation under the throwback rules where an accumulation distribution is made to beneficiaries other than charities.

The technique of making trapping distributions is important to the minimization of income taxes. Where it is desirable to do so, some estate income can be deflected to the trust, or trusts, each year by making appropriate distributions that would be characterized as principal under local law. Of course, income splitting can be extended to the trust's beneficiaries where the distribution it receives from the estate includes items that are properly characterized as income of the trust and that can be distributed to the beneficiaries of the trust.

> **Example 12-26.** T's estate will have a taxable income of about $75,000 this year if none of its income is carried out by way of distributions. After giving effect to the $600 personal exemption the estate would be subject to an income tax of $31,774 at 1982 rates. If the estate distributes $37,500 of principal to a residuary trust the distribution would carry out an equivalent amount of income, thereby reducing the estate's income tax liability to $12,814. If the trust had no other income for the year, it would be subject to an income tax of $12,961 if it was a simple trust and therefore eligible to claim a $300 exemption under §642(b). By making the distribution the overall income tax liability would be reduced by $5,999 (from $31,774 to $25,775). The reduction would be more dramatic if the estate's income were split with more than one trust.

When a trapping distribution is made the income tax liability imposed on the trust should be charged to the trust account to which the distribution is allocated under the local law. Thus, the income tax is appropriately paid from the principal account where the trapping distribution is characterized as principal. Conversely it is chargeable to income where the distribution is characterized as income. In the latter case, it may be necessary to make an equitable adjustment to the principal and income accounts where the tax liability is initially paid from principal. Estate of Holloway, 327 N.Y.S.2d 865 (Sur. Ct. Nassau Cty. 1972), *modifying*, 323 N.Y.S.2d 534 (Sur. Ct. Nassau Cty. 1971).

G. PAYMENT OF ESTATE TAX

§12.35. Introduction

The next section reviews the rules that govern the allocation of the estate tax burden. Succeeding sections examine the options that are available to the executor in making payment of the federal estate tax, most of which involve deferral of payment of the tax. Payment of the tax may be deferred under §6161 for reasonable cause. In addition, portions of the tax may be deferred under §§6163 and 6166. Finally certain issues of United States Treasury bonds ("flower bonds") may be redeemed at par in payment of the estate tax imposed by reason of the owner's death. The last section (§12.43) is a checklist of post-mortem matters.

§12.36.   Source of Payment of Estate Tax

The federal estate tax must be paid by a decedent's executor. §2002. (The term "executor" is defined in §2203 to refer to the decedent's executor or administrator or, if none, any person in actual or constructive possession of the decedent's property.) The executor in turn must be sure that the proper parties bear the burden of the tax. A person is generally free to designate in his or her will or trust the source of funds that should be used to pay the tax. When no source is designated, the state law determines how the tax should be paid. Many states have a form of apportionment law, which allocates the burden among the beneficiaries according to the value of the property each of them receives from the decedent. *See* UPC §3-916 and §4.25, *supra.* The common law of other states generally requires the tax to be paid from the residuary estate in the absence of contrary direction by the decedent. However, courts in a few states have required equitable apportionment of the Federal estate tax.

Four Code sections deal with the question of where the federal estate tax burden will fall, subject to contrary direction by the decedent or the local law. Under the first, §2205, if a person other than the executor pays any portion of the tax, that person may be entitled to reimbursement from the estate or contribution from the other beneficiaries of the estate. The provision is intended primarily to assure the tax is paid from the appropriate source, whether payment occurs prior or subsequently to distribution of the estate. The section recognizes rights to reimbursement, but it does not attempt to establish a particular rule of contribution by the beneficiaries.

In the absence of a contrary direction in the decedent's will, the second section allows the executor to collect a proportionate part of the estate tax from the beneficiary of life insurance proceeds that were included in the gross estate. §2206. If there is more than one beneficiary, the amount recoverable from each is calculated according to this formula:

$$\frac{\text{Proceeds of Policy}}{\text{Taxable Estate}} \times \text{Total Tax} = \text{Amount Recoverable}$$

However, the section does not apply to proceeds received by a surviving spouse for which a marital deduction is claimed and allowed.

The third section similarly allows an executor to recover a proportionate part of the estate tax from persons who receive property that was included in the decedent's estate under §2041 by reason of the exercise, nonexercise, or release of a power of appointment. §2207. Under it the right to recover from the recipients exists, "unless the decedent directs otherwise in his will." As in the case of §2206, however, it is inapplicable to the extent the property qualifies for the marital deduction.

Under the final section the executor has the right to recover from the recipients of qualified terminable interest property any additional estate tax imposed because the property was included in the decedent's estate under §2044. §2207A. The provision also extends to penalties and interest attributable to the additional estate tax incurred by reason of the inclusion of the property. §2207A(d). Subsection 2207A(a)(2) provides that the executor's right of recovery "shall not apply if the decedent otherwise directs by will." Thus, the surviving spouse (the "decedent" under §2207A) can assume the responsibility for payment of any additional tax. For that reason care must be exercised regarding the type of tax clause included in the surviving spouse's will.

Note that the sections do not restrict the *government's* right to collect the tax from any person who received property from the decedent. For example, in Horne v. United States, 519 F.2d 51 (5th Cir. 1975), the government recovered a portion of the unpaid estate tax by levying upon all of the insurance proceeds paid to the decedent's minor daughter although his will directed that the tax be paid from his probate estate. The court pointed out that the daughter's right to contribution from other recipients of the decedent's property was fundamentally a question of state law.

§12.37. *Extension for Reasonable Cause*

The 1976 Act substituted a "reasonable cause" standard for the "undue hardship" standard that previously applied for purposes of the discretionary 10-year extension of time to pay the estate tax. §6161(a)(2). Under that provision an extension may also be granted with respect to the payment of any installment of tax deferred under §6166 or former §6166A. The explanation prepared by the staff of the Joint Committee of Taxation states that "for this purpose, the term 'reasonable cause' is to have the same meaning as the term is used for granting discretionary extensions of up to twelve months (regs. §20.6161-1(a))." General Explanation of the Tax Reform Act of 1976, 546 (1976). The regulation referred to in the quotation provides that an extension may be granted if an examination of all the facts and circumstances shows that there is reasonable cause. Reg. §20.6161-1(a). The regulation also presents several helpful examples of situations that are recognized as constituting reasonable cause for this purpose.

An extension may be applied for by submitting a request that must include a statement of the period of the extension requested and a declaration that it is made under penalties of perjury. The request should be made on Form 4768 (Application for Extension of Time to File U.S. Estate Tax Return and/or Pay Estate Tax) and filed with the internal revenue officer with whom the estate tax return must be filed. Reg. §20.6161-1(b).

If an extension is granted the district director may require the executor to furnish bond for payment of the deferred amount of the tax. Reg. §20.6165-1(a). However, the bond may not exceed double the amount of the deferred tax. Interest is charged at the annually adjusted rate under §6621 on the amount of the unpaid tax.

§12.38. Deferral of Tax on Reversions and Remainders

Where a reversionary or remainder interest in property ("the future interest") is included in the decedent's gross estate, the executor may elect to defer payment of the estate tax attributable to the future interest until 6 months after all of the precedent interests terminate. §6163(a). The election is made by filing a notice with the district director before the date prescribed for payment of the tax. The notice may be in the form of a letter to the district director accompanied by a certified copy of the will or other instrument under which the future interest was created. Reg. §20.6163-1(b). Where the duration of the precedent interest is dependent upon the life of any person, the notice must also show the date of birth of that person. Again, interest is charged at the annually adjusted rate on the amount of tax that is deferred.

Regulations issued under §6165 require payment of the tax and accrued interest to be secured by a bond equal to double the amount of the tax and accrued interest for the estimated duration of the precedent interest. Reg. §20.6165-1(b). If the duration of the precedent interest is indefinite, the bond must be conditioned upon the principal or surety promptly notifying the district director when the precedent interest terminates and upon his or her notifying the district director in September of each year as to the continuance of the precedent interest.

Where the decedent's estate includes both a future interest and other property, the amount of tax that can be deferred is determined by this formula:

$$\frac{\text{Adjusted value of future interest}}{\text{Adjusted value of gross estate}} \times \text{Estate tax} = \begin{array}{c} \text{Tax that} \\ \text{may be} \\ \text{deferred} \end{array}$$

For purposes of the calculation the value of the future interest is reduced by (1) the amount of outstanding liens on the interest, (2) losses deductible under §2054 with respect to the interest, (3) amounts deductible in respect of the interest as charitable transfer under §2055, and (4) amounts deductible in respect of the interest as a marital deduction under §2056. Similar reductions are made in the value of the gross estate.

§12.39. Estate Tax Deferred under Former §6166A

In the case of decedents dying prior to 1982, an executor could elect to pay the estate tax attributable to the decedent's interest in a closely held business in equal annual installments over a period not to exceed 10 years. Under this provision the first payment had to be made when the estate tax was regularly due (*i.e.*, 9 months after death). Interest is payable each year on the unpaid balance of the tax at the annually adjusted rate determined under §6621. (In the period between 1978 and 1983 the rate ranged between 7 and 20%.) Deferral was available under §6166A only where the value of the business interest included in the decedent's estate exceeded 35% of the decedent's gross estate or 50% of the decedent's taxable estate. §6166A(a).

The time for payment of the deferred portion of the estate tax is accelerated in certain instances described in §6166A(h). In particular, acceleration occurs if 50% or more in value of the business interest is (1) withdrawn from the business or (2) sold, exchanged, or distributed. Transactions affecting the business should of course be carefully planned in order to avoid the inadvertent acceleration.

§12.40. Deferral of Estate Tax under §6166

In the case of decedents dying after December 31, 1981, the estate tax attributable to a closely held business interest can be paid in 10 installments, the first of which is due 5 years after the federal estate tax return is due. Deferral under this section is allowed if the value of the closely held business interest exceeds 35% of the decedent's gross estate less the amount of deductions allowable under §§2053 and 2054. (The percentage requirement was 65% for decedents dying between 1976 and 1982.) For purposes of §6166, the decedent's interests in 2 or more businesses may be aggregated if 20% or more of the value of each of them is included in the decedent's estate. In essence, the 1981 Act made the more impressive benefits of §6166 available to estates that met the less onerous percentage requirement of the former §6166A. For a more detailed discussion of §6166, *see* §§11.26 to 11.32, *supra*.

Interest is paid each year on the unpaid amount of the tax. However, the tax on the first $1 million in value of the business interest is subject to interest at only 4%. §6601(j). The maximum amount subject to this special rate is $345,800 less the amount of the unified credit allowable under §2010(a). The remainder of the tax is subject to the annually adjusted rate. Deferral of more than the 4% amount is not particularly attractive when the floating rate is high.

The maximum amount of tax that can be subject to the 4% rate is:

Year	Tax on $1 million	Unified Credit	Amount at 4%
1982	$345,800	$ 62,800	$283,000
1983	345,800	79,300	266,500
1984	345,800	96,300	249,500
1985	345,800	121,800	224,000
1986	345,800	155,800	190,000
1987	345,800	192,800	153,000

The 1981 Act also made the more lenient acceleration provisions of former §6166A applicable to tax that is deferred under §6166 by estates of decedents dying after December 13, 1981. See §6166(g) and §12.39, supra. Tax deferred by the estates of persons dying prior to 1982 are subject to acceleration if one-third or more in value of the business interest is (1) withdrawn from the business or (2) sold, exchanged, or distributed.

§12.41.   Payment of Estate Tax with "Flower Bonds"

Certain United States Treasury bonds issued prior to March 31, 1971, are redeemable at par, plus accrued interest, in payment of the federal estate tax on their owner's death. Reg. §20.6151-1(c). The bonds all carry low interest rates as a result of which bonds that will not mature for some time generally sell at substantial discounts. Redeemable bonds are called "flower bonds" because they "blossom" into full value upon the owner's death. However, the bonds are redeemable only to the extent they are included in the decedent's gross estate. Also, the bonds may be redeemed at par only to the extent of the net amount of the federal estate tax after taking all allowable credits into account. Rev. Rul. 76-367, 1976-2 C.B. 259.

The redemption of bonds held in trust or in joint ownership at the time of the decedent's death is restricted by Treasury Circular No. 300, 31 C.F.R. 306.28 (1973). Under it bonds held in joint ownership are redeemable only to the extent that (1) the bonds became property of the decedent's estate or (2) the surviving joint owner was required to contribute toward payment of the federal estate tax on account of the bonds and other jointly owned property. Bonds held in trust are redeemable under Circular 300 "(a) if the trust actually terminated in favor of the decedent's estate, or (b) if the trustee is required to pay the decedent's Federal estate tax under the terms of the trust instrument or otherwise, or (c) to the extent the debts of the decedent's estate, including costs of administration, State inheritance and Federal estate taxes, exceed the assets of his estate without regard to the trust estate." Because of these limitations it is particularly important to exercise care in drafting trusts and in purchasing flower bonds.

Bonds Purchased by an Agent for an Incompetent Principal. The government has vigorously resisted redemption of bonds purchased for an incompetent individual by another person acting under an ordinary (*i.e.*, nondurable) power of attorney. It has argued that the bonds purchased pursuant under such a power of attorney were not part of the principal's estate because the agent's authority terminated when the principal became incompetent. The validity of the actions taken by the agent is, of course, a question of state law. Campbell v. United States, 657 F.2d 1174 (Ct. Cl. 1981). *Campbell* and most other cases have found that actions taken by an agent for a comatose principal are voidable and not void. Hence, they have allowed redemption of the bonds. *See* United States v. Manny, 645 F.2d 163 (2d Cir. 1981). The most famous case upheld the estate's claim for damages as a result of the government's refusal to redeem $4.7 million in bonds tendered by the estate of Arthur Watson, the late chairman of IBM's board. Estate of Watson v. United States, 48 A.F.T.R.2d 81-6288 (Ct. Cl. 1981). Bonds purchased by an agent acting within the scope of a durable power of attorney for a comatose principal would not be vulnerable to the government's argument. *See* §4.33, *supra.*

A bond that is redeemable at par in payment of the estate tax is includible in the decedent's gross estate at its redemption value plus accrued interest whether or not it is submitted for redemption. Bankers Trust Company v. United States, 284 F.2d 537 (2d Cir. 1960), *cert. denied*, 366 U.S. 903 (1961); Rev. Rul. 69-489, 1969-2 C.B. 172. However, flower bonds in excess of the amount redeemable in payment of the estate tax are valued at their fair market values, not their par values. *Id.* Bonds are also valued at par that could have been redeemed in payment of an estate tax deficiency that was determined after the estate disposed of the bonds it held in excess of the amount of the tax as shown on the estate tax return. Estate of Fried v. Commissioner, 54 T.C. 805 (1970), *aff'd*, 445 F.2d 979 (2d Cir. 1971), *cert. denied*, 404 U.S. 1016 (1972); Estate of Elfrida G. Simmie, 69 T.C. 890 (1978), *aff'd*, 632 F.2d 93 (9th Cir. 1980). However, an unreported district court decision held that the disposal of the "excess" bonds prior to issuance of a deficiency made them unavailable for use in payment of the deficiency and, therefore, it was proper to include them in the gross estate at their market value instead of at their redemption value. Colorado National Bank of Denver v. United States, 71-1 U.S.T.C. ¶12,781, 27 A.F.T.R.2d 71-1827 (D. Colo. 1971).

Income Tax Consequences. Under §1014, the estate's basis in a bond is increased to its estate tax value. Accordingly, the estate does not recognize any gain when the bond is redeemed at its par value. The surviving spouse's one-half interest in a redeemable bond is not stepped up under §1014(b)(6) to the estate tax value of the decedent's one-half interest. Instead, the survivor's basis is the fair market value of her interest in the bonds on the federal estate tax valuation date. Ann F. Neuhoff, 75 T.C. 36 (1980); Rev. Rul. 76-68, 1976-1 C.B. 216.

Community Property Aspects. Only one-half of a bond owned as community property may be redeemed upon the death of a spouse. However, it may be unnecessary to purchase double the amount of the bonds that may be redeemed upon the death of one spouse. Instead, the bonds to be used to pay the tax on one spouse's death can be purchased with separate property created by partitioning some community property into 2 equal units of separate property. Of course, in such a case there is no step up in the value of the surviving spouse's separate property (just as the survivor's one-half interest in community property bonds would not be increased to their par value). Under another approach one spouse can give to the other spouse his or her community property interest in the bonds or in funds to be used to purchase the bonds.

Flower bonds or other property purchased on the separate credit of one spouse are the separate property of that spouse. For an illustration of how the credit extended by a cooperative bank can cause the bonds that were purchased for a decedent to be characterized as separate, see Ray v. United States, 385 F. Supp. 372 (S.D. Tex. 1974), *aff'd per curiam,* 538 F.2d 1228 (5th Cir. 1976).

List of Redeemable Bonds. The following is a list of the bonds that are redeemable in payment of estate taxes:

Series	Issue Date	Due
$3\frac{1}{4}$'s 1978-83	May 1, 1953	June 15, 1983
$3\frac{1}{4}$'s 1985	June 3, 1958	May 15, 1985
$4\frac{1}{4}$'s 1975-85	April 15, 1960	May 15, 1985
$3\frac{1}{2}$'s 1990	Feb. 14, 1958	Feb. 15, 1990
$4\frac{1}{4}$'s 1987-92	Aug. 15, 1962	Aug. 15, 1992
4's 1988-93	Jan. 17, 1963	Feb. 15, 1993
$4\frac{1}{8}$'s 1989-94	April 18, 1963	May 15, 1994
3's 1995	Feb. 15, 1955	Feb. 15, 1995
$3\frac{1}{2}$'s 1998	Oct. 3, 1960	Nov. 15, 1998

Procedure for Redemption. Bonds should be submitted for redemption with Form PD 1782, Application for Redemption of Treasury Bonds for Federal Estate Tax Credit, to a Federal Reserve Bank, the Office of the Treasurer, or to the Bureau of the Public Debt. *See* Rev. Proc. 69-18, 1969-2 C.B. 300. The executor may request redemption as of the date the federal estate tax is due or as of a date prior or subsequent to that date. The bonds and Form PD 1782 should be submitted a month prior to the date requested for redemption. Bonds received after the redemption date requested on Form PD 1782 will be redeemed as of the date of receipt. Inquiries regarding redemption of bonds should be addressed to:

> Bureau of the Public Debt
> Division of Loans and Currency
> Treasury Department
> Washington, D.C.   20226

Problem 12-5. T, a widower, is terminally ill and is not expected to live more than 30 days. The assets that will be includible in his gross estate have a value of about $800,000, including cash of $100,000. T has not made any taxable gifts and will not make any gifts prior to death. If no deductions or credits will be available to T's estate other than the unified credit, what would be the overall tax impact if T purchased flower bonds with a par value of $100,000 at a cost of $80,000? What steps should be taken to purchase the bonds if T were married and his estate consists solely of his interest in community property that has a total value of $1,600,000?

§12.42. *Release from Liability for Taxes*

An executor or other fiduciary of a decedent is personally liable for the payment of the federal taxes of the decedent and the decedent's estate. Their personal liability is based upon §§3466 and 3467 of the Revised Statutes, 31 U.S.C. §§191, 192 (1976). Section 3466 provides that when an estate is insufficient to pay all debts of the decedent, the debts due the United States must be paid first. The priority established by §3466 is enforced by §3467, which subjects an executor or other fiduciary to personal liability for debts due the United States if other debts of the decedent are paid "before he satisfies and pays the debts due to the United States." The matter is of concern to fiduciaries because federal tax liabilities are considered to be debts due the United States and the regulations treat the distribution of property to a beneficiary as the payment of a debt. Reg. §20.2002-1. Funeral expenses, costs of administration, a family allowance, and a limited number of other items are not considered to be debts. *See, e.g.,* United States v. Weisburn, 48 F. Supp. 393 (E.D. Pa. 1943) and Malcolm D. Champlin, 6 T.C. 280 (1946) (estate administration expenses). Accordingly, they may be paid without risk. On the other hand, expenses of the decedent's last illness are considered to be debts. The risk of personal liability naturally discourages fiduciaries from distributing estate property before the tax liabilities are settled. The problem is relieved somewhat by §2204, which permits the executor or other fiduciary to apply for prompt determination of the estate tax liability. Also, §6905 establishes a procedure under which the executor can obtain a discharge from personal liability for the decedent's income and gift taxes.

Section 2204. Section 2204 allows an executor or other fiduciary to apply for prompt determination of estate tax liability and discharge from personal liability for the tax. In the case of an executor, the IRS is generally required to notify the executor of the amount of the tax within 9 months of the time request is filed. The executor is discharged from personal liability upon payment of the amount of which he or she is notified (other than any amount the time for payment of which is extended under §§6161, 6163 or 6166) and upon furnishing any bond that may be required for any amount, the payment of which has been extended. A fiduciary other than an executor can obtain a release from personal liability for estate tax on essentially the same terms. §2204(b). An agreement that meets the requirements of §6324A (relating to the special lien for estate tax deferred under §6166) is treated as the furnishing of a bond for purposes of §2204.

By filing an application for prompt determination of estate tax, the estate tax liability of the estate may be fixed within 18 months following a decedent's death. Many executors and other fiduciaries file requests under §2204 in order to facilitate the early distribution of assets from estates and trusts. However, some planners are reluctant to file a request under §2204 because they believe it would increase the probability the decedent's estate tax return will be audited.

Section 6905. An executor can also apply for discharge from personal liability for the decedent's income and gift tax liability under §6905. If such a request is filed, the executor is released from personal liability if he or she is not notified of the amount due within 9 months of the receipt of the executor's request. Otherwise, the executor is released upon payment of the amount of which he or she is notified.

Section 6501(d). An executor may limit the assessment of any deficiency for income or gift taxes by filing a request for prompt assessment under §6501(d). The provisions of §6501(d) require that income or gift tax liabilities of a decedent must be assessed within 18 months after receipt of a request for prompt assessment. In the ordinary case, if the 18 months pass without an assessment being made, the executor cannot be held personally liable for the taxes unless he or she had personal knowledge of the liability, or had such knowledge as would put a reasonably prudent person on inquiry. Again, the filing of such a request may trigger an audit of the decedent's income or gift tax returns.

§12.43. Checklist of Post-Mortem Matters

I. Income Tax
    A. Decedent's final income tax return
        1. Joint return with surviving spouse, §6013(a)(2), (3), §12.4, *supra* _____
        2. Medical expenses paid within 1 year of death, §§213(d)(1), 2053, §12.5, *supra* _____
        3. Accrued interest on Series E bonds and similar obligations, §454, §12.6, *supra* _____
    B. Estate's income tax return
        4. Election of tax year, §441(b), §12.9, *supra* _____
        5. Estate administration expenses, §642(g), §12.15, *supra* _____
        6. Estate selling expenses, §642(g), §12.15, *supra* _____
        7. Distributions of estate assets (carryover of excess deductions in final year), §642(h), §§12.30 to 12.34, *supra* _____
        8. Distribution of installment obligation to obligor, §691(a)(5), §9.6, *supra* _____
        9. Redemption of stock under §303, §§11.14 to 11-21, *supra* _____
      10. Quarterly payment of income tax, §6152(a)(2), §12.9, *supra* _____
    C. Other income tax elections
      11. Terminate Subchapter S status, §1372(e)(1), §12.7, *supra* _____
      12. Partnership election to increase basis in assets in which decedent had a proportionate interest, §754, §12.7, *supra* _____
      13. Waiver of the personal representative's fees, Rev. Rul. 66-167, 1966-1 C.B. 20, §12.10, *supra* _____
      14. Rollover of lump sum payments to surviving spouse, §402(a)(7), §12.21, *supra* _____

II. Estate Tax
      15. Alternate valuation, §2032, §12.17, *supra* _____
      16. Special use valuation, §2032A, §12.18, *supra* _____
      17. Marital deduction, qualified terminable interest property §2056(b)(7), §12.19, *supra* _____
      18. Estate administration expenses and expenses of selling estate assets, §642(g), items 6 and 7 above _____

BIBLIOGRAPHY

I. General:

Brackney, Post-Mortem Tax Planning for Estates, 15 Wake Forest L. Rev. 581 (1979)

Clapp, Post Mortem Planning, 1 Prob. Law. 1 (1974)

Ferguson, C., Freeland, J. & Stephens, R., Federal Income Taxation of Estate and Beneficiaries (1970) (with annual supplements)

Hawk, Post Mortem Tax Planning — Advanced Techniques, 58 Taxes 165 (1980)

Johnson, Post-Mortem Tax and Estate Planning Elections, 42 Montana L. Rev. 199 (1981)

Report, Post Mortem Tax Planning, 7 Real. Prop., Prob. & Tr. J. 798 (1972)

Walsh, Postmortem Estate Planning. N.Y.U. 37th Inst. Fed. Tax., Ch. 44 (1979)

TABLE OF CASES

(references are to sections)

TABLE OF 1954
INTERNAL REVENUE CODE SECTIONS

TABLE OF TREASURY REGULATIONS

TABLE OF INTERNAL REVENUE RULINGS

(references are to sections)

TABLE OF STATUTES

(references are to sections)

§§970 *et seq.* 4.25
§1120.6 4.22

Revenue and Taxation Code

§13671 *et seq.* 3.20
§13724 6.25
§§16700-16950 2.26

Colorado

Revised Statutes

§39-23.5-106 2.26

Florida

Statutes Annotated

§710.02 4.15
§726.08 10.9

Idaho

Code

§14-402(5) 3.20
§15-2-201(a) 3.31
§15-2-201(b) 3.31
§15-6-201 3.26
§32-906(1) 3.24
§32-906A 3.23

Illinois

Annotated Statutes

Ch. 110-½, §4-5 4.19, 6.69
Ch. 110-½, §202 4.15

Indiana

Annotated Code

§6-4.1-3-6 6.25
§27-1-12-16(B) 6.69

§27-1-12-16(C) 6.69
§27-1-12-16(E) 6.69
§30-1-9-14 10.9

Kansas

Statutes Annotated

§58-2414 (1976) 10.9

Louisiana

Civil Code Annotated

Art. 2336 3.28
Art. 2339 3.24
Art. 2341 3.28
Art. 2443.1 3.28

Maryland

Estates & Trusts Code Annotated

§11-106(a) 12.16

Michigan

Statutes Annotated

§25.131 4.18
§26.155(118) 10.9

Nevada

Revised Statutes

§111.064 3.26, 3.29
§111.065 3.11
§123.070 3.25
§123.230(2) 7.6
§§163.220 *et seq.* 4.19
§163.280 4.22

MODEL ACT

Business Corporation Act

UNIFORM ACTS

Anatomical Gift Act

Disclaimer of Transfers under Non-testamentary Instruments Act

Disposition of Community Property Rights at Death Act

Durable Power of Attorney Act

Gifts to Minors Act

Limited Partnership Act

Parentage Act

Principal and Income Act, Original 1931 Draft

Principal and Income Act (1962 Act)

Principal and Income Act (Revised 1962 Act)

INDEX

(references are to sections)

A

ADEMPTION, 4.13

ANATOMICAL GIFTS, 4.9, 4.34
Action by others, 4.34
Donees, 4.34
Donor card, 4.34
Planning, 4.34
Revocation and amendment, 4.34
Ways of making gifts, 4.34

APPRECIATED PROPERTY ACQUIRED FROM A DECEDENT, 3.29

ATTORNEYS
Assisting client's decision, 1.6
Associating others, 1.1, 1.5
Competence, 1.5
Conflicts. *See* CONFLICTS OF INTEREST
Continuing supervision or services, 1.9
Fees
allocating the fee, 1.18
fee schedules, 1.15
for estate administration services, 1.15
for lifetime estate-planning services, 1.14
income tax deductibility, 1.17, 1.19, 12.15
informing client, 1.13
satisfying the fee, 1.16

AUTOMATION IN ESTATE PLANNING
Document production, 1.8

B

BARGAIN SALES
Charity, to, 8.28

GIFTS

L

Q